ONE &

A History of
The Duke of Cornwall's Light Infantry

Hugo White

HUGO WHITE

TABB HOUSE

First published 2006

TABB HOUSE
7 Church Street
Padstow, Cornwall, PL28 8BG

Cased ISBN 9781873951 200
1873951 205
Limp 9781873951 453
1873951 450

PUBLISHER'S NOTE

The history of the Duke of Cornwall's Light Infantry is the main concern of this book. General topics, such as the political background or wider military events and strategies that put the position of the DCLI into context, are set to a wider measure and in a smaller typeface, to distinguish them from the principle subject.

As a general rule, maps are set at the start of the chapters to which they refer.

* * *

Permission by the trustees of the Duke of Cornwall Light Infantry's Museum to use material in their possession for reproduction as illustrations to the book is gratefully acknowledged.

CONTENTS

ACKNOWLEDGEMENTS

This book could not have been written had it not been for the generous help of many officers and NCOs who have given me the benefit of their first hand experiences or their profound knowledge of regimental matters. I thank them all; and must mention in particular Major-General David Tyacke, who has given a great deal of his time to read large chunks of manuscript, and has used his enclyclopaedic knowledge to correct numerous inaccuracies that would otherwise have gone unremarked. Similarly, Lieutenant-Colonel Geoffrey Sharland has put me right on many points of post-war history which were originally incorrectly reported in *One & All*. I am also most grateful to Major Colin Robins, a leading expert on the Crimean War, who kindly read my draft and gave me much valuable information on that Campaign. Last but certainly not the least of my principal experts has been Mr Frank Grigg, a stalwart member of the 5th Battalion throughout the whole of the Second World War. As the Line Serjeant in the Signal Platoon, Frank was in the thick of every single battle fought by that proud Battalion in North West Europe, and, by reason of his appointment, was in the privileged position of knowing what was happening in the fog of war.

Among the many others who have given me information and assistance, I am particularly indebted to Mrs Debbie Fisher and Mrs Kath Lockhart.

I owe special thanks to two successive Regimental Secretaries, Majors Richard Vyvyan-Robinson and Trevor Stipling for their help, and for enduring my long-standing take-over of the Regimental Library in the Keep at Bodmin.

The book has been embellished with drawings of badges by Mr Endean Ivall from his and Professor Charles Thomas' book *Military Insignia of Cornwall* and I have pleasure in thanking them for their use.

I am grateful to the trustees of the Duke of Cornwall's Light Infantry Museum for encouraging me in the writing of *One & All*, and also to them and the trustees of the Piet Mendles Foundation for their generous financial support, without which the publication of *One & All* would have been impossible. I trust I have not let them down.

Finally, credit for the production and publication of this work must rest with Caroline, my wife. The writing. I have learnt, is just the beginning; the read hard toil lies in the multitude of often frustrating tasks which have to be completed before a pile of A4 sheets is transformed into that wonder of our civilization - a book.

ILLUSTRATIONS

MAPS by Hugo White

For some regions it has not been possible to map a number of places named in the text, but some places not mentioned have been included, to give an idea of the local geography.

INTRODUCTION

THE BRITISH ARMY

Britain has always disliked and distrusted a large standing army. It represents a powerful armed force which can destabilise the lawful democratic government; it is seen as a serious drain on the economy, which in peacetime provides nothing in return; finally, in the days before barracks, its regiments roamed the country, commandeering accommodation and disrupting the even tenor of rural life. As any reader of Kipling will be aware, the nineteenth century peace-time soldier was regarded as the dregs of society, who could find no other employment. This is summed up by the infamous notice that is alleged to have been displayed outside respectable inns: 'Dogs and soldiers not admitted'.

Apart from the latter part of the Great War (1916-18), the whole of the Second World War (1939-45) and the period of world tension following the war (1945-63), Britain has always relied on a volunteer army. Although a very few regiments can claim that their roots go back before the Restoration of King Charles II in 1660, this date marks the true birth of the British Army as we know it today. Originally the standing army was very small (the infantry consisted of only two regiments of foot guards and eight regiments of the line; the cavalry was considerably smaller) but, as Britain grew in power and became increasingly involved in Continental wars, additional regiments were raised when the need arose. However, armies were expensive, so although regiments were raised for specific campaigns, they were just as easily disbanded when their services were no longer required. One therefore finds that, particularly in the eighteenth century, regiments sprang up and disappeared after only brief lives.

In the seventeenth and eighteenth centuries a national bureaucracy did not exist in Britain that was capable of maintaining an army of any size through a centralised system of control. Individual regiments were therefore raised and maintained by men of substance under the delegated authority of the Crown. A gentleman, often a Peer of the Realm, would be granted a Royal Warrant investing him with the Colonelcy of a particular regiment. He was periodically credited with a lump sum of government money with which he was required to finance the recruitment, clothing, training, and payment of his regiment. His regiment carried his name and was virtually his private army. Upright colonels looked after their men with a high degree of benevolent paternalism; those less honest could run their regiments at minimum cost and pocket the balance.

In 1715, colonels lost the complete autonomy that they had previously enjoyed; regiments were henceforth known by a numeral that indicated their seniority in the army. Recruiting was carried out by the regiment itself from the area in which it happened to be stationed (if a regiment was abroad, it normally left a depôt company at home to recruit and train reinforcement drafts). Large numbers of recruits came from Ireland, and up to the middle of the nineteenth century about a third of the English infantry was made up of Irishmen. The regimental system was still extremely flexible, allowing regiments to be raised or disbanded as the national requirement for soldiers varied from war to peace.

In 1782, in an effort to rationalise recruiting, most regiments were given a county title in addition to their number. The idea was that regiments should recruit as far as possible from their counties. It is difficult to ascertain whether this system ever worked in practice. Certainly eighteenth and nineteenth century muster rolls show men who came from every corner of the British Isles, with Irishmen still forming the largest single group.

In 1881 the British Army underwent the most radical and far-reaching reorganisation since its birth in 1660. Every senior officer had long been acutely aware that under the existing system, once a regiment had been committed to foreign service, there was no way of providing any but the meagre reinforcements that its depôt company could drum up. Regiments on foreign service wasted away, usually through disease, till they became non-effective; the survivors were then brought home where a crash programme to obtain and train recruits was undertaken to bring the regiment back to operational efficiency. This was recognised as an inefficient system but no man, politician or soldier had had the courage to force through the necessary radical reforms in the face of powerful reactionary lobbies. In 1868 Edward Cardwell became Secretary of State for War to the Gladstone Administration. Described as 'the least warlike of men', he brought to his office not only a brilliant analytical mind but also the courage and tenacity to augment his reforms in the face of entrenched opposition. The basis of his plan was that every infantry regiment should have two regular battalions. At any time, one of these should be serving abroad while one remained at home. The 'home' battalion was therefore available to send drafts out to its sister battalion abroad, allowing it to remain on station for long periods without the disruption of being forced to return home at frequent intervals to recruit. In addition to the two regular battalions, Cardwell envisaged that each regiment would have a depôt in the county of its title, where all recruits for that regiment would be trained. He also brought the Militia and Volunteers into the framework of the new regiment (previously these bodies had been totally divorced from the regular army). Thus, under the Cardwell System every infantry regiment (with a very few exceptions) was to consist of the following:

2 regular battalions
1 militia battalion
2 volunteer battalions
1 depôt

Having formulated his plan for the organisation of the new regiments, Cardwell then carried out a detailed review to determine how many regular battalions were needed to carry out Britain's world commitment at the end of the nineteenth century. The answer came to a total of 142 battalions of infantry, and from this figure he was able to work out the necessary number of large new regiments. Generally speaking, these were formed by amalgamating the old regiments in pairs. This system, although initially unpopular, served the nation well, and it remained virtually unaltered until the run down of the Army in the 1950s. Although Cardwell was no longer Secretary of State for War when this reform was finally enacted in 1881, it is always known by his name. Cardwell is rightly acknowledged to have been a monumental influence in bringing the Victorian army into the twentieth century.

Before leaving Cardwell, one should consider another of his major military reforms. Before he came to office, officers of the cavalry and infantry had been required to purchase their initial commissions and all subsequent promotions up to the rank of Lieutenant-Colonel. This was a policy of extreme antiquity. It had been reinforced by the prevailing mood after the Civil War when it was perceived that 'soldiers of fortune', who led troops for their own personal gain, were a menace to the stability of the Kingdom. Officers must be men of substance, men who had a stake in the land and whose interests corresponded to those of the nation. To ensure this, officers were required to pay for the privilege of holding their Sovereign's Commission. The purchase system had much to recommend it in the seventeenth and eighteenth centuries, not least because it absolved the Treasury from paying officers' pensions. On resignation an officer 'sold out', being paid back the official purchase price of his original commission plus the price of all subsequent promotions; this lump sum was given back in lieu of a pension. However, the system had serious and scandalous disadvantages. Because promotion depended on an officer's financial means rather than on his military ability, highly experienced but impoverished officers were frequently passed over by their more wealthy colleagues. One of the few ways that cavalry and infantry officers could rise without payment was by being appointed to a vacancy occurring through death, hence the officers' toast, 'A short war and a bloody one'. The stumbling blocks to the abolition of purchase were first, the entrenched reaction of many in the military establishment and second, the parsimony of the Treasury, which would have to repay all serving officers their purchase money and instigate a realistic system of pensions. It needed all Cardwell's courage and tenacity to force through his Act, abolishing the purchase of Commissions. This was, however, enacted in 1871. It cost the Treasury seven million pounds (a large sum in the monetary values of that age) but represented a major advance in the modernisation of the British Army. Henceforward officers were promoted on merit, and a system of exams for certain stages of promotion was instituted.

No apology is made for dwelling at length on Cardwell. Any understanding of the history of the British Army must involve the immense importance of his many radical reforms (of which only two are mentioned above). He can be seen as the pivotal point dividing the old army from the new army that we have known until today.

In 1899 Britain embarked on one of the most ill-conceived and humiliating wars in her history. Trained to fight against a poorly armed savage foe who could normally be beaten by a combination of robust courage and rock steady discipline, the generals in South Africa looked upon the Boer farmers with contempt. They were soon to receive a rude awakening. Three disastrous defeats in a week shocked the British public and caused a rapid reappraisal of military tactics in the age of the high velocity rifle and smokeless ammunition.

After the South African War a committee known as 'The War Office (Reconstruction) Committee' was convened in 1903 to investigate the shortcomings of the British Army and to make recommendations as to how these could be rectified. The most prominent member of this Committee was Lord Esher. Esher was the Liberal MP for Falmouth and Penryn, who had become Lord Hartington's private secretary in 1878. He had thus been intimately involved in the Hartington Committee of 1890, which had made many recommendations on the reform of military high command, all of which had fallen under the dead hand of the Commander-in-Chief, the ageing Duke of Cambridge, and never been implemented.

Esher believed that the office of Commander-in-Chief was archaic and should be replaced by an Army Council. This, he advised, should consist of a politician, a civil servant and seven senior officers: the Minister for War, the Permanent Under-Secretary for War, the Chief of the Imperial General Staff, the Adjutant General, the Quartermaster General, the Director of Artillery, and the Inspector-General of Fortifications. Thus, for the first time in history, the workings of the British Army – political, financial, strategical, tactical and logistical – would be under the control of a seven-man Council, in which each member would be conversant with the operation of the whole. 'The War Office (Reconstruction) Committee Report', commonly known as 'The Esher Report' was published in 1904. It now fell to the Liberal Secretary of State for War, Richard Haldane, to implement these recommendations and take on the task of putting the army onto an efficient footing to fight a modern industrialised war.

Every single aspect, from the composition of the General Staff to the design of soldier's equipment, was examined in the most minute detail. Where necessary, changes were made. Haldane was a Scottish lawyer with a penetrating intellect and a logical brain. He stands beside Cardwell as one of the great men who influenced the advancement of the British Army. He was convinced, even in the early days of the twentieth century, that Britain would one day become embroiled in a continental war, and he saw how unprepared the army was to enter any such conflict. Together with Major-General Douglas Haig, the Director of Staff Duties at the War Office, he reorganised the British Army on a basis that was far more efficient than anything that it had known before. It was thanks to Haldane and Haig that Britain was able to despatch an expeditionary force to France in 1914 which, although tiny compared to continental armies, was arguably the finest regular army that has ever taken to the field. Amongst the more visible changes that Haldane made was the further integration of the Volunteer battalions into the regular army under the new title of Territorial Force, and the formation of reserve battalions from the old Militia. In the event of European war, the primary role of the Territorial Force would be the relief of the very large part of the regular army tied down to garrison duties in India. The role of the reserve battalions was to form training units capable of dealing with the vast influx of recruits that would be required on mobilisation.

The regular army that sailed for France in August 1914 bore little resemblance to that which had existed before 1881. Its new regimental system, to which it rendered unswerving loyalty, had been fashioned by Cardwell; its tactical organisation had been rewritten and refined to a most exact degree by Haldane. It was a proud and, above all, a highly professional army.

Compared to the principal continental armies that took the field in 1914, the British regular army was minute. However, its performance in the early months of the war had an effect on German strategy that was quite out of proportion to its size. Having fought a delaying action on the Mons-Condé Canal in Belgium, the British Expeditionary Force carried out what is perhaps the most remarkable fighting withdrawal in military history. Maintaining contact with the enemy, always in danger of being outflanked, it pulled back 240 miles in 14 days. Then, with only a single day's rest, it counter-attacked alongside the French, driving the Germans back north of the Aisne. In order to rationalise the deployment of the French and British armies, the BEF was then moved back north to Belgium to secure the Allied left flank at Ypres. It was exhausted, outnumbered and occupying far from ideal positions, and it was only by its superb discipline and expert musketry that it prevented the vast hordes of the enemy from breaking through to the sea. The Kaiser had called the British Expeditionary Force 'that contemptible little army'; the 'Old Contemptibles' became a proud epithet for those regular soldiers who had fought at Mons and Ypres. They did their job; they held back a German army that was numerically vastly superior, but their losses in dead and wounded were appalling. It is true to say that the pre-war regular army was virtually destroyed in those first critical months of the war.

Meanwhile in Britain a great citizen army was being assembled. Field-Marshal Lord Kitchener called for volunteers, and the volunteers poured in. So successful was this call to arms that the administrative and training organisation was swamped. Uniform, equipment, weapons and accommodation soon ran out. Men trained as best they could, wearing their own clothes in which they had enlisted, while an inadequate number of officers and NCOs wrestled with unprecedented problems of administration. These volunteers represented the cream of British manhood; many had left comfortable homes and secure jobs for reasons of patriotism. Weapons, equipment and clothing may have been in short supply but their enthusiasm was unbounded. The 'New Army' battalions started to cross over to France in the early summer of 1915. Compared with the old regular army, they were inadequately trained and it would certainly have been desirable not to have committed them to battle for another year. This, however, was not an option. Britain desperately needed to put large numbers of men into the field to support the hard-pressed French. One of the great tragedies of the war was the slaughter of an irreplaceable section of our nation in the mud of the Ypres Salient and the Somme. By the end of 1915 the initial flood of volunteers had dried up. In January 1916, for the first time in the history of the British Army, men were conscripted. By that stage in the war, weapons and equipment were no longer in short supply. Efficient training units, run in most cases by the regimental reserve battalions, had been established and the process of turning the new generation of conscripted recruits into trained soldiers proceeded without the traumas that had attended the formation of the original Kitchener armies. In truth, these conscripts who fought the great battles of 1916-18 made excellent soldiers. They benefited from the fact that, by the latter period of the war, the training and administrative organisations had become outstandingly efficient, and the supply of munitions was more than adequate.

As has already been said, the majority of the Territorial Force battalions were sent out to India to relieve regulars. During the course of the war many of these were committed to the various Middle East campaigns being waged against the Turks in Mesopotamia, Palestine and Greece.

Thus the British Army of 1914-18 consisted of three different parts, each with its own individual character; the old pre-war Regular battalions; the wartime 'Kitchener' Service battalions (both volunteer and conscript); and the Territorial Force battalions. In spite of the very high casualty rates that necessitated continued reinforcement from a common pool, these Regular, Territorial and Service battalions never lost their own individuality.

By the Armistice of 1918 Great Britain had forged the largest and probably the most efficient army that she has ever possessed. After taking the brunt of the German Offensive in March 1918, it brought the German army to a halt, consolidated its position, re-trained for open warfare and launched a text-book attack that broke through the enemy line and won the war. This final phase was carried out almost entirely by British and Dominion troops. The French were, by this stage, a broken and exhausted army; the Americans, arriving in increasing numbers, were inexperienced and ill trained; only the British Army was capable of fighting those last decisive battles. It was a very great military achievement which is not generally recognised, but which should certainly be regarded as one of the proudest chapters of our history.

From 1920 to 1937 this fine army was remorselessly emasculated. The defence budget was reduced each year, with the result that little new equipment was introduced and realistic formation training was seldom carried out. The nation that had invented the tank failed to maintain its lead in either the quantity or quality of its hardware, and utterly failed to formulate any tactical policy for the use of armour. It must be pointed out that this situation arose as the direct result of Government parsimony and was not in any way due to the shortcomings of British officers. Indeed many officers made their feelings known as they watched with apprehension the rise of a modern German army.

Britain only really woke up to the threat of a second European war in 1937. Two years of frantic rearmament was insufficient to make good sixteen years of apathy. The British Expeditionary Force that sailed for France in September 1939 was proud and highly motivated; it was, however, ill equipped and untrained to fight a mobile battle in which tanks were to play a prominent part. In spite of the general inadequacy of much equipment, Britain led the world in one important respect: the BEF went to France without a single horse. Every other nation relied on draft horses for the movement of much of its artillery and transport. Indeed, the German army still used horses for this purpose throughout the war.

The British Expeditionary Force was outmanoeuvred and driven out of mainland Europe. The evacuation of the majority of its manpower in June 1940 may have been a triumph of British improvisation but it was an undoubted defeat, attributable in large part to the neglect with which successive governments had treated the Army in the inter-war years. Apart from minor Commando forays, Allied troops were not to set foot on French soil for another five years.

It was not only in Europe that British armies suffered ignominious defeat. Hong Kong fell to the Japanese on Christmas Day 1941. Far worse was to follow when, on 15th February 1942, Singapore surrendered. 130,000 British soldiers were taken prisoner in the greatest single defeat in our history. By the end of May 1942, the Japanese Army occupied all but a small part of Burma.

After the fall of France, the immediate priority became the defence of Britain and the re-equipping of her army. The entire industrial capacity of the nation was put on a war footing and, as new munitions factories were built and new military units raised, Britain started on the long haul that was to culminate in victory six years later. From the first, the policy of relying on volunteers was discarded. Conscription was introduced four months before the outbreak of war in April 1939, and although at this stage there was only the most basic equipment available, the framework of a citizen army was established in an orderly manner, quite unlike the near chaos that had accompanied the formation of the New Armies in 1914.

The Second World War was to be fought on many fronts. It was a mobile war, usually dominated by the use of armour, which never deteriorated into the slogging trench battles of 1914-18. Less infantry was required and although rates of attrition in certain operations (notably Normandy, 1944) reached Great War proportions, British casualties were far lower over the extended period of this war. However, with the advent of large scale bombing (and latterly of rockets), civilian casualties, which in the Great War had been negligible, constituted a significant proportion of the total. It is estimated that 60,159 British civilians died from German air bombardment.

THE DUKE OF CORNWALL'S LIGHT INFANTRY

Having looked at the history of the British Army, let us now put the story of the Duke of Cornwall's Light Infantry into context. The DCLI was formed in 1881 by the amalgamation of two much older regiments, the 32nd (Cornwall) Light Infantry and the 46th (South Devonshire) Regiment of Foot. Because these two regiments were originally totally separate, it will be necessary to deal with their histories individually.

After the formation of the Duke of Cornwall's Light Infantry, the histories of its 1st and 2nd Battalions are given, and of all the other battalions including Volunteers, Territorials and Pioneers, during the periods when the size of the Regiment was greatly swollen because of the exigencies of the Great War and the Second World War.

The Somerset and Cornwall Light Infantry

An account of the Regiment after its amalgamation with the Somerset Light Infantry as the composite Somerset and Cornwall Light Infantry, until that regiment's absorption into the Light Infantry, is given in an Appendix.

HONI SOIT QUI MAL Y PENSE
THE DUKE OF CORNWALL'S LIGHT INFANTRY

PART 1

Fox's Marines
the 32nd Regiment of Foot
the 46th Regiment of Foot

& the
Duke of Cornwall's Light Infantry

32
DIEU ET MON DROIT

Chapter 1

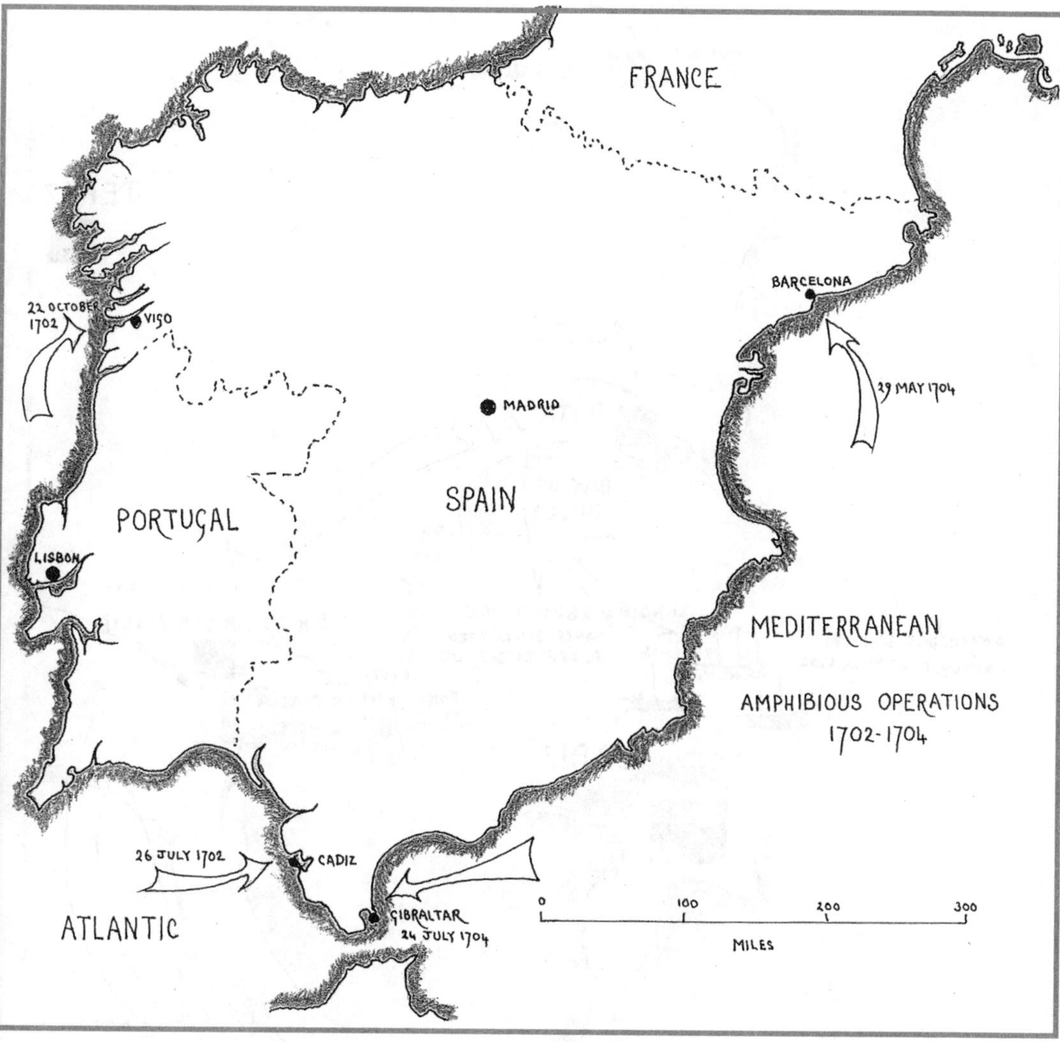
FRANCE
22 OCTOBER
1702
VIGO
MADRID
BARCELONA
29 MAY 1704
SPAIN
PORTUGAL
LISBON
MEDITERRANEAN
AMPHIBIOUS OPERATIONS
1702-1704
26 JULY 1702
CADIZ
GIBRALTAR
24 JULY 1704
ATLANTIC
0
100
200
300
MILES

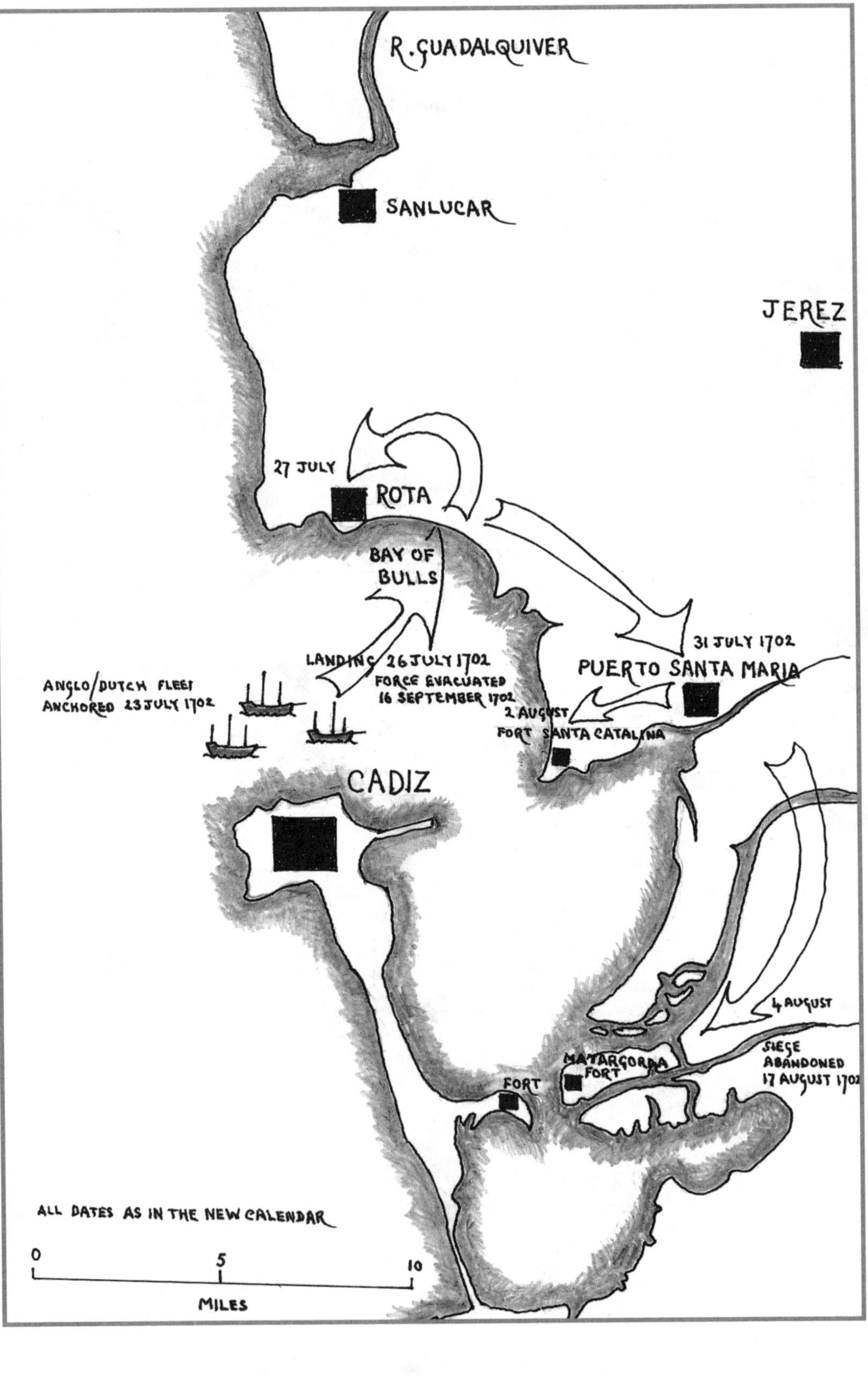
R. GUADALQUIVER
SANLUCAR
JEREZ
27 JULY
ROTA
BAY OF BULLS
LANDING 26 JULY 1702
FORCE EVACUATED 16 SEPTEMBER 1702
ANGLO/DUTCH FLEET ANCHORED 23 JULY 1702
31 JULY 1702
PUERTO SANTA MARIA
2 AUGUST
FORT SANTA CATALINA
CADIZ
4 AUGUST
MATARGORDA FORT
FORT
SIEGE ABANDONED 17 AUGUST 1702
ALL DATES AS IN THE NEW CALENDAR
0
5
10
MILES

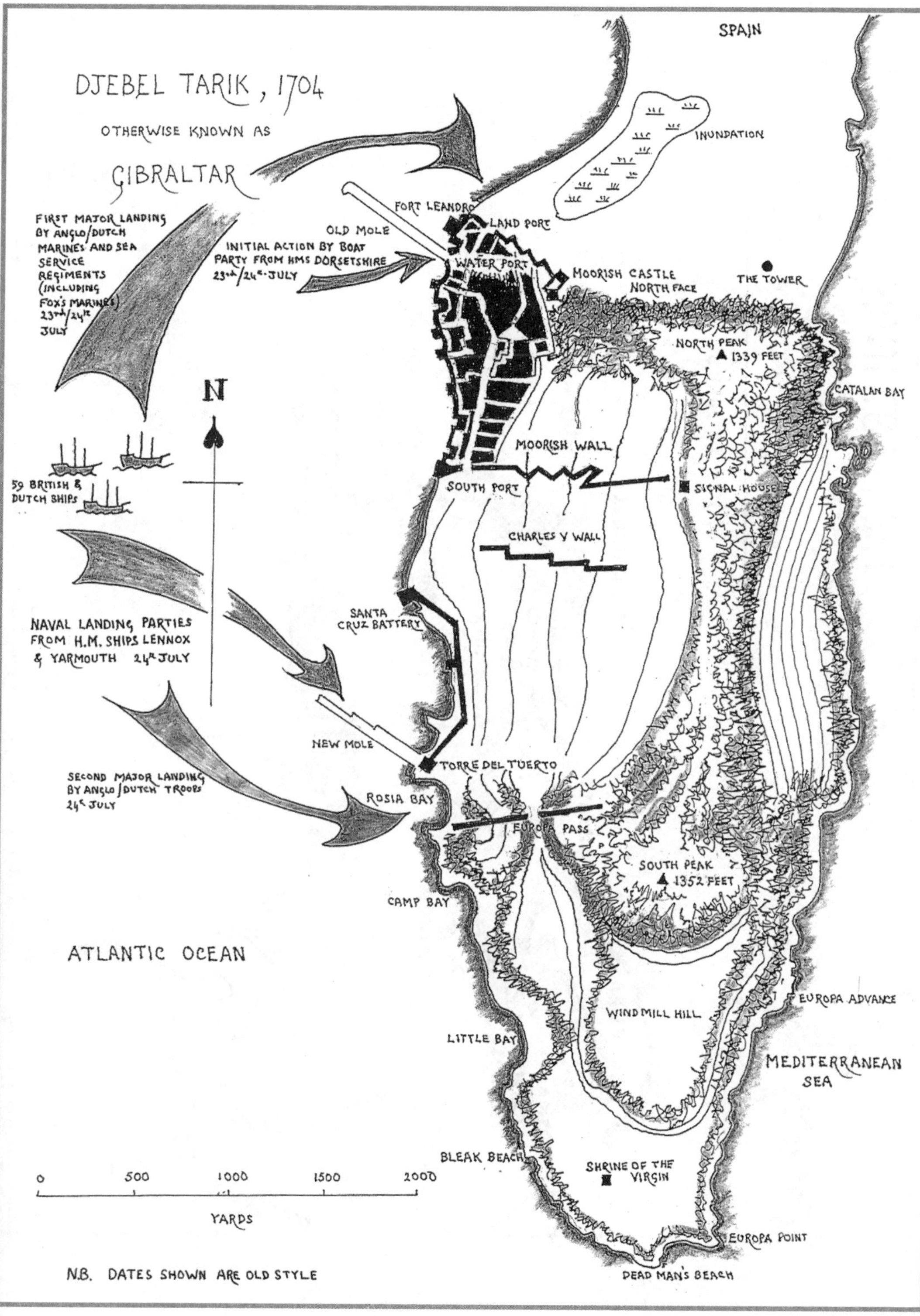
DJEBEL TARIK, 1704
OTHERWISE KNOWN AS
GIBRALTAR
SPAIN
INUNDATION
FORT LEANDRO
LAND PORT
OLD MOLE
WATER PORT
MOORISH CASTLE NORTH FACE
THE TOWER
FIRST MAJOR LANDING BY ANGLO/DUTCH MARINES AND SEA SERVICE REGIMENTS (INCLUDING FOX'S MARINES) 23rd/24th JULY
INITIAL ACTION BY BOAT PARTY FROM HMS DORSETSHIRE 23rd/24th JULY
NORTH PEAK 1339 FEET
CATALAN BAY
N
MOORISH WALL
SOUTH PORT
SIGNAL HOUSE
59 BRITISH & DUTCH SHIPS
CHARLES V WALL
SANTA CRUZ BATTERY
NAVAL LANDING PARTIES FROM H.M. SHIPS LENNOX & YARMOUTH 24th JULY
NEW MOLE
TORRE DEL TUERTO
SECOND MAJOR LANDING BY ANGLO/DUTCH TROOPS 24th JULY
ROSIA BAY
EUROPA PASS
SOUTH PEAK 1352 FEET
CAMP BAY
ATLANTIC OCEAN
EUROPA ADVANCE
WINDMILL HILL
LITTLE BAY
MEDITERRANEAN SEA
BLEAK BEACH
SHRINE OF THE VIRGIN
0 500 1000 1500 2000
YARDS
EUROPA POINT
N.B. DATES SHOWN ARE OLD STYLE
DEAD MAN'S BEACH

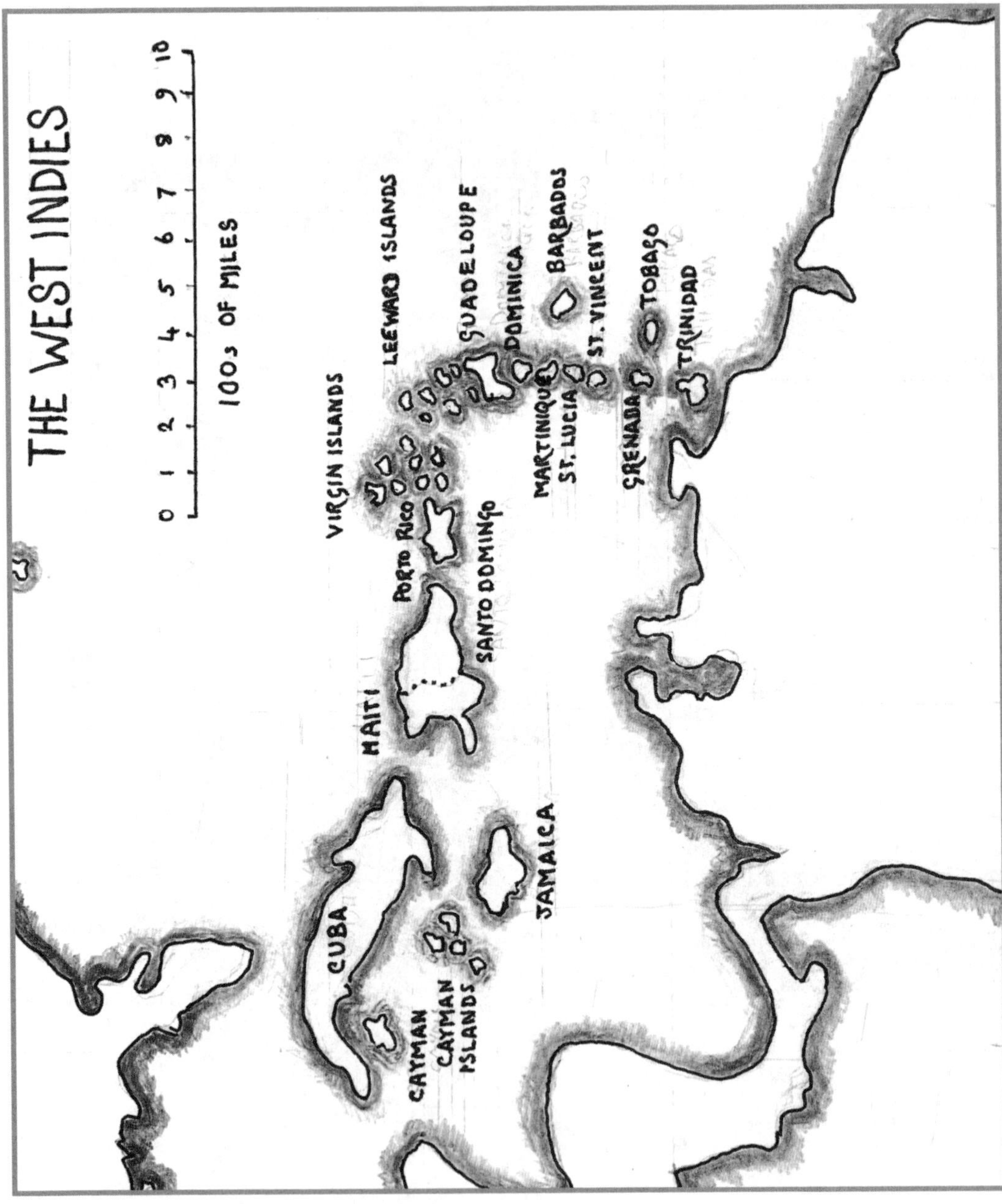
THE WEST INDIES
0 1 2 3 4 5 6 7 8 9 10
100s OF MILES
CUBA
CAYMAN
CAYMAN ISLANDS
JAMAICA
HAITI
SANTO DOMINGO
PORTO RICO
VIRGIN ISLANDS
LEEWARD ISLANDS
GUADELOUPE
DOMINICA
MARTINIQUE
ST. LUCIA
ST. VINCENT
BARBADOS
GRENADA
TOBAGO
TRINIDAD

I. FOX'S MARINES
& THE 32ND REGIMENT OF FOOT

* * *

1
1702-1807

FOX'S MARINES: THE WAR OF THE SPANISH SUCCESSION 1702-1713

Throughout the latter part of the seventeenth century Britain's foreign policy was aimed at maintaining a balance between the two great European powers, France with her Bourbon King, Louis XIV, and the Austro-Hungarian Holy Roman Empire of Leopold I. If either of these nations were to acquire Spain and her Italian empire, this fragile balance would be destroyed.

Charles II, King of Spain, was a weak epileptic whose early death was eagerly anticipated by both Louis and Leopold. Both monarchs had sons who were nephews of Charles II and therefore claimants to the inheritance.

In 1698 William III, King of Great Britain, negotiated a secret treaty with Louis XIV of France whereby, on the death of Charles II of Spain, Joseph-Ferdinand, Prince of Bavaria (and also a nephew of Charles II) would succeed to Spain, while the Italian empire would be split between France and Austria. However, no sooner was the ink dry on this first Partition Treaty than the principle participant, Prince Joseph-Ferdinand, died. A second Partition Treaty was therefore quickly put together. In this new draft the Archduke Charles, son of the Emperor Leopold I of Austro-Hungary, was to succeed to Spain, while the Dauphin of France would get Italy. This treaty was probably agreed by Louis XIV as a sop to Perfidious Albion, for even while it was being negotiated, Louis XIV's most skilful ambassador to the Court of Madrid, Le Marquis d'Harcourt, was persuading Charles II to make a new will bequeathing both Spain and Italy to Phillipe Duc d'Anjou, grandson of Louis XIV. Thus France, Spain and Italy would become united as a single great power block, a situation totally unacceptable to Great Britain, Holland and Austro-Hungary.

On 1st November 1700 Charles II died. Because of the conflicting treaties, war was now inevitable. In the autumn of 1701 Austria Hungary attacked the French in Italy, and on 15th May 1702 Great Britain and Holland declared war on France.

In North West Europe the field was dominated by John Churchill, First Duke of Marlborough, arguably the greatest military commander ever produced by Britain.

Leading a combined Anglo-Dutch army, he advanced 250 miles from Flanders to the Rhine. By building up a sound administrative structure, using his brilliant diplomatic skills to maintain an amicable relationship with his allies, and outmanoeuvring the French at every move, he was able to win a succession of great battles, the names of which still resound in the annals of our history: Blenheim, Ramillies, Oudenarde and Malplaquet.

The Spanish half of the enemy alliance could best be attacked from the sea, using the superiority of the British and Dutch navies. Squadrons of allied ships constantly prowled the coast of Spain, looking for opportunities to land marines and sea-service regiments at vulnerable naval bases.The object was to inflict the maximum destruction before re-embarking and putting to sea while the enemy was still attempting to muster his forces to react effectively.

The Raising of Fox's Marines, 1702

It was to meet the requirement for amphibious soldiers that a Colonel Fox was ordered to raise a Regiment of Marines in 1702. His Regiment was destined, after several changes of title, to become the 1st Battalion the Duke of Cornwall's Light Infantry 179 years later.

Edward Fox was born in about 1660, during a traumatic period for Britain that saw the restoration of the Stuart monarchy, the disbandment of Cromwell's New Model Army and the formation of a new, and much smaller, Royal Army in its place. Fox purchased a commission in one of these new regiments, the King's Holland Regiment, later to become the 3rd Regiment of Foot (the Buffs). He saw active service with them under King William III in Flanders, where it is recorded that their work in repairing the defences of Bruges earned them a gift of 600 barrels of beer from the grateful City Burghers; a singularly unwise gift one would have thought for English soldiers, notorious for their drunkenness.

In 1702 Fox was charged with raising a regiment of marines, the warrant of authorisation being signed by Queen Anne on the 13th March of that year. Recruiting around the towns and villages of Sussex met with such success that by the 13th May the new Regiment was up to a viable strength. Few barracks existed at that time, troops normally being billeted in taverns, inns, or occasionally, private houses. During the two months of its formation, Fox's Marines were successively billeted at Arundel, Midhurst, Liphook, Halleck, Steyning, Terring, Godalming, and finally Guildford. One must presume that these towns and villages mark the progress of this fast expanding regiment around its recruiting area.

When at full establishment, an infantry regiment of the early eighteenth century consisted of 12 companies, each of 100 men, with 44 officers and a Marshal (who equated to the present day Regimental Serjeant-Major). The Colonel was often merely the titular head of his regiment, selected from the Peerage or a wealthy landed family for his prestige and authority rather than for any military attributes, who delegated actual command to a Lieutenant-Colonel. However, in the case of Fox's Marines, Fox exercised full command himself. We know the names and appointments of the founding officers of the Regiment, which were as follows:

Captains

Colonel Edward Fox
Lieutenant-Colonel P. Howard
Major Jacob Borr
Captain Humphrey Corey
Captain Frank Foulk
Captain Robert Kempe
Captain Jonathon Wildbore
Captain Richard Oxenden
Captain Jonathon Gignoux
Captain Richard Cobham
Captain William Helmsley (Grenadier Company)
Captain Charles Monger

First Lieutenants

Captain-Lieutenant William Lee
Lieutenant James Steward
Lieutenant Charles Bourgh
Lieutenant Daniel Sinault
Lieutenant Henry Harris
Lieutenant Richard Mullins
Lieutenant Richard Allison
Lieutenant Barnaby Bowtell
Lieutenant Adrian Van Alphen
Lieutenant Rixton Darby
Lieutenant Thomas Browne

Second Lieutenants

2nd Lieutenant Thomas Skinner
2nd Lieutenant Henry Brooks
2nd Lieutenant Peter Colborne
2nd Lieutenant Thomas Pretty
2nd Lieutenant Isaac Duplex
2nd Lieutenant Isaac Drouart
2nd Lieutenant R. Collingwood
2nd Lieutenant Edward Atkinson
2nd Lieutenant Frank Gincks
2nd Lieutenant Jonathon Dowier
2nd Lieutenant James Collyar
2nd Lieutenant Thomas Porte

Staff Officers

Quarter-Master Richard Mullins
Adjutant Henry Harris
The Rev. Thomas Heskith (Chaplain)

What immediately springs to one's notice in this list is that the Colonel, the Lieutenant-Colonel and the Major are listed as Captains. Although it seems illogical today, it was the custom in the early eighteenth century for three of the twelve companies to be nominally commanded by the Colonel, the Lieutenant-Colonel and the Major, who drew the pay for both their appointments. A company was normally commanded by a captain, aided by two subalterns (although that term was not then in use), who were either first or second lieutenants. As there were only nine captains on establishment, this meant that three of the companies were actually commanded by three first lieutenants, the senior of whom was appointed a captain-lieutenant.

To the present-day observer, the army of Queen Anne would appear remarkably lacking in any uniformity as regards dress, equipment, weapons or drill. Officers' dress was particularly idiosyncratic, as nothing was laid down until the first officers' dress regulations of 1742. These regulations were published under the ponderous title of *A Representation of the Clothing of His Majesty's Household and all the Forces upon the Establishment of Great Britain and Ireland*, which became known more simply as *The 1742 Book*, *The Clothing Book* or *The Cumberland Book*. Up to that time, officers tended to wear a deep-skirted coat and waistcoat of the current civilian style. This was usually, but not always, of some shade of red. Certain regiments appear to have anticipated the 1742 regulations, and required their officers to wear a scarlet coat of similar style to that worn by the soldiers. Whatever their dress, offices could usually be distinguished by a crimson silk sash (or scarf as it was originally called) worn over the left shoulder and knotted on the right hip. The official officer's weapon was the spontoon, a pole-mounted axe-cum-pike, similar to that still carried by the Corps of Gentlemen at Arms. Authorised in 1700, the spontoon remained the symbol of an officer's authority for many years but, although carried on ceremonial parades, was singularly unfitted for use on the battlefield. In keeping with gentlemanly practice of the age, officers invariably armed themselves with swords, though the design of these was left entirely to personal taste, until the introduction of the first standard military pattern in 1786.

The infantry soldier of the early eighteenth century wore a red coat, flared out from the waist and reaching to just above his knees, similar in cut to the civilian style. In the field, high gaiters protected his stockinged legs. The standard head-dress also followed civilian fashion, consisting of a black felt tricorn hat, except for the soldiers of the Grenadier Company who wore a tall brimless cap to enable them to sling their muskets when throwing grenades. Up to 1715 the British Army had no standard firearm, government contracts for muskets and bayonets being granted to numerous gun makers in Britain and Holland, who produced weapons that varied widely in design and quality. Every infantry soldier was issued with a flintlock musket of some description.

Although contemporary paintings depict soldiers wearing scarlet coats, this owes much to artistic licence. Scarlet dye was expensive, and up to the latter part of the nineteenth century the rank and file made do with cloth usually described as 'brick red'. Regiments were distinguished by the colour of the facing cloth on the deep, turned-back coat cuffs and collars. In the case of Fox's Marines, the facing colour was green. The muskets issued to Marines and Sea Service Regiments were generally of a somewhat cruder and more robust character than those carried by normal infantry, the better to stand up to rough usage in the confines of a ship, while the metalwork was often painted black as protection against the salt air.

On 13th May 1702 Fox's Marines (for such was the Regiment's title in accordance with the custom of that time) was ordered to march from Guildford to Portsmouth, where it was to draw tentage and field stores from the ordnance depôt before embarking for the Isle of Wight. There, on 2nd June 1702, the Regiment was reviewed by Prince George of Denmark, who passed the Regiment 'Fit for Service', remarking in his comments that the men 'performed their exercises uncomparably well'. That Fox's Marines was so judged after only two and a half months of existence implies either that its officers and soldiers were of remarkable quality, or that the standards required were very basic.

Whatever the quality of the Regiment, events were moving fast. Within a month of being passed 'Fit for Service', Fox's Marines embarked for operations against Spain. The Anglo-Dutch naval squadron was commanded by Admiral Sir George Rooke, the composition of the military force being as follows:

Lloyd's Dragoons (later 3rd Hussars)	275
Detachments of combined 1st and Coldstream Guards	755
Bellasis' Foot (later 2nd or Queen's Regiment)	834
Churchill's Foot (later 3rd or The Buffs)	834
Seymour's Foot (later 4th or King's Regiment)	834
Columbine's Sea Service Foot (later 6th or Royal Regiment)	724
O'Hara's Foot (later 7th Fusiliers)	313
Erle's Sea Service Foot (later 19th or 1st North Riding Regiment)	724
Hamilton's Sea Service Foot (later 20th or East Devon Regiment)	724
Villiers' Marines (later 31st or Huntingdonshire Regiment)	520
Fox's Marines (later 32nd or Cornwall Regiment)	834
Lord Donegal's Sea Service Foot (later 35th or Dorsetshire Regt)	724
Lord Charleville's Sea Service Foot (later 36th or Herfordshire Regt)	724
Lord Shannon's Marines (later disbanded)	834
Total British Troops	9,653
Total Dutch Troops	3,924
Total Allied Military Force	13,577

The British military element was commanded by General the Duke of Ormond, while the Dutch were under the joint command of Major-General Baron Sparre and Brigadier-General Pallant. The first objective was to be Cadiz. Admiral Rooke's orders were 'to reduce and take the town and island of Cadiz, or if this appeared for any reason impossible, Vigo, Ponte Vedra, Corunna or any place belonging to Spain or France as shall be judged proper'.

The whole force, together with thirty British and twenty Dutch ships assembled at Spithead, and sailed for Spain on 12th July 1702.

Attack on Cadiz, 1702

On 23rd July the Allied Fleet anchored off the Spanish coast just north of Cadiz. The Duke of Ormond wished to land the military force immediately, thus denying the enemy valuable time to deploy his defences. Admiral Rooke however overruled this decision on the grounds that, lying on a lee shore with worsening weather, he might well have to put to sea, leaving the soldiers stranded in enemy territory. There followed three days of argument and indecision, but on 26th July the troops went ashore near the town of Rota, seven miles north of Cadiz. The landing was unopposed, but twenty men were drowned in the heavy surf. The force marched south the following day, arriving at Port St Mary, which was found to be deserted. Discipline seems to have collapsed as the abandoned town was given over to pillage. Jerez, the centre of the Spanish sherry industry, lies only a few miles away, so that the countryside was liberally endowed with bodegas and wine stores. Soon a large part of the force were incapable of taking part in any serious military operations. To add to the Duke of Ormond's problems, Admiral Rooke announced that he was unable to provide the naval gun-fire support, so vital to any successful attack on the fortress, due to the roll of his ships in the heavy swell, while these ships would present sitting targets for the shore-mounted batteries in Cadiz. Amidst increasing acrimony, the attack was aborted and a somewhat disorderly body of frustrated soldiers made its way back to the original landing place, whence they were re-embarked between the 25th and 28th August. During this withdrawal Colonel Fox commanded the rear-guard, which included his own regiment. So effective was he in carrying out this duty that very few casualties were inflicted on the main force, either in the withdrawal or during the subsequent re-embarkation. The *London Gazette* of 2nd November 1702 stated:

> By the extraordinary good conduct of Colonel Fox, who had the management of the whole disposition made by His Grace, a better could never have been, considering the advantage the Spaniards had over him.

Thus, in an otherwise deplorable operation, Fox's Marines gave a creditable performance in their first engagement with an enemy.

Plunder of the Spanish treasure fleet in Vigo Bay, 1702

Having been at sea for a few days, some of Admiral Rook's ships put into Lagos to replenish their supplies of water. While there they learnt that a French fleet of fifteen warships and seventeen galleons loaded with bullion from the West Indies was lying in Vigo Bay. Sail was immediately set. The fleet arrived off Vigo on 17th October, and, without any loss of time Ormond's troops went ashore with the aim of silencing the Spanish land-based batteries. This was done with commendable speed, and on the success signal being received by the fleet, the leading British ship *Torbay* smashed through the chain boom laid across the mouth of the bay. The rest of the Allied ships poured through the gap, laying alongside the enemy, whom they greatly outnumbered. After a brief fight the ships and treasure estimated to be worth £2,000,000 (perhaps a hundred times that in today's value) were captured.

The news was received in England with extravagant joy. A state service of thanksgiving in St Paul's Cathedral was attended by Queen Anne and both Houses of Parliament. All the infantry regiments that had taken part in the landing received a bounty of £561 10s., while each man was awarded a silver medal (probably the first example of a campaign medal issued to all ranks, an example of which is displayed in the DCLI Museum).

First attack on Barcelona, 1704

1703 was a quiet year for the Regiment, which returned to its old recruiting grounds in Sussex, being billeted in Arundel, Horsham and Crickfield.

However, late that year it again embarked in an Allied fleet commanded by Admiral Rooke. Prince George of Hesse Darmstadt was the military commander, having under him:

Seymour's Foot (later 4th or King's Regiment)
Sanderson's Foot (later 30th or Worcestershire Regiment)
Luttrell's Foot (later 31st or Huntingdonshire Regiment)
Fox's Marines (later 32nd or Cornwall Regiment)
Shannon's Sea Service Foot (later disbanded)
Holt's Sea Service Foot (later disbanded)
Mordaunt's Sea Service Foot (later disbanded)

On 21st May 1704 the fleet anchored off Barcelona. 1,600 troops were put ashore the next day to the east of the town without incident. The fortress was surrounded and the defenders called upon to surrender, which they declined to do. After a desultory bombardment from the sea, Admiral Rooke deemed his situation at anchor off an enemy coast too dangerous to continue, and called upon Prince George to re-embark his troops. This they reluctantly did.

On 28th July Admiral Rooke received a despatch urging him to attack Cadiz, which intelligence sources believed to be in a vulnerable state following the withdrawal of most of its garrison to fight the Portuguese in the north. He refused to do this, unless he could be reinforced by a large force of Portuguese sent down by sea from Lisbon.

At about the same time further despatches were received, stating that a French fleet was on passage from Brest to Toulon. Admiral Rooke was ideally placed to confront this fleet but, knowing that Sir Cloudesly Shovel was expected in this area, declined to do so until he could rendezvous with Sir Cloudesly's squadron.

The capture of Gibraltar, 1704

As the fleet set sail for home, Admiral Rooke can have been under no illusions as to his likely reception in England. He had failed in his initial task of destroying the dockyard facilities at Barcelona; he had failed to act in accordance with the wishes of his superiors, to attack Cadiz while it was in a temporarily vulnerable state; and had failed to confront a French fleet on passage from Brest to Toulon. It was vital that he achieved some success before returning to England.

Prince George suggested that a landing might be made at Gibraltar. It was not anticipated that this mighty fortress could be captured, but it was considered that Allied troops could hold the shoreline for sufficient time to accomplish the destruction of dockyard facilities.

On 31st July 1704 Admiral Rooke's fleet anchored in Gibraltar Bay. The following morning 2,300 Allied troops, including Fox's Marines, under Prince George, were put ashore on the narrow isthmus connecting the north face of Gibraltar with the mainland. Advancing to the Land Port, which they proceeded to break down, the soldiers met little opposition apart from a brief appearance of Spanish cavalry, who were quickly sent scuttling back to safety. During that night three Dutch bomb ketches moved in close to the western flank of the Rock, and started firing incendiary shells into the town. As dawn broke the whole fleet took up the cannonade, quickly creating a breech in the walls. Immediately, using their own initiative and without waiting for orders, Captain Jumper of *Lenox* and Captain Hicks of *Yarmouth* put sailors ashore, who quickly established a beach head. Shortly afterwards the main force of some 3,000 soldiers landed at Rosia Bay. While the sailors were preparing to advance a magazine blew up, killing forty and wounding a further sixty of the party from *Lenox*. Sad as was this considerable loss, it represented almost the only casualties suffered by the Allies in this operation.

On 3rd August a demand was sent to the Governor, Don Diego de Salinas, to surrender. At dawn the following morning two emissaries rode out of the fortress to meet Prince George, requesting that an officer accompany them back to the fortress to discuss the terms of surrender with Salinas. Colonel Fox was selected to negotiate the exact terms, which included the safe conduct of the garrison and the civilian population across the isthmus to the mainland.

Immediately the French received news of the capture of Gibraltar, they despatched their fleet from Toulon with the intention of mounting a quick counter attack before the defences could be repaired. The French fleet, newly out of the dockyard, was in excellent shape, fully provisioned, amply supplied with ammunition and with clean hulls. Admiral Rooke's ships had been at sea for many months with the consequence that their hulls were heavily fouled with weed; furthermore, they were seriously short of ammunition. Admiral Rooke, having replenished his water supplies at Ceuta, immediately sailed to intercept the French. It was an unequal struggle, but Admiral Rooke more than vindicated himself by fighting a skilful and aggressive battle. No ships were lost, but damage was considerable and casualties were heavy on both sides. The French aim of retaking Gibraltar was thwarted.

Admiral Rooke then returned to Gibraltar to effect repairs. In early September, having landed sixty of his ship's guns, he embarked some 3,000 of the troops and sailed for home. The garrison left behind numbered about 2,300, and included Fox's Marines.

Thus it was that the capture of this natural fortress, which was to play such an important part in Britain's domination of the Mediterranean, came about almost by accident. If Admiral Rooke had shown a more aggressive spirit earlier in the campaign, he would not have had to exonerate his name by attacking Gibraltar. Once this decision had been made, luck played into his hand. By the improvidence of the Spaniards the garrison had been reduced to a mere fifty regular soldiers while further detachments of militia, volunteers and invalids brought the whole total up to some 450. Considering its enormous significance and the casualties usually inflicted in eighteenth century battles, the capture of Gibraltar was an almost bloodless victory. Three officers and fifty-eight men were killed on the Allied side (all but one killed by the blowing up of the magazine), while the Spanish lost sixty killed.

Borr's Marines & the first siege of Gibraltar, 1704-1705

The Spanish were not slow to react to the capture of their beloved rock. The Marquis de Villadarias assembled an army of 12,000 men and, with the support of a French fleet, on 22nd October 1704 laid siege to Gibraltar. There was now a very real danger that the Allies would be caught in the same predicament that had befallen the Spanish in August. The total Allied garrison of only 2,300 were now besieged by an army of 12,000, supported by a large French fleet. The bombardment from the sea carried on almost continuously by day and night, inflicting severe damage on the defences. On the 9th November Colonel Nugent, the Governor, and Brigadier-General (as he then was) Fox, overall military commander, were both killed by cannon fire. Command of the garrison and, in particular, Fox's Regiment, was assumed by Major Borr, who was promoted to Colonel.

Jacob Borr was an officer of great bravery but uncertain temper. Before transferring to Fox's Marines he had held an appointment in the Earl of Barrymore's Regiment (later 13th Somerset Foot).

The crisis of the first siege occurred the very next night. A major assault was planned to take place during the hours of darkness, in which a mass attack would be thrown against the west face of the fortress. A few hours before this a party of 500, led by Colonel de Figueroa, landed on the east side of the Rock, in an area now known as Catalan Bay. With great dexterity, this party scaled the near vertical east face, and established themselves near the crest overlooking the fortress. Unfortunately for Figueroa, the main attack failed, leaving his party marooned in its eyrie. As day dawned, Colonel Borr led a spirited counter attack, killing 200 and capturing a further 190 prisoners (including Colonel Figueroa). The remainder managed to scramble down the east face to safety.

The siege continued throughout the winter of 1704-05. Attacks and bombardments became routine; casualties from fighting and disease weakened the already depleted garrison, reducing it to a mere one thousand men. Morale seems to have reached a dangerously low level; indeed, a group of officers actually formed a mutinous conspiracy to yield up the fortress.

But however bad conditions were for the Allies, they were no better for the Spaniards. The winter rains of 1704-05 filled their entrenchments with water, and attack after attack on the walls of the fortress was driven off with heavy casualties. It was the enemy who first gave way. On 18th April, having suffered 10,000 casualties, the French Commander-in-Chief raised the siege. On 3rd August 1705 a fleet under the command of Admiral Sir Cloudesley Shovel put into Gibraltar with a relief garrison of eight battalions. The old garrison of about 6,000 men (including Borr's Marines), which had borne the heat of the siege, was embarked under command of the Earl of Peterborough. Two days later the fleet set sail for Barcelona.

Second attack on Barcelona, 1705

The fleet, under Sir Cloudesley Shovel, arrived off Barcelona on 22nd August. Once there, Peterborough prevaricated and delayed, and it was not till 10th September that he was finally persuaded to land his force. By this time the Spaniards had had ample time to gather their forces. The fighting was fierce but on 4th October the garrison surrendered, leaving the British free to complete the destruction of shipping and dockyard facilities. The ferocity of the action does not seem to have deterred Colonel Borr from picking a quarrel with a brother officer, Lieutenant-Colonel Rodney of Holt's Marines, whom he challenged to a duel, and killed. Even in the somewhat more tolerant early years of the eighteenth century, the authorities did not look kindly on this sort of behaviour. Colonel Borr was temporarily relieved of his duties for such time as his Regiment remained in Barcelona.

The Treaty of Utrecht, 1713

By 1712 the nations involved in the War of the Spanish Succession were weary. The war had reached a stalemate in which the maintenance of considerable fleets and armies was steadily draining the participants white. A congress of all parties assembled in Utrecht on 29th January 1712, determined to bring peace to Europe. On 10th July that year King Philip V of Spain was persuaded to sign an agreement renouncing all rights to the throne of France, thus effectively removing the cause of war. There was still, however, much to be negotiated, not least the sovereignty of Gibraltar. Strange as it may have seemed to later generations, neither the Royal Navy nor the British Army wished to retain the Rock. Firstly, the bay and harbour presented a lee shore to the prevailing westerly winds on which a fleet could all too easily find itself trapped, unable to take action against enemy shipping. Secondly, the Navy realised that any military garrison on the Rock was extremely vulnerable and would require the constant presence of warships in the area for its support – ships that could not easily be spared. Thirdly, before the construction of the Suez Canal many years later, Britain had no particular interest in controlling trade routes through the Straits. Likewise, the Army had no wish to tie down valuable troops on the Rock. Garrisons, shut up in a fortress for long periods, idle for most of the time and deprived of the benefits of living alongside a civilian population, were well known for their unruly behaviour. Furthermore, troops in Gibraltar were quite incapable of dominating the Straits, as no gun then in existence had the necessary range. In short, the retention of Gibraltar did not appeal to the sober stability of the newly elected Whig oligarchy. It would seem that it was only the fickle power of public opinion, demanding the retention of Gibraltar, that swung a reluctant government into sealing the British claim in the Treaty of Utrecht. The Dutch, who had played a major part in both the capture and subsequent defence of Gibraltar, were conveniently sidelined. The rock was to be British, and British alone. In the light of today's political manoeuvrings, it is interesting to read the relevant extract from the Treaty:

> The Catholic King does hereby, for Himself, His heirs and successors, yield to the Crown of Great Britain the full and intire propriety of the Town and Castle of Gibraltar, together with the port, fortifications, and forts thereunto belonging; and He gives up the said propriety, to be held and enjoyed absolutely with all manner of right for ever, without any exception or impediment whatsoever.

Change of title to 32nd Regiment of Foot, 1715

Following the Treaty of Utrecht, action was immediately taken to reduce the size of Britain's army. Among the first regiments to be disbanded (or broken, in the language of the day) were the marines and sea service regiments. These were struck off on 9th November 1713, the men being issued with travel warrants back to their homes, and allowed to retain their uniforms, belts and knapsacks.

The history of Borr's Marines during the next eighteen months is confused by a lack of reliable documentation. It appears that the Regiment never entirely ceased to exist, but was placed on the Irish Establishment. Certainly in 1715 we find it still operating in its marine role, and still under the command of Brigadier-General Borr. On 23rd March 1715 the Regiment ceased officially to be designated by the name of its Colonel, and became instead the 32nd Regiment of Foot. However, old customs die hard in the army, and for the next few years it was variously referred to either by its number or by the name of its current Colonel.

Brigadier-General Borr died in 1723, his place being taken by Brigadier-General Dubourgey, described as 'An old military gentleman of diplomatic merit, who spells rather ill', a criticism that could be levelled at certain officers to this day. Dubourgey died in 1732 and was succeeded by Colonel Thomas Paget, a veteran of the Duke of Marlborough's campaigns on the Rhine and the great-grandfather of one of the Duke of Wellington's most trusted officers, Field-Marshal the Marquis of Anglesey.

* * *

THE 32ND REGIMENT OF FOOT: THE WAR OF THE AUSTRIAN SUCCESSION 1740-1748

In October 1740 The Emperor Charles VI of Austria died, leaving the succession to his daughter, Maria Theresa. This was immediately challenged by a coalition of France and Spain, with the support of Prussia and Bavaria. Once again, Britain was threatened by the development of an overwhelming and hostile power block in Europe.

Unlike other European nations of the eighteenth century, Prussia, under Frederick the Great, maintained a large standing army of 100,000 superbly trained and well equipped troops. He was thus able to take to the field while his adversaries were still involved in the long process of raising recruits and training them for war. On 16th December 1740, without any declaration of war, the Prussian army crossed the frontier into Silesia. It met little opposition, and by the end of the year Frederick had occupied all but a small part of that country, dispersing his army to winter quarters in the towns and villages. By February 1741 the Austrians had succeeded in collecting a sufficiently large field army under Count Neipperg to start the reconquest of Silesia. Heavy snow made it difficult for Frederick to concentrate his forces but, on 10th April, he beat the Austrians decisively at the battle of Mollwitz. Europe suddenly realised that Prussia was a major military power, and that summer France sent Marshal Belleisle to Frederick the Great to negotiate a formal alliance. What had started a few months earlier as the Silesian Adventure had developed into the War of the Austrian Succession: a war that was to engulf all Europe for the next seven years.

The political manoeuvrings during these eighteenth century dynastic wars were so convoluted that it is impossible to describe their ramifications in a few short paragraphs. The part played by the Anglo-Dutch armies may have been modest compared to the vast turmoil that took place in Central Europe, but it is the only part that is strictly relevant to this history of the 32nd Foot.

Dettingen, 1743, & Fontenoy, 1745

A British army, commanded by the Earl of Stair, was despatched to the Low Countries in the summer of 1742. This force, numbering in all about 160,000 men, consisted of 8 regiments of cavalry, 3 regiments of foot guards, 13 regiments of foot (including the 32nd) and a train of artillery. Lord Stair quartered his troops in Ghent and Bruges during the winter of 1742, intending to move towards the Rhine with his Dutch allies the following spring.

It soon became obvious that the Dutch were reluctant to take to the field. Frustrated by their lack of enthusiasm, Lord Stair moved to Coblenz, where he crossed the Rhine to its east bank before starting his long march up the river. There he was soon joined by his King, George II, who took personal command of the British army. However, the great victory at Dettingen on 27th June 1743 owed more to the tenacious courage of the British rank and file than to the leadership of their King. The other great British battle of the war was Fontenoy, fought on 30th April 1745. Thanks to the total lack of support promised by the Dutch, the battle proved an undoubted defeat. However, the discipline and courage of the British infantry ensured that it never became a rout. Indeed, the name of Fontenoy was to become symbolic of the extreme steadiness of British infantry under heavy fire.

As always, disease claimed more deaths than battle. In the autumn of 1747 a soldier of the 32nd wrote:

> We have an Epidemical Disorder Throughout all our allied army which is the Bloody Flux carried several off in a Day, they say the French has the same distemper but more violent. At the end of October the Army went into winter Quarters, many officers proceeded on leave to England.

The Bloody Flux was almost certainly dysentery, caused by poor hygiene and drinking polluted water. At the end of the campaigning season it was fully accepted that the majority of officers disappeared back home. Not so the soldiers who were left to live (or die) in crowded and unsanitary camps.

The Treaty of Aix-La-Chapelle, 1748

The War of the Austrian Succession was brought to an end by the Treaty of Aix-la-Chapelle, which was signed on 24th April 1748. Reading the many complex provisions of the treaty, one is immediately struck by the futility of the war. There was to be a general restitution of all conquests, and the right of Maria Theresa to the Hapsberg succession was confirmed. For Britain, the Treaty of Aix-la-Chapelle signalled the reduction of her army; soldiers were an expensive luxury in peace-time. Fortunately for the 32nd, it was not affected by these cuts.

1753-1807

Internal Security Duties in the Scottish Highlands, 1753-1763

After a tour of garrison duty in Gibraltar from 1749 to 1753, the Regiment returned to Scotland for the next ten years. The Highlands of Scotland remained a seething cauldron of hatred towards all things English. Although no major battles were fought during this period, soldiering there cannot have been a very relaxed occupation.

West Indies, 1763-1773

In 1763 the 32nd crossed the Atlantic to the West Indies, where it remained for a further ten years. Britain was again at war with France, and the islands of the West Indies were strategically important as bases, which had to be denied to any enemy intent on mounting raids against our American Colonies. The French could be beaten in battle; against yellow fever and malaria, however, there was then no defence. These two diseases decimated regiments, leaving even the survivors unfit for further service. No accounts of the state of the 32nd when it returned to England in 1773 now exist. It is probable that an almost entire new complement of recruits would have been needed and that these would have had to be trained from scratch. The Regiment was billeted around Wells, Bath and Salisbury, whence recruiting parties scoured the countryside for suitable young men. After two years, the 32nd was 'Reviewed'. This did not merely consist of a ceremonial parade to demonstrate the bearing and discipline of the new soldiers, but included an extremely comprehensive inspection of every aspect of the regiment's knowledge of tactics, skill at arms and administration, to ensure that it was 'Fit for Service'.

Internal Security Duties in Ireland, 1775-1782

In 1775 the 32nd moved to Ireland. On the way there, the *Rockingham Castle* which was carrying the headquarters, the flank companies and all the women and children was wrecked as she approached Cork harbour. 122 officers and men, 12 women and 14 children, together with the entire crew drowned. The Commanding Officer, Lieutenant-Colonel Campbell, and Captain Edward Parker had transferred to the pilot cutter shortly before the disaster so as to arrive at Cork before the Regiment, in order to supervise the arrangements for its reception. They thus escaped death. In the wreck of the *Rockingham Castle* all the regimental records were lost. Regimental records were required to be produced at each annual inspection, and the absence of those before 1775 had been the subject of repeated adverse comment. Commanding officers appear to have repeatedly written to Horse Guards requesting a copy of the duplicate which should have been held in their archive. One can imagine clerks searching in vain for the missing documents until the matter was finally brought to an end by the Adjutant General, who wrote:

Horse Guards, 24 July 1815

Sir,

I have the honour to acknowledge the receipt of your letter of 22nd inst. with its enclosures, and to state in reply, for the information of the Secretary at War, that under the circumstances therein stated, the Record Book of the 32nd Regiment should commence from the year 1775, with reference to the circumstances therein stated which occurred in that year of the wreck of the Head-Quarter transport, by which the books of the Regiment were lost.

H. Calvert, Adjutant General

Thus the detailed history of the 32nd before the wreck of the *Rockingham Castle* was deemed irretrievably lost.

Affiliation with Cornwall, 1782

In 1782 the 32nd was affiliated to the County of Cornwall, becoming officially known as the 32nd (Cornwall) Regiment of Foot. The idea was that recruits for a regiment would primarily be drawn from specific county areas. The success of this scheme is difficult to assess but, from surviving rolls, it appears that regiments continued to recruit from the areas in which they happened to be stationed when in the British Isles, and that up to a third of all recruits to English regiments came from Ireland (the many Irish regiments recruited entirely from their homeland). The full significance of the Cornish connection was not to be fully realised for another century until, in 1881, the 32nd became the 1st Battalion the Duke of Cornwall's Light Infantry, with its depôt in Bodmin.

West Indies & England, 1792-1800

In 1796 the 32nd returned to the West Indies, spending a year in St Domingo protecting the English population from an uprising of the slaves who were held by the French on their plantations. The Regiment then moved to the Bahamas, today thought of as a tropical paradise, but then ravaged by malaria and yellow fever.

Eroded by disease, the 32nd returned to England to recruit, being stationed at Abingdon, Launceston and Bridgwater in 1800.

Ireland, 1802-1807

From England the Regiment moved to Ireland which, following the success of the French Revolution, was in a state of considerable ferment that culminated in the Irish Rebellion of 1803.

After landing at Waterford towards the latter part of 1802, the Regiment was brought up to the full establishment of 1,000 rank and file by the drafting in of volunteers from English fencible regiments. It then marched to Kilkenny and thence to Dublin in February 1803, where it was quartered when the long-expected rebellion finally exploded in that city on the night of 23rd July. In August the 32nd was ordered to Eniskillen, at the same time detaching its Light Company to Armagh. In the latter part of the eighteenth century and the early nineteenth century light companies were as often as not concentrated into light infantry battalions for operational purposes. Thus it was that for operations against Irish rebel bands the Light Company of the 32nd formed part of the 3rd Light Battalion, commanded by Lieutenant-Colonel Edward Barnes of the 79th Foot.

In July 1805 the 32nd was re-united with its Light Company and marched to Monkstown where, under Lieutenant-Colonel Samuel Hinde, it embarked for passage to South America. After the Regiment had remained on board the transports for a considerable time, the whole plan was changed, the operation was called off and the troops disembarked. For the next two years the Regiment continued in Ireland, being quartered at Kinsale and Charles Fort, and sending occasional detachments to Bandon and Clonakilty. During this period the first draft of 124 men under the command of Captain John Wood arrived from the newly formed 2nd Battalion in England.

Finally, in June 1807 the 32nd, together with the 50th and 82nd Regiments (which formed a brigade commanded by Major-General Sir Brent Spencer), again embarked at Monkstown as part of the force destined to capture the Danish fleet at Copenhagen. This time there was to be no change of plan.

The Army of the Late Eighteenth & Early Nineteenth Centuries

The late eighteenth and early nineteenth centuries saw steady improvements in the British Army, largely brought about by The Duke of York, who had been appalled at the inadequacies of the force that he had commanded in the Low Countries in 1793-94. As Commander-in-Chief he set major reforms in motion, of which perhaps the most important was the much-needed imposition of discipline on the officer corps, whose appalling behaviour was running out of control. An almost universal lack of any concern for the well-being of their soldiers, and their drunken and dissipated style of living were clearly unacceptable.

By 1797 an infantry battalion at full strength consisted of 44 officers, 52 serjeants, 50 corporals, 20 drummers and 950 privates. The organisation allowed for a small headquarters, eight battalion companies, a grenadier company and a light company. The Colonel of the Regiment never commanded in the field, always delegating this to his Lieutenant-Colonel. There were now two majors (the junior one being known as the Second Major), and each company was commanded by a captain. The perk of the colonel, lieutenant-colonel and major drawing the pay for command of three of the companies was abolished, thereby allowing three extra captains to be held on establishment. Finally, the appointment of Serjeant-Major, which had existed under various guises for many years, was officially authorised in 1798.

Officers were required to turn out in strict regimental dress. This consisted of a short-tailed, double-breasted, scarlet coatee (a coat cut to waist level at the front), usually trimmed with gold or silver lace (the 32nd wore gold). A sword belt was worn over the right shoulder on which was mounted a metal 'breast plate', an oval, or later rectangular, gilt or silver plate about 3½in x 2½in, which bore the regimental number. From 1796 all infantry officers carried a standard pattern straight thrusting sword but, in 1803, the grenadier and light infantry company officers were authorised to use a sharply curved Light Cavalry pattern weapon. Up to 1812 officers' head-dress consisted of the black felt cocked hat worn 'fore and aft', but in that year they fell into line with the soldiers, adopting a felt and leather shako which came to be known as the 'Waterloo pattern'. A crimson silk sash was worn round the waist, knotted over the left hip.

Soldiers wore a single-breasted coatee, made from coarse brick-red woollen cloth, with the regimental facings showing on collar and cuffs. There were normally ten strips of regimental lace running horizontally across the chest (the design of this lace was unique to each regiment, and was often of extremely complex design). The rank and file soldier was armed with a flintlock musket officially known as the New Land Pattern Musket, but usually referred to as 'Brown Bess'. The calibre was approximately that of a 12 bore shotgun, but was deliberately made slightly larger than the standard French calibre, so that our troops could use captured French ammunition, whereas they could not use ours. The musket could be fitted with a 17 in. triangular socket bayonet, which was, in practice, invariably fixed throughout any action. Serjeants, whose task in battle was to command rather than become involved in the complicated process of re-loading, carried a nine foot pike. Ammunition and bayonet were carried on the right and left hips respectively, supported by broad buff leather straps, which crossed in the centre of the chest. A regimental breast plate similar to that worn by officers was positioned where the two straps crossed. A large wooden water canteen hung on a separate shoulder strap just behind the bayonet. A stiff, rectangular, black-painted canvas knapsack carried on the soldier's back contained all his spare clothing and worldly goods, while to it was strapped his blanket and mess tins.

Soldiers discarded their cocked hats in 1800, when they were issued with the First Pattern Shako, a heavy cylindrical leather cap with a peak and a neck flap, which could be worn either hooked up or let down to protect the neck against rain and snow. In 1806 this was superseded by a similar but lighter pattern made of felt, which soldiers often painted to render it waterproof. Finally in 1812 the so-called Waterloo Pattern, with its upstanding leather front, was introduced. All these patterns of head-dress were deliberately made cylindrical rather than bell-topped, so that, in the thick fog of battle, British soldiers could be instantly distinguished from their French enemies.

By the time of the Napoleonic Wars British infantry was renowned for its discipline in battle and for its exceptional standard of musketry. The British usually fought in ranks only two deep, thereby being able to employ every single musket against the enemy (as opposed to the French who fought in solid blocks of men in which only the leading two ranks could fire their weapons). The two-deep line, although presenting the maximum firepower, was vulnerable to being broken, unless the individual soldiers showed great courage and discipline. It is to the credit of the officers that they appear to have shown absolute confidence in the ability of their soldiers to fight in this seemingly fragile formation.

Cavalry attacks were met by the formation of a square, presenting an impenetrable fence of bayonets on each of its sides. The square was, however, desperately vulnerable to canon fire, so that immediately the cavalry threat was past, battalions quickly re-deployed into line. The speed of changing formations over rough ground in the smoke and chaos of battle was of paramount importance. A battalion caught by the enemy in a state of flux could all too easily be annihilated. The British infantryman was trained first on the barrack square and then in open countryside, to a very high degree of skill, enabling him to perform these complex drills with speed and precision.

Mention has been made of the smoke and fog of battle. It must be realised that so long as black powder was used as the propellant for small-arms and cannon, the discharge of these weapons produced dense clouds of white oily smoke. On still days a battery of guns or a battalion of infantry would be totally enveloped in a thick impenetrable fog after the first few rounds. Friend and foe would often only become visible to each other when very close, hence the importance of immediately identifiable uniforms. In spite of these safeguards, cases of friend firing upon friend were not uncommon.

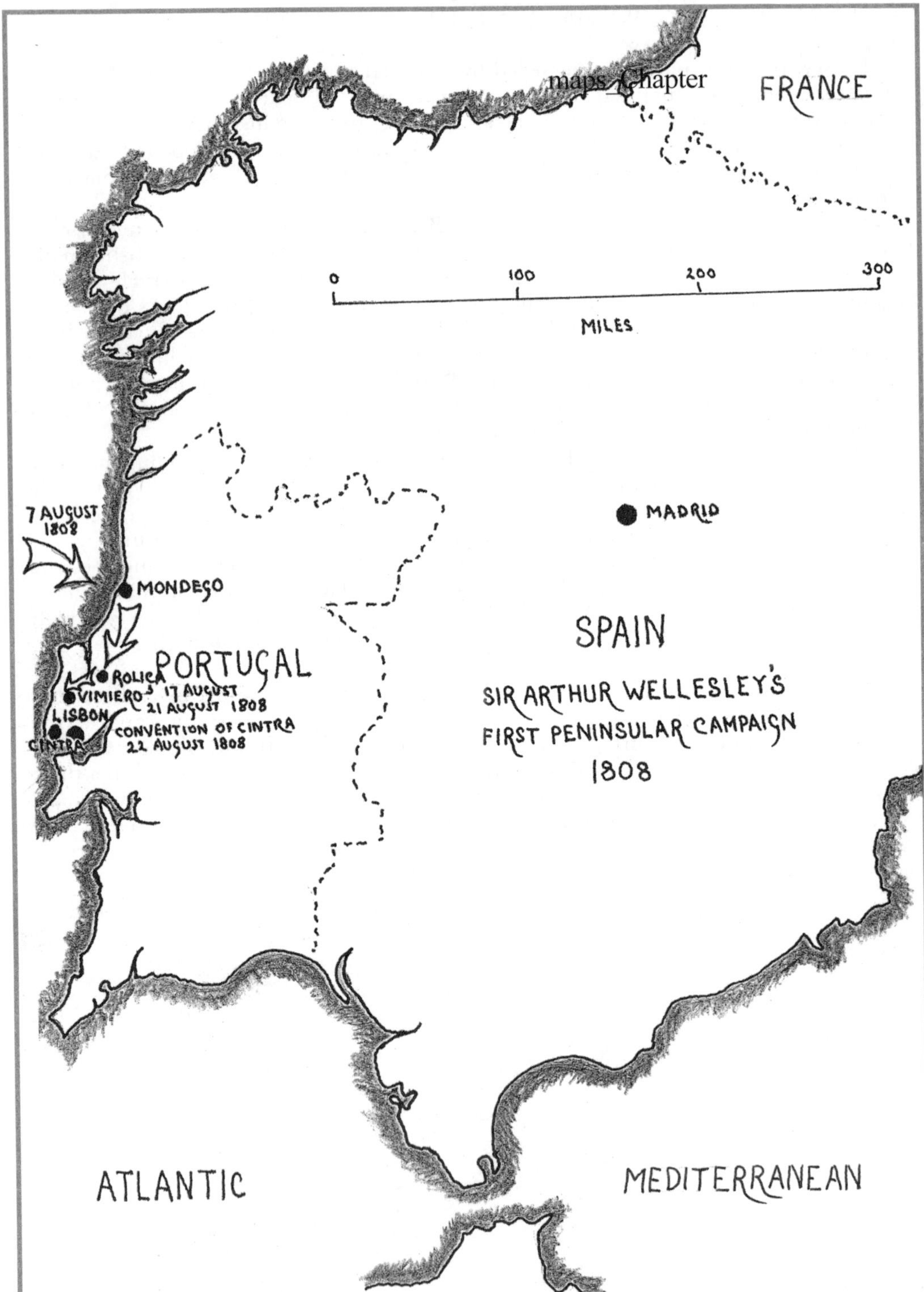
maps_Chapter
FRANCE
0
100
200
300
MILES
MADRID
7 AUGUST
1808
MONDEGO
SPAIN
PORTUGAL
ROLICA
VIMIERO
17 AUGUST
21 AUGUST 1808
LISBON
CINTRA
CONVENTION OF CINTRA
22 AUGUST 1808
SIR ARTHUR WELLESLEY'S
FIRST PENINSULAR CAMPAIGN
1808
ATLANTIC
MEDITERRANEAN

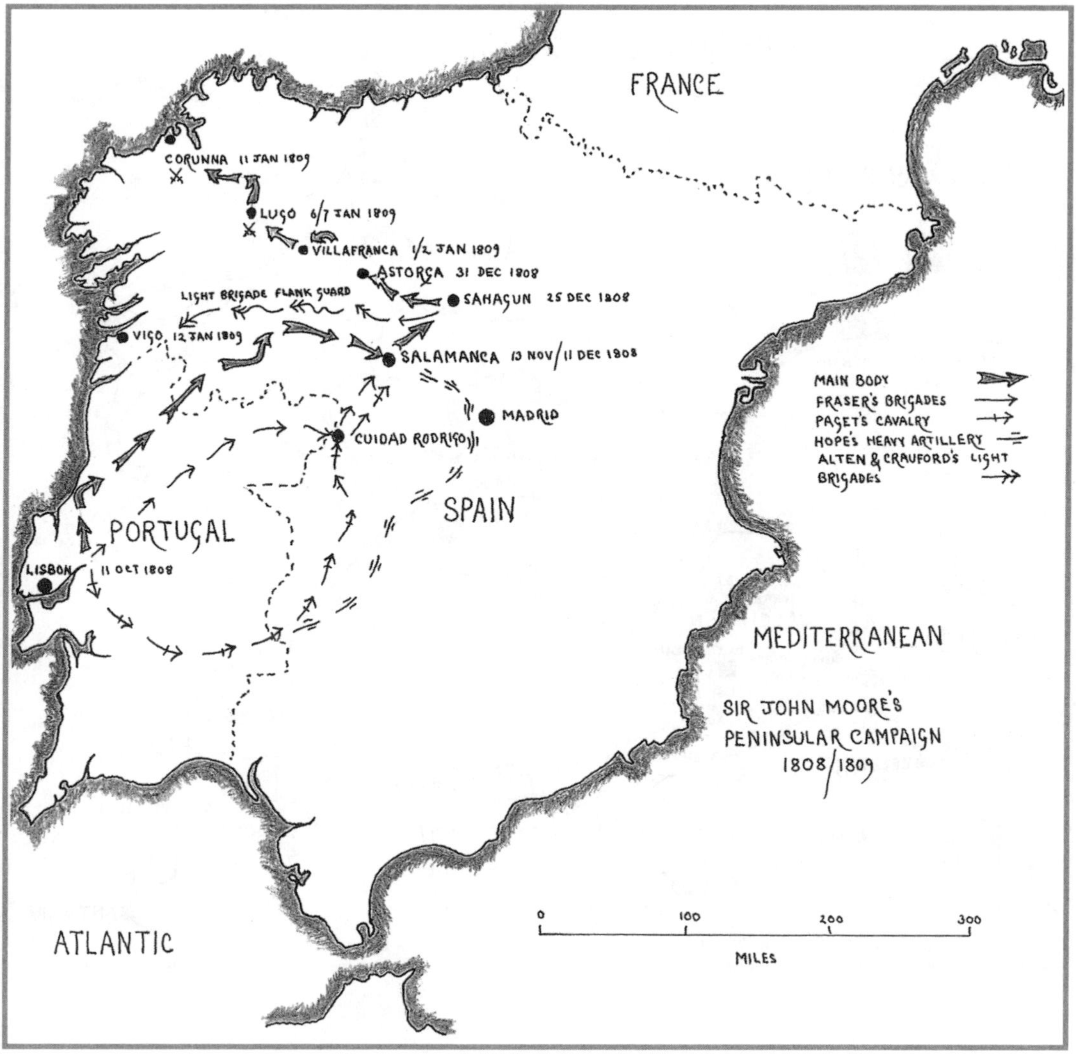

FRANCE
CORUNNA 11 JAN 1809
LUGO 6/7 JAN 1809
VILLAFRANCA 1/2 JAN 1809
ASTORGA 31 DEC 1808
LIGHT BRIGADE FLANK GUARD
SAHAGUN 25 DEC 1808
VIGO 12 JAN 1809
SALAMANCA 13 NOV/11 DEC 1808
MADRID
CUIDAD RODRIGO
PORTUGAL
SPAIN
LISBON
11 OCT 1808
MAIN BODY
FRASER'S BRIGADES
PAGET'S CAVALRY
HOPE'S HEAVY ARTILLERY
ALTEN & CRAUFORD'S LIGHT BRIGADES
MEDITERRANEAN
SIR JOHN MOORE'S PENINSULAR CAMPAIGN 1808/1809
0
100
200
300
MILES
ATLANTIC

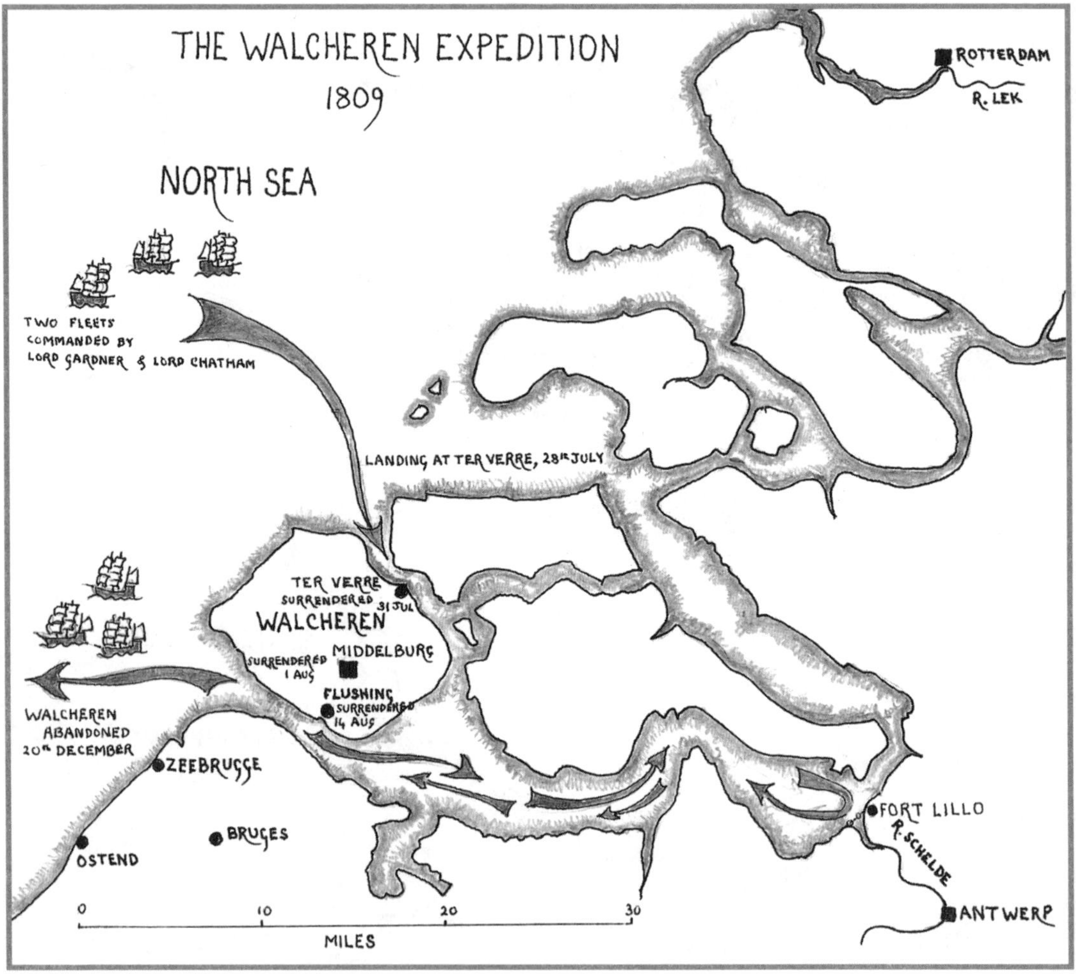
THE WALCHEREN EXPEDITION
1809
NORTH SEA
TWO FLEETS
COMMANDED BY
LORD GARDNER & LORD CHATHAM
LANDING AT TER VERRE, 28TH JULY
TER VERRE
SURRENDERED 31 JUL
WALCHEREN
MIDDELBURG
SURRENDERED
1 AUG
FLUSHING
SURRENDERED
14 AUG
WALCHEREN
ABANDONED
20TH DECEMBER
ZEEBRUGGE
BRUGES
OSTEND
ROTTERDAM
R. LEK
FORT LILLO
R. SCHELDE
ANTWERP
0
10
20
30
MILES

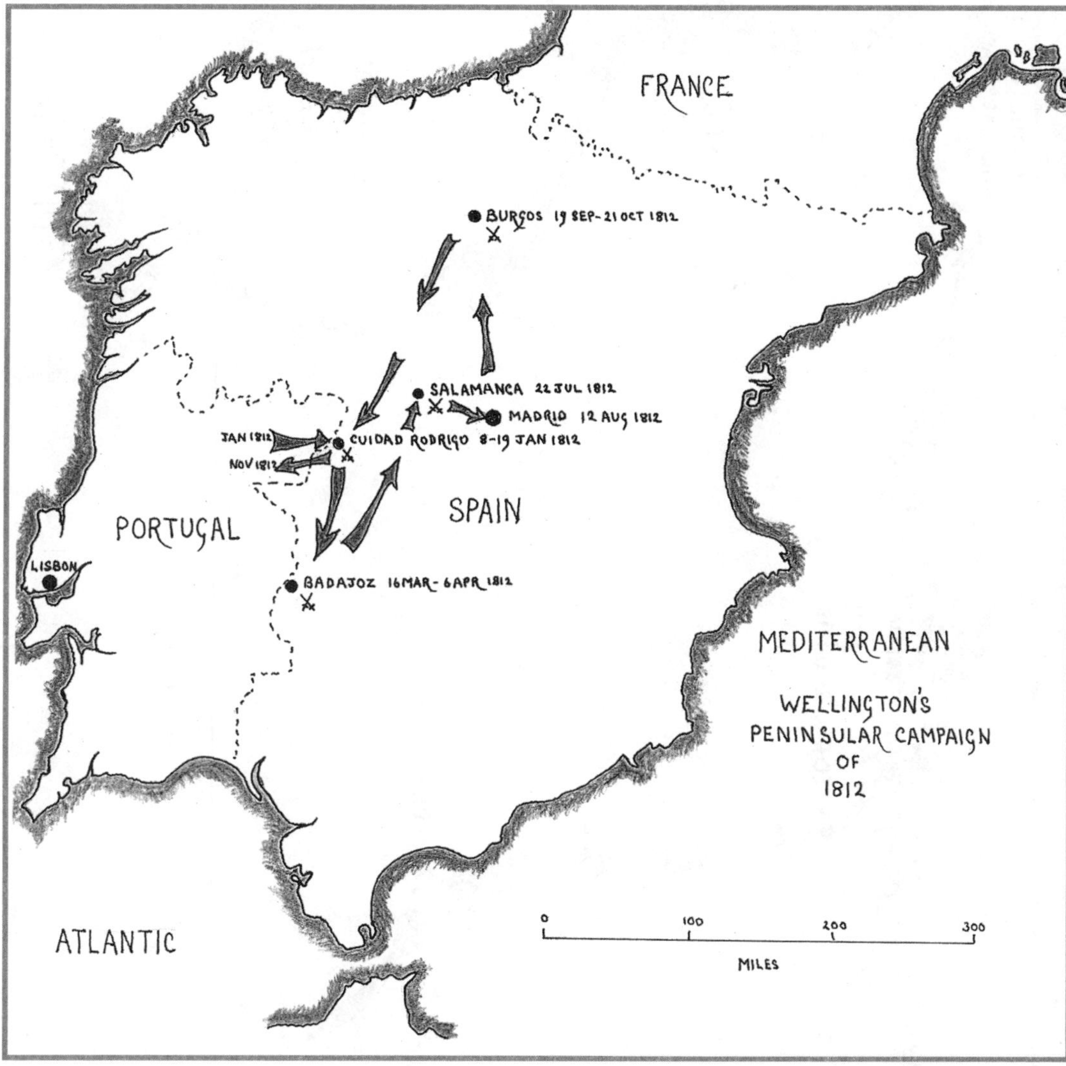
FRANCE
BURGOS 19 SEP-21 OCT 1812
SALAMANCA 22 JUL 1812
MADRID 12 AUG 1812
JAN 1812
CUIDAD RODRIGO 8-19 JAN 1812
NOV 1812
SPAIN
PORTUGAL
LISBON
BADAJOZ 16 MAR-6 APR 1812
MEDITERRANEAN
WELLINGTON'S
PENINSULAR CAMPAIGN
OF
1812
0
100
200
300
MILES
ATLANTIC

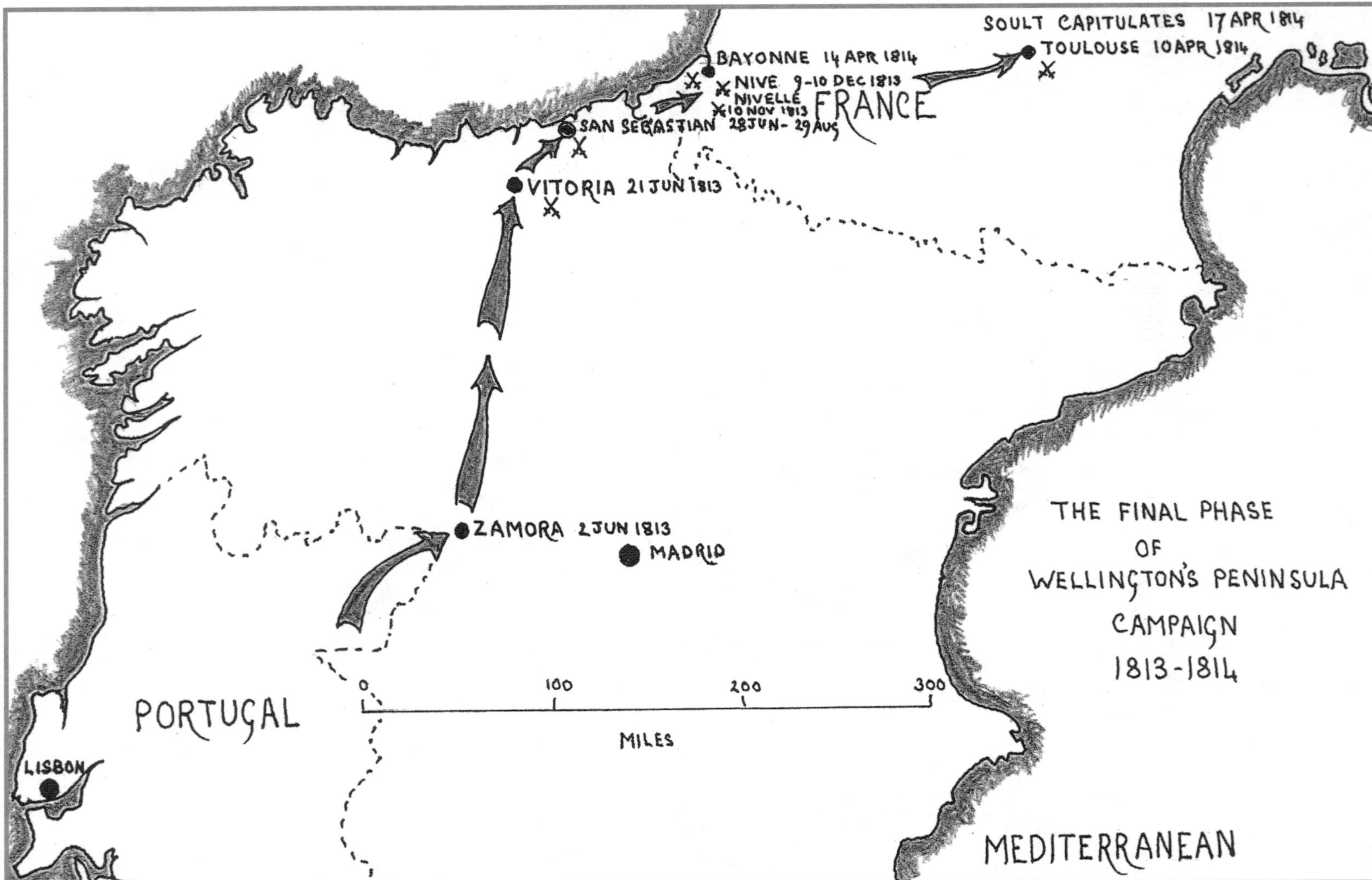
SOULT CAPITULATES 17 APR 1814
TOULOUSE 10 APR 1814
BAYONNE 14 APR 1814
NIVE 9-10 DEC 1813
NIVELLE 10 NOV 1813
FRANCE
SAN SEBASTIAN 28 JUN - 29 AUG
VITORIA 21 JUN 1813
ZAMORA 2 JUN 1813
MADRID
PORTUGAL
LISBON
0
100
200
300
MILES
MEDITERRANEAN
THE FINAL PHASE
OF
WELLINGTON'S PENINSULA
CAMPAIGN
1813-1814

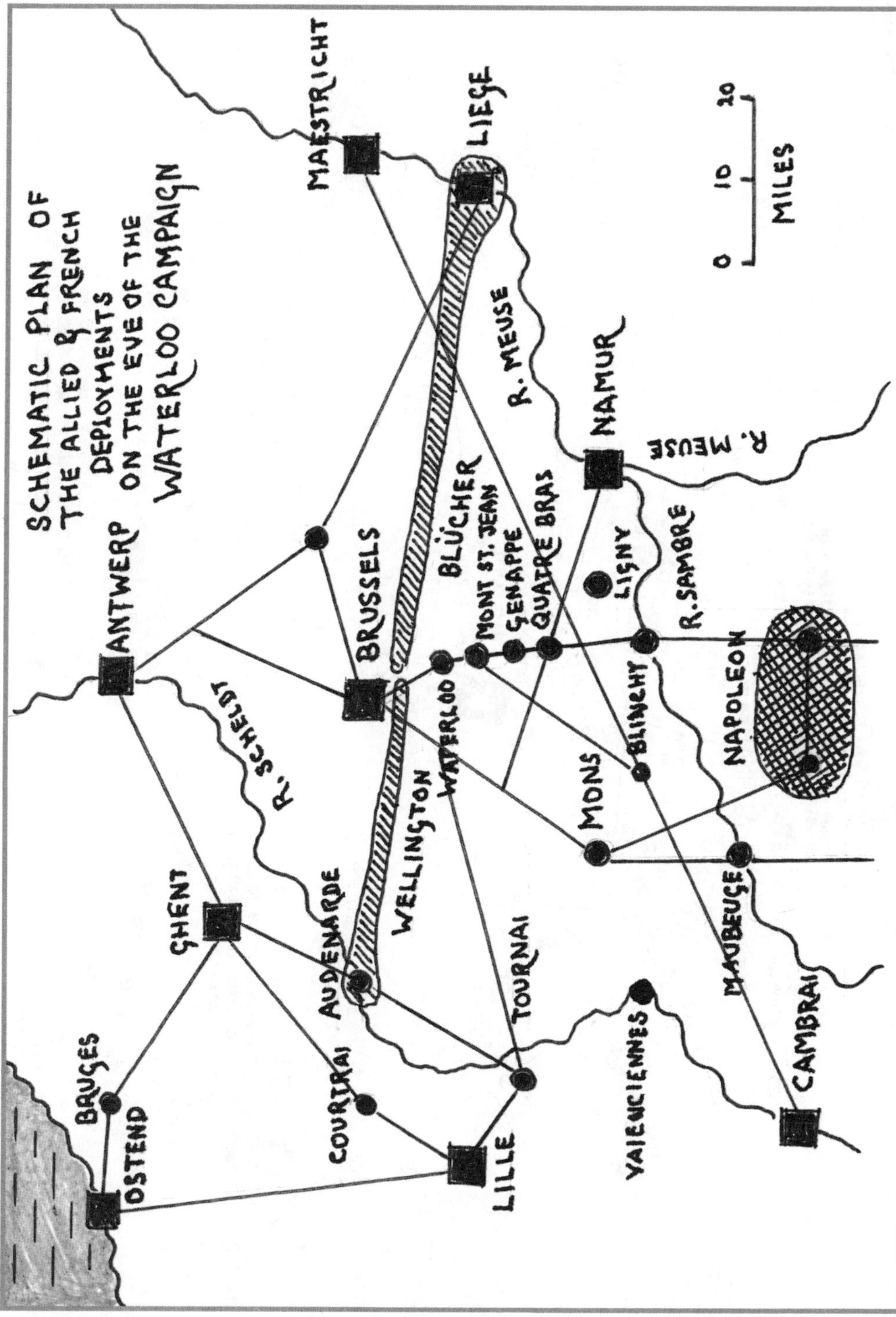
SCHEMATIC PLAN OF
THE ALLIED & FRENCH
DEPLOYMENTS
ON THE EVE OF THE
WATERLOO CAMPAIGN
MAESTRICHT
LIEGE
ANTWERP
BRUSSELS
BLÜCHER
R. MEUSE
NAMUR
R. MEUSE
MONT ST. JEAN
GENAPPE
QUATRE BRAS
LIGNY
R. SAMBRE
R. SCHELDT
WATERLOO
WELLINGTON
MONS
BLINCHY
NAPOLEON
GHENT
AUDENARDE
TOURNAI
MAUBEUGE
BRUGES
OSTEND
COURTRAI
LILLE
VALENCIENNES
CAMBRAI
0
10
20
MILES

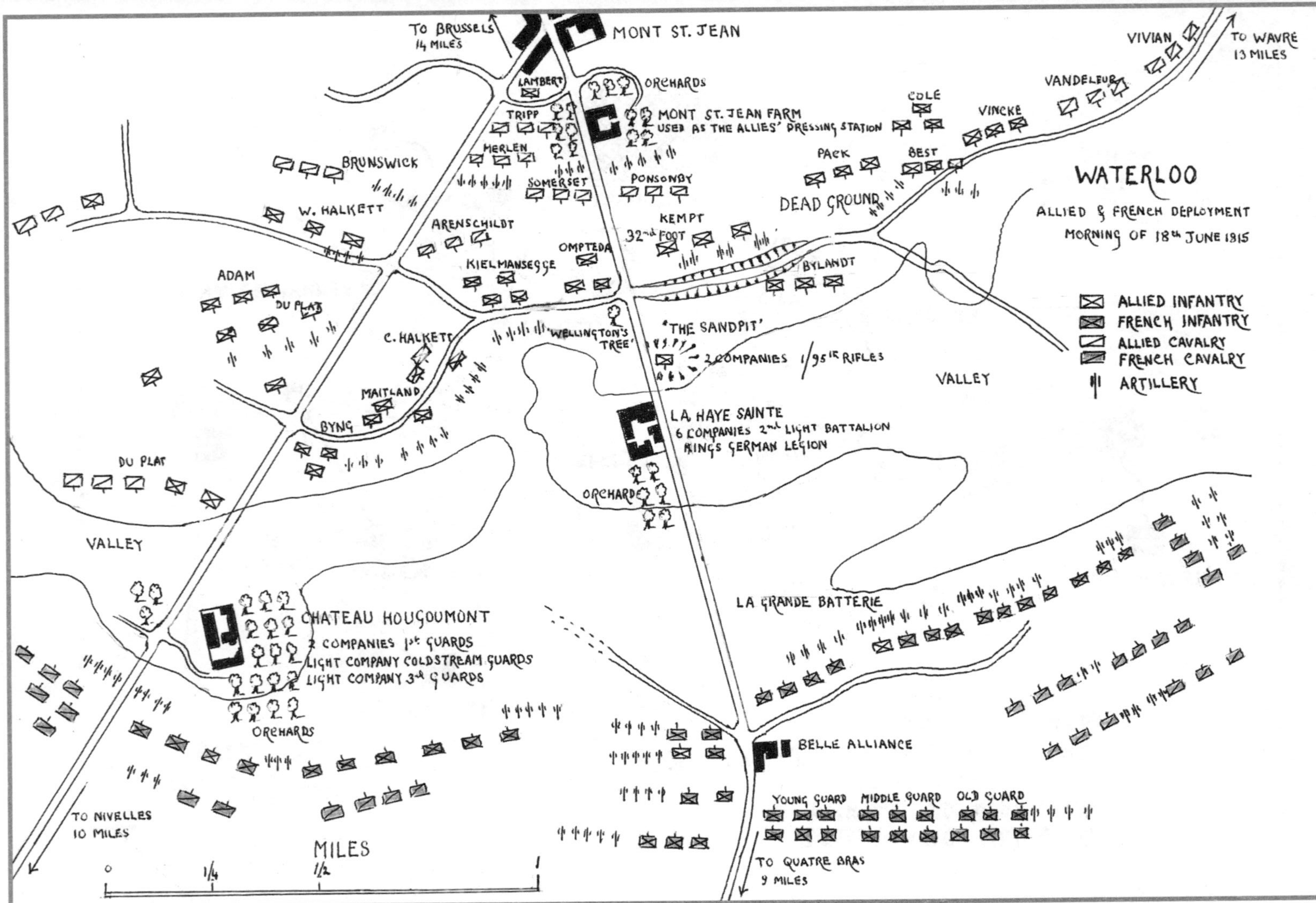
WATERLOO
ALLIED & FRENCH DEPLOYMENT
MORNING OF 18th JUNE 1815
ALLIED INFANTRY
FRENCH INFANTRY
ALLIED CAVALRY
FRENCH CAVALRY
ARTILLERY
TO BRUSSELS 14 MILES
MONT ST. JEAN
TO WAVRE 13 MILES
VIVIAN
VANDELEUR
VINCKE
COLE
BEST
PACK
LAMBERT
ORCHARDS
MONT ST. JEAN FARM
USED AS THE ALLIES' DRESSING STATION
TRIPP
MERLEN
SOMERSET
PONSONBY
BRUNSWICK
W. HALKETT
ARENSCHILDT
KEMPT
32nd FOOT
DEAD GROUND
OMPTEDA
KIELMANSEGGE
BYLANDT
ADAM
DU PLAT
'THE SANDPIT'
C. HALKETT
'WELLINGTON'S TREE'
2 COMPANIES 1/95th RIFLES
VALLEY
MAITLAND
BYNG
LA HAYE SAINTE
6 COMPANIES 2nd LIGHT BATTALION
KINGS GERMAN LEGION
DU PLAT
ORCHARD
VALLEY
LA GRANDE BATTERIE
CHATEAU HOUGOUMONT
2 COMPANIES 1st GUARDS
LIGHT COMPANY COLDSTREAM GUARDS
LIGHT COMPANY 3rd GUARDS
ORCHARDS
BELLE ALLIANCE
YOUNG GUARD
MIDDLE GUARD
OLD GUARD
TO NIVELLES 10 MILES
MILES
0
1/4
1/2
1
TO QUATRE BRAS 9 MILES

2
The Napoleonic Wars, 1807-1815

As a result of French aggressive military might on the Continent, the British Army was considerably expanded by the formation of 2nd Battalions. The 2/32nd was raised at Launceston in 1804. It was primarily used for garrison duties, particularly in Guernsey and Ireland, but also provided large reinforcement drafts to the 1/32nd throughout the Napoleonic Wars. The 2/32nd was disbanded in 1814, having performed a vital, if unspectacular role for ten years.

The 1/32nd took part in operations throughout the Napoleonic Wars and fought in every phase in which the British Army was involved in Europe. These phases can best be summarised as follows.

Expedition to Copenhagen, 1807

Although not at war with Denmark, a British amphibious force, which included the 1/32nd, landed at Copenhagen in early August 1807, with the aim of seizing the Danish Navy and all naval stores held in the dockyard. Lieutenant-General Lord Cathcart, who commanded the land troops, captured Copenhagen on 6th September without undue difficulty. On 21st October the force re-embarked and returned to England, taking with it all the Danish ships loaded with all the stores from the dockyard. The value of the ships and stores was estimated at £4.5 million (equivalent to about £900 million today), but because Britain was not at war with Denmark, the British Government refused, in its usual parsimonious way, to grant prize money to those responsible for the capture.

Gibraltar & Sicily, 1807-1808

In December 1807 the 1/32nd embarked on a Secret Expedition. Whatever the mission of this expedition may have been is now irrelevant, because shortly after setting sail the transports were scattered by a violent storm. Most eventually found sanctuary in various Channel ports, but the ship carrying Lieutenant-Colonel

Hinde and his headquarters managed to make Gibraltar, where they were subsequently joined by other ships carrying small groups of the Regiment. In March 1808 those who had reached Gibraltar embarked for Sicily, where the whole expedition had originally been destined as a major reinforcement. While in Sicily this element of the 1/32nd was stationed in Palermo, Messina and Syracuse.

Meanwhile the main body arrived in Gibraltar under the command of Major William Johnson, where it was employed in garrison duties. At last, in June of that year the Battalion was re-united in Gibraltar. How one sympathises with Lieutenant-Colonel Hinde, who for seven months had had his command scattered he knew not where! The Battalion moved by sea for the short journey to Cadiz, arriving there on the day that Spain went to war against France, and thus witnessing the Spanish shore batteries opening fire on the French ships in the harbour. After remaining in Cadiz for six weeks, it re-embarked to join Major-General Sir Arthur Wellesley's army at Montego Bay in Portugal.

THE FIRST PENINSULAR CAMPAIGN, 1808-1809

Battles of Roliça & Vimiera, & the Convention of Cintra

The 1/32nd was actively involved in the fighting throughout the first and second Peninsular campaigns, being reinforced when necessary with drafts from the 2/32nd at home.

Under Lieutenant-General Sir Arthur Wellesley a British Expeditionary Force, including the 1/32nd, landed at Montego Bay in Portugal at the beginning of August 1808. Moving quickly inland, it made contact with the French army at Leira on 15th August, where a minor skirmish took place. Two days later Wellesley attacked the French in earnest at Roliça (Roleia). Inspite of holding an extremely strong defensive position, the French were driven off, albeit with heavy losses to both sides. Wellesley continued the advance and again caught up with the French army at Vimiera. The French took the initiative, driving in simultaneous attacks on several parts of the British line. These were all held until such time as the French were seen to be tiring, whereupon the British counter-attacked with such determination that the French were routed, abandoning thirteen of their twenty-three guns and much of their transport. Wellesley immediately prepared to pursue the beaten enemy to Torres Vedras, where he planned to destroy it. However, by this time General Sir Harry Burrard, an officer senior to Wellesley, had arrived on the scene. He advised caution, especially as General Sir Hew Dalrymple was known to be on his way from Gibraltar to take command of the army. Wellesley had to defer to his superior officer. When

Dalrymple arrived on 22nd August, he immediately despatched a flag of truce to the retreating French army, offering safe conduct back to France with all its baggage, transport, guns and horses. This pact, known as the Convention of Cintra, was perhaps the most pusillanimous in the entire history of the British Army. It allowed the defeated French army to withdraw intact and thus prolonged the campaign to free Spain from her oppressor. To add insult to injury, the Royal Navy was ordered to transport this French Army back to France. The Convention of Cintra outraged British opinion. The three generals, Dalrymple, Burrard and Wellesley, were immediately ordered home to face an enquiry. They were greeted with hissing and booing whenever they appeared in public. However, Wellesley, who had from the first counselled offensive action, was eventually exonerated from blame.

Advance to Madrid, 1808

In September 1808 General Sir John Moore was sent out from England to take command of the Army in Portugal, with the task of liberating Madrid. Cautiously he advanced into Spain. In the middle of December news reached him that a much larger French army was moving round his flank with the aim of cutting his line of communication to the sea. Moore took the only sensible course open to him and at Sahagun, on Christmas Day 1808, turned about and started the 250 mile retreat to Corunna. The mountains through which his army had to move are daunting even in the summer; as winter closed in they became desolate wastelands of unimaginable misery. Torrential rain turned to sleet and then to snow as the weary soldiers toiled up through the narrow passes. With soaked, frozen clothing, hundreds died of hypothermia. Discipline all but collapsed, and every village was sacked in a frantic search for drink. Only the rear-guard, constantly in contact with the pursuing French, maintained their disciplined fighting spirit. Little is known of how the 32nd Foot fared in the retreat. It undoubtedly experienced a full share of the appalling suffering, but this may possibly have been alleviated by the fact that their brigade commander was Major-General Roland Hill, a brilliant soldier, who was later considered by Wellington to be one of the few senior officers in whom he could trust implicitly.

The battle of Corunna, 1809

The army reached Corunna on 11th January 1809 but had to wait three days for the arrival of the transports with their naval escorts. Embarkation was immediately commenced and by 16th January all the sick and wounded had been put aboard. At midday the reserve brigades moved down to the docks, leaving only a thin defensive line on the high ground commanding Corunna. A few more hours and Moore and his army would have made their escape. This was not to be. Suddenly the French attacked and the reserve were hurriedly marched back to the heights. Gone was the ill discipline of the retreat; at last the British were to fight their opponents in a pitched battle.

The battle, fought on the high ground overlooking Corunna harbour, lasted from early afternoon till late evening. Casualties on both sides were heavy and Moore, who had led the army to safety, was mortally wounded. The French, however, had been fought to a standstill so that, leaving their fires burning, the British army could steal away to the waiting ships.

Back in England, both Houses of Parliament passed a resolution praising the 1/32nd 'for its distinguished discipline, firmness and valour in the Battle of Corunna'.

The Walcheren Expedition, 1809

The Regiment assembled at Horsham, was re-equipped and brought up to strength with drafts from the 2/32nd and the Militia and was passed 'Fit for Service'. It did not have long to wait, for in July 1809 an amphibious force of 40,000 soldiers, with some 100 naval vessels, was despatched to destroy the French garrison on the island of Walcheren off the Dutch coast. Although the British achieved their aim, the cost in terms of human life was high. In the nineteenth century the low-lying areas of Holland provided an ideal breeding ground for the anopheline mosquito. Losses from enemy action in the campaign were insignificant but losses from malaria were appalling, even by the standards of the day. The 1/32nd were not affected as badly as many regiments; even so, between 1st August and 20th December 1809, it lost about 350 men from malaria out of a total strength of 579. On its return to England it was quartered on the Sussex Downs and then in Guernsey, where it again received considerable drafts from the 2/32nd and the Militia, which brought its strength up to more than 600 men. As is now well known, malaria is a disease which, once it has affected an individual, will reoccur for many years. The contamination of the British Army with malaria was to have a profound effect on its future health in the second Peninsular campaign. A very high rate of sickness was always to bedevil Wellington's army. The ailment from which the soldiers suffered in the Peninsula was then referred to as 'the ague'; today it would be called recurring malaria.

THE SECOND PENINSULAR CAMPAIGN 1811-1814

On 24th June 1811 the 1/32nd again embarked for service in the Peninsula. Wellesley, now Lord Wellington, had been completely exonerated from the fiasco of the Convention of Cintra and was in command of the British Expeditionary Force. It would not be an overstatement to call Wellington a military genius. He never moved his army till he had secured his lines of communication and a firm logistic base; he was never frightened of retreating should the tactical situation demand it; and, above all else, he was a master of the battle-field with an almost uncanny feel for a battle, which enabled him to be in exactly the right place to influence events.

The battle of Salamanca, July 1812

The fortress of Salamanca was stormed on 27th June 1812. When a breach had been smashed in the defences by heavy cannon, a party of volunteers, known as the 'Forlorne Hope', was called upon to lead the assault. Although casualties were often catastrophic, there was never a shortage of volunteers. At Salamanca, Ensign Newton of the 1/32nd led the Forlorne Hope, which achieved complete success. The fortress surrendered that evening and the French then retired north behind the River Douro.

Although later overshadowed by Waterloo, the Battle of Salamanca was perhaps Wellington's greatest victory, demonstrating his outstanding powers of generalship. The battle is also of special significance to the current Light Infantry as all its forebears except the Somerset Light Infantry were involved. It is today celebrated as the principle battle honour of the Regiment.

Wellington was opposed by the skilled and experienced Marshal Auguste de Marmont. The Allied army was 51,939 strong, slightly larger than Marmont's 49,647 men, but not significantly so, bearing in mind that Wellington's force included 21,359 comparatively unreliable Portuguese and Spanish troops.

On 17th July Marmont had crossed the Douro, and started his forty-five mile march down the Guarena valley towards Salamanca. Wellington was initially caught off balance by Marmont, who crossed the river at the least expected point, but quickly recovered, closely shadowing the French column as it moved south. Both armies marched on parallel courses, often less than a mile apart, watching each other intently, each ready to exploit the slightest error made by their adversary. Wellington and Marmont were, however, far too experienced to commit tactical mistakes, so apart from some skirmishing on 18th July, the opposing columns continued on their ways without making actual contact. During the march Wellington came under pressure from his generals to attack, but not a man to be unduly influenced by his subordinates, he bided his time. If a suitable opportunity arose he would indeed attack; if not, he would abandon Salamanca and fall back to the fortress of Ciudad Rodrigo in Portugal. In anticipation of this latter course, he ordered his baggage train to start withdrawing to the west. The French were quick to observe this operation, interpreting it as the preliminary to a general retreat. Marmont therefore decided that he would cross the River Tormes, outflank Wellington to the south and then swing north, thereby cutting his line of retreat. In this lay the seeds of Marmont's defeat.

The two armies crossed the Tormes simultaneously a few miles east of Salamanca on the evening of 21st July. As darkness fell, the area was hit by a violent storm. Captain Harry Ross-Lewin of the 32nd described this night of misery:

> With the darkness the rain descended in torrents, and a terrific thunderstorm burst over our head; peal succeeded peal with increasing vehemence; the electric fluid absolutely hissed through the air; and such was the vividness of the flashes, that at one time I was deprived of sight for a few moments. The horses of the 5th dragoon guards became dreadfully frightened, broke their pickets, and ran over the men who were stretched on the ground, inflicting severe injuries on several of them.

Nevertheless, Wellington's army appear to have been little disheartened by their soaking, and the hot sun of the following morning soon dried their clothing. Marmont continued his move south, closely shadowed by Wellington. The countryside over which the Allies were manoeuvring consisted of a rolling grassy plain, bordered on the east by a low undulating ridge and on the south by a similar ridge, the Monte de Azan. Between these two right-angled ridges stood two very much more prominent features: the Lesser Arapile, and the Greater Arapile half a mile further south. When Wellington had conducted his reconnaissance in the heavy dawn mist of 22nd July, he had failed to appreciate the tactical importance of the Greater Arapile. Its significance was not lost on Marmont, who promptly ordered General Bonnet to occupy it with his 8th Division. Shortly afterwards Marmont established his headquarters on this hill, from which he believed the whole of the Allied positions should have been visible. Wellington, however, by the skilful use of ground, was still able to hide much of his army from French observation.

Early in the afternoon Marmont despatched General Maucune's 5th Division to swing west along Wellington's south flank. The 5th Division was to be followed by Brigadier-General Thornière's 7th Division, which was presumably intended to secure the ground between Maucune and Bonnet. However, for reasons never established, Thornière pressed on west past Maucune. Marmont and Wellington both realised the significance of this error. The moment that Wellington had been patiently awaiting for the last six days had arrived. Seeing the gap opening between Maucune and Bonnet, he is alleged to have thrown a chicken leg he happened to be eating over his shoulder, exclaiming "By God, that will do, and I'll attack them directly." Mounting his horse, he galloped off to brief his divisional commanders personally, and to set the battle in motion.

For his part, Marmont had sent aides-de-camp hurrying to General Clausel with orders to bring his 2nd Division forward at all possible speed to close the gap, while he himself prepared to mount his horse to sort out the situation on the Monte de Azan. This was never to happen, for at that moment Marmont was severely wounded by a shell. Soon after, Clausel arrived on the summit to take command, only to be wounded himself. Thus at this critical moment the French were deprived of their high command.

The subsequent battle was fought with typical Wellingtonian precision. Sadly, Ensign Newton was killed leading the advance party in the initial stage of the battle. Slowly and remorselessly the 2nd, 5th and 7th Divisions were driven back, off their high ground, retreating in disorder to the scrub-covered hills to the south east. General Ferey's 3rd Division attempted to stem the retreat, making a gallant rear-guard stand on a steep grassy ridge known as El Sierres. The 32nd played a prominent part in driving him off this exceptionally strong position. Ross-Lewin later wrote:

It was half past seven when the 6th Division, under General Clinton was ordered to advance a second time, supported by the 3rd and 5th Divisions. The ground over which we had to pass was a remarkably clear slope, like the *glacis* of a fortification – most favourable for the defensive fire of the enemy, and disadvantageous to the assailants, but the division advanced towards the position with perfect steadiness and confidence. A craggy ridge, on which the French infantry was drawn up, rose so abruptly that they could fire four or five deep; but we had approached within two hundred yards of them before the fire of musketry began, which was by far the heaviest that I have ever witnessed, and was accompanied by constant discharges of grape. An uninterrupted blaze was then maintained, so that the crest of the hill seemed to be a long streak of flame. Our men came down to the charging position, and commenced firing from that level, at the same time keeping their touch to the right, so that the gaps opened by the enemy fire were instantly filled up. At the first volley that we received, about eighty men of the right wing of my regiment fell to the rear in one group; the commanding officer immediately rode up to know the cause, and found they were all wounded.

Ross-Lewin was himself seriously wounded in the arm during this fight. His account speaks of an experienced and highly disciplined regiment, which had been continuously in action for seven hours, carrying out a bold and bloody assault.

The battle was over. Only General Foy's 1st division, holding the French right had not been in action. Now it provided a rear-guard which allowed the disintegrating remnants of the French army to escape. Marmont's army had been routed, suffering 12,435 casualties, not including some 4,000 prisoners. Wellington's total casualties amounted to 4,809.

The 32nd lost 137 men, killed and wounded, out of an initial strength of 609. The Regiment captured an enemy howitzer and a field gun on the El Sierres height, besides recovering its bass-drum, which had been lost during the retreat to Corunna. In his despatches Wellington gave unusually high praise to the 32nd, writing: '. . . particularly Colonel Hinde of the 32nd Regiment and Ensign Newton, of the 32nd Regiment, who distinguished himself in the attack on the night of the 23rd instant, and volunteered to lead the advanced party in the attack of the 27th.'

*

In August 1812 the fortress of Burgos was besieged. In spite of three assaults, no progress could be made and, hearing that a very large French relieving force was approaching, Wellington broke off the siege and withdrew to the more secure defensive position of Salamanca. The entire British force, complete with guns and baggage, withdrew on the night of 21st-22nd October 1812 under the noses of the French garrison. It was a dark night, straw and dung had been spread on the bridges to deaden the sound of wheels and horses, and, with the rear-guard firing the occasional shot, the French were unaware of the British withdrawal until too late.

The British army spent the winter of 1812 secure behind the lines of Salamanca.

Battle of the Pyrenees, 1813

The following spring Wellington advanced again and by mid July 1813 had arrived at the foothills of the Pyrenees. On 28th July the British Army fought the Battle of the Pyrenees, their last battle on

Spanish soil. The 1/32nd played a crucial role, racing for command of a ridge as the French advanced up the other side. They reached the crest first and were able to pour a devastating volley into the enemy. During the ensuing fighting their Commanding Officer, Lieutenant-Colonel John Wood, was killed. On 2nd August 1813, the vanguard of the British army moved into France.

Battles of Nivelle, Nive & Orthes, 1813-1814, & Ireland, 1814

The year of 1813 was crowned by two further victories, at Nivelle and Nive, in both of which the 1/32nd was heavily involved. Finally on 27th January 1814 the Regiment went into action for the last time at Orthes. It had been continuously in the field for two and a half years and was by this time dressed in rags and ill equipped. It therefore moved back to the ordnance depôt that had been established at St Jean-de-Luz. Having received new clothing and equipment, it set out to rejoin the army at Toulouse (a march of about eight days). However, the last battle of the war had been fought and France had sued for peace. This magnificent army that Wellington forged, with which he had beaten every enemy force opposed to it in the field, was about to be dispersed.

The 32nd, now authorised to emblazon its Colours with the battle honours Roleia, Vimiera, Salamanca, Pyrenees, Nivelle, Nive, Orthes and Peninsula, made its way back to the French coast and thence to Cork in Ireland. There the 1/32nd and 2/32nd amalgamated. The 2/32nd had carried out a vital, if unspectacular role. Quite apart from providing garrison troops on the vulnerable Channel Islands, it had carried out a continuous recruiting campaign which had enabled it to despatch drafts to the 1/32nd in the Peninsula totalling 6 officers and 881 soldiers.

The American War of 1812-1814

Since 1809 the United States of America had followed a policy laid down by the so-called 'Non-Intercourse Law', under which trade with Great Britain was forbidden. Although this operated to the detriment of a large part of the rural population, the elections of 1811-12 led everywhere to the return of members determined not merely to continue the enforcement of the trade embargo, but actually to declare war on Great Britain. James Madison, the natural Presidential successor to Thomas Jefferson, was virtually blackmailed by this group, who made it known that they would not support his nomination unless he would guarantee his intention of going to war. Madison was elected and, perhaps against his better judgement, war was declared on 18th June 1812.

War against Great Britain was synominous with attacks against Canada. However, it soon became apparent how ill prepared was the United States' army. Political appointees, whose knowledge of soldiering was minimal, filled the commissioned ranks, while the rank and file were ill trained and ill disciplined. The opening battle on the Canadian border resulted in General William Hull's army surrendering, and disaster after disaster followed for the next two years. Not only was the United States army incapable of aggressive action, but proved itself unable to defend its coastline from attack. A British amphibious expedition met little effective resistance in 1814 when it landed and burned the city of Washington.

In April 1814 the abdication of Napoleon released large numbers of well trained and highly experienced troops who became available to bring the American war of 1812-14 to a conclusion. Thus it was that the 32nd, stationed at Cork, came under orders to sail for Canada. This, however, was not to be.

THE WATERLOO CAMPAIGN, 1815

On 1st March 1815, having escaped from Elba, Napoleon landed in France. His old soldiers flocked back to him, and by 20th March he was able to reinstate his rule in Paris. In order to reinforce his authority he needed a quick European victory and, to this end, he determined to re-conquer the Netherlands. An alliance was immediately formed against him consisting of Britain, Prussia, Hanover, the Netherlands and Russia (Russia failed to mobilise before the Allied victory so need not be considered in this brief account). Two Allied armies were concentrated in the Netherlands over the next three months: first, the British-Netherland-Hanoverian army under the Duke of Wellington and second, the Prussian army under Marshal Gebhard von Blücher.

Napoleon's force was numerically inferior to the combined Allied armies, so he needed to strike swiftly, in order to destroy each army individually before the two had time to concentrate. He therefore (successfully) spread a smoke screen of false intelligence. None the less, by the evening of June 18th, he had been defeated.

The campaign was in large part won by the tenacity and stamina of British infantrymen, typical of whom were the men of the 32nd (Cornwall) Regiment of Foot.

For the Cornwalls, encamped a few miles to the west of Brussels, the epic drama of this battle opened at 10 p.m. on 15th June, when the drummers beat 'the call to arms'. Wellington had misjudged Napoleon's intentions, believing that his main thrust would be delivered in the area of Mons. Instead, Napoleon fought the Prussians in a bloody engagement that drove them back, and was at that moment advancing up the Brussels road. Now it was imperative that every regiment should make its way to the tactically vital cross-roads of Quatre Bras at all possible speed.

The Cornwalls marched into Brussels at about 3 a.m., and from there were directed down the single *pavé* road leading to Quatre Bras. They hurried south, through the Forêt de Soignes, Waterloo, Mont St Jean and Genappe, arriving at Quatre Bras in the early afternoon of 16th June.

Battle of Quatre Bras, 16th-17th June 1815 & withdrawal to the ridge of Mont St Jean

Brigade by brigade, Wellington's army arrived on the scene. They must have been tired; none had slept the previous night; some, like the 32nd, had marched several miles to the concentration areas in Brussels and then a further twenty-five miles to Quatre Bras. However, the Prince of Orange was already here, conducting a spirited defence with the meagre resources he had under his command, and this was not a time to rest. As each regiment came onto the field it was immediately committed to the battle. The 32nd was involved from an early stage and was almost constantly engaged in the fighting from about 2 p.m. on 16th June.

Throughout that night great efforts were made to recover the wounded and load them onto wagons bound for Antwerp. The weather was hot and humid; water canteens were empty, and soldiers queued patiently to refill them at the single available pump.

The following morning (17th June), fighting continued in a desultory fashion. At about midday Wellington broke off contact to withdraw. It is difficult to estimate exact casualties in the Regiment because many officers and men wounded at Quatre Bras subsequently died within the next few days. The official casualty return for the first day of the battle reported 21 killed and 227 wounded. During one of the engagements a shell burst immediately over the Colours, ripping the Regimental Colour to shreds and killing or wounding a large number of men. (Remarkably, Ensign James McConchy, who was carrying the Regimental Colour, escaped with only minor wounds.)

Owing to a remarkable saga of confusion, the French had failed to bring all their available troops into action against Wellington. Now however, with Blücher's absence from the field, there was little to stop Napoleon outflanking Wellington and cutting the Brussels road. Wellington therefore decided to withdraw to a strong defensive position which he had previously reconnoitred for just such an eventuality. This was the ridge of Mont St Jean, a few miles south of the village of Waterloo. The ridge ran across the line of the narrow Brussels-Quatre Bras road and was backed by the Forest of Soignes, which presented an impenetrable barrier to formed troops. Most importantly perhaps, it allowed Wellington to place his troops behind the crest line (his favourite reverse slope position) so that the enemy had no clear idea of his dispositions and his own troops could not be subjected to direct fire.

The British infantry started to withdraw at about 6 p.m. on 17th June, leaving only a rear-guard of cavalry. The French appear to have been oblivious of this, until it was too late to take effective action.

All that afternoon the weather had become closer and more humid; thunder rumbled, and as the French at last made a move to pursue their foes, the heavens opened.

The rainstorm on the night of 17th-18th June was reported as being the heaviest in living memory. Its effect was to be critical to the conduct of the French advance and indeed to the whole outcome of the battle the following day. The rain turned the fields of rye on either side of the road into quagmires in which horses floundered up to their hocks, and the rear-guard of British cavalry merely had to fight delaying actions on the narrow front of the single road. Thus it was that Wellington's infantry was able to retire to the ridge of Mont St Jean without any interference from the French, and that on the evening of 17th June, soaked to the skin, hungry and exhausted, the 32nd were shepherded into their allotted assembly areas, where they lay down on the sodden ground and slept.

Waterloo, 18th June 1815

Wellington, in his headquarters at Waterloo, was up at 3 a.m. anxiously awaiting news from Marshal Blücher. No messenger came. At 6 a.m. the rain ceased, allowing Wellington's soldiers to clean and dry their muskets. At 8 a.m., regiment by regiment, the Allied army deployed into its previously reconnoitred reverse-slope battle positions. The 32nd were part of General Sir Thomas Picton's 5th Division, occupying a particularly strong position in the centre, on the reverse slope of the ridge, with a deep sunken road to their front. There they were to stand and fight all through this long day.

Napoleon had intended to attack at 9 a.m. but his army, hindered by the atrocious weather, was not yet fully deployed by that hour. Shortly after 11 a.m. a mud bespattered staff officer reported to Wellington from Blücher. The Prussian army was on the move and hoped to arrive by late afternoon. Still Napoleon tarried, waiting for the now hot sun to dry out the ground. Each hour of delay was a bonus to the Allies, for each hour brought the Prussians some four miles closer to the battle-field. At last, at 11.25 a.m., eighty-four French guns opened fire from across the valley and continued pounding the ridge for two hours. The first phase of Napoleon's attack was directed at Hougoumont Château, a walled farm that guarded the Allied right flank. Gallantly defended by the light companies of the British Foot Guards, it was to hold out against almost continued onslaughts throughout the day.

Unable to turn the Allied right flank, Napoleon then concentrated on the centre of the line, and at 1.30 p.m. launched 16,000 infantry. It was here that some of the bitterest fighting of the day took place, and it was here that General Sir Thomas Picton, leading his division forward in a counter attack, was killed. Two serjeants of the 32nd carried his body to the rear. During the ensuing savage hand to hand fighting, the French infantry and the 32nd fought it out with the bayonet. For a brief period the 32nd King's Colour fell into the hands of a French officer before he was despatched by Serjeant Switzer, the serjeant of the escort, and Ensign Birtwhistle, who simultaneously ran him through with pike and sword. The critical situation was only retrieved by the charge of the Union and Household Brigades of heavy cavalry under General Lord Uxbridge. Alas, in saving the Allied centre Wellington's heavy cavalry was virtually destroyed.

At 2.30 p.m. the first men of the Prussian advance guard could be seen through the telescopes of Wellington's staff, as they anxiously scanned the landscape out to the left of the Allied line. If their defence could hold for just a few more hours, the Prussians would fall on the flank of the French army and Napoleon could be beaten.

The opening of the third phase of the French attack came at 3.45 p.m. Napoleon threw in 4,500 cavalry (almost his entire cavalry force) into the centre and left of the Allied line, preceded by yet another prolonged artillery barrage. As soon as the barrage lifted the Allied infantry re-deployed into battalion squares, the classic formation invariably used against cavalry, which presented a four-sided fence of bayonets. These squares were sited in chequer board fashion so that each square could fire across the face of its neighbour. As soon as the cavalry withdrew and artillery opened up, the infantry moved back into line and lay down. To achieve the necessary precision in these manoeuvres, under fire and with considerable speed, required the highest standards of training and discipline. From 3.45 p.m. till 5 p.m. the French cavalry threw themselves onto the unyielding squares. Meanwhile the Prussian army drew ever nearer.

At 6.30 p.m. the walled farm of La Haye Sainte, the key to Wellington's centre, which had been held all day by a battalion of The King's German Legion, fell to the French.

The crisis of the battle came at 7 p.m. when Napoleon, now harassed on his right flank by the Prussians, committed the Imperial Guard to battle. These élite veteran soldiers had never been known to fail; they had however never come up against Wellington. In the next half hour they were pounded by artillery before meeting the lethal musketry of the Guards and the 52nd Light Infantry. Few survived. Wellington, riding to the centre of the line, waved his hat three times towards the French. The signal was instantly understood and the whole army advanced from its tenaciously held position. Hemmed in from the front, rear and flanks, the French army dissolved into a state of chaos. The Allies closed in with the bayonet, and little quarter was given by men who had endured nine hours of almost continuous battering on the ridge of Mont St Jean.

The British, who had played the major part in the battle, were in no state to mount an immediate pursuit. They had barely rested or eaten for three and a half days, during which time they had fought two major battles and marched some forty miles. Having driven the French off the field, the regiments lay down wherever they happened to be to sleep.

The 32nd had suffered heavy casualties and the roll call on the morning after the battle must have brought great sadness to this victorious occasion. The Regiment had gone into action on 16th June at a strength of 746 all ranks; of these only 169 answered their names on 19th June. Of those missing 53 had been killed; the majority of the remaining 540 had been wounded. Remarkably enough, most of these survived the crude medical attention of that era. By the time that Wellington's army had arrived in Paris many of the 32nd wounded and strays had rejoined their Regiment, bringing the total to 386 all ranks.

The Regiment was encamped at Neiully, near Paris, where it was to remain till 28th October when the camp was struck and the troops went into winter billets in the village of Carrières St Denis, on the banks of the Seine. Lieutenant-Colonel John Hicks, who had commanded during the battles, was appointed one of the Commandants of Paris, Major Felix Calvert being promoted Brevet Lieutenant-Colonel in his place.

3
1816-1846

England, 1816-1817

Arrangements having been made for the formation of the Army of Occupation, the regiments that had suffered most heavily at Waterloo were sent home. Their reception was not what they might have hoped for. So fickle was public opinion as regards the army, that those who only a few months previously had been cheering the news of victory at Waterloo now saw soldiers merely as an expensive inconvenience. The regiments returning from the Continent met with a frigid, if not openly hostile reception when they disembarked on British soil. An officer of the 3/14th Foot, which landed at Dover a few days after the 32nd, described his experience as follows:

> Public feeling had undergone a great revulsion in regard to us soldiers. The country was saturated with glory, and was brooding over the bill that it had to pay for the article. Waterloo, and Waterloo men were at a discount. We were made painfully sensible of the change. If we had been convicts disembarking from a hulk, we could not have met with less consideration. 'It's us pays they chaps' was the remark of a country bumpkin, as we came ashore. It was a bitter cold day when we landed; no cheers welcomed us home. The only persons who took any notice of us were the custom-house officers, and they kept us under arms for hours, in the cold, while they subjected us to a rigid search.

The 32nd had returned to England in 1816 and, after a period of recruiting and retraining, sailed for the Ionian Islands the following year.

The Ionian Islands, 1817-1825

The Regiment embarked for Corfu on 21st June 1817 where, on arrival, it was quartered in Citadel Barracks. During the next seven years the movement of the various companies around the Ionian Islands was almost continuous, and many soldiers can have seen little of their base at Corfu. The attempt to exercise control over companies spread over such a wide area of sea must have been their commanding officer's nightmare. Today with modern transport it would be difficult; then, relying on sailing ships and the vagaries of the wind, it must have been impossible. During the Regiment's tour, the companies served at various times in Cephalonia, Cerigo, Santa Maura, Ithaca, Paxa and Calamos. Corfu itself was apparently an unpopular station with the soldiers, on account of the oppressive discipline imposed by the Major-General; they were doubtless delighted to get away to the outlying islands. The inspection reports of this period indicate that this severity may have been needed when the Regiment first arrived in the Ionian Island. The inspection report of 1820 mentions the great improvements that had taken place in all aspects of field drill, and the interior economy and discipline that had been achieved since Lieutenant-Colonel the Hon. John Maitland assumed command. This would assume that its previous state was far from perfect. By the time the Regiment was due to leave in 1825 the general's praise had become positively lyrical. In his final report he stated:

> Approving as the Lieutenant-General [he had been promoted] does of the whole deportment and conduct of the Regiment, he must select one particular by which it has been peculiarly distinguished; the orderly, tranquil, and creditable conduct of the officers and men in their quarters, and their kind and friendly behaviour towards all the inhabitants in all the islands in which it has been stationed; a deportment which he wishes to hold out as an example, because nothing can tend more to raise the British name, or to conciliate the affections and respect of the population who are protected by the British Crown.

On 22nd and 23rd July 1825 the transports *Princess Royal* and *Diadem* arrived with the relief regiment, the 7th Fusiliers. On 29th July the 32nd set sail for Portsmouth.

It is perhaps interesting that while the Regiment was serving in the Ionian Islands, infantry battalions were officially reduced from the war establishment of about 1,000 (a figure seldom achieved) to the peace establishment of 726 (another figure seldom achieved).

Ireland, 1826-1831

The Regiment was quartered for a brief time in the Royal Citadel, Plymouth, before marching to Manchester and thence to Liverpool for embarkation to Limerick. The next five years were spent engaged in almost constant movement around Ireland, during which time much energy was employed in recruiting. It is ironic that a population subjected to a despotic rule by the British should have supplied such a very high proportion of its soldiers. Many of these young men undoubtedly enlisted to escape the grinding poverty of their rural economy, but the Irishman's love of a scrap was probably a powerful draw. Catholics were outlawed from holding an officer's commission, but a quick glance at an Army List of this period shows how a quite disproportionate number of the Irish Protestant gentry held commissioned rank in English regiments.

Canada, 1831-1840

The rebellion of 1837

Between 11th May and 8th June 1831 the 32nd was split into three groups which embarked on the transports *Britomart*, *Perseus* and *Hebe* for passage to Canada; there it was reunited as part of the Quebec garrison, together with the 15th and 24th Foot. At the time of the American War of 1812, Lower Canada, that is to say the area north of the Ottawa river, had been largely populated by French peasant farmers. In spite of their comparatively small numbers and sparse distribution, they had formed effective militia units which had fought with great determination and courage, eventually defeating all three of the American incursions. Britain was not slow to recognise the vulnerability of the long Canadian border, and the paucity of men to defend it against the land-hungry Americans. However, after the defeat of Napoleon's forces in the Peninsula, large numbers of experienced British troops became available to bolster the defence of Canada. At the same time, large-scale immigration was strongly encouraged. Many of those making the journey across the Atlantic were middle-class merchants who saw an opening for their entrepreneurial skills in the vast Canadian spaces.

The original French settlers viewed the appropriation of their commercial interests with increasing alarm. The political expression of this discontent was voiced by Les Patriotes, an organisation formed in 1826 under the radical leadership of M. Louis-Joseph Papineau. In the elections of 1834 Les Patriotes won a landslide victory. The nation was becoming split into two bitterly opposed camps: the largely peasant, French speaking, Catholic farmers, and the educated, entrepreneurial, English speaking, Protestant merchants. Rebellion became inevitable. The revolt against the established order started peaceably as an economic boycott of all British-made goods, but as tempers became ever more strained, the French population itself tended to split into two groups: the extreme radicals, known as the 'wolves', who were centred around Montreal, and the more cautious 'lambs' who were grouped in the Quebec area. The wolves were determined on a course of armed insurrection.

A disastrous harvest in 1837 brought increased poverty to the French farmers. Militant speakers toured the towns and villages preaching revolution, while radical newspapers were widely distributed in both Upper and Lower Canada. The crisis came to a head on 29th June when a rally was held in Montreal with a view to forming armed revolutionary bands capable of taking military action. In September a new association was raised by a certain Dr Robert Nelson. Known as Les Fils de la Liberté, it was from the first an overtly military organisation which drilled and carried out field exercises in full view of the public. That Autumn the 32nd, under the able command of Lieutenant-Colonel the Hon. John Maitland, with the 1st and 24th Regiments of Foot, was moved to Montreal in an attempt to contain the situation. The first blood was spilt on 16th November 1837 when fifteen men of the Royal Montreal Volunteer Cavalry were attacked after attempting to arrest Papineau. Outnumbered ten to one, the horsemen were forced to beat an ignominious retreat after two officers and a trooper had been wounded. The rebels, greatly heartened by this minor skirmish, immediately established armed camps around Montreal. There they trained their force, and carried out hit and run raids whenever the opportunity arose.

On 22nd November the Deputy Quarter Master General, Colonel Charles Gore, led a column of the 24th, 32nd and 66th Regiments, together with a 12 pdr field gun, from his base at Sorel, to attack a group of rebels known to be holding the town of St Denis. During the early part of the twenty-six mile approach march the rain came down in torrents. The rain turned to snow, and then, as the skies cleared, a hard frost set in, freezing the men's wet clothing to their backs. With great determination the column pressed on, led by the 32nd Light Company under Captain Frederick Markham.

The rebels had assembled some eight hundred men in the solidly constructed and strongly barricaded stone houses of St Denis. As Markham's frozen and exhausted Light Company approached the village, they were welcomed by a volley of fire. Gore, having sent flanking parties round to the east and west, attacked from the front. Three times they charged the position and three times they were driven back by the rebels, well protected in the robust stone buildings. By 3 o'clock that afternoon, running critically short of ammunition, Gore ordered a withdrawal. The 12 pdr gun became stuck in the mud and was abandoned, together with some twenty wounded. The 32nd lost 2 killed, 5 wounded and 4 missing. The gallant Markham was hit twice in the neck during the battle. As he was carried to the rear by Serjeant Allcock and an anonymous private, he was hit twice more in the calf and knee. Remarkably, he survived the rigours of the return march.

While this had been taking place, Lieutenant George Weir of the 32nd had been sent from Montreal with despatches for Gore. Missing him at Sorel, he had hastened on to St Denis. Taking a more direct route, he had arrived there before the column, only to fall into enemy hands.

On 30th November Gore again set out for St Denis with an enhanced force of the 24th, 32nd , 66th and 83rd Foot, and a 12 pdr howitzer. Initially the column attempted to advance up the Richlieu river by steam boat, but the ice proved too thick and it was forced to take to the road. On arrival at St Denis, the town was found to be empty. The 12 pdr gun was recovered intact, but a grisly discovery was made when the horribly mutilated corpse of Lieutenant Weir was discovered concealed under boulders in the river. So infuriated were Gore's men that they set fire to the town, destroying every single building. The following day was spent searching for the surviving British wounded, and burying the dead. Three companies of the 32nd with the recaptured 12 pdr gun, under the command of Major Henry Reid, were left to garrison the gutted buildings of St Denis while the main body returned to Montreal, where it received a rapturous welcome.

On 13th December a strong column totalling about 2,000 men under Major-General Sir John Colborne, a highly experienced officer and a veteran of the Peninsular and Waterloo campaigns, marched on St Eustache, which was known to be occupied by a considerable body of rebels. Colborne's column consisted of the 1st, 32nd and 83rd Regiments of Foot, the Royal Montreal Volunteer Cavalry, the Montreal Volunteer Rifles, Globenski's St Eustache Loyal Volunteers, Leclerc's Volunteers, five field guns and a rocket battery. As news of the advance of the column reached the town, the majority of the rebels fled and, on seeing the leading elements approaching, many more took to their heels, including the self styled 'General' M. Girod, who had a sleigh standing by for just such an eventuality. This mass exodus left the rebels with a force of barely 200 men. With a numerical superiority of about ten to one, and with overwhelming artillery fire power, Colborne could afford to fight a careful and methodical battle, driving the remaining brave defenders into an ever decreasing perimeter around the church. The result was inevitable. By 6 p.m. the rebel garrison surrendered. The 1st had lost 1 man killed and 8 wounded; the 32nd had 1 man wounded. The rebels lost about 70 dead, while a further 120 were captured.

Colborne then marched to St Benoit. This town had become infamous over the past few years as the centre of revolutionary intrigue; it was known to be occupied at this time by a considerable rebel force, led by 'General' Girod who had joined it after his flight from St Eustache. As the British advanced, they spread the word around the countryside that any town or village that was found to be harbouring rebels would be burnt. On arrival at St Benoit, none but the innocent civilian population remained; this however did not stop the troops torching the town and indulging in an orgy of destruction which totally destroyed every building. With night temperatures dropping to -30° Fahrenheit (62° of frost), the desperate situation to which the citizens were reduced is not difficult to imagine.

Colborne's column then spread across the whole area, rounding up rebels who were escorted back to Montreal. The 32nd was detached and ordered to occupy the villages of Ste Scholastique and Ste Thérèse. Both surrendered their supplies of arms and ammunition without a fight while, to their credit, the men of the Regiment took no revenge on either persons or property.

Thus ended the Canadian Rebellion of 1837. Its failure can be largely put down to the poor leadership of the rebels. However, the remarkable speed with which it was quashed must reflect credit on British senior officers like Colborne who showed themselves capable of taking quick and resolute action. Added to this must be the efficiency of the Quarter Master General's department, which succeeded in clothing and equipping the British forces in Canada, enabling them to take the field in the most bitter winter conditions. Last but by no means least was that factor which ultimately wins all wars and campaigns: the courage, fortitude and skill of the regimental officers and soldiers.

American incursions, 1838

The internal rebellion had barely been crushed when a new and potentially more dangerous external threat arose from across the border in America. During the winter of 1837 the rebel leader of Lower Canada, William Mackenzie, had fled to America where he was greeted with enthusiasm as a patriot who was endeavouring to throw off the tyranny of British rule. Very soon he had gathered round him a following of American and Canadian malcontents determined to forment rebellion in Upper Canada. On 15th December he and his gang of desperados had attacked the United States Army arsenal, equipping themselves with modern arms and ammunition, including artillery. They had then stolen an American paddle steamer, the *Caroline*, and occupied Navy Island, three miles from Niagara and part of Canadian territory. There Mackenzie proclaimed himself chairman of a 'Provisional Canadian Republic', promising land and money to every man who would join him.

Volunteers soon arrived, one of whom was Rensselaer Van Rensselaer, the son of an American General who had fought in the American War of Independence. Enthused with the vision of a new war of independence for the people of Canada, he now took command and proceeded to bombard the Canadian village of Chippewa. This stung the British into action. The *Caroline*, lying on the American bank of the river, was boarded by the Royal Navy and destroyed. At the same time, military reinforcements were requested from England, while those regiments already in Canada were rushed to the scene. Amongst these was the 43rd Light Infantry which, using sleighs, made an epic march of 370 miles in 18 days during the depth of the Canadian winter. The temperature on two of the nights was recorded as -24° and -30° Fahrenheit (56° and 62° of frost respectively).

Early in January 1838 the 32nd embarked for passage up river from Montreal, but after only a few days the boats became firmly frozen in. The Regiment therefore had to take to its feet and march the remaining 150 miles or so across the broken ice. Arriving at Toronto, half was quartered in that town while the other half continued to New London. Reading of these remarkable marches across vast frozen wastes, one cannot but be amazed at the obvious efficiency of the logistical support provided. There are no accounts of columns running out of food, forage or the warm clothing that was vital to their survival. The lessons of the Duke of Wellington regarding sound administration, which he had drummed into his staff, appear to have been well remembered in this cold, desolate wasteland. How different was the army's experience to be in the Crimea sixteen years later!

Meanwhile, urgent requests were being received at Horse Guards in London to reinforce Canada by bringing the strength of the cavalry up to 500, and that of the infantry up to 10,600 men.

In February a body of American 'brigands' (as the enemy had become known to the British) captured Pelée Island at the head of Lake Erie and proceeded to loot the settlement. The 32nd and 83rd Foot, with a detachment of Volunteer Cavalry and two field guns, set out from Amherstburg on the morning of 1st March under the Command of Lieutenant-Colonel Maitland, 32nd Foot. Travelling by sleigh over the frozen lake, the column covered the 40 miles in about 30 hours. On arrival at Pelée, Maitland detached two companies of the 32nd with the Volunteer Cavalry under Captain George Browne, to the south of the village, while he attacked with the remainder of his force from the north. The Americans withdrew, only to find Browne and his men barring their way. Far outnumbering the British force, the Americans attacked in formation, preceded by a swarm of skirmishers firing from behind the tumbled blocks of ice on the lake. Browne, finding himself outflanked, formed his two companies up in line and charged with the bayonet. The Americans did not wait for the attack to be driven home, but fled across the ice to the woods on the lakeside. There their sleighs were waiting, enabling them to make their escape, leaving over 70 of their number killed or wounded. Browne's companies of the 32nd suffered over 30 wounded, two of whom died later. In recognition of his skill and courage at this engagement, Captain Browne received a brevet majority.

Although the 32nd remained in Canada until July 1840, it took no part further in any major fighting. It was quartered initially in Amherstburg and later in New London, from where the companies patrolled the surrounding areas and carried out operations to seek out rebel fugitives. Sadly, the Commanding Officer, Lieutenant-Colonel Maitland, who had led the Regiment with such distinction throughout the worst days of the campaign, died during the winter of 1839-40. He was succeeded by Lieutenant-Colonel Thomas Wingfield. In July the Regiment embarked on the transport *Appollo*, landing at Portsmouth on 17th September 1840.

England & Ireland, 1841-1846

The 32nd returned to England in 1841, being stationed at St Helens, Portsmouth, Leeds and Manchester. This was a period of severe social unrest at home, necessitating the deployment of troops in the industrial areas of the North and Midlands. In 1844 the 32nd sailed for Dublin under the command of Lieutenant-Colonel Frederick Markham, a hard disciplinarian but an excellent soldier who looked after the welfare of his men. Dublin was considered perhaps the most convivial of all military stations by both officers and men; guard duties were infrequent by the standards of that time, and there was plenty of entertainment for a young man in a red coat; the drink flowed freely and the girls were accommodating. While in Dublin, the Regiment was presented with new Colours by Miss Cecelia A'Court, daughter of Lord Heytesbury, Viceroy of Ireland. After the ceremony the officers entertained the social élite of Dublin to a grand dinner and ball, while the soldiers sat down to a special dinner paid for by the company captains. The following day the Regiment reluctantly left its happy hunting ground and marched to Athlone, the first stop on the long journey which was to take it to India. After resting a few days in Athlone, the march continued to Fermoy where the Regiment went into barracks for six weeks, waiting for the officers and soldiers who had been on leave in England to rejoin. On 3rd May 1846 it marched to Cork; here the final preparations were made for embarkation. One can imagine these long marches through the Irish countryside, always conducted at a leisurely pace (for the weight carried by a soldier was considerable and the roads often appalling). The passage of a regiment through the rural landscape must have provided a colourful and stirring experience: the mounted field officers; the band and drums between them providing almost constant music; the Colours, carried in their black leather protective cases by two Ensigns; the columns of red-coated soldiers plodding forward through the mud or the dust; the heavy creaking carts piled up with the regimental baggage on which the wives and children were precariously perched; and finally the assorted dogs which, if the artists of the period are to be believed, appear to have accompanied every regiment on the march.

To India, 1846

The main body of the 32nd embarked on the steam transport *Aboukir* on 29th May, sailing from Cork later that day to the sound of the band and the cheers of the 67th (South Hampshire) Regiment, which had become close companions since Dublin days.

The passage to India necessitated sailing south for 1,500 miles to the Cape of Good Hope, and then turning north-east towards Calcutta, a further 4,700 miles away. If all went well the voyage was expected to take about five months. Even by contemporary standards, accommodation on a troop transport was very cramped. When the weather was warm and fine, life could be pleasant. Men spent most of their time on deck, whiling away the hours with their comrades, listening to the drums and fyfes, playing games, organising concerts or dances, or just sleeping. Lieutenant-Colonel Markham was notable for doing all in his power to keep everybody happy in those long lazy days. In foul weather, the situation cannot have been more different. The misery and squalor of the troop decks defies description. The chaos of every loose article slithering across the vomit-soaked decks was accompanied by a well-founded dread that the ship would be overwhelmed by the sea. All too often ships sank without trace, but the thought of a quick death by drowning must often have seemed preferable to the terrible incapacitating nausea of seasickness.

On 10th September 1846 the *Aboukir* tied up against the quay in Calcutta. She had been at sea for 103 days, having survived a near capsize in the Atlantic, a collision with another troop ship off the Azores and the loss of her fore topmast in the Bay of Bengal. Nobody appeared to view this chapter of disasters as anything out of the ordinary.

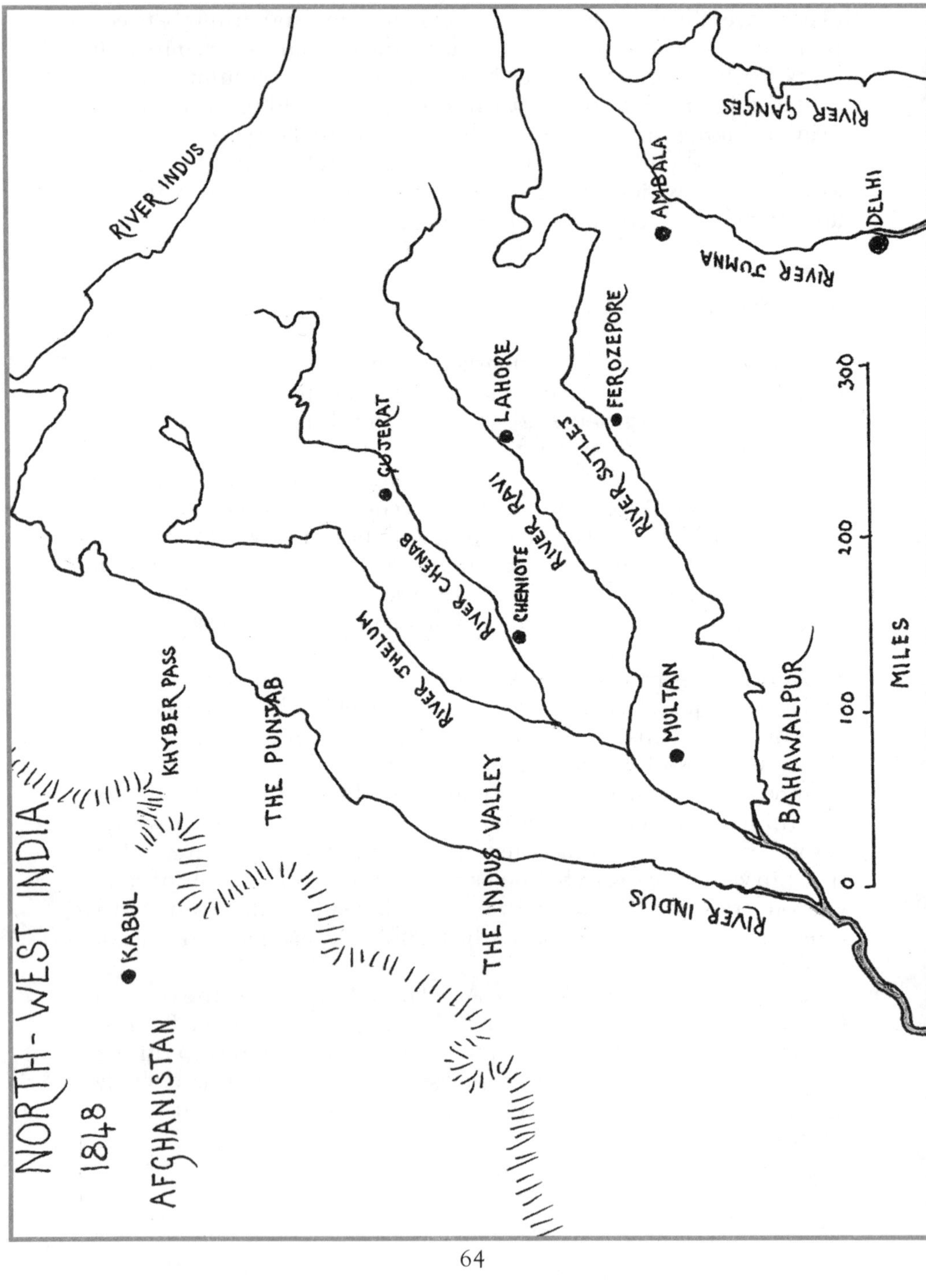
NORTH-WEST INDIA
1848
AFGHANISTAN
KABUL
KHYBER PASS
THE PUNJAB
THE INDUS VALLEY
RIVER INDUS
RIVER JHELUM
RIVER CHENAB
CHENIOTE
RIVER RAVI
GUJERAT
LAHORE
RIVER SUTLEJ
FEROZEPORE
MULTAN
BAHAWALPUR
AMBALA
DELHI
RIVER JUMNA
RIVER GANGES
RIVER INDUS
0
100
200
300
MILES

4
India, 1846-1856

THE SECOND SIKH WAR, 1848-1849

On 11th December 1845 the Sikh army had crossed the Sutlej river in defiance of the treaty of 1804, thereby in effect declaring war on Britain. The British had however anticipated this act of aggression, and deployed a considerable force under the command of Lieutenant-General Sir Hugh Gough to meet this incursion.*

Four hard-fought battles at Moodkee, Ferozeshah, Aliwal and Sabraon achieved victory, albeit at the cost of heavy casualties.

For two years after the battle of Sabraon the Punjaub (or Punjab) remained a British protectorate under the able control of Sir Henry Lawrence, who was appointed Resident at Lahore. On the surface peace appeared to have been re-established, but British intelligence was aware of the undercurrents of intrigue stirred up by the Rani and her ministers. The Sikh army, composed as it was of the fiercest warriors in India, smarted under their recent defeat, and was determined to seek retribution.

On 19th April 1848 a ceremony had been arranged at Mooltan (or Multan) in which power was to be transferred from Dhuleep Singh, the Dewan (or Governor) of Mooltan, to the younger Khan Singh. Trouble was not expected as it was believed (probably correctly) that Dhuleep Singh had salted away a considerable fortune and wished to retire. Two East India Company officers, Mr Van Agnew of the Bengal Civil Service and Lieutenant Anderson of the Bombay Fusiliers, were instructed to oversee this transfer. Arriving before the gates of Mooltan with a very small escort, they were welcomed with courtesy, but during the ceremony they were attacked by Sikhs loyal to Dhuleep Singh and seriously wounded. They made their escape, only to be subsequently hunted down and murdered. The deaths of Van Agnew and Anderson sparked off the Second Sikh War.

* Hugh Gough, first Viscount Gough, was a tough, impetuous, brave, fighting soldier with all the characteristics, both good and bad, of his fellow Ulstermen. Commissioned into the 87th (Prince of Wales' Irish) Regiment of Foot in 1794, he probably saw more active service than any other general officer of his day. The long litany of battles in which he took part include: the capture of the Cape of Good Hope (1795); the capture of Surinan, in the West Indies (1796); the battle of Talavera (1809), at which he was severely wounded; the defence of Cadiz (1810), at which he was slightly wounded; the battles of Barrosa (1811); Vittoria (1813); and Nivelle (1813), at which he was again severely wounded. He commanded the land forces in the China War of 1840-42, and was appointed Commander-in-Chief India in 1843. Gough's battle tactics owed little either to imagination or subtlety, his preference being for the straight forward frontal attack at bayonet point. As a result he became famed for sacrificing soldiers' lives, often to little effect. His appalling 'butcher's bill' at the battle of Chillianwallah aroused severe misgivings back in England, which resulted in his replacement by Sir Charles Napier. Always in the thick of the fighting, he would wear a loose white coat, like a cricket umpire's coat, over his uniform so that he could be immediately recognised.

Lawrence's assistant in the Derajat, Lieutenant Herbert Edwardes, immediately advanced on Mooltan with a hastily raised force of Pathan levies. On 18th June (auspiciously the anniversary of Waterloo) his ragged band crossed the Chenaub river and confronted Dhuleep's army. The young Herbert Edwardes, an almost legendary figure in the colourful history of the North West Frontier, put in an immediate attack. By a remarkable display of charismatic leadership he inspired his Pathan tribesmen with a sense of their invincibility. Always in the thick of the fighting, Edwardes led his men forward until Dhuleep's Sikhs retreated back to Mooltan. There they ensconced themselves behind the formidable fortifications and prepared for a lengthy siege.

In spite of the fact that Edwardes had now been joined by a second column under a Colonel Van Costland, he was entirely lacking in heavy artillery, and his combined force was still quite inadequate for a siege. All he could do was to isolate the fortress and pray for the timely arrival of reinforcements. Fear of the very real danger that the Sikh rebellion, at present confined to the area of Mooltan, could quickly sweep across the whole of the Punjaub promoted increasingly urgent calls to the Commander-in-Chief, General Lord Gough, to despatch a strong expeditionary force without delay. Gough, however, was at that time relaxing in the comforts of the hill station at Simla. He appears to have remained oblivious to the critical nature of the situation, deciding that any major movement of troops must await the start of the cool weather. Sir Henry Lawrence, the only man with a sufficiently forceful personality to influence the Commander-in-Chief, was away on leave in England. His post was occupied by another who had little of the drive or authority of his late master, and thus failed to spur Gough into action. However, a field force under General Sir William Whish, commanding the East India Company Bombay Army, was despatched north. His column moved up the River Indus in barges towed by steam tugs, arriving at Mooltan on 18th August 1848, where it was joined by a large force of Sikhs under Shere Singh.

The march to Mooltan, 15th May-25th August 1848

At the first news of the murders of Van Agnew and Anderson the 32nd, quartered in barracks at Umballa, was ordered to prepare to move north to Ferozepore, thereby making it more readily available to go to the aid of Edwardes should this be required. This march, which started on 15th May 1848, must have been one of the most hellish experiences that the Regiment has ever been called upon to endure. Each morning the 'Assembly' was beaten by the drummers at between 1 a.m. and 2 a.m., so that the day's march could be completed before sunrise. In spite of the early hour the heat was well nigh intolerable; the dust rose in clouds, caking sweating bodies and clogging dry throats. Water was always scarce and often unobtainable, and the thirst suffered by the soldiers was often made more intolerable by their propensity to loot raw spirit from the villages through which they passed. Hundreds would fall out from the line each day; the majority of these would stagger into the camp long after the camp had been pitched, but many died by the road; one soldier shot himself rather than endure the agonies of thirst. At midday, when the Regiment was attempting to obtain rest, the temperature in the tents regularly reached 130° Fahrenheit. It is little wonder that Lord Gough had precluded any idea of moving the Army of the Indus in the hot weather.

The garrison of Ferozepore was reached on 27th May. The distance marched was just short of 164 miles, during which one officer (Captain Gardiner), a serjeant and six privates had died of heat exhaustion. Although Ferozepore boasted a modern barracks built in 1846, this was already occupied by a part of the 14th Light Dragoons. The 32nd therefore had to double up, many of the soldiers having to sleep on the brick floors. Private Wheeler, who has left the best account for this war from the soldier's point of view, described Ferozepore as follows:

> The barracks was infested with all kinds of reptiles, scorpions, centipedes, triantilopes, snakes, etc, several of our men received some severe bites. Scarcely a day passed without a dust storm. It would often come thick and fast for hours, so that we would have to light the lamps before we could see anything, and the country for miles around was nothing but a barren sandy plain, neither tree or cottage to greet the eye; but we knew we were destined not to stay long so we made the best of a bad situation.

Indeed, their stay in this most insalubrious place was happily to be brief. A few days after the Regiment's arrival in Ferozepore, orders were received to join Edwardes at Mooltan. The advance party of 4 officers, 5 serjeants, 4 drummers and 120 rank and file departed for Mooltan on 1st August; the main body, under Lieutenant-Colonel Frederick Markham, followed ten days later.

The first day's march took them to the small village of Ghat on the banks of the Sutlej River. Here, sixty-five flat-bottomed barges towed by steam tugs were waiting to take them up the river for the second leg of the journey. For the next week life could almost be described as idyllic. Camp was pitched on the river bank each evening at about 5 p.m.; thirst was a torment quickly forgotten, and men could wash themselves and their filthy, sweat-ingrained clothing for the first time in three months.

On 18th August the 32nd disembarked and once again took to its feet for the last lap of the long journey to Mooltan. The wheeled transport having been left at Ghat, the baggage was loaded onto camels. Throughout the next week, the old routine of marching in the early hours of the morning and attempting to rest during the heat of the day was resumed. At dawn on 25th August the formidable walls and bastions of the great fortress of Mooltan came into view.

General Whish and his staff rode out to meet the Regiment, the band struck up some lively airs, and the 32nd marched into their camping area in some style.

It had been on the move for 95 days, marching a total of 220 miles, and covering a further 100 miles by river. All this had been undertaken in the hottest season of the year, an achievement that many old Indian veterans would have considered an impossibility for a European regiment. The cost in life had however been high, twenty-two men having died of heat exhaustion.

The camp, which had been prepared by the advance party, was well sited just out of cannon range from the fortress. There was plenty of good water available, but the rations of scraggy mutton were fiercely criticised by the soldiers of the 32nd, who considered that a man's daily rations should include a full pound of good beef. The fortress itself stood on a slight mound dominating the flat plain. Although native built, its design owed much to European practice, and, with its massive forty-foot walls of burnt brick, it was considered to be the most formidable native fortification in the whole of India.

It is perhaps interesting to consider the remarkable efficiency of the staff work which must have existed to make this concentration of troops possible. The Punjab is immense, its total land area being far greater than the entire British Isles. Communications were tied to the speed of a horse; yet rations, boats, steam tugs and camels all seemed to have appeared at the right place at the right time.

The siege & capture of Mooltan
30th August 1848-21st January 1849

The first few days in the camp below Mooltan were spent cleaning weapons and equipment in preparation for an inspection by General Whish. On 30th August the 32nd, together with 10th Foot and the 8th, 49th and 72nd Native Regiments, paraded for the General. With him was Lieutenant Edwardes, of whom all had heard so much. He was described as being dressed in Afghan robes, and with his long black beard and weather-burnt face could easily have been mistaken for one of his wild Pathan tribesmen.

It is difficult to estimate the approximate size of General Whish's force encamped around Mooltan as the various sources vary greatly. Indeed, because Edwardes' Pathans and Shere Singh's Sikh elements were not part of either army or that of the East India Company, it is doubtful that the exact strength was ever known. Colonel Swiney's history puts the total force at rather more than 14,000 infantry and 8,000 cavalry. As yet the heavy artillery was still making its laborious way north. However, on 4th September the guns started to arrive at the encampment; four days later the siege started.

On the night of 7th September 450 men of the 32nd and a lesser number of the 10th moved forward to within musket range of the fortress and dug the first line of trenches. For the next few days work progressed, not only on the network of trenches, but on throwing up earthworks to protect the heavy guns.

By the morning of 12th September all was in place for the first attempt to storm and capture the outworks. Private Waterfield describes the subsequent battle with great relish, almost as if it was a particularly tough game of football. It is worth quoting part of his diary to illustrate the excitement and relish of a private soldier who, having endured terrible hardship on the long approach march, was finally unleashed against the enemy. Waterfield wrote:

> About 8 o'clock we received the word 'forward', and with a true British cheer, we advanced. When within fifty yards of the enemy's entrenchments we lay down to receive their first volley, and scarce a man was wounded. We instantly rose, and with repeated cheers dashed boldly forward till we came to a *nullah* some eight or nine feet deep. We soon crossed this but several of our men got winged, which stayed their further progress and now commenced the sport in proper style! Colonel Pattoun shouted, 'Fetch them fellows out of the trees!' (The ground hereabouts was covered with large trees) and from these we dislodged the discomfited enemy in dozens. My company (the Grenadiers) was led by Captain King, and our gallant Lieutenant Williams, as fine a bit of British mettle as ever faced an enemy. We dashed on to a large *Sammee* or *Dhurum Dalluh* house (or as some would call it, a picquet house). This building was entrenched on all sides and enclosed by loop-holed walls some 10 or 12 feet high. From this place the enemy peppered us in grand style when advancing. We were not long in bursting open the doors of the refuge place, and the massacre which took place in it was frightful; our Grenadiers soon had the place covered with the dead and dying. In the interior of the building was a narrow staircase. The enemy rushed up here followed by the Grenadiers, and in the gallery we had to close upon them, and the struggle for life and death was desperate. We hurled them over the banisters where they were dashed to pieces on the marble floor beneath.

By that evening the objective had been secured and several large guns moved forward. Waterfield's Grenadier Company had 13 wounded, several of whom subsequently died. Altogether the 32nd had 39 killed and 216 wounded. The following morning the Regiment withdrew into reserve, after being relieved by the 10th Foot.

Alas, this battle had been in vain. The day that the 32nd came out of the front line Shere Singh and his 5,000 Sikhs slipped away from their encampment and joined the rebels. With the departure of this large part of his force, General Whish was no longer capable of continuing siege operations. Reluctantly he withdrew to Sovrej-Khoond, about four miles from Mooltan, to await the tardy arrival of Lord Gough's Army of the Indus.

Life in the new camp quickly developed into a steady routine. The Sikhs made occasional forays towards the perimeter, but General Whish always seemed to anticipate their movements, and invariably prevented them from pressing home any attack. As always, when the soldier of that period was not fully occupied in fighting, he turned to his other great activity – drinking. Drunkenness, which threatened both the maintenance of discipline and the security of the camp, became endemic. In order to stop men storing up their daily ration of rum for a great binge, a general order was passed that every man was to drink his tot at the point of issue under the eyes of an officer. Undeterred by this, the more ingenious soldiers went to quite remarkable lengths to beat the system.

At last, on 27th December, Lord Gough's army appeared on the scene. Once more the siege could be resumed and by the 29th December the heaviest guns had been dug in, a mere eighty yards from the walls of the fortress. Three days later a mortar shell penetrated the roof of the main magazine, which was said to contain 400,000 lbs of powder. The resulting explosion caused major damage and considerable loss of life in the fortress, not to mention the destruction of a large part of the Sikh ammunition supply. The disaster seemed merely to increase the determination of the defenders, who sent word that they still had ample powder left and that they dared the attackers to do their worst. The following day a range of store houses was set on fire. They contained vast quantities of *ghee* and grain which burnt furiously all that night, casting a lurid light across the whole grisly scene of carnage.

On 2nd January 1849 the engineers reported that two breaches had been blasted through the walls. The first in the Khoone Bhoori bastion was steep but practical for a major assault, the second at the Delhi Gate could be used as a diversion. The assaults took place at 3 p.m. that afternoon. The advance to the Delhi Gate was covered by the 60th Rifles, with the 32nd leading the way, followed by the 49th and 72nd Native Infantry. The breach was found to be totally inadequate, so that this assault party was withdrawn and redirected to the Khoome Bhoori breach. This had already been carried by the 9th Foot and the 1st and 4th Native Infantry. The 32nd poured across the wall into the narrow streets of the Fortress, led, as always, by the Grenadier Company. The Sikhs quickly withdrew into the citadel, an immensely strong fortress within a fortress.

On 21st January two practical breaches had been blasted in the walls of the citadel and the assault parties were formed up ready for the final attack. Just before the call to advance was sounded a party of Sikhs was seen approaching through one of the breaches under a white flag. They had come to negotiate terms of surrender. Lord Gough, however, remained adamant that nothing short of unconditional surrender would be acceptable, and after two hours the garrison agreed. Thus ended the siege and capture of the fortress of Mooltan, the bloodiest in the history of the British conquest of India. British army and East India Company losses amounted to just over 10,000 killed and wounded. The 32nd came through with remarkably light casualties, only 2 officers being killed and 11 wounded, while a serjeant and 16 men were killed and 3 serjeants and a 103 men were wounded.

The privations suffered by the women and children in Mooltan had been grim. Even the hardened Private Waterfield, watching the trail of sparks from the shells as he did duty in the trenches at night, had written:

> They would appear like comets or meteors chasing or trying to outstrip each other, seeing which should first deprive the mother of her children or the child of its parents. It often caused me to think of the happy homes of old England, hoping the same fate might never befall it. All women and children should have free egress from town, city or fort during war, not to be exposed to all the dangers and privations attendant upon besieged places.

Written eighty years before the aerial bombardments of cities in the Second World War, this comment has a prophetic ring.

The 23rd January was given over to the looting of Mooltan, accompanied by considerable drinking of the new native spirit. However, by the next morning good order and military discipline appear to have been restored, and on the 27th January General Whish's force once more set out on the road to join Lord Gough, who had already moved to do battle with the Sikh army at Chillianwallah. By this time of year the weather was cool and good water was plentiful. The long marches of up to twenty-five miles per day therefore presented these toughened veterans with little hardship.

Cheniote, 8th- 9th February 1849

The fortress of Cheniote lay on the route. It had recently been occupied by a rebel leader, Narain Singh, with about 3,000 Sikhs, most of whom had been coerced into following him. However, another force under command of the loyal Shaik Eman-ood-deon had succeeded in occupying the high ground around the fortress, thereby barring any movement in or out of its gates. Arriving on 8th February, General Whish immediately sent a message to Narain Singh demanding surrender. This was accepted. At 9 a.m. the following morning the 32nd were formed up flanking the main gate, waiting for the defenders to emerge. Private Waterfield, probably expressing the views of many of the soldiers, fervently hoped that there would be no surrender so that 'We might have the pleasure of storming the place, for which we were quite ready.'

Apart from the thought of a good battle after so many weary days of marching, there was also the anticipation of the considerable quantities of loot if the fortress was sacked. However, this was not to be. Wiser councils had prevailed and, at exactly 9.30 a.m., Narain Singh emerged from the gate with his staff, followed by the defenders who laid down their weapons in piles.

The march to Chillianwallah, 10th-13th February 1849

There was to be no loot and no respite. The day after the surrender of Cheniote the forces of Whish were again on the march, covering eighteen to twenty-three miles each day. On arrival at Chillianwallah, they were met by scenes of the most appalling carnage. Although the battle had taken place on the 21st November, the still unburied corpses of men and horses were lying in grotesque attitudes. Lord Gough, as was not unusual for him, had incurred heavy casualties in achieving a limited victory. The field hospitals were crowded with the wounded, but many of these men were early recipients of one of the greatest blessings known to medicine; chloroform was used in the field for the first time. Providing this drug was available, the appalling pain suffered by soldiers undergoing amputation without anaesthetic would be an experience of the past.

The march to Gujerat, 15th-20th February 1849

Having rested for a day, during which many of the 32nd took the opportunity to get gloriously drunk with their comrades of the 53rd (Shropshire) Regiment, the column was once more on the move heading for Goojerat, where contact would at last be made with Lord Gough and the Army of the Indus. Doubtless with throbbing hangovers, the march was continued.

At 9 a.m. on 20th February the 32nd marched into Lord Gough's camp with drums beating and Colours flying, to be greeted with rousing cheers. The 10th (North Lincolnshire) Regiment, which had arrived the previous day, had a substantial hot breakfast waiting, which was greatly appreciated. That afternoon the combined force, which was now complete, marched some four miles nearer Gujerat. That evening, on the eve of battle, the next day's ration was cooked and issued out. Private Waterfield noted that he wrote a letter to his parents. He was probably not alone in this, for one of the great benefits enjoyed by soldiers on active service in India was that, for the first time, they were entitled to send mail home for one penny.

Battle of Gujerat, 21st February 1849

At dawn on 21st February the camp was struck, the baggage loaded onto the wagons and the army moved off by brigades to the scene of action.

At about 9 a.m. the enemy opened fire, with fifty-seven or more well concealed and well dug-in guns. Lord Gough deployed his infantry into line and ordered them to lie down, while he brought his hundred or so guns forward. The 32nd, as part of Colonel Markham's 2nd Brigade, was in reserve about 300 yards behind the firing line. For the next three and a quarter hours, there followed what was perhaps the fiercest artillery duel in nineteenth century history. The Sikhs, masters as always of the art of gunnery, gave courageous account of themselves, but in spite of their skill and bravery the odds against them told. One by one their guns were knocked out and the crews killed. At 12.30 p.m. the fire fight had been won; the buglers sounded the advance and the infantry moved forward. Witnesses remarked on their precision, saying that it was worthy of a review in Phoenix Park, Dublin. Infantry and Artillery leap-frogged though each other, the guns engaging with grape and canister shot while the infantry lay down, before advancing again. As the battle lines closed, Lord Gough ordered his flanks to wheel inwards, thus enveloping the enemy position and inflicting heavy casualties, but although few remained to fight it out with the bayonet, their officers refused to accept defeat and perished in the attempt to rally survivors.

As the Sikh army finally crumbled, the fugitives were pursued by Lord Gough's cavalry who cut them down without mercy.

The 32nd had taken no part in the actual fighting, but had had a better overall view of the battle than most of the active participants. The Regiment was now given the task of securing the ground and collecting the abandoned guns, which remained on serviceable carriages, and bringing them back to Lord Gough's headquarters. Later, three companies under Major William Case, together with a further two companies of the 51st Native Infantry, secured the eight gateways into the city of Gujerat.

The battle had been won and, with this victory, the war was over. In the next few weeks all the Sikh chieftains agreed to total submission, over 16,000 of their troops laying down their arms. The enemy casualties at Gujerat have never been accurately established, but were undoubtedly exceptionally high. Lord Gough's force was made up of a total of 24,000 British and East India Company troops and, because of his almost two-to-one preponderance of artillery and its skilful employment, he was able to win this final battle with remarkably few casualties. His losses amounted to only 96 men killed and about 700 wounded. The 32nd had one man killed and an officer and four men wounded. Lord Gough ordered that the enemy corpses should not be buried, but should lie as a grisly reminder *pour encourage les autres* not to defy the might of the British Raj.

Thus was the greatest military race in India finally subjected to British rule. During the two Sikh wars, each side had developed a profound respect for the fighting qualities of the other. When eventually beaten, they had, like the Ghurkhas in 1815, maintained a deep admiration for their conquerors. In the next few years they were to rebuild an army loyal to Britain. This army was to be a vital factor in the suppression of the coming Sepoy Mutiny of 1857. In the second part of the nineteenth century and the first part of the twentieth century, Sikh soldiers were to serve Britain in numerous imperial wars and throughout the two World Wars.

Two years in cantonments, 1849-1851

The 32nd took no part in the pursuit of the remnants of the defeated Sikh army, which was carried out by a 'flying column' under Major-General Sir Walter Raleigh Gilbert. Instead it moved by a succession of the now familiar long marches to Jullundur, where it took over barracks on 17th April 1849.*

The Regiment had been in the field for eleven months and its clothing and equipment were in tatters, so that the first urgent task was the renewal of almost everything worn or carried by the soldiers. Colonel Markham, commanding the 2nd Brigade, ordered that the regimental canteens should remain open for three days, during which he appears to have tolerated the fact that there was hardly a sober man available for duty. The garrison of Jullundur housed the depôt

* Walter Raleigh Gilbert was commissioned into the Royal Artillery in 1831. He is of interest to Cornishmen in that he lived out his retirement in Bodmin's Priory House. His life is commemorated by the massive obelisk that stands at the top of the beacon overlooking the town.

of the 61st (South Gloucestershire) Regiment. Private Waterfield observed that

> The Depôt of Her Majesty's 61st Regiment lay here, with all their women, and this being the attractive mart for all who were foolish enough to squander their money there was no lack of fools. Many who had some hundreds, and even thousands of rupees, did not stop till the last gold mother was in the possession of some fair dame of the 61st.

One wonders how these women explained their sudden unaccustomed wealth when their husbands returned!*

Looking back on the Second Sikh War, one cannot but be amazed at the extraordinary robustness of the British soldier. Uniforms of this period show how comparatively small men were, yet in full marching order the weight carried was about fifty-six pounds. Sometimes (but by no means always) some of this was carried on the baggage wagons, but invariably each man would have his musket, bayonet and a hundred rounds of ammunition with him. In the Duke of Marlborough's campaigns, a day's march was considered to be about twelve miles, along reasonable roads, in a temperate climate. During the Sikh War, double this distance was often accomplished, very often across country devoid of roads, in conditions of near intolerable heat. The fact that so many men died of heat exhaustion is not surprising, though deaths would undoubtedly have been greatly reduced if the army could have been persuaded to be more abstemious; indeed, the consumption of brandy during these campaigns, and the drop in morale if brandy was not available, remains a constant source of amazement. Another aspect of the mid-nineteenth century soldier was his enthusiasm for battle. In spite of the knowledge that medical facilities were of the most primitive should he be wounded, he anticipated battle with the greatest relish, and the more bloody the better. He had supreme confidence in his comrades, his regiment and his race. He fought like a lion while respecting a brave and determined enemy. Looking at these men, one ceases to be surprised that a numerically miniscule British army was able to conquer and hold down such a vast sub-continent.

* * *

* The soldiers of the 61st Regiment were away with Major-General Walter Raleigh Gilbert's flying column. It is perhaps fortunate that the 32nd had left Jullunder before the 61st returned.

Operations on the North West Frontier, 1852-1856

The Regiment's time in barracks at Jullunder passed only too quickly. Lieutenant-Colonel John Inglis had taken over command from Lieutenant-Colonel Henry Brooke in 1849.

Brooke had not been popular, but Inglis made it his duty to get to know every soldier in his Battalion, and, although a strict disciplinarian, was well liked for this. Ample room, a plentiful supply of compliant women, with abundant spare time provided a haven for the soldier serving in India.

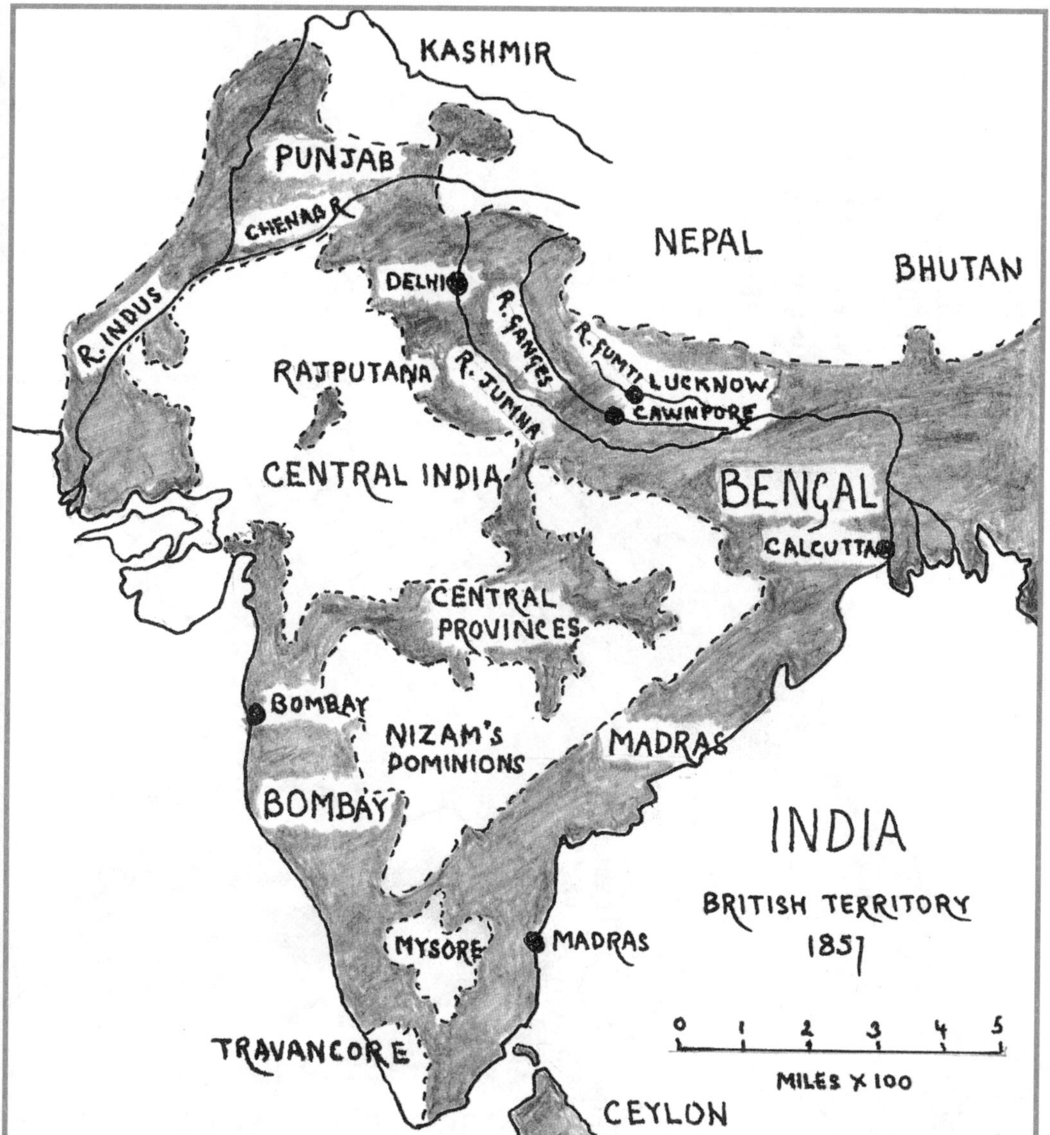
KASHMIR
PUNJAB
CHENAB R.
NEPAL
BHUTAN
DELHI
R. INDUS
R. GANGES
R. GUMTI
LUCKNOW
RAJPUTANA
R. JUMNA
CAWNPORE
CENTRAL INDIA
BENGAL
CALCUTTA
CENTRAL PROVINCES
BOMBAY
NIZAM'S DOMINIONS
MADRAS
BOMBAY
INDIA
BRITISH TERRITORY 1857
MYSORE
MADRAS
0 1 2 3 4 5
MILES X 100
TRAVANCORE
CEYLON

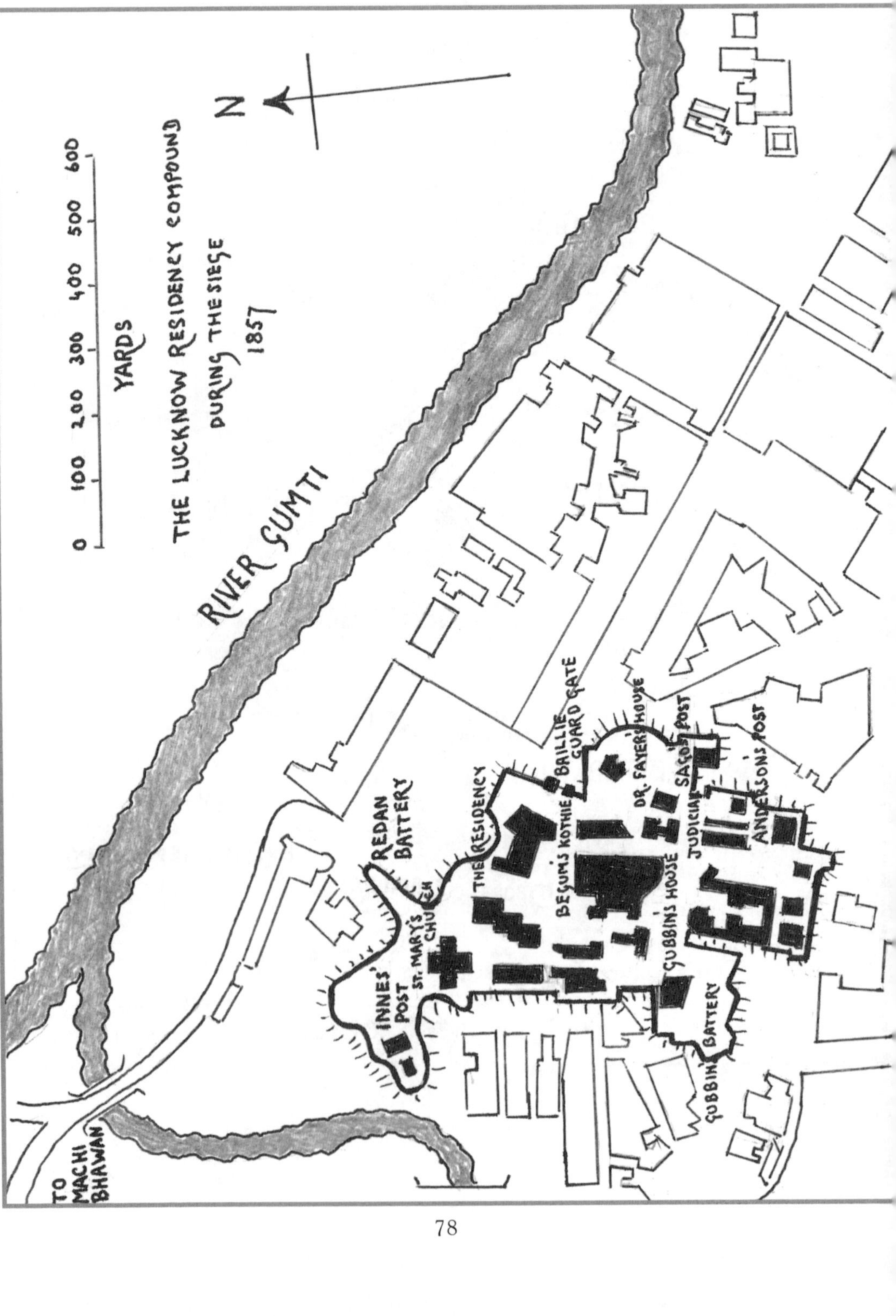
THE LUCKNOW RESIDENCY COMPOUND
DURING THE SIEGE
1857
YARDS
0 100 200 300 400 500 600
N
RIVER GUMTI
TO MACHI BHAWAN
REDAN BATTERY
INNES' POST
ST. MARY'S CHURCH
THE RESIDENCY
BAILLIE GUARD GATE
BEGUM'S KOTHIE
DR. FAYER'S HOUSE
SAGO'S POST
JUDICIAL
ANDERSONS POST
GUBBINS HOUSE
GUBBINS BATTERY

5
The Indian Mutiny, 1857-1858

The conquest of much of the sub-continent of India by the British was not originally carried out as a policy of imperialist expansion. In 1600 a Royal Charter had been granted to the Honourable East India Company, giving it a virtual trade monopoly together with authority to raise troops to guard its trading posts. The subsequent wars pursued by the Company were aimed at driving out first the Dutch and then the French, in the interests of ever greater commercial gains.

By 1773 the East India Company had become not merely a trading company, but the instrument by which the British Government implemented its rule in India. The Company maintained three very considerable armies (Bengal, Madras and Bombay) and built up a bureaucracy under which it controlled a population of 150 million. In 1833 the Company was ordered to close its commercial interests and to assume an official role as the British governing body in India. The East India Company armies consisted of a large numbers of regiments of all arms, each made up of three native units and one recruited at home. This force was augmented by the British Government, which allocated a number of British Army regiments to Indian service. The proportion of these British Army soldiers to native soldiers was originally set at one to three, but due to the withdrawal of numerous regiments to fight the Crimean War of 1854-55 and the parsimony of the British Government in failing to replace them after the war, by 1856 the proportion had fallen to one to six. This was to have dire consequences.

The term 'Indian Mutiny' is a misnomer. It never spread across the whole sub-continent of India (much of which was in fact not under direct British rule) and, generally speaking, was confined to the native soldiers belonging to the East India Company army in the Province of Oudh. Indians today call the 1857 uprising 'The First War of Indian Independence'. This is a much more apt description for, whatever the many contributory factors that may have driven Indian soldiers to attack their officers, the basic cause was that an increasing number of their countrymen saw themselves to be under the yoke of a foreign, infidel power.

One of the ironies of the Indian Mutiny was that many of the East India Company officers had a genuinely warm-hearted affection for their soldiers, which blinded them to the events unfolding in 1856-57. It seemed to them inconceivable that mutiny could occur in their regiments, which they knew and loved so well. Preparations were therefore seldom made to meet such an eventuality.

The first signs of trouble within the native units of the East India Company army were becoming evident in January 1857 and, by February, outright mutiny had broken out in the garrisons of Barrackpore and Berhampore. On 15th May the city of Delhi fell to the rebels, giving them a vast stock of arms and ammunition that had been stored within its walls. On 30th May the native regiments in Lucknow mutinied, leaving the British garrison isolated and surrounded by a vastly superior rebel force. The 32nd Foot was the only complete regiment within the garrison, and, as such, played a crucial part in the famous siege, which was to last till 17th November 1857. First, however, a tragedy was to unfold at Cawnpore, thirty miles away.

Cawnpore, May-July 1857

Cawnpore lies on the River Ganges about 1,000 miles north of Calcutta. In 1857 it was a bustling trading post guarded by a strong military garrison. This garrison was commanded by a sixty-seven year old officer, Major-General Sir Hugh Wheeler, who had been commissioned into the East India Company at the age of fourteen and had served in India ever since. Like many of the older East India Company officers, he had become integrated into Indian life, marrying a native woman and regarding his soldiers as much loved children. This was to have tragic consequences, for he was one of those who refused to believe that his soldiers would ever turn against their officers.

Mutiny struck the Cawnpore garrison in May 1857. By 6th June almost all the native troops had deserted to the rebel leader, Nana Sahib, who had surrounded the barracks with a force of about 3,000 well armed men. Wheeler had rather less than 900 within his fragile defensive perimeter, two thirds of whom were civilians, women and children.

Wheeler had finally decided to dig an entrenchment linking the various barrack buildings, but this was shallow, had no protection against the searing heat of the sun and was not connected to the barrack pump – the only source of water. Day-time temperatures rose to 138 ° Fahrenheit. Life in the trenches became utterly appalling, with little protection against either the constant bombardment or the sun. One of the few officers to show true leadership in this hour of crisis was Captain John Moore, who commanded a detachment of the 32nd. Moore, a tall handsome Irishman, virtually took over the defence of the barracks from the ailing hands of the old General. He was indefatigable in his efforts to maintain a fighting spirit amongst the soldiers, and repeatedly led sorties against the enemy. His gallant efforts were to no avail. Every day increasing numbers of children, women and men died from enemy action and exhaustion. The end was inevitable. On 25th June Nana Sahib offered Wheeler terms under which his garrison would be given safe passage down the Ganges to join the British in the south.

Captain Moore persuaded General Wheeler to accept and, on 27th June, the surviving men, women and children left the entrenchments and made their way down to a muddy creek where boats had been assembled. As they were embarking the surrounding jungle erupted to a storm of musket and cannon fire. Scarcely had this died down than rebel cavalry rode into the shallow water hacking at the survivors with their swords. About 600 were killed; a few men and about 125 women and children were taken prisoner; 4 men made their escape.

It is not known who was responsible for this carefully planned act of treachery, but it was almost certainly not the work of Nana Sahib, who had gone to some trouble to organize the safe passage.

The prisoners, many of whom had been wounded, were herded back to the barracks. In early July news was received that Brigadier-General Havelock's relieving column was approaching Cawnpore. A rebel council of war argued at great length over the fate of the survivors, and it was finally agreed that, so long as they remained alive, the British were bound to attack Cawnpore to save them. However, if they were killed, Havelock would have nothing to gain by re-taking the town, and would therefore bypass it, making for Delhi or Lucknow. Accordingly, on 15th July, orders were given that the prisoners should be shot. All the men were executed by firing squad, but the rebel soldiers refused to despatch the women and children. Nana Sahib's wife, incensed by their insubordination, ordered two Mohameden butchers into the house where some 200 women and children were incarcerated (their numbers had increased by the addition of wives and children rounded up by rebel cavalry patrols). There the most appalling slaughter took place as the butchers set about with their knives and meat cleavers.

The massacre of the women and children at Cawnpore changed the whole aspect of the mutiny. From that time on native soldiers who, for two hundred years had fought alongside their British comrades, were regarded as savage animals. No quarter was given to captured rebels and there is no doubt that terrible atrocities were committed in revenge.

Lucknow, May-November 1857

We must now return to the centre of this drama – Lucknow. Lucknow, a large and splendid city on the River Gumti, the seat of the government of the Province of Oudh. In 1857 Brigadier-General

Sir Henry Lawrence was the Commissioner. A man of great experience, he had long warned his superiors of the simmering discontent amongst the native regiments. Ignored by them, he set about building up supplies of food, ammunition and weapons within the Residency compound, which he feared would inevitably have to stand a siege. The Residency compound occupied a commanding position in this city of palaces, gardens and narrow streets, providing a natural defensive fortification with an area of about 400 by 600 yards. Although its two dozen or so buildings were constructed only of light brick and stucco, the Residency itself was built over a large underground room, proof against cannon fire, and an underground tank, which was to provide plentiful supplies of water for the garrison.

The majority of the native troops in Lucknow mutinied on 30th May 1857. Lawrence immediately put his carefully prepared plans into operation and withdrew his force into two defensible areas: first, a fort known as the Muchee Bhowun, and secondly, the Residency compound itself. It is difficult to give an exact figure of the garrison as so many were women, children, civilians and loyal Indian soldiers who had refused to join the rebels. The approximate strength was probably:

107	British officers, of whom 25 were 32nd Foot.
782	British NCOs and soldiers, of whom 493 were 32nd Foot
51	Eurasian Drummers
153	British civilians, who were formed into an *ad hoc* cavalry squadron
680	Indian civilians
712	Loyal native officers and soldiers*
510	Women and children, of whom about 40 were 32nd Foot
50	Boys from the Martinière School†
3,045	approximately

*Elements of three East India Company regiments, the 13th, 48th and 71st Bengal Native Infantry, remained loyal to the British throughout the siege of Lucknow. This was in spite of being subjected to continuous taunts and entreaties made by their former comrades, who were entrenched only a few yards outside the Residency. Furthermore, they were under no illusions of the terrible fate that awaited them should the garrison fall.

After the reconstruction of the old East India Company Army into the new Indian Army in May 1861, these three loyal regiments were amalgamated to become the 20th Bengal Infantry. Three months later it was renumbered as the 16th Bengal Infantry, and in 1864 was granted the honour of being designated the 16th (The Lucknow Regiment) of Bengal Infantry. At the same time, the *pagri* badge was altered to one depicting the Baillie Gate surmounted by the words 'Defence of Lucknow' entwined with the numeral 16. The title was again changed in the Indian Army reorganisation of 1903, when it became the 16th Rajputs (the Lucknow Regiment).

† The Martinière School lies south east of Lucknow about two and a half miles from the

Although this strength of over three thousand looks formidable at first sight, it must be realised that the 32nd Foot was the only formed unit and that 1,370 of the garrison were non-combatants who ate rations but took little if any part in the defence. Furthermore, 712 were native officers and soldiers whose loyalty came under increased strain as they were entreated to desert by their former comrades.

Battle of Chinhat

On 29th June intelligence reports indicated that a rebel force, estimated as being some 550 strong, was advancing on Lucknow from the east. Although Lawrence's own spies put the enemy figure at nearer 3,000, he reluctantly agreed to sally out with over half his available troops and fight a pre-emptive battle. Owing to confusion in organising the operation, the column did not move out of Lucknow and cross the River Gumti till the sun was well up on the morning of 30th June. All that night the soldiers had been awaiting orders and many had passed the time in heavy drinking. Under the blazing summer heat, and suffering from their excesses, men started falling out almost immediately. The route followed a good metalled road across flat country in which no enemy was encountered. Ten miles from Lucknow the column was confronted by the Kukrail, a narrow but deep river with near vertical banks, which was impassable to men or horses except by a single narrow bridge.

On the far side of the Kukrail lay an open grassy area bounded on one side by the river and on the other three sides by jungle. It seems almost inconceivable that the British force should have been drawn into such an obvious trap.

Residency. The impressive Italianate building was originally the house of a wealthy French officer, Major-General Claude Martine who, on his death in 1800, left a considerable endowment for his house to become a school for Christian boys of European or mixed extraction.

At the time of the Mutiny the staff consisted of the Principal, the Headmaster, 3 teachers, the Matron and the Purveyor, together with 58 pupils between the ages of about 8 and 15. On 13th June 1857 the staff and boys were evacuated to the comparative safety of the Residency compound, where they were to remain until the British force withdrew from Lucknow on 22nd November. During the siege some of the older boys were instructed in the use of the musket and did duty alongside soldiers of the 32nd. The remainder acted as messengers and carried out the multitude of domestic tasks in the garrison, thus releasing able-bodied adults for more military duties.

All the staff and boys who were present at the siege received the Mutiny Medal with clasp 'Defence of Lucknow', while the Martinière School was awarded the Battle Honour 'Defence of Lucknow'. This is unique in the history of the British Army. The School returned to their original home in 1859. It continues to flourish there to this day, and their Cadet Force wear a cap badge depicting the ruins of the Residency.

On the jungle edge across the Kukrail lay the village of Chinhat. No signs of military activity could be seen from the near side of the river and, without even sending out scouts, the British force crossed the narrow bridge and advanced towards the village. Scarcely had it deployed on the far bank than some six thousand rebels, concealed in jungle and high grass, opened a devastating fire with cannon and musket. For a short time the British rallied, conducting an orderly withdrawal, but when Lieutenant-Colonel William Case, commanding the 32nd was killed, discipline began to collapse. As the enemy were seen moving round the flanks to capture the bridge, that slender link between safety and annihilation, retreat became rout as every man joined in a wild race to cross back over the Kukrail. It must be said that amongst this chaos many acts of gallantry were performed, by both British and loyal Indian soldiers; however, the lasting picture is of an appallingly ill considered and ill led operation from which few emerged with any credit. The Lucknow garrison, which even before the battle of Chinhat was already dangerously outnumbered, had suffered very heavy losses: 118 British and 175 loyal Indian soldiers had been killed and a further 78 wounded, many of the Indian soldiers had deserted and several pieces of artillery (including an 8 in. howitzer which was to prove highly effective in enemy hands) had been abandoned. As the last of the defeated column straggled in through the Residency compound gates, thousands of mutineers could be seen closing in from every direction. By nightfall, the Residency and the Muchee Bhowun Fort were completely surrounded.

As dawn broke on 30th June 1857 the Lucknow garrison must have felt despair. Reduced to a fighting strength of 1,640 active men after a humiliating defeat, and hemmed in by a victorious army probably ten times as strong, any possible option of withdrawal was now firmly closed.

The siege, 28th June-23rd November 1857

Because of the severe losses incurred at Chinhat, the following morning Lawrence made the decision that he must concentrate his much reduced force in a single defensive position, and the Muchee Bhowun Fort must therefore be evacuated before being blown up. There was no shortage of explosives to achieve this object; the Muchee Bhowun Fort was a major arsenal containing 240 barrels of gunpowder and nearly a million rounds of assorted ammunition. That morning orders were transmitted to the Fort by semaphore. It was to be prepared for demolition, those guns on field carriages were to be made ready for evacuation and those that could not be moved were to be spiked. The garrison, complete with women and children, were to be waiting ready to move that night, immediately after which the fort was to be blown up. At 10 p.m. all was ready; the guns were limbered up, the column formed up and the roll was called. Every man answered his name except for one Irish soldier of the 32nd, who could not be found. At precisely midnight the sentries joined the column and a minute or so later the gate was opened and the garrison sallied out, making for the Residency. The fuses on the demolition charges were lit. Remarkably, no opposition was encountered during the fifteen-minute march to the Residency. As everything had gone so smoothly, the column arrived at the Baillie Guard Gate earlier than was expected. The leading officer called out "Open the gate", which was mistaken by the gunners covering the approaches as 'Open with grape'. Only the quick action of an officer within the defences prevented a tragic accident. No sooner had the last of the column entered the Residency compound than the Muchee Bhowun Fort blew up. So great was the force of the explosion that ornate ceilings in the Residency collapsed and masonry fell from walls. It transpired that the soldier missing at roll call had been sleeping off a heavy bout of drinking. He was blown clean out of his hiding place, and, being dead drunk, landed in some soft earth still blissfully asleep. The following morning he awoke to find himself in the smoking ruins, none the worse for his experience. Slightly bedraggled, he made his way back to the Residency, arriving unmolested at the Baillie Guard Gate leading a bullock with an ammunition cart, which he had found wandering in the street.

The garrison commander, Brigadier-General Sir Henry Lawrence, the Chief Commissioner of Oudh, was a severe and devout Christian, who eschewed the fripperies of fashionable social life. Born in Ceylon and educated at home in Ireland, he was commissioned into the Bengal Artillery at the age of seventeen. After almost continuous active service under the Indian sun, his weather-beaten face and ragged beard made him look far older than his fifty-one years. He was not a tactician but an administrator, who could identify the essential elements of a situation, and plan accordingly.

As a result of the death of Lieutenant-Colonel Case at Chinhat, command of the 32nd was assumed by Lieutenant-Colonel John Inglis. Inglis had been born in Nova Scotia in 1814, the son of the Bishop of Nova Scotia, and was commissioned into the 32nd at the age of nineteen. Since then he had seen active service during the Canadian Rebellion and throughout the Second Sikh War. At forty-two he was a competent regimental officer, though not over-endowed with either intellect or ability. His outstanding qualification, rare in officers of that period, lay in the fact that he knew every one of his soldiers and was, in return, respected by them.

As soon as the men and families from the Muchee Bhowun Fort were safe inside the Residency compound, frantic activity took place to improve the fortifications. Strong points were constructed that were linked around the perimeter by a trench system.

On 1st July Sir Henry Lawrence was in a room in the Residency with his secretary, Mr George Couper, when a shell, fired from the 8 in. howitzer captured by the enemy at Chinhat, crashed through the window. Amid the falling rubble Lawrence was virtually untouched, although his companion was killed. His officers tried to persuade him to move to less exposed quarters, but he merely replied "Sailors always consider the safest place in a ship to be that where the shot has made the last hole." Alas, he was wrong. The following day a second shell from the same 8 in. howitzer hit his room. This time it exploded with devastating results. Lawrence was mortally wounded; he died forty-eight hours later.

As the senior surviving officer, Lieutenant-Colonel John Inglis took over command of the garrison, handing command of the 32nd to Major Edward Lowe. His immediate problem was how to deploy his very limited force to best effect. With so few troops available, it would have been impossible to man the entire perimeter while also maintaining a reserve to meet emergencies. He therefore constructed a number of defensible posts, each of which was heavily defended and mutually supported by its neighbours. These posts became self-contained garrisons. The occupants normally remained under cover during daylight hours, and commanders were expected to use their initiative in dealing with attacks. Officers and men took their turn on sentry duty without distinction of rank. The women and children were kept under cover as far from the perimeter as possible, and were given various administrative duties; four women volunteered to work under the surgeon in the hospital.

Rations were adequate, though the sole means of preparation produced a greasy stew, thickened with ship's biscuit, which was not exactly *haute cuisine* and became extremely monotonous. There was an ample, perhaps too ample, supply of alcohol available.

Enemy action, cholera, small pox and malaria all took their toll, and within the first week claimed between fifteen and twenty dead per day. In the summer heat bodies had to be disposed of without delay. They were buried each night, but the physical effort involved in digging so many graves placed a severe strain on the already exhausted defenders.

As July wore on, life in the Residency Compound began to assume an orderly routine. The civilians learnt their military duties and gradually became inured to the deprivations, discomfort and dangers of active service.

One of the more sinister aspects of the siege was the constant mining and counter-mining operations that were carried out by both sides. The mutineers continually attempted to drive galleries under the Residency defences, and the defenders dug their own tunnels to intercept these works. Miners would lie with an ear pressed to the earth listening for the tell-tale clink of pick and shovel, while beside them lay a ready primed barrel of gunpowder to blow in the enemy works: a truly terrifying game of cat and mouse which required a high degree of cool courage.

Every night the enemy made attempts to advance their siege line and establish gun positions from which the defences could be bombarded at close range. These guns posed a very serious threat, and had to be destroyed at any cost. Sorties were mounted, which under covering fire from the posts, would rush out and drive an iron spike into the touch hole of the cannon. The projecting head of the spike was then broken off, making it impossible to fire the cannon. Although 'spiking' was simple in itself, the sorties were invariably carried out against stiff opposition that led to savage hand to hand fighting. Of the four Victoria Crosses awarded to members of the Regiment, three were for outstanding gallantry displayed in such sorties. They were Private William Dowling from Thomastown in Ireland, Lieutenant Henry Browne from Newtown in Ireland, and Lieutenant Samuel Hill Lawrence from Cork in Ireland. The fourth, Corporal William Oxenham from Tiverton in Devon, was awarded his Victoria Cross for rescuing a civilian from the wreckage of a building under heavy close-range fire.

Another officer who repeatedly displayed outstanding courage in leading sorties was Captain Bernard McCabe. McCabe was an Irishman who had enlisted in the 31st Foot in the last days of 1839, and joined his Regiment at Agra on 3rd March 1840. From that day he was seldom far from the violent action that was shaping British Imperial India in the mid nineteenth century. He took part in the 700 mile march to relieve Jellalabad, and in the Kabul campaign, fighting at Marzina, Jugdulluk, Tezea and Haft Kotel. By the time of the First Sikh War in 1845 he was a serjeant. That December the 31st Foot provided the Divisional vanguard on the forced march to Modkee, covering 149 miles in 7 days before going straight into action against the Sikh army. There followed the battles of Ferozepore, Badowal, Aliwal and Sabraon. In the last named, the Ensign carrying the Regimental Colour was killed as he scrambled up the breach in the earthwork. With complete disregard for his own safety, McCabe picked up the fallen Colour and, rushing forward, planted it on top of the rampart. His action was considered to have been a major factor in securing the decisive British victory by which the First Sikh War was brought to a triumphant conclusion. When the 31st sailed for England, McCabe preferred to remain in India, and therefore transferred to the 18th (Royal Irish) Regiment, taking part in the Canton expedition of April 1846. The following month his gallantry at Sabraon was officially recognised by the granting of an Ensign's Commission. He was subsequently promoted Lieutenant in April 1847, transferring to the 32nd Foot that summer. Officers commissioned from the ranks often led a lonely life, failing either to fit into the closed club-like intimacy of the officers' mess, or to gain the respect of their soldiers. McCabe never appears to have suffered in this way. All accounts testify that he was popular and highly regarded by both his fellow officers and his men. After the battle of Chinhat he was promoted to fill a Captain's vacancy. Throughout the siege his conduct was of the highest order; he led many sorties outside the walls of the Residency to spike cannon or destroy mine shafts, and was constantly in the thick of the fiercest fighting. On 29th September 1857 he was mortally wounded while leading a sortie against an enemy gun battery. He died two days later. Had McCabe survived, there seems little doubt that he would have joined that select band of Victoria Cross recipients. At that time, however, this highest award for valour could not be granted posthumously.

Siege operations tend to follow the same general pattern. The besiegers advance their trenches ever closer to their objective, while their guns blast the walls in an attempt to create a breach. The defenders, for their part, sally out to drive the enemy from their forward trenches and destroy their guns, and while operations are being conducted above ground, work goes on below the surface, where both sides mine under their adversaries' positions, with the aim of placing explosive charges to blow their occupants to kingdom come. The planning and execution of these aggressive operations is not only tactically necessary, but also raises the morale of men who would otherwise feel themselves passive victims of an all-encompassing enemy. At Lucknow Inglis was determined that everybody, whether soldier or civilian, man or woman and European or Indian, should feel that they were playing a full part in the defence. Even the boys from the local Martinière School were employed as messengers (forerunners of Baden-Powell's 'scouts' at Mafeking).

* * *

The first relief, 25th September 1857

On 7th July 1857 a small Movable Column of about 1,200 British and 300 Sikhs set off from Allahabad, over a hundred miles south east of Lucknow, commanded by Brigadier-General Henry Havelock. Havelock was a diminutive sixty-two year old, with a weather-beaten face and a white beard, who had probably seen more active service in India and Burma than any other officer in the army. A teetotaller and zealous evangelical Christian, he had been considered decidedly eccentric by his brother officers in the 13th Light Infantry, but even they appreciated his military skill and remarkable physical courage. Although described as 'an old fossil dug up and only fit to be turned into pipe clay', Lady Canning, the Viceroy's wife, saw him for his true worth, remarking, "no doubt he is fussy and tiresome, but his little, old, stiff figure looks as fit and active for use as if it were made of steel."

It is to Havelock's great credit that although fully aware of the desperate numerical weakness of his column, he pushed steadily ahead, determined to relieve Cawnpore and Lucknow. His sound military skill, together with his inspirational leadership, won battle after battle against overwhelming odds. On 16th July, after heavy fighting around the villages of Beebiapore and Suktipore, his victorious little band of British and Sikhs entered Cawnpore. He was too late. Quite apart from the tragedy which confronted him, he was now isolated with barely 1,000 men fit for action, no hope of immediate reinforcement and woefully short of ammunition.

A second relief column had meanwhile been assembled at Allahabad under Major-General Sir James Outram, consisting of 2,300 British infantry, 250 Sikh infantry, 80 cavalry and a variety of artillery pieces. The two columns met at Cawnpore on 5th September. The total force was still numerically very weak in comparison to the rebel army, which was rapidly gathering to oppose any movement toward Lucknow. On 5th September Havelock and Outram set off across the Ganges, and for the next twenty days the combined columns were almost continually in action against ever increasing opposition.

News of this advance was received in Lucknow on 12th September, and more encouraging messages were smuggled through the lines on succeeding days. On 23rd September the garrison could distinctly hear heavy firing from the west.

There followed forty-eight hours of frustrating anxiety. Sometimes the firing seemed closer, sometimes more distant and sometimes there was silence. On 24th September the garrison was subjected to the heaviest bombardment yet. It seemed that this was to be the prologue of a final attempt to storm the Residency before Havelock's force could arrive. All through the 25th September heavy firing could be heard in the city itself and, a few minutes after 5 p.m., men of the 78th Highlanders were seen fighting their way forward towards the Baillie Gate. An hour later, to the accompaniment of tumultuous cheers, the first of Havelock's men scrambled over the walls into the Residency. It was the eighty-seventh day of the siege.

With the numbers of defenders doubled, the situation in Lucknow suddenly appeared more optimistic. The perimeter was enlarged and the defences improved. Most important of all, Havelock's troops brought news that the main British force under General Sir Colin Campbell was moving north.

The final relief, 17th November 1857

Campbell had with him 3,400 men, including a naval brigade with eight heavy guns and two rocket launchers. These were joined by a third column from Delhi, bringing his total strength to more than 5,000 men with nearly 40 cannon; a formidable force, though still outnumbered by the rebels. By 7th November Campbell was within signalling distance of Lucknow (a semaphore system had been set up for this purpose), and preparations were made within the garrison for the final evacuation to take place on 13th November.

This was not to be. Sir Colin Campbell was never famed for his speed of manoeuvre, and in this case he appears to have fully lived up to his nickname of Sir Crawling Camel. It was not till the afternoon of 17th November that a strong sortie party from the Residency made contact with the relieving force.

Evacuation, the night of 22nd-23rd November 1857

During the night of 18th November Campbell deployed men of the Naval Brigade to secure the escape route to Secundrabagh, erecting canvas screens along the most vulnerable sections. At midday on 19th November the evacuation started. The women and children moved out first, followed after dark by the sick and wounded. While this movement was taking place, the guns of the garrison and of the Naval Brigade maintained a heavy covering fire. Only when these groups were safely away were preparations for the withdrawal of the garrison put in hand. By this time the rebels were fully aware of what was happening; detailed planning and the highest standard of discipline were therefore vital to success. During the afternoon of

22nd November every soldier was briefed. Each man was allotted to a group; each group in turn would withdraw through the proceeding groups, never more than one moving at any time while the others remained firmly established on the ground. The Naval Brigade would move along the flanks, and the 78th Highlanders (the men who had led the relief) would be given the honour of providing the rear-guard.

Sharp at midnight of 22nd-23rd November the leading group filed out of the Baillie Guard. The lamps were left burning and all was quiet. Remarkably, in spite of the fact that the rebels knew of the evacuation of women, children, sick and wounded on 19th and 20th November, they appear to have had no idea that the garrison itself was to be pulled out. It is a fine testimony to the skill and discipline of those involved that some 9,000 British and Indian soldiers together with cannon made their way through enemy lines to safety.

It was only then that Sir Colin Campbell first saw the 32nd drawn up as a regiment. "On my honour, Brigadier", he said to Inglis, "you have a motley crowd to command." Indeed their uniforms, of those who still had them, were in complete rags, and their beards were long and matted. They had been in the field continuously for almost exactly six months.

Award of the title 'Light Infantry', 14th May 1858

The 32nd underwent a hurried programme of reinforcement and re-equipping before being deployed back into the final and often brutal stages of the campaign, which crushed the Indian Mutiny in 1858.

On 14th May that year the Regiment received the following message from Buckingham Palace:

> Her Majesty, in consideration of the enduring gallantry displayed in the defence of Lucknow, has been pleased to direct that the 32nd Regiment be clothed, equipped and trained as a Light Infantry Regiment from the 26th February last.
>
> Her Majesty has also been pleased to command that the word 'Lucknow' shall be borne upon the Regimental Colour in commemoration of the enduring fortitude displayed in the defence of the Residency for 87 days.

The granting of the title 'Light Infantry' was indeed a very great honour. Historically the role of Light Infantry had called for an exceptional class of soldier. Light Infantrymen were not only required to achieve a high standard in their close-order battle drills, but also had to possess above average physical fitness, intelligence and initiative, to allow them to skirmish in widely dispersed formations. They were trained to make quick individual decisions, to move fast, to make use of cover and to be expert marksmen. By 1858, as a result of the replacement of the old smooth bore musket by the new, considerably more accurate Enfield rifle, the whole infantry was adopting Light Infantry tactics. The title of Light Infantry therefore became an accolade of excellence rather than an indication of a separate role. The outward symbols of a Light Infantry regiment were the dark green head-dress and the incorporation of the bugle horn (the traditional emblem of light troops) in its badge. (A brief history of British Light Infantry is contained at Appendix 2.)

6
The 32nd Foot until Amalgamation, 1881

SERVICE FROM ENGLAND TO MAURITIUS 1859-1877

The 32nd returned in triumph to England in 1859, landing at Portsmouth in August, where it was inspected by Queen Victoria before moving to barracks in Dover Castle. After further tours in Aldershot, the Plymouth Citadel, Devonport, the Curragh and Dublin, the Regiment was once again brought up to full establishment and sailed for Mauritius in 1866. There it was to remain for the next decade, sometimes with a detachment in South Africa. In the twenty-first century Mauritius epitomises the tourist's ideal of South Sea islands with its palm trees, white sand, transparent sea and encircling coral reef; in the nineteenth century it was a coaling station, vital to Britain's line of communication with India, which needed to be securely guarded. Malaria was endemic and, in the absence of effective drugs, often lethal. The many 32nd gravestones on Mauritius mark those ten years of garrison duty.

The Sad Tale of Patrick McCafferty, 32nd Foot, 1861

In the 1860s the majority of infantry recruits were trained at one of the twenty-three depôt battalions dotted around the United Kingdom. In 1861 an Irish recruit of the 32nd Foot by the name of Patrick McCafferty (or M'Caffery; the spelling varies) was undergoing training at Fulwood Barracks, Preston. On the morning of 13th September McCafferty was doing duty as picquet sentry near the officers' mess when the Adjutant, Captain John Hanham (of the 62nd Foot), emerged from the mess and ordered him to clear away children from the soldiers' married quarters who were playing nearby, and to take their fathers' names. Captain Hanham became angry at what he considered to be the casual manner that McCafferty was carrying out this order, and placed him in close arrest. The following morning McCafferty appeared before his Commanding Officer, Colonel Hugh Crofton (late of the 20th Foot), on a charge of insubordination. He was awarded fourteen days Confinement to Barracks. He left the Orderly Room, went to his barrack room where he collected his rifle, loaded it and waited for the Adjutant, whose habit it was to walk across the barrack square on his way to the mess for lunch. He duly appeared; McCafferty took careful aim and fired. Unfortunately on this occasion Captain Hanham was accompanied by Colonel Crofton. The single bullet passed through both these officers, mortally wounding them both.

McCafferty immediately walked quietly to the guard room and gave himself up. He appeared before the Liverpool Assizes in December 1861, where he was very poorly defended by Lord Charles Russell. The jury took only ten minutes to find McCafferty guilty of the murder of Captain Hanham and guilty of the manslaughter of Colonel Crofton. Mr Justice Channell pronounced the death sentence. He was hanged outside Kirkdale Gaol, Liverpool at 12 noon on Saturday, 11th January 1862. All that morning excursion trains had been arriving in Liverpool bringing in spectators. It is estimated that there were between 30,000 and 40,000 people present at the execution. As McCafferty stood on the scaffold, a priest handed him a small crucifix which he kissed, then, calling out "Blessed Jesue, Mary and Joseph, I give you my heart and soul. Jesus and Mary have mercy on me," the bolt was withdrawn. Patrick McCafferty went to meet his Maker.

McCafferty was born in Mullingar in 1843 or 1844. His family had moved to Carlow and then to Kildare. While there, his mother died and his father, who was employed as a lunatic asylum master, ran off to America on account of some scandal. Patrick McCafferty found his way to Stalybridge in Lancashire, where he was employed in a cotton mill. In October 1860 he enlisted in the 32nd Foot, and was sent to the depôt barracks at Preston. McCafferty never conformed to the popular image of the wild Irishman. All the evidence from the trial indicates that he was studious and quiet, a bookworm who sat up late at night reading and shunned the coarse fellowship of his comrades.

Captain Hanham was a veteran of the Sikh Wars in which he had been wounded, leaving him with a deeply scarred face. He was a harsh disciplinarian, notorious for meting out heavy punishments for trivial offences. Not surprisingly he was most unpopular with the soldiers. Colonel Crofton on the other hand was a gentleman who was admired by his men.

Soon after McCafferty's death, the following ballad began to be sung in the Irish pubs around Liverpool. It still is.

When I was just nineteen years of age,
To the British Army I did engage,
I left my home with good intent
To join the thirty-second regiment.

To Fulwood Barracks I did go.
To serve my time in that depôt,
From troubles then I was never free:
My captain took a great dislike to me.

When posted on duty at the Barrack gate,
Some soldiers' children came to play;
From the officers' mess my captain came
And ordered me to take their parents' name.

I took one name instead of three;
'Neglect of duty' they did charge me;
Well, I've no mother to break her heart;
I've no father to take my part.
I have only one friend, and a girl is she;
She'd lay her life down for McCafferty.

Come all you young officers of the present day,
Just treat your men with civility,
For if you don't, there's sure to be
Another hard case like McCafferty.

AMALGAMATION OF THE 32ND & 46TH REGIMENTS 1877-1881

In 1877 the Regiment returned to Cornwall, where it was quartered within the massive defences of Tregantle Fort. That same year saw the introduction of a series of radical reforms that were to change the organisation of the British Infantry out of all recognition. The final chapter of the Cardwell Reforms has already been covered in pages 2 to 4. It was bitterly opposed by the military establishment and had therefore to be introduced over a period, which would render it more palatable to officers, particularly of the older generation. The new two-battalion regiments were therefore established in two distinct phases, the first one comparatively painlessly. In 1877 it was decreed that all infantry regiments with only one existing battalion would be linked with a similar sister regiment. Thus the 32nd (Cornwall) Light Infantry was linked with the 46th (South Devonshire) Regiment of Foot. The individual regimental badges, dress distinctions and traditions were not altered, but officers and soldiers could henceforth be crossposted between the two Regiments.*

In this way a certain degree of cross fertilisation took place; officers and soldiers made close friends across the old regimental divide and came to realise that theirs was not the only regiment in the army to have claim to efficiency and companionship.

* As soldiers were now liable to be posted between regiments that displayed different facing colours, it became necessary for regimental tailors to be able to change facings with the minimum of work. A system was therefore introduced under which all infantry tunics were identical, the facings being indicated by patches of cloth sewn onto the front of collar and cuffs. After the amalgamations of 1881, all battalions of the same 'large' regiment wore the same colour facings. There was therefore no requirement to alter a soldier's uniform when he was posted between battalions. The old system of more permanent facings was therefore re-introduced.

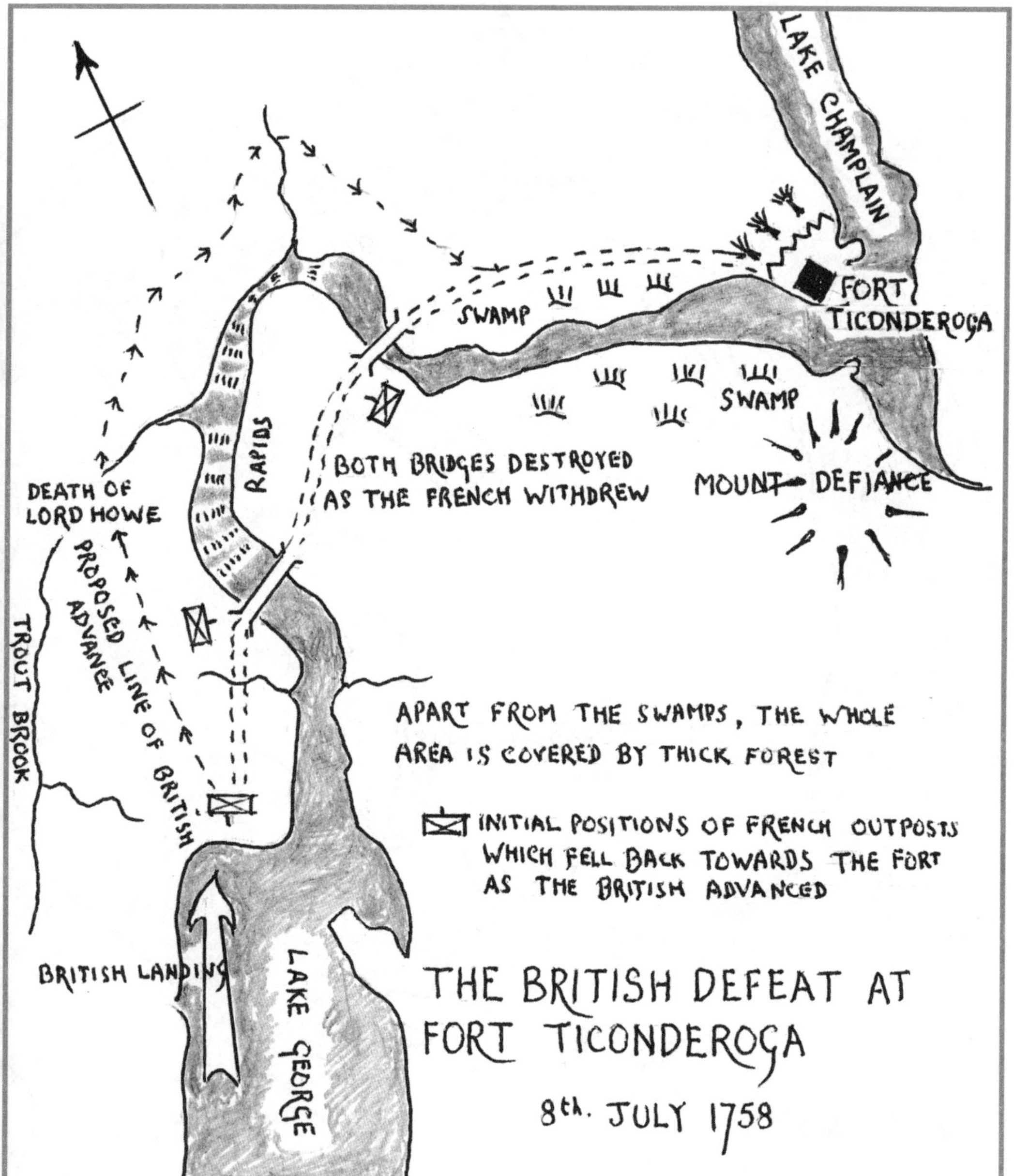
LAKE CHAMPLAIN
FORT TICONDEROGA
SWAMP
SWAMP
RAPIDS
BOTH BRIDGES DESTROYED AS THE FRENCH WITHDREW
MOUNT DEFIANCE
DEATH OF LORD HOWE
PROPOSED LINE OF BRITISH ADVANCE
TROUT BROOK
APART FROM THE SWAMPS, THE WHOLE AREA IS COVERED BY THICK FOREST
INITIAL POSITIONS OF FRENCH OUTPOSTS WHICH FELL BACK TOWARDS THE FORT AS THE BRITISH ADVANCED
BRITISH LANDING
LAKE GEORGE
THE BRITISH DEFEAT AT FORT TICONDEROGA
8th. JULY 1758

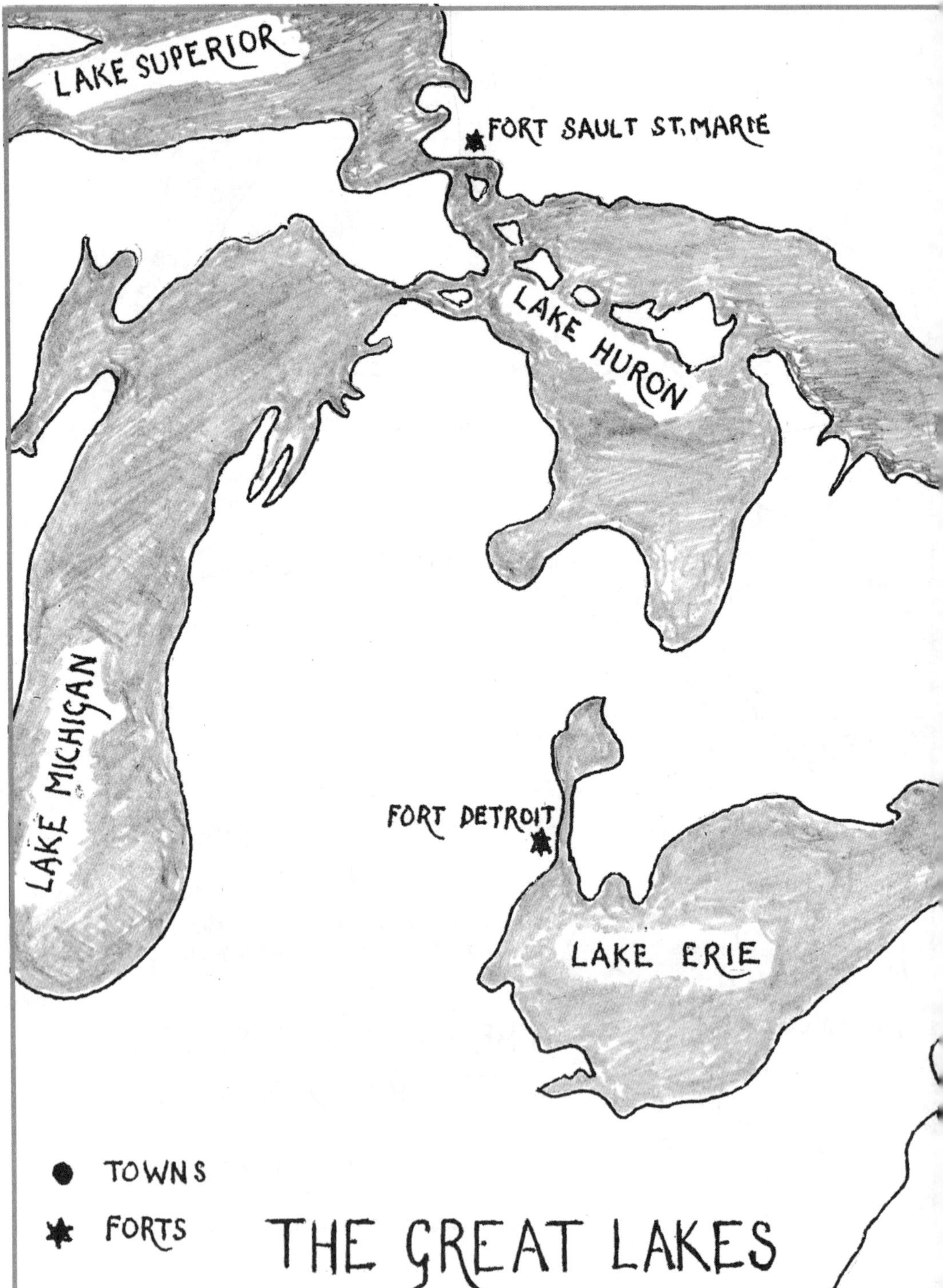
LAKE SUPERIOR
FORT SAULT ST. MARIE
LAKE HURON
LAKE MICHIGAN
FORT DETROIT
LAKE ERIE
TOWNS
FORTS
THE GREAT LAKES

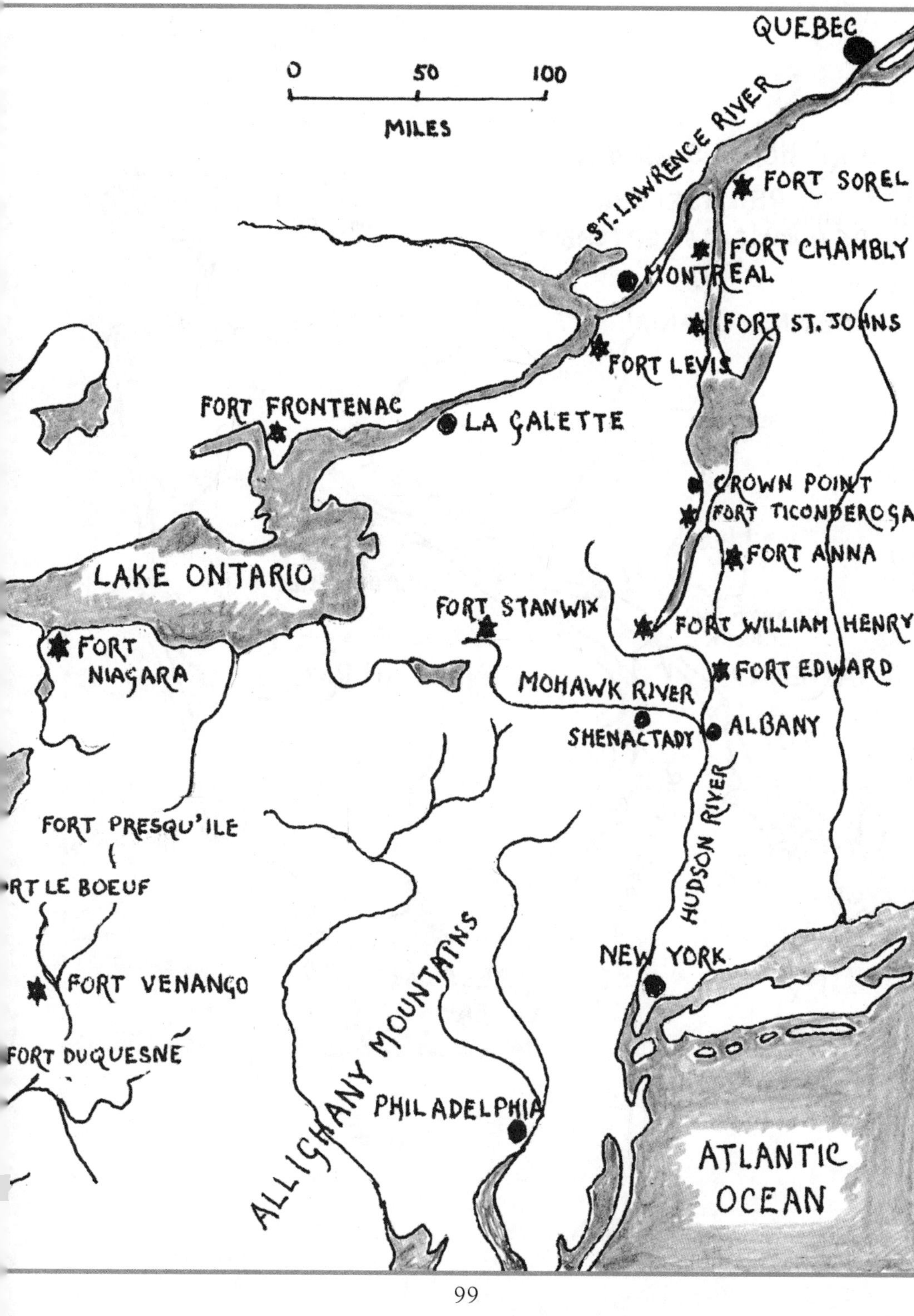
QUEBEC
0 50 100
MILES
ST. LAWRENCE RIVER
FORT SOREL
FORT CHAMBLY
MONTREAL
FORT ST. JOHNS
FORT LEVIS
FORT FRONTENAC
LA GALETTE
CROWN POINT
FORT TICONDEROGA
FORT ANNA
LAKE ONTARIO
FORT STANWIX
FORT WILLIAM HENRY
FORT NIAGARA
FORT EDWARD
MOHAWK RIVER
SHENACTADY
ALBANY
HUDSON RIVER
FORT PRESQU'ILE
FORT VENANGO
FORT DUQUESNE
NEW YORK
ALLIGHANY MOUNTAINS
PHILADELPHIA
ATLANTIC OCEAN

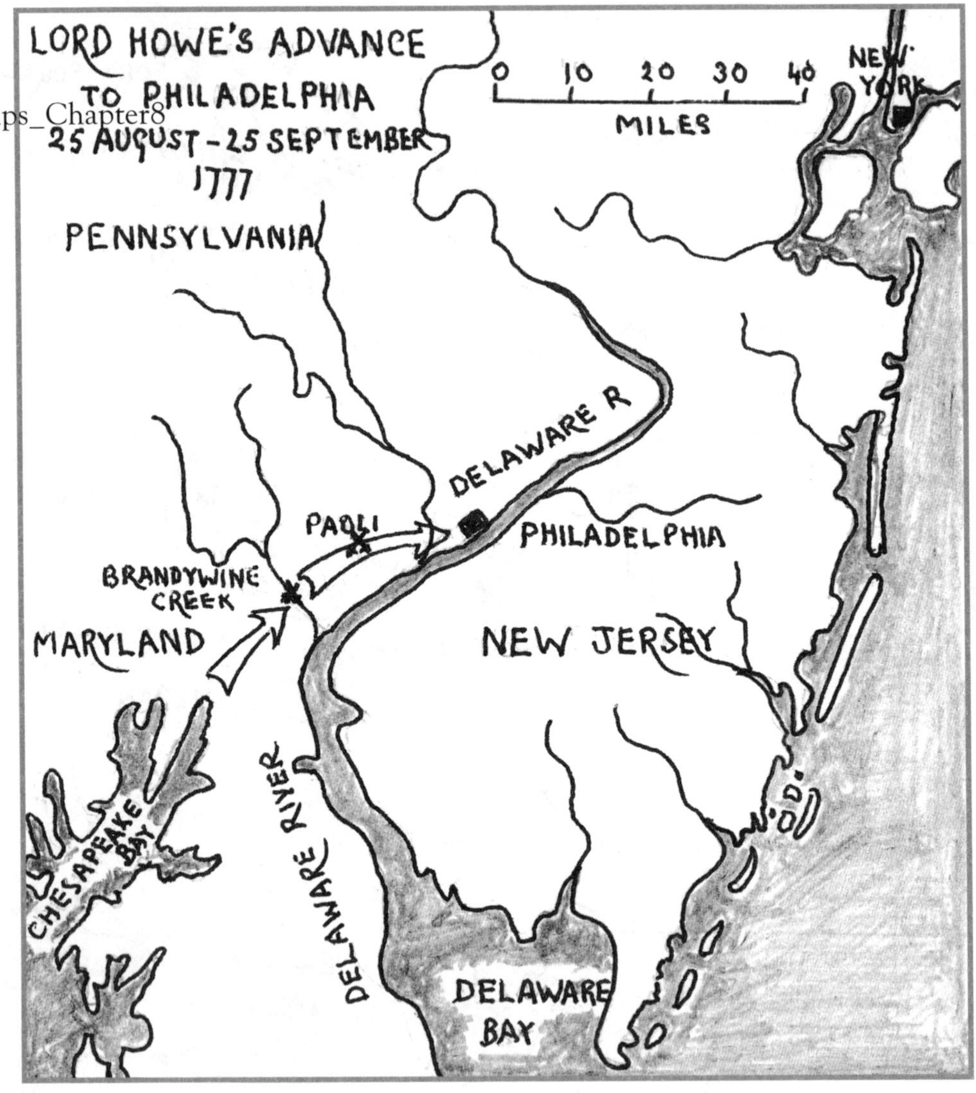
LORD HOWE'S ADVANCE
TO PHILADELPHIA
25 AUGUST - 25 SEPTEMBER
1777
0 10 20 30 40
MILES
NEW YORK
PENNSYLVANIA
DELAWARE R
PAOLI
PHILADELPHIA
BRANDYWINE CREEK
MARYLAND
NEW JERSEY
CHESAPEAKE BAY
DELAWARE RIVER
DELAWARE BAY

Chapter 7

II. THE 46TH REGIMENT OF FOOT

* * *

7
1741-1854

The raising of Price's 57th Regiment of Foot, 1741

The War of the Austrian Succession, which has already been mentioned in connection with the 32nd Foot, led to an expansion of the British Army. Amongst the new regiments that were authorised was Colonel John Price's, raised at Newcastle-on-Tyne on 13th January 1741, and initially numbered the 57th of Foot. The Regiment was stationed for the first four years of its existence at Berwick on Tweed as part of the large English garrison deployed in Scotland. In 1743 the Hon. Thomas Murray, late of the Third Foot Guards, took over the Colonelcy. He was, by all accounts, a stickler for smartness and his Regiment became known as 'Murray's Bucks'.

The Jacobite Rebellion, 1745

The Jacobite Rebellion of 1745 saw the 57th right in the centre of the conflict. France had pledged her support to the Young Pretender, Charles Edward Stuart, grandson of King James II, guaranteeing a substantial military force for the invasion of Scotland. This force was in the process of assembly at Dunkirk when the majority of the transports were wrecked in a gale. Nothing daunted, Charles proceeded alone, except for a small band of followers, arriving in the Highlands towards the end of July 1745. There he was joined by some of the Highland clans. The English Commander-in-Chief assembled all the available troops (numbering a mere 1,400 men) at Stirling, thus leaving the south of the Country unprotected. Charles immediately exploited this opportunity, and crossing the Forth on 13th September 1745, entered Edinburgh, where he had himself crowned King of Great Britain and Ireland on 17th September. Meanwhile the English force had marched to Inverness, where ships were waiting to move it south to cut off the Highlanders. The force landed at Dunbar, twenty-seven miles east of Edinburgh, where it was joined by two additional regiments of dragoons. From there the English advanced towards Edinburgh, camping near the hamlet of Preston Pans on the night of 20th September. During that night the Highland army, which outnumbered the English by about three to one, moved up silently. At about 3 a.m. the Highlanders fired a volley, threw down their muskets, and with a blood curdling cheer charged home with their broad swords. The English were taken completely by surprise and, after a brief skirmish, fled the field in total disorder. About 400 were killed or wounded and more than 1,200 captured. It was an inauspicious start for the 57th Foot.

Following the disaster of Preston Pans, the Duke of Cumberland assumed command of the English army. After receiving reinforcements, he reimposed discipline and reorganised training. Charles Edward Stuart's Highland army was conclusively defeated at Culloden in 1746. The 57th did not, however, take part in this battle, though it was almost certainly involved in the subsequent vicious retribution that was meted out to the defeated Highlanders.

The Treaty of Aix-La-Chapelle, 1748

1748 saw the conclusion of the War of the Austrian Succession by the Treaty of Aix-la-Chapelle. The army was immediately reduced in size by disbanding several regiments. The 57th escaped disbandment, but as a result of this reorganisation was renumbered the 46th.

Ireland, 1749-1757

During this period relations between the troops and the local Irish must have been excellent, for it was particularly noted that, whereas it was the usual practice for shopkeepers to raise their prices when soldiers descended on a community, no such thing happened on this occasion. Indeed, when the names were drawn of the wives and families who were to accompany the regiment to America, the citizens of Cork raised money by public subscription to provide for those left behind.

The 46th sailed for Nova Scotia in 1757, after eight years of garrison duty in Ireland.

* * *

The Canadian War, 1757-1761

On 25th April 1757 a long awaited convoy of warships and transports appeared off the Head of Kinsale, and the following morning anchored in Cork harbour. The force, commanded by Major-General the Earl of Loudoun, which consisted of the 2nd Battalion the 1st Royals, the 17th, 22nd, 27th, 28th, 42nd, 43rd, 44th, 46th, 48th, and 55th Regiments, and the 2nd and 4th Battalions the 60th Royal Americans, immediately embarked. There were 15 escorting warships and 45 transports. The 46th was allotted passage in the transports *Essex, John & Samuel, Mediterranean, Ward, Fair American* and *Heron*. The *Essex* was by far the largest vessel at 602 tons, while *Mediterranean* was the smallest at a mere 183 tons (considerably smaller than a modern fishing trawler).

The international situation existing in North America at this time can be broadly summarised as follows. The British held thirteen colonies along the Atlantic seaboard that formed a continuous chain from Georgia in the north to Maine in the south. The French disposition was considerably more complex. They controlled large swathes of territory to the west of the British possessions, based on chains of forts strategically sited on the major rivers and the Great Lakes. Quebec in the north was the French centre of operations, with the forts of Sorel, Montreal, La Galette, Frontenac, Niagara, Presqu'ile and Detroit stretching south west along the St Lawrence river, Lake Ontario and Lake Erie, while far into the hinterland lay Sault St Marie at the junction of Lake Superior and Lake Huron. Two subsidiary strings of forts ran due south; the first, along the Richlieu river from its junction with the St Lawrence river at Sorel, ran through Lake Champlain, and included Chambly, St Johns, Crown Point and Ticonderoga; the second, from Presqu'ile on Lake Erie, included Le Boeuf, Venango and Duquesne. To the far south lay the French territories of New Orleans in the Gulf of Mexico, while to the far north west was the natural harbour of Louisbourg on the western shores of Cape Breton Island. Here the French had assembled a formidable garrison and fleet, which presented a serious threat to the British seaboard colonies.

The strategic aim of the French was to link Quebec in the north to New Orleans in the south, to prevent any expansion of the British colonists to the west. The aim of the British was: first, to destroy the military and naval base at Louisbourg, thereby removing the threat of a seaborne attack on the east coast colonies; and second, to harass, capture or destroy the French forts, thereby disrupting their defensive chain and frustrating their whole strategy. In this conflict, both sides made full use of the native American Indians. The various tribes which comprised this ethnic race possessed unsurpassed forest skills; they were also greatly feared for their cruelty.

Loudoun's force disembarked at Halifax, and immediately set about throwing up defensive earthworks to protect the town from French marauders from Louisbourg, who might try to pre-empt his own operations. This being done, he left the small original garrison ashore while he re-embarked his main force to capture Louisbourg. However, while his ships were still at anchor off Halifax, a captured French schooner was brought in. Her master brought the disturbing intelligence that there were now 22 ships of the line and 3 frigates, together with a reinforcement of an additional 7,000 soldiers in Louisbourg. Against such odds, Loudoun had no hope of conducting an opposed landing. Reluctantly he called off the operation.*

A rapid change of plan was made. Loudoun's force was split up, and the major part, which included the 46th, was despatched by sea to New York. Arriving there on 31st August 1757, it learnt that General Montcalm had attacked Fort William Henry, a stronghold at the head of the Hudson river, and captured it. Burning the stockade and buildings, he had then withdrawn, whereupon the 'red skins' had moved in and slaughtered the survivors, including the women and children. Loudoun immediately set off north up the Hudson river to avenge this atrocity by attacking the French-held fort of Ticonderoga, which commanded the junction of Lakes George and Champlain. In the event this came to nothing. His force was ill prepared for such an operation, lacking the specialist training and equipment needed to fight in forests. Furthermore, the last of the warm summer weather was rapidly passing, and there was no fur clothing yet available that was essential if men were to survive out of doors in the bitter winter weather. Loudoun considered it expedient to call off the operation. His force was dispersed, the 46th marching to Schenectady, a Dutch trading station on the River Mohawk. From there the Regiment deployed detachments to the forts Herkiner, Hendrick and Hunter. The barracks at Schenectady had the reputation of being the worst in the whole of North America. The soldiers seem, however, to have spent little time in barracks, for alarms were frequent and the Regiment was frequently turned out to chase off 'red skins' who invariably melted away into the thick forest.

In December 1757 the hapless Lord Loudoun was recalled to London by Pitt. Although Loudoun's decisions to abort the operations against Louisbourg and Fort Ticonderoga were almost certainly militarily sound, politicians demand success from their generals. Excuses for failure are seldom accepted and the penalty is all too often ignominious dismissal. In Loudoun's place, Pitt appointed Major-General Abercromby, a fifty-two year old officer

*The Earl of Loudoun was later severely criticised for his actions. The fault, however, lay with the Government which had kept him hanging about in Cork for eight weeks. Had be been able to sail earlier, he would have arrived before the French reinforcements, and would thus have captured Louisbourg without undue trouble.

described as 'Prematurely aged and heavy of body and mind.' He owed his appointment to political influence that could not be disregarded, but Pitt let it be clearly understood that Abercromby was only in nominal command, and that his second-in-command, Brigadier-General Lord Howe, would be expected to exercise control. Howe was an outstanding officer who had immersed himself in the tactics of forest fighting. He was a strict disciplinarian, but loved by his soldiers.*

By mid June 1758 Abercromby's force, including the 46th, had moved out of New York to its assembly area at Albany. Boats had been built and a large detachment had been trained to man this flotilla. Meanwhile at Fort Ticonderoga, news of the British build up reached the ears of Colonel Bourlamaque, the commander, who immediately made plans for detailed deployment of his force in and around the fort. The fort itself was approximately square enclosed by a double rampart, each about ten feet thick, built of two outer skins of substantial tree trunks held together by transverse tree trunks, dove-tailed at both ends. The space between the two skins was filled with stones and earth. Within the ramparts lay stone magazines and barrack quarters. All approaches to the fort were covered by a tangle of felled trees which made ordered movement impossible. By this time General Montcalm had arrived at Fort Ticonderoga, and wasted no time in making further improvement to the defences. Nature and man had between them made the fort virtually impregnable.

After a less than trouble-free approach march, during which Abercromby's column became lost in the thick pine forest, the troops arrived before Fort Ticonderoga on 8th July 1758. The fort was sited on a spit of land projecting into the lake and was thus almost entirely surrounded by water. The only landward approach was very strongly defended. Because of the extreme difficulties attending the movement of anything but infantry through the forest, the British force had no artillery. However, because intelligence had been received that a French force of a further 3,000 men was on its way to the fort, General Abercromby determined to attack immediately. The attack was a disaster. The British force suffered heavy casualties and was forced to withdraw.

Since it was raised, the Regiment had thus taken part in two actions that had ended in catastrophe. However, its fortunes were about to change for the better. In July 1759 the 46th took part in the siege and capture of Fort Niagara, a stronghold not dissimilar to Fort Ticonderoga, situated in a commanding position at the junction of the Lakes Ontario and Erie. As before, intelligence reported the

* See pp. 109-110

movement of a strong French relieving force so that the attack had to be carried out without delay. This time, however, it was entirely successful and the Fort surrendered on 25th July 1759.

Campaigning against the French continued in Canada throughout the summer months until 1761.

The West Indies, & return to Canada, 1762-1767

War having been declared against Spain in 1762, a considerable force under command of the Earl of Albermarle was despatched from England in March of that year to capture the wealthy port of Havannah on the north coast of the island of Cuba. Three months later, the 46th, together with a miscellany of American independent companies embarked at New York to join Albermarle's expedition. The 46th was accommodated in HM Ships *Intrepid* and *Chesterfield*, and the transports *Masquerade*, *Amherst* and *Lyon*, all of which sailed on 11th June. The voyage to Havannah was not without incident. On 24th July HMS *Chesterfield* and four of the transports ran aground on the Cayos Romanos, a group of small sandy islands in the Old Bahamas Straits some 300 miles short of their destination. Fortunately there was no loss of life, everybody managing to get ashore in the ships' boats. Thus it was that, for several weeks, the 46th became split up, initially only those aboard *HMS Intrepid* reaching Havannah.

The siege and capture of the port demanded very hard labour in building supply lines through the virgin jungle and constructing trenches and gun batteries in the rocky soil. From the first landing, yellow fever and malaria began to take a heavy toll. Havannah was eventually captured but it proved to be a Pyrrhic victory, for on 3rd November 1762 the Treaty of Paris was signed at Fontainbleau. Under the terms of this treaty, France agreed to surrender all her territories in North America except New Orleans. In exchange, Britain gave France the islands of Martinique, Guadeloupe, St Lucia and Marigarlante. Spain ceded East and West Florida in exchange for Havannah. The considerable loss of life from battle and disease had all been in vain.

The Spanish were not slow to reassert their authority in Havannah. The new British Commander-in-Chief, Major-General the Hon. William Keppel, was anxious to remove his troops from this disease ridden place, but waited in vain for orders. Each day more men fell sick and died. The devastation by disease during the British brief occupation of Havannah can be judged by the muster rolls of the four regiments, which numbered 252, 208, 212 and 257 respectively.

Impatient of the delay, Keppel embarked the force and set off back to England. However, while in mid Atlantic, his fleet of transports was intercepted by a sloop of the Royal Navy bearing the long awaited orders. All would continue east to England except the 15th, 28th, 40th and 46th of Foot, which were to return to New York. One can imagine the feelings of the officers and men of these four regiments when, with their home shores so close, they turned back west for America.

Their future role was to operate against the native North American Indians, who were staging a major and very bloody rebellion against the Europeans.

The ships reached New York on 29th July 1763, and an advance party of the 46th was soon despatched by boat up the Hudson river to Fort Niagara. The main body, probably because it needed to do some urgent recruiting, did not arrive till 13th September, when it took over from a battalion of the 60th (Royal American) Regiment. Lieutenant-Colonel William Browning, the Commanding Officer, wrote to the Commander-in-Chief, General Sir Jeffery Amherst, imploring him to provide drafts to bring his regiment to a viable strength, capable of carrying out its duties in and around the fort.*

His plea seems to have had some effect as far as numbers were concerned, but the quality of the drafts that arrived left much to be desired. In the Colonel's words they were made up of '. . . old and worn out soldiers which no corps would have accepted unless forced by necessity to do so.' On 19th October a motley battalion of 600 all ranks, mainly consisting of these old time-expired men, left the safety of Fort Niagara with the object of crossing Lake Erie, to relieve Detroit. A sudden storm blew up on the night of 7th November, sinking many of the boats. Two lieutenants, the surgeon, four serjeants and sixty-three rank and file were drowned. Most of the provisions and all the ammunition was lost. The expedition was aborted and the battalion returned to Fort Niagara.

The following year, the new Commander-in-Chief, Major-General the Hon. Thomas Gage, noted in a memo that 'Captain Hopkin's [American] Independent Company has been disbanded, and its officers and men transferred as near as their numbers admitted [to] the 46th Regt. at Niagara.' Poor Browning must have had a remarkably mongrel battalion, mainly composed of the scrapings of time-expired soldiers from many regiments together with an assortment of men from the disbanded local American Independent Companies.

*William Browning was the last of the officers who had served continuously with the 46th since its raising in 1741.

Jeffery Amherst: see Appendix 2, pp. 534-535

The 46th finally left the area of the Great Lakes in 1766, arriving back in New York at the beginning of July. Numbers were so depleted that a party of four officers, four serjeants, four corporals and four drummers was immediately despatched to England to recruit men in preparation for the Regiment's anticipated return home.

The Regiment then returned to the never ending round of garrison duties in Ireland.

Ireland, 1767-1775

Ireland, with its seething rebellious element, offered a vulnerable flank to any French invading force. Every English politician was acutely aware of the doggerel couplet:

> He who would England win
> Must in Ireland first begin.

Troops were continuously deployed in Ireland throughout the eighteenth and nineteenth centuries, in numbers out of all proportion to the size of the country, to combat armed insurrection and to provide a defence against invasion.

The Origins of the Light Infantry

The years of campaigning in Canada and North America during the mid eighteenth century are not only of interest because of the involvement of the 46th Foot, but also because they witnessed the effective development of Light Infantry.

After the Peace of Aix-la-Chapelle in 1748, the British Army was appreciably reduced in size. Thousands of ex-soldiers who had served their country with great honour found themselves destitute and unemployed. It was to the credit of the Government that a scheme was set up to offer free passage to any of them who wished to emigrate to Nova Scotia, where they would be offered a grant of land. The French reaction to these newcomers was predictable. Fomenting the native 'Indians' to make war against the British, they set about the construction of forts on the Ohio river, thus barring all but French trade from moving to the sea. The largest and most important of these was Fort Duquesne.

In 1755 The Duke of Cumberland despatched General Braddock to bring the confrontation to a conclusion. Both these men were firm disciples of Frederick the Great, whose military concept was based on 'drill, more drill and still more drill, never an ounce of initiative'. In the flat open plains of northern Europe this ethos had proved formidable; in the forests of Canada it was to be useless. It is ironic that, from his first arrival in Nova Scotia, General Braddock was surrounded by settlers who had adapted to the local conditions and were fully conversant with Indian warfare in the forests. If he had listened to their advice he could have set about re-training his army for its forthcoming role, and made use of the existing, highly experienced local militia units. Instead he chose to believe that these ill-armed savages could be quickly put to route by the awesome fire power of disciplined battalions standing shoulder to shoulder, three ranks deep in their perfect drill formations. At his first battle on the Monongahela river on 9th June 1755, Braddock was to be dramatically disillusioned. As his men were steadily picked off by an unseen enemy, the survivors fled in total disorder. As far as numbers were concerned, it was a minor battle, but proportionately it was a disaster. The British force had been 1,473 strong, but in only a few hours fighting had suffered 977 casualties. The French and Indians had been about 900 strong and suffered 39 casualties. The battle of Monongahela river, seldom remembered today (for obvious reasons), was to prove a turning point in British tactical doctrine.

The fiasco at Monongahela river had an immediate effect on The Duke of Cumberland, who was quick to grasp its significance. Hearing of the British difficulties, a Swiss soldier of fortune, M. Jacque Prevost, made himself known to the Duke. He offered to raise a four-battalion regiment, manned by American colonists but officered by gentlemen of various nationalities who had seen active service in the recent European wars. This was agreed and, after a sum of £80,178 16s had been made available, this new regiment, known as the Royal Americans, was officially raised on 4th March 1756. The nucleus sailed for Pennsylvania, where it was known that the large colony of English, Swiss, Tyrolese and German backwoodsmen would provide excellent recruit material. The Royal Americans, originally numbered 62nd in the Line (later to become the 60th) were the first true Light Infantry to be included in the British standing army.

There were many British officers who realised the folly of applying barrack-square tactics to the forest. In 1757 Colonel Lord Howe arrived in North America with his regiment, the 55th Foot. Being a practical man, he at once set himself to learn the art of forest warfare. He joined the irregulars and Indians in their scouting parties, lived in the forest, adopted their dress, shared their hardships, and totally immersed himself in the conduct of this most unconventional form of soldiering. Having thoroughly schooled himself, he proceeded to teach the lessons to his regiment. He cut the long heavy skirts off their coats and the brims off their broad tricorn hats; he abandoned the use of pipe clay, pomade and hair powder; he trained and equipped his men to move with stealth and speed, taking advantage of every piece of cover. A far cry from the Prussian rigid lines of battle. Many of the more imaginative officers watched the Royal Americans and Lord Howe's 55th Foot with interest, becoming convinced that this new tactical employment of troops represented the future of infantry – if not in Europe, certainly in America.

In 1758, probably due to Lord Howe's influence, a new regiment known as the 80th Regiment of Light Armed Foot was raised by Colonel Gage, and the following year the 90th Irish Light Infantry was raised by Colonel Morgan.

During the advance to Louisbourg and the capture of the town in 1758, full use was made of light troops. A battalion with a strength of 550 men, known simply as the Light Infantry, was formed by taking suitable soldiers from the currently available regiments in North America. This battalion, commanded by a Major Scott, played a prominent part in the Canadian war from that time until the peace. That same year,

Lord Howe was killed during the first unsuccessful attack on Fort Ticonderoga; however, his tactical doctrine was now so firmly established that additional light infantry battalions were being raised. At the taking of Quebec on 13th-14th September 1759 General Wolfe relied heavily on his Light Infantry troops; indeed, it was a carefully picked group of twenty-four light infantrymen under the command of Major Sir William Howe (youngest brother of the late Lord Howe) who led the way, silently creeping up the 200 foot cliff to the Plains of Abraham.

The Peace of Paris in 1763 saw the inevitable reduction of the British army, most of the recently formed Light Infantry being disbanded. However, perhaps in anticipation of some necessary future expansion of the light infantry arm, a light company was authorised for every battalion of the line. Alas, these companies seem to have been regarded as penal settlements into which battalions could crosspost all their worst characters. So useless did light companies become that in 1774 George III ordered a school of instruction to be set up at Salisbury under General Sir William Howe, to train a selected seven light companies.

AMERICA, 1775-1778

In 1775 rebellion erupted, not in Ireland but in the American Colonies. Large reinforcements were despatched across the Atlantic. These included the 46th, which landed in North Carolina early in April 1776.

The war that was fought in America between 1775 and 1778 is believed by many (including most Americans) to have been a black and white affair, conducted on one side by Americans determined to throw off the shackles of colonialism, and on the other side by a British army sent by its government to maintain the suppression of a prosperous nation. As is the case in most wars, the truth is more complex. If the entire population of America had risen up in arms, no force that Britain could have put into the field would ever have even aspired to success. In fact, the America of 1775 was a deeply divided nation, large parts of its population not merely remaining loyal to Britain, but actually taking up arms against the rebels. In truth, the American War of Independence might well be called the First American Civil War.

British operations during the War of American Independence are often depicted as demonstrating the incompetent intransigence of her senior commanders, whose insistence that inappropriate European style tactics should be employed led to successive disasters. The truth was rather different. The remarkable fact is not that the British Army, operating at the end of a 3,000-mile line of communication and neglected by a parsimonious government, finally lost the war, but that she nearly won it. At the opening of the War of American Independence the sad lack of highly trained and motivated light troops had become all too apparent. At both Lexington and Bunker Hill the British sustained unnecessarily heavy casualties under the command of General Gage, who appeared to have forgotten all his previous experience with Light Infantry. But in 1776 General Gage was relieved of his command by General Sir William Howe, an officer experienced in American warfare. He had commanded a battalion under General Wolfe, who had described it as 'the best trained in all America', high praise indeed from a man who was known never to give undue credit. Howe immediately took the light companies away from their respective battalions and organised them into specialised light infantry battalions.*

It was while operating in this manner that the Light Company of the 46th Foot fought with such success throughout this war.

Capture of Brooklyn & New York, September 1776

The 46th were initially involved in the siege and capture of Brooklyn, followed by the capture of New York. The rest of the army then proceeded to enlarge their territorial gains while the 46th remained on the River Hudson, using an old transport ship as a barracks. During the winter of 1776 the Regiment was employed on the line of communication to the advanced winter quarters of the Army and were involved in frequent skirmishes with the rebels, who operated with comparative freedom behind the British lines.

Attack on Peek's Hill, 1777

In March 1777 the 46th formed part of an amphibious force that landed at the naval dockyard of Peek's Hill and destroyed the rebel magazines, barracks and dockyard facilities. During that spring and summer, the royal forces were constantly trying to tempt the rebels to fight a pitched battle, but without success. Being highly competent guerrillas, they limited their operations to hit-and-run attacks against the vulnerable British line of communication.

* It is not clear whether these light infantry battalions always operated as such. It seems more likely that the light companies were often reallocated to their own regiments. It is evident, however, that the organisation existed by which light companies could be brought together at very short notice.

Battle of Brandywine Creek, September 1777

The Army, under General Lord Howe, brother of the Lord Howe killed at Ticonderoga, determined to move south west and capture the wealthy city of Philadelphia. Its route was barred by General George Washington, who had established his army in an almost impregnable position at Chad's Ford, one of the few crossing places of a major obstacle known as Brandywine Creek. Soon after dawn on 11th September 1777 Lord Howe put in a frontal attack with great vigour and noise. This, however, was merely a feint, for at the same time he delegated General Lord Cornwallis to lead the larger part of his army around the left flank to take the rebels in the rear. The 46th were part of this flanking force, which carried out a forced march of eighteen miles before falling on the unsuspecting rebel rear in the early afternoon. After fierce fighting Washington was forced to withdraw, leaving small detachments to delay the British advance.

Battle of Paoli, September 1777

As he withdrew, Washington ordered Colonel Anthony Wayne to move a large force of his Pennsylvania Continentals around behind the British and conceal them in the woods near a building known as the Paoli tavern. Their task was to let the main body of the British army pass by and then cut its line of communication. Unbeknown to Wayne, news of this plan reached Lord Howe, who immediately ordered General Charles Grey (later Earl Grey) to take the light companies from a number of regiments and attack Wayne.

The Light Company of the 46th formed part of this *ad hoc* battalion. The plan was that the troops should move out at dusk on the evening of 20th September and advance through the woods to attack Wayne's camp during the night. Surprise was absolutely vital; a single accidental shot from a musket would compromise the whole operation. General Grey therefore gave the order that every soldier was to remove the flint from his musket, thereby rendering it inoperative. When contact was made, the British would have to rely solely on the bayonet. Soon after midnight General Grey attacked the rebels. Surprise was complete, and terrible slaughter was inflicted, every man who could not escape being bayoneted. 460 enemy dead were counted the following morning; the British losses amounted to 1 officer, 1 serjeant, and 1 private killed, and some 17 wounded. The American rebels were appalled, considering the bayoneting of men in cold blood (for many of them had been sleeping) as an act of barbarism. They immediately named this action the Paoli Massacre, and swore that from henceforth no quarter would be given to British prisoners. General Grey's men, perhaps wishing to protect the rest of the army who had played no part in the attack, but also undoubtedly proud of their own highly successful operation, let it be known that they, and they only, were responsible. In order that the rebels should recognise them, they dyed their hat feathers red. From that day the 46th Foot and their various successors have worn red in their head-dress, sometimes as red feathers, a red chaco tuft, a red pugree or simply a red backing to the cap badge. This last symbol of Paoli is today worn by every Light Infantry soldier.

Attack on New Bedford, September 1778

In 1778 the 46th were once more embarked for amphibious operations, and on 5th September carried out a raid on the strong naval dockyard at New Bedford. The attack was successful: all opposition was easily swept aside, seventy ships were destroyed, the fort was demolished, the magazine blown up and an immense quantity of naval stores removed. The troops then advanced to Martha's Vineyard, destroying the defences, capturing the militia arms, and looting and burning the houses. It was there that the 46th removed a bible from the house of an old man by the name of Batholomew West. It is commonly believed that this bible was the one on which the young George Washington had sworn his Oath of Apprenticeship into the Masonic Order, and that it was originally inscribed with his name on the flyleaf. The 46th appropriated the bible as their Masonic Bible. It led an eventful life, for the Americans captured it shortly afterwards, and the French captured it in 1805. In both cases it was returned under a flag of truce. The bible is now held in the Duke of Cornwall's Light Infantry Museum.*

* The authenticity of the claim that the bible was once inscribed on its flyleaf with the signature of George Washington is open to doubt. The popular explanation for its disappearance is that it was stolen from the officers' mess of the 2nd Battalion the Duke of Cornwall's Light Infantry at some time when wives and guests had been invited back to the mess after Sunday church parades. The station at which this theft is alleged to have taken place is severally given as Gibraltar in 1905-06, and Burmuda in 1907-08. The disparity of time and place does not endow this story with credibility. Furthermore, a close examination of the bible discloses no sign of a page ever having been forcibly removed. The bible was re-bound in Ireland in about 1835; if the flyleaf did indeed disappear, it is more likely that it was removed at that time. Over the years the so-called 'Washington Bible' has been the subject of numerous claims for its return made by descendents of Nathaniel West. However, the retention or return of the 'spoils of war' is a complex legal matter, and while the trustees of the Regimental Museum may feel sympathy for the West family, they are under no obligation to return the Bible. Certainly, at the present time, in 2005, there is no intention of so doing.

Philadelphia & St Lucia, December 1778

The 46th returned to Philadelphia, hoping to settle down for the winter in the comparative comfort of the town. However, in early December news was received that a large French force had crossed the Atlantic, with a view to helping the American rebels in their struggle for independence. The security of the West Indies, which might have provided vital naval bases for the French, therefore became of paramount importance. Under General Prescott the 46th was immediately despatched with three other regiments to St Lucia. The French did indeed land at La Vigie in St Lucia on 18th December, but after a sharp action they were driven back to their ships, leaving some 400 dead and 1,100 wounded. British losses amounted to only 10 killed and 130 wounded.

The 46th remained in the West Indies till 1782. By then it had been wasted by malaria and yellow fever, and by casualties suffered in six years of hard campaigning, and the Regiment returned home to recruit and re-train.

1782-1818

Home service & Gibraltar, 1782-1792

In 1782 the 46th was affiliated to South Devonshire and this was reflected in the change of the full title to the 46th (South Devonshire) Regiment of Foot. After being stationed at Plymouth and in Ireland the Regiment moved to Gibraltar in 1792.

More service in the West Indies, 1794-1811

War with France again broke out in 1794, and the 46th was once more despatched across the Atlantic to the West Indies. These continuous campaigns to maintain supremacy in the West Indies caused the most appalling attrition of the British Army. Malaria and yellow fever could kill off half a regiment in a couple of years, necessitating its return home to recruit and re-train. During the years 1794-1811 the 46th served in Martinique, St Vincent, Dominica and Guadaloupe, with one home tour to recuperate between 1797 and 1805. The Regiment particularly distinguished itself in Dominica in 1794 when the island was attacked by a French force of some 4,000 men, which landed at Roseau supported by ten warships.

1. Silver statuette depicting the original uniform of Fox's Marines, presented to HRH Prince Charles, Duke of Cornwall, 1952.

2. A Private of Fox's Marines, 1707.

3. The Anglo-Dutch landing at Gibraltar, 1704.

4. An officer of the Light Company, 32nd Foot, 1800.

5. The death of Sir Thomas Picton at Waterloo, with men of the 32nd Foot.

6. Soldiers of the 32nd Foot in the trenches before the Fortress of Mooltan, 1848. By John Dunlop, Assistant Surgeon to the Regiment.

7. General view of the attack on the fortress of Mooltan, 1848. By John Dunlop.

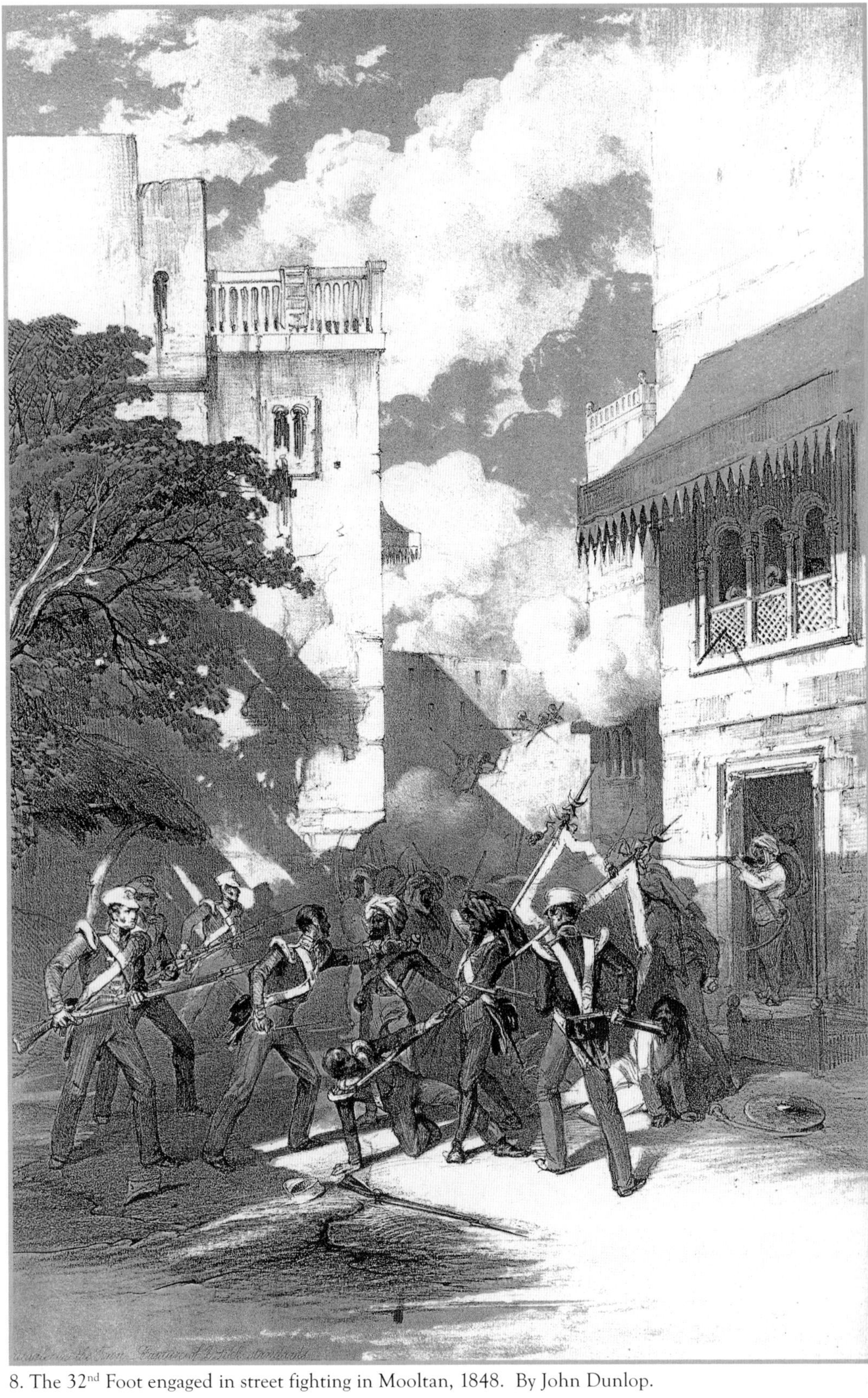

8. The 32nd Foot engaged in street fighting in Mooltan, 1848. By John Dunlop.

9. Maj-Gen. Sir John Inglis, late 32nd Foot.

10. 'The Cawnpore Battery' in the Baillie Guard, Lucknow, 1857.

11. The death of Capt. McCabe, 32nd Foot, 29th September 1857.

12. The first relief of Lucknow by Gen. Havelock's column, 25th September 1857.

13. A Private of the Light Company, 46th Foot, 1777.

14. A loyal American Light Infantryman, 1777. An early depiction of the dress and equipment of Light Infantry of that period. Note the musket, carried at the trail, and the axe.

15. The attack at Paoli on the night of 20th-21st September 1777, by the Light Company, 46th Foot.

16. Pte. William Dicker, 46th Foot, c. 1857.

17. Officers of the 46th Foot in the Crimea, 1855. From left to right: Capt. T.D. Forde, ADC to Col. Garrett Col. R. Garrett, KH, Brigade Commander; Maj. A.R. Garrett, Brigade Major; Lt.-Col. A. Maxwell, CO 46^{t}

After five days of heavy fighting in the south of the island, the enemy withdrew and re-embarked. The following morning a similar landing was mounted at Morne Daniel in the north of the island. During the ensuing action a strong French column advancing up a defile was confronted by a small party consisting of a serjeant and four men of the 46th with a 3 pdr gun, five men of the 1st West Indian Regiment and a few men of the St George's Regiment of Militia. This little group put up a valiant resistance, fighting to the last man and the last round. After failing to achieve any success in the north the whole French force again re-embarked and this time sailed away, leaving many dead and prisoners. In spite of the heavy fighting the 46th only lost 1 serjeant, 1 drummer and 10 rank and file killed, and 1 captain and 7 rank and file wounded. The citizens of Dominica showed their gratitude to the Regiment by the presentation of a magnificent set of table silver. Some of this is still used by one of the present Light Infantry battalions while the remainder is displayed in the Museum of the Duke of Cornwall's Light Infantry at Bodmin.

New South Wales, 1814-1818

After a period of recuperation in England, on 23rd August 1813 the 46th embarked for New South Wales, arriving at Sydney in February the following year. This was to be the start of one of the more remarkable tours of duty in which the Regiment was deployed in very small groups, tracking down bush rangers (Australian outlaws who lived in the 'out back' and terrorised the scattered homesteads). If anyone believes that the nineteenth century soldier was not fully capable of using his initiative and operating with little supervision, they should read the Historical Record of the 46th. I will quote just two examples:

In May 1815, Serjeant Robert Broadfoot and six men, stationed at Hobart Town, were despatched into the desert to deal with a gang who were carrying out terrorist activities. The party captured the two ringleaders, Irishmen by the names of Maguire and Burne, who were both tried and executed.

In February 1816, Corporal Justin McCarthy and seven men were despatched to deal with a similar gang. After chasing them for six months, the corporal's party, now reduced to himself and five men, finally brought the gang to bay. The bushrangers numbering eleven, all of whom were heavily armed, fought for an hour and a half. When the ringleader, a deserter from the 73rd Foot called Geary, was mortally wounded, his followers attempted to escape; two however were captured, tried and executed. Corporal McCarthy's party received £100 for Geary and £25 for each of the other two. Very sizable sums in 1816.

On the subject of money, it is interesting that a member of the 46th, Serjeant Jeremiah Murphy, was the first individual to open an account in the newly founded Bank of New South Wales, when he deposited £50 on 8th April 1817.

India, 1818-1833

The 46th were probably sorry to leave Australia, where their duties gave scope for the display of initiative and imagination among the junior ranks. However, in 1818 the Regiment sailed for Calcutta to start a tour in India, which was to continue for the next fifteen years. The Regiment was stationed at Vellore, Madras, Bellary, Cannanore, Secunderabad and Masulipatan; during this time it took part in the occupation of Hyderabad and the suppression of a native mutiny at Fort Kittoor. Indian soldiering in the early nineteenth century was a debilitating occupation. Throughout the summer, the day-time heat made it impossible to carry out training. Drill was conducted in the very early morning before the sun was high, after which the men were incarcerated in their barrack rooms to pass the long, hot hours as best they could. This was usually accompanied by heavy drinking of crude spirit sold by the native contractor. Hard drinking had always been the British soldier's downfall but, in the unforgiving climate of India, this vice often proved fatal. It would not be for another thirty years that Henry Havelock of the 13th Light Infantry, by introducing regimental coffee rooms and organising teetotal societies, made any real effort to curb the problem.

Home service, 1833-1839

The 46th returned to Canterbury in 1833 to begin the usual round of recruiting and training. Two years later it moved to Ireland, where it was involved in duties in aid of the civil power in Belfast and Enniskillen.

The West Indies & return to Canada, 1842-1848

After a tour of garrison duty in Gibraltar the 46th once more crossed the Atlantic and was stationed in Barbados and St Vincent until

1845. The rest of the overseas tour was spent in Canada at Halifax, Nova Scotia and Montreal. Contemporary pictures show men looking more like Arctic explorers than soldiers, heavily wrapped against the elements in thick animal furs. For the first time in the regiment's history, the troopships in which the 46th travelled were described as steamers. The advent of the steamship revolutionised the speed and reliability with which troops could be deployed across the seas.

Home service, 1848-1854

On its return from Canada in 1848 the 46th landed at Dover. There followed a period of home service during which the Regiment was successively quartered in Liverpool, Chester, Hull, Preston and Manchester. It must be remembered that this was a time of considerable unrest in England, when troops were not infrequently called out in aid of the civil power.

In 1852 the 46th crossed to Ireland where it saw service in Belfast, Dublin and Kilkenny. If a brooding atmosphere of discontent had hung over the industrial midlands of England, that in Ireland was infinitely worse. The famine caused by the potato blight had killed nearly a million of the Irish peasantry in the previous five years. The famine was followed by widespread agitation for land reform under the legend of The Three Fs: 'Fair rent, Free sale and Fixity of tenure'. It was far from a pleasant time for a soldier to serve in the Emerald Isle.

In early 1854 the 46th returned to England and was quartered in barracks at Windsor. While at Windsor there occurred an unedifying episode in the Regiment's history, and one that not only incurred the wrath of the Commander-in-Chief and the contempt of the general public but profoundly affected its deployment to the Crimea in the forthcoming war. There were at that time in the mess of the 46th two subalterns of very different character, Lieutenant Thomas Greer and Ensign James Perry. Greer was a heavily built, somewhat uncouth young man, a bully, a gambler and a womaniser; Perry was a small, unprepossessing individual, the son of a paymaster and perhaps disdained by some of his brother subalterns on account of his humble social background. One night, as a result of an altercation over a game of cards, Greer attacked Perry who responded by striking his assailant with a candlestick. Greer fell to the floor, unconscious and bleeding profusely. The Orderly Officer was called, who in turn summoned the Regimental Surgeon, Dr Walter Breslin. Although Greer's injuries proved not to be serious, the incident was entered in the Orderly Officer's report. Perry was called before Lieutenant-Colonel Robert Garrett the following morning to explain his conduct. To understand the situation as it stood at that moment, it must be remembered that in the 1850s drunken altercations between officers in the mess were not uncommon. Commanding Officers were usually loath to wash their dirty linen in public, and, if it were possible, confined disciplinary action to the close circle of the regiment. It would therefore have been expected for Garrett to have administered a sharp rebuke to Perry, and to have delivered some unofficial punishment to which Commanding Officers have always had recourse. Instead, Garrett ordered that Perry should be formally charged. A succession of Courts Martial followed, the unsavoury details of which were eagerly reported by *The Times*. The Commanding Officer angrily demanded that *The Times* should be excluded from the courtroom. This illegal request was naturally ignored, and *The Times* continued to print full and highly sensational reports. *Punch* joined the fray with a cartoon showing an officer of the 46th standing outside the barrack gate, saying to a yokel "Can I offer you a commission in the 46th?" – to which the yokel replies "Thank 'ee kindly zur, but oi be used to mixing with gentlemen." The Regiment should have formed part of the original expeditionary force to the Crimea. However, because the Courts Martial directly involved the Commanding Officer and many of the regimental officers as witnesses, it was unable to move. Two companies together with four officers, who were not required as witnesses, were despatched to the Crimea at the end of July 1854, to be attached to the 68th (Durham) Light Infantry. On 9th August Lieutenant George Dallas embarked at Plymouth on the steam transport *Harbinger* with thirty more NCOs and men of the 46th, detailed to furnish the guard of honour for the arrival of the new General Officer Commanding the 4th Division, Lieutenant-General Sir George Cathcart. In his letters Dallas describes the vicissitudes of mid nineteenth century trooping. Attempting to make passage through the Straits of Gibraltar, *Harbinger* came against storm- force easterly winds which drove her back into the Atlantic. There she wallowed in mountainous seas, waiting for the wind to subside.

It was not till 14th October that the main body of the 46th under Lieutenant-Colonel Garrett left England for the theatre of war on the transport *Prince*.

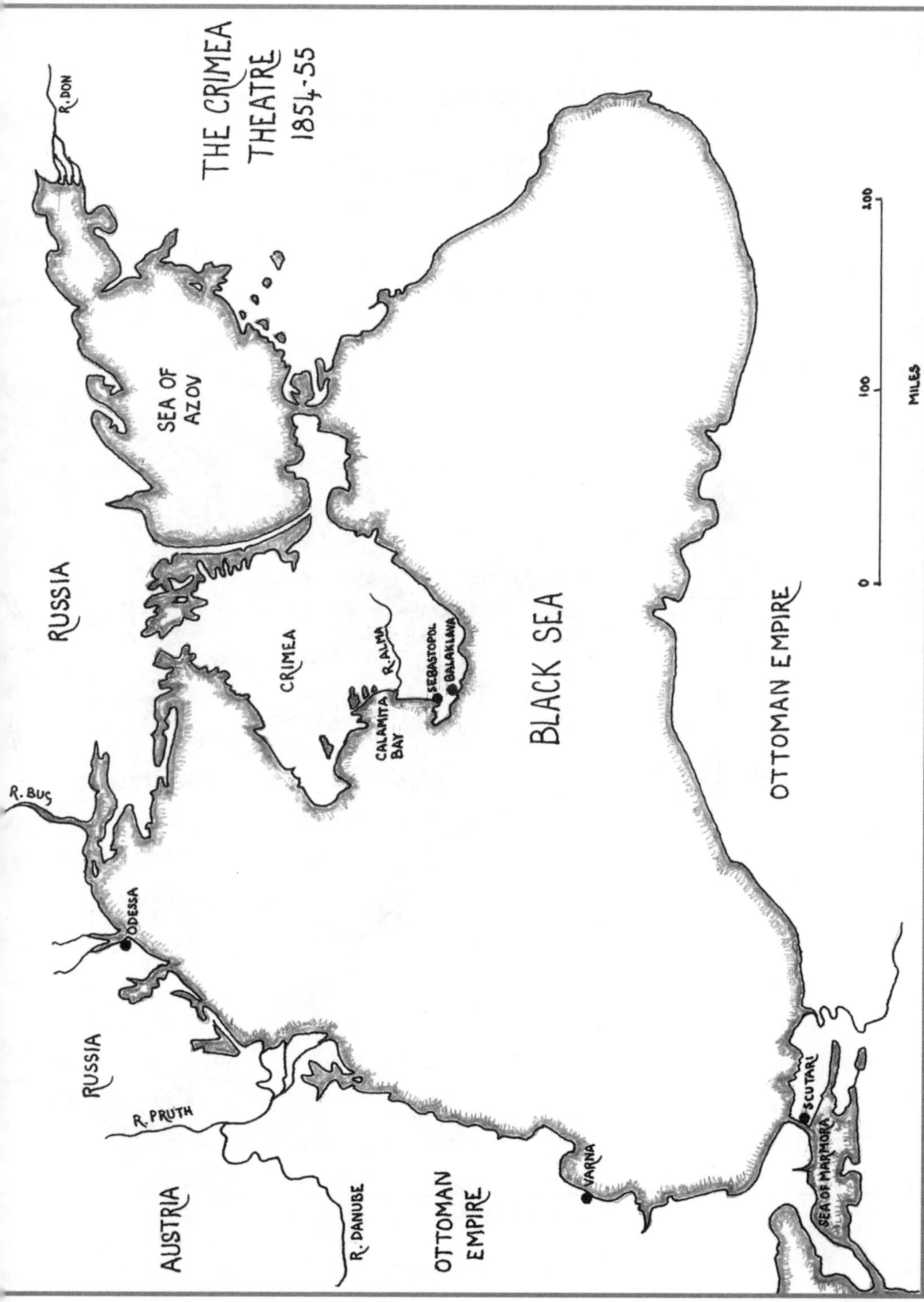
THE CRIMEA THEATRE 1854-55
R. DON
SEA OF AZOV
RUSSIA
CRIMEA
R. ALMA
SEBASTOPOL
BALAKLAVA
CALAMITA BAY
BLACK SEA
OTTOMAN EMPIRE
0
100
200
MILES
R. BUG
ODESSA
RUSSIA
R. PRUTH
R. DANUBE
AUSTRIA
OTTOMAN EMPIRE
VARNA
SCUTARI
SEA OF MARMORA

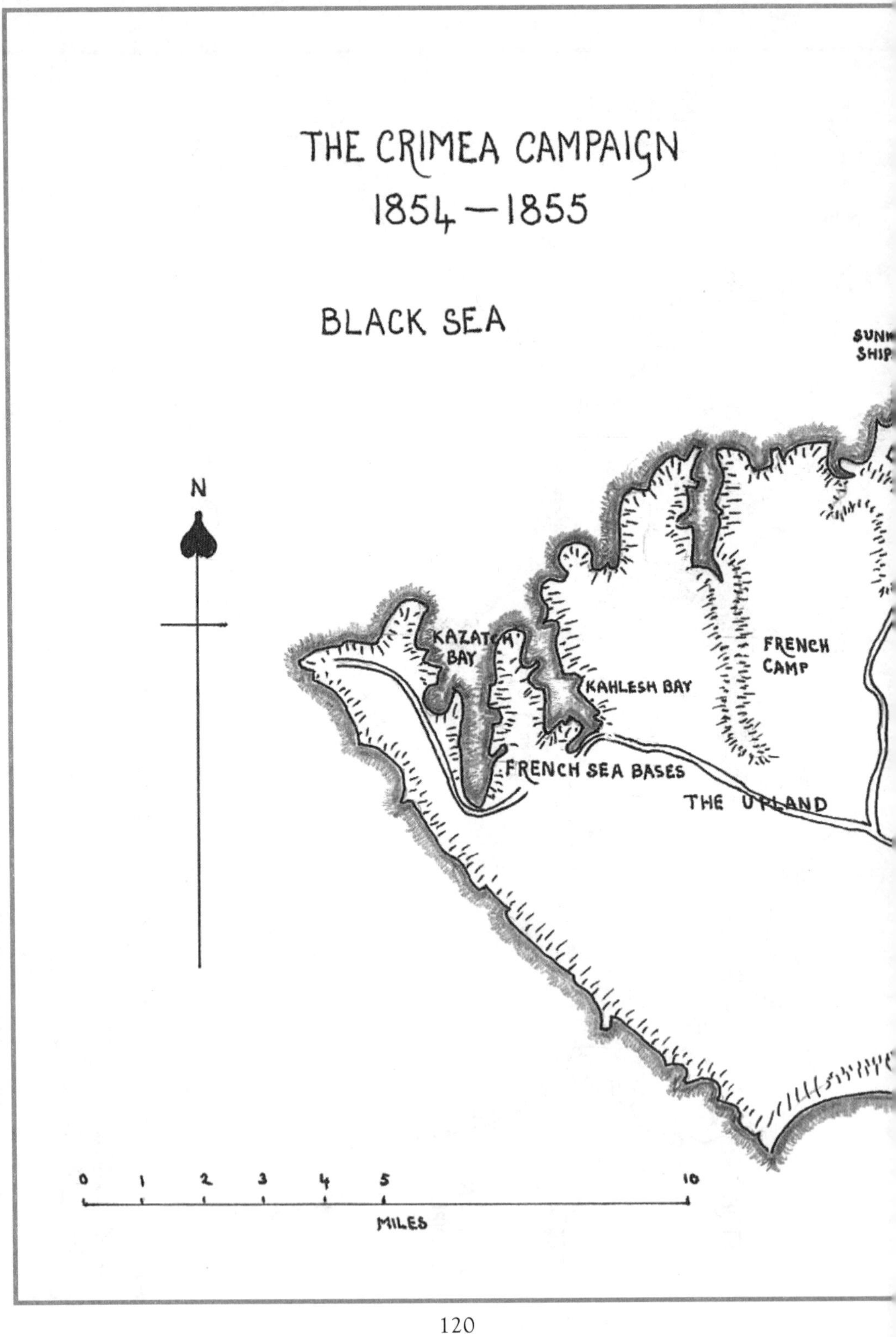
THE CRIMEA CAMPAIGN
1854—1855
BLACK SEA
N
KAZATCH BAY
KAHLESH BAY
FRENCH CAMP
FRENCH SEA BASES
THE UPLAND
0 1 2 3 4 5 10
MILES

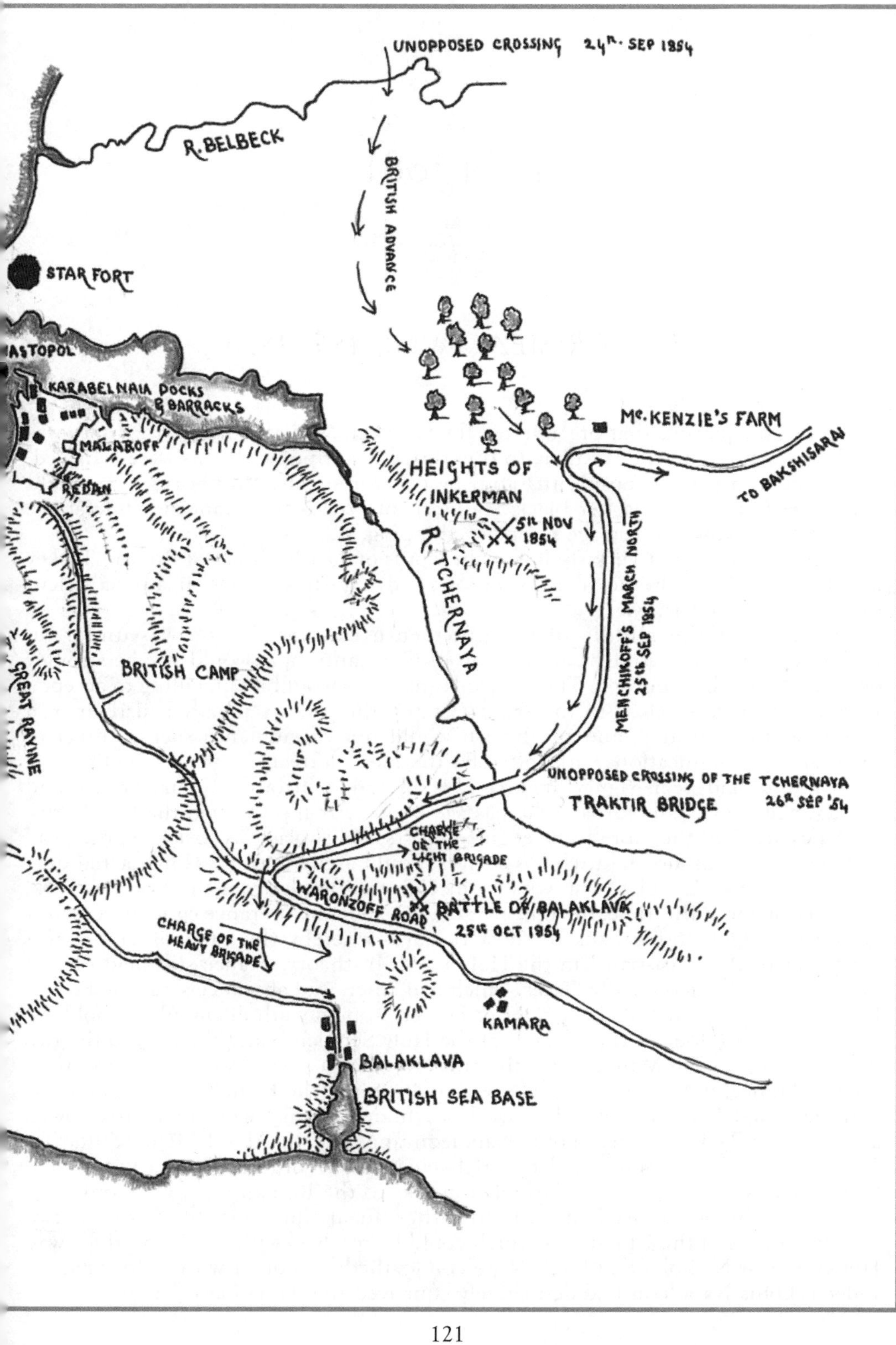

UNOPPOSED CROSSING 24th SEP 1854
R. BELBECK
BRITISH ADVANCE
STAR FORT
ASTOPOL
KARABELNAIA DOCKS & BARRACKS
MALAKOFF
REDAN
Mc. KENZIE'S FARM
TO BAKSHISARAI
HEIGHTS OF INKERMAN
5th NOV 1854
R. TCHERNAYA
MENCHIKOFF'S MARCH NORTH 25th SEP 1854
BRITISH CAMP
GREAT RAVINE
UNOPPOSED CROSSING OF THE TCHERNAYA
TRAKTIR BRIDGE
26th SEP '54
CHARGE OF THE LIGHT BRIGADE
WARONZOFF ROAD
BATTLE OF BALAKLAVA
25th OCT 1854
CHARGE OF THE HEAVY BRIGADE
KAMARA
BALAKLAVA
BRITISH SEA BASE

8
1854-1881

THE CRIMEAN WAR, 1854-1856

Whatever the quarrels that precipitated the Crimean War, the underlying cause was the long-nurtured desire of Russia to occupy Constantinople. If this were achieved, she would control the Bosphorus and, by controlling the Bosphorus, she would secure the free passage of her Black Sea Fleet into the Mediterranean, while at the same time denying the passage to enemy shipping.

Constantinople was Turkish, but in the words of Tsar Nicholas of Russia, 'Turkey is falling to pieces. The sick man of Europe is dying'. It was time, in Russia's view, to carve up her territory.

However, by the middle of the nineteenth century, Russia was under no misconception that a straight annexation of Constantinople would not be strongly opposed by much of Europe. The Austro-Hungarians would be unwilling to accept a Russian presence so close to the Balkan States, the French already had their own ambitions for that area, and the British would not countenance such a threat to their land communications with India. Furthermore, a treaty known as the Protocol des Detroits had been signed in July 1841 by Great Britain, Russia, France and Turkey, which expressly forbade the passage of any warship through the Bosphorus.

An excuse had therefore to be engineered. Tsar Nicholas was, *ex officio*, the head of the Greek Orthodox Church. As such he could argue that it was his sacred duty to free the Christian places of worship in Constantinople from the heathen Turk. However, at about this time, the Emperor Louis Napoleon of France chose to resurrect an ancient right dating back to the Crusades, whereby the ruler of France was 'Protector of the Christians' in the Holy Land. In theory, France still held certain privileges regarding the Holy Places, which had fallen into abeyance since the French Revolution. These included the right of French Roman Catholic monks to hold the key to the main door of the Church of the Holy Sepulchre and the keys to the two doors leading to the Manger; also the right to place a silver star, bearing the royal arms of France, in the Sanctuary of the Nativity. Since the French Revolution, these privileges had been assumed by Greek Orthodox monks who, of course, owed allegiance to Tsar Nicholas. Louis Napoleon appealed to Abdul Mejid, Sultan of Turkey who, judging Louis Napoleon's rights inalienable, ordered that the keys should be handed over by the Greek Orthodox monks to the Roman Catholic monks.

One might be excused for thinking that an arcane squabble between two denominations of the Christian Church could be resolved without the need for war. However, Tsar Nicholas and Louis Napoleon loathed each other with a bitter hatred. Indeed, Louis Napoleon had deliberately contrived the 'Holy Places' affair to humiliate Tsar Nicholas. The Tsar was not slow to act; moving two army corps south to the frontier with the Turkish principalities of Wallachia and Moldavia, he despatched Prince Menschikoff to Constantinople. Menschikoff presented two demands to Abdul Mejid: first, that the authority recently accorded to the Catholic monks in regard to the Holy Places should be rescinded; secondly, that Russia should be granted a protectorate over the Christians in Constantinople. The first of these demands was agreed, the second refused.

Six weeks later, on 22nd June 1853, two Russian army corps invaded the Turkish provinces of Wallachia and Moldavia. Turkey immediately declared war on Russia.

Great Britain was from the first reluctant to be drawn into this war. *The Times*, echoing public opinion, thundered against any British involvement. The Prime Minister, Lord Aberdeen, informed Russia that so long as her troops did not cross the Danube or attack any Black Sea Port, there was no *causa belli*. Notwithstanding, the Russian Navy bombarded the Turkish fleet, virtually annihilating it. Public opinion underwent an immediate change. On 27th March 1854 Great Britain and France (later to be joined by Sardinia) declared war on Russia.

The British Army of the Mid Nineteenth Century & The Crimea

At this stage it is worth looking at the mid nineteenth century home-based British army. At the time of Waterloo it had formed the most formidable fighting machine in the world. Since then it had rested on well-earned laurels, until now it had become a mere shadow of itself in terms of operational efficiency. The pride and discipline of its individual regiments were never in doubt, and these regiments were adequately trained to carry out field exercises at battalion level. In almost every other respect the British army was sadly lacking. In particular, there was an extreme dearth of senior officers with either the experience or energy to command and administer formations in the field. Most of the senior officers lacked imagination, and having last seen field service under the late Duke of Wellington half a century before, were well past their prime. Instead of looking forward they looked back, forever asking what the Great Duke would have done. But in all their preoccupation with Wellington, they signally failed to realise that the secret of his victories lay in meticulous administrative planning. The administrative services that he had so patiently assembled had been allowed to decay. The British army, magnificent on the barrack square, was quite unprepared for war.

An infantry battalion of that period had an establishment of 1,113 all ranks organised into a small headquarters, a grenadier company, a light company and six battalion companies. At the beginning of the forthcoming war, the infantry was armed with a mix of two types of small arm. Although the French-designed .702 in. Minié rifle had been authorised for service in 1851, many of the soldiers still had the old .75 in. smooth bore 1842 pattern musket. Large numbers of Minié rifles were quickly despatched to the expeditionary force, and by the time it reached the Crimea, three out of four infantry divisions were probably fully equipped with 'Minneys'. *The Times* later wrote: 'It is a king of weapons . . . the volleys of the Minié cleft them [the Russians] like the hand of the destroying angel and [they] fell like autumn leaves before it.'

However, in 1853 an even more effective soldier's firearm had already gone into production. This was an all British weapon (albeit built using American machine tools) known as the '53 pattern Enfield rifle. With a bore, small for its day, of only .577 in., it was a beautifully finished weapon that was surprisingly accurate up to 1,000 yards. Enfields started to arrive in the Crimea in mid 1855, immediately being distributed around the regiments; however it was not till the latter part of that year that the 4th Division received theirs.

The infantry was clothed in what was basically the dress of 1829, a swallow-tailed scarlet coatee that owed everything to sartorial splendour and nothing to practicality. The stand collar was a full four inches high, reinforced, in the case of soldiers, by a stiff leather stock. Officers wore extremely expensive gold bullion epaulettes or wings, and had their coatees cut so closely that they can surely not have been able to use their sword arms effectively. The head-dress for all ranks consisted of a heavy and uncomfortable leather chaco with a peak to both the front and rear. Allegedly designed by Prince Albert and known as the Albert chaco, it was universally detested. Most were to be discarded at the earliest opportunity on arrival in the Crimea.

A British Expeditionary Force was despatched. The regiments, marching through the seaport towns to embark, were cheered on by dense crowds. By the end of April the first troopships were arriving at Scutari on the Bosphorus; in June the army moved north to Varna, a filthy, verminous and disease-ridden port on the west coast of the Black Sea. Here they were well positioned to reinforce the Turkish army holding the key fortress of Silistria, should the need arise. The need, however, did not arise. On 23rd June 1854 the Russians, threatened by superior forces and mounting pressure from Austria, withdrew. Here then was a British expeditionary force that had come to fight a war against an enemy which had evaporated without a shot being fired, marooned in the most squalid conditions, and lacking any military aim. Now, to add to its troubles, cholera struck the British lines.

Britain had gone to war against Russia to support Turkey in her defence of the Danube provinces. Subsequent invasion of the Crimean peninsula and the destruction of the Russian naval base at Sevastopol had never been a declared aim of either the British or French governments (although it had been freely discussed in the press of both nations). However, with two great armies now sitting idly on the west coast of the Black Sea, the prospect of action in the Crimea was viewed with growing enthusiasm. Thus it was that the British Government ordered the invasion of the Crimea. However, this order was couched in such indecisive terms that the whole onus for the operation was laid on Lord Raglan. After long consideration, a final council of war was held at Varna on 24th August 1854 to decide whether or not to invade the Crimea. When asked by the Commander-in-Chief, General Lord Raglan, for his opinion, Major-General Sir George Brown, commanding the Light Division, replied:

> You and I are accustomed, when in any great difficulty, or when any important question is proposed, to ask ourselves how the great Duke [of Wellington] would have acted under similar circumstances. Now I tell your Lordship that without more certain information than you appear to have obtained with

> regard to this matter, that great man would not have accepted the responsibility of undertaking such an enterprise as that which is now proposed to you. [He then added] But if you won't, then they'll send someone who will [invade].

The message to Raglan was clear, but the responsibility was disgracefully shifted by the government onto his shoulders. On 1st September 1854 the army started to embark amid scenes of the utmost confusion. The fleet was to convey the army to an enemy country of which virtually nothing was known.

The space in the ships had been seriously underestimated so that, as the soldiers were crammed in ever more closely, vital stores had to be off-loaded and left behind. As each ship was filled, it moved away from Varna to anchor in Balchik Bay. Cholera was now rife and spread like wildfire in the unsanitary conditions of the grossly overcrowded troop decks. Every day more corpses were committed to the depths but, being inadequately weighed down with weights attached to their legs, rose up again as their bodies putrefied, floating head and shoulders above the surface, ghastly witnesses to the developing tragedy.

By 7th September the British transport fleet was all loaded and assembled in Balchik Bay. It was a magnificent spectacle. Over 600 ships lay at anchor: transports, escorting warships and tugs, some steam driven, others relying on their sails. The outward magnificence of the scene hid the appalling squalor below decks.

The British fleet sailed north to the mouth of the Danube to rendezvous with the French. Once again, anchors were dropped and the fleets waited. The reason for this delay was simple. No decision had yet been made on where the troops should land. It was not till 11th September, when Lord Raglan's steam yacht returned from carrying out a reconnaissance of the Crimean coast, that there could be any movement. On the evidence of a cursory examination of the beaches through telescopes, it had been agreed that the armies should land at the inauspiciously named Calamita Bay, about forty miles north of Sevastapol. The British army was to land on the left flank, the French on the right flank; a buoy was to be positioned to mark the boundary between the two armies. This having been decided, the combined fleets set sail due east to invade a country about which almost nothing was known.

On 14th September the majority of the infantry disembarked. Many of the men had been cooped up below decks for a fortnight with insufficient food and water amidst the filth associated with cholera, enteric fever and seasickness. They were certainly glad to be ashore, but were considered to be too weak to carry their knapsacks. Instead each man carried his rolled blanket bandolier fashion, in which he carried his meagre possessions. Even before the first man landed, acrimony broke out between the British and French. The British sector of the beach proved inadequate for the numbers: the French were accused of moving the marker buoy to their advantage but replied that if the buoy had moved, it was due to the ineptitude of the Royal Navy for not mooring it securely. Altercations of this nature were to dog Allied relations throughout the campaign.

On the shore, a most serious shortage of fresh drinking water had developed. The wells proved brackish and, with only one meagre stream to supply the wants of some 27,000 men and several thousand horses, the error of attempting to carry out a major military operation without sufficient intelligence became brutally apparent. After a great deal of confusion, the armies finally moved from their beach-head on the morning of 19th September. Marching south, their first objective was to secure a crossing of the River Alma twenty miles away. With its steep valley, this feature offered a perfect natural defensive position that would undoubtedly be fiercely contended by the Russians.

The 46th in The Crimea

The two companies of the 46th Foot had landed with the rest of the infantry at Calamita Bay on 14th September 1854. The first night ashore, the dull sultry weather turned to torrential rain. The men huddled under their sopping blankets, the officers ruefully brooding on the price they had paid for their gold bullion epaulettes, now rapidly losing their pristine brilliance in the mud.

The regiment formed part of the 2nd Brigade of the 4th Division which, to their bitter chagrin did not accompany the main body towards the Alma. Instead it was employed in cleaning up the camp, and re-embarking the mass of stores that could not be moved forward due to the lack of horses and wagons. When the 2nd Brigade did finally move, it would appear that the 46th companies had been sent inland to find a source of fresh water. To catch up with their Division, they attempted to take a short cut. Rather than saving time, they became lost.

The battle of the Alma, 20th September 1854

The battle of the Alma was fought on 20th September. Alas, the two companies of the 46th took no part in the battle. After finally regaining their direction, they marched with all possible speed towards the sounds of firing. They were too late; all was over by the time of their arrival in the Alma valley. Despite their absence from the actual fighting, they all eventually received the clasp 'Alma' when the Crimean War medal was issued. However, in spite of repeated appeals, Alma was, not unnaturally, never granted as a Battle Honour. In the final letter on this subject, written on 5th May 1881, the Deputy Adjutant General wrote somewhat testily

> . . . that you will be so good as to refer the Officer Commanding to the reply that was then made, a copy of which will no doubt be found in the Orderly Room of the 46th Regiment dated 17th January 1856, from which His Royal Highness sees no reason for departing.

The march to Balaklava, 23rd-27th September 1854

For the next two days the army laboured to bury the dead on the Alma battle-field and provide what limited medical aid was available to the wounded. The British had lost 381 killed and 1,621 wounded; the total of French casualties was 1,340, while that of the Russians was 5,709.

The advance towards Sevastopol continued on the morning of 23rd September. No resistance was met and, after halting for the night on the 25th, the outlying picquets were within sight of the church domes of Sevastopol. It seems remarkable that up to this point no firm decision had been made as to whether the goal of the whole campaign should be attacked from the north or south. After lengthy consultations with the French, it was decided that Sevastopol should be by-passed, and that the small sheltered harbour of Balaklava, eight miles to the south, should first be captured. Having thus secured a firm base, Sevastopol would be attacked from the south. The advance continued. There now occurred one of the most ludicrous incidents of the whole campaign.

Up to then the route had lain across rolling grassland. Soon however the army entered woods, where, without maps or the benefit of any previous reconnaissance, it inevitably became lost. The tactical order of march became totally confused, and no less a person than the Commander-in-Chief found himself leading the column, followed closely along the narrow woodland track by the guns and wagons of C Troop, Royal Horse Artillery. As the Commander-in-Chief emerged into a clearing, he came almost face to face with a strong Russian column crossing his front from right to left. This was General Prince Menschikoff's army moving out of Sevastopol to secure his line of communication with the Russian mainland. Both sides were equally amazed to see each other. Without any cavalry or infantry immediately available, Lord Raglan was powerless to take any offensive action. The Russians passed on, fortunately unaware that what they had assumed was a small patrol, was in fact the British Commander-in-Chief at the head of his entire army! After pausing briefly at what is now known as McKenzie's farm, the British army turned south down the Bakshisaras road to cross the River Tchernaya at Traktir Bridge.

Once again, Sir George Cathcart's 4th Division (of which the two companies of the 46th formed part) was not involved. It had been left behind at Katcha, seven miles south of the Alma, to transfer the sick and wounded to British ships, and provide a rear-guard to the main column. It was not till the 26th September that it started to move inland and follow the route of the main column.

It had originally been intended that the British and French should share the port of Balaklava. On arrival there, however, it was obvious that it was totally inadequate to serve both armies. A second additional anchorage at Kameish (or Kahlesh) Bay, six miles west of Sevastopol, was therefore selected. It was agreed that the French should make use of Kameish Bay as their base, while the British remained in Balaklava. This meant that the French army, which had been operating on the Allied right flank, was henceforth deployed on the left flank.

Arrival on the heights above Sevastopol, 27th September 1854

On the 27th September the British army reached the area selected for its encampment, on the firm high ground just south of Sevastopol. For the men of the 46th war must have seemed a pleasant activity. So far they had not seen a shot fired in anger, they were still free of cholera and, apart from the first night of rain, the week had remained warm and sunny.

Quite why the Allied armies did not stage an immediate assault on Sevastopol, while the defenders were ill-prepared, remains a mystery. Sir George Cathcart declared that his 4th Division could 'walk into Sevastopol almost without the loss of a man'. Sir George held a dormant commission to take over command of the force should Raglan be killed or wounded and was therefore incensed that his advice was ignored. Indeed, he was not even consulted in the formulation of the operational plan. In the event no action was taken, and it was left to the Russians to make the first move.

Battle of Balaklava, 25th October 1854

On the 21st October 1854 intelligence had been received that the Russians were about to carry out a wide encircling movement around the Allied right flank, and attack Balaklava from the rear of the British position. If successful, this would cut off the British from their only supply base, rendering their position on the heights above Sevastopol untenable. Various troop deployments were made by Lord Raglan to meet this threat (including the move of the 4th Division) but, as the day wore on and all remained peaceful, the units were ordered back to their encampments. On the morning of 24th October a further intelligence report again indicated a forthcoming Russian attack on Balaklava. Lord Raglan, believing this to be just another false alarm, took no action. Just before dawn on 25th October a major Russian force of 22,000 infantry, 3,400 cavalry and 78 guns was reported to be converging on the eastern approaches to the Balaklava Plain. The battle that followed has become famous for the charges of the Heavy and Light Cavalry Brigades, and for the action of the 93rd Highlanders who were holding the mouth of the defile. The 4th Division was late in moving from its encampment on the heights, largely due to an acrimonious dispute between Sir George Cathcart and Lord Raglan. Once again those two companies of the 46th missed the battle.

Battles of Inkerman, 26th October & 5th November 1854

The 46th, however, had not long to wait for action. On the afternoon of the day after the battle of Balaklava, about 5,000 Russians carried out an attack on what became known as the Inkerman Heights, which lay on the extreme right flank of the British lines. They were beaten off with heavy loss. We now know that this was a reconnaissance in force mounted as a prelude to a much greater battle. This was not appreciated by the commanders at the time. No senior officer visited the area, nor did anyone in authority appear to be in the least concerned by the weaknesses of the existing defence works on this flank. Nine days later, on 4th November, steady rain fell throughout the day. That evening the rain cleared and a thick fog enveloped the front. As night came on, the routine of withdrawing the forward outlying picquets to the safety of the main position was effected. It was then that a certain Serjeant-Major Williams, acting on his own initiative, walked back to the crest and lay down to listen. What he heard, although muffled by the fog, was undoubtedly the sound of many iron shod wheels. He returned to his battalion and reported this information, only to be told that it was merely the routine movement of carts and wagons bringing supplies to Sevastopol. In fact what he had heard was the movement of 134 guns and limbers moving round the British right flank in preparation for the greatest Russian attack of the war.

The plan devised by Prince Menschikoff was over complicated and relied on very exact timings, to be maintained by a vast force of 35,000 infantry and 134 guns operating across extremely steep and rocky terrain. If all had gone well, Menschikoff could have split the British army in two, and using his considerable preponderance of men and guns, annihilated it piecemeal. However, due to a vagueness in his orders and the fog, there was confusion in the Russian ranks almost from the start. Far too many men were crammed into too small an area and the fog, although initially giving them the benefit of surprise, made their progress over unfamiliar broken ground against a largely invisible enemy peculiarly difficult.

The Russians attacked at about 6 a.m. on 5th November, driving in the British picquets. Heavy guns, waiting in readiness to move forward, were soon bombarding the 2nd Division camp. Throughout the British lines bugles were sounding the Assembly. Many, just returning from their twenty-four hours duty in the forward trenches, found themselves parading with their units before marching to the noise of battle. They joined the fight, sometimes by brigades, but more often as individual battalions or even companies. The fighting was bloody and confused. Men, separated from their units, coalesced into mixed groups and fought for their lives with bullet, butt and bayonet. Inkerman has been described as the 'Soldiers' battle'. This is very apt, for in the fog little command or control was possible. The battle of Inkerman was to prove perhaps the finest example of the dogged determination of the British rank and file when chaos reigned and they were outnumbered by the enemy.

The two companies of the 46th, attached to the 68th (Durham) Light Infantry, were slow to join the battle. As soon as his Division was assembled, Sir George Cathcart marched it off towards the noise of the guns. All seemed utterly confused. In answer to his query as to where his men were required, he received the singularly unhelpful answer "Everywhere!" Men were therefore deployed in penny packets to meet the many urgent calls for help. Thus it was that Sir George was left with only some 600 men when he was begged by The Duke of Cambridge to come to the aid of his hard pressed 1st Division, which had been heavily engaged from the start. Sir George's remaining force consisted of three companies of the 68th Light Infantry, two companies of the 46th and a company of the 20th. With hindsight, he should have used these meagre resources to reinforce the exhausted men of the 1st Division, gallantly hanging on to the high ground barring the Russian advance up the Tchernaya valley. Instead, he saw his chance to deal the enemy a decisive blow by carrying out a right flanking movement, and then plunging down off the high ground to attack the Russian column in its rear. He did indeed take the enemy in the rear, but no sooner had his men left the security of the high ground than they found that they themselves had been taken in the rear by Russians, who had infiltrated up onto the heights which they had so recently quit. As his situation became ever more desperate, Sir George Cathcart turned to Lieutenant Dallas of the 46th and made what must rank as the most memorable understatement of the war. "I fear we are in a mess!" he exclaimed, "We must try the bayonet!" As the troops moved forward, he shouted "Well done the 46th!" So saying, he was shot through the heart and died instantly.*

In leading his men down into the valley, the hapless Cathcart had all but lost the whole battle. It was only by the indomitable

*The Durham Light Infantry dispute this, claiming that Cathcart's last words were "Well done the 68th!"

spirit of the British soldiers, the belated arrival on the scene of two 18 pdr guns, and, most importantly, the timely arrival of French reserves that the initiative was regained. Slowly the Russian advance was brought to a halt, they wavered, and finally withdrew. By 2 p.m., eight hours after the first shots had been fired, the battle was over. The British were too exhausted to mount a pursuit.

So ended the battle of Inkerman, a battle perhaps like no other in history, a battle of confusion and errors fought in a haze of fog and gunpowder smoke, in which only the conduct of the regimental officers, non-commissioned officers and soldiers deserves credit. Major James Patullo of the 30th Foot wrote:

> No orders were given from first to last but to advance. No attempts to reform shattered battalions, no plan of operations. I feel gratitude to the courageous British soldier who fought all day, replenishing his ammunition from his wounded comrade's pouch without a direction or hint from superior authority, only the example of his officer who was left equally without guidance, not to the generals who in my opinion have not distinguished themselves.

Arrival of the main body of the 46th Foot, 8th November 1854

The main body of the 46th arrived at Balaklava in the steamship *Prince* on 8th November 1854 (three days after the battle of Inkerman). The regiment was in good heart, and as yet unaffected by the cholera that had swept through the expeditionary force. Before the troops disembarked new Colours were presented at a simple ceremony on the upper deck of the *Prince.* That afternoon the 46th marched the six miles up to the camp of 4th Division, where they rejoined their already veteran comrades. For much of the year the Crimea enjoys an idyllic climate, and October had been warm, dry and sunny. The tents of the 4th Division stood in neat rows on firm, high ground overlooking the Allies' objective, the Russian naval base of Sevastopol. Although by early November the evenings were becoming cool, few anticipated the terrible rigours of the coming winter. The 46th had barely had time to settle in, when on the evening of 14th November a violent storm swept across the Black Sea. Hurricane force winds, accompanied by torrential rain, created chaos and misery in the camps. Every tent was destroyed, stores ruined and men left soaked to the skin, desperately trying to hold onto their blankets. Even more importantly, twenty one ships in or near the harbour of Balaklava were sunk and eight others disabled. The steamship *Prince,* which had carried the 46th from England, was sunk with all hands, and with her went much of the army's supply of blankets, great-coats, winter clothing and boots. As the night wore on, the torrential rain turned to sleet and snow. In the next few hours many of the 46th were to die of hypothermia. The Great Storm, as it became known, was a disaster from which the army was never fully to recover. Weakened as many of them were from the effects of dysentery, they were in no state to live without shelter, dry clothing, or firewood. By the end of that winter these shortcomings had largely been rectified, but by then it was too late. By February 1855 the 46th had been reduced to an effective strength of 95 all ranks. There was talk of evacuating the survivors but, in the event, the remnants of the Regiment remained in the Crimea till after the fall of Sevastopol, too weak to take any significant part in the actions. In the forty years since Waterloo, Wellington's superb field army had forgotten the basic lessons of war, particularly the vital need for efficient logistical support.

The fall of Sevastopol, 8th September 1855

On 8th September 1855, after a day of bloody fighting, Sevastopol finally fell. The 4th Division, including the 46th Foot, remained in reserve during this last battle, taking no part in the actual assaults.

It is not necessary to recount the course of events on that terrible day in great detail, but rather to show how they demonstrated the serious shortcomings of the British infantry after a year of debilitating siege operations, and the dogged determination of the Russian soldier facing inevitable defeat against overwhelming odds.

The two vital elements of the Russian defence consisted of the Malakhov bastion on the Allied right flank and the Redan bastion half a mile to its left. Of these two, the Malakhov was the more important. Not only did it dominate all approaches to the town and dockyard, but it had been cleverly sited to provide devastating fire support across the front of the Redan. The task of capturing the Malakhov was assigned to the French under the command of General Pélissier. When and only when the Malakhov had been secured were the British under General Codrington to attack the Redan.

These two forts were subjected to a very heavy preliminary bombardment. Large quantities of shot and shell had been stockpiled, enabling the guns and mortars to fire continuously throughout the 5th, 6th and 7th September. It was a bombardment that presaged those of the Great War sixty years later, and like those, the Generals believed that nothing could survive such a weight of fire. So confident were the Allies of easy victory that a large crowd of spectators – men, women, soldiers and civilians – had assembled to watch this grand finale.

Intelligence had revealed that the Russians changed the guard on their defences at noon each day and that for a brief minute or so, while this change was taking place, the defences were not manned. The French therefore attacked the Malakhov at exactly midday. Their leading assault wave of Zouaves leapt from their trenches, dashed across the narrow space which separated them from the Russian ramparts, and consolidated inside the bastion. Not a shot had been fired. The enemy, however, was not slow to react. The Russians poured out of their subterranean shelters, intent on killing the intruders. A desperate hand to hand battle was fought, every traverse being contested with savage intensity. It was not till 4 p.m. that the tricolour was to be seen flying above the Malakhov. In those desperate four hours the French had lost 7,567 killed and wounded, including no fewer than five general officers killed and a further four wounded.

Even before the Malakhov had been fully secured by the French, the British attacked the Redan. This was a result of an understandable breakdown of battle communications, but was to have the most dire results, for the Malakhov was positioned to provide enfilade fire across the Redan.

Now it was the turn of the British. The Redan itself was an exceptionally formidable stronghold which the British had already attempted to capture that June, with a singular lack of success. To understand the difficulties of the operation, one must look at the defences of this bastion. Unlike the French front-line trenches which were close up against their objective, those of the British were separated by a glacis: an area of flat ground, devoid of any cover, of no less than 450 yards. Those who succeeded in crossing the glacis were confronted by an abbatis, an entanglement of felled trees laid side by side with their sharpened branches pointing towards the attackers. Having negotiated this obstacle, they then had to cross a ditch some ten feet deep and twenty feet wide. From this rose an earth embankment topped by gabions, large wickerwork cylinders filled with earth and stones. The face of the embankment had been pulverised by the ceaseless cannonade, making it exceedingly difficult to climb. If these physical defences were not enough, it must be realised that the British, unlike their French allies, did not have the advantage of surprise. The Russian defenders knew full well that their turn would come just as soon as the Malakhov was neutralised. The Redan was fully manned with every cannon loaded with canister.*

It had been decided to use the 2nd and Light Divisions in the initial assault, with the 3rd and 4th in reserve. The 2nd and Light Divisions were selected as being the most battle-hardened. Battle-hardened they may once have been, but it was precisely because of this that their past casualties had been exceptionally heavy, so that they now contained a preponderance of drafts made up of untried young soldiers, barely out of recruit training. The only active service that these men knew had been their periods of duty in the trenches where a soldier's major consideration was to look after his own safety, not an experience to infuse them with the fiercely aggressive spirit needed for a desperate assault.

As the leading British soldiers, many burdened with heavy eighteen-foot scaling ladders, arose from their trenches, they were met by a murderous hail of musketry and canister shot. Advancing across those 450 yards of flat, open ground, the carnage was terrible. As the survivors reached the ditch, most tried to seek shelter rather than go forward, and as subsequent waves of attackers joined them, the ditch took on the hideous aspect of a slaughter house. Dead and living became increasingly backed together as the Russians poured down musket fire from above. Officers and

* Canister, or case shot as it was sometimes known, consisted of a tin plate cylinder loaded with several hundred musket balls.

NCOs behaved with great valour, haranguing and imploring their men to close with the enemy. All was to no avail. Time and time again officers and NCOs would succeed in climbing up over the gabions, to find that only a very few brave soldiers were following them.

Captain Colin Campbell of the 46th wrote: 'The fact is only the officers and the best men ever reached the battle; a good many of the men did not behave well at all. The army does not consist of anything like so fine a set of men as those that fought at Alma and Inkerman.' Lieutenant Boscawen Griffith of the 23rd Foot echoed these words, writing 'Disease had all but wiped out the older veterans who had fought like lions at Inkerman. Much of those remaining were fresh faced young boys who had only served in the trenches.'

The walking wounded and stretcher bearers, making their way to the rear along the narrow trenches, blocked the reserves attempting to move forward. Chaos ruled. Gradually those who had made it to the Redan started drifting back. By dusk the attack was abandoned for that day, plans being rapidly prepared for its resumption the following morning with fresh troops.

During that night, however, dramatic events were taking place. It was the French who first reported signs that the Russians were withdrawing from their forward defence works. All through that night their magazines in the various forts were blown up, and fires were started all over the town. Soon after daybreak a massive explosion shook the town. As the reverberations died away it could be seen that the bridge of boats across the harbour had been cast adrift and the last of the Russian troops were climbing the northern slope.

So ended active operations in the Crimea. Lord Wolseley, who served as a young officer with the 90th Light Infantry in the Crimea, perhaps best summed up the war by his damning indictment written many years later:

> The officers still living who passed the winter of 1854 in the trenches look back, I am sure, with intense pride of race and commendable regimental spirit to the noble endurance of our rank and file. In all the misery the private soldier fought well, and for the honour of England he met his death from want without a murmur. He knew that no stars or ribands could by any chance fall to his lot, yet he fought like a hero, and suffered with the steadfastness of a martyr. The history of his devotion to duty, of his determination to maintain at all costs the credit of the British Army, is beyond any praise I can find words for. Indeed, the whole story of the private soldier's conduct throughout that disastrous winter is so heroic, so pathetic, that to me it is far more glorious and worthy of record than the most dramatic of those daring feats which waved the pages of our military history.
>
> We had also much to complain of during the progress of the war on account of the military ignorance of many of the Generals set over us. But we all know that our wretched conditions in front of Sebastopol could not be entirely laid at their doors. The report of the 'Select Committee', which investigated this matter in 1855, put the saddle on the right horse, and condemned the Cabinet of 1854 as the real authors of our misery.
>
> Our sufferings had their origin in the folly, criminal ignorance, reckless parsimony and ineptitude of the gentlemen who were Her Majesty's Ministers. See the Parliamentary report of this 'Select Committee'. It is little read now,

though full of useful military information, and intensely interesting. The crass ignorance of the Cabinet which ordered our army to the Crimea was only equalled by the baseness with which it afterwards endeavoured to shift the blame of our winter misery from its shoulders and place it upon Sir Richard Airey and the military authorities in the field. We now know also that our superior officers' want of military knowledge was less their fault than the result of our monstrous military system, which allowed useless and ignorant men to command regiments and to become Generals.

Strong words indeed.

*

The casualties of the 46th speak for themselves. For the most part, men did not die from enemy action but as a result of cholera and dysentery, which raged through an army already desperately weakened by cold, wet and malnutrition. Of the original fighting strength of 706 men of the 46th, 19 were killed in action (mostly men of the advance party at the battle of Inkerman), 4 died of wounds received in action, and 481 died of disease.

Postscript to The Crimea

Serving in the Crimea with the 46th was an officer who was to make a major and lasting contribution to the humane treatment of the wounded in war. The name of Charles John Burgess has been generally forgotten but the organisation of which he was a founder member, The British Red Cross, lives on.

Burgess, like so many others, was appalled by the terrible sights of the wounded, both friend and foe, left to die on the battle-fields through lack of medical attention. As a young subaltern, he could then do nothing to alleviate their suffering. However, in 1862 during the Austro-Hungarian war, the terrible aftermath of the battle of Solférino shocked all Europe. For many days thousands of wounded lay where they had fallen; without any medical attention, most of them died a lingering death. A certain M. Dunant, who had witnessed the scenes, produced a pamphlet titled '*Un Souvenir de Solférino*', in which he urged the necessity for the formation of a permanent 'Society for the Aid of the Wounded'.

Amongst those who read this pamphlet was the President of Le Societé Genevoise d'Utilité Publique, M. Gustave Moynieu, who immediately invited M. Dunant to address the society in Geneva. The members were greatly impressed, passing a resolution that an organisation to be known as Le Comité International de la Croix Rouge should be set up without delay.

The following year Le Societé Genevoise held a conference in Geneva, attended by the representatives of thirty-six European nations, at which the treatment of the wounded in war was debated. As a result, a declaration, known as The Geneva Convention of 1864, was signed by all the thirty-six nations. There is no doubt that this convention, still in large part valid today, formed a momentous turning point in the treatment of soldiers wounded in battle. The plight of those wounded in the Franco-Prussian war of 1870 was greatly alleviated by both sides observing the Geneva Convention, and by the action of volunteers recruited by Le Comité International de la Croix Rouge.

In August of that year Burgess (now a retired Major and Adjutant of the Honourable Artillery Company) attended a meeting of the Croix Rouge in Geneva, at which individual countries were urged to form their own national organisations. Burgess returned to England where he set about forming The National Society for Aid to Sick and Wounded in War, soon to be renamed The British Red Cross. In this great endeavour he was joined by a Mr John Furnely and a Major Henry Brackenbury of the 61st Foot. Later still, the committee was expanded to include Lieutenant-Colonel Robert Loyd-Lindsay, VC of the Scots Fusilier Guards (later to become General Lord Wantage). Sadly, a serious clash of personalities appears to have developed between Burgess and Loyd-Lindsay, which resulted in the former publishing numerous letters of bitter recrimination in the newspapers. Much of the honour for the success of the British Red Cross was accorded to its high profile member, General Lord Wantage, and it was only towards the end of Burgess's life that he received due recognition, being awarded decorations by France, Germany, Bavaria and Belgium. What may have given him the most pleasure was his appointment by the King as a Military Knight of Windsor in 1902. Burgess died in 1905. A plaque in Mitford church states unequivocally:

> In memory of Charles John Burgess. Sometime an officer in Her Majesty's 46th Regiment of Foot, and afterwards Major of the Honourable Artillery Company of London. The Founder of the National (Red Cross) Society for the Aid to the Sick and Wounded in War.
>
> 10th June 1836-15th July 1905

The war in the Crimea was the first in which the appalling hardships suffered by the army became widely known to the British public. Previously, the civilian population had known little about the closed world of the military and probably cared less. Suddenly all this was changed. With the advent of steam ships, fast railway communications and a consequent proliferation of cheap newspapers, the conduct of far-away wars became a subject of deep and widespread interest. Civilians developed a new found awareness of their army, and the realisation that soldiers were not merely anonymous pawns, but flesh and blood human beings. From this sprang a general feeling of outrage that soldiers should be subjected to a system maintained by politicians and senior officers who were so palpably incompetent. Anger towards the Government erupted in Parliament.

On 29th January 1855 the Commons divided on a motion proposed by John Roebuck, QC that 'a Select Committee should enquire into the conditions in the Army'. In the subsequent debate, the Secretary at War stated: 'The responsibility [for the administrative chaos] lies with that collection of regiments which calls itself the British Army, and not with the Government'.

The opposition replied with fury against this outrageous criticism of regimental officers who had carried out their duty with honour and courage. Lord Aberdeen's government fell.

The Roebuck Committee sat for many months, producing a lengthy report highlighting the outdated, inefficient, inept and corrupt systems by which the army was commanded and administered. However, so powerful was the entrenched hierarchal structure that little reform was immediately possible. It was not until that great reforming zealot, Edward Cardwell, became Secretary of State for War in 1868, that many of the Roebuck recommendations were finally put into effect.

Possibly the most visible reform emanating from the Roebuck Committee was the radical change in the appearance of the British infantryman. During the war the French were shown to be, in many respects, a far more professional army; now the style of their uniform, if not their ethos, was eagerly copied. Gone for ever was the skin-tight swallow-tailed coatee, which was now replaced by a loose fitting, long skirted, double breasted tunic that provided far better protection from the elements. The new garment was far more comfortable; the collar was rounded off at the front and considerably reduced in height, while the officer's extremely expensive gold bullion epaulettes or wings were abolished in favour of a simple twist of crimson cord worn on the left shoulder to retain the sash. Officers' badges of rank were transferred to the collar, where they would have been easily distinguishable had not the fashion for beards often rendered them invisible. In place of the tall, heavy chaco, a far more comfortable French style kepi was introduced. A battalion may no longer have looked quite so magnificent on the barrack square, but for those who were required to carry out their daily work in uniform, the change must have been more than welcome.

In fact, by the end of the campaign many shortcomings had been addressed. The Commissariat was functioning more efficiently; there was at last some semblance of order in Balaklava harbour, and a railway had been built by civilian contract from the harbour to the British encampment; prefabricated huts had supplanted the rotting canvas; and, last but not least, the famous French chef, M. Soyer, whose patent stove is still in military use, had been co-opted to advise on the provision of palatable food for soldiers.

OTHER POSTINGS, 1856-1868

Corfu, 1856-1858

In 1856 the remnants of the Regiment sailed for the island of Corfu, a station with a temperate Mediterranean climate that was judged beneficial to the health of soldiers. The 46th remained in Corfu for two years before moving on to India.

India, 1858-1868

When the 46th disembarked at Karachi in 1858, the Indian Mutiny had only just been crushed. The Mutiny had delivered a rude shock to a complacent Britain, and the British relationship with India was about to undergo a profound change. On 1st November 1858 a proclamation was published, which abolished the long-established East India Company and disbanded its army. A new Indian Army was about to be raised, whose men would be soldiers of the Queen and not of a trading company. The establishment of the British Army in India was set at 80,000 men and, although this figure was never achieved, the actual strength of about 62,000 was considerably greater than it had been before the Mutiny. This additional commitment therefore meant that British soldiers were henceforth to spend a greatly increased proportion of their service in India.

Between 1858 and 1868 the 46th were stationed in Karachi, Mooltan, Jullunder, Cawnpore, Shahjahnpore, Lucknow, Allahabad, Jubblepore and Poona.

AMALGAMATION WITH THE 32ND LIGHT INFANTRY, 1881

The impact of the Cardwell Reforms on the army have already been recounted in the chapter covering the history of 32nd. The 46th undoubtedly felt bitter at the loss of its identity following the Cardwell amalgamation in 1881. The new title, The Duke of Cornwall's Light Infantry, made no reference to South Devonshire while the long established distinction of wearing yellow uniform facings was abandoned in favour of the standard English white facings of the 32nd. In a *cri de coeur*, the Colonel of the 46th requested that the new regiment might be allowed to continue the honour of wearing the Paoli red feathers. This was granted, and the new regiment was given the necessary authority. When red feathers were considered impractical, a small patch of red cloth was worn behind the cap badge, a custom that is still observed today.

The 46th became the 2nd Battalion the Duke of Cornwall's Light Infantry. Although crosspostings between the two battalions became common, they retained their individuality for many years to come.

III. THE DUKE OF CORNWALL'S LIGHT INFANTRY

* * *

9
The New Regiment

THE ARMY OF THE LATE NINETEENTH CENTURY

The final twenty years of the nineteenth century saw major changes in both organisation and tactics in the British Army. The former were in large part a result of the sweeping reforms enacted by the Secretary of State for War, Edward Cardwell; the latter were the result of advances in military technology, principally the development of the breech-loading rifle and the advent of a smokeless propellant.

Battalion establishments varied according to the part of the world in which the particular battalion was stationed. These ranged from the Indian establishment of 1,032 all ranks to that of the Home Battalion, which was not supposed to fall below 801 but almost invariably did.

The Colonel of a regiment no longer played any active part in its command. The appointment was usually given to a distinguished general officer as a reward for his past services. Up to 1881 it had carried a salary of £1,000 per year, but became entirely honorary after that date. A battalion was commanded by a lieutenant-colonel, with two majors, eight captains, seventeen subalterns, a quartermaster, a pay master and a medical officer. Most of the regimental officers owed their original commissions and subsequent promotions to purchase, but in 1871 this system was abolished, to be replaced by one based on seniority, examination and selection.

Up to 1881 the serjeant-major of a battalion was merely the senior non-commissioned officer. He was appointed by his commanding officer, who also had the power to demote him. Henceforth, the serjeant-major was given a new status of Warrant Officer. He now held a Royal Warrant confirming him to his rank, giving him both greater security of tenure and additional prestige in this extremely important appointment. To mark this change, the old rank badge of four chevrons was changed to that of the Royal Arms, and he was referred to as the Regimental Serjeant-Major.

An infantry battalion was organised into eight companies, each commanded by a captain with a colour-serjeant as his right hand man. The companies were split into two half-companies, commanded by subalterns; and each half-company was further divided into two sections, commanded by serjeants. All the companies were of equal status, the élite flank companies (Grenadier and Light) having been abolished in 1855. For tactical purposes, the battalion could be manoeuvred as two wings, each commanded by one of the two majors on establishment.

From 1874 all infantry soldiers were armed with the .45 in. Martini-Henry single-shot breech-loading rifle. It was a robust, reliable weapon, which gave excellent service. Although sighted up to 1,000 yds, its low velocity required that the firer should be able to judge ranges with a fair degree of accuracy, hence the custom of putting out 'range posts' in front of a defensive position. The Martini-Henry had two noticeable shortcomings: first, the exposed barrel became too hot to touch after only ten rounds; secondly, the black powder propellant produced clouds of oily white smoke that not only concealed the target but gave away the firer's position. In 1893 the Martini-Henry was superseded by the .303 in. Lee-Metford bolt-action magazine rifle, a weapon that was to remain in service, with a change of name and important although not radical modification, for the next seventy years. At first the propellant used was black powder, but this was soon changed to cordite. The change to smokeless powder was of profound significance, which was to utterly change infantry tactics in the coming years. In 1897 the Lee-Metford gave way to the Lee-Enfield, an almost identical weapon except for the profile of the rifling, which was modified to suit the use of cordite. The Lee-Enfield was sighted up to 1,800 yds, but was also equipped with an additional sight by which targets could be engaged with collective fire up to the remarkable range of 2,900 yds. A large part of a soldier's training was devoted to the use of his rifle, and the British army became renowned for its rapid and accurate small-arms fire.

While the soldier's rifle was undergoing these changes, an entirely new weapon was introduced that was eventually to dominate the infantry battle, the machine-gun. Early machine-guns such as the Gatling, Gardner and Nordenfelt had all relied on the operator winding a handle, but in 1887 the American inventor, Hiram Maxim, perfected a gun that relied on recoil for its operation. The following year the Maxim machine-gun entered service with the British Army. One battalion in each brigade was henceforth issued with two such guns.

Another major innovation was the training of mounted infantry. From 1880 each infantry battalion was required to include an officer and thirty-two men trained in horsemanship. Men picked for this role merely attended a week's course at Aldershot, Shorncliffe or the Curragh, before returning to their units to continue their normal duties. The War Office was most emphatic that this scheme was not designed to produce additional cavalry on the cheap, but to enable an infantry soldier to ride a horse sufficiently well to give him considerably increased mobility. He was invariably to fight on foot, using his rifle.

With the advent of the accurate breech-loading rifle, the carrying of Colours in battle became suicidal. The War Office issued a directive in 1882 advising Commanding Officers that Colours need not be taken on active service, but even before then the futility of the practise had been recognised; the last recorded example of Colours being carried in battle was by the 58th Foot at Laing's Neck in January 1881.

Although Infantry training manuals advocated the employment of tactics using open formations combined with fire and movement, much of the experience of field commanders consisted of action against savage races, lacking modern firearms but of vast numerical superiority. Often the only defence against such an enemy was reversion to the old drills of shoulder to shoulder formations; hence one can find plenty of photographs of troops manoeuvring in close order right up to the 1890s. This was not nostalgia for a military past, but a skill that was still of vital importance in certain situations.

Military dress remained conservative. An officer was required to possess a bewildering array of uniforms. Foremost in his wardrobe was the full dress scarlet tunic, an extremely expensive garment that was only worn for important ceremonial occasions (it was certainly never worn in the field, whatever the director of the film *Zulu* may have thought!) For daily wear in barracks and on active service he had the scarlet serge frock (a much cheaper version of the tunic) or blue patrol. In the field he carried his sword, revolver, binoculars, water bottle, blanket, etc. on a Sam Browne belt. Soldiers also had a scarlet full dress tunic which, like those of the officers was expensive and consequently only worn on important ceremonial occasions, and never taken abroad. His normal dress was the scarlet frock made of comparatively coarse woollen cloth. Up to 1878 a French-type chako was worn by all ranks, but as a result of the ascendancy of the Prussian Army, a modified pattern of *pickelhauber*, crowned with a spike, was introduced that year.

The pattern of the infantry soldier's equipment varied slightly over the period, but was always (apart from the Rifle regiments) made of buff leather, incorporating a waist belt, bayonet frog, cartridge pouches and various straps to secure blanket or great-coat. At home it was pipe-clayed white, but on active service was invariably left in its natural matt colour.

Although various forms of khaki uniform had been worn by British troops on active service since at least the days of the Indian Mutiny, nearer home soldiers had to sweat in their scarlet serge. The battle of Tel-el-Kebir in Egypt in 1882 is probably the last time that the British fought in scarlet. Thereafter khaki dress was always worn on active service. In spite of this, scarlet, complete with full dress helmet, remained in use for troops exercising in Britain. It was only after the winter of 1899, when the army fighting the Boers in South Africa suffered severely from the lack of a warm uniform, that khaki serge was hurriedly introduced.

THE FORMATION OF THE DUKE OF CORNWALL'S LIGHT INFANTRY, 1881

On the formation of the Duke of Cornwall's Light Infantry all the former diverse units became part of a single County Regiment. The subsequent change of titles can be summarised as follows.

OLD TITLE	NEW TITLE
32nd (Cornwall) Light Infantry	1st Battalion the Duke of Cornwall's Light Infantry
46th (South Devonshire) Regiment of Foot	2nd Battalion the Duke of Cornwall's Light Infantry
The Royal Cornwall Rangers (The Duke of Cornwall's Own Regiment of Militia)	3rd (Militia) Battalion the Duke of Cornwall's Light Infantry

1st Cornwall Rifle Volunteers	1st Volunteer Battalion the Duke of Cornwall's Light Infantry
2nd Cornwall Rifle Volunteers	2nd Volunteer Battalion the Duke of Cornwall's Light Infantry

In addition, a regimental depôt was established in the newly built Victoria Barracks, Bodmin at which all recruits were trained and the Militia Battalion headquarters was stationed.

It was a new experience for soldiers to have a permanent base in the county, and the Depôt soon came to be regarded not merely as a training unit but as the established home of the Regiment. Close social contacts were made within the county which henceforth looked upon the Duke of Cornwall's Light Infantry with pride and affection.

10
The 1st Battalion, 1881-1914

Gibraltar, Devonport & Ireland

The implementation of the Cardwell Reform on 1st January 1881 found the 1st Battalion the Duke of Cornwall's Light Infantry fulfilling the role of Home Battalion, quartered in barracks at Aldershot. From the very first day of the formation of this new regiment no one was left in any doubt as to its implications for, on the morning of 1st January, 140 all ranks paraded on the snow-covered square, destined for the 2nd Battalion in Gibraltar. The draft travelled to Portsmouth by train and by that afternoon were safely on board HM Troopship *Himalaya*, bound for warmer climes.*

From contemporary accounts it would appear that these men were happy to be despatched to their sister battalion, knowing that they were not leaving the regimental family and would continue to wear their familiar badges and facings. It also seems that, on their arrival with the Second, they were accepted in the same spirit.

The following year, 1882, the Battalion moved to Devonport and then in 1883 to Ireland, where it was stationed first in Cork and then in Dublin. Ireland remained a fruitful source of recruits, accounting for about one third of the total intake to the English infantry. These tours were therefore regarded as excellent opportunities to bring a regiment up to establishment.

Malta, 1885-1888

In 1885 the First commenced an overseas tour that was to take them to Malta for the first three years. The Second should have returned to the United Kingdom by this time to assume the duties of Home Battalion; however, war had broken out in Egypt, making

* The *Himalaya* was one of several Royal Naval troopships built, commissioned and manned by the Royal Navy especially for this role. These were introduced as a result of the transport fiasco during the Crimean War when the army had to make do with hastily hired and often unsuitable vessels. See also *Crocodile* (pp.144-145).

this impossible. While such minor wars were being fought the numerous garrisons of the far-flung British Empire still had to be manned, thus pinning down large numbers of troops. Cardwell, when drafting his reform, had estimated that 142 infantry battalions were needed to fulfil Britain's world role; at any one time 71 would be stationed in the United Kingdom, while the remaining 71 would be deployed overseas. Very quickly it became obvious that Cardwell had been over optimistic in his calculation. Right from the start, unanticipated wars and campaigns threw the carefully prepared arms-plot into confusion, with the result that, all too often, regiments found themselves with both their regular battalions serving overseas. Had it not been for the regimental depôts, the situation could well have reverted to the unsatisfactory state of affairs that had existed before 1881. As it was, the depôts provided a degree of flexibility which allowed drafts to be held after their initial recruit training until such time as they could be despatched overseas to one of their battalions.

In 1886 the troopship bringing the Second Battalion home from Egypt called in at Malta. This was the first time that the two battalions of the Duke of Cornwall's Light Infantry (or indeed their predecessors, the 32nd and 46th, had ever met). It must have been an interesting foregathering; while the celebrations were taking place in the various messes and canteens, each battalion would undoubtedly have been sizing up the other, noting its similarities and idiosyncrasies, its strengths and weaknesses. Although there was crossposting between the two, both battalions resolutely maintained their links with the past, and, because their paths so seldom crossed, they were always to retain their distinct individuality.

The two and a half years in Malta appear to have passed happily. The *One and All*, the regimental journal, recounts an apparently continuous programme of dinners, dances, concerts and other entertainments. Owing to the considerable presence of the Royal Navy and Royal Marines, together with the garrison of four infantry battalions and a large element of the Royal Artillery, Malta probably provided as full a social programme for all ranks as any overseas station. By day football, cricket, swimming, athletics, tug of war and polo filled the off duty hours. Most of the events would be familiar to today's soldiers, but one at least needs explanation. Swimming matches usually included the 'fifty yard pipe match'. On the starting pistol being fired, each competitor had to light his pipe, enter the water, swim fifty yards and emerge at the finishing point with his pipe still alight! The footballers complained long and loud at the broken beer bottles and glasses on the pitch, a cry echoed by the rugger players of the Somerset & Cornwall Light Infantry seventy-five years later concerning their pitch at La Linea.

Military training consisted of a great deal of shooting, much of it in competition with other units, the inevitable drill and ceremonial parades, and occasional field days. In Malta these took on a flavour of their own as they usually involved an invasion of the island. Sometimes the Battalion would enact its part in the overall scheme of defence; sometimes it would be allotted the more exciting role of attack. On these occasions the invading force would be embarked in a number of HM ships which would sail out of sight of land before returning at speed to a beach not previously notified to the defenders. Boats would be lowered and the troops would carry out their assault. There was much rivalry between attackers and defenders as to who could outwit the other.

On 30th June 1887 Lieutenant-Colonel George Swiney handed over temporary command to Major John Ballard. Swiney was an unusual officer to find in command of an infantry battalion in the late nineteenth century. Born in 1840, he had been commissioned as a Cornet into the Bengal Cavalry of the East India Company at the age of seventeen. After the Mutiny he became a Lieutenant with the 5th Bengal European Cavalry, from which he exchanged in 1863 to the 8th King's Royal Irish Hussars, and then immediately to the 6th Dragoon Guards. It was not till 1866 that he exchanged to the 32nd. Between 1870 and 1873 he was employed as the ADC to the Governor of the Cape of Good Hope. Swiney was an efficient and popular officer who had commanded the 1st Battalion almost from its inception. He was an avid historian who founded the The *One and All* in 1886. It was a magazine which, apart from enforced gaps during the two World Wars, continued publication under the title until the demise of the Duke of Cornwall's Light Infantry in 1959. He also wrote the standard reference work on the history of the 32nd entitled *Historical Records of the 32nd (Cornwall) Light Infantry*, a scholarly account to which the author of this book owes a very great deal.

On about 15th July Lieutenant-Colonel David Bond arrived in Malta to take over command from Major Ballard again, on a temporary basis. Finally, on 1st December, Lieutenant-Colonel John Stopford joined the Battalion to take over command on a more permanent basis.

The 1st Battalion at this time was largely recruited from London and the Midlands with a considerable proportion still coming from Ireland. The Army Recruiting Return for 1887 stated: 'Fewer recruits are raised in Cornwall than in any other county in the three kingdoms'. During the same period Cornwall was providing far more than its share of recruits for the Royal Navy.

Early in January 1888 the 1st Battalion was warned for service in

India. The scale of baggage allowed to be conveyed at public expense by troopship was published, with dire warnings of what would happen to anything in excess of the official scales. The Commanding Officer was allowed 18 cwt. This weight allocation decreased according to rank, with the senior NCOs and the Schoolmistress being granted 3 cwt each. All married soldiers were allowed an additional 1 cwt for their wives, but an unmarried Private soldier had to rely on stuffing his entire worldly goods into the equipment he carried on his back. It is interesting that the officers' mess was allocated no less than two and a half tons, which presumably included a considerable quantity of carefully crated silver and the inevitable vast dining-room table which at that time followed a battalion around the world.

HM Troopship *Crocodile* steamed into Malta docks on 17th February 1888, bringing the 1st Battalion the Dorset Regiment from England. Throughout the disembarkation of the Dorsets and the loading of the Cornwall's baggage, the rain poured down in sheets. As the Battalion marched down to the docks the following morning, lead by the 1st Battalion the Black Watch, it continued unabated. On the quayside, before actually going aboard, HRH The Princess Louise inspected the Battalion, walking down each rank of each company, talking to soldiers, apparently quite unperturbed by the remorseless torrents of rain.*

It has not been mentioned that during its stay in Malta the Battalion had acquired a quite remarkable number of widely assorted dogs. The gangway sentries had therefore been given strict orders that a total of five dogs only were to be allowed onto the troopship. The sentries appeared to have performed their duties with diligence until, with *Crocodile* at sea and the island of Malta fading over the horizon, no less than twenty canine friends were found to be sharing berths in the various troop decks.

India, 1888-1890

En route to Bombay

Crocodile was one of the rare breed of troopships existing at the end of the nineteenth century that sailed under the white ensign, being officered by the Royal Navy with a civilian, mainly Lascar, crew. Although a steamer, she was rigged as a barque and made full use of her sails when the wind was favourable.

* Princess Louise was the 4th daughter of Queen Victoria.

18. The Tirah Expedition of 1897. Picquet overlooking the Bara Valley, occupied by men of the 1st Battalion. This illustrates the scale of the heights: physical fitness was vital for officers and soldiers operating in the mountains of the North West Frontier.

19. Charkatra, 1894. Although the drills for fighting in close formation became largely obsolete with the introduction of the magazine rifle in 1893, they were still occasionally used into the 20th century when operating in 'Savage Wars'. This shows the 1st Battalion formed into a square that would not have been out of place at Waterloo.

20. Lady Inglis, widow of General Sir John Inglis, laying the foundation stone of the Lucknow Memorial in the grounds of the Residency at Lucknow on 5th April, 1896. (The granite for the obelisk came from the De Lank quarry in Cornwall.)

21. Men of the 2nd Battalion rowing whalers up the Nile in the attempt to relieve General Gordon at Khartoum, 1884-85. (On one of the stretches of the river, a prize was offered to the crew attaining the fastest time. The Cornwalls, in spite of their presumed familiarity with boats, came in last.)

22. It is said that after the Egyptian campaign of 1882 Queen Victoria requested photographs showing the dress of all those who had taken part. It is believed that this was the one submitted by the 2nd Battalion. 4th from left: Sgt-Maj. George Carr.

23. The officers of the 2nd Battalion photographed at Raglan Barracks, Devonport before embarking fo South Africa. Although khaki drill uniform was worn in the field, cold weather khaki serge had yet to be authorised: these officers are wearing undress scarlet frocks under their athol-grey greatcoats.

24. In the long drawn-out final stages of the South African War, chains of forts such as this helped curtail th mobility of the 'Commandoes'.

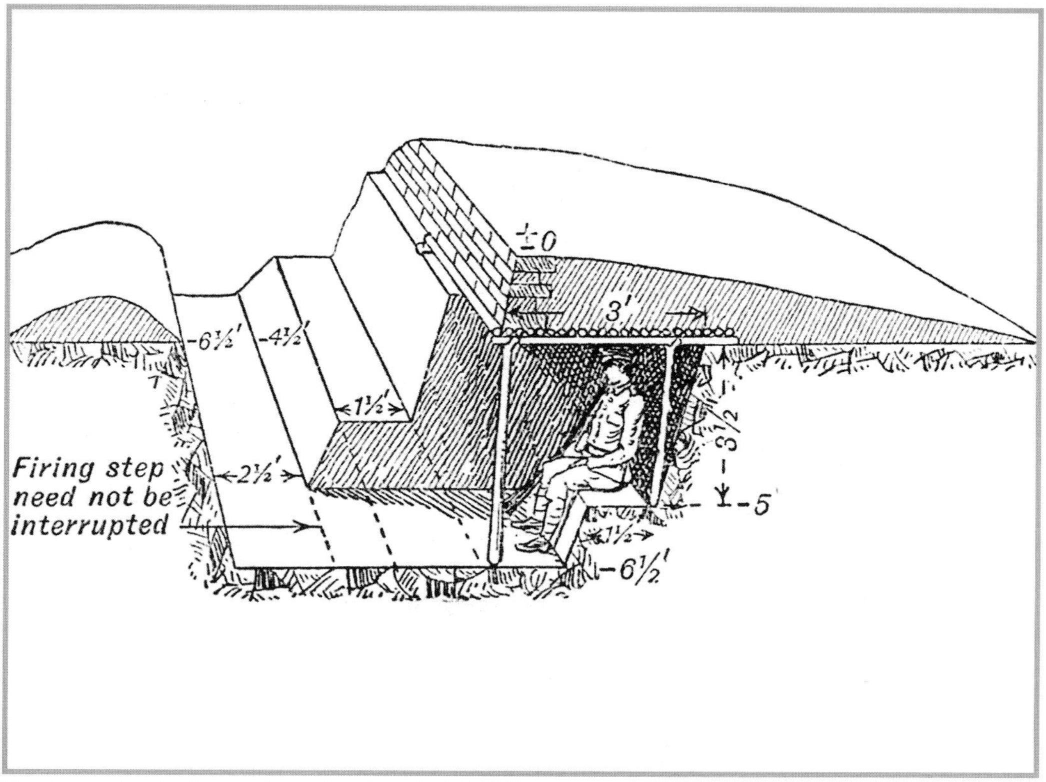

25. A trench – in theory, from *The Manual of Field Engineering, 1912*
& 26. – all too often the reality, probably in the Ypres Salient, 1915.

27. The 1st Battalion leaving the Curragh Camp railway station, 13th August 1914. Within a few months

many of these soldiers would be dead, and the women waving farewell widowed.

28. NCOs and soldiers of the 1st Battalion, taken at Neuve Eglise in January 1915. No proper cold weather clothing had yet been introduced.

29. This photograph of barbed wire demonstrates why infantry attacks so often failed.

On this passage to India *Crocodile* was carrying about 1,800 soldiers, their wives and children (and dogs). For a ship of 5,000 tons, this entailed crowded conditions. The daily conditions and routine would not have been unfamiliar to anybody who had trooped by sea in the years immediately following the Second World War. Officers were accommodated comfortably enough in cabins, albeit in cramped conditions. They were served excellent food and drink in a well-appointed dining saloon by an army of Lascar stewards. The men had to make do with crowded troop decks in which they slung their hammocks. In these troop decks they lived, ate and slept. Food was collected by the mess orderlies from the main galley and eaten off tables, which were rigged each morning as soon as the hammocks had been stowed. The daily routine was: stow hammocks, 6.30 a.m.; breakfast, 7 a.m.; troop deck cleaning by the mess orderlies, 9 a.m., during which time all those not involved made their way up to the weather deck; Captain's Rounds, 10 a.m.; dinner, midday; 'Porter Call', 12.30 p.m., when each man queued up to be issued with his daily pint of porter; games and sports on deck, forenoon; tea, 4 p.m.; hammocks rigged, 5 p.m.; a concert involving the band and all available talent, evening; lights out, 10 p.m. Sundays were observed as days of rest when, apart from the obligatory morning church parade, there were no duties other than those essential to the safe running of the ship.

Crocodile anchored for a day at Port Said to take on coal, all ranks being allowed ashore to sample the dubious delights of the town. Then off down the Suez Canal and out into the Red Sea. There the hot, sticky conditions made life almost unbearable in spite of canvas plunge baths being rigged on deck. There were therefore no regrets when the ship passed Aden and headed east into open sea on the last leg of her passage to Bombay. The only excitement occurred on 1st March when a *felucca*-rigged *dhow* was sighted wallowing in the swell with a broken rudder. She was carrying, to quote the Regimental Journal, 'a large number of niggers', and was bound for Aden from Zanzibar. Strongly suspecting (probably correctly) that she was a slave ship, *Crocodile*'s Captain ordered her to be boarded. Finding her papers in order, the broken rudder was repaired, a supply of water transferred, and the *dhow* was allowed to proceed on her way.

India & Weston-super-Mare

On arrival at the Sassoon Dock, Bombay, on 7th March 1888 the 1st Battalion entrained for the 120-mile journey to Poona. As the train steamed into the station it was met by the band of the 2nd Battalion

Durham Light Infantry, which was stationed there. During the next few days there was considerable cleaning up to be done together with a major sorting out of baggage, for the Battalion was to be split into two wings over 300 miles apart. The Headquarters, together with B, D, E and F Companies under the command of Lieutenant-Colonel Stopford were to be stationed at Bellary up in the hills, while A, C, G and H Companies under Lieutenant-Colonel Bond would occupy the more humid and therefore less pleasant quarters in Madras. The companies were periodically moved between Bellary and Madras.

In Bellary during the summer months the day time temperature frequently exceeds 90° Fahrenheit. Most activity was therefore confined to the periods before 10 a.m. and after 4 p.m. Military training was usually conducted in the cool of the morning before breakfast; games and sports occupied the late afternoon; and concerts and dances took place after sunset. The barracks boasted a splendid theatre which, in the absence of any local entertainment, was in almost continuous nightly use. Snakes were numerous and frightening but of little danger unless provoked. The E Company 'Snake Patrol' killed nineteen snakes in a single month, thirteen of them cobras, the largest of which was 6ft 3in long. A cobra was discovered living in the officers' mess wine cellar. When disposed of, its stomach was found to contain two large rats, so perhaps it would have been better left alive as a guardian against these vermin.

*

At his home in England, at Weston-super-Mare, on 10th April 1889 Thomas Palmer, late of the 32nd, died a few weeks short of his hundredth birthday. He had enlisted in 1807 and seen service at Copenhagen, Corunna, Flushing, Badajos, Salamanca and Toulouse. Almost certainly the oldest retired soldier in the British Army, his mind remained astonishingly clear, although his eyesight became weak. A member of the Rifle Brigade, who died in 1966, remembered reading the newspaper to him each morning and hearing his reminiscences of the Peninsula War; two overlapping lives that covered the ages of the flintlock musket and the nuclear bomb.

*

Back in India, in May 1889 the guard mounted by the Battalion on Government House in Madras experienced an incident that must have made dramatic reading in the usually mundane guard report. That morning a group of young Band Boys reported seeing a large alligator moving down a drain and entering a subterranean pipe that ran under the main gate, where it was lying concealed in some two and a half feet of mud and water. Immediately the guard commander,

Lieutenant Charles Evelegh, together with Captain Edward Sharpe (an officer on the General's staff), a DCLI Colour Serjeant and two hapless natives set out in pursuit. Evelegh led the advance, pushing a stout wooden board in front of him. The alligator attacked, severely injuring both the natives (who had presumably been sent down the other end of the tunnel to act as beaters). Sharpe fired four shots, scoring two hits in the mouth and two in the head. A Sub-Contractor, James Grant, who had appeared on the scene, hit it four more times. Still the animal appeared very much alive. The following day Sharpe, with great courage, entered the tunnel armed with two steel hooks attached to ropes, which he managed to attach to the wounded beast. Waiting DCLI soldiers hauled it out and finally despatched it. Its length was found to be 11 ft 5 ins.

Burma, 1891

Burma had been annexed by Britain in 1886 after a period of savage chaos that accompanied the demise of the Burmese monarchy. However, for the next decade, British troops had constantly to be called upon to restore law and order and to crush incipient rebellions.

In 1891 the 1st Battalion was moved from India to Burma for the purpose of quelling an uprising by a tribe known as the Tsawbaws. Contemporary accounts concentrate on the roughness of the terrain, the heat, the humidity and the mosquitoes, which were described as 'fine and large'; it is therefore difficult to unravel the course of the military operations. It appears that the column to which the DCLI was attached consisted in large part of 105 men of the 2nd Devon Regiment, 150 men of the 1st DCLI (of which 100 of these were Mounted Infantry), a battalion of the locally raised Shwebo Military Police and 2 guns of the 2nd Mountain Battery Royal Artillery. Slowly the rebels were driven back into the strongly stockaded defensive position near the provincial capital of Wunthoo. In the ensuing attack the stockade was stormed against a hot fire, the defenders clanging a heavy bronze bell and keeping up a chant of "Slay, slay the dogs". However, once inside the stockade, the rebels fled at the sight of the fixed bayonets. Seventy-six dead were counted within the stockade, and many more who had been wounded probably died in the surrounding jungle. The column then moved on to occupy Wunthoo itself without any further resistance.

When the DCLI detachments rejoined the main body of the Battalion at Mandalay, they took with them booty taken from the stockade and from the temple at Wunthoo. Two statues of the

Buddha, removed from the temple, are now on view in the Regimental Museum, while the bell which had provided a brazen accompaniment to the battle was presented to the Bodmin Town Council. These actions cannot perhaps be condoned today, but one must remember that soldiers had been killed in the storming of the Wunthoo stockade and that, by the ethics of the nineteenth century, property taken from an enemy who had offered resistance was regarded as the legal spoils of war.

India & Ceylon, 1894-1901

Chakrata & Meerut, 1894

In early 1894 the First Battalion returned to India, where it was stationed at Chakrata, a military garrison in the foothills of the Himalayas, some 150 miles north of Delhi. The cool, clean air must have been most welcome after the oppressive humidity of Burma. In September that year the Battalion moved to Meerut by march route, where it was accommodated under canvas. Meerut is 35 miles north-east of Delhi, and its distance from Chakrata is just over 140 miles. These long marches by which units were regularly moved across India might strike today's soldiers with considerable apprehension, but in fact they were carried out at a very leisurely pace. Chakrata to Meerut took the Battalion twelve days – an average daily march of only about eleven and a half miles. Tents would be struck each morning and loaded onto the battalion wagons, which would immediately set off under the quartermaster to the next camping ground. When the column arrived there at about midday, the men would find the tents pitched and a hot meal waiting. During the afternoon the officers would leave camp to shoot game, thereby providing a welcome addition to the army rations. At the same time the considerable convoy of native ox-drawn carts carrying the Battalion's extensive baggage would wend its slow way into the camp and prepare for the night. The Band and Bugles invariably accompanied the marching column, and if the night's camping area happened to be close to a permanent military station, the occupying unit would despatch its band and drums to play the visitors in for the last mile or so, and out the following morning. It was a soldier's way of life that had hardly changed for two centuries.

In Meerut the Battalion distinguished itself by losing a number of rifles. The theft of weapons and ammunition had always been a skill of the locals in northern India, who over the years had brought it to a fine art. Accordingly, strict orders were invariably issued concerning the security of arms, which included the chaining and padlocking of the soldiers' rifles to the tent pole at night. Snap checks were frequently made by the orderly officer to check that this order was obeyed. However, for obvious reasons, the rifles of the guard were kept at immediate readiness in an arms rack in the guard tent. One night the soldier standing sentry outside this tent was jumped by a gang of ruffians. He managed to hold onto his weapon, but in the ensuing confusion five rifles disappeared. The NCOs of the guard must have had some explaining to do the following morning!

The regimental journal makes frequent mention of meetings of the Army Temperance Association. The First Battalion mustered no fewer than 430 members at this time. One hears so much of the drunkenness that afflicted the army at this time that it is interesting to see almost half the Battalion were members of the Temperance Association.

Lucknow, 1895-1897

On 8th February 1895 the First Battalion moved to Lucknow. Once again, it marched every yard of the 350 or so miles, covering the distance in thirty days. Lucknow was of course a station of particular historical interest to the First Battalion, whose forefathers had won glory in its defence in 1857. Much time was therefore given to conducting 'battle field tours' of the area. In the cool winter weather field training, including elaborate field firing exercises involving cavalry, artillery and infantry, were carried out. Curtailed as we are today by ever more stringent safety 'templates', the conduct of field firing in India at the end of the nineteenth century makes one gasp with astonishment. Presumably the luckless inhabitants of the areas picked for these exercises beat a hasty withdrawal from their fields when they got wind of what was to happen.

During the Battalion's tour at Lucknow each company in turn was sent up to Ranikhet, 200 miles north in the mountains, where it lived in a primitive camp with similar detachments from the other arms. The aim appears to have been to toughen everybody up, and train them to fight in these wild mountainous areas. To this end they were almost continuously employed either in hard field exercises or physical activities, which usually involved races up and down the *khud*. The camp was called 'Standing Camp', which seemed ironic as nobody was ever given a minute's rest to stand still. As the reader will doubtless guess, the moves to and from Ranikhet were carried out on foot.

While in Lucknow the Battalion was issued with the new magazine

Lee-Metford rifle in place of the single shot Henry-Martini. Although the Lee-Metford was in fact already obsolescent (having been replaced at home by the Lee-Enfield), it was a major improvement that gave the soldier a far higher rate of fire.

Tirah, 1897-1898

In 1897 the tribesmen of the Tirah attacked across the Kohat-Peshawar border. A division of British and Indian troops was quickly organised to mount a punitive expedition into the Tirah to exact reparation for this unprovoked aggression. Initially the Battalion was allotted to the Reserve Brigade at Rawal Pindi, but later in the campaign was involved in skirmishing in the mountains overlooking the Bara valley. The skills and physical fitness acquired at Ranikhet stood the Battalion in good stead.

Lucknow, 1899-1900

On return to Lucknow the Battalion was honoured with a visit by Lady Inglis, widow of Major-General Sir John Inglis, late of the 32nd Foot, who had commanded the garrison of Lucknow during the siege. On 5th April 1899 the successors to the gallant Defenders of Lucknow paraded in their white summer uniforms to witness Lady Inglis lay the foundation stone of the 32nd Foot Memorial. The granite had come from the Bosaham Quarry in Cornwall and had been paid for by all ranks of the Regiment, both past and present. It was a solemn and moving occasion.

Dum-Dum, 1900-1901

After many orders and counter orders, the 1st Battalion set out from Lucknow on 10th January for Dum-Dum, a garrison town in the south of Bengal near Calcutta. Doubtless to the relief of the soldiers, their long journey was carried out by rail except for the final march from Calcutta to Dum-Dum. Even so it took thirteen days, with frequent pauses at military bases on the route where everybody could take some exercise.

Ceylon, 1901

By the beginning of 1901 the problem of accommodating Boer prisoners-of-war in South Africa was becoming acute. A policy was therefore implemented to establish two large prisoner-of-war camps, one in Canada and one in Ceylon. The 1st Battalion was tasked with running the one in Ceylon.

On 21st December the Battalion left Dum-Dum in two troop trains for Kiddepore Docks in Calcutta. There it embarked in SS *Clive*. The coolies who were supposed to be loading the baggage gradually drifted away until only the long-suffering soldiers were left. These men worked on through the night, allowing the ship to cast off on schedule at 8 a.m. the following morning.

Christmas Day, 1901 was celebrated at sea. The short voyage was calm, and boredom was kept at bay with deck sports and nightly band concerts. On the evening of 27th December the *Clive* entered the breakwater of Colombo harbour, and the following day tied up against the quay.

The prisoner-of-war camp, consisting of rows of neatly laid out wooden huts, was situated at Diyatalawa in the Badulla District about 4,500ft up in the mountains. The climate was excellent. The prisoners slept fifty-six to a hut, were well clothed, well fed and, apart from having to remain within the wire perimeter, were allowed to live their lives undisturbed. Being enterprising men, they cultivated gardens, set up markets in which they sold the produce, and used their considerable skill in making intricate ornaments from the local ebony. There seems to have been no sense of animosity between captor and captive. The camp was run efficiently and humanely – a far cry from the notorious concentration camps back in South Africa.

THE LAST DAYS OF PEACE, 1906-1914

The 1st Battalion remained in South Africa till 1906 when it returned to Plymouth, where it was stationed in Crownhill Barracks. The following year it moved to Woolwich, then to Gravesend in 1908, to Tidworth in 1911 and finally to the Curragh, County Kildare, in 1913. Regardless of the individual views of officers, the British Army has a proud record of keeping clear of any active involvement in politics, but this ethos was about to be severely tested. The rejection by Ulster of Asquith's Home Rule Bill in January 1914 threw Ireland to the verge of civil war. Ulstermen formed an irregular army under Lord Carson, who made it clear that armed force would be used to oppose home rule from Dublin. The British garrison at the Curragh was mobilised to move on Ulster. However, many British officers came from the Protestant landed families of Ulster, and were not prepared to take up arms against their kith and kin. They would not refuse a direct order, but they would resign their commissions were that order to be given. This unprecedented situation, which became known as 'The Curragh Mutiny', caused a major crisis in both the political and military worlds. It was only brought to an end by a far greater crisis; the mobilization of Great Britain for war against Germany. Looking at the impassive faces staring out of the regimental photographs of this period, it is difficult to imagine the drama that was being played out in Ireland. What were the views held by the officers of the 1st Battalion? Alas, no record appears to have survived, and one can only guess at the animated meetings, discussions and arguments which must have dominated mess life that year.

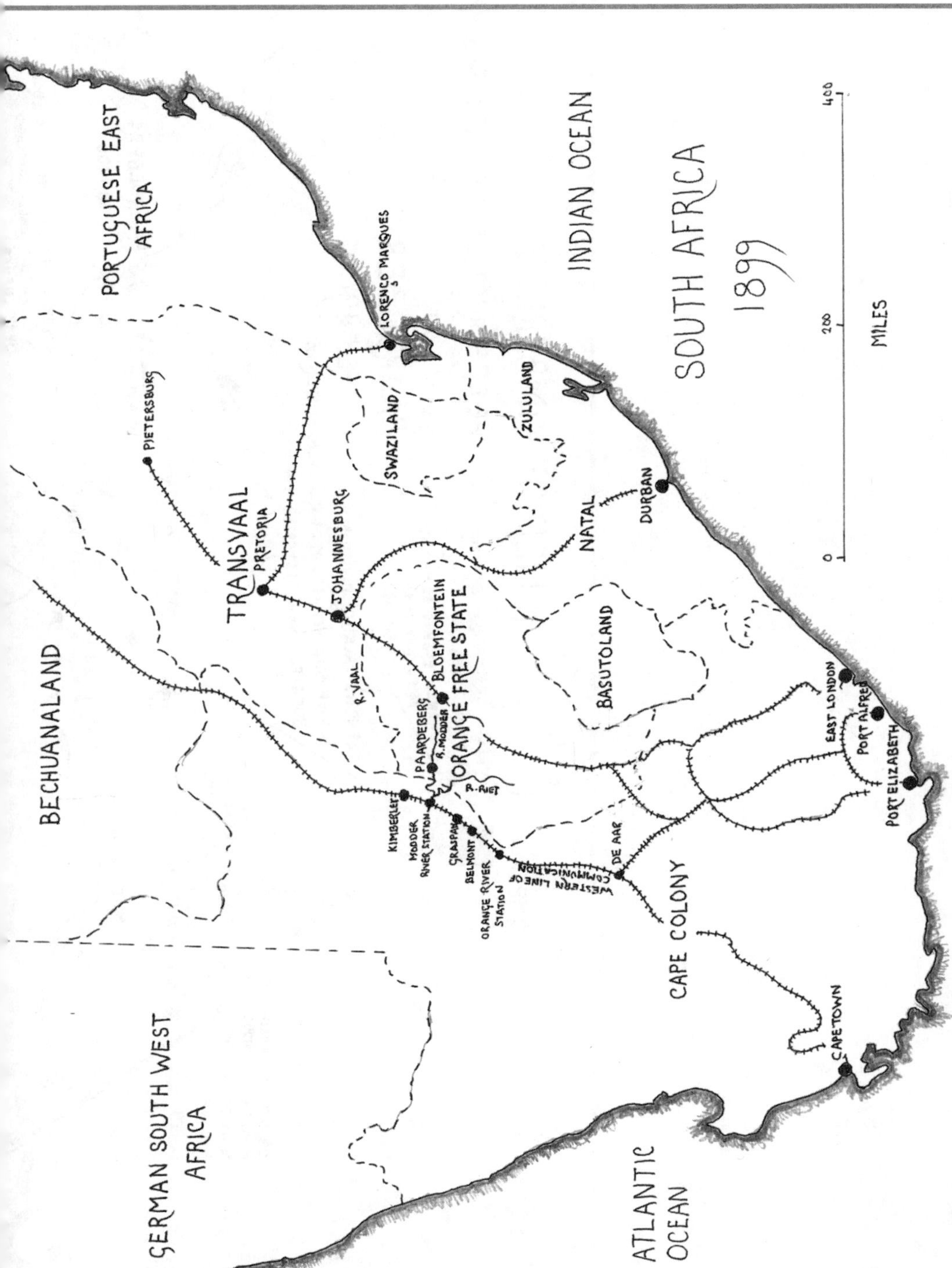
SOUTH AFRICA
1899
PORTUGUESE EAST AFRICA
INDIAN OCEAN
LORENCO MARQUES
PIETERSBURG
TRANSVAAL
PRETORIA
JOHANNESBURG
SWAZILAND
ZULULAND
DURBAN
NATAL
BLOEMFONTEIN
ORANGE FREE STATE
BASUTOLAND
BECHUANALAND
R. VAAL
PAARDEBERG
R. MODDER
R. RIET
KIMBERLEY
MODDER RIVER STATION
GRASPAN
BELMONT
ORANGE RIVER STATION
WESTERN LINE OF COMMUNICATION
DE AAR
CAPE COLONY
EAST LONDON
PORT ALFRED
PORT ELIZABETH
CAPETOWN
GERMAN SOUTH WEST AFRICA
ATLANTIC OCEAN
0
200
400
MILES

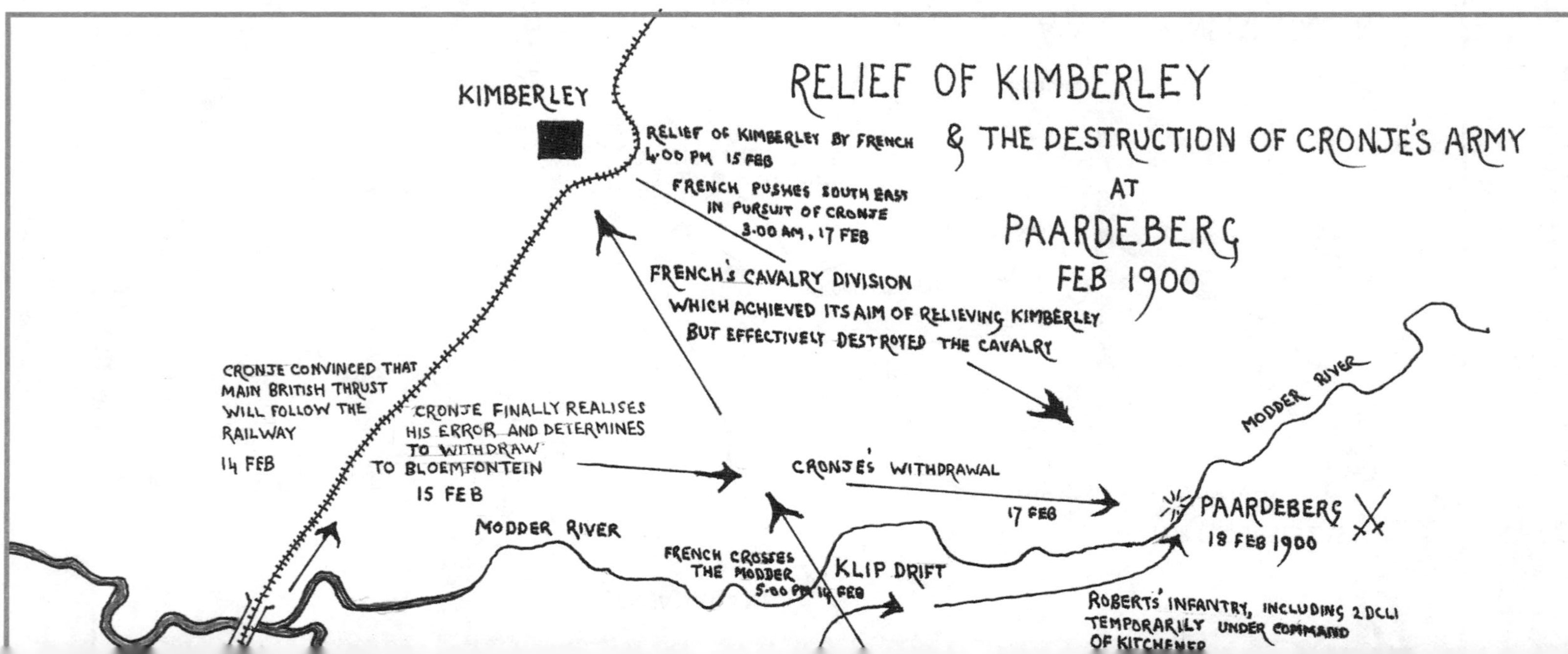
RELIEF OF KIMBERLEY
& THE DESTRUCTION OF CRONJE'S ARMY
AT
PAARDEBERG
FEB 1900
KIMBERLEY
RELIEF OF KIMBERLEY BY FRENCH 4.00 PM 15 FEB
FRENCH PUSHES SOUTH EAST IN PURSUIT OF CRONJE 3.00 AM, 17 FEB
FRENCH'S CAVALRY DIVISION
WHICH ACHIEVED ITS AIM OF RELIEVING KIMBERLEY BUT EFFECTIVELY DESTROYED THE CAVALRY
CRONJE CONVINCED THAT MAIN BRITISH THRUST WILL FOLLOW THE RAILWAY
14 FEB
CRONJE FINALLY REALISES HIS ERROR AND DETERMINES TO WITHDRAW TO BLOEMFONTEIN
15 FEB
CRONJE'S WITHDRAWAL
17 FEB
MODDER RIVER
MODDER RIVER
PAARDEBERG
18 FEB 1900
FRENCH CROSSES THE MODDER 5.00 PM 14 FEB
KLIP DRIFT
ROBERTS' INFANTRY, INCLUDING 2DCLI TEMPORARILY UNDER COMMAND

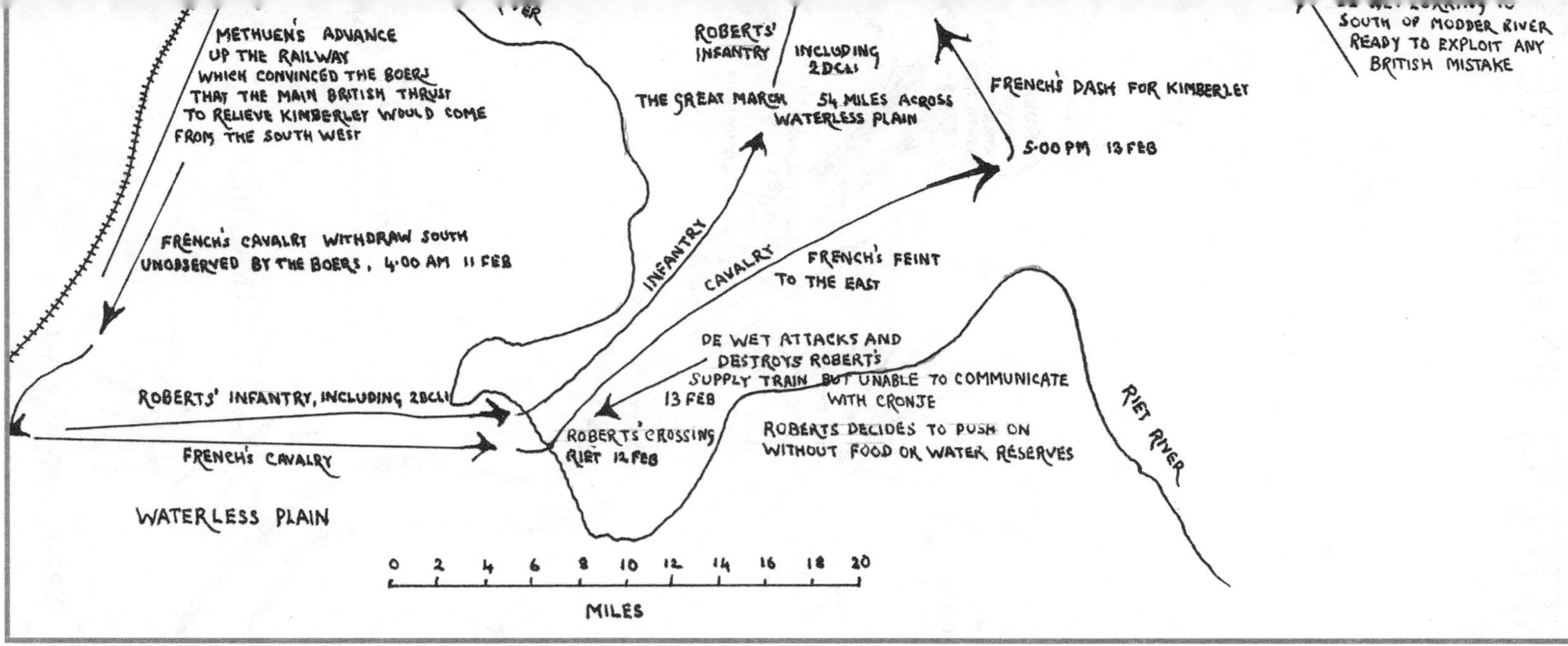

METHUENS ADVANCE UP THE RAILWAY WHICH CONVINCED THE BOERS THAT THE MAIN BRITISH THRUST TO RELIEVE KIMBERLEY WOULD COME FROM THE SOUTH WEST
FRENCH'S CAVALRY WITHDRAW SOUTH UNOBSERVED BY THE BOERS, 4.00 AM 11 FEB
ROBERTS' INFANTRY, INCLUDING 2DCLI
FRENCH'S CAVALRY
WATERLESS PLAIN
ROBERTS' INFANTRY
INCLUDING 2DCLI
THE GREAT MARCH 54 MILES ACROSS WATERLESS PLAIN
INFANTRY
CAVALRY
FRENCH'S FEINT TO THE EAST
FRENCH'S DASH FOR KIMBERLEY
5.00 PM 13 FEB
DE WET ATTACKS AND DESTROYS ROBERTS SUPPLY TRAIN BUT UNABLE TO COMMUNICATE WITH CRONJE
13 FEB
ROBERTS' CROSSING RIET 12 FEB
ROBERTS DECIDES TO PUSH ON WITHOUT FOOD OR WATER RESERVES
RIET RIVER
SOUTH OF MODDER RIVER READY TO EXPLOIT ANY BRITISH MISTAKE
0 2 4 6 8 10 12 14 16 18 20
MILES

THE BATTLE OF PAARDEBERG,

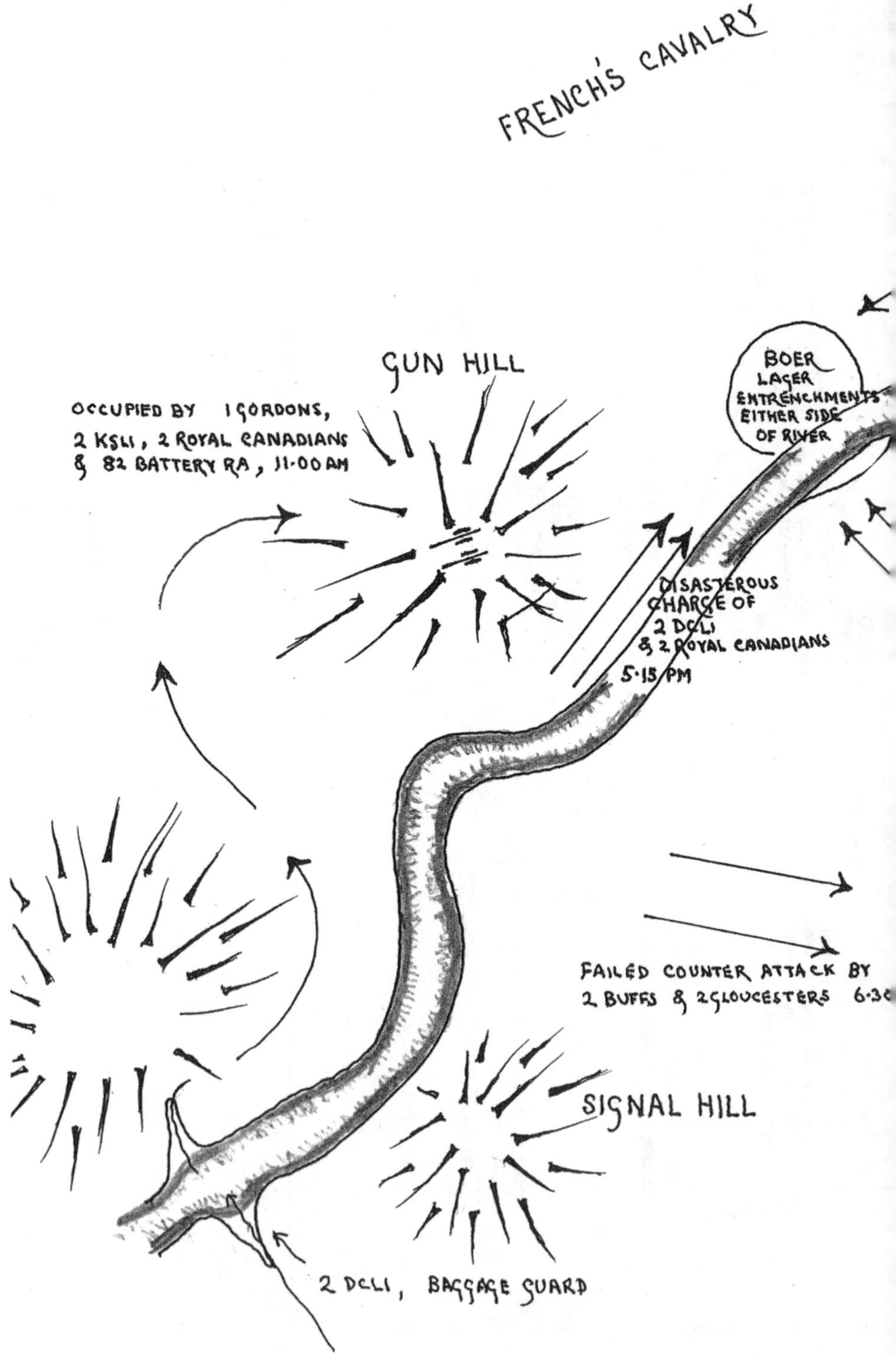

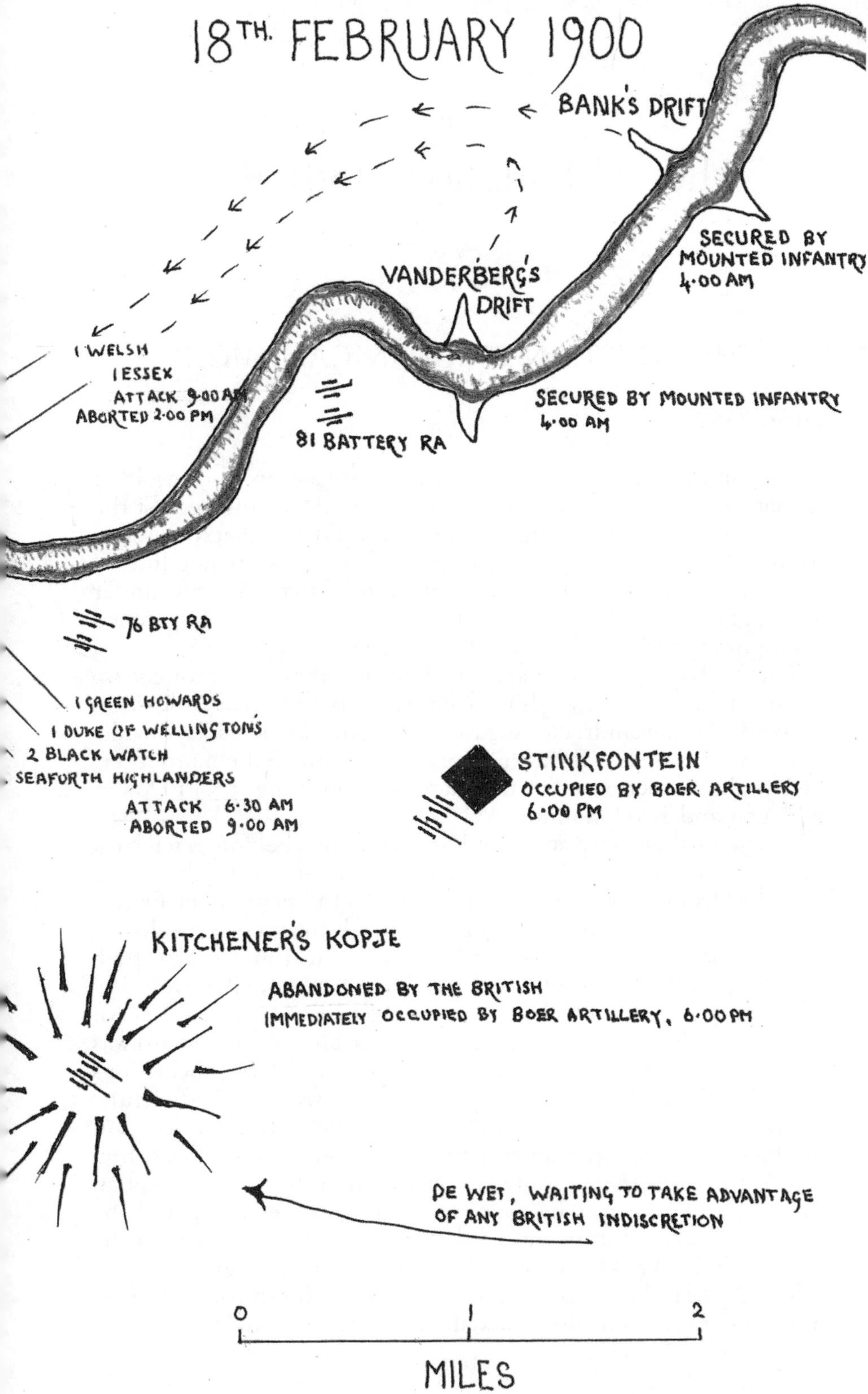
18TH. FEBRUARY 1900
BANK'S DRIFT
SECURED BY MOUNTED INFANTRY 4.00 AM
VANDERBERG'S DRIFT
1 WELSH
1 ESSEX
ATTACK 9.00 AM
ABORTED 2.00 PM
81 BATTERY RA
SECURED BY MOUNTED INFANTRY 4.00 AM
76 BTY RA
1 GREEN HOWARDS
1 DUKE OF WELLINGTON'S
2 BLACK WATCH
SEAFORTH HIGHLANDERS
ATTACK 6.30 AM
ABORTED 9.00 AM
STINKFONTEIN
OCCUPIED BY BOER ARTILLERY 6.00 PM
KITCHENER'S KOPJE
ABANDONED BY THE BRITISH
IMMEDIATELY OCCUPIED BY BOER ARTILLERY, 6.00 PM
DE WET, WAITING TO TAKE ADVANTAGE OF ANY BRITISH INDISCRETION
0
1
2
MILES

11
The 2nd Battalion, 1881-1914

THE EGYPTIAN & SUDAN CAMPAIGNS

Egypt, 1882

The Second did not have to wait long to taste action. In June 1882 the nationalist leader Arabi Pasha led a popular rising against the established government of Egypt. Any political action that threatened Britain's free use of the Suez Canal, a vital link in her line of communication to India, could not be tolerated. A force under General Sir Garnet Wolseley was hastily assembled and despatched to support the army of the Khedive of Egypt.

The 2nd Battalion, then stationed at Gibraltar, was brought up to war establishment by a draft from the 1st Battalion at Aldershot, and landed at Alexandria in August. Moving quickly across to Ismailia on the Suez Canal to form the flank protection to the main force, the Battalion experienced its full share of skirmishing at Kafr Dower, El-Magfar and Tel-el-Mahuta.

After a further sharp action at Kassassin, the rebel forces fell back on their carefully prepared defensive position at Tel-el-Kebir, sixty-five miles from Cairo. On the night of 12th-13th September British and Indian forces carried out a silent night advance across the desert, attacking at dawn. The ensuing battle was short and sharp. By 6 a.m. all opposition had collapsed. British-Indian casualties were 459 killed and wounded, while the rebels lost almost 2,000. An immediate follow up was ordered and the cavalry advance guard was at the gates of Cairo by the following evening. 15,000 rebel troops surrendered. The rebellion had been crushed swiftly and efficiently.

The Egyptian Campaign of 1882 was probably the last occasion on which British troops fought in their traditional scarlet. The scarlet serge 'kersey' jacket was unsuited for service in the heat of the Egyptian summer, and accounts by contemporary witnesses compared the filthy sweat-soaked uniforms of the British unfavourably with the light, washable khaki drill worn by their Indian comrades.

The 2nd Battalion returned to barracks in Alexandria, where all ranks were presented with a medal, known as the Khedive's Star, in the presence of the Khedive himself. At the conclusion of the parade the Battalion exercised its Light Infantry tradition by doubling past. Alas, the medals were only loosely pinned on, and many fell into the dust of the barrack square. After being dismissed men could be seen crawling about, searching for their lost medals. As these were not engraved with the recipient's name, there must have been some heated altercations.

The Sudan Campaign, 1884-1885

Even while the British were fighting Arabi Pasha's rebels in Egypt, a far more serious threat was developing in the Sudan. There the fanatical Muslim fundamentalist, Raouf Pasha, proclaimed himself Mahdi. Tribesmen flocked to his banner, and in a pre-emptive strike his army of Dervishes captured 20,000 rifles, 19 field guns and a large supply of ammunition. A small, poorly trained force of 10,000 local levies under an Indian Army Officer, Colonel William Hicks, moved out into the desert from Khartoum to confront the Mahdi. Caught, weak from thirst, at Kashgil, it was totally annihilated. In December 1883 this tragedy was repeated when a force under General Baker was routed at El-Teb, losing over two thirds of its men killed. These appalling defeats at the hands of tribesmen prompted a decision by the British Government to evacuate the Sudan. Accordingly, General Charles Gordon was despatched to Khartoum to oversee this operation. It was not to be. The town was quickly invested by a strong rebel force, and yet another relief force, which was to include the 2nd Battalion, had to be assembled and despatched. Khartoum is situated on the junction of the Blue Nile and the White Nile, 1,650 miles south of Cairo by river. Speed was of the essence, yet the logistical problems of moving and supplying an army along this immense line of communication through enemy dominated country were, to say the least, daunting.

Whale boats, capable of negotiating the many cataracts, were constructed in England and shipped out to Egypt, while some 3,000 camels were hired locally together with their drivers. The boats and camels were assembled at Wadi Halfa on 14th October 1884, and by Christmas Day 2,200 men had reached Korti, beyond which lay the most difficult section of the river.

Meanwhile, Gordon had sent back four steamers, down the Nile as far as the depth of water permitted, to meet the approaching relief force. These joined up with the vanguard on 24th January 1885, and a small force of 20 British and 280 Sudanese soldiers under Colonel Sir Charles Wilson was immediately embarked, setting off on the final phase of the advance to Khartoum. It was obvious that time was fast running out for Gordon and his beleaguered garrison, and that speed was now vital. However, frustrations continued to dog the expedition and one of the steamers grounded twice, thereby losing a further twenty-four hours. On 28th January Khartoum was sighted, but it soon became clear that the town was in enemy hands. The steamers turned and started to make their way back down river under heavy enemy fire. Both were wrecked, but the troops and crews managed to get ashore, where they succeeded in holding out against repeated attacks until relieved.

Gordon had been killed on the morning of 26th January. The relief force had arrived forty-eight hours too late. On 24th February orders were received for withdrawal, this extremely hazardous operation being carried out with commendable efficiency. A further advance was planned for the end of the summer, but events in India demanded the move of many units of the army in Sudan to the borders of Afghanistan. On 22nd June the whole operation was called off indefinitely.*

A HOME TOUR, 1886-1898

The 2nd Battalion returned to the United Kingdom in 1886 for a home tour, being stationed at Devonport in 1886; Plymouth in 1888; Pembroke Dock in 1889; Dublin in 1891; Newry in 1894; and at Devonport in 1898.

As has already been mentioned, home battalions were often little more than holding units that received recruits from the depôt, and provided continuation training to bring them up to the standard required by operational battalions before arranging for their drafting overseas. Home battalions were thus usually well below establishment. An amusing insight into life with the 2nd Battalion in Plymouth is given in *Recollections of Three Reigns* by Sir Frederick Ponsonby:†

> I was gazetted to the 46th Regiment of Foot (Duke of Cornwall's Light Infantry) and joined them at the Citadel at Plymouth. It was an ideal regiment. It had practically no men. There was an officers' mess, a band, some charming officers,

* After the withdrawal of the 1895 Nile Expeditionary Force it was another thirteen years before Khartoum was recaptured by an Anglo-Egyptian army, under Major-General Sir Herbert Kitchener.

† Sir Frederick Ponsonby, 1867-35, Assistant Private Secretary to Queen Victoria and Private Secretary to King Edward VII and King George V.

a certain number of excellent NCOs and a sprinkling of old soldiers, but otherwise nothing but recruits. It was what Lord Wolseley described as a 'squeezed lemon'. As soon as a recruit was sufficiently trained, he was packed off to India to feed the other Battalion. Of course, I had to spend the first few months doing recruits' drill, but after that I had a wonderful time and was away practically every day merely attending a parade on Saturdays.

THE SOUTH AFRICAN WAR, 1899-1902

(The Second Anglo-Boer War)

The causes of the Boer War have been a matter of dispute among historians ever since the Boer army crossed the frontier into Natal on 12th October 1899. Undoubtedly an important factor behind the conflict was the earlier war against the Boers in 1881. Under the pretext of bringing law and order to the Boer Republic of the Transvaal, Britain had annexed it in 1877 and two years later declared it a Crown Colony. Since it was precisely to escape the hated British rule that the Boers had originally trekked north and established themselves north of the Vaal river, this aroused their bitterest feelings.

In 1881 the Boers had taken up arms, inflicting four decisive defeats on the British at Brokhorst-Spruit, the Ingogo River, Laing's Nek and Majuba Hill. A much subdued Britain quickly negotiated peace and the Transvaal was granted independence.

In October 1899 the Boers, believing that another attempt was to be made to re-annex their territory, and convinced that they could repeat another lightning victory against the British garrison of only 20,000 men, launched their 45,000 strong army across the border into Natal in a pre-emptive strike.The garrisons of Kimberley and Mafeking were cut off and came under siege on 16th October 1899, and that of Ladysmith a fortnight later.

The Boers nearly achieved their aim and the British, under General Sir Redvers Buller, were repeatedly outmanoeuvred and out-fought.

The 2nd Battalion DCLI was quartered in Raglan Barracks, Devonport in 1899. Being a home battalion, it then existed in little more than cadre form. As soon as it was warned for active service in South Africa immediate steps had to be taken to bring the Battalion up to full war establishment. This was done in two ways: first, all available Reservists were immediately recalled to the Colours; secondly, the Battalion carried out a recruiting march across Cornwall, bivouacking in the grounds of the large country houses each night. The physical standard of many recruits and reservists was appalling and, in spite of the urgent need for soldiers, a huge proportion was found unacceptable for service. This failure of so many men to reach even minimal standards of fitness shocked a complacent nation into a realisation of the true state of the working man's health.

The 2nd Battalion entrained at Devonport on the evening of 4th November 1899. It marched to the railway station in pouring rain, arriving at the Royal Albert Docks in London the following dawn. Their troopship, HMT *Somosa*, was old and the voyage was not memorable for comfort.*

When the Battalion disembarked at Cape Town on 29th November it must have quickly become aware of a sense of despondency. British troops were flooding into South Africa but, in spite of their apparent military superiority, they were being outmanoeuvred by bands of untrained farmers. Whereas the majority of the British army was restricted to the speed of marching men, the Boers were all mounted on tough, wiry ponies and could literally run rings around their adversaries. Rhodes had been surrounded and was besieged at Kimberley, as was General White at Ladysmith.

The nadir came in 'Black Week', 9th-15th December 1899, when the Boer army inflicted three humiliating defeats on the British at Stormberg, Magersfontein and Colenso.

General Buller was replaced by Field Marshal Lord Roberts, an officer with considerable experience of guerrilla operations in Abyssinia, Afghanistan, India and Burma, who fully appreciated the importance of light mobile forces.

Relief of Kimberley, 15th February 1900, & pursuit

Field-Marshal Lord Robert's plan for the relief of Kimberley and the subsequent operation to bring General Cronje's Boer army to battle was a masterly example of military subterfuge. Lieutenant-General Lord Methuen's 1st Division, together with Lieutenant-General French's Cavalry Division, were to push steadily north towards Kimberley along the axis of the railway. When Cronje was sufficiently convinced that this was the main British thrust, French was to slip away to the south and carry out a wide sweeping movement to the east, crossing the Riet and Modder rivers before making a final dash for Kimberley from the south east. Meanwhile Roberts' 6th and 9th Divisions would also cross the Riet River and march at all possible speed north east to cut off Cronje. It was anticipated that Cronje would retire east towards Bloemfontein, crossing the Modder River at Paardeberg.

* HMT stands for Hired Military Transport.

French's lightning cavalry dash succeeded, and, on 15th February 1900, Kimberley was relieved.

Cronje, finally realising that he had been duped, set off east on the ninety-mile march to Bloemfontein, intending to cross the Modder River by the drift at Paardeberg. Meanwhile, Roberts' 6th and 9th Divisions had also crossed the Riet River and were heading across the waterless veldt towards Paardeberg. The race was on.

Initially, 2 DCLI had been principally engaged in the vital but less than exciting task of securing the lines of communication on the main north-south railway, based at isolated tin-shack hamlets such as De Aar, Orange River Station, Belmont and Graspan. Suddenly all was changed as the Battalion joined Lord Roberts' flanking force in pursuit of the Boers.

The day after the marching infantry had crossed the Riet River De Wet's mobile commando, which was lurking to the south ready to exploit any British error, struck at the slow-moving ox-drawn column as it attempted to make the crossing. It was destroyed, and the infantry were left without any reserves of food and water. It would be hard to exaggerate the suffering experienced by the soldiers as the columns moved across the veldt. There was little water and less food. Hungry and parched with thirst, roasted by day and frozen by night, these indomitable men somehow kept going, covering immense distances, often with worn out boots and occasionally without boots at all. Luckily De Wet's men were far too engaged in plundering the baggage train to pay attention to Roberts' infantry column. The British, however, were buoyed up by the knowledge that Cronje was not far ahead of them and that if he could be forced to turn and fight he would be destroyed.

The battle of Paardeberg, 18th February 1900

On 17th February the advance guard made contact with Cronje's army, forcing it to halt and deploy into a defensive position near Paardeberg on the Modder River. Roberts himself, severely indisposed (probably with enteric fever), handed over command to his Chief-of-Staff, Major-General Lord Kitchener, rather than the more senior officer commanding the 6th Division, Lieutenant-General Kelly-Kenny. From that moment almost anything that could go wrong did go wrong. Kitchener launched unco-ordinated attacks without any consultation with his divisional or brigade commanders. Each of these attacks was repulsed with heavy and unnecessary casualties. To crown the disasters of the day, Kitchener abandoned a tactically important kopje to the south of the river (known afterwards as

Kitchener's Kopje), which was immediately occupied by De Wet's artillery, who commenced to shell the British from their rear.

At the outset of the battle 2 DCLI had been guarding the baggage train of Major-General Sir Henry Colvile's 9th Division, to the south west of Cronje's position on the south bank of the Modder River (the opposite side to Cronje's position). The initial attacks from the south and east having failed disastrously, Kitchener ordered Colvile to attack from the south west. However, Kitchener had already removed the Highland Brigade from this Division (without telling Colvile), leaving insufficient troops to carry out this proposed attack. Kitchener therefore ordered Battalion Headquarters and three companies of 2 DCLI to cross the Modder River and form the right flank for the attack. He failed to inform the Brigade Commander, Brigadier-General Horace Smith-Dorrien, who was, to say the least, somewhat surprised to see part of his command, which should have been guarding the baggage train south of the river, rise up from the grass to the north of the river and advance in a suicidal attack across open veldt. The Commanding Officer of 2 DCLI, Lieutenant-Colonel William Aldworth DSO, late of the Bedfordshire Regiment, had led his men across the river and brought them forward to the firing line of the Royal Canadians. They fixed bayonets and then, in the words of the Adjutant, Lieutenant Fife:

> The Colonel gave the order to "advance", "prepare to charge", "charge". The men gave a tremendous shout and rushed pell mell through the firing line. We got about 300 yards through a terrific hail of bullets, pom-pom shells and shrapnel, men falling at every yard. At last I saw the Colonel discharge his rifle, and then I was struck on the left shoulder and bowled clean over. I believe the Colonel was hit simultaneously; he was about 15 yards to my left and slightly in front. I never heard the Colonel give any more orders, though some say he gasped out "charge" with his last breath.

No DCLI soldier succeeded in getting to within 300 yards of the Boer entrenchments. In the minute or so before the charge was brought to a halt, 28 men had been killed and 52 wounded. The survivors, including the wounded, lay under the blazing sun till nightfall, the slightest movement inviting the quick response of a sniper's bullet.

It was only with the return of Roberts on the following morning of 19th February that order was restored. The plan, originally proposed on 17th February by Lieutenant-General Kelly-Kenny, was implemented. Cronje surrendered with his army on 27th February (the anniversary of the British defeat at Majuba). This was the first decisive victory of the war.

Later stages of the war

The war was, however, still far from over. With the surrender of Cronje and his 4,000 strong army, the Boers split into commando bands and it was to be another two years before the Boer Republic finally surrendered, during which time the British army waged a frustrating and increasingly pitiless campaign. The commandos depended on their farms and womenfolk to supply food and other vital supplies; the natural response was therefore to burn the farms, destroy all crops and move the women and children to 'concentration camps'. Conditions in these camps became appalling, resulting in the deaths of thousands. It is a sad indictment of Britain that these concentration camps, originally set up for purely tactical reasons and intended to be administered with humanity, should, forty years later, have become synonymous with those of the brutal Nazi regime. However, commandos continued to operate across the area, harassing isolated posts and destroying military communications. The tactical solution was to build a network of forts across the country. These forts, each of which was within sight of its neighbour, could immediately report any attempted movement of a commando through the net. There were over 8,000 of these built, mostly sited along railways so that troops could be brought up with great speed to deal with any incursion. The forts themselves were some twenty feet in diameter, built of two skins of corrugated iron with the gap filled with stones and earth. Barbed wire entanglements discouraged intrepid enemy patrols from creeping up too close at night. Photographs in the Regimental Museum at Bodmin clearly show one such fort with its detachment of a serjeant and fourteen men. Life must have been almost unbearably tedious, cooped up in these tin boxes, with only night patrols between neighbouring forts to alleviate the boredom.

A more exciting form of soldiering was experienced by the Mounted Infantry companies. Each infantry battalion provided one such company; these were deployed away from their parent units, ranging over very wide areas and seeing considerable action. One cannot relate the story of the 2 DCLI Mounted Infantry Company because it operated independently and left no records; however, the medal rolls show the wide variety of the clasps awarded to these mounted soldiers, which indicate the vast scope of their movements during the latter stages of the war.

In mid 1903 the 2nd Battalion moved by train to Durban to embark for England. Shortly before departing from South Africa the two regular battalions briefly met. This was a rare occasion in the post-Cardwell army.

During the three years of the South African War 13 officers and 143 soldiers of the 2nd Battalion had been killed or had died of disease. By the terrible standards of fighting in which the world was soon to be engulfed, these figures could have represented a single day of battle. At this time, however, the British Army was not used to accepting casualties on this scale, particularly if they had been inflicted by bands of semi-organised farmers.

Throughout the war the German high command had kept a very close eye on British operational methods and on the effects that casualties had on morale. On both these counts Germany dismissed the British Army as not constituting a viable force capable of conducting prolonged operations in a full scale European war. This disparagement of Britain's fighting ability undoubtedly led the German high command to underestimate her true resolve.*

The remark is attributed to the Kaiser, in August 1914, that if the British Army got in his way he would order the police to arrest it. Although this was obviously intended as a joke, it demonstrated how Germany despised our 'Contemptible Little Army'. Many German soldiers were to experience a rude shock in August 1914.

1903-1914

The 2nd Battalion was stationed at Crownhill Barracks, Plymouth for the next two years. After the many reservists had been discharged back into civilian life, the severely reduced battalion resumed its old routine of receiving recruits from the Depôt, providing them with further continuaton training and drafting them out to the 1st Battalion in South Africa.

All this changed in 1905 when it again assumed the role of an overseas battalion. After being brought up to establishment by retaining depôt drafts it sailed to Gibraltar, where it was quartered in the Casemates and South Barracks.

Two years later it again moved to Bermuda (one of the plum peace-time stations). In 1910 it returned to South Africa, this time as part of the British Army of Occupation in the Transvaal. It must have now been a pleasant peace-time posting, in a country with a wonderful climate and unlimited opportunity for sport.

In 1913 the British Army of Occupation was dissolved and the Battalion sailed for Hong Kong, for a final period of carefree soldiering before the world was plunged into war.

* This was not a difficult task for German intelligence. As was the custom, all units rendered monthly operational reports, not only to the War Office but to their Colonels and Colonels-in-Chief. In the case of the 1st (Royal) Dragoons, the Colonel-in-Chief happened to be the German Emperor, HM Kaiser William II.

PART 2

The Great War, 1914-1919

& its Aftermath

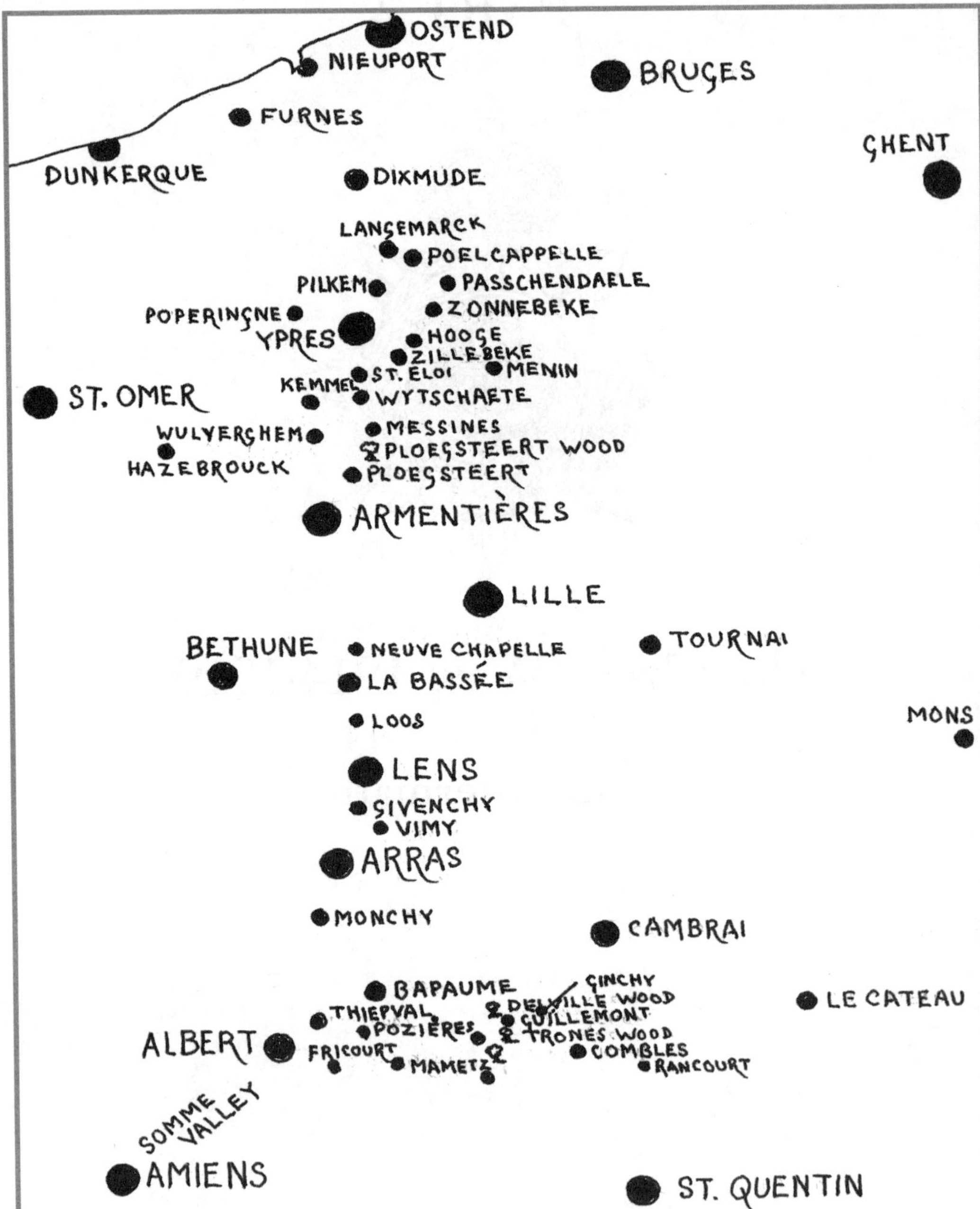

THE BRITISH & COMMONWEALTH SECTOR OF THE WESTERN FRONT

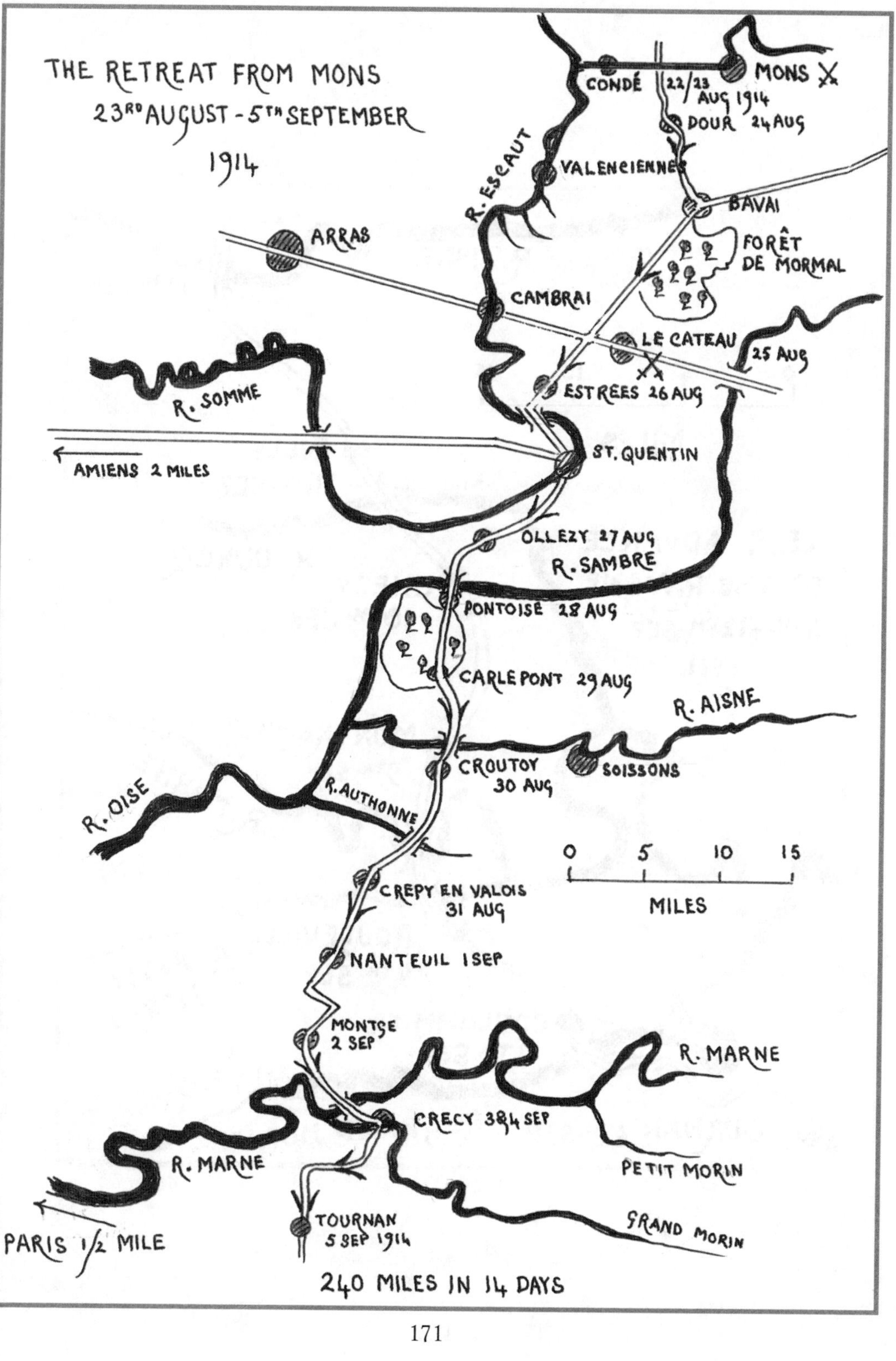
THE RETREAT FROM MONS
23RD AUGUST - 5TH SEPTEMBER
1914
CONDÉ
22/23 AUG 1914
MONS
DOUR 24 AUG
VALENCIENNES
R. ESCAUT
BAVAI
ARRAS
FORÊT DE MORMAL
CAMBRAI
LE CATEAU
25 AUG
R. SOMME
ESTREES 26 AUG
ST. QUENTIN
AMIENS 2 MILES
OLLEZY 27 AUG
R. SAMBRE
PONTOISE 28 AUG
CARLEPONT 29 AUG
R. AISNE
CROUTOY 30 AUG
SOISSONS
R. OISE
R. AUTHONNE
0 5 10 15
MILES
CREPY EN VALOIS 31 AUG
NANTEUIL 1 SEP
MONTGE 2 SEP
R. MARNE
CRECY 3&4 SEP
R. MARNE
PETIT MORIN
GRAND MORIN
TOURNAN 5 SEP 1914
PARIS 1/2 MILE
240 MILES IN 14 DAYS

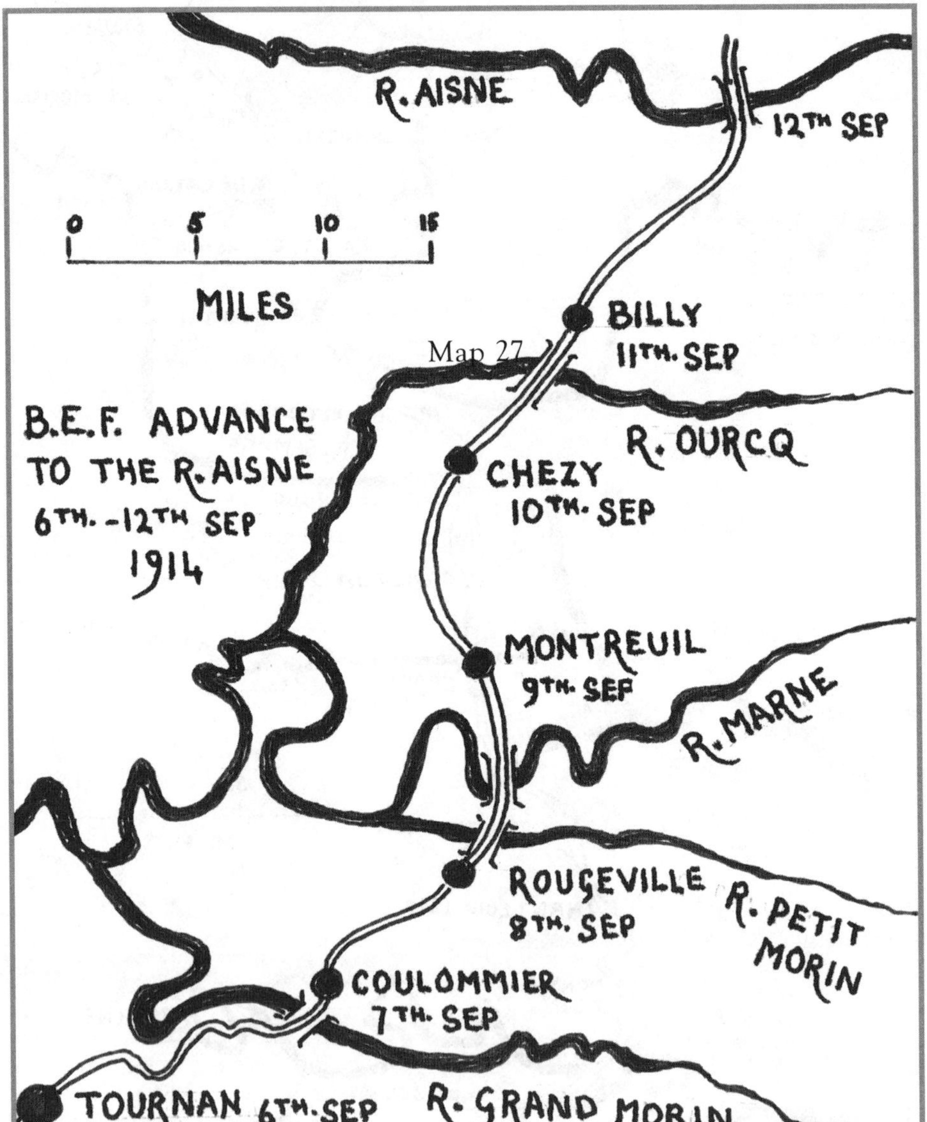
R. AISNE
12TH SEP
0 5 10 15
MILES
BILLY
11TH. SEP
B.E.F. ADVANCE
TO THE R. AISNE
6TH. -12TH SEP
1914
R. OURCQ
CHEZY
10TH. SEP
MONTREUIL
9TH. SEP
R. MARNE
ROUGEVILLE
8TH. SEP
R. PETIT
MORIN
COULOMMIER
7TH. SEP
TOURNAN 6TH. SEP
R. GRAND MORIN
Map 27

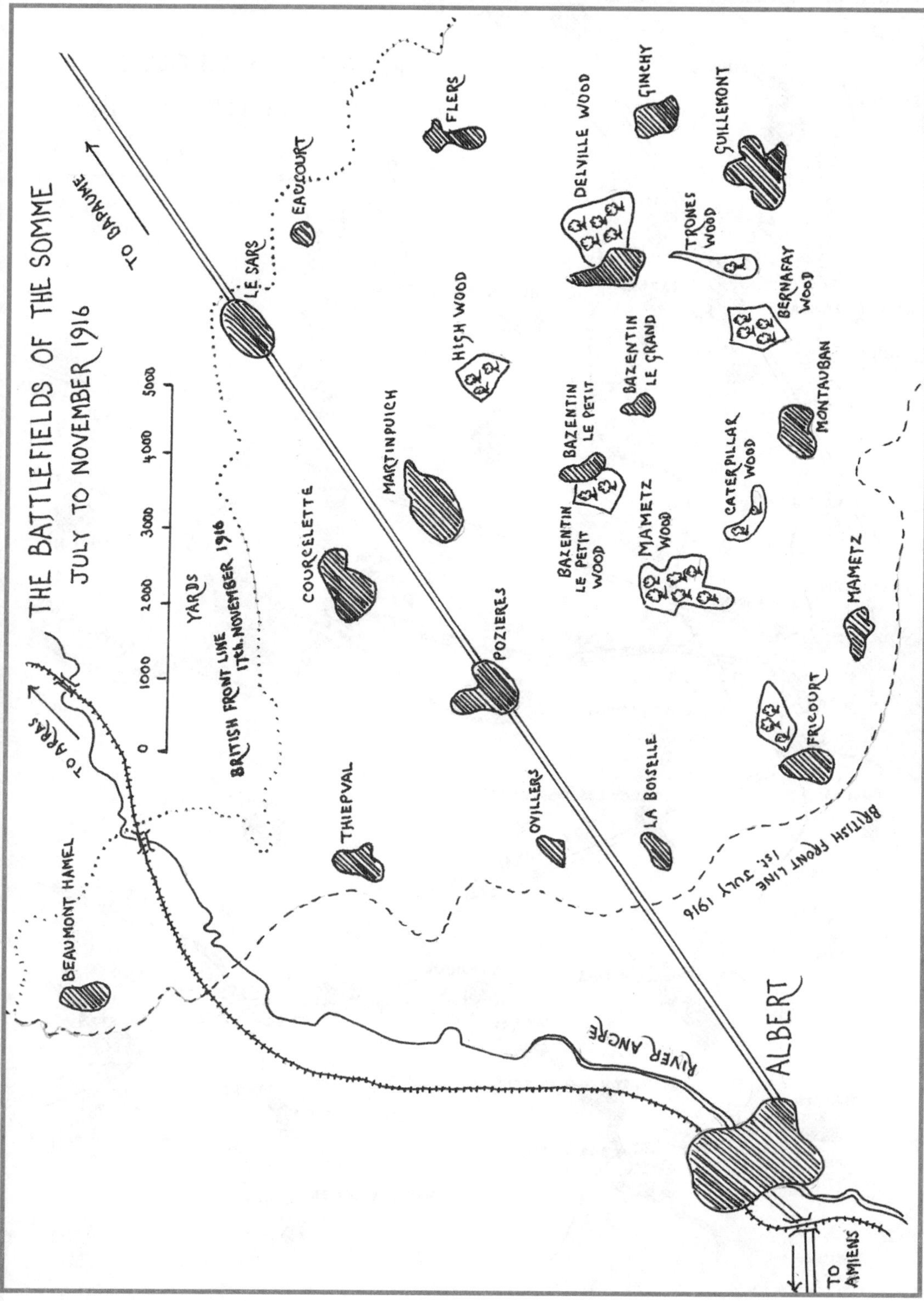

THE BATTLEFIELDS OF THE SOMME
JULY TO NOVEMBER 1916
0 1000 2000 3000 4000 5000
YARDS
TO ARRAS
TO BAPAUME
TO AMIENS
BRITISH FRONT LINE 17th. NOVEMBER 1916
BRITISH FRONT LINE 1st. JULY 1916
BEAUMONT HAMEL
THIEPVAL
OVILLERS
LA BOISSELLE
POZIERES
COURCELETTE
MARTINPUICH
LE SARS
EAUCOURT
HIGH WOOD
FLERS
BAZENTIN LE PETIT WOOD
BAZENTIN LE PETIT
BAZENTIN LE GRAND
MAMETZ WOOD
CATERPILLAR WOOD
MAMETZ
FRICOURT
MONTAUBAN
BERNAFAY WOOD
TRONES WOOD
DELVILLE WOOD
GUILLEMONT
GINCHY
ALBERT
RIVER ANCRE

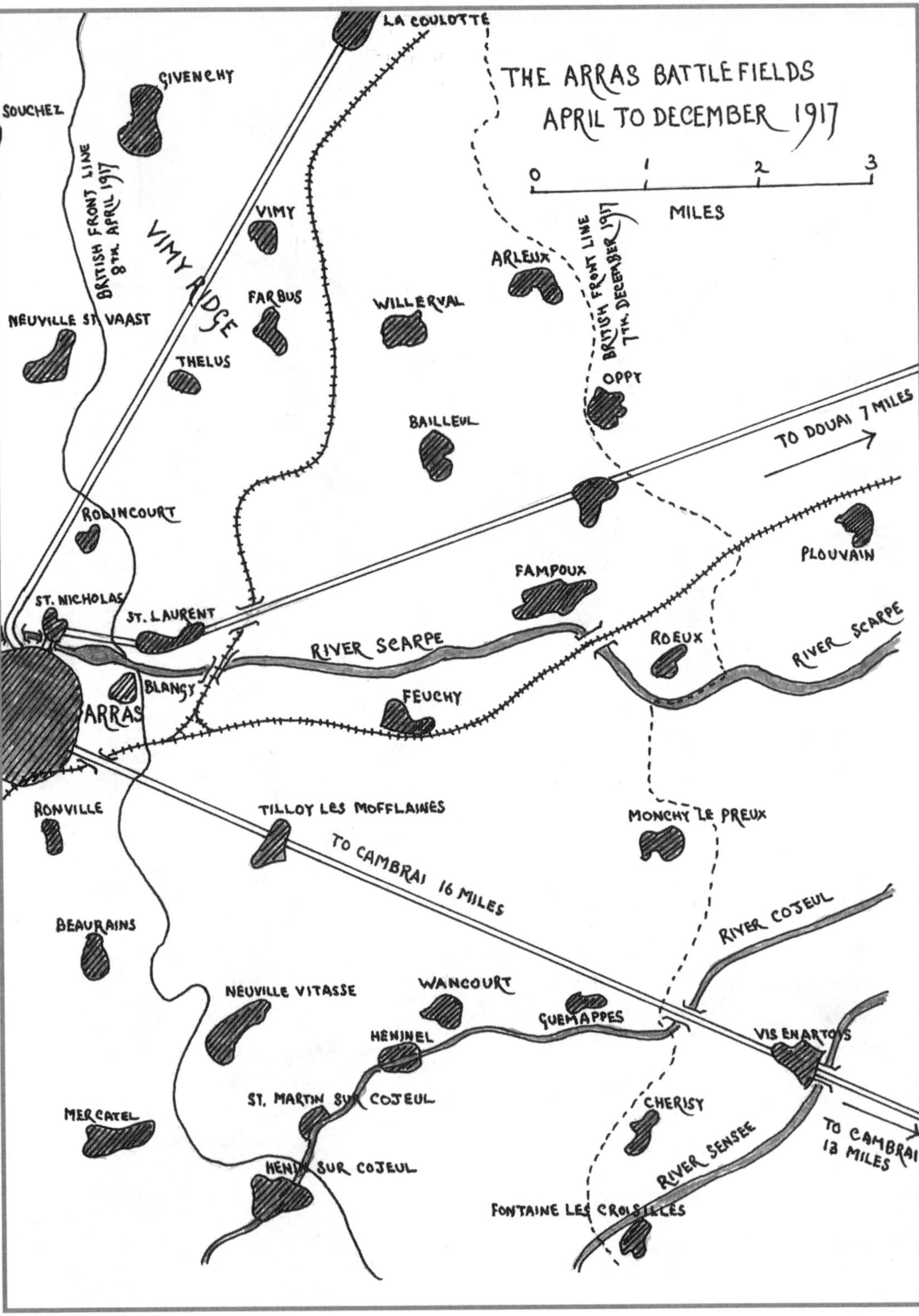
THE ARRAS BATTLEFIELDS
APRIL TO DECEMBER 1917
0 1 2 3
MILES
LA COULOTTE
GIVENCHY
SOUCHEZ
BRITISH FRONT LINE 8TH. APRIL 1917
VIMY RIDGE
VIMY
ARLEUX
BRITISH FRONT LINE 7TH. DECEMBER 1917
FARBUS
WILLERVAL
NEUVILLE ST VAAST
THELUS
OPPY
BAILLEUL
TO DOUAI 7 MILES
ROCLINCOURT
PLOUVAIN
FAMPOUX
ST. NICHOLAS
ST. LAURENT
RIVER SCARPE
ROEUX
RIVER SCARPE
BLANGY
ARRAS
FEUCHY
RONVILLE
TILLOY LES MOFFLAINES
MONCHY LE PREUX
TO CAMBRAI 16 MILES
BEAURAINS
RIVER COJEUL
NEUVILLE VITASSE
WANCOURT
GUEMAPPES
HENINEL
VIS EN ARTOIS
ST. MARTIN SUR COJEUL
CHERISY
MERCATEL
TO CAMBRAI 13 MILES
RIVER SENSEE
HENIN SUR COJEUL
FONTAINE LES CROISILLES

I. INTRODUCTION

* * *

12
August 1914

THE CAUSA BELLI

A brief mention should be made here of the complex chain of events which in 1914 plunged Europe into an apocalypse of such destruction that it is still known as 'The Great War'. Prince Otto von Bismarck had gloomily predicted that if Europe was ever to be thrown into war again it would be ignited by 'some damned foolish thing in the Balkans'. How right he was. On 28th June 1914 the Archduke Franz Ferdinand, the Austrian heir apparent, was carrying out a state visit to Sarajevo in Serbia when he was assassinated by a Serbian nationalist. Austria-Hungary used this incident as an excuse to invade Serbia. Russia immediately declared war on Austria-Hungary, mobilising her vast army, whereupon Germany declared war on Russia. France had a treaty with Russia guaranteeing mutual support should either be in danger. Honouring that agreement, France declared war on Germany. Germany therefore attacked France. The German military plan for the conquest of France, which had been formulated by Field Marshal Count von Schlieffen in 1891, depended on a wide flanking advance through Belgium, the isolation of France by the capture of her Channel ports, and finally the envelopment of Paris from the rear. Belgium's neutrality was, however, guaranteed by a long standing treaty with Great Britain. When on 4th August 1914 German troops crossed the border into Belgium, Great Britain issued an ultimatum that unless they were withdrawn by midnight she would declare war on Germany. Thus it was at 4 p.m. on 5th August that the Prime Minister announced to a packed House of Commons that a state of war existed between Great Britain and Germany.

THE INFANTRY ON THE EVE OF THE GREAT WAR

A battalion serving abroad was, as far as possible, maintained at the full establishment of 1,007 all ranks. The infantry had just been reorganised on what was known as the 'square' system: four battalions to a brigade, four companies to a battalion, four platoons to a company and four sections to a platoon. A battalion by a lieutenant-colonel with a major as his second-in-command, and a lieutenant or captain as his Adjutant. Also in his headquarters were the Signals Officer, Transport Officer and Quartermaster (the last named usually being an ex-warrant officer of considerable experience). The old rank of Serjeant-Major had been upgraded to a new appointment of Regimental Serjeant-Major, holding the rank of Warrant Officer Class I. He and the serjeants played a large part in the routine running of the battalion in peace time, and thus learnt to accept responsibility with equanimity. With the exception of the Commanding Officer, the Regimental Serjeant-Major probably carried more power and influence than any other man in the battalion.

The only non-regimental officers in battalion headquarters were the Medical Officer who was seconded from the Royal Army Medical Corps, and the Padré who came from the Army Chaplain's Department. Apart from his routine duties at daily sick parade, the Medical Officer was responsible for the training and operational deployment of his team of stretcher bearers and orderlies provided by the battalion band, and most importantly for implementing rigid standards of hygiene and sanitation.

Companies were each commanded by a captain with a lieutenant as Second-in-Command. A new rank of Company Serjeant-Major had been established. In the same way that the Regimental Serjeant-Major played a very prominent part in the running of the battalion, so the Company Serjeant-Major had an equally important role at company level, particularly as regards discipline and routine. These men held Warrant rank, being graded as Warrant Officers Class II. The Colour-Serjeants (or Company Quartermaster-Serjeants) now looked after stores, accommodation, feeding and pay, and were divorced from their old disciplinary duties.

Platoons were each commanded by a lieutenant or second lieutenant, aided by a serjeant. Sections were commanded by a corporal. Although the infantry soldier still 'walked out' and appeared on ceremonial duties resplendent in his traditional scarlet, he took to the field in a drab khaki uniform, infinitely more practical than that of any other European army of the period. Khaki had been worn by the British on active service since 1882, and the current pattern had been authorised in 1902. With this uniform went a radical new type of canvas webbing equipment, introduced in 1908. The ammunition pouches allowed 150 rounds to be carried snugly against the body, while a couple of disposable light cotton 50 round bandoleers meant that every soldier could go into action with 250 rounds for his rifle. The standard service rifle for all arms was the excellent .303 in. Short Magazine Lee-Enfield No. 1 Mk III* with a 17 in. sword bayonet. In skilled hands it was extremely accurate and capable of very rapid fire. Soldiers practised engaging targets at 800 yards and every man was required to fire 15 aimed rounds per minute at closer ranges. Officers were armed with a .455 in. revolver and sword, which were carried on the leather Sam Browne equipment, from which could also be hung such items as a haversack, binoculars, prismatic compass, map case, verey pistol and water bottle.

With hindsight, there was one field in which the British infantry was sadly lacking: automatic weapons. Most officers believed that the very high standard of musketry achieved by the British infantryman was quite sufficient to provide more than adequate fire power for any phase of any war. The Maxim machine-gun had been introduced into service with the infantry in 1901 on a basis of two per battalion. Certain far sighted officers, particularly Brigadier-General McMahon, DSO (known as the 'Musketry Maniac') who was Chief Instructor at the Small Arms School, Hythe from 1905-14, pleaded with the War Office to raise the battalion machine-gun establishment to six. He had no success. In 1912 the Maxim was replaced by the Vickers, arguably the finest machine-gun ever used by any army, and one which was to remain in service, virtually unchanged, for the next half century. In spite of its excellence, the War Office however refused to issue more than two per battalion. Light machine-guns were unknown. In the United States a certain Colonel Lewis had designed a light machine-gun, but had failed to find any government backing. Certainly in the British Army, the ability of a rifleman to fire fifteen aimed rifle shots per minute far outweighed the concept of a light automatic weapon in the minds of most senior officers.

On the eve of Armageddon the British Army was in excellent shape. It had experienced the humiliation of the South African War but had learnt its lessons well and incorporated them into virtually every aspect of its organisation, training, equipment, weapons and administration. Unlike every other European army, it consisted entirely of volunteers; the conscript European armies were vast by comparison. This was something that was to have the most profound significance in the years ahead.

The County Regiments

At the outbreak of hostilities most county infantry regiments consisted of two Regular battalions, two Territorial Force battalions and a Reserve Battalion (existing only in skeleton form). Very soon after Britain's declaration of war, Field Marshal Lord Kitchener instigated the raising of additional Service battalions. These were initially recruited entirely from volunteers, but conscription was introduced on 27th January 1916.

In the case of the Duke of Cornwall's Light Infantry, the two Regular battalions were numbered 1st and 2nd; the Reserve battalion was numbered 3rd and became the principle training unit for the Regiment; the Territorial Force battalions, originally numbered 4th and 5th, were expanded to the 1/4th, 2/4th, 3/4th, 1/5th and 2/5th; finally, eight Service battalions were raised which bore the numbers 6th to 13th.

The Duke of Cornwall's Light Infantry

We have seen that the two regular battalions of the Regiment were able to enjoy the final days of peace-time soldiering in congenial stations. Lord Haldane's reforms had been implemented, producing a highly professional army capable of despatching an expeditionary force to mainland Europe at very short notice.

The 1st Battalion

The 1st Battalion, at the Curragh, was a Home Battalion and therefore far below full establishment. From group photographs, its total strength appears to have been little more than 400. However, because regular soldiers enlisted for an initial engagement of five years with the Colours and seven years on the Reserve, a very large Reserve existed from which the home battalion could be quickly brought up to war establishment if the necessity arose.

The 2nd Battalion

The 2nd Battalion was at full establishment at the outbreak of the Great War, serving in Hong Kong.

The 3rd (Reserve) Battalion

The 3rd Battalion, previously the Militia Battalion, had in 1907 became the Reserve Battalion. It was based at the Depôt in Bodmin where it existed only in cadre form. However, in the event of war it had the capability of expanding into a major training and holding unit.

The 4th & 5th Battalions (Territorial Force)

The two Volunteer Battalions had become the 4th and 5th DCLI battalions of the new Territorial Force, inaugurated by Lord Haldane in 1907. The 4th recruited from West Cornwall with its headquarters in Truro; the 5th was recruited in East Cornwall with its headquarters in Bodmin. Both battalions were still organised on the old eight-company establishment. Compared to the regular army, their training and state of readiness left much to be desired. More importantly, by Act of Parliament their role was confined to one of home defence, except for those individuals who had volunteered for Imperial Service. These men had an obligation to serve overseas in time of war, and for this they received a small increment of pay. Photographs of this period show the silver 'Imperial Service' badge being worn on the right breast by these volunteers. Territorial Force soldiers were issued with the final version of the old .303 in. Long Lee-Enfield and wore equipment of various obsolescent patterns.

II. THE REGULAR BATTALIONS

* * *

13
The 1st Battalion

MOBILIZATION

In chapter 10 we left the 1st Battalion at the Curragh in Ireland. It was a home battalion with the principle role of receiving recruits from the Depôt, and giving them some continuation training before despatching the majority as drafts to the 2nd Battalion (the overseas battalion) stationed in Hong Kong. It was accepted that home battalions were invariably far below full strength; however, thanks to the extremely efficient Reserve system, these battalions could be quickly brought up to full war establishment.

On 4th August 1914, the 1st Battalion had just returned to the Curragh, having completed a period of internal security duties in Newry and Dundalk. At 5.25 p.m. that day the order to mobilise was received; immediately the recall notices were sent off to the Reservists. These men first travelled to the Regimental Depôt at Bodmin where they were kitted out before being despatched by rail and sea to the 1st Battalion. By 6th August 650 Reservists had reported to the 1st Battalion. Of all the recall notices sent out, only two men failed to report; both were serving at sea. These figures speak volumes, not only for the remarkable efficiency of the system, but for the dedication of the Reservists themselves. The next week was given up to a period of intense training, much of which consisted of route marches designed to wear in new boots and harden men's feet for the trials that lay ahead.

The Battalion was ably commanded by a remarkable officer, Lieutenant-Colonel M.N. Turner. Truly a soldier's soldier, he had run away from home in 1885 to enlist as a Private in the Gordon Highlanders. After seeing considerable active service on the North West Frontier of India, he was recommended for a Commission, attended the Royal Military College Sandhurst, and was gazetted to the Duke of Cornwall's Light Infantry in July 1890.

CROSSING TO FRANCE, 13TH-15TH AUGUST 1914

On the morning of 13th August the Battalion, with an all ranks strength of 1,023, entrained at the Curragh. That evening it sailed from Dublin in the steamer SS *Lanfranc*, arriving at Le Havre on the morning of 15th August.

MOVE INTO BELGIUM, 17TH AUGUST

After an uncomfortable couple of days bivouacked in the pouring rain, the 1st Battalion entrained in the early hours of 17th August, packed into a train that meandered slowly north to Le Cateau. From thence the move was continued on foot.

The Battle of Mons, 23rd August

The 1st Battalion formed part of the 14th Brigade of the 5th Division, which moved into a defensive position on the Mons-Condé Canal on the afternoon of 22nd August. Standing patrols were immediately pushed forward north of the canal while the main body dug breastworks covering the principal crossing. At about 6 a.m. the following morning a German cavalry patrol, quite unaware of their proximity to British troops, rode into a forward DCLI three-man standing patrol. One of these men, Private Sambrook, fired at and killed the German officer, whose helmet is in the Regimental Museum at Bodmin. This was the first shot fired by the Duke of Cornwall's in the Great War, and possibly the first shot fired by any infantryman.

By 11 a.m. the German advance guard was pressing the British along most of the front, but it was not until about 4.45 p.m. that the DCLI was fully involved, when the Germans attacked near Le Petit Crépin, marching forward in massed columns shoulder to shoulder. The DCLI opened up with rapid rifle fire, inflicting terrible casualties.

The retreat from Mons, first phase, 24th-26th August

At about midnight on 23rd-24th August, the British position on the Mons-Condé Canal became untenable and a general withdrawal was ordered. Thus started one of the most famous operations in British military history, the Retreat from Mons.

Battle of Le Cateau, 26th August

The Germans followed close on the heels of the withdrawing British. II Corps, which included the DCLI, reached Le Cateau in the early hours of 26th August. Few had slept for the past two days, and all were soaked by the heavy rain that fell incessantly. The Germans had by this time occupied the high ground to the flank, which effectively rendered any further withdrawal by daylight impossible. Lieutenant-General Sir Horace Smith-Dorrien, commanding II Corps (he had previously commanded the brigade in which the 2nd Battalion had fought at Paardeberg in 1900) decided to stand and fight. The battle was both complex and confused. The Germans were surprised that what they believed to be a beaten enemy should suddenly turn and fight; the British, as was inevitable in the middle of a withdrawal, and with only very basic communications, were caught off balance. The 1st Battalion became split up, officers and men often having to use their own initiative in the fog of war. By that evening the Germans had been decisively fought to a standstill. That night contact with the enemy was skilfully broken off and the withdrawal continued.

The retreat from Mons, second phase, 27th August-5th September

For the next ten days the British Expeditionary Force conducted a masterly withdrawal, for the most part in contact with the enemy. The 1st Battalion reached the village of Tournan, south of the River Marne, on 15th September, having marched 240 miles in 14 days. It should be remembered that over half the Battalion were Reservists who were not fully hardened to marching and were wearing new boots. To have performed this feat in peace-time with practised soldiers would have been praiseworthy; in the circumstances under which it was performed, it rates as an epic.

* * *

Advance to the Aisne
6th-12th September 1914

The 1st Battalion were doubtless looking forward to a well earned rest when the retreat ended at Tournan. This was not to be. The German army had outrun its supply line and left its flanks dangerously exposed. Thus it was that after a single night's rest the British Expeditionary Force, together with the 5th and 6th French Armies, launched an offensive with the aim of driving back the Germans to the north of the River Aisne. During the next week the 1st Battalion marched a further eighty miles, fighting several minor engagements and crossing five rivers, including the opposed crossing of the Aisne itself a few miles east of Soissons. The Battalion suffered heavy casualties including Lieutenant-Colonel Turner, who was severely wounded; Major T.H.F. Price assumed command. Once the Allies had established their positions north of the Aisne, both sides dug in; a foretaste of the static trench warfare that was to grip the Western Front for three and a half years.

The Race to the Sea
25th September-18th November

It was obviously illogical that the British Expeditionary Force should be sandwiched between two French armies, thereby complicating logistics and command. Accordingly it was agreed that the British should be withdrawn from the Aisne and moved up to the north flank, where its lines of communication to the Channel ports would not only be shorter, but would not have to cross those of the French. This extremely intricate manoeuvre was carried out with such secrecy that the Germans were unaware of it having taken place until they were confronted by British troops on their northern flank. As yet this flank hung in the air. However, immediately the fighting in the south became bogged down, both sides made strenuous efforts to outflank their adversaries in the north. Thus started the operation which was to become known as 'the Race to the Sea'.

The 1st Battalion withdrew from its position on the Aisne on 25th September 1914, and on 1st October started its move north. The first major action took place at La Bassée on 21st-22nd October. Casualties on both sides were heavy, but more particularly within the German infantry, which stuck to their tactical policy of attacking shoulder to shoulder, even though this formation offered such a splendid target to the British rifleman. When the 1st Battalion was withdrawn for rest in the early hours of 23rd October its fighting strength was so reduced that the four companies were reorganised into just two.

As the two armies moved northwards into Belgium on roughly parallel axes, the British found themselves not only heavily outnumbered, but always twenty-four hours behind their adversaries. As a result, the Germans were able to seize the more favourable tactical ground – a factor which was to bedevil British actions for the next four years.

The First Battle of Ypres 19th October-13th November

The great battle, which came to be known as the first battle of Ypres, was launched on 19th October by the German 4th and 6th Armies. The newly formed, ill-equipped and poorly led 4th Army was thrown into an attack north of Ypres, designed to drive the Belgians from the line of the Yser river and capture the ports of Dunkirk and Ostend. This attack failed, partly due to the inefficiency of the German planning, and partly due to the stoic resistance offered by the exhausted Belgian troops. Eight days later the lock gates at Nieuport were opened, flooding the low-lying country west of the Yser, and thus denying the Germans any hope of further advance in that sector. At the same time, the more experienced 6th Army met strong resistance from the French south of Ypres. A new formation, named after its commander, von Fabeck, consisting of six divisions and 250 heavy guns, was thrown into the battle on 29th October. Its task was to cut the Menin road at Ghelvelt, destroy the leading elements of Haig's 1 Corps and occupy the city of Ypres itself. Some of the fiercest fighting of the whole war then ensued, but the line still held, and by 13th November the Germans had effectively shot their bolt. On 25th November they abandoned any thought of a further immediate advance and were ordered to dig in and secure the ground that they held.*

In truth the losses suffered by both sides were unsustainable. Of the 84 British infantry battalions which had gone to war that August, each with some 1,000 men, 75 could muster less than 300, while 18 of these had fewer than 100 all ranks. German casualties were no

*The 2nd Battalion the Worcestershire Regiment won immortal glory by carrying out a brilliant counter attack near Ghelvelt.

less appalling, and it is estimated that their losses between 19th October and 13th November 1914 were in the region of 80,000.

By 1st November the 1st Battalion had crossed the French border into Belgium, and by 18th November were facing the enemy on the Messines ridge some six miles south of Ypres.

It was here, near the village of Wulverghem, that Bandsman T.E. Rendle, acting in his wartime role as a stretcher bearer, won the Victoria Cross for his outstanding gallantry under heavy fire. The citation read 'For conspicuous bravery on 20th November near Wulverghem when he attended to the wounded under very heavy shell and rifle fire, and rescued men from the trenches in which they had been buried by the blowing in of the parapet by the fire of the enemy's heavy howitzers.' What is not mentioned is that Bandsman Rendle was accompanied on this most hazardous action by Lieutenant R.R. Wingate. Not only did Wingate apply first aid to the injured, but he deliberately placed himself in the open in order to offer some protection to Rendle while he dragged Lieutenant Colebrooke to safety. It was Wingate who recommended Rendle for the Victoria Cross. Although Wingate was Mentioned in Despatches for bravery later in the war, his act of heroism at Wulverghem went unrecognised. It was the accepted ethos of officers that they should lead by example, regardless of danger, and without thought of reward.

The ancient city of Ypres is surrounded by low-lying farmland overlooked from the north, east and south by ridges. These ridges, although of no great height, completely dominate the city and the area around it. Twenty-two miles to the north west lies the sea – the German objective. The low-lying ground is artificially drained. Once fighting began, artillery soon destroyed the drainage system, and the land became a vast swamp. It was in these conditions that the British were destined to fight all too often in the next three and a half years. The war of movement was finally over; now a continuous line of trenches ran from the Belgian coast to Switzerland.

That first winter the British Expeditionary Army endured conditions that have seldom been more terrible. The weather was atrocious, and thigh boots and sheepskin coats were not yet available. British battalions, apart from being greatly outnumbered by the Germans, were by this time very weak in numbers (our First Battalion was reduced to about 300 men). This meant that men spent a disproportionate period in the front line trenches, and even when 'resting' were required to carry out heavy manual work digging defences and carrying up ammunition and stores.

All through that winter the old Regular Army held the line against near impossible odds. They did so at a heavy price, for by the following spring few of the original officers or men were left. The Kaiser had referred to them as 'that contemptible little army'. The British survivors turned these words into an epithet of pride, calling themselves 'The Old Contemptibles'.

The Somme, August 1915

In August 1915 the 1st Battalion left the Ypres Salient, doubtless without regret, and took over part of the French line on the north side of the River Somme. At that period of the war there was little action in this sector. Nevertheless, during the winter of 1915-16 the war of attrition continued. Even during the quietest times artillery, sniping, and the extensive mining operations that both sides conducted below ground, claimed a sad stream of casualties. However, reinforcements made up of volunteers who had answered Lord Kitchener's call to arms, were now arriving in an increasing stream. By the spring of 1916 the 1st Battalion was again not far short of its full establishment. The 14th Brigade, to which the Battalion had so far belonged, had been reorganised on 12th January to become the 95th Brigade.

March 1916 saw the 1st Battalion in the line near Arras, thirty miles north of the Somme. The War Diary repeatedly reports the weather as 'glorious'. It was a quiet sector of the front, and the Battalion appears to have enjoyed a rare respite before being plunged into the terrible battles of the Somme.

Quiet or not, the steady stream of casualties continued, and on 16th April Lieutenant-Colonel H.T. Cantan was killed. He was replaced by Lieutenant-Colonel H. Fargus.

The Battles of the Somme, 1st July-18th November 1916

Never before in the history of warfare had the preparations for a forthcoming battle been planned with such meticulous attention to detail. Each of the divisions ear-marked for the initial attack was withdrawn to an area well behind the front line, where it rehearsed attacks against replica German trenches and field defences based on ground and air reconnaissance. The Royal Engineers and infantry pioneer battalions laid many miles of new railway lines and sidings, built to facilitate the swift movement of men and the vast tonnage of ammunition and supplies to the front. Forward command posts were constructed together with their web of deeply buried telephone lines. Casualty clearing stations and field hospitals were established, and hospital trains assembled. Last, but by no means least, preparations were made for what was to be the greatest artillery bombardment ever envisaged. Guns of every calibre, from the giant 12 in. railway-mounted howitzers to the light Royal Horse Artillery 13 pdr field guns, were dug in and camouflaged. Over the preceding month fire plans were formulated and targets registered. The battle plan depended on a continuous bombardment to be fired over the unprecedented period of fourteen days. For this, enormous quantities of shells had to be stockpiled in the gun positions and at readily available ammunition points immediately to their rear. Indeed, much of the British plan depended on the catastrophic effect of an intense and protracted bombardment. It was firmly believed that when the whistles blew for the infantry to attack, the defenders would be either dead or totally demoralised. The error of this belief led to the carnage of that first day's fighting. With hindsight, it is apparent that the intelligence reports submitted by patrols should have alerted the staff to the exceptionally deep concrete bunkers which the Germans had constructed beneath their trenches, providing a fair measure of protection. Those that did survive, although battered by the ceaseless concussion of high explosive, demonstrated the highest traditions of German military discipline and bravery. As the barrage finally lifted, they emerged from their shelters, manhandling the machine-guns into firing positions in the cratered chaotic wasteland which had once been their trenches.

The British-French Somme offensive of 1916 opened on 1st July and dragged on till 18th November, when weather and exhaustion forced operations to a halt. The Somme has become deeply ingrained in the British mind as an appalling experience that epitomises all that is most tragic in twentieth century war. The campaign was originally conceived as a limited operation in order to relieve pressure on the fortresses of Verdun to the south, where the French were near to collapse. The British Commander-in-Chief, General Sir Douglas Haig, was strongly opposed to attacking on the Somme where the German defences were known to be exceptionally strong. However, political considerations outweighed military expediency, and Haig was ordered to attack on this particular sector of the front where he would be seen to be acting in the closest co-operation with the French on his right flank. As so often happens in such events, the ensuing battle generated its own momentum, making it impossible to disengage from what had become a life or death struggle. The terrible cost of human life in the Somme battles has perhaps blinded us to the fact that not only did they achieve the aim of relieving the Verdun fortresses, but they wore down the German army to an extent that was to prove critical in the final years before the Allies' victory. The scale of conflict was greater than anything previously experienced by the British. At 8 a.m. on 1st July about 60,000 British and Commonwealth troops crossed the start line; by that evening 57,540 of these men were casualties. On that first day 22,000 British and Commonwealth soldiers died; more than the total number killed in action during the five years of Wellington's Peninsular war. These battles were made more hideous by the fact that they were fought in a very small arena. One can drive a car down the Albert-Bapaume road, across the centre of the battlefield, in a few minutes. The entire width of the British front line never exceeded eleven miles, and the maximum depth of the advance was about seven miles. Many of the woods and shattered villages which were fought over with such ferocity were only a few hundred yards apart. Today, with this landscape returned to peaceful farmland, one can barely comprehend the enormity of the slaughter that it witnessed during those four and a half months in 1916.

* * *

High Wood & Delville Wood, 19th July 1916

The 1st Battalion was not committed on the Somme until 19th July, when it moved into the line near Delville Wood. Some of the survivors of the previous year had seen this area before, but it was now barely recognisable. The rich farmland had been turned into a cratered moonscape, the villages destroyed and the woods reduced to a tangle of splintered timber. Delville Wood and the rubble which had once been the adjoining village of Longueval had been captured by the British on 15th July, but a subsequent German counter attack had retaken the northern part of these two objectives. The German front line now ran north west from Delville Wood for about 1,500 yards to High Wood. Both these woods had been reduced to a shambles of smashed trees, made even more impenetrable by a heavy lacing of barbed wire. Fighting for these three mutually supporting strong points continued day and night from 15th July to the final recapture of Delville Wood on 3rd September. It was arguably the most savage battle of the entire war.

The 1st Battalion took part in the attack on High Wood on 23rd July, but was repulsed with heavy loss. It was relieved that night, and from then until 1st August spent about forty-eight hours in reserve followed by a similar period in the front line around Delville Wood, subject to almost continuous heavy shelling. On 1st August 14 Brigade finally marched back to billets around the village of Meaultre. In the thirteen days that the 1st Battalion had been in action it had suffered 500 casualties, including 22 officers. It was now in urgent need of rest and an uninterrupted period in which reinforcement drafts could be absorbed.

Guillemont, 26th August

On 26th August 1916 the 1st Battalion, now brought up to strength of 29 officers and 794 soldiers, returned to the front line near the village of Guillemont. Like Delville Wood, a mile to the north east, it had been fought over for many weeks and been virtually razed to the ground, leaving only rubble in which even the streets were indistinguishable. Three unsuccessful attacks had been made at great cost of life. The Battalion was in reserve on 2nd September, but that night moved up to the assembly trenches for the fourth and final attack. The leading elements assaulted at 9 a.m., followed by the Cornwalls about an hour later. The attack was conducted in textbook fashion, and all objectives were captured with little loss of life. However, four young subalterns who had recently joined the Battalion were killed, leading their platoons forward: Kitson, Teague, Hitchens and Forbes. The last named was the only son of the Newlyn artist, Stanhope Forbes.*

Winter 1916-Autumn 1917

The Winter of 1916-1917

The 1st Battalion was withdrawn from the Somme battle-field after the capture of Guillemont in September 1916. Following a period of rest, it moved back into the line at La Bassée, an area that the few remaining survivors of The Old Contemptibles knew well from 1914. This was now a quiet sector of the line, in which battle-exhausted German formations were sent to recover their strength. But, however much both sides might have wished to adopt a 'live and let live' attitude, this was not to be. The Divisional policy was that the weary German units should be given no peace. Constant harassment was the order of the day; aggressive patrolling must take place to ensure the domination of no man's land, while trench raids on a larger scale were to take place at least twice a week. By November winter had set in, with snow and hard frosts. The British Army was however now better clothed to withstand the cold and wet, which continued well into April 1917.

The German withdrawal to the Hindenburg Line, 14th March 1917

On 14th March 1917 the German army started a major tactical withdrawal to a new, previously prepared defensive position between ten and twenty miles to its rear. The withdrawal, which was conducted with great skill over an eighty mile front between the River Scarpe in the north and the River Aisne in the south, resulted in a significant shortening of the front line. The Chief of the German General Staff freely admitted that this withdrawal became an absolute necessity due to the severe attrition suffered by his formations in the Allied offensive of 1916, thus at last vindicating the terrible sacrifices made by the Allies in those titanic battles. The German withdrawal came as a much needed boost to the war-weary British and French armies, who saw it as the first crack in their enemy's invincibility.

This new German line, known to the Allies as the Hindenburg Line and to the Germans as the Siegfried-Stelling Line, was of immense defensive strength.

* Stanhope Forbes's fine portrait of his son, painted on his last home leave, was acquired by the Regimental Museum about eighty years later.

The three battles of the Scarpe, 9th April - 4th May & the subsidiary attack at La Coulotte, 23rd-24th April

On 16th April 1917 the French army attacked on the River Aisne and in Champagne, suffering heavy casualties without making any significant progress. Haig was therefore again called upon to mount a limited offensive on the Arras front to draw German divisions away from the French. The resulting British operations, which included the battle of Vimy Ridge and the three battles of the Scarpe, did not directly affect the 1st Battalion; however, during the second battle of Scarpe it was involved in a much smaller subsidiary attack around the village of La Coulotte, just to the south of Lens.

In order to achieve surprise, there was no preliminary artillery barrage. The assaulting troops were able to assemble without interruption from the enemy but, shortly after 'going over the top' at 4.45 a.m., they met thick belts of uncut wire which speedily brought the attack to a halt. A fierce bombing fight developed between the two sides but no further progress was possible. That evening the Battalion was back in its original trenches, where it was relieved during the night.

The Summer of 1917

Although the series of very bloody battles, known by the generic term as the third battle of Ypres, opened on 7th June 1917, the 1st Battalion remained in the Arras area until 7th September. There life, although by no means quiet, was positively peaceful compared to the maelstrom erupting in the Ypres Salient. However, in order to discourage the Germans from denuding the Arras front in order to reinforce the Salient, the British mounted a series of minor, but important attacks. The nightly routine of aggressive patrolling ensured that the enemy could never feel secure.

On 28th June the 5th Division carried out an attack on a prominent feature known as Oppy Wood which, because of its commanding position, had become the home of a multitude of observation posts, machine-guns and mortars. It was heavily defended by infantry in carefully sited trenches. The 1st Battalion remained in reserve throughout the subsequent battle, but were well placed to watch its progress. The preliminary artillery barrage was awesome even to the eyes of the most experienced soldiers.

The War Diary states 'The whole of the trenches (after our barrage had fallen on them) were soon enveloped in a dense smoke and all that could be seen was our flame shells which, when they burst, sent up showers of golden rain.'

The 'flame shells' mentioned were the British answer to the German *flammenwerfer* (flame thrower). They consisted of cylinders of petrol-oil mixture together with a small bursting charge, which were projected from mortars. They produced a terrifying effect.

The attack was a complete success and was achieved with very few casualties. The German defenders appeared demoralised by the ferocity of the artillery bombardment, 143 surrendering.

On 1st July 1917 the Battalion came out of reserve and moved into the front line. It was commanded by Captain (acting Major) A.J.S. Hammans, MC, who had taken over from Lieutenant-Colonel H. Fargus, DSO, temporarily detached to command a brigade. Hammans, who had served in France since the arrival of the Battalion in August 1914, was considered to be a quite exceptional officer. While visiting a digging party in the front line he was killed by a 4.2 in. howitzer shell.

In those days, when life was cheap, a man's death tended to go unremarked by those outside his immediate circle. The death of Hammans, however, was deeply felt throughout the Battalion and beyond. He had assumed the appointment of Adjutant on 16th January 1915, replacing Captain A.N. Acland, who had succumbed to illness. Acland was to become a brilliant staff officer destined to rise to the top of his profession, but within a fighting battalion he lacked that vital spark of *rapport* with young officers and soldiers. Hammans was very different – an outstandingly brave man, he had already been awarded the Military Cross, the Legion d'Honneur and been mentioned in despatches three times. As Adjutant, he made it his business to leave the headquarters and make frequent visits to the forward positions. Wherever the danger was greatest or the conditions most foul, there Hammans could be found, putting new heart into tired and frightened men by his quiet confidence, humour and courage. He was intensely admired and respected by all ranks.

Hamman's funeral on 6th July was a remarkable affair for those times. Not only was it attended by the 1st DCLI, but also by officers and men from every unit in the 5th Division. His death probably occurred as he would have wished - in the front line with his beloved soldiers. In recording the incident, the War Diary finishes with a sentence unique in entries through four years of war: 'General dismay throughout the Battalion'.

The Battalion remained in its sector of the Arras front until 7th September. Minor operations continued with the aim of harassing the enemy and discouraging him from moving his divisions north. The weather was deteriorating; mud and water filled the trenches, and life became increasingly uncomfortable.

On 7th September the 5th Division handed over to the 31st and 63rd Divisions. It had been almost continuously in action since the previous April, and was in need of training and proper rest. The 1st Battalion went into billets in Ambrines for eleven days. During this period a Divisional small arms meeting was held. Thirty-six teams completed, the Cornwall's team winning with a score of 96 points out of 100.

The Third Battle of Ypres, October 1917

Battle of Broodseinde, 4th October

The 1st Battalion remained in the Arras sector of the line throughout the summer of 1917. However, on 2nd October it entrained for a move that would take it north back to the loathsome Ypres Salient. If much of this area had resembled a quagmire when the Battalion had last operated there in the winter of 1914-15, conditions were now infinitely worse. Trenches being virtually impossible to maintain, the Germans had developed a new defensive system based on mutually supporting concrete blockhouses sited in considerable depth. These veritable fortresses, with walls three foot thick, were proof against anything less than a direct hit by medium artillery. Entirely new tactics were required to deal with them.

The Battalion arrived in the Salient on 3rd October, and prepared to take part in the battle of Broodseinde the following day. That night it moved up into the assembly area, and it is an indication of the severity of the fighting that enemy shelling accounted for sixty casualties during this initial phase. At 6 a.m. on 4th October the Battalion started its advance across the shell-torn wasteland, in which villages and woods had been reduced to mere names on the map. In this desolation, the carefully sited concrete blockhouses (or 'pill-boxes' as the British soldiers called them) proved their extreme effectiveness in defence, each one necessitating a separate co-ordinated attack to knock it out. Conditions were appalling, with knee-deep mud. Wounded men often sank into this morass and drowned. All through that day the enemy shelling continued unabated and casualties were heavy. At 10.30 p.m. the Cornwalls were relieved. In spite of heavy shelling, machine-gun fire, mud and the confusion that is inevitable under these conditions, the Battalion had doggedly clawed its way forward and had achieved all its objectives. Enemy prisoners disclosed that the British attack at 6 a.m. that morning had thwarted a German attack which was scheduled to go in a quarter of an hour later. Thus the enemy had plenty of guns and ammunition immediately available. The German fire programme, designed to support their own attack, was quickly switched to one of defence. This accounted for the unusually heavy artillery concentrations on the British positions the previous night and for the continuing bombardment throughout the day.

Battle of Poelcapelle, 9th October 1917

Four miles north west of Broodseinde lies the village of Poelcapelle. It was now necessary to take this village in order to secure the flanks for the final advance onto the tactically important ridge, in the centre of which stood the hamlet of Passchendaele. The 1st Battalion moved up into the line on 9th October but remained in reserve during the ensuing battle until relieved on the night of 11th-12th October.

The first battle of Passchendaele, 12th October 1917

The name of Passchendaele is emotive in itself, and has become synonymous with the worst horrors of the Great War. The two battles are viewed with what can only be described as morbid fascination, not only because of the heavy casualties suffered by both sides but, perhaps even more, because of the appalling conditions in which the fighting was conducted. By this time winter had set in, bringing almost incessant cold torrential rain. Not only did the wet and cold make the lives of the men involved inexpressibly miserable, but all movement, particularly of guns and their attendant ammunition limbers, became virtually impossible. Operations were called off after the first day when mud and flooded streams made it obvious that the planned objectives were unattainable. The 1st Battalion was in reserve, so perhaps escaped the worst of the misery.

The second battle of Passchendaele, 26th October-10th November 1917, & attack on Polderhoek Chateau, 6th November

By mid October the rain appeared to have abated, and on 26th October it was considered that the attack was once again a viable operation of war. The terrible slogging battle, carried out through a wilderness of mud and flooded shell craters, need not concern us here, for the Battalion remained in reserve for most of the battle. However, on the night of 5th November it moved up into the front line, ready to take part in the attack on Polderhoek Château the following morning. In spite of their most valiant efforts, heavy German shelling together with machine-gun fire from numerous concrete block houses brought all movement to a halt. That afternoon the Battalion received orders to fall back on its original assembly position. Some idea of what it had experienced in those few hours can be gathered by the Battalion strength returns. Before going into action in the morning of 6th November, the fighting strength was 16 officers and 300 soldiers; by that afternoon it was reduced to 5 officers and 177 soldiers, barely a full company's worth.

On 7th November the remnants of the 1st Battalion marched back to billets for much needed rest, reinforcement and training.

MOVE TO ITALY, 12TH DECEMBER 1917

By 15th November the 1st Battalion was occupying billets in Escoeville, well away from the mud and horror of the Passchendaele ridge. Reinforcements were arriving each day, bringing the Battalion back to a viable fighting strength. Hard training was intermixed with football matches and other recreational activities. All thoughts of the future rested on the belief that within a very few weeks the green countryside of Escoeville would give way to the churned up, stinking morass of the dreaded Ypres Salient. However, this was not to be. The situation on the Italian front was looking critical and it was believed that the Italian army would not long continue the fight unaided. If Italy collapsed, many German divisions would become available for employment on the Western Front; it was therefore decreed that five British and seven French divisions (including the 5th British Division to which the 1st Battalion belonged) should be moved to Italy to reinforce the Italian army. Accordingly, on 12th December the 1st Battalion entrained for a long and extremely slow journey to this new theatre, arriving at Carmignand di Brenta five days later. In the event, the situation on the front had stabilised, with the Italians holding strong defensive positions in considerable depth, sited on near impregnable knife edge ridges. The British and French troops remained as a formidable reserve but were never actually employed in the front line. The clear, cold weather in the mountains acted as a tonic, while plenty of sport and long route marches through this unfamiliar landscape toughened up the newly joined drafts.

* * *

MOVE BACK TO FRANCE, 2ND APRIL 1918

The German Spring Offensive

Winter gave way to spring, but while the 1st Battalion was leading this near-idyllic life in Italy, much more serious events were taking place on the Western Front, which saw the British army being remorselessly driven back to the sea. In 1917 the events of the Russian Revolution had led to the withdrawal of the Russian Army from the Eastern Front, releasing a substantial part of the German Army for service in Belgium and France. Germany had thus been able to plan a massive offensive there, which was launched in the spring of 1918. So it was that at the beginning of April the 1st Battalion retraced its journey by train to northern France, arriving at Frevent on 7th April 1918. After several days of order and counter order, it moved into the line just east of Merville on 12th April. This was to be the extreme westerly point reached by the German army in its offensive. Although the Germans had outrun their effective logistical capability, they were still fighting with great determination. The 1st Battalion therefore had a taste of the final traumatic days of this great trial of strength. The battle that raged in that final phase on 13th April was both highly confused and bloody. Companies repeatedly found themselves outflanked, necessitating complex manoeuvres being carried out with great skill under heavy fire. The Regimental Serjeant-Major, C.W. Willis, was awarded the DCM for his gallant conduct in one such critical situation.

That night, both sides dug in about 200 yards apart, but at 5.30 a.m. on 14th April the Germans again put in a determined attack. However, during the night, four machine-guns had been brought up to cover the DCLI front and these, with the Lewis guns and rifles of the Battalion, produced such carnage that the Germans were unable to press home their attack. The crisis had passed. The Germans were beaten and made no further attempt to prolong the battle.

On the night of 15th-16th April 1918 the 1st Battalion was relieved, and withdrew into Divisional Reserve near Le Touquet. So ended the great German offensive of March 1918, which had come so dangerously close to success.

Consolidation, 29th April-21st August 1918 & action at La Becque, 28th June-July, 1918

The months of May, June and July 1918 were comparatively uneventful. Field-Marshal Sir Douglas Haig's policy was to consolidate the existing line, while at the same time allowing the maximum number of units out of the line for rest, retraining and reinforcement. Offensive operations were to be limited to local attacks, aimed at capturing specific enemy positions that threatened the security of the newly established line. One such operation involved the 1st Battalion in a Divisional attack on a sector of the German lines at La Becque (about twenty-seven miles west of Lille). The attack was meticulously planned and thoroughly rehearsed. The Battalion moved from its billets to the assembly position during the night of 27th-28th June, and 'went over the top' just after 6.00 a.m. All objectives had been captured by 7.30 a.m. In spite of the Battalion War Diary stating that 'when our troops left their trenches and advanced towards the enemy's front line, they met with little or no opposition and all objectives were taken without the slightest difficulty', about 40% of the battalion became casualties. Lance-Corporal C. Bailey was awarded the DCM for conspicuous gallantry and devotion to duty in leading forward the remnants of his platoon after all the officers and serjeants became casualties. Captain E. Hare, who was wounded, and Company Serjeant-Major J. Phillips were both awarded the MC.

Advance to Victory, 8th August-11th November 1918

The British Army was becoming enthused with a spirit of real optimism. It had fought the Germans to a standstill in their great spring offensive; it had consolidated its line and brought its units back up to fighting strength; now it was poised to deliver a crushing blow that could lead to a quick victory. However, very few members of the British army had experienced the sort of mobile operations that were anticipated once a break-through had been achieved. For this reason a large part of the training during the summer of 1918 was directed towards this aspect of war.

The great Allied offensive, which was to lead to final victory, opened on 8th August 1918 on a 40 mile sector of the front east of Amiens. By nightfall an advance of 7 miles had been consolidated and 13,000 prisoners and between 300 and 400 guns had been captured. General Ludendorf called the 8th August 'The black day of the German Army in the history of the War'. The attack continued for a further 4 days, bringing the advance to a depth of 12 miles and adding a further 22,000 prisoners. The German army, which just a few months earlier had itself been so close to victory, now saw its hopes fast fading. The number of prisoners taken was a clear indication of the collapse of German morale.

Battle of Albert, 21st-23rd August 1918

The 1st Battalion entered the fray on 21st August, near Albert north of the River Somme. It had moved into the village of Coigneux before first light on the previous day to make final preparation for the forthcoming attack. The weather was warm and sunny. That evening the Battalion moved forward into the front line, but during that night heavy fog enveloped the area. The attack, supported by tanks and a very heavy creeping barrage, went ahead as planned and in spite of poor visibility was a brilliant success. Fighting continued for three days. Large numbers of prisoners were taken, whose morale appeared to be at a very low ebb, many freely admitting that Germany had lost the war.

Second battle of Bapaume, 31st August 1918

At 5 a.m. on 31st August the Germans put in a strong attack on the New Zealanders to the right of the DCLI position, driving the New Zealanders back and exposing the DCLI flank. The situation looked serious until a determined counter attack by the New Zealanders and two companies from the 1st Battalion drove the Germans out of their newly gained trenches, leaving many dead. The 1st Battalion was relieved in the front line during the night of 3rd-4th September and marched back to billets and bivouacs between the villages of Biefvillers and Bihucourt that morning.

Battle of the Canal du Nord, 27th September 1918

The 1st Battalion returned to the front line on 20th September and on the 28th September took part in one of the many subsidiary engagements within this great advance. The 95th Brigade, consisting of the 1st East Surreys, 1st Devons, 1st DCLI and 12th Gloucesters, attacked and captured Beaucamp. It is perhaps of interest that although British brigades on the Western Front had been reorganised on a three-battalion basis since the 1st February 1918, the 5th Division had managed, because it had been serving in Italy, to retain each of its brigades at the old four-battalion establishment. After this battle the Division was ordered in no uncertain terms to reduce its brigades by one battalion each. On 29th September the second phase of the attack took place, and in spite of a certain lack of co-ordination with the artillery, the 1st Battalion captured all its objectives and took 100 prisoners and 30 machine-guns. 79 officers and soldiers were killed or wounded.

* * *

Battle of Selle, 12th October-23rd October 1918

By this stage, operations had become very much more fluid. Although the Germans were still fighting with considerable skill and tenacity, major advances were now being made. The battle of the River Selle involved an immense striking force of twenty-four British and two American divisions. Although numerically outnumbered, the Allies had won a significant victory, capturing 20,000 prisoners and 475 guns. Field Marshal Sir Douglas Haig appreciated that this was a critical moment of the war. If the Germans were allowed to break off contact and withdraw to a shorter line of defence, they would be in a position to prolong the war through yet another winter. He therefore determined to deliver the final *coup de grace* at the earliest opportunity.

The battle of the Sambre, 4th-11th November 1918

The 1st Battalion moved into the battle area on 4th November. In doing so it crossed the Roman road that runs in a dead straight line from Bavay, past Le Cateau, to Estrées. In August 1914 the Battalion had trudged south down this road, relentlessly pursued by the German army, and had fought the ever memorable battle of Le Cateau. Now, a little over four years later, the Battalion found itself crossing the Roman road, this time pursuing a beaten German army eastwards. Nevertheless, fighting was still hard, the battalions of the 95th Brigade leap-frogging forward, advancing distances of some 2,000 yards in each phase. By 8th November the 1st Battalion was held up by heavy opposition near Le Quesnoy. That evening it was relieved and marched back to billets at St Rémi.

Victory

The Armistice, November 1918

It was at St Rémi that the 1st Battalion received the following signal:

Hostilities will cease at 11.00 hours today, 11th November. Troops will stand fast on line reached at that hour which will be reported by wire to Corps Headquarters. Defensive precautions will be maintained. There will be no intercourse of any description with the enemy. No Germans are to be allowed to enter our lines, any doing so will be taken prisoner.

As *The Duke of Cornwall's Light Infantry History* records,

> . . . the Great War was over. Of wild cheering and frantic outbursts of joy, of temporary madness such as seized upon the civilian population of almost every country in the world, there was none in the battle area of France and Flanders. Only a great silence fell upon the battle-field, a silence pregnant with things which none dare mention, which indeed no one had had time to think about – a silence which left one dazed and wondering. For so long, death and destruction and the awfulness of living, as it were upon the very edge of the grave, had been the soldiers' dreadful companions, that when they were suddenly torn from him as eleven o'clock boomed on the morning of the 11th November, it was at first impossible to believe that Peace had come, that the incredible had happened.

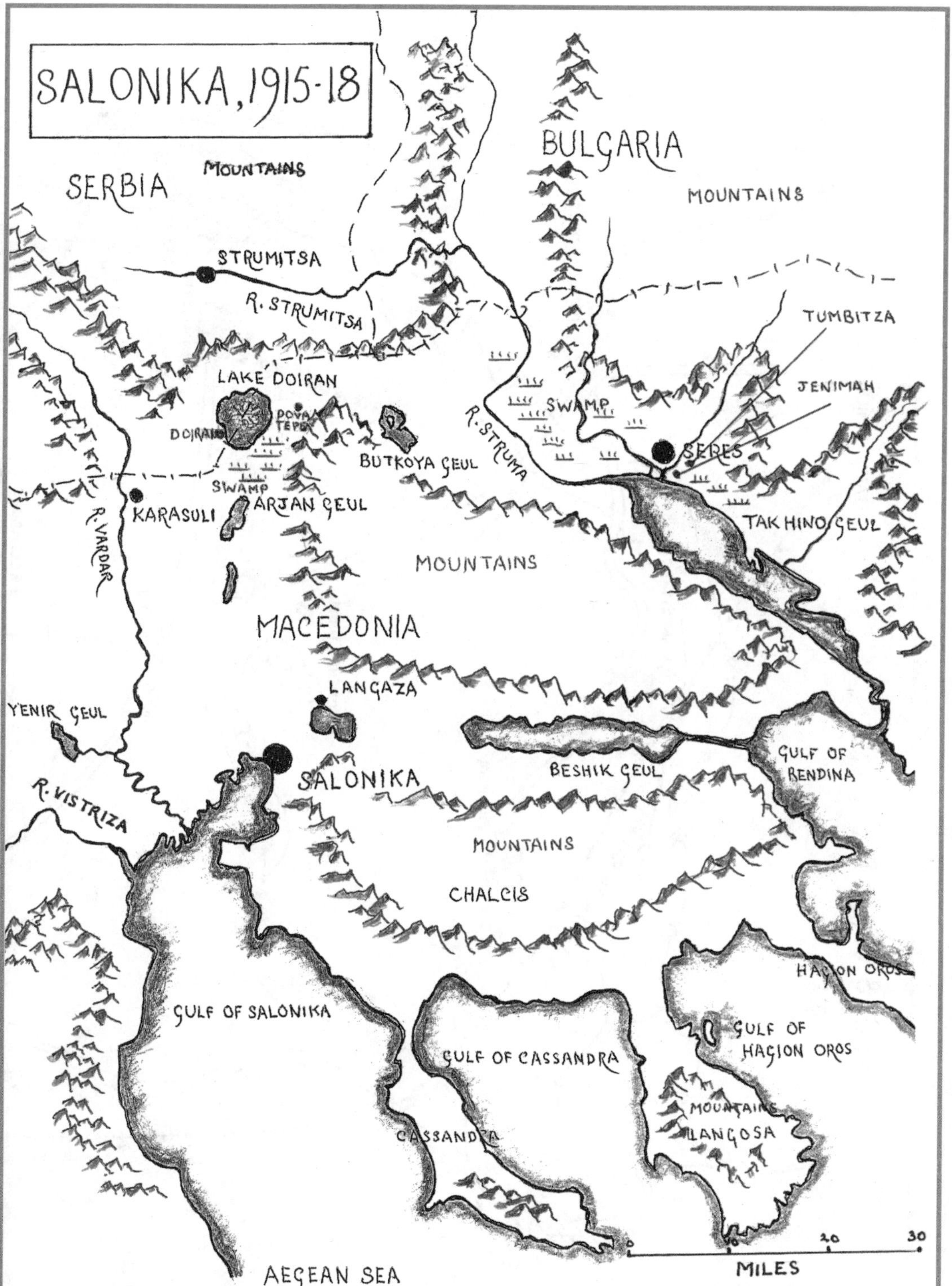
SALONIKA, 1915-18
SERBIA
MOUNTAINS
BULGARIA
MOUNTAINS
STRUMITSA
R. STRUMITSA
TUMBITZA
JENIMAH
LAKE DOIRAN
DOIRAN
SWAMP
R. STRUMA
SERES
BUTKOYA GEUL
SWAMP
KARASULI
ARJAN GEUL
R. VARDAR
TAKHINO GEUL
MOUNTAINS
MACEDONIA
LANGAZA
YENIR GEUL
SALONIKA
BESHIK GEUL
GULF OF RENDINA
R. VISTRIZA
MOUNTAINS
CHALCIS
HAGION OROS
GULF OF SALONIKA
GULF OF CASSANDRA
GULF OF HAGION OROS
MOUNTAINS
LANGOSA
CASSANDRA
0
10
20
30
MILES
AEGEAN SEA

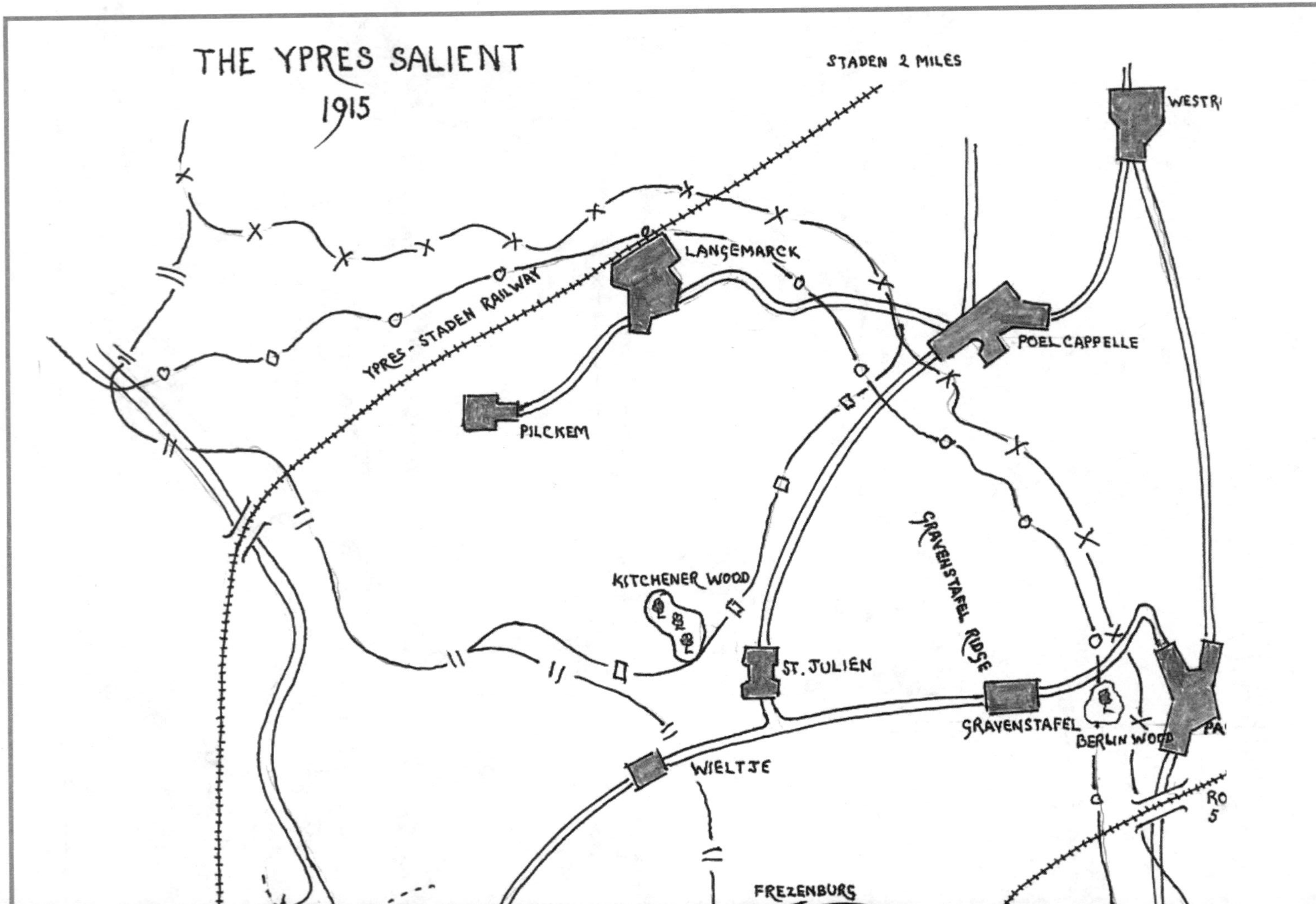
THE YPRES SALIENT
1915
STADEN 2 MILES
WESTR
LANGEMARCK
POEL CAPPELLE
YPRES - STADEN RAILWAY
PILCKEM
KITCHENER WOOD
GRAVENSTAFEL RIDGE
ST. JULIEN
GRAVENSTAFEL
BERLIN WOOD
WIELTJE
FREZENBURG
RO
5

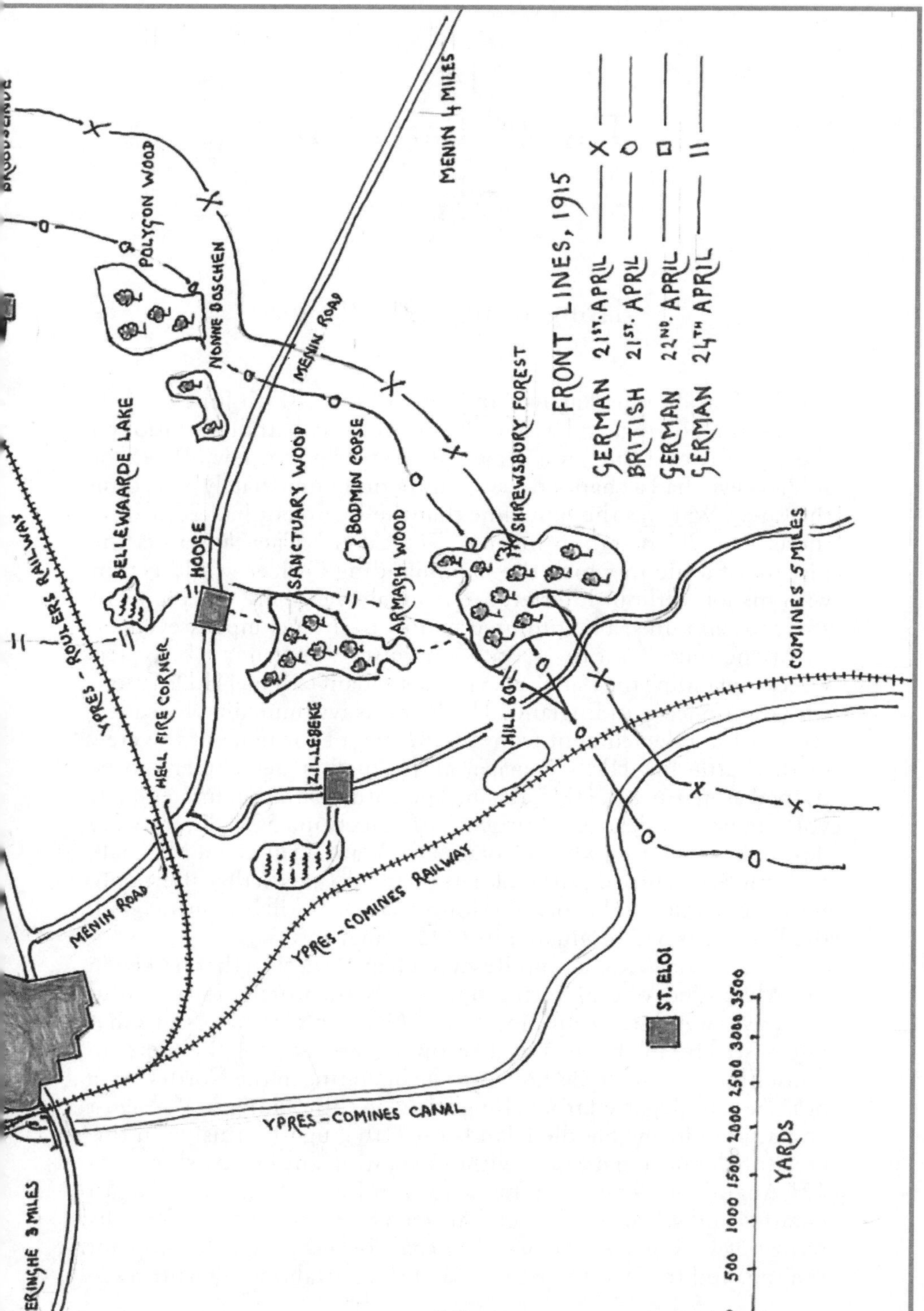
FRONT LINES, 1915
GERMAN 21ST. APRIL
BRITISH 21ST. APRIL
GERMAN 22ND. APRIL
GERMAN 24TH APRIL
POLYGON WOOD
NONNE BOSCHEN
MENIN ROAD
MENIN 4 MILES
BELLEWAARDE LAKE
HOOGE
SANCTUARY WOOD
BODMIN COPSE
ARMAGH WOOD
SHREWSBURY FOREST
HILL 60
ZILLEBEKE
YPRES - ROULERS RAILWAY
HELL FIRE CORNER
MENIN ROAD
YPRES-COMINES RAILWAY
COMINES 5 MILES
YPRES-COMINES CANAL
POPERINGHE 8 MILES
ST. ELOI
0 500 1000 1500 2000 2500 3000 3500
YARDS

14
The 2nd Battalion

Hong Kong, 1913-1914

The 2nd Battalion had arrived in Hong Kong on 13th June 1913. It was a plum posting, and with only one infantry battalion stationed there at any one time, was a part of the world that few officers or soldiers ever had a chance to see. This period immediately preceding the Great War was the only time that the Regiment had done duty there. The 2nd Battalion journal, *The Cornish Chough*, paints the picture of a life in which the Commanding Officer would get on with his job without interference from above. There was plenty of sport for all ranks, albeit limited mainly to inter-company events.

At the outbreak of war on 4th August 1914 Major P.B. Norris was commanding the Battalion, vice Lieutenant-Colonel H.D. Tuson, who was on leave in England. The Royal Navy immediately made a request for a detachment from the Regiment to augment the crew of the battleship HMS *Triumph*, and a further detachment to be trained as marines in HMS *Tamar*. The entire Battalion immediately volunteered and, after a process of selection, 50 soldiers were despatched to *Tamar*, while Captain E.B. Ward, Lieutenant Marshall, Serjeant Blackburn and 105 soldiers boarded *Triumph* that afternoon. It was an example of history repeating itself for, it will be remembered, the Regiment had originated in 1702 as marines.

HMS *Triumph* was an old Reserve Fleet battleship that had been quickly called out of retirement to steam north. Its two-fold objectives were first, rounding up any German merchant ships that might still be in the area and second, searching for the German cruiser *Emden*, which was known to be operating in the North China Sea. *Triumph* departed from Hong Kong on the evening of 4th August and arrived in the Saddle Islands on 11th August, cruising in this area for the next eight days without sighting any enemy ships. On 19th August she set out for Tsing Tao, and on 21st and 22nd August boarded and captured the merchantmen SS *Hanametal* and SS *Frisia* respectively. On 24th August *Triumph* docked at Wei-hai-Wei for coaling, and this was to be the end of the Battalion's adventures as marines for the Captain, Captain M. Fitzmaurice, announced that his soldiers were urgently required back in Hong Kong and that he must reluctantly bid them farewell. Amid high praise from the Royal Navy the Cornwalls transferred to SS *Frisia*, and arrived back in Hong Kong on 26th August, where they found scenes of the greatest activity while Hong Kong was put into a state of defence. (Sadly, HMS *Triumph* was sunk in the Dardanelles on 26th May 1915, during the Gallipoli campaign).

Return to England, 21st September-3rd November

On 21st September 1914 the 2nd Battalion embarked in the troopship HT *Nile*, bound for England. During the first part of the passage she was escorted by the French cruiser *Dupleix*, and for the final part by the Russian cruiser *Askold*. The Battalion landed at Devonport on 3rd November and moved straight to Winchester, where it became part of the 82nd Brigade in the 27th Division (a formation composed of Regular units which, like 2 DCLI, had been serving overseas at the outbreak of the war). The first priority was to re-equip all units, for foreign service kit was quite unsuitable for winter in the trenches of France and Flanders. This was hampered by serious shortages, and an inspection report of 23rd November noted that the Battalion was still short of great-coats, packs, blankets, tools, signalling equipment and harness.

FRANCE, 1914-1915

Move to France, 19th December 1914

By 18th December all the equipment shortcomings had been made good. The following day the Battalion marched to Southampton, with a strength of 902 all ranks, and embarked that night on several ships bound for Le Havre. Having disembarked in the early hours of 21st December, the Battalion moved by train to Arques, and thence marched to Wardrecques where it was billeted in two factories.

The Ypres Salient, 12th January-26th May 1915

After a short period of training in trench warfare, the 2nd Battalion took over a sector of the front line at St Eloi, a small village in the extreme south of the salient. It is interesting to note the normal routine that governed the continuous cycle of duty in the front line. Brigades would usually do four days in the front line, one in support (a few hundred yards behind the front line) and two in reserve (a thousand or so yards further back); after about a fortnight they would be pulled from the battle area where proper rest could be obtained, training carried out and reinforcement drafts absorbed. However, this was largely dependant on the tactical situation, and could vary considerably.

On 15th February the 2nd Battalion had their first taste of real action, when it mounted a counter attack to recapture a portion of the line from which a battalion of Leinsters had been driven back.

Although by the standards of the Great War, this was a minor operation, it was carried out with text book precision. Within half an hour of the leading companies going over the top, all objectives had been captured with the loss of only forty-one casualties. The Corps Commander, Lieutenant-General Sir Horace Smith-Dorien (who had commanded the brigade in which 2 DCLI had served throughout the South African War), sent a personal signal congratulating the Battalion on 'the most ably planned and gallantly carried out successful counter attack.'

The Mound, 14th-15th March 1915

On 14th March the 2nd Battalion was occupying a forward position in front of the village of St Eloi. Part of the line included an artificial feature known as the Mound, which consisted of a spoil heap about thirty feet high. Although elsewhere a feature of this size might appear insignificant, it was of considerable tactical importance in this low-lying countryside.

During the morning of 14th March it was noted that enemy artillery were registering on the Battalion position. This soon stopped, peace and quiet descending on the line, before being rudely shattered at 5 p.m. by the detonation of mines underneath the Mound itself and the adjoining trenches. Immediately the enemy guns opened up, putting down heavy concentrations on the Battalion front line. This was followed by a closely co-ordinated infantry assault, which included bombing groups carrying a large number of grenades, but otherwise unarmed. Very fierce fighting ensued, but gradually the DCLI, still shocked and confused by the detonation of the mines, was driven out of its front line trenches. The few survivors on the Mound put up a particularly gallant fight, in recognition of which Company Serjeant-Major T. Hanwright, and Privates J.F. Lock and

A.J. May were each awarded the DCM. Casualties were severe, amounting to 144 all ranks killed and wounded; this figure included seven officers killed. Lieutenant-Colonel Tuson received a letter from the Divisional Commander saying:

> I must express my admiration at the manner your Battalion stuck to its back trenches during the afternoon of the 14th inst. I fear you must have had heavy losses in your forward trenches, which I deeply deplore. I congratulate you on the steadiness of your Battalion.

Mining, in the context of Great War operations, consisted of driving tunnels underneath the opposing lines, into which were packed very considerable explosive charges. The results could be devastating. Both sides became highly proficient in this form of warfare, using charges of immense weight. (The heaviest of these was detonated by 185 Tunnelling Company, Royal Engineers at La Boiselle on 2nd March 1916. It blew a crater 450 feet in diameter and represented the greatest explosion in military history until the advent of the nuclear bomb.) The mining of the 2nd Battalion position at St Eloi was probably the first occasion in which British troops experienced the horrors of this tactic.

Battle of Gravenstafel Ridge, 22nd-23rd April 1915, & the first use of poison gas

Intelligence reports were being received in early April 1915 that the Germans were contemplating the use of poison gas. Unfortunately it was believed by both the British and French GHQs that not even the Germans would so flagrantly break the Hague Convention; consequently, no protective measures were taken by the Allies.

At 5 p.m. on 22nd April the Germans released chlorine gas against the French holding the Gravenstafel ridge, about four miles north east of Ypres. The attack fell on two French divisions, one a Breton territorial division and the other made up of French Colonial soldiers from North Africa. They had no protection whatsoever, and as their trenches were inundated with the lethal, greenish cloud, they had no choice but either to choke to death or run. Simultaneously the Germans put down a heavy artillery barrage behind which their leading troops, wearing protective gear, advanced. The situation facing the Allies was potentially catastrophic. Within minutes, a four and a half mile stretch of the front line had seen total collapse, and there now seemed little to stop the Germans pushing straight through to Ypres and beyond. The reserves of every British division in the Ypres Salient were immediately ordered to move up towards the front line.

On 22nd April the 2nd Battalion, resting in billets to the west of Ypres, received the order to move at 2.30 a.m. on 23rd April. Shortly afterwards the Battalion was formed up, and having passed through

Ypres and out onto the Menin road, arrived to the rear of Divisional Headquarters at Poltijze Chateau at 4.30 a.m. From there the Battalion was despatched to Wieltje as part of a composite detachment hastily assembled under the command of Colonel Geddes of the Buffs (the East Kent Regiment). Meanwhile, the Cornwall's Commanding Officer, Lieutenant-Colonel Tuson, had been ordered to organise an *ad hoc* brigade, leaving Captain Dene to command the Battalion. A lull then took place on the battle-field as it became apparent that the Germans had been surprised by the success of the gas attack, and had been unable to exploit their initial breakthrough. At 2.40 p.m. Tuson's *ad hoc* brigade consisting of 2nd DCLI, 9th Royal Scots, 4th Rifle Brigade and part of 5th King's Own, was ordered to form the right wing of an attack by three *ad hoc* brigades mustering a total of eleven battalions. The objective was to drive the Germans out of the captured French trenches and to restore the integrity of the front line. The daunting magnitude of the task can be judged by the fact that this hastily collected eleven-battalion force was opposed by forty-two German battalions with a preponderance of at least five to one in artillery.

The 2nd Battalion attacked in perfect extended order, as though it was taking part in a peace-time exercise. The sight was magnificent, but soon the attacking lines were hidden by the dust and smoke of battle. The attack, which must to a certain extent have caught the Germans by surprise, was put in with the greatest determination. By 7 p.m. the line had been re-established and all companies were digging in. The casualties were however high, the Battalion suffering a total of 278 men killed or wounded.

For those who survived, St George's Day 1915 was always remembered with enormous pride. It was the day when they and their comrades in that hastily assembled counter-attack force snatched victory from defeat, at one of the most critical moments of the war.

Battles of St Julien & Frezenberg Ridge
24th April-25th May 1915

For two more days the 2nd Battalion held the makeshift line that they had established on 23rd April. Captain Dene having been wounded, Captain Crawley-Boevey took over command. In the early hours of 27th April the Battalion was withdrawn to form part of another *ad hoc* brigade, to support the Indian Corps in a further attack north west of Wieltje. This brigade, which was again commanded by Lieutenant-Colonel Tuson, consisted of 2nd DCLI,

1st York and Lancaster, 5th King's Own and 2nd Duke of Wellingtons. No attack, however, took place and on 28th April the brigade was split up, Lieutenant-Colonel Tuson resuming command of the Battalion. From then until the final German attack on 24th May the Cornwalls were almost continuously on the move, attached to various brigades which were constantly switched about the front to meet the ever changing threats. Although the 2nd Battalion saw little actual fighting in the latter part of this great battle, it was involved in the most exhausting manoeuvring, and was, for most of this period, under enemy artillery fire. The second battle of Ypres demonstrated two formidable attributes of the old pre-war regular army: first, the almost unbelievable stamina of the British soldier which enabled him to keep going in conditions of extreme adversity; second, the extreme flexibility of the British system of command and control which made it possible for units to be hurriedly grouped into *ad hoc* formations, and to be rapidly moved to meet each new threat. Commanders of today, with all the sophisticated communications equipment now available, would surely find this difficult. One can only marvel at what was achieved by those commanders of April 1915 who, exhausted from lack of sleep and with virtually no communications except despatch riders, runners and vulnerable telephone lines, deployed their meagre resources with such skill, and fought a superior German force to a halt.

The Armentières Area, Summer 1915

The 2nd Battalion was pulled out of the Ypres Salient on 26th April for a period of much needed rest and the training of reinforcement drafts. All had expected to be committed again to the Salient, so it came as a pleasant surprise when orders came to relieve the Leinsters at Le Touquet in the Armentières area on 9th June. This section of the line was, at that time, comparatively quiet, being described by the Battalion as 'a haven of rest'. It is, however, indicative of the war on the Western Front that even this haven of rest was subjected to desultory shell-fire and sniping, which inevitably claimed a steady toll of casualties.

All that summer the 2nd Battalion moved in and out of the line, relieving and being relieved by other units of the 82nd Brigade. However, on 27th October, the startling news was received that the 27th Division was to be transferred from the Western Front to join the Mediterranean Expeditionary Force in Greece.

* * *

SALONIKA, NOVEMBER 1915-AUGUST 1916

The strategic aim of the Greek campaign was to drive north from Salonika in order to support the beleaguered Serbian army in its fight against Bulgaria. This action would, it was hoped, not only save Serbia, but draw German troops from the hard pressed Italian front. Neither of these aims was achieved; indeed, the British were themselves initially penned into a highly vulnerable enclave around Salonika.

Move to Salonika, 27th October 1915

The Battalion sailed from Marseilles on 26th November 1915, landing at Salonika on 5th December after an uneventful voyage. As it disembarked the men were cheered by the 8th Battalion, who had arrived a few days earlier and who supplied their Bugles for the march to the tented camp at Lembet. Life there was far from comfortable. Tentage was in short supply, the weather was bitterly cold and the battalion transport and horses were not due to arrive till the New Year. If its living conditions were spartan, its role was certainly less than exciting. Although the country was criss-crossed by a web of donkey tracks, there was no metalled road leading from Salonika into the hinterland; thus, before any major advance could be made, roads capable of supporting a modern army had to be built from scratch. All through that winter the 2nd Battalion laboured with pick, shovel and wheelbarrow, constructing what was to be the sole British line of communication through this inhospitable, barren and rocky terrain. On Boxing Day 1915 the Battalion moved camp ten miles north to an insalubrious village by the name of Gradobor. There Lieutenant-Colonel Price left for Egypt, handing over command to Lieutenant-Colonel J.W.C. Kirk. It was at this remote little village that an air attack was first experienced, when a working party was bombed on 7th January 1916 by a single German aeroplane.

The winter of 1916 merged into spring. Apart from the daily grind of constructional work, little of interest took place. As the weather became warmer dense swarms of flies and mosquitoes came out of hibernation. Bivouacs were moved to positions a clear half mile from water, and quinine was issued. In spite of all precautions malaria and enteric fever became a serious problem in all units.

Advance to the Struma Valley, August 1916

By August 1916 preparations were complete for an advance to a new line, running roughly along the Serbian border from Lake Ohrid in the west to Lake Doiran in the east. The 2nd Battalion moved off from Lembet on 29th August. All transport had been withdrawn and pack mules substituted, with the result that only bare essentials could be carried. The few villages were so filthy and verminous that any thought of their use as billets was quickly discarded. For the rest of this campaign, officers and men alike were to live with only the protection of their groundsheets. The Struma valley, where the Battalion found itself, consisted of a wide expanse of reed covered swamp, densely inhabited by anopheline mosquitoes. The 2nd Battalion took over the front line (so far as any established line existed) on 9th September 1916. Patrolling and minor offensive operations across the Struma became routine, but this strange and largely unmapped area of scrub and swamp could not have been more different to conditions on the Western Front. On 15th November and 1st December two minor battles were fought at Tumbitz, a group of hovels on a patch of high ground rising out of the swamp, a few miles north of the Struma. The attacks were not successful and the British force withdrew back across the river, the 2nd Battalion having suffered seventy casualties.

However, the chief enemy was not the Bulgar army; it was the mosquito. Disease, principally malaria, accounted for far more casualties than battle. The Commanding Officer, Lieutenant-Colonel Kirk wrote 'The mosquitoes were the largest that I have ever seen and a "finer brand" than in any other part of the valley: and the numbers of them appalling. By the end of September, the sick of the Battalion were numbered in hundreds.'

The War Diary states '26th, 27th and 28th September 1916. Nothing to report except serious outbreak of malaria in the Battalion. Many were incapacitated in addition to those admitted to hospital.'

The figures of those sent to hospital in those three days alone were 11, 27 and 44. On a march carried out on 30th September, 60 sick were left behind and a further 100 men dropped out in the course of the day. Nor was evacuation to the hospital in Salonika either swift or easy along forty miles of makeshift roads.

The winter of 1916-17 was particularly cold and wet, heavy snowfalls being intermixed with torrential rain. The Struma became a raging torrent, which made it impossible to cross. Little was seen of the enemy and the Battalion's efforts were principally aimed at improving the defences, and keeping warm and dry.

In March the weather improved, and with this improvement patrolling and raiding operations were intensified. However, at the end of May orders were issued to implement a major tactical change. All battalions were to be withdrawn from the Struma valley onto the high ground behind the river. Only small standing patrols and machine-gun sections would henceforth cover the crossing places to deny Bulgar infiltration. An officer of the 2nd Battalion, Major Williams, bitterly noted in his diary: 'All troops are being withdrawn from the left bank of the Struma. The last nine months' work appears to have been wasted.'

The reason for the withdrawal was not the Bulgars, but our old friend the anopheline mosquito. With the sickness that crippled every unit each summer in that swampy valley, it had become imperative to move the army back onto the healthier high ground. The Battalion War Diary showed a very marked improvement in the sickness rate, and in August 1917 the fighting strength was recorded as 20 officers and 700 men.

Early in October 1917, as the weather grew colder, it was considered safe to re-occupy the valley. Patrolling across the Struma once more became the principal role of the Battalion. New Year's Day of 1918 dawned with heavy snow blown by fierce winds. The Battalion was in reserve in the extreme east of the British line near Lake Doiran, but it was not until 14th February that it went into the front line. In May Lieutenant-Colonel Kirk departed to take over command of the 1st Battalion in France. He was replaced by Lieutenant-Colonel W.P. Rushbrooke of the Northumberland Fusiliers.

One of the great differences between soldiering in France and soldiering in Greece was that in the former there were towns and bright lights where men could relax during periods of rest, while in the latter no recreational facilities of any kind existed. Leave camps were therefore established on the Aegean coast. It was to one of these camps that the 2nd Battalion moved at the end of June, where for a fortnight bathing and games were the order of the day. Very little of any significance happened throughout that spring and early summer, and it was not until 5th August 1918 that orders were received of a British offensive. The 27th Division were to capture an enemy salient centred on a feature known as the Roche Noir.

Battle of Doiran, 14th-18th September 1918

On the morning of 14th September 1918 the Allied artillery bombarded the eighty miles of Bulgar line from Monastir in the west to Lake Doiran in the east. The following day French and Serbian troops attacked along the western sector of the front, followed on the 18th September by the British thrust to the west and north east of Lake Doiran. The 2nd Battalion played only a small part in this battle; indeed the War Diary makes no mention of the offensive having opened! However, on the 19th September, the Battalion took part in the pursuit of a beaten and demoralised enemy.

Capitulation of Bulgaria, 30th September 1918

On 30th September 1918 news was received that Bulgaria had capitulated. For the 2nd Battalion the war was over.

Operations in Greece could not have been more different to those in France and Flanders. There were no great battles, and the casualties inflicted by the enemy were minimal. The British army was operating in a desolate, inhospitable terrain without the benefit of any modern infrastructure. Roads, such as there were, had to be constructed by the troops, and in the forward areas all supplies had to be brought up by pack mules. The lack of adequate roads and wheeled transport also meant that the evacuation of wounded and sick to Salonika became a nightmare for those involved. The filthy, verminous condition of the few villages meant that there was nowhere for troops to be billeted when out of the line, and certainly nowhere that they could find recreation. Above all, the ubiquity of the anopheline mosquito in the swamps of the Struma valley posed a far greater threat than the enemy. Besides making life hellish for the soldiers, mosquitoes were capable of infecting complete battalions with malaria, rendering them unfit to play any active part in the campaign. The Mediterranean Expeditionary Force was a forgotten army, never being involved in any great set piece battles or covering itself with glory. But it carried on quietly and doggedly and, in spite of a bleak and barren country, an atrocious climate and the constant scourge of malaria, beat its enemy into submission.

III. THE OLD MILITIA & THE TERRITORIAL BATTALIONS

* * *

15

The 3rd (Reserve) Battalion

On the formation of the Duke of Cornwall's Light Infantry in 1881 the 3rd Battalion had been created from the old County Militia. This ancient force, now no longer manned by conscripts of somewhat dubious value, consisted of a volunteer special reserve, with a permanent headquarters staff stationed at the Depôt in Bodmin. Under Lord Haldane's Territorial and Reserve Forces Act of 1907 all Militia battalions were re-designated as the reserve battalions of their county regiments.

Mobilization and move to Falmouth, August 1914

At the outbreak of war the Headquarters of the 3rd Battalion, together with the special reservists, moved to a tented camp at Falmouth, where it prepared for the reception of the anticipated influx of recruits. It had not long to wait. Within days of the call for volunteers by Field-Marshal Lord Kitchener on 7th August 1914 it became obvious that the Depôt had neither the resources to administer and train the resulting flood of recruits, nor the space in which to accommodate them. The surplus of recruits, which could not be dealt with by the Depôt, was therefore initially despatched to the 3rd Battalion at Falmouth.

Between March and August 1915 elements of the Battalion carried out recruiting marches, covering the whole of Cornwall. Every town and many larger villages were visited by the band and some thirty men. This party included Lance-Corporal T.E. Rendle, VC, who had won his award as a bandsman stretcher-bearer at Wulverghem for rescuing the wounded under very heavy shell-fire. The tour was extensively reported in the local press, with details of exactly how many recruits were obtained from each town.

Move to Freshwater, Isle of Wight, May 1915

Meanwhile, the main body of the 3rd Battalion had moved to Freshwater on the Isle of Wight, where it occupied the old fort and an adjoining hutted camp. There it was to remain till the end of the war, carrying out the vital task of training recruits and preparing them for drafting to the various operational battalions of the Regiment. Most officers and soldiers passed through Freshwater. Regrettably no records and practically no photographs appear to have survived; it is therefore almost impossible to give any details of the life in this Battalion or of the training syllabus that was required to turn a civilian into a trained infantryman. It would appear that basic recruit training lasted from between twelve and sixteen weeks, although this period seems to have varied according to the urgency of the demand for reinforcements in France and Flanders.

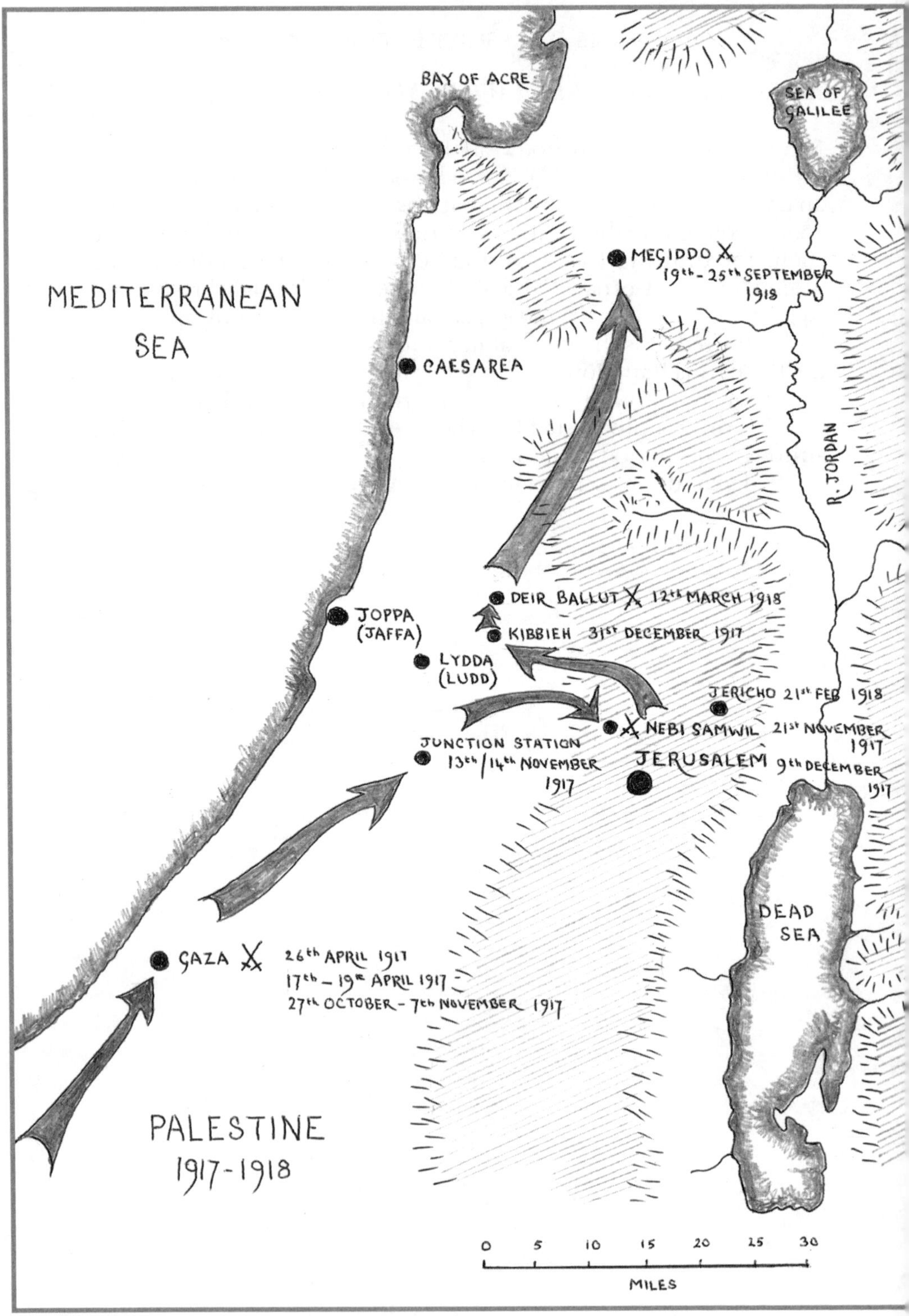
BAY OF ACRE
SEA OF GALILEE
MEDITERRANEAN SEA
MEGIDDO
19th - 25th SEPTEMBER 1918
CAESAREA
R. JORDAN
DEIR BALLUT 12th MARCH 1918
JOPPA (JAFFA)
KIBBIEH 31st DECEMBER 1917
LYDDA (LUDD)
JERICHO 21st FEB 1918
NEBI SAMWIL 21st NOVEMBER 1917
JUNCTION STATION 13th/14th NOVEMBER 1917
JERUSALEM 9th DECEMBER 1917
DEAD SEA
GAZA
26th APRIL 1917
17th - 19th APRIL 1917
27th OCTOBER - 7th NOVEMBER 1917
PALESTINE 1917-1918
0 5 10 15 20 25 30
MILES

16
The 4th Battalions

THE 1/4TH BATTALION (TERRITORIAL FORCE)

Generally speaking, although certain individuals had volunteered for overseas service in the event of war, the Territorial Force as a whole was under no obligation to serve outside the United Kingdom. However, by the end of August 1914, so great was the need to recall regular units from India to fight in France and Flanders that the Government made a plea for territorial soldiers to volunteer to take their place overseas. The response was immediate. On 2nd September a composite DCLI battalion was formed from the existing 4th and 5th Battalions. This was initially known as the 4th (Foreign Service) Battalion DCLI (Territorial Force) but, in accordance with War Office policy, was quickly re-designated the 1/4th Battalion DCLI (Territorial Force).

Having moved from its home base at Truro to a tented camp on Perham Down near Bulford, it was quickly re-equipped for Indian service and put through a crash course of training. On 17th September the Devon and Cornwall Brigade, of which it was part, was inspected by Field-Marshal Lord Kitchener, and on 25th September by His Majesty the King. Lieutenant-Colonel the Hon. H.W. Hepburn-Stuart-Forbes-Trefusis was nominally in command but, as he was away in Japan at the outbreak of war, temporary command in these exciting weeks fell on the shoulders of Major G.E.S. Smith (a fact that must have delighted the orderly room clerks, absolved from repeatedly typing their Lieutenant-Colonel's name).

Move to India, 4th October 1914

On 4th October 1914 the Battalion embarked in HMT *Assaye*. Apart from some rough weather in the Bay of Biscay, the voyage was uneventful and the Battalion arrived at Bombay on 10th November.

That night it entrained for the 937 mile journey to Bareilly, which was to be the home of most of the 1/4th for the next few months (part of the Battalion was detached to Lucknow for three weeks). The culture shock for these Cornish soldiers, many of whom had previously barely moved from their home parishes, must have been traumatic. We are indebted to the diary, conscientiously maintained by the Battalion's Serjeant Tailor, Serjeant T.H. Heard, which records with excited delight the new sounds, smells and sights which assailed him from every quarter. It should not be forgotten that, although soldiering in India could be tough in the extreme, the humblest British Private was accorded a degree of personal service to which he could never in his wildest dreams have aspired at home. Serjeant Heard was allotted a three-roomed bungalow which he shared with his Corporal Tailor. He enjoyed the exclusive services of a native *dooley*, who performed every domestic duty that his master might require, all for 1 rupee (1s. 4d.) per week. It is perhaps interesting that right up to the Second World War British soldiers in India continued to luxuriate in the perks offered by native servants. Not only were their barrack rooms cleaned and their boots polished, but barbers could shave a man before reveille without waking him from sleep!

The Kitchener Test, 26th-27th March 1915

The tempo of training increased throughout that winter in preparation for what was known as the Kitchener Test. All new units arriving from England were subjected to this gruelling exercise, which was designed to test the endurance and military skills of all ranks. It lasted forty-eight hours and consisted, on the first day, of a long approach march, immediately followed by a battalion attack, using live ammunition. The next day was devoted to a fighting withdrawal over a distance of some fifteen miles. The weather was extremely hot, and it was deemed wise to cancel the night patrolling programme, which should have taken place at the end of the first day, to allow the Territorials some rest before completing the final and most arduous part of the test on the second day. In spite or perhaps as a result of this, Brigadier-General Woodyalt, who was conducting the exercise, expressed himself very well pleased with the Battalion's performance.

During the summer of 1915 two companies at a time were sent up to the hill station of Ranikhet where they could find some relaxation in the comparative cool. The Battalion also sent drafts to reinforce the 4th Dorsets in Mesopotamia, most of whom ended their war in Prisoner of War camps, after the surrender of General Townsend's force at Kut-el-Amara. Although it is not strictly part of the history of the 1/4th DCLI, the exploits of one of its officers, Lieutenant Ellis, who was transferred to the 4th Dorsets are worthy of note. Escaping from his prison camp at Yozard he, with 8 other British officers, walked 330 miles across the Taurus Mountains to Pershembre on the Mediterranean, and stole a Turkish motor boat in which they navigated their way to Cyprus 120 miles away. Lieutenant Ellis was awarded the MC.

Move to Aden, 2nd January 1916

On 8th January 1916 the 1/4th Battalion was warned for active service in Aden, where it was due to relieve the 1/4th Battalion of the Buffs. The DCLI entrained on 19th January for the long rail journey back to Bombay, which was reached on 22nd January. The Battalion embarked in HMT *Elephanta*, which sailed that night. The passage took six days, and was far from comfortable. The accommodation was extremely crowded, even by wartime standards, particularly as much of the living space had been converted to stables. On landing at Steamer Point nobody could be left in doubt that they were entering an operational area. Military stores were stacked on the quayside, while Indian cavalry disembarked their horses, and wounded men were ferried out to a waiting hospital ship.

Quickly the 1/4th DCLI took over the quarters and duties of the 1/4th Buffs. The new role was far from exciting, consisting as it did of guarding numerous vulnerable key points in the Colony such as the fresh water distillation plant, the passes through the mountains, the searchlights, the headquarters of the Eastern Telegraph Co. and the several forts.

Operations in Aden, 28th January 1916-8th February 1917

For the next year life settled down to the routine of guard duties intermixed with minor operations with the Aden Field Force in the Sheikh Othman area. A desultory war was being fought with the Turkish army which, in a somewhat half-hearted manner, was attempting to capture the vitally important British staging post of Aden. British and Indian troops spent much of their time digging field defences along the front line north of Sheikh Othman, with the occasional raid or fighting patrol into the Turkish positions to dispel any feelings of boredom. The largest operation in which the 1/4th took part was a major reconnaissance carried out at brigade strength on 15th November 1916. The 1/4th Battalion crossed the start line at 6.30 a.m. and advanced towards the village of Uzeli. It came under heavy shrapnel and small arms fire until 9 a.m. when, according to plan, a withdrawal was made to a covering ridge. Just after 2 p.m. a final withdrawal was made to the defences of Sheikh Othman. The DCLI casualties amounted to thirteen killed and wounded. Unimportant as these minor operations were in themselves, they provided an excellent preparation for more serious fighting in the future, and gave all ranks experience of being under fire.

Move to Egypt, January 1917

Soon after the New Year the Battalion received warning that it was to be relieved by a battalion of the East Surrey Regiment and would proceed to Egypt, where it was to join General Allenby's Egyptian Expeditionary Force. Although operations by the Egyptian Expeditionary Force are henceforth described as British it must be remembered that an Australian/New Zealand cavalry division, an Australian infantry corps and an Indian infantry brigade formed a very significant portion of General Allenby's army.

The Battalion embarked in HMT *Egra* on 8th January 1917, 746 strong, arriving at Port Tewfik on the morning of 13th January. From there it moved by train to Cairo, and from Cairo marched to Polygon Camp, Abbassia, which was to be its home for the next two months. The weather was bitterly cold with occasional heavy rainstorms, and the Battalion, used to the hot humid climate of Aden, and dressed in tropical khaki drill, found life far from pleasant.

Palestine

The Sinai Desert, March 1917

By this time General Allenby had advanced 140 miles east through the Sinai Desert; no mean logistical feat; and was confronting the Turks at Gaza, a town near the coast on the south west corner of Palestine. There was thus an urgent need for extra troops to guard his vulnerable line of communication, which included a standard gauge railway that had been laid across the desert as the troops advanced. On 15th March 1917 the 1/4th moved to a tented camp at Kantara, on the east bank of the Suez Canal. Five days later it entrained and crossed the Sinai Desert, the first complete unit to use the newly laid railway. The Battalion took over lines of communication duties from the 10th Battalion the King's Shropshire Light Infantry. The work was extremely heavy because, apart from manning innumerable picquets, deep dug-outs had to be constructed as a protection against air attack. From this time the 1/4th came under command of 234 Brigade in the 75th Infantry Division.

Battle of Gaza, 27th October-7th November 1917

Desert training was carried out throughout the summer of 1917, and on 18th August the Battalion moved up to the front line in the Sheikh Abbas sector. The Turks, however, were not the principal enemy. In common with each of the Middle Eastern campaigns, disease claimed far more casualties than battle. By 24th August 15 officers and 246 soldiers had been evacuated to hospital, mostly suffering from sand-fly fever, leaving a seriously depleted battalion to carry out front-line duties.

The arrival of the 1/4th in the front line coincided with the start of the British offensive towards Jerusalem, which now lay forty miles to the north east. The battle opened on 27th October, with the aim of driving the Turks out of Gaza. Although the 1/4th were not directly involved in the actual battle, the Battalion held part of the front line to the east of the town. Turkish shelling was heavy, causing a few casualties. On the night of 6th-7th November patrols reported that Gaza had been evacuated, whereupon the Battalion was moved forward into the northern defences of the town. Further patrols found no trace of the enemy and, by the evening of 8th November, the British force had moved on towards Jerusalem.

Battle of Nebil Samwil, 19th November 1917

It would be difficult to exaggerate the logistical difficulties attending the supply of the army across the barren, rocky hills east of Gaza. The railway had followed the line of the British advance through the flat coastal plain of the Sinai Desert, but any question of extending it into the hills would have involved a lengthy, major civil engineering operation that was quite impractical. Henceforth, supplies had to be off-loaded from the railhead at the village of Kerne and carried by mule or camel up the stony tracks to the forward troops. Water was very scarce. Previously, the men and animals had had recourse to pipe lines which were laid by the Royal Engineers, but now movement was strictly curtailed by the need to capture wells. These were few and far between; most had been damaged by the retreating Turks and required Royal Engineer repair work. Meanwhile the Turkish army had been split in two, their 8th Army withdrawing due north up the coastal plain, while the 7th Army fell back into the Judean hills towards Jerusalem.

General Allenby was loath to become involved in fighting a battle in the Holy City itself, first, because the inevitable damage and destruction of historical shrines, central to the faith of Christians, Jews and Arabs, would not be politically acceptable; second, because fighting in the ancient streets and alleys of the old city would have been extremely costly in soldiers' lives. He therefore decided to outflank Jerusalem and cut the Turkish line of communication in the north. Thus it was that the 1/4th found themselves in hot pursuit of the 7th Turkish Army across the abominable terrain of the Judean hills. The New Testament tells of Christ's forty day vigil in this rocky wilderness; Allenby's soldiers found it unchanged. Contact was made with the Turks a few miles to the north west of Jerusalem near the village of Nebil Samwil. Fighting was hard, the Turks being driven from successive ridges.

While this battle was taking place, the weather added to the tribulations of those involved. The temperature dropped and the rain came down in torrential sheets. Life for the soldiers, dressed in tropical khaki drill with only their groundsheets for cover, became grim. To add to their miseries, the camels and their Egyptian drivers, which had up till then served them stoically, carrying supplies in the hot coastal plain, became demoralised by the unfamiliar cold and wet of these inhospitable hills. On 22nd November the Turks made a series of strong counter attacks against the ridges held by the 75th Division. One of these was repulsed by the rifle fire of the 1/4th, inflicting heavy losses on the enemy.

During a pause in the battle a complete Turkish battalion was seen marching up the hill in column of fours with their rifles slung. The DCLI, assuming that these men wished to surrender, sent an officer and twelve men to bring them in. The Turks, who were presumably completely lost, were equally non-plussed by the arrival of this unexpected British party, whom they presumed were trying to surrender to them. Neither spoke the other's language, so, after what must have been a quite remarkable altercation, both sides made a hurried withdrawal to safety! By this time the fighting strength of the Battalion was reduced to two companies, commanded by Major A.P. Coode and Captain C.H. Kendall respectively. Particularly heavy fighting occurred on 22nd November around a mosque sited on a vital ridge known as El Jib. This feature was attacked by the 1/123rd

Rifles and 1/4th DCLI, supported by 231st Machine-gun Company, 2/4th Hampshires and 3/3rd Gurkha Rifles. The objective was captured in spite of heavy Turkish artillery and machine-gun fire, but all through that day the enemy made repeated and determined counter attacks. At one time the 3/3rd Gurkha Rifles completely ran out of ammunition but continued to hold their position with kukri and bayonet. Seeing how desperate was their situation, Captain T.A. Kendall led a small party of men from his depleted company across the bullet-swept gap, carrying boxes of ammunition. The Commanding Officer of the 3/3rd Gurkha Rifles, Lieutenant-Colonel G.K. Channer, DSO wrote 'My signals for reinforcements and ammunition resulted in the former not being able to get through the incessant gun fire, but Captain Charles Kendall, 1/4 Battalion the DCLI, with a handful of men brought up the much needed ammunition. A gallant achievement.'

The capture and retention of the El Jib feature proved a critical, possibly the critical, factor in the victory at Nebi Samwil, which in its turn led to the capture of Jerusalem.

The 1/4th Battalion had gone into action on the morning of 22nd November with a fighting strength of just over 200 officers and men. During the next two days of fighting it had lost a total of 111 casualties. At times, completely cut off from their flanking units, these Territorial soldiers had fought with the skill and determination of veterans. Extraordinary acts of gallantry were carried out, as witnessed by the award of the MM to Lance-Corporal S. Noel, while Serjeant J. Bartlett, Private A. Jane, Private T. Hambly, Private W. Penlerick and Private P. Trethewey received the DCM.*

These awards were a just tribute to a fine battalion in which all performed beyond the call of duty. In particular the stretcher bearers carried out their task of mercy, bringing back the wounded to comparative safety, often under heavy artillery and machine-gun fire. It is good to see two of those often unsung heroes of the battle-field receiving recognition for their selfless gallantry.

*The Distinguished Conduct Medal was the oldest gallantry decoration in the British Army, pre-dating the institution of the Victoria Cross by many years. It was awarded only to NCOs and men who had performed acts of 'conspicuous gallantry in the face of the enemy' (officers were not eligible), and was thus a very highly prized decoration, the proud recipients being held in great esteem throughout the army. The award of five DCMs to a single battalion for actions in a single engagement is certainly very rare indeed, and possibly unprecendented. It is therefore instructive to look at the citations published in the *London Gazette* in respect of these gallant Territorial soldiers.

The citations for the recipients of the DCM are as follows:

Serjeant J. Bartlett from Delabole, Cornwall

For conspicuous gallantry and devotion to duty. When his officer and senior NCO had become casualties,

Capture of Jerusalem, 9th December 1917

XX Corps, in which the 1/4th Battalion was serving, had born the brunt of the operations up through the Sinai Desert and in the Judean hills. It had suffered heavy casualties from disease and battle, and was now in urgent need of rest and reinforcement. On 27th November General Allenby started the complex operation of relieving XX Corps by XXI Corps.

The General's actions did not go unobserved by Field-Marshal von Falkenhayn, the German Commander-in-Chief, who had recently come from the Western Front to take over command of the Turkish Forces. He immediately threw his forces into a series of hard-fought counter attacks along the whole front line. After confused and bitter fighting, the final advance on Jerusalem was not made till 8th December. The city surrendered the following day. The manner in which the most serious military operations can sometimes mutate to comedy is well illustrated by the story of the first British soldiers to enter Jerusalem. Two mess cooks from the 2/20th Battalion the London Regiment became lost as they were searching for water during the night of 8th-9th December. As dawn broke they found themselves in the outskirts of Jerusalem, and were quickly surrounded by a large crowd out of which appeared the Mayor carrying the keys of the city, which he wished to surrender. Not feeling themselves equal to the occasion, the two private soldiers fled back to their battalion!

The 1/4th took no part in these latter operations. Reduced to a strength of 12 officers and 497 men, it had marched out of the hills

on the defence of his post devolving on him, he maintained it for many hours, though himself wounded, displaying a fine fighting leadership. On one occasion, leaving his cover, he rushed out into the open, bombed the enemy who were collecting under cover, preparatory to rushing the post, and dislodged them.

Private A. Jane from St Germans, Cornwall

For conspicuous gallantry and devotion to duty. After being wounded, he displayed great courage and coolness in keeping his machine-gun in action under heavy fire.

Private T. Hambly from Camelford, Cornwall

For conspicuous gallantry and devotion to duty. Though wounded, he kept his Lewis gun in action with great courage and determination under heavy fire.

Private W. Penlerrick from Helston, Cornwall

For conspicuous gallantry and devotion to duty. He, as a stretcher-bearer, showed great gallantry and endurance in collecting wounded under fire consecutively for thirty-six hours. On one occasion he volunteered to proceed from a post to the front line under extremely heavy and intense fire over an area in which several of his comrades had been wounded, but was recalled by order of his medical officer in the interests of the unit. His courage and utter indifference to danger were beyond all praise.

Private P. Trethewey from Grampound Road, Cornwall

For conspicuous gallantry and devotion to duty. He, as a stretcher-bearer, showed great gallantry and endurance in collecting wounded under fire consecutively for thirty-six hours. On one occasion he volunteered to proceed from a post to the front line under extremely intense fire over an area in which several of his comrades had been wounded, but was recalled by order of his medical officer in the interests of the unit. His courage and utter indifference to danger were beyond all praise.

to a bivouac area at Beshshit on 27th November 1917. Here, fresh fruit and vegetables were available in abundance and, perhaps even more importantly, the men's threadbare khaki drill was exchanged for winter clothing. On 1st December, 6 officers and 48 men rejoined from hospital and on 17th December a further 3 officers and 84 men arrived with a reinforcement draft, bringing the Battalion up to a viable fighting strength.

The following day the 1/4th returned to the front line, relieving the 2/3rd Gurkha Rifles at Kibbieh. Heavy rain continued all that week, making life thoroughly miserable. A further reinforcement draft of 1 officer and 127 men joined on Christmas Eve, and yet another draft of 1 officer and 89 men joined on 30th December. Most of these drafts came from the sister battalion, the 2/4th, stationed in India.

Pursuit of the Turkish Army, January-March 1918

There was little to report during January apart from the severity of the weather. The rain continued unabated, causing abject misery to the troops who, for the most part, were without any shelter other than their ground sheets. The Quartermaster's staff worked miracles in their efforts to provide hot food but, with roads washed away and the wadis deep in swirling water, their task at times became physically impossible. Camels, such excellent beasts of burden in the dry desert, became near useless as they attempted to stumble through the slippery mud and swollen streams.

Action at Tel Asur, 8th-12th March 1918

General Allenby's intention was now to push eastwards across the Jordan. The 75th Division was required to continue its advance due north through the hills, in order to secure the westerly flank of Allenby's main force. During this advance the 1/4th were involved in a sharp engagement at Tel Asur. During this action, on 12th March 1918, C Company became split up while crossing a particularly steep and rocky wadi. One platoon, under Second-Lieutenant J.M. Cowls, continued towards the objective, picking up stragglers on the way. Unable to make any contact with the rest of his company, he decided to make the attack with his platoon alone. As he was approaching the strongly held objective, the Turks made the error of leaving their trenches and attacking with the bayonet. Cowls immediately led a counter charge, which not only drove the Turks back, but drove them right out of their position. Cowls was awarded the MC for his initiative and gallant leadership throughout this action.

During the following weeks the 75th Division slowly worked its way northwards over the rocky ridges, which were proving ideal ground for the defenders. Mention is made in the diaries of the first issue of steel helmets. These must have saved many lives in terrain where every bullet and exploding shell produced hundreds of jagged rock splinters.

Rest & training, 8th May-17th September 1918

On 8th May the 1/4th moved back into Divisional Reserve for much needed rest, returning to the front on 27th May. On the night of 22nd-23rd August it again moved back for rest. Rest however there was none, for every available man was employed in heavy manual work, building a road that was to form the Divisional line of communication. On 31st August the Battalion marched to Beit Nebala, where a fortnight's intensive training was carried out, which concluded with a hard brigade exercise.

On about 15th September the Division marched west to a new part of the line on the coastal strip. No tears were shed as the Battalion bade farewell to those bleak, cold, wet hills.

Battle of Sharon, 19th-25th September 1918

The battles that led to the final collapse of the Turkish army were primarily cavalry actions. What had so often been attempted on the Western Front without success became feasible in this land of vast desert spaces. In the 75th Divisional area the infantry broke through the Turkish front line, to allow the cavalry to exploit success. The 1/4th were in Brigade reserve throughout this final battle, so enjoyed a ring-side seat for the engagement. As the Battalion moved up to consolidate the defence of the captured Turkish position it was to witness a sight never to be seen again, a divisional cavalry charge. First came the Australian cavalry, closely followed by Chasseurs d'Afrique and Spahis, moving at full gallop through the Brigade position with drawn swords.

* * *

The Armistice, 31 October 1918

This was the final action in which the 1/4th took part; Turkey was to sign an armistice on 31st October 1918. It was certainly a very different battalion to that which had left Southampton just over four years previously. Then they were enthusiastic amateurs; now they were war-hardened veterans, who had seen action in the humid heat of Aden, the harsh waterless desert of the Sinai, and the cold, rain swept, stony hills of Judea. 148 of their number were dead, either killed in action or through disease. For the first time in their history Territorials had taken to the field, not just as groups of volunteers attached to Regular units, but as fully fledged Territorial formations. In four years of hard service they had become highly professional soldiers.

THE 2/4TH BATTALION (TERRITORIAL FORCE)

In September 1914 the 2/4th Battalion DCLI (Territorial Force) was formed at Truro from men of both the 4th and 5th Battalions who had volunteered for overseas service. It sailed for India the following month as part of the 2nd Wessex Division (later to be re-named the 45th Division).

The initial role of the 2/4th was to relieve troops of the Regular army, so that they could be brought back to Europe to fight in France and Flanders. Latterly it provided reinforcement drafts, not only for its sister battalion the 1/4th, which served in Aden and Palestine, but for many other regiments in Palestine, Gallipoli and Mesopotamia. Its role, never in any way spectacular or exciting, was nevertheless vital, both for the security of India itself and for the maintenance of the fighting strength of many units operating in the Middle East.

THE 3/4TH BATTALION (TERRITORIAL FORCE)

The 3/4th Battalion DCLI (Territorial Force) was a third line Territorial battalion raised at Bodmin in March 1915. This date coincided with the enactment of an amendment to the Territorial

Regulations, which made all recruits liable to foreign service. Its role was to train reinforcements for the 1/4th and 2/4th Battalions, both of which were serving in India. In October 1915 it moved to Bournemouth; in spring of 1916 it again moved, to Hursley Park near Winchester, where it absorbed the 2/5th Battalion and became the 4th (Reserve) Battalion DCLI. It was subsequently commanded by an ex 2/5th Officer, Lieutenant-Colonel W.F. Parker.

THE 4TH (RESERVE) BATTALION (TERRITORIAL FORCE)

The 4th (Reserve) Battalion DCLI (Territorial Force) was born of an amalgamation of the 2/5th and 3/4th Battalions at Hursley Park near Winchester on 1st September 1916. As previously mentioned, it was commanded by a 2/5th Officer, Lieutenant-Colonel W.F. Parker. Its role was to provide reinforcements for the three DCLI Territorial Force battalions serving abroad. In October 1916 it moved to Bournemouth; in March 1917 to Sutton Veny; in October 1917 to Larkhill; and finally, in April 1918 to Buncrana in Ireland. While in Ireland the Battalion initially formed part of the 15th Brigade and latterly the 27th Brigade.

Chapter 17

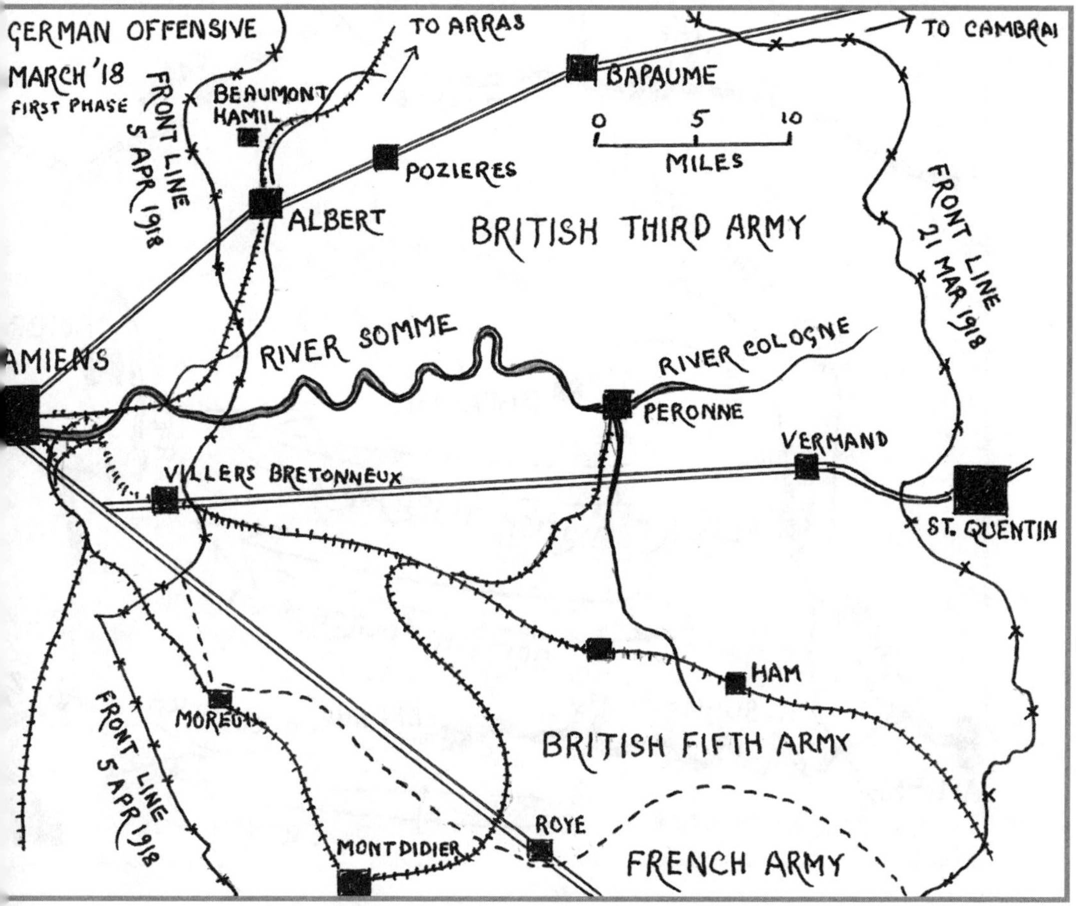
GERMAN OFFENSIVE
MARCH '18
FIRST PHASE
FRONT LINE
5 APR 1918
BEAUMONT HAMIL
TO ARRAS
BAPAUME
TO CAMBRAI
0 5 10
MILES
POZIERES
ALBERT
BRITISH THIRD ARMY
FRONT LINE
21 MAR 1918
AMIENS
RIVER SOMME
RIVER COLOGNE
PERONNE
VERMAND
VILLERS BRETONNEUX
ST. QUENTIN
HAM
MOREUIL
BRITISH FIFTH ARMY
FRONT LINE
5 APR 1918
ROYE
MONTDIDIER
FRENCH ARMY

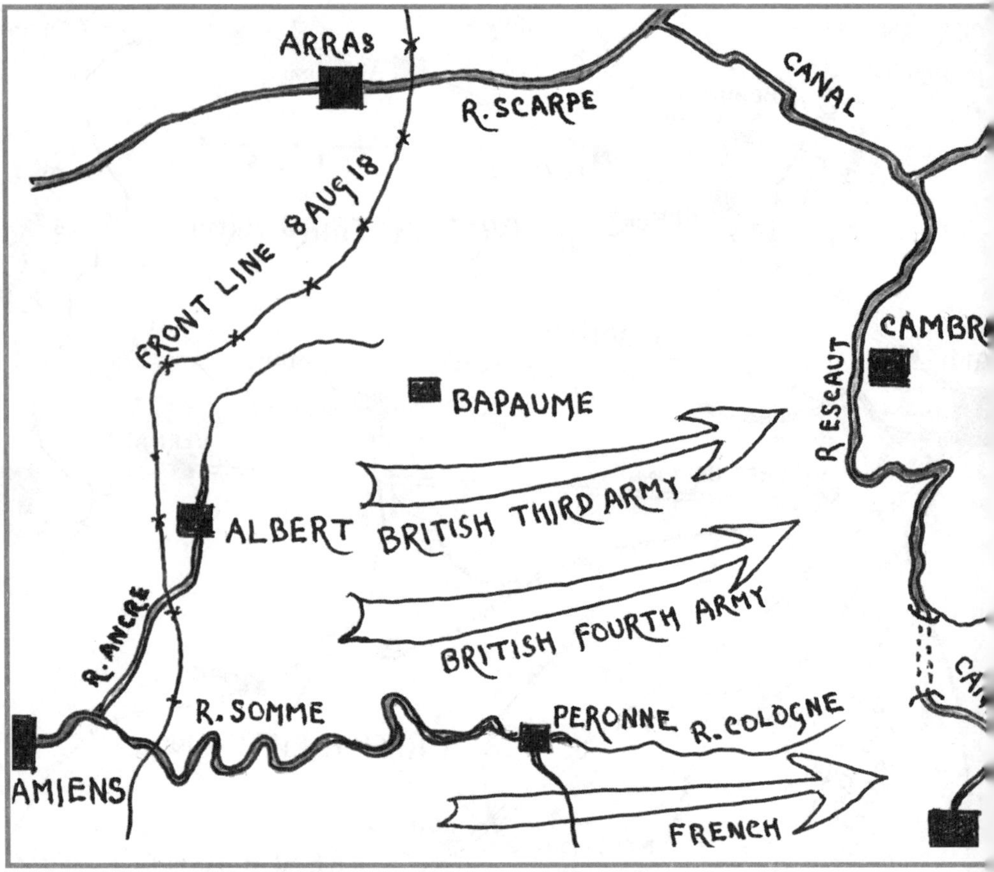
ARRAS
CANAL
R. SCARPE
FRONT LINE 8 AUG 18
CAMBR
BAPAUME
R. ESCAUT
ALBERT
BRITISH THIRD ARMY
R. ANCRE
BRITISH FOURTH ARMY
R. SOMME
PERONNE
R. COLOGNE
AMIENS
FRENCH

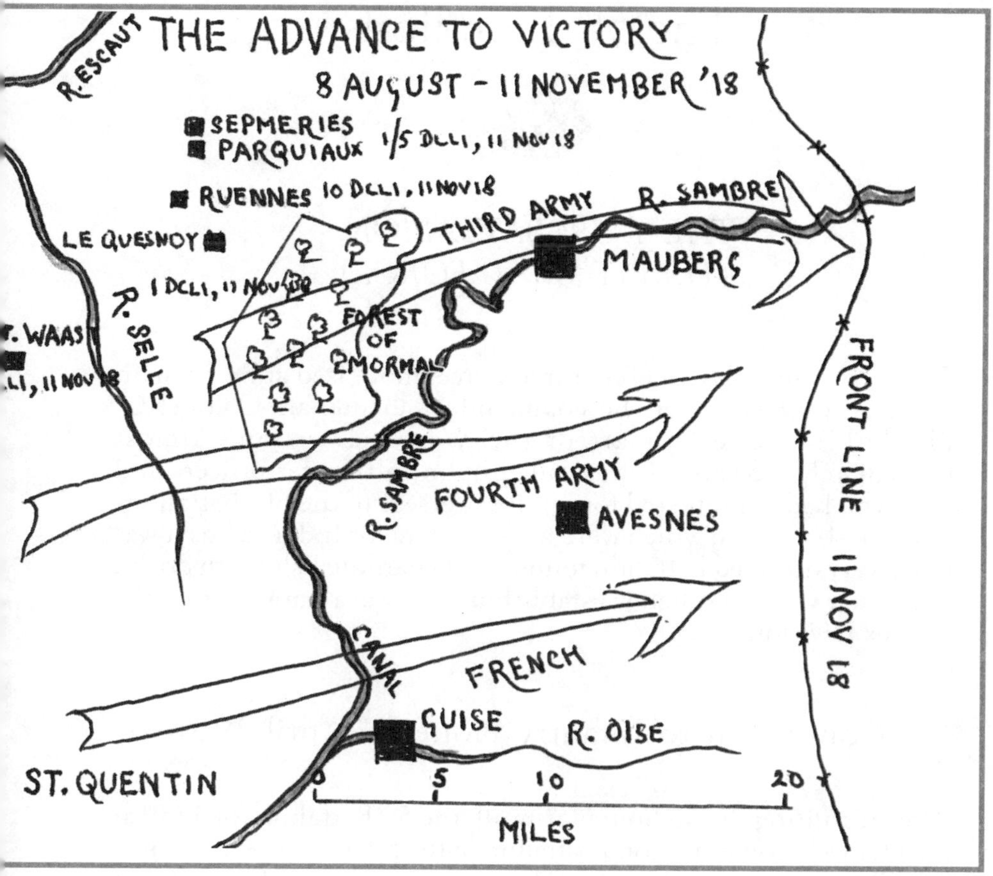
THE ADVANCE TO VICTORY
8 AUGUST - 11 NOVEMBER '18
R. ESCAUT
SEPMERIES
PARQUIAUX 1/5 DLI, 11 NOV 18
RUENNES 10 DLI, 11 NOV 18
LE QUESNOY
1 DLI, 11 NOV 18
R. SELLE
THIRD ARMY
R. SAMBRE
MAUBERG
FOREST OF MORMAL
R. SAMBRE
FOURTH ARMY
AVESNES
FRONT LINE 11 NOV 18
CANAL
FRENCH
GUISE
R. OISE
ST. QUENTIN
0 5 10 20
MILES

17

The 5th Battalions

THE 1/5TH BATTALION, (TERRITORIAL FORCE)

The 5th Battalion DCLI (Territorial Force) mobilised at Bodmin on 4th August 1914, under the command of Lieutenant-Colonel G. Pleydell-Bouverie, as part of the Wessex Division. Almost immediately, however, it was called upon to transfer officers and men who had volunteered for service overseas to the two battalions of the 4th Battalion, which were under orders for India. Thus it was that a very depleted battalion found itself guarding Falmouth docks. Because it was so far below establishment it was removed from the Wessex Division.

Conversion to Infantry Pioneers, April 1916

After recruiting throughout Cornwall, the 5th Battalion (or 1/5th as it had now become, a second battalion of the 5th having been recently raised) found itself back in the Falmouth area, training for service in France. However, by this point of the war, it had already become obvious that the Royal Engineers were unable to cope on their own with the vastly increased field engineering commitment required of static trench warfare. Accordingly, certain infantry battalions were re-trained as Infantry Pioneers, and allotted on a basis of one per Division. Most Infantry Pioneer battalions were created from Service (or Kitchener) battalions. The 1/5th DCLI (Territorial Force) was one of the few exceptions to this rule. Thus it was that the 1/5th was moved to Salisbury Plain in April 1916 for conversion to an Infantry Pioneer battalion, destined for the 61st Division.

* * *

The Role of Infantry Pioneers

The primary role of Infantry Pioneer battalions was to support the Royal Engineers. This included the building and maintenance of roads, light railways and bridges, the construction of command posts, dug-outs and other defensive works, and the erection of the vast hedges of barbed wire that encompassed the forward defensive lines. Much of this work was carried out in or near the front line, always within artillery range and often under small arms fire. Machinery of any kind was seldom available and, even if it had been, could not have been used so close to the enemy. Pioneers were therefore required to be men of strong physique, capable of carrying heavy loads, and working long hours with pick and shovel. Quite apart from their field engineering duties, all Infantry Pioneers were trained and equipped as infantrymen. They were fully capable of taking their place in the fighting line. This they did on many occasions, acquitting themselves with great honour. For all this, Infantry Pioneers were paid, regardless of rank, an extra 2d per day. Infantry Pioneer battalions were made up, at least in theory, of 50% tradesmen (particularly smiths, carpenters, bricklayers and railway gangers) and 50% 'pick and shovel' men (men used to doing heavy manual work in all weathers). Cornwall was an ideal county for finding such soldiers, with the tin mines in the west and the clay pits in the east providing exactly the sort of man-power required.

France, 1916-1918

Move to France, 21st-22nd May 1916

On 21st May 1916 the 1/5th, with a strength of 34 officers and 998 men, embarked at Southampton. It was commanded by Lieutenant-Colonel W.A. Bawden. Disembarking at Le Havre the following morning, it marched to a tented camp a few miles from the port at Sanvic. A few days later the Battalion entrained for a move by rail to the town of Merville. Here it came under command of the 61st Division with which it was to remain (except for brief detachments) for the rest of the war. Groups of officers and men were immediately detached, on a temporary basis, to more experienced Infantry Pioneer Battalions to learn more of their trade.

At about this time Private Stevens was awarded the Military Medal for advancing alone into no-man's-land under heavy fire, to rescue a wounded comrade who had been partially buried by an exploding shell. Sadly, Stevens was killed two months later.

The Laventie Area, Summer & Autumn 1916

For the remainder of the summer and autumn of 1916 the 61st Division remained in the sector of the line between Neuve Chapelle and Armentières, the 1/5th being based in the village of Laventie.

The great battles of the Somme, sixty miles to the south, had been launched on 1st July. Although the 61st Division played no direct part in the offensive at this stage, it was required to put in a strong diversionary attack in the area just east of Laventie on 19th July. This was timed to coincide with the attacks on Delville Wood, Longueval and High Wood in the Somme area, and was intended to dissuade the Germans from moving men away from the comparatively peaceful Laventie sector to the raging inferno of the Somme. No ground was taken, and losses were heavy. The battle did however achieve the intended aim of tying up significant German formations that could have usefully been employed to the south. It was during this action and in the subsequent weeks that the 1/5th found themselves holding portions of the line in their infantry role.

The Battles of the Somme, 28th October-20th November 1916

On 28th October 1916 the Battalion started its march south towards the Somme. It was a pleasant and surprisingly leisurely move, through countryside untouched by war. When the Battalion reached Beaumetz, commandeered buses and charabancs took it to a hutted camp near Aveluy whence, on 17th November, it marched to dug-outs between Contalmaison and Posières (four miles east of Albert). These dug-outs were, for the most part, merely large shell craters roughly covered with corrugated iron. The weather was by now cold and very wet, and these dug-outs did little to provide shelter from the elements. Although the great battle of the Somme was breathing its last exhausted gasps, there was still much work for Infantry Pioneers. The laconic entries in the War Diary stating 'The Battalion did pioneer work as usual' hide the reality of the nightly labour carried out under fire at the cost of many casualties.

On 11th November Lieutenant-Colonel Bawden, who had commanded the Battalion since its early days in England, handed over to Major T. Carus-Wilson. All through that winter the 1/5th worked unceasingly on the massive engineering work required to create some order out of the chaos, and it was with a considerable sense of relief that, on 3rd February 1917, the Battalion marched back to Acheux, where it entrained for the village of Longpré for training and well earned rest. Unlike the shell-torn wasteland of the

Somme battle-field, the countryside in this area was green and untouched by war. At last officers and men had a chance to rid themselves of the mud and grime ingrained in their clothes and bodies, catch up with sleep and take part in games of football. Reinforcements arrived from England, bringing the Battalion back to an effective strength.

All too soon this period came to an end. On 23rd February the 1/5th moved back to the Somme battle-field, being billeted in the ruined village of Herleville. Here it was engaged in the installation of trench drainage pumps, reinstatement of dug-outs and command posts and the repair of railway tracks, bridges and roads. Herleville itself was a verminous slum, of which an officer of the 1/5th wrote 'if Herleville was ever famous for anything it must have been rats. There were millions of them and they possessed such powers of assimilation that books, valise straps and clothing soon disappeared with comparative ease.'

On the day that the Battalion moved into Herleville, Private C. Lowther and two other men were digging a channel for a pump hose across the parapet of a trench when one of them struck an old French hand grenade with his shovel. It immediately began to smoke. With complete disregard for his own safety, Lowther unearthed the grenade and threw it into a nearby shell hole where it exploded. But for his very prompt action, all three men would probably have been killed. Lowther was awarded the Military Medal.

The German retreat from their old line on the Somme to the newly prepared Siegfried-Stellung Line (or Hindenburg Line as the British called it) commenced on 14th March 1917. They moved back in good order, leaving the maximum havoc in their wake. Bridges were blown, trees felled across roads, and roads and railways cratered. In the 1/5th's area of operations the British follow-up covered a distance of about twelve and a half miles, in which there was a vast amount of engineering work that had to be carried out without delay. Royal Engineers and Infantry Pioneers worked round the clock to open up communications to the front. A new skill had to be learnt, and learnt quickly, for the Germans had liberally laid booby traps to kill or maim the unwary. The neutralisation of these devices became an urgent priority and a highly dangerous task.

The third battle of Ypres, 9th August-14th September 1917

The third battle of Ypres is now commonly known as the battle of Passchendaele. Although the 61st Division was held in reserve, this did not mean that there was much rest for the Pioneers. As the battle raged ever more fiercely, so did the requirement for field engineering work increase. Most of this involved the laying and constant repairs of plank roads, the construction of a light railway, the digging of trenches for telephone lines and the erection of barbed wire defences. Nowhere was safe in the Ypres Salient, where every road and track was subject to heavy artillery fire or aerial bombing. Barbed wire and picquets had to be brought forward by night, carried by mules or pack horses. These poor animals did not take kindly to the shelling, and the task of persuading them to move in the required direction was never a popular duty.

The 61st Division remained in the Ypres Salient until mid September, when it moved back to the Arras Sector.

The Battle of Cambrai, 20th November 1917

The Arras sector was at that time extremely quiet. Two companies occupied dry and comfortable dug-outs in the railway cutting near Athies while the other two companies worked in the forward area, constructing a new road that was to form the principle line of communication should the Germans retire. This situation was, however, too good to last. On 20th November the now famous tank attack was launched in the Cambrai area, in which six infantry divisions supported by 420 tanks were to smash a hole through the German line at a point where it was least expected. Initially the British attack met with unprecedented success but, as so often in the battles of the Great War, the reserves were not able to exploit the break-through quickly enough.

By 30th November the Germans were sufficiently recovered to mount a series of counter attacks against the British salient. The 61st Division were hurriedly moved from the comfort of Arras to the battle-field of Cambrai, where the 1/5th was put to work digging trenches and erecting barbed wire for the hard pressed infantry to fall back on. The work was hard and dangerous, and the weather bitterly cold with heavy snow storms. The Battalion left the Cambrai salient on Christmas Eve 1917 without any regrets.

The German Offensive, First Phase

Battle of St Quentin, 21st-31st March 1918

After leaving the Cambrai salient, the 61st Division moved south to relieve troops in the St Quentin area on the Hindenburg line. During the early part of the year all was comparatively quiet, although rumours abounded of the expected major German offensive. Trench lines were constructed at intervals, many miles back from the front, in case of the need for withdrawal. In February a number of officers were posted in from the 6th Battalion, which had been disbanded as a result of the reorganisation of infantry brigades from four to three battalions.This coincided with a similar reduction in the establishment of a Pioneer battalion from four to three companies, with the result that, almost for the first time in the war, the 1/5th had a welcome surplus of officers.

On 20th March 1918 a warning was circulated to all forward troops that intelligence sources had reason to suspect that the long awaited offensive might be opened the following day. That night was, however, exceptionally quiet, made more so by a thick ground mist which covered the front.

At 5 a.m. on 21st March every German gun and mortar on the Somme front opened up with high explosive and gas. The signal 'Man battle stations' was sent out at 5.30 a.m. The Battalion, less B Company, quickly assembled and moved into a line of redoubts immediately behind the forward trenches. B Company was in the meantime lost (all communications having been destroyed). All through that day the fog persisted. The men manning the reserve line peered into the murk, listening to the noise of battle but unable to see anything and ignorant of the situation ahead of them.

At about 1 p.m. on 22nd March, A and C Companies and Battalion Headquarters were ordered to withdraw to a position north east of Germaine, where they began to dig in. This task had just been completed when orders were received to withdraw again to Canizy, about fifteen miles west. They arrived there at about 8 p.m. and proceeded once again to dig in. At about 3 a.m. on the 23rd March the position was subject to machine-gun and artillery fire. Thick fog still covered the ground, making it impossible to take stock of the situation. Stragglers from various units were making their way back through the Cornwall's position, many of whom appeared to be headquarters clerks, laden with books and files. Nobody, however, was able to give any accurate picture of what was happening in the front line. New orders were received at about 5 a.m. for the 1/5th to withdraw to a cutting on the line of the Nesle-Ham railway, and to dig in. There they found the Battalion Headquarters of 7 DCLI, together with many stragglers from the 61st Division.

At about midday on 23rd March the 1/5th, less B Company, was ordered to mount an immediate counter attack on the village of Verlaines, together with part of 2/4th Battalion the Oxfordshire and Buckinghamshire Light Infantry and stragglers from various other units. There was no time for reconnaissance, orders or briefing. The composite force moved out of the railway cutting and deployed into battle formation about 4,000 yards from the objective. 7 DCLI was holding this area, and its band played the Regimental March as their comrades from the 1/5th deployed. It seems quite remarkable that at that stage in the war an infantry battalion should have had its band, complete with instruments, right up in the front line. It was perhaps the last time in history that British troops were played into battle. In spite of very heavy fire, the 1/5th pushed forward and captured Verlaines. The Battalion then advanced out of the village and drove the Germans off a dominating ridge to the immediate north. This brilliant action by a battalion of Pioneers was carried out with such bravery and determination that the 1/5th were specially mentioned in Field- Marshal Sir Douglas Haig's official despatch of the German offensive. The cost however had been high, and those killed included Captain N. Tyacke, commanding A Company.*

During the rest of 23rd March several counter attacks were made by the Germans, each of which was beaten off. An enemy aircraft also strafed the position with machine-gun fire, causing many casualties, until shot down with rifle and Lewis gun fire.

On the morning of 24th March the Germans put in attacks against the front and flanks of the Cornwall's position (both flanks were open). It was perhaps lucky that the fog persisted, allowing A and C Companies to fall back to a reserve position at Herly. It was here that B Company, which had become lost on the first morning of the offensive, rejoined the Battalion. In what was literally 'the fog of war' they had found themselves, at dawn, in another brigade position. Peering over the parapets of their trenches, they could see only a few yards ahead. Suddenly the mist rose a few feet, and there, twenty yards to their front, was a solid mass of German infantry advancing in close order. B Company put down rapid fire for ten minutes, causing terrible slaughter in the massed German ranks. However, French Colonial troops on the right flank had given way and B Company was forced to retire, finding, doubtless to their astonishment, that they were mixed up with men from the 183rd Brigade. From there B Company had fought its way back until joining the Battalion Headquarters on 25th March, where it was warmly welcomed by Lieutenant-Colonel Carus-Wilson, who had just returned from leave. Soon after this, in a skirmish, he was mortally wounded while spotting for a Lewis gun. As he was being carried back, he said to his soldier servant Private Stacey "Give my love to the

*The father of David Tyacke, an officer who was to have a distinguished career with the Regiment during and after the Second World War.

Battalion." This was his last message to the 1/5th, for he died in the hospital train two days later. It was a great blow, for he was much cherished by all ranks for his unselfish bravery, kindly disposition and interest in the welfare of his men. It was said of him, "If you want to find Carus-Wilson, you will find him in the line".

On 28th March the Battalion was resting in billets at Marceleave when at 5.30 a.m. it was subjected to heavy shelling. At 1.30 a.m. it moved into trenches on the high ground 2,000 yards south of the village which, by the following dawn, had become the British front line. As the day proceeded the Germans shelled this line unmercifully, driving back the unit to the right of the Cornwalls. This necessitated a withdrawal back to a previously dug line of trenches in front of a feature known as Hangard Wood. No sooner were they secure in these trenches than orders came to counter-attack the high ground. Inspite of the greatest determination of the two battalions taking part, two attacks failed. Nightfall found the 1/5th back in the Hangard Wood trenches, consolidating the position. That night, 30th-31st March, it was relieved by an Australian battalion.

So ended the part played by the 1/5th Battalion in the battle of St Quentin. At a time when the outcome of the entire war hung in the balance, the 1/5th had made a significant contribution to the action which had absorbed, slowed down and finally halted the massive German offensive.

It must be remembered that in the first four days of the battle no one in the Battalion had any proper sleep or hot food. These were not fresh soldiers; they were exhausted men, held together by a sense of pride and comradeship, who fought against overwhelming odds with quite remarkable courage. During the terrible days of the St Quentin battle, these Cornish Pioneers showed themselves truly worthy of the highest traditions of the Duke of Cornwall's Light Infantry. Sadly, the price had been high; between 21st and 30th March the Battalion lost 214 casualties.

While in the rest area, the 1/5th received a draft of 423 men from its sister battalion back in England, the 2/5th. At this stage of the war Britain was scraping the barrel for men, and the standard of drafts being sent to France reflected this serious shortage. The reinforcement from the 2/5th were conscripts who had only had a few weeks service; they were all under the age of nineteen and had done no field training; many were medically downgraded, and few seemed to have the slightest idea of discipline. They were brought out to France by an unfortunate Major in the Oxfordshire and Buckinghamshire Light Infantry who, with the aid of just one experienced warrant officer, succeeded in shepherding this unruly rabble to their new battalion. It is remarkable that this unpromising material was to be thrown into battle within the week, and would acquit itself with great honour.

The German Offensive, Second Phase

Battle of Estaires, 10th-11th April 1918

Foiled in his attempt to break through the Allied line on the Somme, the enemy now turned his attention to the northern sector between the La Bassée and the Ypres-Comines canal. The attacks were launched at dawn on 9th April against a Portuguese division, which soon broke and scattered. The Germans immediately pushed through the gap, turning north and south against the now vulnerable Allied flanks. The situation was serious indeed. Troops which had previously been in action on the Somme were hurriedly despatched north, as quickly as trains could be made available. The 61st Division moved throughout the 10th April, with the 1/5th Battalion leading. On arrival at the northern rail-head, it came under command of 153 Brigade of the 51st Division, and at 2 a.m. on 11th April was ordered forward to take up a blocking position east of Merville. The march was severely hampered by streams of refugees and demoralised Portuguese stragglers blocking the roads, but by dawn the Battalion was reasonably well dug in, in spite of heavy machine-gun fire. The Germans shelled the position all day, and at 6 p.m. put in a determined attack. This was initially held off, but by 7.30 a.m. the following morning (12th April) both flanks had been turned, and the Battalion was forced to withdraw to a line in front of the village of Calonne. Again the flanks were turned, and the Pioneers had to withdraw back across the canal. This was effected under heavy machine-gun and rifle fire, resulting in very heavy casualties. The final line taken up ran west of the village of Le Sart, which the 1/5th held till midnight on the 12th-13th April, when it was relieved by fresh troops moving up from the south, and returned to the 61st Division again. By the 17th April the German offensive had ground to a halt, and after being relieved at midnight on 12th-13th April the 1/5th took no further part in the battle. Its losses had been terrible; no less than 16 officers and 467 soldiers had been killed or wounded. Many of the latest draft that had joined a few days previously were now dead. It had certainly been a rude initiation to war for these young, untrained men. They had played their part with great courage in one of the most critical battles of the war. For forty-eight hours they had performed like veterans, standing firm when their positions were repeatedly outflanked and they were subjected to lethal enfilade fire. In the near chaos of the subsequent withdrawals they had shown discipline that was certainly not apparent when they joined the Battalion. The 1/5th had demonstrated once again that they were not only Pioneers, but very fine infantrymen as well.

Active defence, April-August 1918

For the next few months the 61st Division remained in the area of Ypres, and the 1/5th reverted to its role as Pioneers. The German offensive had been stemmed and there was now an enormous requirement for the construction of defensive works on the newly established line. At this time the Battalion was commanded by Lieutenant-Colonel P. Carew. In recognition of the many acts of bravery performed by officers and soldiers during the recent German offensive, the following awards were made:

MC
Captain R.C. Coatsworth (RAMC)
Captain B.S. Hodge
Captain J. Trehane
Lieutenant J.M.F. Chomley
Second Lieutenant F.H. Edwards
Second Lieutenant A. Green

Bar to MC
Lieutenant L.S. Leverton

DCM
Private H. Hale

MM
Serjeant W.G. Bishop
Serjeant F. Trebell
Corporal H.H. Cradock
Lance-Corporal H. Hooper
Lance-Corporal W.G. Inch
Private T.D. Bennett
Private F.J. Langdon
Private R.L. Matthews
Private W. Osborne
Private T. Penhale
Private W. Redmond

MSM
Lance-Corporal S. Hoblyn
Lance-Corporal F. Treverthan

As has already been stated, the 1/5th Battalion was mentioned in the Commander-in-Chief's despatch. It is believed that this was one of only twelve cases of individual units specifically nominated in the Commander-in-Chief's despatches throughout the war. Praise indeed.

The breaching of the Hindenburg Line, August 1918

The Allied advance that was to lead to victory was launched on 26th August 1918, with the 61st Division in the van. As the Germans withdrew they cratered roads, destroyed bridges, and left a mass of booby traps and delayed-action mines. All this placed a severe strain on the resources of the Pioneers. The searching of houses for booby traps and their subsequent neutralisation called for steady nerves and the quick acquisition of new skills.

Final Advance to Victory

The battle of the River Selle, 17th-25th October 1918

The battle of the crossing of the River Selle marked the last of the actions against a really determined enemy. Although the Germans continued to offer resistance after being driven off this obstacle, they appeared to have lost heart, realising that their position was hopeless. The River Selle, a tributary of the River Escaut, runs north-south along the front about ten miles east of Cambrai. It provided a natural defence line, made more formidable by major field works. The 61st Division was heavily engaged on the northern flank of the British 3rd Army; once again, the 1/5th together with Royal Engineer companies provided considerable engineering support, building bridges and repairing roads.

Battle of Valenciennes, 1st-2nd November 1918 & from the end of the war to December 1919

This was the final set piece battle of the war but, unlike the crossing of the River Selle, was fought against a largely demoralised enemy. By 1st November the Allied line had advanced twenty miles east of the River Selle. For some unexplained reason the battle of Valenciennes was never claimed by the DCLI as a Battle Honour. Be that as it may, the 1/5th undoubtedly performed a very arduous role, building six footbridges across the River Rhonelle just east of Artres, and a further road-bridge north east of the village. Their efforts won the warmest praise from the Commander 61st Division.

In the evening of 2nd November the 1/5th moved back to St Aubert for rest. The Battalion had seen its last action of the war. After the Armistice on 11th November 1918 it moved to Cambrai, Beaumetz, and finally, to Etaples. Here the majority of the soldiers who had been longest with the Battalion were demobilised, while their places were taken by young men from many other regiments. Throughout that winter the 1/5th guarded stores and dumps. With the war over, and every officer and soldier wishing only to get back home, this period of service must have come as a frustrating anti-climax. On 21st July it moved to Namur, and ceased to be part of the 61st Division – the formation which it had served so well. By the anniversary of the Armistice, the Battalion was reduced to a total strength of fifty all ranks. Finally, on 1st December 1919, Lieutenant-Colonel E.B. Ward, Captain G.F. Taylor, Lieutenant Quartermaster F. McAlister and thirty-five soldiers crossed to Dover and returned to the Territorial Headquarters in Bodmin.

THE 2/5TH BATTALION (TERRITORIAL FORCE)

The 2/5th Battalion DCLI (Territorial Force) was a second line Territorial battalion raised at Bodmin in May 1915 as part of the Wessex Reserve Brigade. This was soon after the amendment to the Territorial Regulations had been enacted, which made all recruits liable to foreign service. Its role was to train reinforcements for the 1/5th, and to provide its sister battalion with drafts when it eventually proceeded overseas. It was commanded by Major C.E. Whitford. Initially the Battalion was stationed at Whitchurch Down near Tavistock, but in the spring of 1916 it moved to Hursley Park near Winchester. as part of the Wessex Reserve Brigade. At this point its name was changed to the 5th (Reserve) Battalion DCLI, and Lieutenant-Colonel W.F. Parker, who had previously commanded the Regimental Depôt at Bodmin, assumed command.

IV. THE SERVICE BATTALIONS

* * *

18
The 6th (Service) Battalion

THE ORIGIN OF THE SERVICE BATTALIONS

On 6th August 1914 the Secretary of State for War, Field Marshal Lord Kitchener, persuaded the Cabinet that the existing British military organisation was wholly inadequate to meet the requirements for the prosecution of a war in Europe. That evening parliamentary approval was given for the strength of the army to be raised by 500,000 men; the following morning the newspapers carried the headline 'Your King and Country needs you', under which it was announced that 'an additional 100,000 men to His Majesty's Regular Army is immediately necessary in the present grave National Emergency. Lord Kitchener is confident that this appeal will be responded to by all who have the safety of our Empire at heart'. Men between the ages of nineteen and thirty were asked to volunteer for service.

Lord Kitchener had every reason to feel confident that young men would answer his call. Indeed, even before the newspaper announcement of 7th August, the recruiting officers throughout the country had been overwhelmed by applicants. Those who passed the necessary tests were immediately despatched to the various regimental depôts, where they were met by scenes of frantic activity bordering on chaos. Depôts were established to cope with intakes of some thirty recruits every eight weeks or so, and their small permanent staffs were totally inadequate to deal with such an unprecedented influx. There was insufficient accommodation and an almost total lack of uniform, equipment or weapons. Tents were procured and erected in every open space, married quarters were vacated for use by recruits, and billets were requisitioned near the barracks; old time-expired officers and NCOs were called back, and even police serjeants were drafted in to help the military. The problem of the supply of uniform, equipment and weapons was initially insoluble, and for many weeks these new recruits performed such training as was possible wearing the civilian clothes in which they had enlisted. The one thing that these young men had in abundance was enthusiasm; they certainly needed it in those early days.

On mobilisation the 3rd (Reserve) Battalion DCLI had moved from Bodmin to a tented camp at Falmouth. To ease the strain on the Regimental Depôt, many of the new recruits were sent there; however, by the end of August the pattern of the 'New Army' battalions, for which these young men were destined, was beginning to take shape. They were known as New Army, Kitchener or Service Battalions and were identified by the word Service or the abbreviation S immediately after the battalion number.

THE 6TH (SERVICE) BATTALION

The senior DCLI (Service) battalion was the 6th; which was formed at Watt's Common, Aldershot on 4th September 1914. It was commanded by Lieutenant-Colonel T.R. Stokoe, a regular DCLI officer, who was destined to remain with the 6th throughout its existence. He was a big man, both in physique and courage. It must be understood that these New Army battalions attracted individuals from a very much wider range of society than from those who would previously have enlisted into the Regular Army. Two examples from the 6th Battalion stand out: Second Lieutenant R. McG. Barrington-Ward and Private F.H. (Ben) Keeling.

Barrington-Ward was one of three remarkable brothers, each of whom rose to the top of his selected profession. One became a distinguished QC while another was a leading surgeon. R. Barrington-Ward worked in the field of journalism, becoming the Editor of *The Times* from 1941 until his death in 1948.*

As a Second Lieutenant in the DCLI, he founded and edited the battalion journal, *The Red Feather*, from 1914 to 1916. Although the publishing of these journals was prohibited in war time, *The Red Feather* seems to have evaded the attentions of the Staff for two years. Unclouded by hindsight, *The Red Feather* was published as the great events were unfolding, and so provides an exceptionally clear picture of life in a Kitchener battalion; it is thus an important historical source. The production of the journal was carried out under somewhat rougher conditions than Barrington-Ward was later to find in *The Times* office. For much of the time it was printed on a press that had been discovered broken and abandoned in the rubble of Ypres. Having been laboriously repaired, it was set up in a cellar where it continued to give excellent service. We would like to believe that Barrington-Ward's experience in Flanders helped him up the

* Quite apart from his considerable skills as a journalist, Robert McGowan Barrington-Ward was a fine and dedicated soldier who would doubtless have achieved senior rank had he remained in the army. While serving with the 6th Battalion, he was twice mentioned in despatches and awarded the Military Cross for outstanding leadership in a bloody encounter at Sanctuary Wood on 30th July 1915. On that day the Germans launched a surprise attack on part of the British line, using flame-throwers. In the subsequent counter attack, after Major Jones-Parry had been killed, Barrington-Ward took over command of two companies. Casualties had been very heavy, but against all odds he drove the Germans out of their newly captured position and held it throughout that night, against repeated enemy counter attacks, until relieved by the 6th KOYLI. He was wounded at Bellecourt in 1917 and, after a short period of convalescence, was posted to the staff. During the last year of the war he was awarded the Distinguished Service Order and was mentioned in Despatches for the third time.

ladder of national journalism. Certainly as a result of his work on *The Red Feather*, he came to know and respect another remarkable member of the 6th Battalion whom he appointed Assistant Editor, Private (later Company Serjeant-Major) F.H. Keeling.

Keeling was born in 1886, the son of a modest middle-class solicitor living in the pleasant outskirts of Colchester. From his early childhood he questioned the structure of the society in which he found himself. Educated at Winchester, he stood out as the antithesis of the conventional English public school boy, hating games, but becoming fascinated by modern European history. He already thought of himself as a Socialist, and was by no means timid in making his views known. Although a great upholder of order, he accepted no rule without an examination of its meaning and purpose. As head of his house, he introduced clearly thought-out reforms. Orphaned at the age of seventeen, Keeling was awarded a scholarship at Trinity, Cambridge where he read for the History Tripos. During his years at Cambridge he founded the University Fabian Society, travelling widely in Europe during vacations to study the conditions of the working class. They were brave undergraduates who were prepared to stand up for their beliefs in the Cambridge of that time, and in his memoirs he recounts extraordinary stories of their rooms being wrecked and the vicious riots that were organised by the opposition to break up Fabian Society meetings. After being awarded a First in both parts of the History Tripos, Keeling remained at Cambridge for a further year studying Economics. In 1908 he moved to Walworth in East London, then one of the worst slum areas, where he flung himself into social work. As a result of a meeting with Mr Winston Churchill, he was then employed by the Civil Service organising the first Labour Exchanges. On the declaration of war he immediately joined the Artists' Rifles, a London based officer-producing battalion but, adamantly refusing a commission, enlisted in the Duke of Cornwall's Light Infantry at the end of August. He was posted to the 6th Battalion, just forming at Watt's Common, Aldershot. Keeling's descriptions of his initial reception at Bodmin, and life in a Kitchener battalion, are perhaps the most vivid and perceptive ever written. Having stood out so conspicuously as a rebel at school and university, he loved the atmosphere of order and discipline exemplified by a good infantry battalion, and became determined to make himself an outstanding soldier. His days with the Regiment were perhaps the most fulfilling of his life, and he was quickly promoted through the ranks to Serjeant. In France Keeling was sent on a bombing course, returning to his beloved 6th Battalion as the Serjeant-Major commanding the Bombing Platoon. These men performed perhaps the most dangerous of all infantry tasks. Keeling led from the front and was always to be found where the action was hottest. The end was inevitable; on 18th August 1916 he was killed, leading a bombing party at Delville Wood. Thus died a remarkable man; a courageous, unconventional example of the left-wing intelligentsia. To the end he never accepted rules that he considered unnecessary, and was probably the only British soldier to be allowed a beard (except for pioneer serjeants). In the early days back at Aldershot, when ordered to shave, he allegedly replied that what was good enough for the King of England was good enough for Private Keeling; a fine answer for an avowed Fabian!

France, May 1915-March 1918

Move to France, 22nd May 1915

After a period of intensive training at Aldershot and Witley, the 6th Battalion crossed to France on 22nd May 1915 as part of the 43rd (Light Infantry) Brigade of the 14th Division. The other battalions in this Brigade were the 6th Somerset Light Infantry, 6th King's Own Yorkshire Light Infantry and 10th Durham Light Infantry. It was the first time in history that Light Infantry battalions had been brigaded together, and the close ties of comradeship forged during these years of war were, in due course, to have a profound effect on the relationship between the six English Light Infantry regiments.

Actions at Hooge, July & August 1915

Throughout June and the first half of July the Battalion was attached to the 14th Brigade for trench warfare training. Lieutenant-Colonel Stokoe's remarks, following his familiarisation visit to a front line formation, are of considerable interest and are therefore attached verbatim at Appendix 3. Being a regular soldier with previous operational experience in both India and South Africa, he was by no means uncritical. In particular, he was appalled by the sanitary practices tolerated by units in the line, each one blaming its predecessor for the continuing absence of even the most rudimentary latrines. His service in the South African War, in which enteric fever and other intestinal diseases had claimed more lives than the Boer bullet, had made him acutely aware that the absence of strict hygiene discipline in the cramped and unsavoury conditions of the trenches could have even more devastating results.

On the night of 18th-19th July the 6th took over part of the line near Hooge, two miles east of Ypres, just in time to provide covering fire for an attack by the division on its right; the first shots to be fired by the Battalion against the Germans. This attack roused the enemy into violent retaliation, and the whole line was subjected to heavy artillery and mortar fire for the next week. Casualties were heavy, and included the Commanding Officer, Lieutenant-Colonel Stokoe, who was severely wounded.

The battle of Sanctuary Wood, 30th July 1915

The Battalion was relieved on 26th July, marching back to billets west of Vlamertinghe. They were however not destined for much rest, for at dawn on 30th July the Germans mounted an attack using a previously unknown weapon, the flame thrower. As the front line was driven back the 43rd Brigade were hurriedly moved forward to mount an immediate counter attack. This attack was carried out with great courage and determination against strong opposition on the high ground of Sanctuary Wood. All that day the trenches of Sanctuary Wood were held against repeated counter attacks. Casualties were high, 105 all ranks being killed or wounded (this included the Medical Officer, Lieutenant McG. McCallum, killed; a serious blow to a battalion engaged in such a bloody battle). All through the following day the counter attacks continued, eighty-five all ranks being killed or wounded.

On the night of 31st July-1st August the 6th Cornwalls were relieved by the 6th KOYLI, and moved back to Ypres. They had acquitted themselves in this, their first battle, with great honour, but the casualties in those two days of fighting at Sanctuary Wood had cost a total of 190 killed and wounded. Sadly, this was not the end of the story. Although the cellars and dug-outs of Ypres were comparatively safe, the city was subjected to almost continuous shell-fire, some of which was from very large calibre guns. At 6.30 a.m. on 8th August a 17 in. gun started shelling Ypres, firing for five hours at the rate of one shell every quarter of an hour. Little could stand up to these missiles, and the cellars and cloisters in which the 6th Battalion was billeted were reduced to rubble. The bodies of 2 officers (including the Adjutant) and 18 soldiers were recovered, while 2 officers and 19 soldiers were wounded. The bodies of a further forty soldiers were not recovered from the collapsed cellars of the Cloth Hall until after the war.

* * *

The last of the Ypres Salient, August 1915-February 1916

After the tragic events of 8th August 1915 the 6th Battalion was allowed a short period of respite behind the lines, where it could absorb reinforcement drafts and carry out training. On 29th August the Battalion returned to the front line in the Ypres Salient, where, even without much enemy activity, life was always hellish. The battlefield had become one vast stinking swamp, in which waterlogged trenches collapsed and the front line often consisted merely of half flooded shell holes. Men were perpetually wet, and as the winter months drew in, they also suffered from the bitter cold. Conditions in the salient tested men beyond the limits of normal human endurance, and made it the most loathed and feared sector of the entire Western Front. No tears were therefore shed when orders were received on 18th February 1916 that the 14th Division was to take over part of the front line from the French south of Arras. On that day Lieutenant-Colonel Stokoe, having recovered from his wounds, rejoined the Battalion. The new sector could not have presented a greater contrast to the salient. The trenches were dry, deep and well constructed. Equally important was the fact that this was perhaps the quietest part of the Western Front at that time.

The Battles of the Somme, 1st July-18th November 1916

The battle of Delville Wood, 15th July-3rd September 1916

The great Allied offensive on the Somme was launched on 1st July 1916 but it was not until the 15th August that the 6th Battalion was committed to the cauldron of battle.

The name of Delville Wood summons up all the most terrible images of the many Somme battles. Known by the soldiers as 'Devil's Wood', it was a piece of ground vital to the German defence, and it was fought over by day and night for almost seven weeks. On 18th August the 6th took part in one of the many attacks on the wood, capturing a small portion of the German position.

Of special note was the action of Second Lieutenant Jessup who, with the bombing platoon of twenty men led by CSM Keeling, was ordered to hold a position on the left flank of the battalion. Although subjected to repeated attacks, he and his dwindling band held their ground until relieved after twelve hours of almost continuous fighting. Second Lieutenant Jessup was awarded the DSO. For a subaltern this was a very rare decoration, indicating that he had almost certainly missed the award of a Victoria Cross by only a narrow margin. It was here that Keeling, who was perhaps as responsible as anyone for the determination of this gallant stand, was killed. A few days earlier he had been recommended for the award of the Military Medal, which was confirmed after his death. The Battalion had suffered heavy casualties, with 14 officers and 283 soldiers killed and wounded. It would be grossly invidious to differentiate between officer and soldier casualties in human terms, but officers took an appreciable time to train, and suitable material was becoming increasingly hard to find. The heavy attrition of officers, particularly in the infantry, was becoming a serious threat to the effectiveness of battalions in battle. It should be noted that since coming to France in May 1915 the 6th Battalion had lost a total of 31 officers.

The battle of Flers/Courcelette, 15th-22nd September 1916

The 6th Battalion remained out of the line throughout August and first part of September. During this period considerable progress had been made in securing the vital ground on the British right flank, with the capture of Delville Wood and Ginchy. Now it was time to exploit this success by driving the Germans off the next dominating ridge in the centre of the line, between the villages of Flers and Courcelette. This battle saw the first employment of two very important innovations: the tank, which for the first time provided a means of effectively crushing barbed wire; and the creeping barrage, behind which the infantry could be supported by artillery right up to the enemy trenches.

The 6th Battalion moved into the front line south east of Flers on 16th September and was straight away involved in an attack on the neighbouring village of Gueudcourt, which claimed very heavy casualties. 20 officers and 550 soldiers had gone into action at 9.25 a.m. that morning; by the evening 15 of those officers and 294 soldiers had been killed or wounded. The Battalion was relieved at 5 a.m. on 17th September and moved back to a rest area at Sus St. Leger. It was in no state to play any part in the final Somme battles.

The Battles of Arras

First battle of the Scarpe, 9th-14th April 1917

During the winter of 1916-17 the 6th Battalion was principally employed in a quiet sector of the front near Arras, and in training the new draft that were arriving to make good the losses suffered at Flers/Courcelette.

However, in April 1917 the British launched a series of attacks to capture Vimy Ridge and the Arras sector erupted in fierce fighting. The 43rd Brigade was placed on the right flank with the task of advancing up the line of the River Scarpe. The German positions were sited in considerable depths with a web of reserve trenches protected by broad belts of barbed wire. For this reason, the whole area was subjected to an exceptionally heavy bombardment for the four days before the actual attack. At 5.30 a.m. on 9th April, as the infantry advanced out of their trenches, the artillery bombardment was stepped up to what was described as 'a tornado of shell-fire'. Resistance was initially minimal, with large numbers of the enemy surrendering. Although the battle became somewhat confused during the next three days, considerable progress was made. On the afternoon of 11th April the Battalion was relieved, withdrawing to billets in Warluzel.

Back to Ypres

The third battle of Ypres, 31st July 1917

In May 1917 the 6th Battalion moved back to the dreaded Ypres Salient, in preparation for the coming British offensive. The Battalion was not involved until 22nd August, when it took part in two days of fierce fighting in which every attack was followed by counter attack without any appreciable gain of ground. The Battalion was withdrawn on 24th August, having suffered 350 casualties in two days.

The 6th took no further part in the actual fighting during the Ypres offensive. However, it was employed at the second battle of Passchendaele, between the 26th October and 10th November 1917, in the humble but absolutely vital task of carrying ammunition forward to the leading troops. By this time the whole battle-field had become so deep in churned up mud that men could drown if they slipped off the narrow duck-board tracks. Apart from the ever present danger from enemy fire, the back-breaking work and the freezing rain called for the greatest stamina, and demanded a high quality of leadership.

Battalions of the same regiment seldom met in the field, so it was quite an occasion when the 1st Battalion passed through the 6th at Kruisstraathoek on their way up the line on 28th October 1917.

* * *

The Ypres Salient, December 1917

The 6th Battalion remained out of the line throughout November, fully occupied with training. On 6th December it was warned to be ready to take over part of the front line in the Meetchaele-Passchendaele sector.

The physical conditions in this area were utterly appalling. No trenches existed, as the waterlogged ground made digging impossible. Men therefore lived as best they could in shell holes, from which there could be no movement during daylight hours. When night fell, carrying parties laboriously floundered through this featureless desolation, in an attempt to locate the shivering men in their shell holes with supplies of food, water and ammunition. Hot food was seldom available. It would appear from diaries that a battalion would spend about three days in the line, followed by two days in a rest area where men would attempt to clean themselves up.

The period of duty in the Ypres Salient had not been remarkable for any fighting, but the hardships had tried the officers and men to the very limits of human endurance. Belgian civilians watching columns of mud encrusted soldiers, singing bawdy songs as they marched back out of the line, never ceased to be amazed at the extraordinary robustness of the British infantrymen.

On 20th December the 43rd Brigade went into reserve. This brought little rest, for the reserve battalions were responsible for providing the carrying parties in support of the front line troops. At last however, on 26th December, the Battalion marched to Brandhoek where it entrained for Wizernes, and thence to comfortable billets in Boisinghem.

The Somme, 3rd January-1st February 1918

The 6th Battalion entrained at St Omer on 2nd January 1918 for a return to the Somme. The Battalion arrived at Bray-sur-Somme early in the morning of 3rd January, where it settled into billets. It was not till 21st January that the 6th moved forward into the front line, taking over trenches between La Fère and St. Quentin from the French. There it remained, without incident, till relieved by the 6th KOYLI on 1st February.

As the men got back to their billets, they heard sad news; the 6th Battalion was to be disbanded. Even with the introduction of conscription in 1916, the supply of suitable man-power had become insufficient to maintain the existing formations at a viable strength. At the end of March 1918, it was therefore decreed that infantry brigades should be reduced from an establishment of four to three battalions. The implementation of this reduction was extremely controversial at the time, Field Marshal Sir Douglas Haig and his formation commanders being in unanimous agreement that the 'square' brigade of four battalions provided the most effective fighting formation. Under normal conditions of trench warfare, this organisation allowed various permutations whereby battalions could be rotated between the front line and the rest area. With the reduction of brigades to three battalions, there remained the same requirement for front line duty with the result that battalions had less time out of the line to rest, re-equip and absorb reinforcement drafts. It is believed that it was not politically expedient to announce in Parliament that the critical shortage of man-power was resulting in the disbandment of brigades. However, in spite of military logic, the reduction of the brigade establishment from four to three battalions could be slipped through without the risk of political storm. Accordingly the 6th was disbanded, the majority of the officers and soldiers being crossposted to the 1/5th, 7th and 10th Battalions of the Regiment. Although they still belonged to the same regiment and wore the same cap badge, it was a bitter blow. Few of the original 6th who had crossed to France in May 1915 remained (32 officers and 696 soldiers had been killed, and many times that number had been wounded) but, despite such appalling casualties, the original spirit of this remarkable battalion survived to the end. The 6th was not only pre-eminent in battle, it was also a very happy and close-knit band of brothers.

19
The 7th (Service) Battalion

The 7th Battalion DCLI, the second of the Kitchener or Service battalions to be raised by the Regiment, was formed at Bodmin on 22nd September 1914, under the command of a retired DCLI officer, Brevet-Colonel H.G. Morrish.

It immediately moved to a camp near Woking, becoming part of the 61st (Light Infantry) Brigade of the 20th Division (the other battalions being the 7th Somerset (Light Infantry), the 7th King's Own Yorkshire Light Infantry and the 12th Kings).

Move to France, 25th July 1915

After a period of concentrated training the 7th crossed to France, arriving at Boulogne on the morning of 25th July 1915. Lieutenant-Colonel H. Ross-Johnson had just taken over command, which he sadly had to relinquish very shortly after arrival in France, due to ill health. Lieutenant-Colonel G.N. Colvile, DSO, late of the 2nd Battalion the Oxfordshire and Buckinghamshire Light Infantry took over command.

Initially the 61st Brigade was deployed with the 82nd Brigade for training and experience in trench warfare. The 7th was billeted at La Bolanderie near Armentières. On 5th September 1915 the Battalion took over front line trenches for the first time near Petillon. Two officers were wounded during this first tour of duty, the first of many casualties.

The Battle of Loos, 25th September 1915

The 7th Battalion played only a very small part in this battle, providing a noisy diversion to draw the enemy away from the main British thrust. The Germans reacted by shelling the Cornwall trenches, inflicting thirteen casualties.

The Winter of 1915-1916

The 7th Battalion remained in the area of Armentières during the winter. Although the enemy was extremely active, the chief concern of all ranks turned to the task of keeping warm and dry in the rapidly deteriorating weather conditions. Rain fell incessantly, flooding dug-outs and trenches, and making life utterly miserable. However, goat skin coats and thigh boots were becoming available, together with pumping equipment.

Less welcome was the reduction of the daily rum ration from two and a half to one and a half ounces. 'Typical of the orders emanating from old women at home' as it was described in the official War Diary.

The Ypres Salient, January-July 1916

On 1st January 1916 the Battalion moved north to the Fleurbaise sector of the Ypres Salient. If conditions had been bad at Armentières, they were infinitely worse in the Salient. The area was so waterlogged that trenches had collapsed, leaving men to shelter in shell craters as best they could. All through that winter the infantry endured terrible hardship. Not only was the weather awful, alternating between snow and rain, but the enemy was exceptionally active. The battalion suffered continuous attrition from the heavy artillery bombardments meted out by the enemy. The desolate landscape was reduced to a vast stinking swamp in which rotted the corpses of men and animals. As can be imagined, the evacuation of casualties became a nightmare. Tours of duty in the front line appear to have lasted four or five days, a long period under such conditions. On 11th April the Cornwalls repulsed the first major German attack, inflicting heavy casualties. One of the problems encountered was that both machine-guns and rifles repeatedly jammed, due to their being covered in mud thrown up by shell explosions. A battalion order was subsequently issued to the effect that the canvas breech covers were to be kept in place till the very last moment. Two officers, Captain W.W. Forestier and Second Lieutenant L.E. Oudin, were awarded the MC for their gallantry in this action.

All through that summer the routine of moving in and out of the line in the Ypres Salient continued. Life in the so-called rest areas was almost as uncomfortable and dangerous as that in the front line. 'Rest' was certainly a misnomer, as large working parties were always in demand to carry ammunition, food, water and defence stores up to the leading troops. Apart from being extremely hard work, the occupation was very hazardous; every road and track junction had been accurately registered by the enemy artillery, which would suddenly put down heavy concentrations of fire at times when carrying parties were likely to be active. Many casualties were sustained in this way.

The Somme, 22nd July 1916

The great Somme offensive opened on 1st July 1916, but it was not till 22nd July that the 20th Division was re-deployed south, ready to be thrown into the maelstrom. The Battalion marched for most of the way and, although feet had grown soft from nine months of comparatively static operations in wet conditions, the men stood up to the march well, completing stages of about sixteen miles on five successive days. Finally at Mailly Maillet the Battalion were accommodated in cellars; that night the position was shelled by a 5.9 in. gun causing many casualties, including two officers killed and one wounded. Later that same day Lieutenant-Colonel Colville was posted from the Battalion, his place being taken by Major R. Mander, a regular DCLI officer.

The battle of Guillemont, 22nd August-3rd September 1916

The 7th Battalion moved into the front line east of Trones Wood, facing the patch of devastated rubble that had once been the village of Guillemont. This, together with the mutually supporting positions of Delville Wood and Ginchy, formed the vital ground which was essential to the German defence. Each of these places was therefore fought over with the utmost ferocity over a long period. At this time the cordon around Guillemont was slowly closing but the enemy were far from beaten, and continued to shell the British line without mercy. During the next few days the operations in which the 7th took part appear to have become ever more confused. Orders and counter orders came in swift succession, each one necessitating weary and hazardous moves. An attack by the 61st Brigade was organised, then cancelled. The 7th Battalion was then hastily switched to the 59th Brigade, with orders to support the 10th King's Royal Rifle Corps and 10th Rifle Brigade. Loaded with digging tools and tins of water, the Battalion set out for Gullimont. The cratered, waterlogged ground made the going difficult and map reading nearly impossible. 10th King's Royal Rifle Corps, who had lost about eighty men earlier that morning from our own artillery, were located, but 10th Rifle Brigade could not be found. Due to the destruction on the ground, it was no easy task for the CO 7th DCLI to locate his ordained position at Guillemont and, as 10th King's Royal Rifles Corps had found to their cost, errors of map reading could have tragic results. However, by that night of 3rd- 4th September, the infantry was firm on the ground and consolidation was going well. The 7th Somerset Light Infantry was immediately ahead of the Battalion, together with groups from the 6th Oxfordshire and Buckinghamshire Light Infantry, which appeared to have become lost. All through the night heavy German shelling was accompanied by equally heavy rain. The following day the 7th was occupied in carrying back wounded men, and collecting the dead bodies of both British and Germans. Thus at long last the vital ground on which Guillemont had once stood was in British hands after one of the bloodiest and most chaotic battles of the war.

The battle of Flers/Courcelette, 15th-22nd September 1916

The village of Ginchy fell on 9th September, giving the British command of all the high ground on their right flank. Now the centre could advance to take the ridge between the villages of Flers and Courcelette. The 61st Brigade was attached to the Guards Division for this battle and saw no action on the first day. On 16th September the Brigade took part in a divisional attack. The 7th suffered heavy casualties before even crossing the start line, six officers being killed or wounded before zero hour. Captain Macmillan (acting CO) reorganised the company dispositions, and at zero hour (9.25 a.m.) the Battalion rushed the German trenches, capturing about a hundred prisoners. These dashed back to the British rear, running into their own artillery barrage, which killed about a third of them. At 10 a.m. the second phase of the attack was launched against very strong opposition, but by evening the ridge had been secured. The following day the 7th was pulled back out of the line. In the two days' fighting it had lost 180 all ranks.

The battle of Le Transloy, 1st-18th October 1917

With the high ground in the centre and left flank of the British position now captured, it became imperative to secure the dominating ground on the right flank around Le Transloy. The 7th Battalion relieved the 10th KOYLI on 29th September in the area of

Gueuedcourt, some 1,500 yards east of Flers and facing the village of Le Transloy, where the Germans were frantically digging in. On 1st October the Battalion moved three groups forward 500 yards, to secure a start line for the forthcoming attack. Each group consisted of ten riflemen, a Lewis gun detachment, two Royal Engineers and five strong men who could dig fast. Although only a minor operation, this was carried out with very great courage, successfully establishing firm posts within yards of the German trenches. That night men of the 11th Durham Light Infantry moved up, and dug trenches connecting these posts, which were then occupied by the main part of the Battalion. On 3rd October, the 7th was relieved and marched back to the reserve trenches in heavy rain, arriving there at 4 a.m.

On 7th October the Battalion returned to the line to take part in the final phase of this battle. In the absence of the senior 7 DCLI officer, Major Simcox, who had taken over command of the 61st Brigade, it was still commanded by Captain Macmillan. The attack went in against only moderate resistance, many prisoners being taken. At one point the remarkable spectacle could be seen of the advancing British line being met by a similar line of German soldiers who had emerged from their trenches with their hands up. Early on 8th October two companies were withdrawn to rest, leaving C Company acting as stretcher bearers. These rejoined the Battalion in billets at Meaulte the following day.

By this time the weather, seldom pleasant at the best of times, deteriorated to almost continuous rain. Trenches became muddy watercourses, and crater-pitted roads became impassable. There was to be one more battle before the Somme offensive closed, but the 7th Battalion was not involved.

In recent years Field Marshal Sir Douglas Haig has been strongly criticised for his conduct of the Somme offensive. It has been pointed out that the advance, which at its maximum point had captured 13,000 yards of ground, had cost the British army some 419,000 casualties. This is to miss the point. The primary aim of the Somme offensive had been to draw German divisions away from the hard-pressed French at Verdun. In this it was admirably successful. It is perhaps an unpalatable fact that by 1917 the war on the Western Front had degenerated into a war of attrition, in which both armies attempted to inflict massive casualties in order to grind down their enemy's capacity and will to fight. We tend to concentrate on the appalling British casualties, forgetting that those in the German army were considerably higher, and that for the first time many were surrendering in the face of infantry assaults. Although the British territorial gains may seem to have been modest, they included all the dominating ground in the newly formed salient, forcing the Germans into an untenable position. The true victory of the Somme offensive did not become fully apparent until March 1917, when the Germans abandoned their existing line and withdrew to the previously prepared Hindenberg Line, some twenty miles to the east. General Ludendorff later wrote:

> The decision to retreat was not reached without a painful struggle. It implied a confession of weakness bound to raise the morale of the enemy and lower our own; but as it was necessary for military reasons, we had no choice; it had to be carried out.

Thus were vindicated the terrible sacrifices and dogged determination of those young British soldiers in the newly raised Kitchener battalions. The tragedy of the Somme offensive was that it destroyed such a large part of the cream of British manhood, those men who had so selflessly volunteered for service in 1914.

The Third Battle of Ypres, July 1917

During April, May and June 1917 the Battalion was involved in various operations aimed at harrying the Germans back to that part of the Hindenburg Line which lay north of Havrincourt Wood. However, on 2nd July it entrained once more for the Ypres Salient. During the next few weeks it worked as pioneers, building a mule track up to the front line.

The battle of Langemarck, 16th-18th August 1917

The 7th was the only battalion of the Regiment to take part in this battle. The 61st Brigade were to attack with the 7th Somerset Light Infantry and the 7th KOYLI in the first wave, followed by the 7th DCLI and 12th Kings, which were to pass through as soon as the initial objectives had been secured. Throughout the night of 15th-16th August the battalions moved forward to the start line. There was heavy enemy shelling which, with the darkness and the cratered landscape of mud and water, caused the 7th to become split up, one and a half companies becoming temporarily lost.

Zero hour was 4.45 a.m., and the Commanding Officer and two and a half companies moved forward, following the 7th KOYLI. A few minutes afterwards most of the remainder of the Battalion, which had been located by Second Lieutenant E.M.C. Denny, arrived on the start line. Floundering about in the mud, and under heavy shell-fire, Denny had done a splendid job in locating these lost sheep and guiding them back to their proper place. He was awarded a well merited bar to his MC.

At about 5.15 a.m. the 7th KOYLI was held up by very heavy fire from a group of concrete pill-boxes to its front. Suddenly the opposition collapsed and British troops were seen around the pill-boxes, as Germans came out with their hands up. The former proved to be a platoon from the 7th DCLI under command of Captain F.C. Eary which, having lost its way, had been in a position to help the KOYLI. Seeing the situation, but still being out of contact with his battalion headquarters, he used his own initiative to move round the KOYLI flank and attack the pill-boxes. He was awarded the MC for this action.

During the afternoon the gains were consolidated, in spite of counter attacks. However, soon after 7 p.m. the 10th Kings on the right of the Battalion were driven back, leaving the 7th Battalion flank open. Serjeant J.N. Mitchell immediately moved a platoon round to face the crisis, which succeeded in holding off the attackers till darkness fell and the line could be restored. Serjeant Mitchell was awarded the DCM for 'his magnificent coolness and courage during the enemy's attempt to turn the flank'. Although only small gains were made in this battle, the village of Langemarck had fallen to the British. The 7th Battalion had recovered from the initial confusion, and gone on to achieve every one of its objectives against considerable resistance. The cost, however, had been high, 179 all ranks being killed or wounded.

As has been noted, the waterlogged state of the ground had made the digging of deep trenches and dug-outs impossible. The German solution to this problem had been the construction of concrete pill-boxes, sited in depth in mutually supporting positions. These strong points, each containing at least one machine-gun, were proof against small arms fire and all but a direct hit by medium artillery. By their nature, they were often capable of holding on even after being by-passed by the attacking line, thus creating mayhem amongst the reserves. The neutralisation of these concrete fortresses required a rapid rethinking of tactics.

The 7th were withdrawn on the night of 17th-18th August, moving by train to a tented camp at Proven. Here a draft of 50 men brought the Battalion's fighting strength up to 380.

The battle of the Menin Road Ridge, 20th-25th September 1917

The 7th were not left long in peace. On 24th August it again moved to Elverdinghe, where it operated as pioneers under the Royal Engineers. The heavy rain added to the discomfort of working in deep mud. On 19th September the Battalion relieved the 17th Royal Welch Fusiliers in reserve, and the following day relieved the 10th

Welch Regiment in the support line near Langemarck. There it came under heavy German artillery fire, which claimed several casualties. During this period in reserve the Battalion was employed on battlefield salvage, recovering the debris of war, including 250 rifles and 2 Lewis guns.

The battle of the Menin Road Ridge took place between 20th and 25th August 1917. The 61st Brigade remained in reserve, standing by at fifteen minutes' notice, but was not used till 23rd August when it moved into the newly captured front line.

The battle of Polygon Wood, 26th September-3rd October 1917

The third battle of Ypres consisted of a number of comparatively small set- piece battles, each with a limited objective, followed by a period of consolidation during which artillery and ammunition were moved forward. Following the capture of Langemarck on 18th August, the next attack was carried out south of the Menin Road. The 20th Division was not directly involved but its units including 7th DCLI, which were in the front line, received their share of heavy shelling and aerial bombing. On the night of 26th-27th September the 7th DCLI was relieved by the 7th KOYLI, the former moving right back to a rest area near Lechelle, which was finally reached on 3rd October. This was to be the end of the Battalion's involvement in the third battle of Ypres. It had been in action for the greater part of 171 days, albeit not always in the front line. At the battle of Langemarck it had overcome the most testing conditions of terrain and played a major part in the outcome of the battle. During this period the Battalion had lost 184 all ranks.

The Battle of Cambrai, 20th November 1917

The 7th Battalion was, however, to be denied rest. The day after arriving at Lechelle it marched to another camp at Haut-Allaines, and then on 8th October to yet another camp at Heudecourt. The following night, in wet and stormy weather, it moved into the front line, taking over from the 13th Green Howards. There were no forward trenches, the line consisting of a number of shell craters each garrisoned by a section. Patrolling of no man's land took place each night, but not a single German was encountered. The enemy artillery, machine-guns and mortars were however active, and made life far from pleasant. On 16th October 7 DCLI moved back into support, and on 9th November moved down to Bray-sur-Somme for training with tanks. It was not till 18th November that the Battalion went back into the line near Cambrai, relieving the 10th King's Royal Rifle Corps. The following day there was great activity as the Commanding Officer and Company Commanders reconnoitred the ground with Tank Corps officers, pinpointing the forming up places for the tanks and deciding on their lines of advance. At 4.30 a.m. on 20th November the assaulting troops were in position, drawn up behind the first wave of tanks on the start line. Complete secrecy had been maintained, and there had been no preliminary barrage. All was unnaturally quiet. 7 DCLI was in the van of the 20th Divisional attack, with A and B Companies in the first wave and C and D in the second. At 6.10 a.m. the first wave, preceded by tanks, started to move forward, followed ten minutes later by the second at zero hour. At that moment, the massed divisional artillery opened fire. Surprise was complete. By that evening success had been achieved on all parts of the line, and throughout the night there was frantic activity to consolidate the gains. The 7th had lost 79 all ranks, which was a modest price for such great success. The following morning it moved back into support.

German counter attack at Cambrai 30th November-6th December 1917

The Germans, however, were certainly not prepared to see the situation rest. Almost immediately German aeroplanes appeared above the newly won position, searching out details of the British deployment, and by the last day in November it became obvious that the Germans were preparing a counter attack on a very considerable scale. On 29th November the 7th DCLI was in support of the 7th Somerset Light Infantry and 12th Kings, ensconced in old German trenches. At 5.30 a.m. on 30th November the German artillery opened fire on the entire Cambrai salient, the heaviest concentrations falling on the 20th Divisional sector, and hence much of it on the 7th Battalion. At about 7.15 a.m. it became obvious that an attack was imminent. Soon afterwards, German infantry were seen advancing. Major J.B. Macmillan, who was commanding the Battalion, ordered two companies forward to positions from which they could put down the maximum fire. During the day the enemy made attacks, each one being met by heavy rifle and Lewis gun fire. However, their numbers told, and the 7th was forced to withdraw a few hundred yards west as the enemy came round both flanks, threatening to surround it. That night the Battalion was relieved. It had suffered about 162 all ranks killed, wounded or missing. Nevertheless, German casualties had been far higher; even after three years of war, they had failed to appreciate the lethal effects of British rapid rifle fire, and continued to attack in massed ranks.

After a short period of rest at Wallon Cappel, the 7th moved back into the Ypres Salient on 6th January 1918. The enemy appeared to be showing little active aggression, and once again the main enemy was the cold, the wet and the mud.

The German Offensive, 21st March-5th April 1918

On the morning of 21st March 1918 when the Germany army launched its massive offensive in Picardy, the 7th Battalion was in billets in Flavy-le-Medleux. It is interesting that at that time the Medical Officer was a doctor seconded from the US Army. The heavy casualties suffered by the RAMC, who were not easily replaceable, had meant that the British army was leaning more and more heavily on the USA. These doctors brought important expertise (including the technique of blood transfusion) to the RAMC. The 7th had recently received a draft from the 6th Battalion, which had been disbanded on 1st February. Amongst this draft was the complete 6th Battalion band.

The German offensive had been fully anticipated by the British, although the exact date was unknown. On the evening of 20th March the Battalion was turned out in fighting order, ready to move at immediate notice. Later that night it was stood down. Next morning the first news of the German attacks began to filter through, and at 7 p.m. the 7th once again turned out in fighting order, each man carrying 220 rounds of ammunition, and marched to a blocking position on the St Quentin canal. Here it dug in. However, the Battalion was not destined to remain in this position long, for at 2.30 a.m. on 22nd March orders were received to withdraw back to Ollezy, and again dig in, forming a reserve line in rear of the 12th Kings and 7th Somerset Light Infantry. During the 23rd these two battalions were heavily involved with the leading German troops, gradually falling back on Ollezy. In order to maintain depth in the defence the Cornwalls fell back again, and once again dug in. At 4.30 p.m. that day the 12th Kings withdrew through the Battalion position, leaving the Cornwalls holding the front line. This they did till 10 a.m. on 24th March, when fresh orders were received to fall back and take up a position between the villages of Gugny and Eaucourt. As the battalion was about to move, the Germans put in a determined attack. The 7th Battalion fought a skilful fighting withdrawal, inflicting heavy casualties on the enemy. Barely was the new defensive line reached than the 7th found itself with both flanks unprotected, making another very fierce rear-guard action imperative. Both sides lost heavily.

While the Cornwalls were still frantically digging in at their allotted position at Villeseive, the French on the right flank withdrew *en masse*, forcing another major fighting withdrawal on the hard pressed 7th, first to Fresnoy Les Roye and then back again to Le Quesnoy. On the morning of 27th March the 7th once more went into Brigade Reserve, behind the village of Beaufort, where on the following day it was relieved by a French battalion. It marched back to a wood near Demuin for rest. By this time units had become mixed up, nobody knowing what had become of a large proportion of the Battalion. An attempt was made to sort things out; stragglers rejoined, and men from other regiments were despatched to their own units. However, the rest period was to be short lived. During that day, news was received that the French had been driven out of their position. The remnants of the 7th DCLI were hastily moved forward to Meziers where they were heavily attacked and forced back to Demuin. The Battalion was driven out of this position and fought its way back to Hangard.

On 1st April 1918 the 7th Battalion was finally withdrawn out of the line for rest and reinforcement. A fleet of motor buses carried the survivors back to good billets at Quevenvillers.

The bare recorded facts of these moves and counter moves can never convey the intensity of the fighting. The British line had been pushed back some thirteen miles in this particular sector, but every foot of ground had been fiercely contested and the Germans had paid dearly for their gains. During that week few officers or men could have had anything but minimal sleep, yet they had stuck together in the face of fearful odds, knowing that the battle they were fighting could lose or win the war.

The 7th Battalion casualty figures speak for themselves. 18 officers were killed, wounded or reported missing, including the Commanding Officer (Lieutenant-Colonel Burges-Short), the Second-in-Command and the Adjutant, while 413 soldiers were killed, wounded or reported missing. Thankfully, many of the missing eventually found their way back to the Battalion or were reported as Prisoners of War.

Period of Regrouping & Active Defence May-August 1918

For the next three months the 7th Battalion carried out a programme of concentrated training, interposed with periods in the front line.

Not only was there an urgent requirement to assimilate some 300 reinforcements who had arrived from England, but new training directives were being issued from GHQ in anticipation of a great Allied advance, which would necessitate the re-learning of the skills required in the conduct of mobile operations by the whole army. Although the Germans were quiescent they were given no peace, being continually harassed by every possible means. During this period the Commanding Officer, Lieutenant-Colonel R. Mander, was severely injured when his horse fell on him. Major A.R. Scott assumed command. Although the Cornwalls were suffering very few casualties at this time fate dealt them a sad blow when, while at rest on 24th July, a German aircraft dropped a bomb on the camp, causing twenty-eight casualties.

Advance to victory, 6th September-17th October 1918

The final advance to victory was initially conducted in the Somme area, and was launched on 6th August 1918. However, it was not until this part of the front was well advanced that operations to the north, in Flanders, could be set in motion. As far as the 7th Battalion was concerned, their part in the Flanders offensive can be considered to have started at midnight on 26th September when two companies took part in a highly successful local attack. Second Lieutenant E.R. Lobb, commanding B Company, was awarded the MC for his coolness and gallantry during fierce fighting, which accompanied the unsuccessful German counter attack. On 1st October Lieutenant-Colonel Scott returned to England for leave, leaving Major D.M. Rose to command the 7th for the last momentous days of the war.

On 31st October 1918 the 61st Brigade was transferred to the Somme front, the 7th Battalion arriving at Bapaume by train early that morning, and then moving to Cambrai by motor transport. During the next eleven days the 61st Brigade remained in reserve, moving up behind the advancing troops. The 7th were to see no action in the last phase. By 11 a.m. on the 11th November 1918 the Battalion had reached St Vasst La Vallée. The war was over.

The 7th (Service) Battalion DCLI had served with fortitude on almost every sector of the Western Front for just under three years and four months. During the war it had taken part in more actions than any other battalion of the Regiment except for the 1st. Contemporary diaries note that when the fighting finally stopped on that November morning there was no wild exultation; just a profound feeling of peace and gratitude.

20
The 8th (Service) Battalion

England & France, 1915

The 8th (Service) Battalion Duke of Cornwall's Light Infantry was formed at Bodmin in September 1914, and immediately moved to Codford in Wiltshire. The Commanding Officer was a remarkable old soldier, Brevet Colonel J.H. Verschoyle who, like many other elderly retired officers, was called back to the Colours to raise a new Service battalion. Verschoyle had been born in 1854, and had been commissioned into the 46th Regiment of Foot. In 1882 he had fought at Tel-el-Kebir on the last occasion at which the British army wore scarlet in battle. By any standard, he was therefore too old to lead a battalion in war. However, at the age of sixty, Verschoyle had other ideas. When the time came for his Battalion to cross to France it was considered that he was so physically fit, his mind so adaptable to modern conditions and his popularity with his officers and soldiers so great, that he should continue in command.

In the following month, November 1914, the 8th moved to Bath, where it was billeted around the city. In May 1915 it moved to a camp at Sutton Veny for the final stage of training. On the night of 21st-22nd September the Battalion crossed to France as part of the 79th Brigade of the 26th Division, and landed at Boulogne. There, orders and counter orders resulted in a series of somewhat puzzling moves, first to Cachy for training in trench warfare until 10th October, then a long march to Larnotte. However, on arrival there the orders were changed and the Battalion marched back to Cachy. Thence, after another series of moves, it arrived on the Somme front near Albert. Two companies took over front line trenches on 29th October, while the remaining two companies were engaged in preparing a reserve line of trenches. The following day the Battalion suffered its one and only casualty in France, when Private Collier was killed.

The Balkans, November 1915-1918

Move to Salonika, 10th November-23rd November 1915

On 3rd November the 8th received orders to stand by for an immediate move to an undisclosed destination. Nine days later the Battalion learnt that it was to be transferred to the Salonika front. It moved by train to Marseilles, embarked on the morning of 23rd, and disembarked at the port of Salonika on the 27th November 1915.

Salonika, 27th November 1915-April 1916

The winter in Salonika brings snow and bitter cold. The War Diary reported on the day of disembarkation: 'Extreme weather. Heavy rain followed by snow and wind, extreme cold the whole time, freezing'.

The Battalion was immediately put onto the unglamorous but vital task of road building. Four British divisions were operating in this theatre, and the lines of communication were almost non-existent. Such tracks as did exist into the mountains were suitable only for mules, and it was therefore essential that roads capable of taking wheeled transport should be constructed without delay. The weather was vile and the work hard. There was no machinery of any sort available in the early days; picks, shovels and wheelbarrows were the only equipment used. During this period the 8th and the 2nd Battalion were working in close proximity. Christmas Day was celebrated by both Battalions in Lembet Camp. The party appears to have got somewhat out of hand, as the War Diary reports: 'A fracas of uncertain origin in which Greeks were concerned: in the promiscuous shooting which ensued, the 2nd DCLI suffered their first casualty in Salonika'.

The New Year brought little change to the grinding routine of road building. German aircraft appeared on the scene in January; it did little damage but caused considerable excitement. Those who could be spared from road building started mountain warfare training. The exercises, which involved the endless picqueting of the hill tops, required extreme physical fitness.

The Struma valley, April-July 1916

As winter gave way to spring the snow melted, but the flies and mosquitoes arrived. The 26th Division was poised to move up to the front in the Struma valley, which meant that the tempo of training was increased. On 19th April the Battalion said farewell to the Commanding Officer, Colonel Verschoyle. Aged sixty-two, and known to all ranks as 'Daddy Verscholye', this much respected and loved officer had shared all the discomforts and hardships of two years of war-time soldiering. The Divisional Commander, Major-General Sir Charles Mackenzie-Kenedy wrote a eulogy to him, which finished: 'A splendid, great-hearted man, to whom and to his like, the Country owes more than it perhaps realises.'

Verschoyle was succeeded by Lieutenant-Colonel F.C. Nisbet, seconded from the 2nd Battalion the Gloucestershire Regiment.

Lake Doiran, July-December 1916

On 20th July 1916 the 8th Battalion started the long march that was to take it to the front line, where it took over the Croix Blanche and St Pierre sectors from the 10th Devons. The Bulgar line was separated from the British position by a valley, some four miles wide. It was a quiet area in which the only military activity consisted of continuous patrolling with the aim of dominating this exceptionally wide strip of no mans land. At the end of October the 8th moved to the Lake Doiran area, relieving French Colonial troops in this very active sector. The Cornwalls occupied a feature in the centre of this front known as La Tortue, which came in for considerable shelling including bombardment from 8 in. guns.

As with all battalions operating in the swampy area of Lake Doiran, malaria took a heavy toll. Very few men who served in the Salonika theatre escaped this most debilitating disease, which not only strikes at the time of first infection but subsequently recurs periodically for many years. There was then no effective way of treating malaria, with the result that it often proved fatal.

Lake Doiran, Winter 1916-1917

Winter brought relief from the mosquitoes, which were replaced once more by the discomforts of snow and rain. The artillery bombardment continued, and was augmented by bombing from the air. On 26th January the Battalion position was attacked by 16 aircraft and the following day by 21 aircraft. Air attack cannot have been very effective as the Cornwall's casualties only amounted to three men wounded. At about this time Privates A. Thompson and H. Thompson were each awarded the MM for gallantry, and Second Lieutenant R.A. Thompson was awarded the MC.

Lake Doiran & Dova Tepe, Spring & Summer 1917

The spring brought renewed activity to the front, with probing attacks being launched, preparatory to a major offensive. Between 25th and 28th April the 8th was involved in one of these somewhat confused battles, the first taste of prolonged fighting in which it had taken part. Although initially held in reserve, the Battalion soon found itself in the thick of the action, mixed up with sub-units of the 8th Oxfordshire and Buckinghamshire Light Infantry and the 12th Hampshire Regiment. For their conduct in this battle, Lieutenant C.M. Maunder and Second Lieutenant J.W. Binge were awarded the MC, while Lance-Corporal W. Cuncliffe, Private J. Mansfield and Private R. Spanton were awarded the MM. Spanton's action deserves special comment. He and three others established a detached post to cover the flank of their platoon. They beat off several counter attacks, losing one man killed. Of the remaining three, two were wounded; yet they refused to withdraw. In the close-quarter fighting that ensued, one of them bayoneted three Bulgars in quick succession.

In August the 8th Battalion was withdrawn from the Lake Doiran sector and moved to the Dova Tepe sector where, on 1st September, it repulsed a heavy attack. Captain C.W. Turner was awarded the MC and Private R.J. Sparks the MM for defending his post single-handed although wounded, and bayoneting two Bulgars. It is perhaps interesting to note that although 'experts' claim that the bayonet was seldom if ever responsible for inflicting casualties, there are many well authenticated examples of its use in this particular campaign.

Ereselli & Lake Doiran, Winter 1917-1918

The Battalion saw in the New Year while out of the line at Ereselli. A splendid meal was served to all ranks, and the celebrations appear not to have provoked a 'fracas of uncertain origin' this time! Patrolling against the Bulgar lines continued. These fighting patrols were usually carried out in considerably greater strength than those on the Western Front, and often amounted to virtual battalion attacks. It became a point of honour for those taking part to withdraw at walking pace, maintaining perfect formation, even when under artillery fire. In fact, as one officer said, 'the high explosive was pretty harmless unless it hit you full toss, as it buried itself in the ground.' The swampy, mosquito infested marsh did have this one advantage.

The Battalion War Diary of that period records the award of the Serbian Order of Karageorge to Lieutenant-Colonel Nisbet, the MC to Captain I.B. Greig and Military Medals to Lance-Corporal W.J. Martin and Private J. Jones. At about this time Lieutenant-Colonel Nisbet left the Battalion to command a brigade, his place being taken by Major H.F. Smith.

Lake Doiran, Spring & Summer 1918

Aggressive patrolling continued but, as the spring of 1918 turned to summer, fewer and fewer Bulgars were met in no mans land. In July a determined effort was made to lure the enemy out of their defences by means of a complex dummy position, which was made to appear highly vulnerable to the enemy. Meanwhile, a large ambush force lay concealed to a flank ready to deal with any attack. Alas, not even this could lure the Bulgars to expose themselves. In June it was announced that Lieutenant-Colonel M.R. Dickson had been awarded the DSO; Captains F. Garland and F.A. Clemo, the MC; RSM A.J.S. Piddington, the DCM; and Serjeant A. Liggitt, the MSM.

Battle of Doiran, 14th-18th September 1918

During August and early September 1918 preparations were made to launch an offensive which, it was hoped, would succeed in knocking Bulgaria out of the war. The offensive was to take place along an eighty-mile front. Initially the French and Serbs would attack and capture the high ground in the centre of the Bulgar line, after which three British divisions would attack between Lake Doiran and Varder on the west, when a fourth would attack on the east flank. After a heavy artillery bombardment along the whole front on the morning of 14th September, the Allied forces started their advance. The 8th was involved in comparatively easy fighting on that first day, but four days later came up against formidable positions held by a well dug-in enemy. The Battalion attacked two objectives at 5 a.m. on 18th September. Although some progress was made against very determined resistance, the resolution and courage of the Cornwalls proved of no avail against the objectives. They hung onto the slopes of bare rock, which offered no cover from shot or shell, for five and a half hours. Furthermore, the temperature rose to about 100° Fahrenheit as the day progressed; their situation must have been similar to that of the 2nd Battalion at Paardeberg eighteen years earlier, when the wounded had lain in the scorching sun throughout the day unable to move. At about midday the Battalion was ordered to withdraw. Casualties amounted to fifty-four all ranks, including Captain R.A. Rendell who was wounded four times during the battle, dying as he was finally carried back on a stretcher. Corporal J. Fidler was awarded the DCM for conspicuous gallantry in this attack. The offensive continued the following day, but by this time the 8th were in reserve.

Capitulation of the Bulgars, 30th September 1918

The 8th again moved forward on 25th September, taking the lead in the Allied advance. It had the honour of being the first battalion to cross the border from Greece into Bulgaria. On 29th September the 8th made their final attack on the withdrawing Bulgars. Next morning it was preparing to continue the advance when orders were received ordering an immediate halt to operations, as the Bulgars were about to sign an armistice.

So ended the war for the 8th (Service) Battalion DCLI. It had played a full part in a campaign of which the public was largely ignorant, and in which there were no great battles to capture popular imagination. The Battalion, doubtless expecting dramatic fights with the Bulgars, had knuckled down to back- breaking manual work, building a road through a rocky wilderness without recourse to machinery. Officers and men had lived with little cover through blistering summers and bitterly cold winters. All had experienced the maddening torment of vicious mosquitoes, and most had succumbed to the debilitation of malaria. Finally, at the end of the campaign, the 8th had shown itself to be a courageous and battleworthy battalion.

21

The 9th (Service) Reserve Battalion

The 9th (Reserve) Battalion DCLI was raised at Falmouth on 29th October 1914 by Lieutenant-Colonel the Hon. H.W.H.S.F. Trefusis. Its role was one of home defence, and it never saw overseas service.

The 9th originally formed part of the 103rd Brigade of the 34th Division but, in May 1915, moved to Wareham where it became part of the 10th Reserve Brigade. It was finally absorbed into the various battalions of the 10th Training Brigade –one of the several large depôts at which infantryman from all over the West of England were trained.

22
The 10th (Service) Battalion (Pioneers)

Although 10 DCLI was destined to become one of the outstanding Infantry Pioneer battalions on the Western Front, little is known of its early history. The reason for this is that, in common with a few other units formed during that period of patriotic fervour in the early days of the war, the 10th was raised not by the War Office but by the Mayor and citizens of Truro. Thus, although it would seem that much of the Battalion's pay, clothing and equipment came from War Department sources, those who shouldered the daunting workload involved in raising a new unit from scratch gave their services free. Although the 10th first saw the light of day on 27th March 1915, no mention of its existence appears in the Army Lists until July of that year. To all intents and purposes it was a private army during those first few months.

The City of Truro appointed Brevet Colonel Dudley Acland Mills to be the first Commanding Officer. Mills had been born on 24th August 1859. He had been commissioned into the Royal Engineers in 1878 and had retired in 1909. Like so many dedicated elderly ex-officers, he put on uniform again to shoulder a formidable burden.

The only other officer in those early days was Sir Arthur Quiller-Couch. Although his father had held the appointment of Surgeon to the Royal Cornwall Militia in the previous century and his son Bevil was a regular officer in the Royal Artillery, Sir Arthur himself, a distinguished academic and writer, had had no military training whatsoever. The name of Mills did not occur in the Army Lists till October 1915, so one must presume that he was not paid during those seven months. Quiller-Couch was never officially gazetted as an officer in spite of the crushing burden of his work, believing only that it was his patriotic duty.

At that time Quiller-Couch was also heavily involved with his academic work at Cambridge, which included setting the English papers for the final degree exams. From March 1915 he was forced to devote all his energies to military matters, combining the duties of Adjutant, Quartermaster and Training Officer, wrestling with the tide of unfamiliar army forms, and attempting to keep one step ahead of his recruits as he instructed them in drill, fieldcraft and musketry. He seldom left his makeshift office before midnight. Dr Joan Coombs summed up his frenetic lifestyle in her book *A Fowey Jig-Saw*:

> Q's own battalion was 210 strong. After a hard morning's drill he describes taking them on a route march in the afternoon. He was considered to be an eccentric leader by his recruits. He insisted on them shaving every day and inspected their chins every morning at 9.30 a.m. The unforgettable eccentricity of this kindly leader was revealed on the day he took his whole company back home for tea after a route march. The day was fine and they sat at tables in the garden of the Haven and Lady Quiller-Couch provided them with teas until 'the cupboard was bare'. Even more bizarre was the day when the company was encouraged to swim in the sea and Q cut the overlong toenails of soldiers himself. No doubt many had feet made more comfortable by this almost biblical tender care.

By June 1915 the 10th Battalion had outgrown its makeshift billets in Truro and was moved to a temporary tented camp at Penzance; then, in October, it again moved to a more commodious hutted camp on the outskirts of Hayle. Anyone remotely familiar with unit moves must marvel at how this was accomplished by just two officers and a very small skeleton staff. They must have felt a great weight slip from their shoulders when, on 24th August 1915, the War Office announced that it would 'take over' the 10th Battalion. From that date a steady stream of officers and senior NCOs was posted in to take care of the many aspects of training, administration and discipline.

By 16th October there were sixteen officers on strength. Colonel Mills continued in command and, although there was still no Second-in-Command, he could boast an Adjutant and Quartermaster (albeit, both newly commissioned war time officers). By January the following year the Battalion was almost up to full establishment, though still lacking a Second-in-Command. Colonel Mills, whose immense labour of love had transformed this privately raised group of Cornishmen into a fully-fledged battalion, stepped down to make way for a new and younger Commanding Officer. Lieutenant-Colonel E.A.B. Alston of the Northamptonshire Regiment assumed command, and it was he that took them across to Le Havre on 20th June 1916, to join the 2nd Division as its Infantry Pioneers.

The role of Infantry Pioneers has already been explained in the chapter dealing with the 1/5th Battalion; it is sufficient to say that this role required physically robust tradesmen and labourers who were also fully trained in the skills of the infantryman. No praise can be too high for those two remarkable officers, Mills and Quiller-

Couch, who laid the basis of all that was to follow in the crucible of battle.

On the night of 19th-20th June 1916 the 10th crossed the Channel to Le Havre, to become part of the 2nd Division.

The battle of Delville Wood, 25th July-10th August 1916

For a month after its arrival in France the 2nd Division was out of the line, allowing the 10th Battalion to become acclimatised to active service conditions. However, the terrible battle of Delville Wood had been raging almost continuously since 15th July and, towards the end of the month, the Battalion moved up closer to this part of the front, being billeted in Vaux-sur-Somme.

Work under the Royal Engineers was carried out at Bernafay (1,500 yards south west of Delville Wood), and on the edge of Delville Wood itself. At 6.10 a.m. on 27th July, medium and heavy artillery opened up a terrific bombardment on the 160 acres of twisted devastation that had once been Delville Wood. At 7.10 a.m. the assaulting troops from the 2nd Division moved forward. Dazed and utterly cowed, Germans rose from the shell craters in which they had been sheltering, and surrendered. The fighting however was far from over; the German artillery continued to shell both Delville Wood, Bernafay Wood and Trones Wood with every available gun, and for the next week the enemy made frequent strong counter attacks. Delville Wood represented vital ground in the German scheme of defence, and was not a position that they were prepared to give up without a very bloody battle. During this period, from 27th July to 10th August, the 10th Battalion was in the thick of the fighting, working around the clock with little rest. Much of the work consisted of carrying ammunition up to the leading troops and digging trenches, but on at least two occasions companies were attached to other battalions to fight as infantrymen. On 10th August the 2nd Division, together with the 10th Battalion, was withdrawn to rest. The battle for Delville Wood (which finally fell on 3rd September) was so bitter and confused that it is difficult to piece the details together. Chance decreed that the 10th should receive their baptism of fire in what was arguably the bloodiest battle of the war – it was certainly one that British infantry soldiers looked back on with horror.

* * *

The battle of the Ancre, 13th-18th November 1916

After the 10th were withdrawn from Delville Wood it enjoyed only the briefest rest at Coigneux, before moving back into the front line on the River Ancre. At that time this was a comparatively quiet sector of the Somme front, which allowed the 10th to get on with the construction of field defences. It had been intended to launch the next phase of the Somme battle in this sector, but the thick mud prevailing around the Ancre valley had so far precluded this. However, by 9th November the weather had changed, and the rain was succeeded by frosts. The battle of the Ancre was launched on 13th November. The Battalion was heavily involved, digging new communication trenches forward to the advancing troops and constructing command posts and dug-outs. The 2nd Division was withdrawn to a rest area on 18th November 1916, but the 10th Battalion was soon back in the Ancre sector, carrying out pioneer work. Its chief tasks were laying trench boards, revetting the new front line trenches, excavating stone for ballasting the light railway tracks and improving these tracks. Most of this work was carried out at night, well within range of the enemy guns.

Throughout December 1916 and January, February and March 1917 pioneering work continued in the Ancre valley. It was an unglamorous task, but the Battalion, largely unseen in the cold wet nights, was performing vital work. But for its efforts, guns could never have been moved forward, nor ammunition, rations and water brought up to the infantry holding the front line.

German withdrawal to the Hindenburg Line, 17th March 1917

Unknown to British intelligence, the Germans had been busy constructing a strong fall-back position, which ran from Arras in the north to Missy in the south. This new line shortened the German front considerably, allowing their battle-weary divisions to be withdrawn for much-needed rest. The withdrawal was carried out with great skill during the nights of 17th-18th and 18th-19th March 1917. As the Germans withdrew they left roads cratered and blocked by trees, bridges destroyed and a mass of booby traps. The situation obviously demanded a huge pioneer effort to allow a quick follow up, and particularly to allow guns and their ammunition forward. The 10th were fully employed in this often dangerous work throughout the latter part of March and April 1917.

* * *

The Battles of Arras, April 1917

In April 1917 it was still vital that the maximum number of Germans should be drawn away from the French, south of the Somme. Much against his will, Field-Marshal Sir Douglas Haig was forced to continue his offensive in the southern part of his front. Thus the battles of Arras were launched on 9th April 1917.

The 2nd Division was not actively involved in the early battles of Arras. However, the 10th was present at the battle of the Scarpe on 23rd April 1917, being awarded 'Scarpe, 1917' as a Regimental Battle Honour.

On 28th April the 2nd Division attacked at Arleux. The Divisional History states:

> To the pioneers fell none of the glories of the front line fighting, but no attacking troops were ever served more faithfully than were the infantry of the 2nd Division by the 10th Duke of Cornwall's Light Infantry. For many hours on end, after strenuous labour on the communications within the Divisional area, these men went cheerfully forward and 'carried' for the battalions in the front line. They had to pass across shell swept areas and at times came within the enemy's barrage, but they stuck to their work with grim and splendid tenacity.

At the end of June 1917 the 10th moved north to the Ypres Salient, where it was detached to the 1st Division. On 17th July the 66th Division relieved the 1st Division, which entailed yet another change of command for the Pioneers. It would appear that the GOC 66th Division attempted to have the 10th Battalion permanently transferred to his command. This resulted in a very strongly worded letter from the GOC 2nd Division. An extract of this letter ran as follows:

> I can hardly believe that such a thing could be contemplated. In my letter through the Corps, I mentioned that the Cornwalls held the line for the Division at Delville Wood to relieve the exhausted infantry and that the deepest ties exist between the Division and their Pioneers.

August began with the usual hard work. Casualties had initially been light, but on 10th August the Battalion came under heavy shell-fire while at rest. During the bombardment Battalion Headquarters received a direct hit from a heavy shell. The Commanding Officer, Lieutenant-Colonel E.A.B. Alston, was killed and the Second-in-Command, Major G.B. Stratton, and the Adjutant, Lieutenant H.L. Slingsby, were mortally wounded. Captain H. Chapman immediately assumed temporary command, and appointed Second Lieutenant B. Crouch as his Adjutant. Lieutenant-Colonel P.D. Ironides took over command on 13th August. All this had been a traumatic blow for the Battalion, made no easier to bear by a steady toll of casualties over this period, which included many senior NCOs. On 1st October Lieutenant-Colonel Ironides was severely wounded, being replaced by Major G.E.A. Brown from the 11th King's Regiment on 29th October. Meanwhile the Battalion had been carrying out work which, even by the standards of the Ypres Salient, was especially hard and dangerous. The battles of Polygon Wood, Broodseinde, Poelcapelle and First and Second Passchendaele followed in quick succession. In that desolate, shell-swept, water-logged landscape, the Cornwalls worked day and night

At last, on 29th October, the 10th was pulled back out of the battle area for badly needed rest and reorganisation.

The Battle of Cambrai 30th November-5th December 1917

The 10th Battalion was heavily involved in the fierce fighting that accompanied the massive German counter attacks which followed the British victory at Cambrai. The initial artillery barrage opened at 8.45 a.m. on 30th November, surpassing anything that had previously been experienced, cutting communications and destroying trenches. Next, the German infantry advanced in mass formations. Every British weapon opened up, creating a prodigious slaughter. As their casualties mounted, the Germans threw more and more men into the maelstrom, with the intention of overwhelming the opposition by sheer weight of numbers. At the height of the battle two companies of the Cornwalls were supporting the 17th Royal Fusiliers, carrying much-needed small arms ammunition and grenades up to the leading elements of that Battalion. They toiled throughout that day under heavy artillery and machine-gun fire, and by their selfless action undoubtedly saved the Fusiliers from being overrun. Meanwhile, further to the left, the other two companies were performing much the same task in support of other units. In this sector these two companies actually held the line during the height of the battle. Thus passed the 30th November, a day of terrible fighting and of heroic deeds.

Christmas, 1917

The 2nd Division was pulled back into reserve on 1st December for four days' rest. On the 4th the Battalion again started work near the front line, digging new trenches and repairing old field defences.

There was to be no pause for much in the way of Christmas celebrations that year.

New Year, 1918

Work continued with the interminable task of digging ever more trenches and burying signal cables. On 5th January a draft of 100 men was despatched to the 7th DCLI while an equal number were posted in from the 1st Royal West Surrey Regiment. The latter were, however, all medically downgraded soldiers who cannot have possessed the robust physique necessary for the work of pioneers. On 10th January the Battalion moved back into the line. The trenches were in atrocious condition, the recent thaw rendering them deep in mud. Intelligence sources let it be known that a major German offensive (referred to earlier) could be expected, which increased the urgency of the need to repair and improved the defences. The Pioneers were allotted a sector of the line which they were to hold, should a major attack develop.

On 8th February the 10th received a draft of 4 officers and 192 soldiers from the 6th Battalion, the 6th having been disbanded on 1st February due to the man-power crisis. (See p. 250-251.)

The German Offensive, 21st March -5th April 1918

The fighting in which the 10th Battalion took part during the next week was exceptionally confused. The War Diary speaks of interminable moves and counter moves, the manning of front and reserve lines, and the haze of exhaustion through which officers and men continued to perform their duty. To chronicle this period would be impossible, partly because the action was so complex, and partly because the War Diary (not without very good reason) is at times of little help.

The War Diary emphasises two points: first, the efficiency of the Battalion cooks, who by careful planning and in spite of the general confusion, always managed to get hot tea and food up to the companies. This may perhaps seem a minor aspect, but anybody who has ever served as an infantryman will know the immense importance of a mess tin of hot, sweet tea and a slab of bully beef at times like this. Second, the morale of the 10th Battalion seems to have risen as the battle progressed. As men became ever more exhausted they seemed to have been gripped by a superhuman determination to hang on and kill Germans. One particular incident should be recalled. A platoon of X Company moving down a sunken lane came face to face with a somewhat larger force of Germans. A few minutes of desperate hand to hand fighting ensued, during which the entire German force was annihilated. All British officers were wounded and about twenty soldiers were killed or wounded. Captain A.W.H. Coysh was awarded the MC for his gallantry in this skirmish.

On 28th March the 2nd Division was withdrawn from the front line to reserve.

Period of active defence, 1st April-20th August 1918

On 31st March 1918 the 10th was billeted at Haute Côte where it received a draft of 208 men. After three days training the Battalion marched to Barly whence, on 13th April, it relieved the 4th Coldstream Guards (Pioneers). Enemy attacks were still anticipated and the Pioneers were allotted positions in the firing line.

On 4th June Captain J.G.G. Noble and Regimental Serjeant-Major W. Cleall were awarded the MC; Serjeant W.E. White was awarded the DCM; and Private F.C. Lister, the MSM.

Advance to Victory

The battle of Havrincourt, 12th September 1918

The British offensive on the Hindenburg Line opened on 12th September. The 10th Battalion was placed in support of the 2nd Highland Light Infantry and 2nd Oxfordshire and Buckinghamshire Light Infantry, which were to carry out a preliminary assault to secure the crossings of the Canal du Nord, over which the main attacking force would cross. Zero hour was 6.15 a.m., and was preceded by the laying of a smoke screen by our artillery. The Pioneers moved forward fifty yards behind the leading assault, with the task of blocking the German communication trenches immediately their front line trenches were captured. The men were heavily laden, not only with their rifles and ammunition but with sandbags, extra grenades, picks and shovels, and, presumably, coils of barbed wire. Casualties were heavy. With hindsight it might have been better if the Pioneers had advanced only when the trenches were captured, but speed was of the essence in cutting off the communication trenches through which the Germans could counter attack; hence the decision to keep the Pioneers well up in the assault.

For the next fortnight the 10th was working with the Royal Engineers, repairing roads on the 2nd Division areas of advance.

The second battle of Cambrai, 8th-9th October 1918

The 2nd Division was one of the attacking formations in this battle, which meant that the Cornwalls were working close up to the front line and were consequently under almost continuous artillery and machine-gun fire. Roads and bridges had to be constantly repaired or rebuilt to allow no slackening in the momentum of the advance. Major H.G. Bigg-Wither was awarded the DSO for conspicuous gallantry, devotion to duty and disregard of personal danger during the construction of a trestle bridge across the Canal de L'Escaut, under very heavy fire. At about the same time Second Lieutenant A.G.L. Burton performed sterling work with his platoon in reinstating a pontoon bridge across the canal, which had been sunk by shell-fire. It should be noted that Infantry Pioneers were not specifically trained in pontoon bridging, yet they completed this particular task without Royal Engineer assistance.

The battle of the River Selle, 17th-25th October 1918

This, the last great battle of the war, saw the 10th working steadily and efficiently just behind the front line, concentrating on their priority task of keeping the lines of communication open – as always, heavy and unglamorous work, but work which was absolutely vital to the Allies, who were now in full pursuit of the Germans.

The Armistice, 11th November 1918

The 10th Battalion left the battle area for the last time on 23rd October when it went into bivouacs just outside the village of Vertain. From there it moved to billets in Ruesnes, and were there when the Armistice was announced on 11th November.

The story of the 10th Battalion DCLI (Pioneers) is allotted more space in Everard Wyrall's history of the Great War than any other battalion except the 1st. This is certainly well merited, because for three years these tough, weather-beaten soldiers had performed massive labours in the face of extreme danger. To the casual observer their work was perhaps unspectacular, but without their contribution no unit of any arm could have functioned for long on those desolate and ravaged battle fields.

The 2nd Division was one of the formations selected to move into Germany after the Armistice. It was fitting and appropriate that the 10th Battalion should have taken part in this final victorious march. The Guards Division, followed by the 2nd Division, started from the village of Bovey, just south of Mons, on 17th November; crossed into Germany at Elsenborn on 12th December; and reached Düren, just west of Cologne, on 14th December.

What thoughts must have gone through the heads of those men, who marched across the Belgian-German frontier on that grey December day in their weather-stained khaki, with bayonets fixed and their band playing? Few of those who had rallied to the call with such youthful enthusiasm in March 1915 remained. By the nature of its work a Pioneer battalion suffered a continuous trickle of casualties as it went about its never-ending work in the front line. 257 had been killed and many times that figure wounded. These casualties must have had a sad impact on Cornwall for, unlike the other Service battalions of the DCLI which were largely recruited from London and Birmingham, the 10th was originally entirely composed of Cornishmen, and even by the end of the war was still predominently Cornish.

23
The 11th (Reserve) Battalion the 12th (Labour) Battalion the 13th (Service) Battalion & also the 1st & 2nd (Volunteer) Battalions

THE 11TH (RESERVE) BATTALION

There is some doubt as to the origins of the 11th (Reserve) Battalion DCLI. Two sources of equal reliability give its date and place of raising as November 1915 at Launceston and March 1916 at Crownhill Barracks, Plymouth. The latter is probably correct. The Commanding Officer was Lieutenant-Colonel W.G. Hatherall, a retired officer of the Indian Army. On 1st November 1916 the 11th Battalion became the 95th Training Battalion, and ceased to be part of the DCLI.

THE 12TH (LABOUR) BATTALION

The 12th (Labour) Battalion DCLI was raised at Plymouth in either March or April 1916, under Brevet Colonel D.A. Mills, a retired officer of the Royal Engineers. Labour battalions performed the vital but unspectacular task of carrying out much of the heavy work on the lines of communication, including the loading and unloading of ships. The Battalion moved to France soon after formation, coming under command of 4th Army. In April 1917 it was reformed as 156 and 157 Companies, Labour Corps, and ceased to be part of the DCLI.

* * *

THE 13TH (SERVICE) BATTALION

The 13th (Service) Battalion DCLI was raised at Cromer on 20th June 1918 but was immediately absorbed by the 6th (Service) Battalion the Somerset Light Infantry.

THE 1ST & 2ND (VOLUNTEER) BATTALIONS

Although the threat of invasion was never as serious in the Great War as it subsequently became in the early years of the Second World War, with her Regular and Territorial armies serving overseas, Britain was undoubtedly vulnerable.

In January 1917 HM The King made a personal appeal to Lord-Lieutenants to assist in the raising of Volunteer battalions within their respective counties. Cornwall raised two such battalions, the 1st commanded by Colonel Adams, retired Indian Army; the 2nd by Colonel C.R. Prideaux-Brune, retired Rifle Brigade. The battalions were recruited from those men who were either too old or medically unfit for service with the Regular or Territorial armies. Their duties were much the same as those performed by the Home Guard in the Second World War: that is to say, guarding docks, railway bridges and other vulnerable points, and patrolling the coast, particularly the more remote creeks in which German submarines could lay up at night in order to effect emergency repairs. The officers and men, who so cheerfully performed this humble and unspectacular role, received a well earned accolade from His Majesty at the end of the war, when he wrote:

> I cannot forget the self-sacrifice and patriotism which inspired as many of my subjects who, from reasons of health or age, were unable to serve abroad, to come forward and train themselves for any eventuality in the hour of the Country's need.

IV. THE INTER-WAR PERIOD 1918-1939

* * *

24
The 1st, 2nd & 3rd Battalions & the 4th & 5th (Territorial) Battalions

By the Armistice of 1918 Britain had, for the first time in her history, built an army on the continental scale. Not only was it of vast size, but its training, its equipment and its command and staff structure were all outstanding. It is too often forgotten that the Allied offensive, which led to final victory, was largely carried out by British and British Dominion divisions.

Exhausted both physically and economically, Britain accepted the concept that she had emerged from 'the war to end all wars'. From 1920 to 1935 the Defence Budget was annually reduced in real terms. Not only were the Service battalions quickly disbanded but the finance available for realistic training and for the development of modern equipment was severely cut. Thus, formation commanders and staff rarely enjoyed the opportunity to exercise large bodies of troops in the field. However, in one important respect the British Army led the world during those inter-war years, as the horse was all but superseded by the petrol engine. Indeed, the British expeditionary force that crossed to France in September 1939 was not accompanied by a single horse.

Under the Haldane Reforms of 1907-08 the original Militia battalions had become Reserve battalions. In 1914 the Reserve battalions had assumed the role of training units, that of the 3rd DCLI moving to the Isle of Wight the following year. During the four years of war the Reserve battalions had trained almost every officer and soldier, assembled them into drafts and despatched them to the operational theatres. In 1919, their work done, they were disbanded.

In this inter-war period the establishment of all regular and territorial infantry battalions was smaller than it had been in 1914 and the Duke of Cornwall's Light Infantry therefore consisted of the following:

Two Regular battalions: the 1st and 2nd DCLI
One Territorial battalion: the 4th/5th DCLI
One Regimental Depôt at Bodmin

THE 1ST BATTALION

The day that the Armistice was signed found the 1st Battalion in billets in Le Quesnoy. From there it moved by a succession of route marches into territory that had previously been occupied by the Germans. The weather did its best to dampen spirits with rain and snow but, not surprisingly, everybody was in good heart and the ample spare time was mainly taken up by football matches, with a certain amount of drill thrown in to remind everybody that they were still soldiers. On 3rd and 4th December 1918 HM The King visited units in the 4th Army area, and the Cornwalls lined the route to give him three cheers as he passed. On 14th December the Colour party, which had been despatched to the Depôt at Bodmin to collect the Colours, rejoined the Battalion at Louvroil. Heavy snow fell in February 1919, while the first of the demobilisation groups were despatched to England. During that month 3 officers and 439 soldiers said farewell to the Battalion, and in March a further 3 officers and 140 soldiers left to join the 1/5th Battalion at Etaples.

Return to England, April 1919

By 17th April the 1st had been reduced to a small cadre of regular officers, NCOs and soldiers. That morning, this much reduced band of brothers entrained at Baulet, changed at Charleroi, and arrived at Antwerp early the next morning. They were comfortably quartered in Nissen huts until 20th April, when they embarked in SS *Pretoria* bound for Tilbury. From there they moved to barracks in Catterick.

Once in Catterick, the majority of those who had not completed their engagement were crossposted to the 2nd Battalion, which was being made up to full establishment preparatory to its posting to India. The 1st remained in Catterick till the end of August, when the few remaining officers and men were crossposted to the 3rd Battalion, which had itself moved to Ballyshannon on the coast of Donegal Bay. There the 3rd Battalion, together with the small cadre from the 1st Battalion, became the new post war 1st Battalion, under the command of Lieutenant-Colonel T.H.F. Price, CMG, DSO. It had as its Regimental Serjeant-Major a man who, by his very appearance, must have turned young subalterns and soldiers cold with terror. This was Walter Bland, MC, who had originally enlisted in the Grenadier Guards, and had transferred to the Welch Guards on their formation in 1915. He was to remain with the 1st DCLI for many years, building up a fine regular Battalion from scratch.

Ireland, 1920-1922

At this time Ireland was in a state of open insurrection. The 1st moved to Ballykinlar in August 1920 where it remained until February 1922, taking part in arduous and unpleasant internal security duties in Belfast. During this period it was warned for a tour of duty in India (at that time it was not unusual for infantry battalions to carry out very long overseas tours lasting for twenty years or more). The 2nd Battalion had originally been destined for India, but due to the political state of flux which followed the defeat of Germany, plans had to be constantly amended to meet changing conditions. In the event, the 2nd Battalion had only completed eleven months in India before being despatched to Iraq.

In February 1922 the 1st Battalion moved south to Dublin, where it spent a short time re-fitting before sailing for India. During that period the two regular battalions found themselves serving in the same city, for the 2nd Battalion had been in Dublin since the previous July, being fully involved in the bitter campaign against the Irish Republican rebels.

India, 1922 until 1941

On arrival in India the 1st Battalion was split into three detachments, quartered at Chakrata, Meerut and Dehra Dun respectively. In December 1923 the Battalion was again concentrated at Lucknow – scene of the most revered battle honour in DCLI history. Four years were spent in Lucknow, after which the Battalion moved to Barrackpore, while in the hot weather Battalion Headquarters and two companies moved to the hill station of Lebong. The Battalion was once again at full establishment, and consisted almost entirely of young men. Group photographs of this period show only the more senior officers and NCOs with Great War Medals. From 1930 to 1934 the Battalion stationed at Bareilly, before moving north to Razmak on the legendary North West Frontier. The move to Razmak was conducted in a manner that would have been familiar to Kipling's soldiers. The standard-gauge railway transported men, horses, mules, carts, and wagons to the terminus at Mari Indus. There all were reloaded onto a steamer, which ferried the Battalion across the great River Indus. From there the journey continued a few more miles by narrow-gauge railway. After that the Battalion took to its feet, marching the final seventy-two miles to Razmak. The road rose steadily to 7,000 feet through some of the most spectacular mountainous country in the world. Remarkable photographs show the long column of troops snaking up the passes through a succession of hairpin bends, followed by a miscellany of animal-drawn transport. Operations on the North West Frontier provided the gruelling test by which an infantry battalion in India was judged. The rocky mountainous terrain may have been spectacular, but it was utterly inhospitable. The climate was blisteringly hot in summer and bitterly cold in winter, when deep snow would block the passes. Above all else, the local tribesmen had perfected the art of mountain tactics, and delighted in a lethal game of harassing British troops. Any stupidity, slackness or lack of vigilance when out on 'column' could result in casualties, and any wounded man who was allowed to fall into Pathan hands could expect no mercy. Soldiering on the North West Frontier demanded the highest professional standards and exceptional physical fitness from all ranks. It was a hard school, perhaps the best possible training for war, to which a certain zest was added by the real element of danger. Even allowing for the total absence of women, soldiers of a good regiment enjoyed the Frontier, developing pride in their military prowess.

In 1935 the Battalion moved to Dinapore in Bihat, with detachments in Marzaffardur, and also the Andaman Islands in the Indian Ocean where there was a penal settlement guarded by British troops. In January 1937 the Battalion moved *en bloc* to Lahore, where it took over from the 2nd Battalion the Royal Scots.

Declaration of war, September 1939

The declaration of war in September 1939 found the 1st Battalion back in Lahore, carrying out garrison duties under the command of Lieutenant-Colonel T.G.L. Elliott. During its long tour of duty in India previous Commanding Officers had been Lieutenant-Colonel A.P. Williams Freeman, DSO, OBE; Lieutenant-Colonel H.D. Goldsmith, DSO; Lieutenant-Colonel A.P. Dene, CMG, DSO; Lieutenant-Colonel A.N. Floyer-Acland, DSO, MC; and Lieutenant-Colonel D.G. Watson, MC.

THE 2ND BATTALION

Salonika, Serbia, Bulgaria, & Transcaucasia, 1918

We left the 2nd Battalion in Salonika after the collapse of Bulgaria. For the next few years it was perpetually on the move. From Salonika the expeditionary force advanced north into Serbia, and thence into

Bulgaria, then across the Black Sea to Transcaucasia which, since the Russian revolution of 1917, had comprised the republics of Georgia, Azerbaijan and Armenia. The occupation of this area by British forces was an attempt to bring stability to a highly volatile area in which Armenia, taking advantage of the power vacuum, had attacked both Georgia and Azerbaijan.

During this period of rapid post-war flux the Battalion was initially commanded by Lieutenant-Colonel H. Fargus, CMG, DSO. He was appointed CB and retired on 8th July 1919, handing over to Lieutenant-Colonel R.M. Wetherell, CMG.

Return to England, 1919

Britain's intervention in Transcaucasia was to no avail, and in August 1919 the greater part of the British force, including the Cornwalls, was withdrawn. The Battalion returned by sea for a brief spell in England where, at Crownhill Barracks, Plymouth, it re-fitted, absorbing drafts from the other battalions of the Regiment, in expectation of commencing a long overseas tour of duty in India. The advance party, under Captain E. Hare, was despatched to Bombay to prepare for the Battalion's arrival.

India, 1919

On 26th September 1919 the 2nd Battalion entrained at Plymouth, travelling to Tilbury that day where it embarked on HMT *China*. The ship sailed for Bombay that evening. The voyage was uneventful, marred only by the death of Serjeant Phillips.

On arrival at Bombay on 14th October it was learnt that the plan had been changed. The Battalion was not to remain in Bombay but was to be stationed at Calcutta, some 1,500 miles east on the opposite side of the sub-continent. However, a 'Prayer of Protest Day' was due to be held in Bombay which, it was anticipated, might lead to serious rioting. The fortuitous appearance of the 2nd Battalion therefore gave the military commander a useful bonus. Consequently it was retained in the area, being temporarily accommodated with the 1st Garrison Battalion the South Staffordshire Regiment in Caliba Camp. In the event the day passed off peaceably, and on 18th October the Battalion entrained for the long three and a half day rail journey to Calcutta. There it was met by motor lorries that transported men and baggage to Fort William, where it was due to relieve the 1st Garrison Battalion the Lincolnshire Regiment and the Brecknockshire Battalion the South Wales Borderers (TF).

Immediately the take-over was complete, A and D Companies moved to Dum-Dum and Barrackpore, a few miles north of the city.

In January 1920 a War Office letter was received, ordering the Regiment to cease wearing the red feathers in its tropical headgear – only the red patch behind the cap badge would in future be permitted. It will be remembered that the red feathers commemorated the action of the Light Company of the 46th Foot against American rebels at Paoli in 1777. From that time the 46th had worn red feathers, plumes or tufts in its head-dress. On the formation of the DCLI from the 32nd and 46th Regiments in 1881 this honour had been granted to the whole of the new Regiment, taking the form of red feathers in the tropical helmet. An order meddling with such a long hallowed custom must have made the feathers fly in more senses than one. The Commanding Officer replied that this was a matter for the Colonel of the Regiment, Lieutenant-General Sir Richard Pole-Carew, and that in the meantime his battalion would carry on wearing their red feathers. Details of the subsequent correspondence are not known; all one can say is that the DCLI continued to wear its red feathers till well after the Second World War.

In February C and D Companies moved to Lebong, and during successive months the rifle companies were rotated through this station in order to get men away from the damp, humid climate of Calcutta. In summer the temperature can rise to 118° Fahrenheit with proportionate humidity, and life becomes almost unbearable. In June the electric generators in Fort William broke down, bringing all the fans to a halt. Apart from those engaged on essential duties, there was little anyone could do but lie on his *charpoi* and sweat it out, waiting for the blessed monsoon to break.

On 17th July 1920 rumours started to circulate that the Battalion's tour in India was to be cut short, and that it would move to Iraq.

Iraq, 1920

After the defeat of the Ottoman Empire Iraq had been established as a new Arab nation, formed from the three former Ottoman *vilayets* of Mosul, Baghdad and Basra. Nationalism in this area had flickered only feebly at the time of the Arab revolt during the Great War. However, after the capture of Baghdad on 19th March 1917, a proclamation had been issued under the name of General Maude which in effect gave the liberated Arabs in Mesopotamia control over their own destinies. All this was, however, in sharp contradiction to an announcement made by HM Government that same month that the formerly occupied territories were 'to be administered by HM Government'. Thus, the end of the war found British policy totally confused.

The Nationalists, having been encouraged by Maude's policy of independence, were deeply angered to learn that they were to remain under the control of yet another foreign power.

The resolution of this dangerous muddle fell on the unfortunate shoulders of the Assistant Commissioner, Sir Arnold Wilson, who firmly believed that the British Government's wish to interfere with the affairs of an Arab nation was damaging to the interests of both the British Empire and the population of Iraq. Events however took their sad and almost inevitable course. Anti-British sentiment was stimulated and pressed into service by the Nationalists. The publication on 3rd May 1920 of the details imposing a British mandate on Iraq merely gave further proof that Great Britain could not be trusted to keep her word.

The Iraq rebellion broke on 30th June 1920 when its leader, Amir Abdullah ibn Hussain, attacked Rumaitha. Strong measures were immediately taken to destroy the roots of dissent. 4,883 British troops and 24,508 Indian troops together with an RAF squadron of bomber aircraft were immediately despatched from India.

As a result of the Iraqi rebellion, on 13th September 1920 the 2nd Battalion left Calcutta for Iraq, destined never to return.

After retracing its journey along the railway to Bombay, on 17th September it embarked on HMT *Conconada*, together with the 2nd East Yorkshire Regiment.

Arriving at Basra on 23rd September, the Battalion spent a fortnight in a tented camp before entraining for the 120 mile journey up the Euphrates to Nasiriyeh. On reaching Iel el Lahm, intelligence sources indicated an intended attack on the railway. The Battalion therefore de-trained to give support to a company of Indian infantry dug in around the station. The following morning, as nothing had happened, the railway journey was continued to Nasiriyeh, where the Battalion was accommodated in native mud huts on the west bank of the river.

Little happened at Nasiriyeh except routine patrolling to maintain security. However, on 9th October the Battalion took part in a punitive expedition against a village in the Khidar area whose occupants had carried out a number of murders and had plundered and destroyed a British river steamer, SS *Greenfly*. The column, under the command of Major A. le G. Jacob, consisted of 2nd DCLI, a Sikh battalion and a battery of Royal Field Artillery. The DCLI lost two killed and five wounded, while the acting Commanding Officer, Major E.B. Ward, DSO, had his horse killed under him (Lieutenant-Colonel Wetherell was sick with sand-fly fever).

The rebellion was broken by the use of harsh measures including the employment of airpower against dissident villages. It finally collapsed completely in October 1920.

* * *

Malta, 1921

The Battalion saw no further action during the rest of its uncomfortable tour in Iraq, and was doubtless glad to be given the news that it was earmarked as one of the resident units in the Malta garrison. On 26th February 1921 it embarked from Basra, first sailing south east to Bombay where it trans-shipped to HMT *Huntsend* which was scheduled for the return journey home. On arrival at Suez the ship picked up the 1st KOYLI who, like the 2nd DCLI, had been told that they were to start a two-year tour in Malta. Valetta was reached on 23rd March, and the Battalion moved into Imtarfa Barracks – comfortable and commodious quarters compared with those that they had known in Iraq.

Plymouth, 1921

Within a week of arriving in Malta news was received that the 2nd Battalion must move again: because of the coal miners' strike in England, considerable reinforcements of troops were required to stand by in case of serious civil disturbance. Thus, on 5th April the Battalion re-embarked on its old friend HMT *Huntsend*, bound for Devonport. There it was quartered in Raglan Barracks, but was not required to take part in any internal security duties.

The spring and early summer of 1921 were given over to the unaccustomed delights of a thriving English city and the lovely surrounding countryside. Many of the 2nd Battalion officers came from that area, for the Regiment had perpetuated the 46th tradition in maintaining close links with South Devonshire; thus they were close to home. In addition of course, the Regimental Depôt was only a few miles across the border in Cornwall, and one can be sure that many old friendships were re-established there. As my reader may have guessed, this situation was too good to last. In early 1920 open rebellion had broken out in Ireland. Troop reinforcements were urgently required. On 1st July 1921 the Battalion sailed from Devonport to Dublin.

Dublin, 1921-1922

After a short time in Raglan Barracks the Battalion sailed for Dublin, on 2nd July 1921. Quelling an Arab rebellion in Iraq was doubtless considered by the soldiers to be all part of the day's work, but the sight of burnt out buildings, barbed wire, armoured cars and bayonets in a British city must have aroused feelings first of incredulity and then of deep bitterness. For the next ten months the 2nd Battalion carried out its unsavoury duties with commendable discipline and efficiency. Known in Ireland as the 'Anglo-Irish War' it was a strange affair, waged by a very small minority of the population. The Irish Republican Army was said to number no more than two thousand, but by widespread acts of terrorism was able to hold down an army and police presence many times its size. The men of the Royal Irish Constabulary, dispersed as they were in the rural areas, made easy targets for murder. The 'Auxiliaries' (known from the colour of their hastily devised uniform as the 'Black and Tans') were quickly recruited in England and sent across to Ireland to reinforce the police. Their brutality and ill discipline quickly made them loathed, and did much to unite the Catholic population against British rule. Regular soldiers were much less vulnerable; only one DCLI soldier, Private Radford, was killed. During this period the 2nd Battalion provided a draft of 500 officers and men for the 1st Battalion stationed at Ballykinlar, Co. Down, which was being brought up to establishment for service in India.

Initially billeted under canvas in Richmond Barracks, the Battalion later moved to more permanent quarters in Wellington Barracks, with companies doing duty by turn at Dublin Castle. The tour, which lasted till the final withdrawal of the British Army on 1st February 1922 from what was to become known at the Irish Free State, must have been a sad and frustrating period for all ranks.

The Irish Free State, with the status of a British Dominion, officially came into being on 16th January 1922 when the Irish Peace Agreement, which had been signed the previous day, was ratified by the Parliament of Westminster. Already Southern Ireland had become a divided nation, with the extreme right Republican party at daggers drawn with the Provisional Government elected to the *Dáil*. The Royal Irish Constabulary was immediately disbanded, but the new unarmed *Garda* took time to organise, and its members immediately became murder targets in the eyes of the extreme Republicans, who saw them merely as an extension of authoritarian rule. An orgy of murder, house burning and general destruction of property was rapidly spreading across this still embryonic nation. Gangs of armed youths roamed the countryside, settling old scores and killing and terrorising fellow Irishmen. The only Irish force capable of maintaining a semblance of law and order was the newly formed Irish Army, but its loyalty to the Provisional Government was often doubtful. Many senior officers in the Irish Army backed the Republican cause, using their authority to continue the armed struggle against Great Britain.

It was in an atmosphere of near anarchy that, on 25th January 1922, the 1st Battalion passed through Dublin on its way to England. This was one of the few times that the two battalions of the Regiment found themselves, for a brief time, quartered in the same city.

On the evening of 30th January 1922 the DCLI guard on Dublin Castle handed over its duties to the Irish Army. The union flag, which had flown for so many years, was finally hauled down, to be replaced the following morning by the green, white and orange tricolour of the Irish Free State. Two days later the 2nd Battalion paraded on the square of Wellington Barracks in field service marching order, ready to move to the docks, where it embarked for England that morning – the last formed unit of the British Army to leave the Irish Free State.

The following day the Battalion arrived at Tidworth. There, during the next seven weeks, it refitted for service with the British Army of the Rhine.

Cologne & Silesia, 1922-1924

The 2nd Battalion staged at Tidworth for refitting, before being posted to Cologne as part of the British Army of Occupation of the Rhine. Almost immediately after arrival in that city a detachment of two companies was despatched to Silesia, to carry out duties in aid of the civil power during the plebiscite to determine whether that country should remain as part of Germany.

Having commanded the Battalion for four years of almost constant movement, Lieutenant-Colonel Wetherell, CMG was succeeded by Lieutenant-Colonel A.P. Williams Freeman, DSO, OBE, who had previously commanded the 1st Battalion. During its tour in Cologne the Battalion won the Rhine Army Infantry Shield, an award made to the infantry unit judged best for its performance in both the military and sporting fields.

Vickers machine-guns had been taken away from all infantry battalions in the summer of 1915, as it was considered that they could best be employed under separate command. Now, with the disbandment of the Machine Gun Corps, these splendid weapons were once more brought back into the integral structure of each infantry battalion. The 2nd DCLI Machine Gun Platoon was evidently outstanding, for in the summer of 1923 it won the Army Rifle Association MG cup, beating the score of the previous winners by a handsome 76 points. Later that year it went on to win a decisive victory at the Rhine Army Championships, scoring 313 points against the 2nd King's Royal Rifle Corps, which came second with a score of only 189 points.

* * *

Guernsey & Alderney, 1924-1927

In 1924 the Battalion moved to the Channel Islands. Battalion headquarters and two companies were stationed in Guernsey and two companies in Alderney. Lieutenant-Colonel A.P. Willams Freeman, DSO was succeeded by Lieutenant-Colonel H.T. Dobbin, CBE, DSO on 6th May 1926.

Aldershot, 1927-1932

In 1927 2nd DCLI at last came home for a protracted tour of home duty for the first time since the war. It was posted to the hub of the British military machine, Aldershot, taking its place with the 5th Infantry Brigade in the 2nd Division. Soldiering in England at that time was not a particularly inspiring occupation. The economic climate could scarcely have been more gloomy; the 'war to end all wars' had been fought and won, so that the Government saw little reason to allocate scarce funds to the army. It was accepted that home battalions would always be below establishment, and in spite of large scale unemployment, this was an especially lean recruiting period. The 2nd Battalion was so reduced in strength that the regimental journal noted that 'shortage of men compelled us to combine our four rifle companies into one company for individual training'. Imaginative collective training barely existed, for this cost money. However, ceremonial drill was cheap and this, together with an orgy of spit and polish, occupied much of the soldiers' working day. This alone might have been demoralising if the Regiment had not thrown itself wholeheartedly into sport. The regimental journal notes what an important contribution 2nd DCLI made in almost every field of sport during this period, and especially to cross country running. Between 1922 and 1929 the Battalion won the Rhine Army or Aldershot Command cup every year, and the Army Cup five times in succession between 1925 and 1929. No other regiment or corps has ever approached this record. They were to become Army champions once more in 1939. During this long tour of duty at Aldershot, Lieutenant-Colonel H.T. Dobbin, CBE, DSO was succeeded by Lieutenant-Colonel W.T. Brooks, MC.

Gibraltar, 1932-1935

In the spring of 1932 the 2nd Battalion was posted to Gibraltar, where it had last been stationed in 1905. Two companies were quartered in South Barracks, an elegant group of buildings dating back to the eighteenth century; and the other two companies in Grand Casemates Barracks, a remarkable warren of cave-like dwellings constructed within the defences of the Fortress. The Battalion's arrival coincided with that of the Atlantic Fleet, which resulted in a close bond of friendship being formed between soldiers and sailors. Social and sporting events were organised with the Royal Navy, and groups of soldiers were taken out to sea during naval exercises. One lucky group was aboard HMS *Nelson* when she carried out gunnery training, finishing up by firing a broadside of all her nine 16 in. guns at night: quite an experience! Sport of every kind played a large part in the soldier's life, with plenty of water sports including keenly contested rowing races in naval whalers. Although military training was limited, the Battalion concentrated on its shooting, sweeping the board in the Garrison Rifle Meetings. It is interesting that the regimental journal mentions 'de-bugging' of beds; a problem that appears to have been endemic in Gibraltar. (The Somerset & Cornwall Light Infantry had to tackle the same problem in 1962.)

Early in the Gibraltar tour the command changed, Lieutenant-Colonel W.T. Brooks, MC handing over to Lieutenant-Colonel W.P. Buckley, DSO.

Blackdown, Shorncliffe & Public Duties, 1935-1939

The 2nd Battalion returned to England in 1935, embarking on HMT *Nevasa* on 16th January. The ship was on its outward journey so that the Battalion was first carried some 1,000 miles east to Malta, where it disembarked for two days, being royally entertained by the 2nd Rifle Brigade. The Battalion was quartered at Blackdown, as part of the 6th Infantry Brigade. After a month's leave it got down to the serious business of training.

The 6th Infantry Brigade had been selected to carry out trials of the new infantry establishment, based on mechanical transport. New vehicles and equipment were gradually arriving, with which every soldier had to be made familiar. The most obvious change was that, for the first time in its history, the 2nd Battalion was to rely totally on motor transport. The vehicles, which included Carden-Lloyd tractors (the forerunners of the ubiquitous Universal Carrier of later years), were slow to arrive; the urgent need to train a large number of drivers from scratch was therefore no easy task. Another important innovation was the replacement of the well-proven Lewis light machine-gun with the Czechoslovakian Zbrojorka Brno light machine-gun (later to be known as the Bren gun).

By the end of April the Battalion mustered some thirty assorted vehicles, while sufficient soldiers had returned from the MT School at Bovington to drive them. On 3rd May a motorised convoy set off across the Tamar to carry out a recruiting tour in Cornwall. Money for recruiting being short, this exercise could only be authorised as 'driver training'.

During 1936, training took on a new state of urgency. The threat posed by Germany had at last alerted a parsimonious government to the threat of another European war. The 2nd Battalion was however still the home battalion, and as such, was responsible for keeping the 1st up to establishment. Although the 1935 tour had brought in a number of Cornishmen, recruiting was still poor, which meant that the 2nd was permanently short of men. In March Lieutenant-Colonel W.P. Buckley, DSO relinquished command, to be replaced by Lieutenant-Colonel A.R. Godwin-Austen, OBE, MC on transfer from the South Wales Borderers.

In 1938 the Battalion moved to Shorncliffe, a town significant to Light Infantrymen as the birthplace of Sir John Moore's Light Brigade in 1802. Politicians and soldiers alike were by now under no illusions concerning the threat of war. The main problem facing the Battalion was, however, still lack of soldiers. The regimental journal notes: 'Year after year we did much the same thing, we had more equipment each year but fewer men, and therefore more work'. During 1939 Universal Carriers replaced the Carden-Lloyd tractors.

As a final fling for peace-time soldiering, the 2nd Battalion moved to the Tower of London in the summer of 1939, to take over London public duties from the Foot Guards. Much of the credit for the immaculate drill and turnout of all ranks must go to Regimental Serjeant-Major A.G. (Sticky) Hill, an outstanding Warrant Officer who was destined for a commission and a very distinguished war record.

Lieutenant-Colonel E.R. Rushton assumed command in July 1939 from Lieutenant-Colonel E.H. Carkeet James, OBE, MC.

The 2nd Battalion returned to barracks at Shorncliffe in early August with the full knowledge that war was imminent. In August the order was received to mobilise. Reservists, who had initially reported to the Depôt in Bodmin, flooded in, bringing the Battalion up to full war establishment for the first time in many years. The inevitable declaration of war came on September 3rd and very shortly afterwards the Battalion moved out to billets in the Lyminge area.

THE 4TH & 5TH BATTALIONS (TERRITORIAL ARMY)

On the demobilisation of the Territorial Force battalions after the Great War, the whole future of the Territorials hung in the balance. It was argued, from the experiences of 1914, that Territorial battalions were unfit to take their place in the line alongside Regulars without considerable additional training. As it was generally agreed that in any future war military conscription would be put into effect immediately mobilisation was authorised, there seemed little point in maintaining Territorials in peace time. The nub of this reasoning was undoubtedly finance. The defence budget was in process of being drastically cut, so the Regular Army argued that every penny spent on part-time soldiers would mean less for its own already meagre budget. To this was added the problem of recruitment. The nation had just emerged from four years of bloody warfare, so that few young men had any inclination to put on khaki to play at weekend soldiers. Thanks to the newly appointed Secretary of State for War, Mr Winston Churchill, the Territorials survived, albeit on a much reduced scale, with newly negotiated terms of service. The new force was to be known as the Territorial Army. Under successive governments during the lean years of the 1920s and 1930s financial backing for the Territorials was further reduced. For several years the War Office had counselled the abolition of Territorial annual camps on the grounds of expense. In 1926 certain camps were cancelled.

1926 brought swingeing financial cuts to an already impoverished Territorial Army. Apart from the cancellation of certain camps already mentioned, the funding for training, building maintenance and clothing was reduced and many units were disbanded. Most damaging of all perhaps was the abolition of the bounty paid to all new recruits and all those re-engaging for an extension of service. In 1931 further financial savings were made by severely limiting recruiting, while in 1932 all camps were cancelled. This was a great blow to the Territorial soldier, for not only was his training geared to this event, but he looked forward to the sociability and opportunity to play games which only camp life could offer. It was only in 1935 that the tide appeared to turn, when a specially constituted Defence Requirements Committee, made up of soldiers and politicians, recommended that an additional £250,000 per year should be spent for the next five years towards modernising the equipment of the Territorial Army. This recommendation was strongly opposed by the Chancellor of the Exchequer, Mr Neville Chamberlain, but was eventually ratified the following year when it became only too obvious that the war clouds were gathering.

> In 1926, in the DCLI, although a nucleus of its Territorials remained intact, the number of Territorial battalions were cut by half, the resulting unit being known as the 4th/5th Battalion Duke of Cornwall's Light Infantry (Territorial Army).

THE EVE OF WAR, SEPTEMBER 1939

A radical reorganisation of the establishments of all arms had been undertaken by a committee in 1931. Their recommendations had been thoroughly tested and revised over the next eight years, so that by the summer of 1939 an infantry battalion at full war establishment consisted of a headquarter company and four rifle companies, giving a total strength of 559 all ranks. Apart from administering battalion headquarters, headquarter company had four specialist platoons: the signal, the administrative, the mortar and the carrier platoons. Each rifle company consisted of a headquarters and three platoons, which in their turn each had three sections.

The same well proven .303 in. No.1 Mk III* bolt action Lee-Enfield rifle, with its formidable 17 in. sword bayonet, was still the weapon with which the majority of soldiers were armed. Officers carried the old .455 in. Webley No.1 Mk VI revolver. The hand grenade was of a type familiar to soldiers of the Great War, known as the grenade No.36. Each section was equipped with two close support weapons: first, the .303 in. Bren light machine-gun (developed from the Zbrojorka Brno), a most excellent magazine-fed weapon which could either be fired in the light role using the integral bipod, or from a heavy tubular steel tripod in the anti-aircraft or medium machine-gun roles (for the latter it could be fitted with a dial clinometer sight, giving it an indirect fire capability). Secondly, there was a newly developed light 2 in. mortar. The mortar platoon had six 3 in. mortars capable of firing a 10 lb bomb to a range of 2,700 yds. With hindsight, by far the greatest gap in the infantryman's armoury was the lack of any effective anti-tank weapon, other than the nearly useless .5 in. Boy's anti-tank rifle. This was to have dire effects the following year.

Mention has been made of the universal carrier. This was a lightly armoured, tracked vehicle with a good cross-country performance. Its concept was unique to the British army, and it was destined to give valuable service for the next twenty years. Each carrier was armed with a Bren light machine-gun (hence its popular name of Bren-gun carrier), which made it ideal for reconnaissance purposes. However, its most important use was to ferry ammunition and supplies across a bullet-swept battle-field. These splendid vehicles were issued on an ever larger scale during the war and came to epitomise the image of the modern infantryman.

A new pattern of webbing equipment was introduced in 1937. The width of the belt was reduced from three to two inches, and two deep rectangular pouches capable of holding grenades, Bren-gun magazines and 2 in. mortar bombs as well as rifle ammunition replaced the ten small pouches of the earlier equipment. Many old soldiers argued, probably with good reason, that this new equipment was less comfortable than the old and tended to ride up round the waist. The steel helmet was very similar to that worn in the latter days of the Great War.

All ranks wore a newly designed 'battle-dress' consisting of a loose-fitting khaki serge, waist-length blouse, with trousers of the same material, tucked into webbing gaiters. Apart from giving little protection from the cold to the lumbar regions, the blouse and trousers were apt to part company, leaving the wearer with a bare midriff. A singularly useless khaki head-dress known as the 'cap, field service' was worn with battle-dress. Soldiers took delight in wearing their caps at ever more improbable angles, secured to their heads only by a liberal application of Brylcream. Their only merit was that they folded flat for stowing away when steel helmets were worn.

It should be noted that the British Army in India was a law unto itself as far as equipment was concerned. Most infantry units were armed with the Vickers Berthier light machine-gun in place of the Bren gun, and still relied very largely on mule transport.

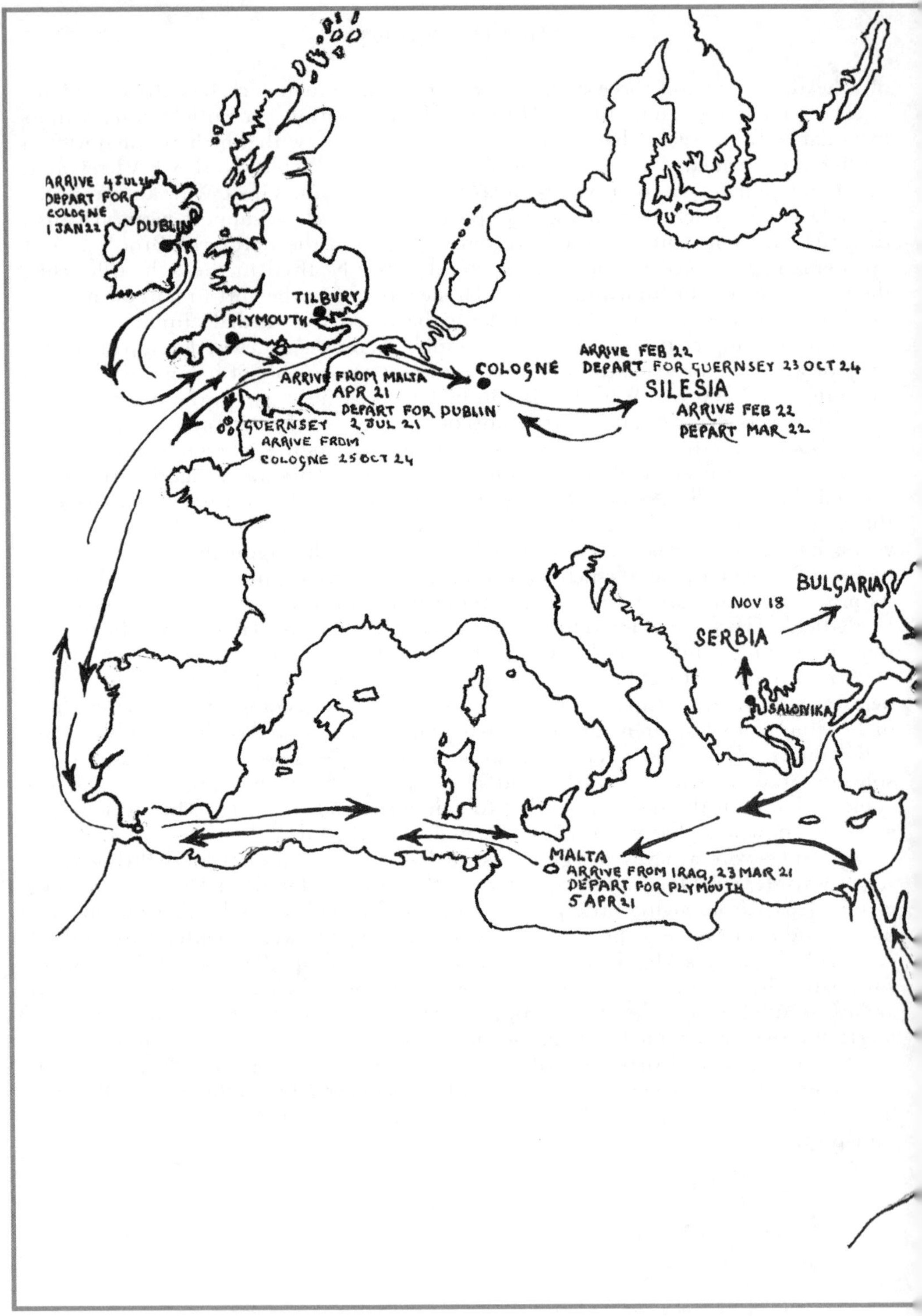
ARRIVE 4 JUL 21
DEPART FOR COLOGNE 1 JAN 22
DUBLIN
TILBURY
PLYMOUTH
ARRIVE FROM MALTA APR 21
DEPART FOR DUBLIN 2 JUL 21
GUERNSEY
ARRIVE FROM COLOGNE 25 OCT 24
COLOGNE
ARRIVE FEB 22
DEPART FOR GUERNSEY 23 OCT 24
SILESIA
ARRIVE FEB 22
DEPART MAR 22
BULGARIA
NOV 18
SERBIA
SALONIKA
MALTA
ARRIVE FROM IRAQ, 23 MAR 21
DEPART FOR PLYMOUTH 5 APR 21

2 DCLI

MOVEMENTS NOVEMBER 1918 TO OCTOBER 1924

THE PERIPATETIC BATTALION

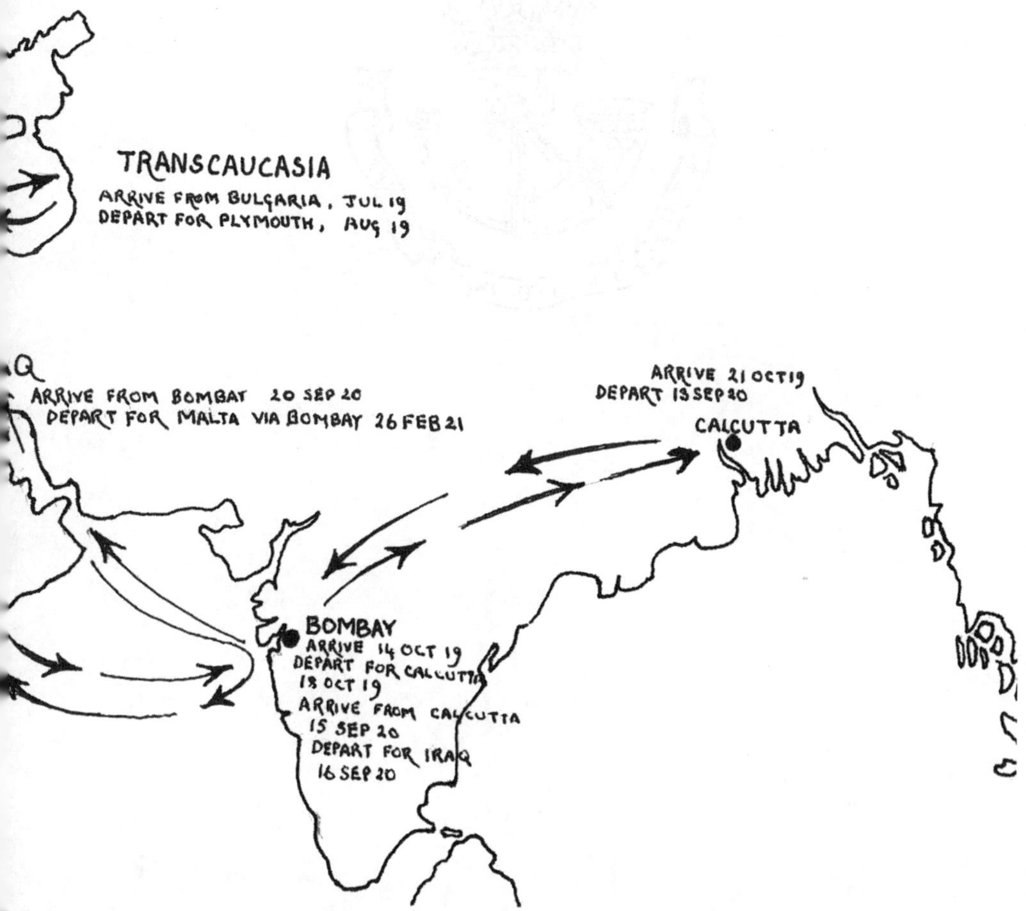

THE
DUKE OF CORNWALL'S
LT INFY

PART 3

The Second World War 1939-1945

& its Aftermath

Chapter 25

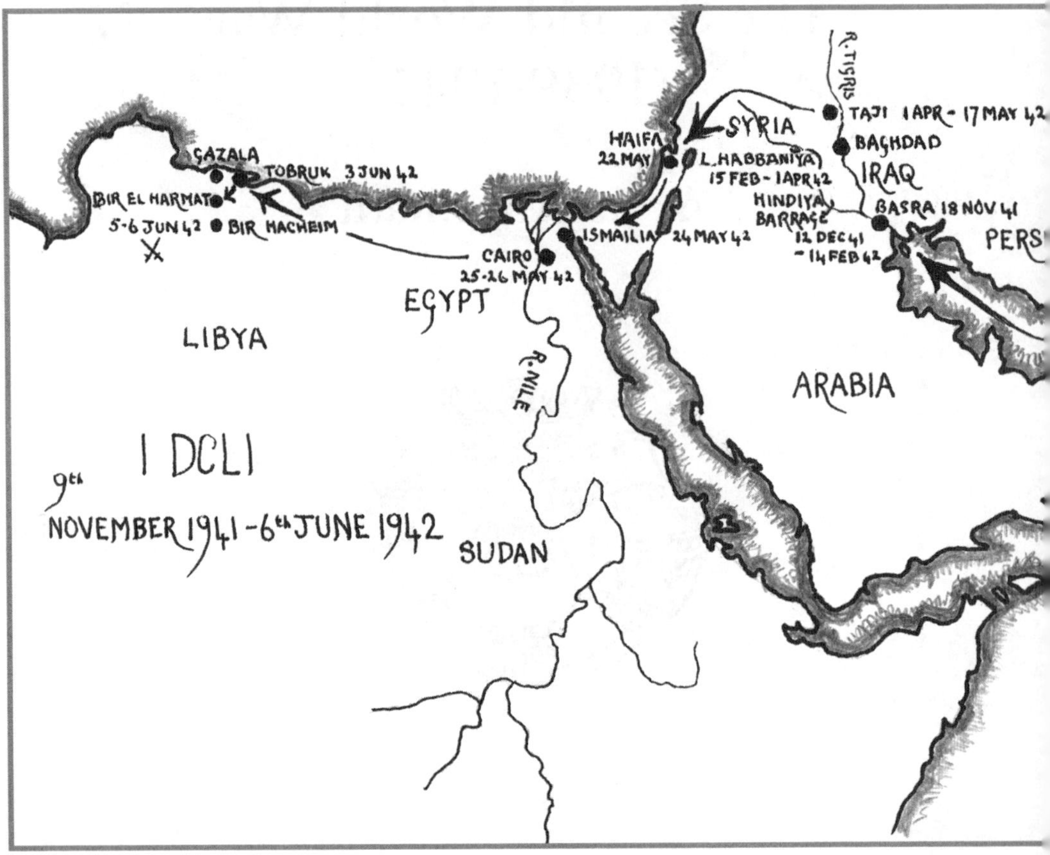
GAZALA
TOBRUK 3 JUN 42
BIR EL HARMAT
5-6 JUN 42
BIR HACHEIM
HAIFA
22 MAY
SYRIA
L. HABBANIYA
15 FEB - 1 APR 42
TAJI 1 APR - 17 MAY 42
BAGHDAD
R. TIGRIS
IRAQ
HINDIYA BARRAGE
12 DEC 41 - 14 FEB 42
BASRA 18 NOV 41
PERS
ISMAILIA 24 MAY 42
CAIRO
25-26 MAY 42
EGYPT
LIBYA
R. NILE
ARABIA
SUDAN
1 DCLI
9th NOVEMBER 1941 - 6th JUNE 1942

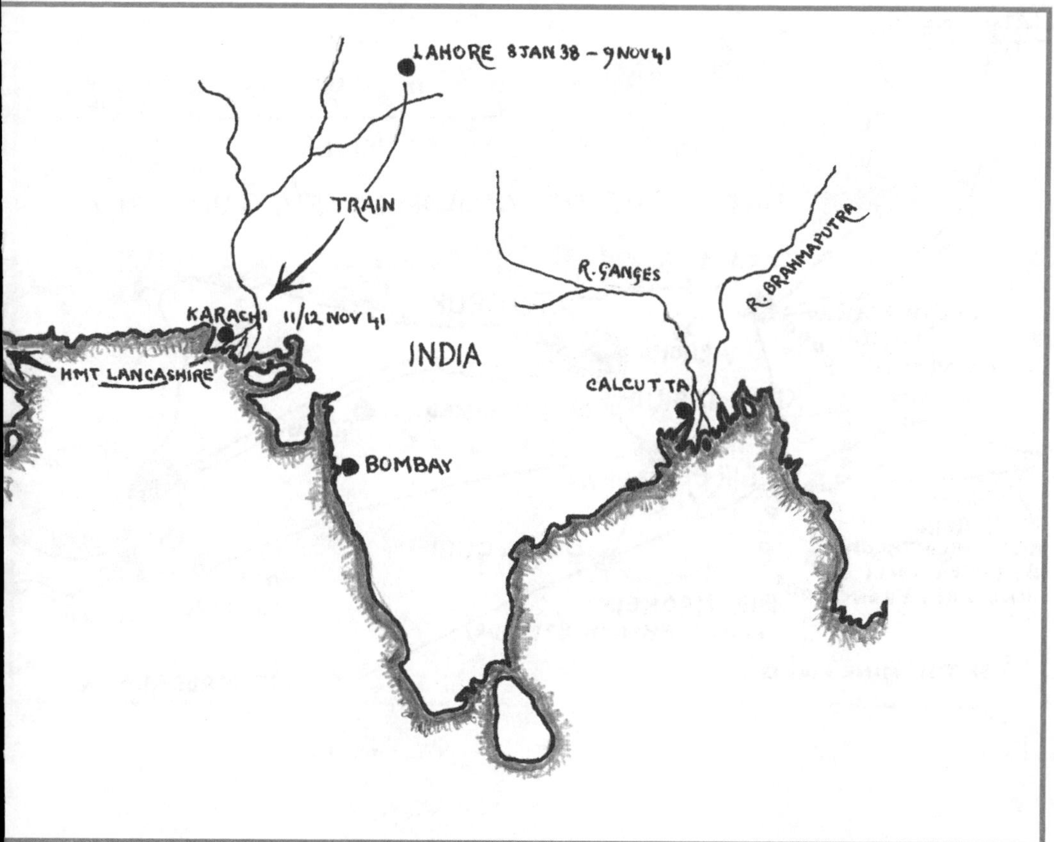
LAHORE 8 JAN 38 – 9 NOV 41
TRAIN
KARACHI 11/12 NOV 41
HMT LANCASHIRE
INDIA
BOMBAY
R. GANGES
R. BRAHMAPUTRA
CALCUTTA

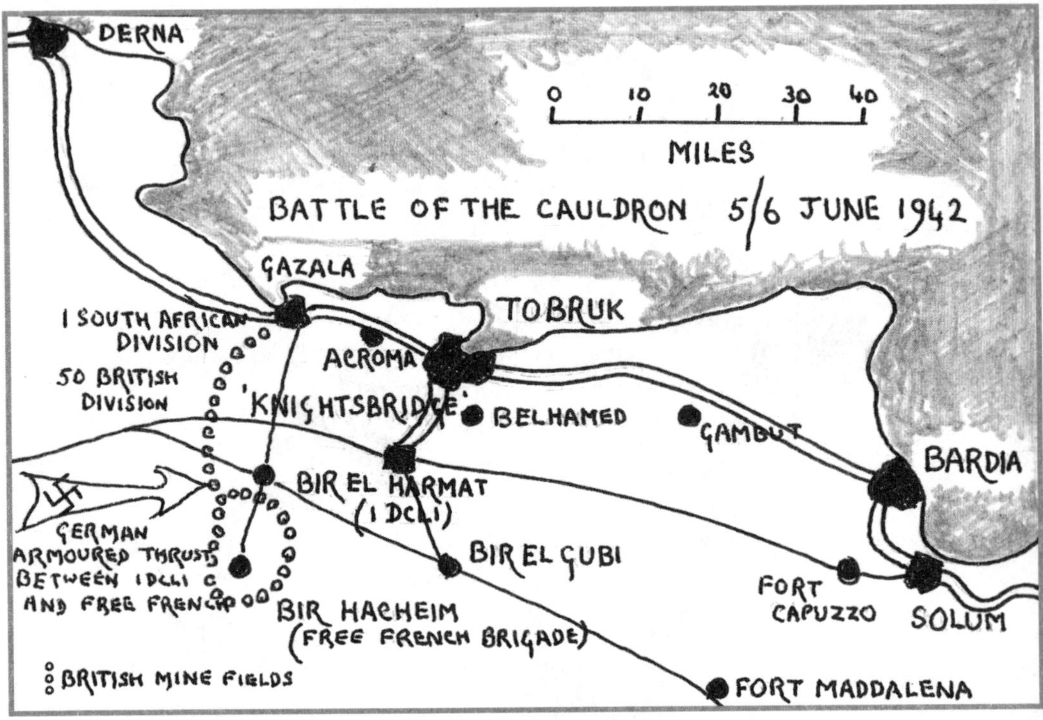
DERNA
0 10 20 30 40
MILES
BATTLE OF THE CAULDRON 5/6 JUNE 1942
GAZALA
TOBRUK
1 SOUTH AFRICAN DIVISION
ACROMA
50 BRITISH DIVISION
'KNIGHTSBRIDGE'
BELHAMED
GAMBUT
BARDIA
BIR EL HARMAT (1 DCLI)
GERMAN ARMOURED THRUSTS BETWEEN 1DCLI AND FREE FRENCH
BIR EL GUBI
BIR HACHEIM (FREE FRENCH BRIGADE)
FORT CAPUZZO
SOLUM
BRITISH MINE FIELDS
FORT MADDALENA

I. THE DCLI AT WAR

* * *

25
The 1st Battalion

Lahore, 8th January 1938-9th November 1941

The outbreak of war on 3rd September 1939 saw the 1st Battalion in Napier Barracks, Lahore, with battalion headquarters and two companies in the Simla Hills at Dagshai. Lieutenant-Colonel T.G.Ll. Elliott was in command.

Initially, the news did little to alter the tempo of life, except that the Lahore rifle companies were involved with the Punjab Police in rounding up male enemy nationals, and providing guards over the temporary detention cages in the Battalion's barracks. Officers on leave in England were ordered to report either to the 2nd Battalion or the Depôt, while a batch of newly joined young officers was sent out to India in their place. The Battalion was reorganised on the Provisional War Establishment. Details of the establishment of the 2nd Battalion in England have been explained in the preceding chapter. That of the 1st Battalion was similar, except that much of the equipment and all the motor vehicles were 'notional', existing only on paper. This was to have a profound effect at a later date when the Battalion went into action against a modern, fully mechanised German army. At this stage each platoon had a pack mule which carried the Vickers Berthier light machine-gun (a weapon similar to the Bren gun issued to troops in India), together with magazines and reserve ammunition. There was also a Carrier Platoon similarly equipped with mules and VBs. Company and forward echelon battalion transport consisted of mule carts, while the Quartermaster relied on a motley string of bullock carts and camels. No wireless sets were issued at battalion level, all communication being carried out by flags, lamp, heliograph, or field telephone. Formation training during the first year of the war showed how inadequate this equipment was for the conduct of modern mobile operations.

In December 1939 any thought of the 1st Battalion seeing early action was dispelled when many officers, warrant officers and NCOs were ordered to return to England to undertake various urgent duties. However, these gaps were later filled by drafts of Reservists together with additional drafts from Territorial battalions and the Militia (the 1939 Militia bore no relation to its namesake of the eighteenth and nineteenth centuries, but consisted of men who had been conscripted for military training shortly before the declaration of war).

In February 1940 the Battalion carried out a week-long exercise in the Ferozepore area, the theme of which was mobility. This once more showed up the shortcomings of the reliance on animal transport.

For the remainder of 1940 and the early part of 1941 the 1st Battalion remained in Lahore, carrying out routine garrison duties. With the war raging in Europe, the situation in India seemed somehow unreal. The social life of the British community in India was unaffected, with hunting, horse shows, point-to-point races, dances, shooting and games of all sorts continuing as though no war existed. While all continued to enjoy themselves, most officers felt a deep frustration. All the military talk was of mobility and fast armoured movement, while the 1st Battalion was still tied to the speed of the pack mule, and many of the weapons carried were dummies.

In the spring of 1941 the Battalion was subjected to a deliberately gruelling brigade exercise in the Jhelum area, designed to prove that British soldiers could operate in extreme heat just as well as Indian troops. The Battalion was required to march to the training area, a distance of 108 miles along the Grand Trunk Road, and then for the next ten days to carry out arduous exercises by day and night. At the end of the fortnight's training the 1st DCLI was the only battalion in the brigade to be at full strength, without a single man dropping out from heat exhaustion. Much of the credit for this performance must lie with the Commanding Officer, Lieutenant-Colonel T.V. Williams, MC whose dictum as regards training was 'You've got to be cruel to be kind'.

Move to Iraq, November 1941

August 1941 brought the first intimation of a move from India. A large draft was received from England, and the long promised motor transport was delivered. It must be remembered that at that time very few soldiers had ever driven a motor vehicle before joining the army, so that in September and October concentrated driver and maintenance training was required.

On 8th November the Motor Transport Platoon, with all the

vehicles, entrained for Karachi, where after a journey lasting two nights and a day, men and vehicles were embarked on HMT *Burnside*. The main body, less B Company, followed on 9th November, embarking on HMT *Lancashire*. B Company had previously been despatched north to collect 200 German and Italian men, women and children from Peshawar. This disparate group arrived that evening and were duly embarked with the main body.

IRAQ & THE MIDDLE EAST, 1940-1942

Burnside and *Lancashire* left Karachi on the night of 11th November and set off westwards, arriving at the mouth of the Shatt-al-Arab on 15th November, where they anchored. So tight was security that at this stage nobody (except perhaps the Commanding Officer and Adjutant) knew where the Battalion was bound. Lucknow Day was celebrated in fine style with lifeboat racing, and a splendid officers' dinner which was attended by members of the German Diplomatic Corps who were amongst the detainees, a unique event in the Regiment's history. The ships weighed anchor again on 17th November and sailed for Basra, which was reached on the following evening. After the detainees had been handed over to the Turkish authorities, the Battalion moved out into the desert to tented camps at As Zubair and Shu'aiba, about fifteen miles from Basra. Here it became part of the 10th Indian Division, commanded by Major-General W. J. Slim, MC.

Arrival in Iraq, December 1941

The operational task allotted to the 1st Battalion was to guard the Hindiya Barrage on the River Euphrates. This barrage provided irrigation for many hundreds of square miles of fertile land, and was thus of vital importance to Iraq. The new defensive position lay about 300 miles to the north west, but such was the configuration of the ground that the actual route was far longer. The move was to begin on 7th December 1941 but, almost at the last moment, orders were received that the Battalion was to take fifty additional 3 ton lorries for delivery to the vehicle depôt near Baghdad. Even today this would present a problem but at that time, in a unit which until recently had relied on mule transport, it seemed an impossible demand. It speaks highly of the flexibility of an infantry battalion that men were found who, after a few days of instruction, managed to drive these extra 3 tonners for hundreds of miles across desert tracks. In spite of drifting sand which obliterated the track, rainstorms which turned it into mud, and novice drivers, the long journey was accomplished in six days. The Cornwalls arrived at the Hindiya Barrage on the afternoon of 12th December.

Hindiya Barrage, December 1941

The Battalion was now part of 21 (Indian) Brigade, which included the 4/13th Frontier Force Rifles and the 2/4th Gurkha Rifles. The defensive line was based on a broad water obstacle known as the Husainiya Canal. For the next few weeks all efforts were directed towards digging field works and laying thousands of yards of barbed wire. Throughout this period, although the weather was pleasantly warm by day, the nights were bitterly cold with hard frosts.

Training at Habbaniya, February 1942

On 15th February 21 Brigade drove to the area of the RAF base at Habbaniya, to carry out a six-week programme of desert training. Much of this involved the practice of complex manoeuvres across open desert in company, battalion or brigade formations. Wireless communication, such as it was, being thoroughly unreliable, control was exercised by the use of flag signals. The whole effect was reminiscent of a naval fleet at sea.

Taji, April 1942

On 1st April the Brigade moved to Taji, a few miles north west of Baghdad, where it again constructed a strong defensive position, bounded by the River Tigris to the east and the Aqua Quf depression to the west. There followed a period of about six weeks of hard digging, revetting and wiring. While at Taji Lieutenant-Colonel T. V. Williams, MC left the Battalion on promotion to Brigadier, and was succeeded by Lieutenant-Colonel H.W. Dean of the Suffolk Regiment, who had joined at Lahore as Second-in-Command.

Move to Egypt, 17th-26th May 1942

Scarcely had Lieutenant-Colonel Dean assumed command than a cryptic order was received: '1 DCLI will move to Egypt by desert route 16 May'. The order could scarcely have come at a more inopportune time; the Commanding Officer was away acting as an umpire on an Army exercise near the Turkish frontier, and many Warrant Officers and NCOs (including the Regimental Serjeant-Major) were also away on courses. The task of the rapid planning for this move initially fell on the shoulders of the Second-in-Command, Major J.B. Peter-Hoblyn. Orders and counter orders flooded in, adding to his problems and frustrations. The heavy baggage was to be left in Baghdad, together with certain vehicles; the machine-guns and motorcycles were to be handed over to a neighbouring Indian battalion; while, at the same time, sufficient 3 and 5 ton lorries to carry the complete Battalion were to be drawn from the Command Vehicle Depôt. These, it was learnt, were to be used for the move before being handed over to the Eighth Army in Egypt; it seemed to be the fate of the Battalion to ferry vehicles around the Middle East. The challenge facing the Battalion cannot be exaggerated. RASC drivers would normally have driven the troop-carrying vehicles, but as these were not available, the comparatively inexperienced DCLI soldiers were again required to perform this duty.

The distance to be negotiated was about 2,000 miles, the first 500 or so being across some of the roughest and most inhospitable desert in the world.

The Battalion was ready to move by 16th May, but it was not till the following morning that the order came to start. After four days of extremely difficult going across the lava belt of the Syrian desert, the column reached the town of Mafraq on the Palestine border. The worst was over, for from there the route dropped down out of the barren highlands to the lush Jordan valley. Soldiers who had lain huddled on lorry floors suddenly came to life, exchanging badinage with the girls in the villages through which they passed.

On 19th May the column reached the port of Haifa on the Mediterranean. Here the Battalion enjoyed a day's rest with a chance to have a proper wash and sample the delights of fresh fruit and vegetables. A nearby Australian Workshop Company moved in and set about servicing the hard-used vehicles.

On 21st May the Battalion turned south and continued on a route parallel with the coast. Two days later it arrived at Bir Asluj, a village with little to commend it to soldiers except a plentiful supply of good water. Here the Battalion again rested for a day before setting off on the last leg of the journey across the Sinai Desert to Ismailia, on the Suez Canal. Meanwhile the Quartermaster submitted demands for vehicle spares and other urgent needs. Brand-new universal carriers appeared as if by magic, so that once again the Carrier Platoon had their vehicles.

Cairo & El Ameriya, May 1942

Early next morning the Battalion set off for Cairo, arriving there at midnight on the 25th-26th May. In contrast to Baghdad, the town was brightly lit as though there was no war. Here Lieutenant-Colonel Dean rejoined the Battalion. It will be remembered that he had been umpiring a major exercise when the original order came to move. Since then he had fallen ill but, although far from recovered, had succeeded in cutting through a mass of red tape to make his own way to Cairo.

The stay in Cairo was brief, for orders were immediately received to continue on for a further 100 miles west to El Ameriya. There it seemed that the Battalion's odyssey was finally over, and that it could look forward to an uninterrupted period of training and administration. This view was reinforced by orders to despatch two officers and six serjeants to Almaza to undergo an anti-tank course.

Here it must be emphasised that, at this time, the Battalion had been given no idea of what its operational role would be. It was known that the two other battalions of 21 (Indian) Brigade were following close behind, and that the remaining elements of the 10th (Indian) Division were also moving towards Egypt. It was therefore assumed that, when the Division was complete and the additional weapons and equipment had been issued, everybody would get down to a period of training. This may indeed have been the original plan; if so, it had been overtaken by events taking place out in the desert beyond Tobruk. On 27th May 1942, the very day that the 1st Battalion arrived at El Ameriya, General Rommel struck at the southern flank of the Allied position. A fierce and confused battle was raging.

The 1st Battalion knew nothing of these events. Orders and counter orders flooded in, unsettling officers and men who were used to acting on clear and concise instructions. One well-remembered priority signal, brought in by a dust-stained despatch rider, ordered the Band to be returned to Cairo immediately. Since the Band was 2,000 miles away in Baghdad, little could be done about that!

Move to Cyrenaica, May 1942

All thoughts of settling down in the El Ameriya area were dispelled when orders were received to dump all tentage and camp equipment and move further west, to El Daba. This last order raised an ugly spectre: if all camp equipment was to be dumped, someone on the staff must be anticipating the early commitment of the Battalion to battle; did that person realise how ill-equipped the Cornwalls were to fight against German armour? Steel helmets, 2 in. mortars, the majority of the wireless sets and, above all, any form of anti-tank weapon were all missing. The men were fit and their morale was high, but this apparent lack of decision on the part of the staff gave the feeling of incompetence.

The camp equipment was duly dumped at El Daba and the Battalion carried on its move, ever westwards to Mersa Matruh. Here it caught up with the advance party, commanded by Major D.Y. Hext, which had been preceding the main body since Taji. They had already been up close to the battle, but had been ordered to move back to the town to Sollum to liaise with the 2nd Queen's Own Cameron Highlanders, whom the DCLI were to relieve.

At long last a clear operational task seemed to have been given; everybody's spirits rose.

On the evening of 27th May Brigade Headquarters of 21 (Indian) Brigade arrived at Mersa Matruh with the other Battalion commanders. Orders were given for the occupation of the defensive position at Sollum, and the column started off again early next morning. Passing through the village of Buq Buq, the Commanding Officer was told that the plan was changed, and that his battalion should pass through Sollum and move to Tobruk, where further orders would be issued. He was also told that eight 2 pdr anti-tank guns were to be collected at Sollum on the way through. This was ironic when one remembers that the two officers and six serjeants, who were to instruct the men to crew these weapons, had been sent back to Cairo where they were kicking their heels! Nevertheless, the eight guns did appear, complete with their 30 cwt 'portee' vehicles. At last the Battalion had a potential capacity to kill tanks. The fact that nobody was trained to use these weapons, and that six of the eight guns were lacking their wheels (so that they could not be dismounted from their portees), and that four of the eight portees were non runners (and had to be towed) seemed of little consequence by comparison.

Sollum, 28th May 1942

That night the Battalion leaguered near Sollum, allowing for a rapid reorganisation. Two officers, sixteen NCOs and thirty men were withdrawn from the rifle companies to form an anti-tank platoon and a medical section (the Band, which would normally have provided the latter, being in Iraq).

The following morning, 29th May, orders were again changed. The Battalion was to take over a sector of the Sollum defensive Bir perimeter from the 2/7th Gurkha Rifles, and all the troop-carrying vehicles were to be despatched to Gambut, forty miles to the west. This indicated that the Battalion would remain at Sollum for an appreciable time, so the opportunity was taken to send the newly formed anti-tank platoon to the nearby anti-tank school at Salt Lake. However, that evening, fresh orders were received to the effect that the Battalion was to move off at first light the following morning towards Tobruk. As the Battalion had obeyed a previous order to send all its troop-carrying transport to Gamut, this appeared impossible. However, the Brigade Transport Company managed to produce a number of vehicles. By means of shedding every item of non-essential kit, the Battalion was eventually squeezed on board, and at 6 a.m. on 30th May the grossly overloaded vehicles took to the road. All through that day and the following night the column moved westwards, along crater-pitted roads that were often obscured by sand storms. During 31st May urgent orders were received to relieve the Highland Light Infantry in the defensive perimeter around Gambut airfield, and to send out patrols to the south to check that Rommel was not outflanking the British position.

Move to Tobruk, 2nd June 1942

On 2nd June 1942 orders were received to hand over the position to a battalion of the Free French army, and to move as fast as possible to Tobruk. The Commanding Officer and Anti-tank Officer were to precede the battalion for briefing by the Tobruk Garrison Commander. This they did, though reconnoitering the proposed new position was far from easy as the minefield maps had been lost in the confusion. The main body of the Battalion had a far greater problem. The orders clearly required it to move to Tobruk as quickly as possible, but the transport, borrowed from the Brigade Transport Company, had by this time been withdrawn. In order to get at least some of the Battalion forward, Major Peter-Hoblyn ordered the Headquarters Company platoons (which had their own transport) to push on ahead. The weather could not have been more vile, with sandstorms reducing visibility to a few yards. Meantime, Major Peter-Hoblyn had persuaded the two Indian battalions to lend some of their 3 tonners into which the remainder of the Battalion were packed. The two groups met at Tobruk that afternoon (3rd June). To everybody's delight the Anti-Tank Platoon, which had dashed the 100 miles from Salt Lake, also appeared with their guns and portees. The complete Battalion then moved forward to the Tobruk defensive perimeter, taking over a sector astride the Tobruk-El Adem road from the West Yorkshire Regiment. The borrowed 3 tonners were then returned to their owners.

Tobruk, 3rd June 1942

The defensive perimeter around Tobruk consisted of a rabbit warren of concrete field works; at intervals, tall wooden towers gave observation over many miles of desert, while belts of barbed wire and mines had been laid in great depth. It was anticipated that, now the Battalion was part of Tobruk Garrison, it would remain there for the foreseeable future.

Once again, all hopes of a period of reasonable stability were soon dashed. Having failed to break through the southern flank of the Allied position, Rommel had withdrawn to regroup. An immediate counter attack by 10th (Indian Division) was ordered by the Commander-in-Chief, General Auchinleck, to re-secure the gaps in the British line. The attack was to be launched at first light on 4th June. The Battalion was to be detached from 21 (Indian) Brigade and attached to 9 (Indian) Brigade as a mobile reserve. Lieutenant-Colonel Dean pointed out that his Battalion could not possibly be in the required position by the following dawn, not least because it had insufficient vehicles.

Move to the Gazala Line, 4th-5th June 1942

During that afternoon there was feverish activity to scrounge extra vehicles, and to draw supplies of water and rations. By the evening the plan was again changed, and the Battalion returned to the command of 21 (Indian) Brigade with orders to move west out into the desert, to rendezvous with a representative of XXX Corps, who would give out further instructions. The Battalion was to move across a featureless desert plain along what was known as the Trigh Capuzzo, marked with oil barrels, each painted with a number. Barrel number 722 was the point at which the XXX Corps representative was to be met.

The Adjutant, Captain S.N. Floyer-Acland, was ordered to move ahead of the main body to Barrel number 722. As described, this may sound simple, but on a dark night it was a slow operation requiring great skill. On passing the airfield at El Adem, the Adjutant requested the Military Police to halt the main body when it arrived so that he could guide it forward. He proceeded to barrel 722; nobody was there. At this point the Commanding Officer, who knew nothing of the new 21 (Indian) Brigade order (as he had been at 9 Brigade Headquarters when the order was issued), despatched Lieutenant C.S. Denman (later Lord Denman, CBE, MC) to contact the main body. This had somehow passed the Military Police post at El Adem without being stopped, but luckily Lieutenant Denman made contact as it was moving west on the Trigh Capuzzo. Unfortunately the rear half of the column had become lost in the darkness. Half a battalion being better than nothing, Major Peter-Hoblyn therefore continued to the new rendezvous ordered by his Commanding Officer. By sheer good fortune the missing half met Lieutenant Denman at barrel number 722. Meanwhile, the lieutenant had managed to make telephone contact with XXX Corps, who gave orders that all available men should move at first light on a bearing of 265 degrees; after nine miles they should reach Headquarters 5th (Indian) Division under whose command they should place themselves.

In visualising the situation, it must be realised that the Libyan desert in which all this was taking place does not consist of sand. Generally speaking, it is very flat, stony ground, scattered with rocks, boulders and clumps of thorny scrub. The surface is cut by the occasional steep wadi running down to the sea. By day, vehicles can motor across the terrain at a reasonable speed; by night, movement is very slow and difficult. In June the surface is extremely dry and dusty, and sudden winds blow up sandstorms, which often reduce visibility to a few yards. There is only one proper tarmac road running from east to west, but there are many desert tracks, some marked on the maps, some not. The Trigh Capuzzo, on which the Battalion was moving during the last stage of its journey, was merely a very broad track, about a mile wide. Although clearly visible by day, its delineation was far from easy to follow in the dark.

The 5th (Indian) Division Headquarters was found without great difficulty, and, at about that time (the exact sequence of events is confused) both halves of the Battalion once more came together. Major Peter-Hoblyn met the GSO1, who gave what must be one of the shortest operation orders in the history of war: "Drive," he said, pointing dramatically to clouds of dust visible in the west, "for about nine miles, and see what you can do."

Bir-el-Harmat

The Battalion motored west, where it was met by guides who led it forward onto a low feature known as Bir-el-Harmat. This formed the centre of a defensive line running from Gazala on the coast to

Bir Hacheim on the extreme southern flank, where the hard desert surface gave way to soft sand. The northern sector of this line from the sea to Bir-el-Harmat was strongly held by units of the 1st (South African) Division and the 50th (British) Division; the area around Bir-el-Harmat, known as the Cauldron, was held by the 5th (Indian) Division. The southern flank position at Bir Hacheim was defended by a Free French formation, but the considerable length of front between Bir-el-Harmat and Bir Hacheim was only covered by a minefield.

The Battle of Bir-el-Harmat (The Cauldron) 5th- 6th June 1942

Lieutenant-Colonel Dean, who had moved ahead of the Battalion, deployed the companies into positions that he had selected. With his headquarters in the centre, D and B Companies were to the west, C Company was to the south, and A Company was to the north. Immediately everybody started to dig rudimentary weapon pits, but the rocky nature of the ground limited these to eighteen inches. Meanwhile the Carrier Platoon, under Captain T.H. Jobson, was despatched to make contact with the Free French to the south. After driving about six miles a column of vehicles, including tanks, was seen moving through an obvious gap in the minefield from west to east. This was duly reported to Divisional Headquarters. Later, another carrier patrol led by Captain Jobson was actually fired on by tanks east of the minefield, and was lucky to get away without casualties. Once more Divisional Headquarters was informed and a request made for artillery fire. The reply came back stating that Captain Jobson's report must be incorrect, and consequently no fire would be brought down on the alleged enemy target.

To clarify the situation, Lieutenant-Colonel Dean sent out a strong patrol made up of the Carrier Platoon and C Company. They became involved in another running battle with large numbers of Germans who had crossed the minefield, and were now well east of the defensive line. Lieutenant-Colonel Dean once more requested urgent artillery support. He was told that a Forward Observation Officer would be sent up to him. No gunner materialised.

After a strike of low level bombing, the Germans attacked from the south into the position held by C Company and Battalion Headquarters. Major Petrie, commanding D Company, immediately led a counter attack. As his men charged in with the bayonet, he himself drove his 15 cwt truck across their front to produce a 'smoke screen' of dust. He was almost instantly killed, as were most of his gallant Company. In the middle of all this, a number of British universal carriers clattered into the Battalion position from the rear. Presuming that these represented reinforcements their arrival was cheered by the hard pressed Cornwalls; hopes were, however, quickly dashed, for they proved to be captured vehicles, from which fire was immediately opened. By late afternoon the battle was virtually over. German tanks and infantry occupied most of the Bir-el-Harmat position, and although spasmodic shooting continued, the Battalion was no longer capable of carrying on the fight. About fifty soldiers lay dead, and as many were wounded. As dusk fell on the confusion of the battle-field, opportunities arose for the bold to make a break for freedom. Lieutenant Denman gathered the survivors of D Company, and led them eastwards. Without either map or compass, he navigated by the stars, and, after dodging German leaguers, succeeded in reaching a friendly headquarters. He was awarded an MC. Sadly, his wounded batman, who had been carried most of the way, died shortly afterwards. Serjeant L. Holt gathered up most of the Carrier Platoon, and driving at full speed through the German lines, also managed to get clear. For this he was awarded the DCM.

By nightfall several hundred prisoners, including most of 9th (Indian) Brigade and a number of British tank crews, had been herded together in the Bir-el-Harmat position. A German general arrived, who asked if anyone present could translate for him, whereupon Major D.V. Holt replied that he could. The general addressed the prisoners, saying "Tell your men that it was a good fight, and but for your bad 'war luck' you might have won. You must sleep the night here where you are as it is not safe to take you through the minefield in the dark, but we will get you back as soon as we can."

The following morning the prisoners of war column was escorted westwards to captivity. As it wound its way through the minefield the British gunners mistook it for Germany infantry and opened fire. As a final indignity, those men, who throughout the previous day had been denied artillery support, now found themselves subjected to British shells.

Regrouping of the survivors, 6th June 1942

It was normal operating procedure for the Commanding Officer to detail a group under the Second-in-Command who, in the event of casualties amongst key members of the Battalion, could re-establish command and control. Lieutenant-Colonel Dean had therefore previously ordered his Second-in-Command, Major Peter-Hoblyn, and a small group of officers and men to move back about three miles, close to the headquarters of the 5th Division. This party would provide a nucleus around which the Battalion could be reformed in the event of disaster. Lieutenant-Colonel Dean's foresight was to prove invaluable for, after the battle, Lieutenant Denman's and Serjeant Holt's parties together with other individuals who had made their escape joined Major Peter-Hoblyn's group to form a cadre Battalion. This, with the other two battalions of 21 (Indian) Brigade, moved back to Gambut airfield on 9th June, where additional equipment was acquired. At Gambut various officers and men who had been attending courses in Iraq rejoined, bringing the total strength of the cadre to about 150. These were quickly organised into two rifle platoons, an anti-tank section and a depleted carrier platoon.

Ameriya & Kassassin, 9th June-17th July

With many alarms and minor battles, this body of officers and men made its way east to Ameriya, where it arrived on 3rd July. By that time about fifty had been lost (mostly captured). There it was deployed as a guard on the airfield for a week, after which it at last moved back to safety to a rest camp at Kassassin, (the site of the 2nd Battalion battle in 1882).

While resting at Kassassin, a draft of 100 men from the Devonshire and the Worcestershire Regiments joined. While the Quartermaster Lieutenant W. Edwards was struggling to draw new clothing and equipment from the Ordnance Depôt at Tel-el-Kebir, news was received that the embryo battalion was to sail for Cyprus as soon as a ship became available. This it did on 17th July.

Cyprus, July-August 1942

Attempted amalgamation to form a new battalion of the King's Own Royal Regiment, 1st September 1942

On arrival in Cyprus Major-General F.I.S. Tuker, CB, DSO, OBE visited the Battalion and announced that it was to be brought up to strength and that the new Commanding Officer, Lieutenant-Colonel C.E. Lewin-Harris, would assume command on 31st July. Morale was very high, and all ranks immediately got down to energetic and imaginative training. However, there seemed to be a jinx on the 1st Battalion that invariably ensured that every order was countermanded almost immediately. On 2nd August the Battalion was told that there had been a complete change of plan; a cadre of two officers and ten soldiers was to return to England to raise a new 1st Battalion. The remaining officers and men were to join an amalgamation of the 1st South Wales Borderers and 1st King's Own Royal Regiment, to form a new battalion known by the title of the latter regiment.

This news sickened and dumbfounded everybody. The British regimental system possesses enormous strengths, in that it deliberately welds all ranks into a close family with a fierce pride. Every soldier is taught from his first day as a recruit, that he is a member of the finest regiment in the army. The regiment, in its turn, demands absolute and total loyalty. Everything in a soldier's life is done to nurture this spirit, and there is no doubt that over the centuries it has given men superhuman strength to carry on against all odds. However, this same regimental system can have grave shortcomings. After training men to look down on all those not lucky enough to wear the same cap badge, it becomes almost impossible to turn that allegiance on its head and post large drafts to another regiment. Individuals or small groups can absorbed, but to attempt to form a new battalion from three large groups, each with its clear cut pride of identity, courts disaster. It must be remembered that in this particular case many of the men were long-serving regular soldiers, into whom the ethos of the regiment had been instilled over many years; furthermore, the three battalions, the DCLI from rural Cornwall, the South Wales Borderers from the Welch coalfields and the King's Own Royal Regiment from the industrial towns of Lancashire, could not have formed a more disparate trio.

The new Battalion was formally inaugurated on 1st September 1942. There was discord from the very start, and soon serious trouble erupted, often of a violent nature. To restore discipline, drastic measures were taken which eventually had their effect. For the old regulars who had survived the hardships of the desert and the dangers of battle, and had been promised that their beloved Battalion would arise Phoenix like from the ashes, this was the final tragedy in a tragic campaign.

Departure of the 1st Battalion cadre to England 26 August 1942

The cadre of two officers and ten soldiers departed from Cyprus on 26th August 1942, bound for England.

The fate of the Prisoners of War

At this stage one must return to the Western Desert. Large numbers of prisoners of war are always an embarrassment to the captors, particularly in a theatre in which supplies of food and water are scarce. It is therefore not surprising that the conditions under which the prisoners were held were far from comfortable; indeed, at times they were little short of barbaric, when the agonies of thirst drove men to the borders of insanity. As shipping became available, the prisoners were sent off to camps in Italy.

When Italy surrendered on 3rd September 1943, many made their escape. For the majority of these, their freedom was short-lived; the Germans were quick to round up the fugitives, who were taken to prisoner of war camps deep in eastern Germany or Poland. A few made good their escape. Some made for the Swiss border; some, like Private H. Gosselin, met up with Yugoslav or Italian guerrilla bands with whom they continued to fight against Germany. A few trudged southwards till they reached the Allied lines. Three such men were Captains G.T.G. Williams, T.H. Jobson and W.P. Pryke. Their epic walk of over 450 miles in 35 days was later recorded by the three in an account entitled 'An unofficial hike in Italy during 1943'. The light-hearted style of this narrative of their escape plays down the physical feat of the endeavour, and the formidable difficulties that they overcame by their determination to reach freedom.*

Tragically, two ships carrying prisoners of war from North Africa to Italy were sunk by British warships. Very few of the men on board escaped, and those who were killed included DCLI soldiers. The sinking of these two vessels, which were in no way marked to indicate that they were carrying prisoners, represented one of the ever-present hazards of war. No guilt can possibly be attributed to the Royal Navy, who were merely carrying out their orders to sink all Axis shipping.

Epilogue

Reading the extraordinary saga of the Battalion's move through Egypt, into Libya and on to the final disastrous battle west of Tobruk, one has every reason to be appalled by the apparent breakdown of all coherent staff work. It would seem that, at every level, the staff

*A fourth officer, Captain Ian Shaw of the Green Howards, was also with this party of escapees for the majority of the journey. Sadly, he was killed near Antwerp in October 1944 while serving in the 52nd (Lowland) Division.

failed to appreciate that the 1st DCLI was totally ill-equipped to fight a modern battle against armour. In defence of the various headquarters it must be realised that they were under intense pressure, attempting to fight a fast-moving armoured blitzkrieg with inadequate numbers of troops. For them, it was no time to look a gift horse in the mouth; any battalion that arrived in the theatre was hastily deployed into battle in an effort to plug the ever widening gaps.

Of the Battalion itself, one can hardly speak too highly. It had left its base in Iraq at very short notice, and had moved entirely under its own resources for some 2,000 miles, the first part of this epic journey being through some of the roughest desert in the world. This alone must stand as a considerable achievement. Given no opportunity to rest, it had continued across Egypt and Libya, always responding with alacrity to a deluge of orders and counter orders from a miscellany of headquarters. Although confused by events, it had never become despondent or lost its high state of morale. Thrown into battle with totally inadequate weapons and equipment, without armour or artillery support, and facing overwhelming odds, few can have doubted what the final outcome must be. They had not long to wait but, during the short battle that raged, the 1st Battalion fought with great gallantry, living up to the proudest traditions of the Duke of Cornwall's Light Infantry.

Helston, 9th December 1942

The 1st Battalion cadre arrived back in England during the autumn of 1942, and was attached to the 6th Battalion, then deployed on coastal defence duties between Falmouth and the Lizard. The cadre consisted of the following: Major J.B. Peter-Hoblyn; Lieutenant (QM) W. Edwards; Regimental Serjeant-Major L.Moore; Regimental Quartermaster-Serjeant H. Walker; Company Serjeant- Majors M. Shelley and G. Jones; Serjeant F. Gundry, Corporals A. Stokes, D. Cennal and W. Harden; and Private T. MacLennan.

The 1st Battalion lives again, 9th December 1942

Shortly afterwards an official announcement was made to the effect that the 6th Battalion, under command of Lieutenant-Colonel G.J. Fletcher, was to amalgamate with this cadre, and was to be re-named the 1st Battalion. On 9th December 1942 a ceremonial parade took place at Helston, in which the acting Colonel of the Regiment, Lieutenant-General A.N. Floyer-Acland, CB, DSO, MC handed

Colours over to the new Battalion. As the Colours in current service with the 1st Battalion were then stored in India, the Quartermaster was despatched to the Parish Church in Bodmin to borrow the 1883 Colours. The next day they were returned to Bodmin. Thus the 1st Battalion arose like a Phoenix from the ashes of the Western Desert.

Although the new 1st Battalion was never to see active service nor, indeed, leave the shores of Britain, it carried out vital if unglamorous duties, providing reinforcement drafts for various overseas battalions. As D Day approached, the Battalion found itself more and more involved in the massive administrative operation which ensured the smooth movement of a vast army to its embarkation areas. Soon infantry casualties in Europe began to outstrip the supply of reinforcements. Anti-aircraft regiments were withdrawn from the Order of Battle, and retrained as infantry reinforcements. The 1st Battalion was given the task of converting these men, who took such pride in the Royal Artillery, into infantry soldiers, for posting wherever they might be needed. This job required not only skill but considerable tact, if morale was to be retained.

Lieutenant-Colonel Peter-Hoblyn assumed command in March 1945, and almost immediately learnt that his Battalion was earmarked for war against the Japanese in the Far East. Jungle training was immediately commenced in deepest Sussex, and it was here that the 1st Battalion found itself when Japan surrendered on 2nd September 1945.

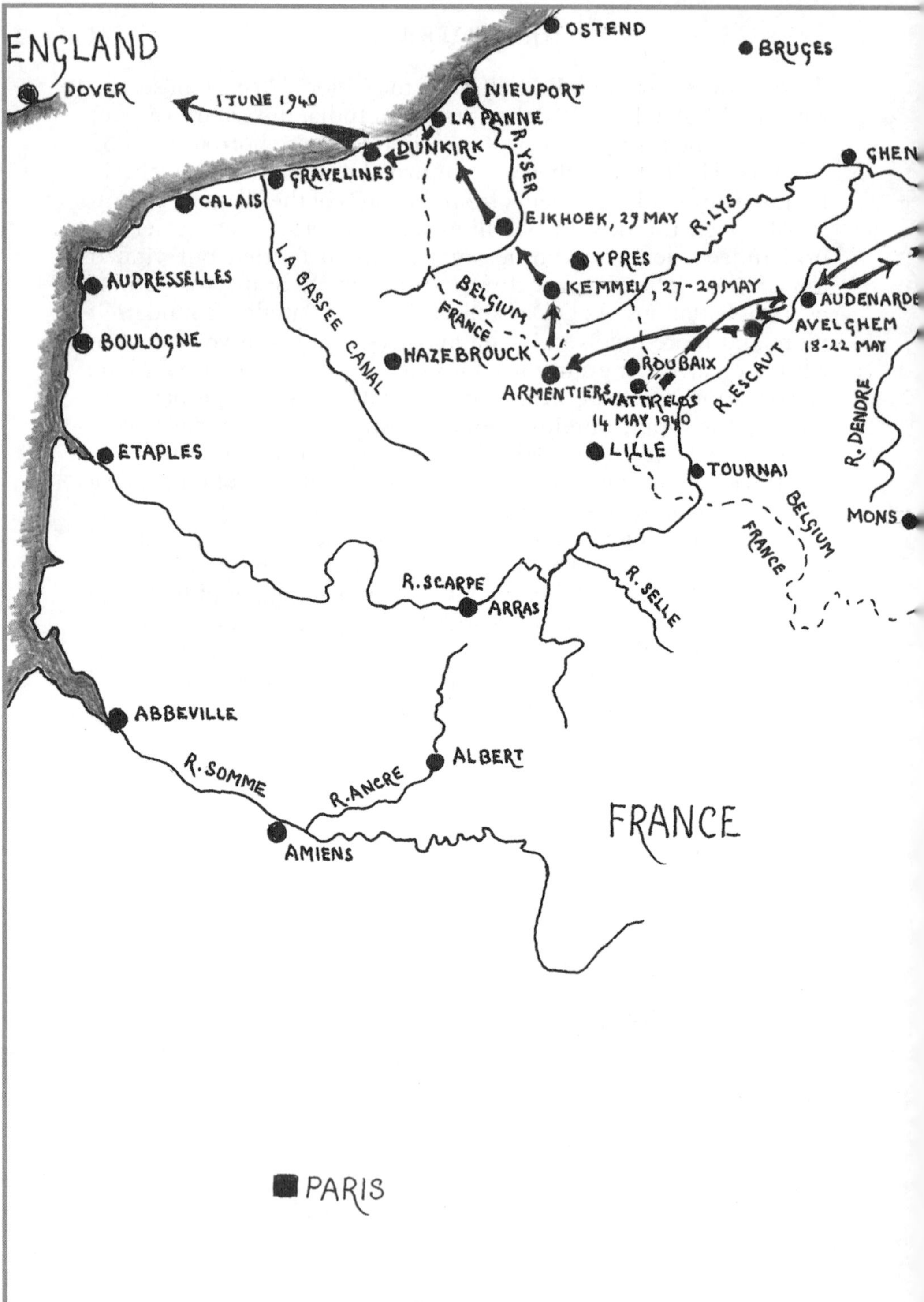
ENGLAND
DOVER
1 JUNE 1940
OSTEND
BRUGES
NIEUPORT
LA PANNE
DUNKIRK
R. YSER
GRAVELINES
CALAIS
EIKHOEK, 29 MAY
R. LYS
GHENT
YPRES
AUDRESSELLES
LA BASSEE CANAL
BELGIUM
FRANCE
KEMMEL, 27-29 MAY
AUDENARDE
AVELGHEM
18-22 MAY
BOULOGNE
HAZEBROUCK
ROUBAIX
ARMENTIERS
WATTRELOS
14 MAY 1940
R. ESCAUT
R. DENDRE
ETAPLES
LILLE
TOURNAI
BELGIUM
FRANCE
MONS
R. SCARPE
ARRAS
R. SELLE
ABBEVILLE
ALBERT
R. SOMME
R. ANCRE
AMIENS
FRANCE
PARIS

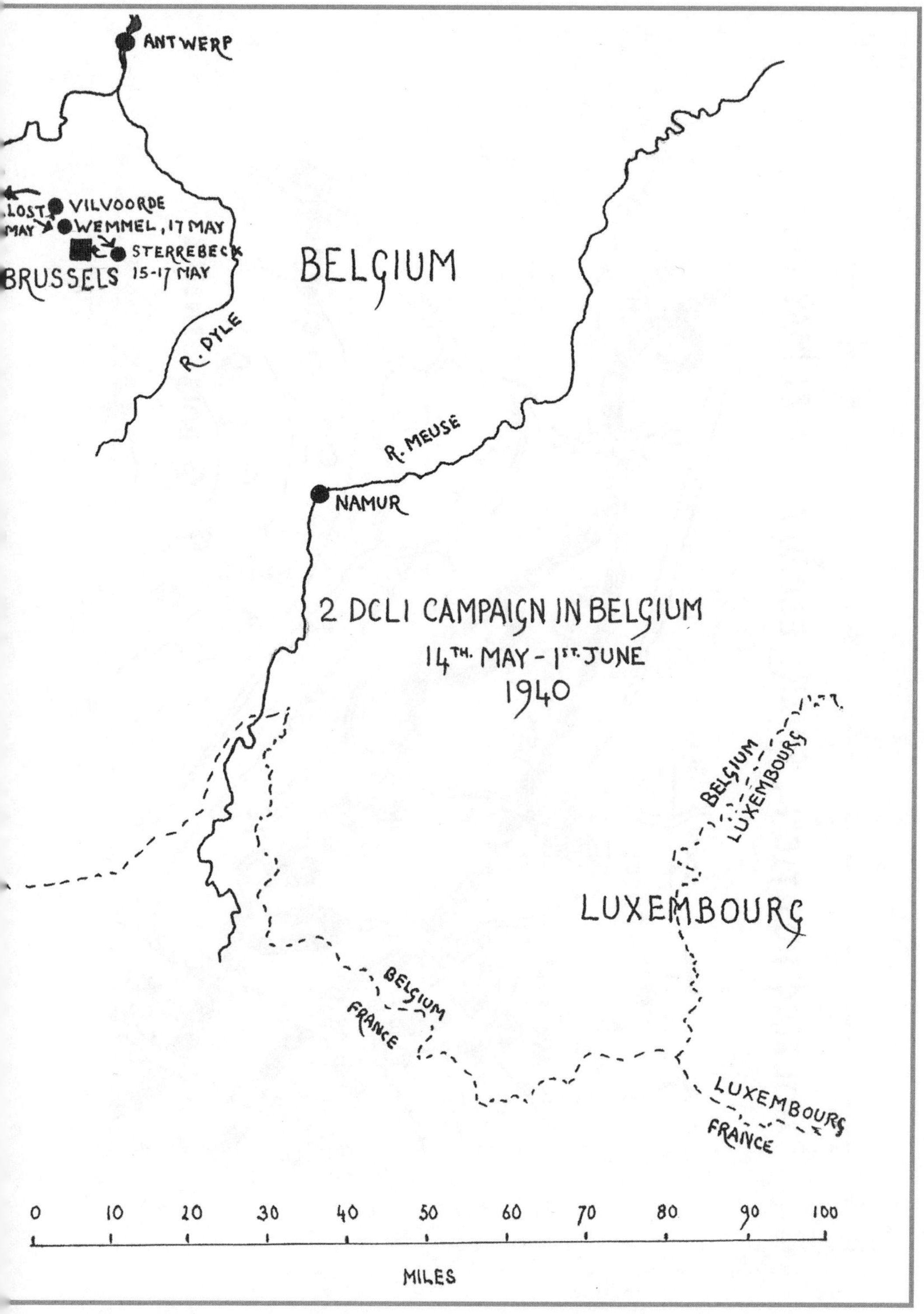
ANTWERP
LOST
MAY
VILVOORDE
WEMMEL, 17 MAY
STERREBECK
BRUSSELS
15-17 MAY
BELGIUM
R. DYLE
R. MEUSE
NAMUR
2 DCLI CAMPAIGN IN BELGIUM
14TH. MAY - 1ST. JUNE
1940
BELGIUM
LUXEMBOURG
LUXEMBOURG
BELGIUM
FRANCE
LUXEMBOURG
FRANCE
0
10
20
30
40
50
60
70
80
90
100
MILES

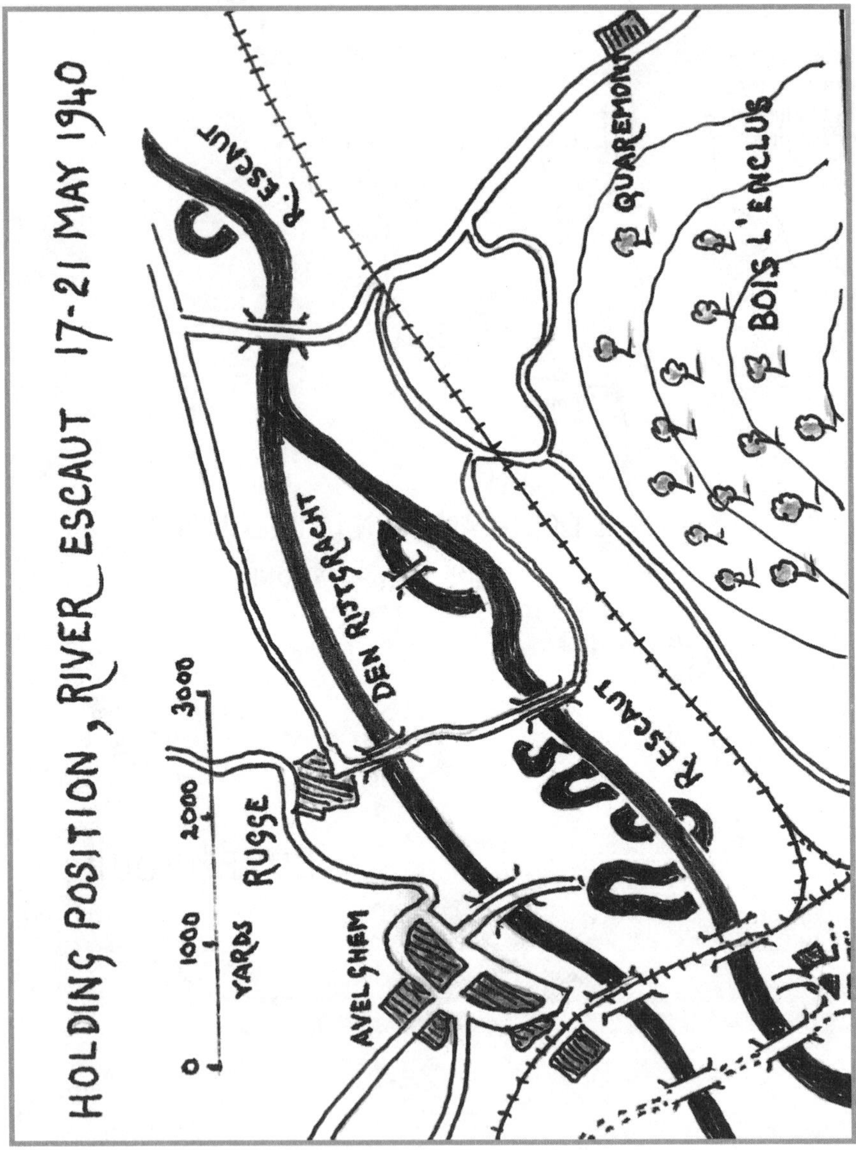
HOLDING POSITION, RIVER ESCAUT 17-21 MAY 1940
0
1000
2000
3000
YARDS
AVELGHEM
RUSSE
DEN RIJTGRACHT
R. ESCAUT
R. ESCAUT
QUAREMONT
BOIS L'ENCLUS

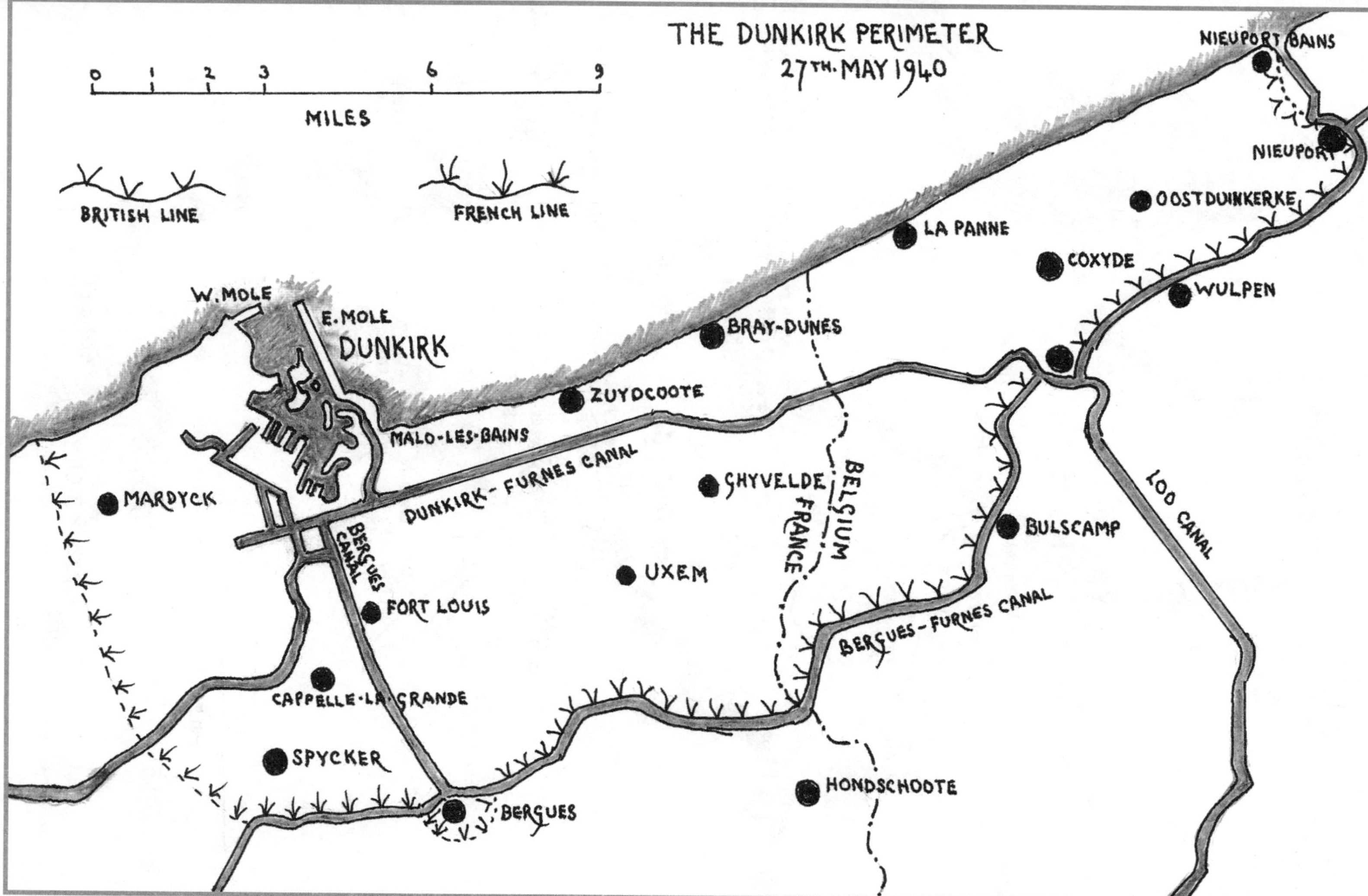
THE DUNKIRK PERIMETER
27TH. MAY 1940
0 1 2 3 6 9
MILES
BRITISH LINE
FRENCH LINE
NIEUPORT BAINS
NIEUPORT
OOSTDUINKERKE
LA PANNE
COXYDE
WULPEN
W. MOLE
E. MOLE
DUNKIRK
BRAY-DUNES
ZUYDCOOTE
MALO-LES-BAINS
DUNKIRK - FURNES CANAL
GHYVELDE
BELGIUM
FRANCE
LOO CANAL
MARDYCK
BERGUES CANAL
BULSCAMP
UXEM
FORT LOUIS
BERGUES - FURNES CANAL
CAPPELLE-LA-GRANDE
SPYCKER
HONDSCHOOTE
BERGUES

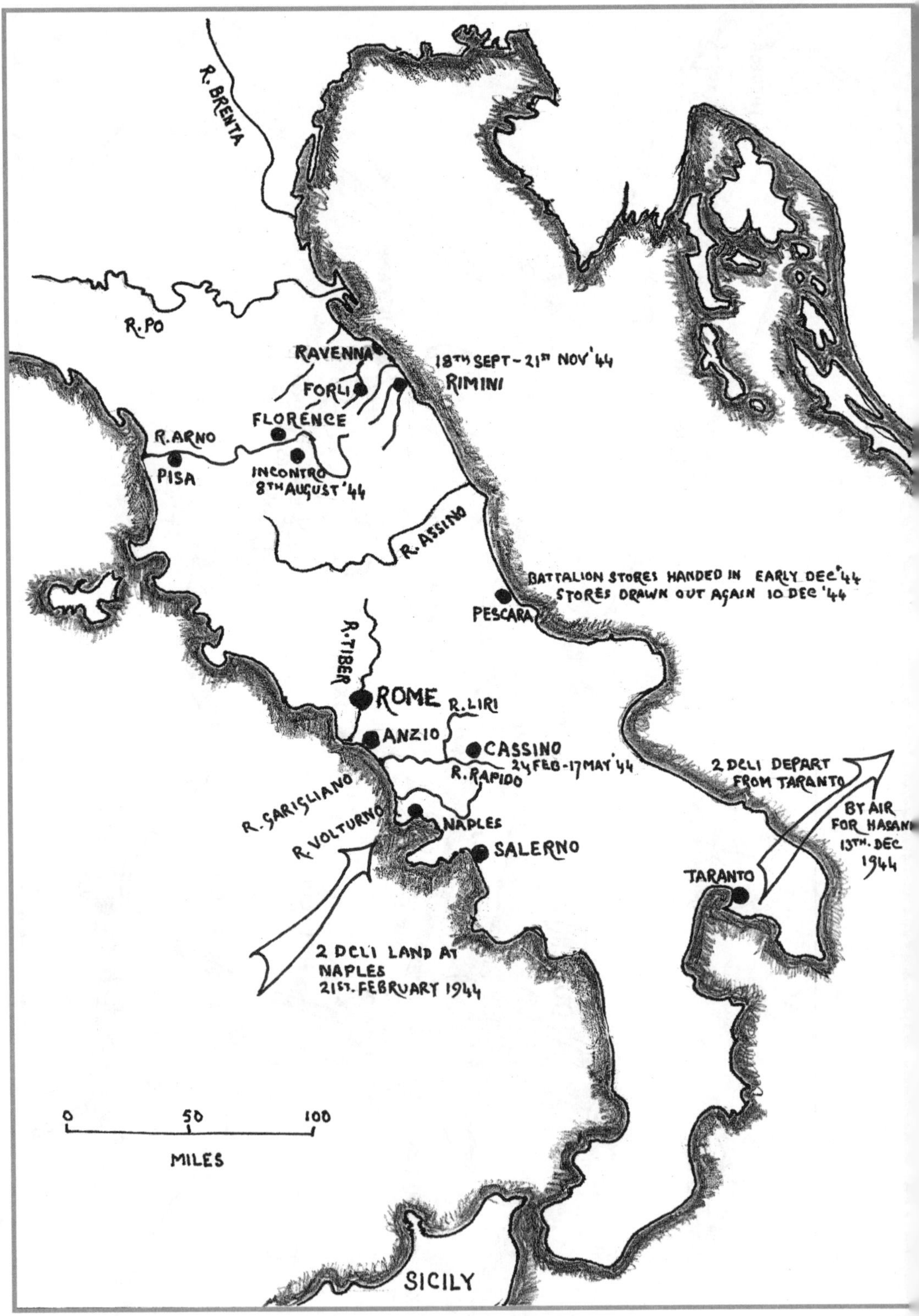
R. BRENTA
R. PO
RAVENNA
18TH SEPT - 21ST NOV '44
RIMINI
FORLI
FLORENCE
R. ARNO
PISA
INCONTRO
8TH AUGUST '44
R. ASSINO
BATTALION STORES HANDED IN EARLY DEC '44
STORES DRAWN OUT AGAIN 10 DEC '44
PESCARA
R. TIBER
ROME
R. LIRI
ANZIO
CASSINO
24 FEB - 17 MAY '44
R. RAPIDO
R. GARIGLIANO
R. VOLTURNO
NAPLES
SALERNO
2 DCLI DEPART
FROM TARANTO
BY AIR
13TH. DEC
1944
TARANTO
2 DCLI LAND AT
NAPLES
21ST. FEBRUARY 1944
0
50
100
MILES
SICILY

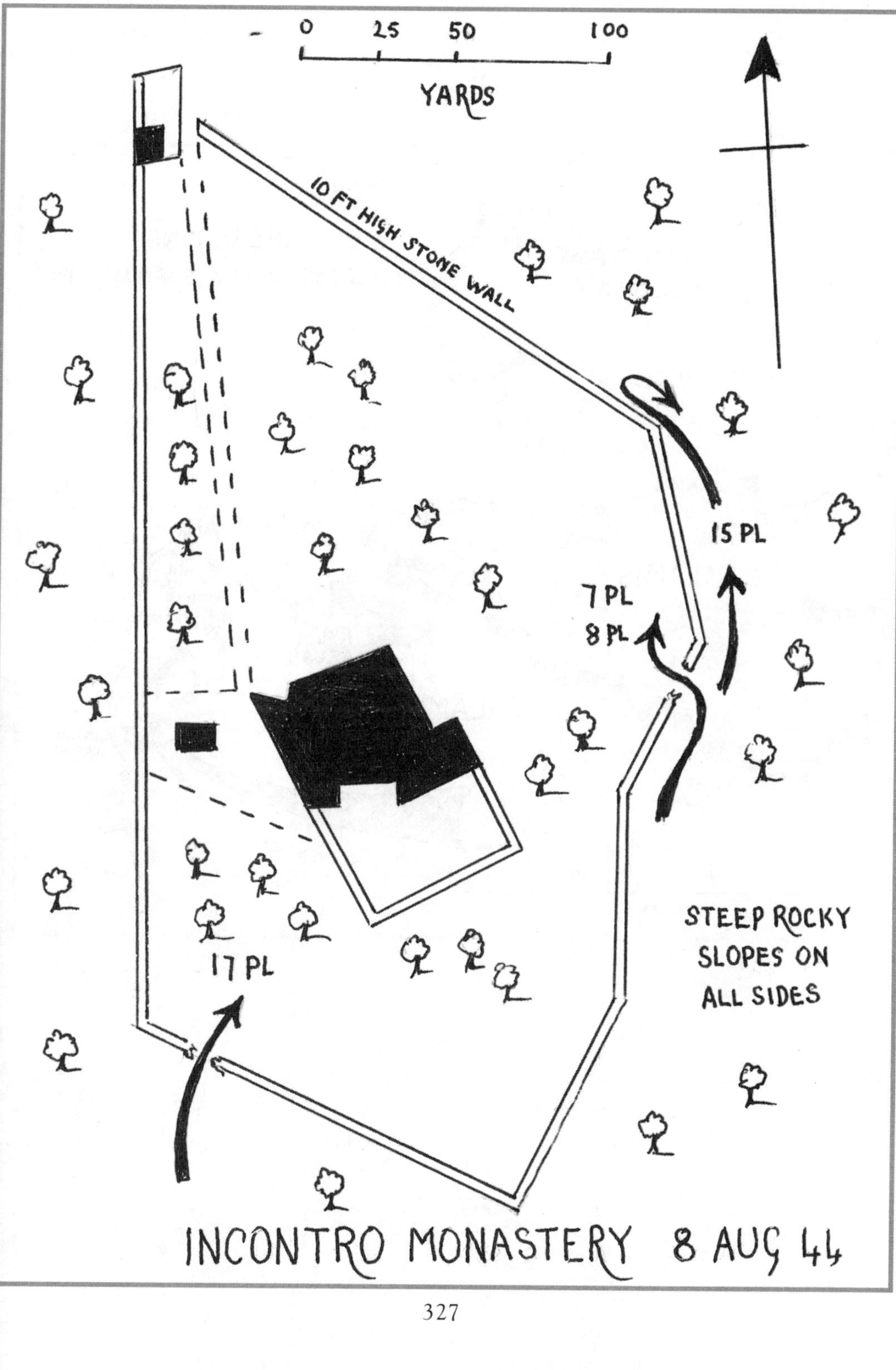
0
25
50
100
YARDS
10 FT HIGH STONE WALL
15 PL
7 PL
8 PL
17 PL
STEEP ROCKY
SLOPES ON
ALL SIDES
INCONTRO MONASTERY 8 AUG 44

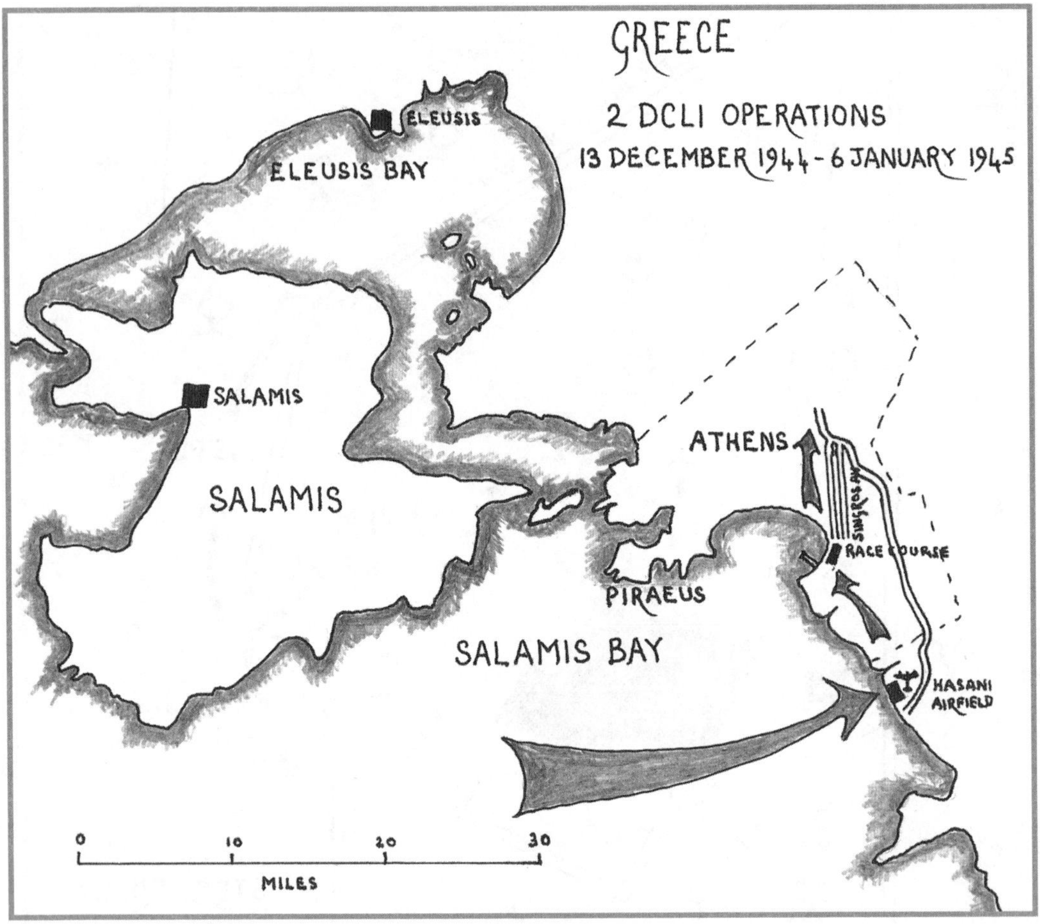
GREECE
2 DCLI OPERATIONS
13 DECEMBER 1944 - 6 JANUARY 1945
ELEUSIS
ELEUSIS BAY
SALAMIS
SALAMIS
ATHENS
RACE COURSE
PIRAEUS
SALAMIS BAY
HASANI AIRFIELD
0
10
20
30
MILES

26
The 2nd Battalion

DECLARATION OF WAR
3RD SEPTEMBER 1939,
& THE BRITISH EXPEDITIONARY FORCE

The declaration of war with Germany on 3rd September 1939 found the 2nd Battalion in Shorncliffe. It was part of 10 Infantry Brigade in the 4th Division and, as such, was due to accompany the British Expeditionary Force (BEF) to France. Within two days the Battalion moved out into billets in Lyminge, as John Moore Barracks was to become a Royal Engineer OCTU.

For the first fortnight training included route marching, exactly as the 1st Battalion had done at the Curragh twenty-five years before. On 21st September the advance party under the Second-in-Command departed for France; two days later the rest of the Battalion moved by rail to Aldershot, where it was quartered in Barossa Barracks awaiting embarkation. The motor transport set off for Newport, Monmouthshire, on 27th September under the command of Captain C.E.B. Acland, where it was loaded into a waiting ship. On that day Their Majesties King George VI and Queen Elizabeth visited Aldershot and the Battalion, with thousands of other troops lining the route. The Commanding Officer, Lieutenant-Colonel E.R. Rushton, had the honour of being presented to Their Majesties.

Move to France, 30th September 1939

The Battalion moved by rail to Southampton docks, where it embarked on the SS *Princess Maud* on the evening of 30th September. That night the ship sailed, docking at Cherbourg early the next morning in pouring rain.

The following day the men started on a long trek, first to the village of Permil near Le Mans where it remained for a week, and then on to the British concentration area around Lille.

Defence of the Franco-German border

It must be explained here that the French had constructed a massive defensive work known as the Maginot Line, which ran along their border with Germany from the Swiss mountains in the south to the Ardennes forest in the north. The Ardennes was considered (incorrectly as it transpired) to be impenetrable; the continuation of the French frontier with neutral Belgium was therefore barely defended in any way. Considering that the German army had attacked through Belgium in 1914, this last omission seemed scarcely wise. General Lord Gort, VC, KCB, CBE, DSO, MVO, MC, Commander-in-Chief of the British Expeditionary Force, would have liked to advance into Belgium without delay, but this course of action would have compromised the neutrality of that country and was politically unacceptable. He was therefore left with the much less effective alternative of constructing a line of field defences along the line of the Franco-Belgian border, which was put in hand as a matter of the greatest urgency.

Wattrelos, & operational experience in front of the Maginot Line, February 1940

The 2nd Battalion's area of responsibility now lay around the border of Wattrelos.

On 16th December 1939, as the result of a tragic accident, the Battalion suffered its first two casualties. Lieutenant E.I. Arnold and Second Lieutenant P.C.S. Milward were attending a course run by the Royal Engineers when an anti-tank mine, being demonstrated in a classroom, exploded. The instructor and all the nine students were killed instantly.

Soon after the BEF arrived in France it was decided that British units, which were digging in on the Belgian border, would benefit from experience in actually facing an enemy. One infantry brigade at a time would serve under French command in front of the Maginot Line for a period of fifteen days, when it would be relieved by a fresh British brigade. The first brigade from the 4th Division to undertake this duty would be the 12th, and a party of three officers was attached to the 1st Black Watch to gain battle experience. The turn of 10 Brigade came at the end of February 1940. At this stage it is necessary to explain the layout of the Maginot defences. On the outbreak of war, the French had advanced several miles forward of their great complex of steel and concrete tunnels and gun emplacements, and established three additional defensive lines. The most advanced of these, *la ligne de contacte*, held by a single battalion, was little more than a line of isolated posts from which patrolling could be carried out. Its function was to monitor German movement and give warning of any impending attack. A supporting battalion held *la ligne de recueil*. Behind this again was a third battalion in *la ligne d'arrêt*, which was intended to act as a buffer to disrupt any enemy advance before it hit the massive fortification of the Maginot Line. It was to the *ligne d'arrêt* that the Battalion was deployed during the night of 25th-26th February 1940, and from which reconnaissance parties moved forward to look at the positions on the *ligne de contacte*, which the Battalion was to occupy. It must be realised that, in all three lines, frontages were very wide, with long gaps between defended localities.

On the 2nd March the Cornwalls took over from the 2nd Bedfordshire and Hertfordshire Regiment in the *ligne de contacte*. The position was not one to inspire confidence. The Battalion was required to occupy a front of some 5,000 yards which ran through heavily wooded, undulating countryside. Not only was mutual support impossible between companies, but often platoons in the same company were out of touch with each other. Because the Battalion was only a short-term tenant in this sector, and was under command of the French, the Commanding Officer was powerless to protest against the obvious impracticality of this defensive layout. In conformity with what had been the practice in the 1914-18 War the battalion holding the *ligne de contacte* was assisted by three so-called 'Battle Patrols', one from each battalion in the Brigade, and operating directly under brigade control. In theory, these patrols were intended to dominate no man's land and to give warning of any enemy movement. These Battle Patrols, each consisting of one officer and twelve men, were billeted together just behind the *ligne de contacte*, irrespective of which battalion was holding that part of the line. Given that the distance between the British and German lines varied between 600 yards and 2 miles, no man's land represented a vast area, broken by hills, valleys and woods. The chances of ever meeting the enemy were therefore slim. General D.N.H. Tyacke, who as a Captain commanded a DCLI Battle Patrol, remembers how night after bitterly cold night he and a few men would move out and lie up watching a track or stream crossing, only to return before dawn with nothing to report. Occasionally artillery would fire a few rounds in the general direction of the enemy, but for most of the time all remained uncannily quiet. Apart from the live ammunition in magazines and pouches, this might have been a very realistic peace-time exercise.

A salutary lesson, 5th March 1940

For 17 Platoon of C Company, this dream was rudely shattered at dawn on 5th March. At 6 a.m. the platoon commanded by Platoon

Serjeant-Major Larcombe had 'stood to'. Of all the incompetently sited positions, this was perhaps the worst. Not only was there dead ground immediately to the front, but there was an undefended wood to the left rear, with direct access to the German lines. So potentially dangerous was the layout of this particular position that the British Brigade Commander had brought up the French Divisional Commander only two days previously to point out its extreme vulnerability. Ten minutes before 'stand down' at 6.50 a.m. German artillery opened fire, putting down a 'box barrage' around the Platoon. After a few minutes this ceased and the Germans attacked. It was all over very quickly; Platoon Serjeant-Major Larcombe and Corporal Killick were killed, and sixteen men were taken prisoner, of whom some were seriously wounded. The Germans left two of their own number dead. This comparatively minor action has been recounted in some detail because it acted as a salutary lesson, which spread far beyond the Battalion, dispelling any illusions about the nature of the war.

Return to Wattrelos, 17th March 1940

Three days after the incident, La Ligne de Contact positions were handed over to another British battalion. The next few days were spent in La Ligne de Recueil before the DCLI moved to billets on the outskirts of Lille, returning to Wattrelos on the Belgian border on 17th March. There the interminable work of digging and wiring continued unabated, as the Allied high command waited in anticipation of a move by the German army.

The German Attack on Belgium & Holland 10th May 1940

On 10th May 1940 the Germans struck, crossing both the Dutch and Belgian frontiers. Fast-moving armoured columns were preceded by heavy air attacks. The city of Rotterdam was virtually destroyed, the Dutch airforce eliminated and all the major bridges captured intact. On 15th May HM Queen Wilhelmina of the Netherlands embarked in a destroyer of the Royal Navy, which brought her to the safety of England. That same day, Holland surrendered. In just five days Germany had secured a firm northern flank and captured the most important port on the North Sea coast. This first move through Holland was, however, merely a feint; the full strength of the German thrust was planned to push through the Ardennes forest further south. As has already been mentioned, this area was considered by the French and Belgian tacticians to be impenetrable by tanks, and was therefore only lightly defended. How wrong they were.

Move into Belgium: advance to the River Dyle, 10th May 1940

A few hours after the German army crossed the Belgian border on 10th May, the leading elements of the British Expeditionary Force also crossed into Belgium, moving east towards Brussels. The 4th Division was in reserve, so did not move till the 14th May. On the same afternoon the 3rd Division first saw action against the Germans, along the line of the River Dyle, while elements of the 4th Division were deployed in depth and on the northern flank. The Battalion found itself near the village of Nosseghem, facing north. Unbeknown to the soldiers on the ground a major drama, which was to shape the whole conduct of the campaign, was unfolding to the south; on 14th May the Germans had unleashed their main thrust through the Ardennes. Meeting little opposition, their armoured columns had quickly broken through, capturing intact the vital bridge across the River Meuse at Sedan. Driving west, they had effectively forced a wedge between the British and French armies, and were in danger of cutting the British line of communication to the port of Le Havre. All this had left the BEF along the River Dyle in an untenable position, with strong German forces to its front and on both flanks. A decision was therefore made on 16th May to withdraw to the next line of defence – the River Escaut.

Withdrawal to the River Escaut, 17th-18th May 1940

The Battalion was ordered to withdraw from its position at Nosseghem on the morning of 17th May, without having made contact with German ground forces (several attacks by Stuka dive bombers had been experienced, and one Stuka had been shot down by rifle and Bren gun fire).

All that hot day and the following night the Battalion marched westwards, arriving in the area of Alost on the morning of 18th May. The roads were crowded far beyond their capacity, not only by the British Expeditionary Force, but by French and Belgian horse-drawn transport and artillery, and by streams of refugees with their pathetic possessions piled on hand-carts and farm wagons.

After what seemed an interminable wait for orders just beyond

Alost, the Battalion was met by RASC motor transport. As the men embussed, the sound of rifle and machine-gun fire could already be heard to the east. The dash back to the River Escaut was going to be a close-run thing.

Defence of the River Escaut line

The Battalion reached its new position near Avelghem on the River Escaut just after midnight on 18th-19th May, and the following morning was able to take stock of its surroundings. The area is flat and low-lying; the Escaut, which at this point is about twenty-five yards broad, runs between high artificial banks. About half a mile behind is a subsidiary watercourse, known as Den Rijtgracht, which runs parallel to the main river. The whole valley is dominated by the Bois L'Enclus, a wooded hill on the south-eastern side, which provides excellent observation over many miles. When the Battalion arrived it found two bridges across the river, one of which had already been destroyed.

Probably as a result of the confusion on the roads, orders for the defence failed to arrive with the Battalion till mid-morning on 19th May. They were to occupy positions on the ridge of the Bois de l'Enclus. The move was in process of being carried out when new orders came to hold the line of the river, with positions on the near side. The Battalion dug in there, but after dark on 20th May it was ordered to occupy new positions on the Rijtgracht, with small patrols established forward on the banks of the Escaut itself, which could be reinforced by night.

Digging and wiring took place all that night and the following day, with little interference from the enemy except for some desultory shelling. The Battalion occupied a front of about 3,000 yards, with the 2nd Bedfords on the right and the 2nd Lancashire Fusiliers (from the next brigade) on the left. The position left much to be desired. Not only was it overlooked by the Bois L'Enclus, but the roads and railway ran on embankments, which effectively cut off each sub-unit from its neighbour. Little or no mutual fire support was therefore possible. As darkness fell on the 20th May, the Germans were seen to be firing Verey lights from the direction of the Bois L'Enclus. The Battalion's supporting battery of 22 Field Regiment Royal Artillery proceeded to shell the ground to the east of the Escaut, to discourage its use as a forming-up point.

The German attacks started at first light on 21st May, and were accompanied by very heavy artillery fire. During that long day of hard fighting much gallantry was displayed. When B Company had almost run out of ammunition the Regimental Serjeant-Major, 'Sticky' Hill, led a carrying party through very intense artillery and machine-gun fire with replenishments. That night Captain E.S.D. Pentreath carried out a highly dangerous reconnaissance of one of the Escaut bridges, returning with vital information. Hill and Pentreath received the DCM and MC respectively, but there were many others who got on with their jobs with cool, unflustered courage. This dedication to duty was perhaps typified by the imperturbable Private Palmer of the Signal Platoon, who was seen whistling merrily, as he sat in full view of the enemy repairing a telephone cable, while shells and mortar bombs exploded round him. All through that day the artillery fire was terrifying, many of the Great War veterans saying that it was the worst they had ever experienced. That night the Battalion was relieved by the 1st Surreys, and fell back into Brigade reserve where it remained for the whole of 22nd May.

Withdrawal to the Franco-Belgian frontier, 22nd-23rd May 1940

On the night of 22nd-23rd May the British Expeditionary Force withdrew from the line of the River Escaut and moved down to the defensive positions on the Franco-Belgian frontier, which had been so laboriously constructed over the previous months. The Germans followed up closely, but were as yet in insufficient strength to mount a serious attack. On the flanks, however, the situation was rapidly becoming catastrophic. In the north the Belgian army had been driven back towards Ypres; in the south, the main German thrust had reached the coast near Abbeville, thereby isolating the BEF and cutting its line of communication to Cherbourg. Its very existence was therefore in extreme jeopardy, and the only course now open to the Commander-in-Chief was to fall back to a fortified beachhead. The area chosen lay around the port of Dunkirk. The withdrawal was to be covered by the rear-guard units then holding the Franco-Belgian frontier, which included the 2nd Battalion, and thus it was that the Cornwalls played a critical part in the fighting during these last desperate days in France.

The main part of the Battalion withdrew stealthily during the daylight hours of 27th May, leaving one platoon per company to simulate the continued occupation of the position. These last platoons were relieved by one Coldstream platoon after dark, and set off in the wake of the Battalion under the command of Major H.F. Joslen.

Withdrawal & move north to Kemmel, 27th May 1940

The 10th Infantry Brigade had been detached to the 5th Division, with orders to plug the gap south of Ypres. As the enclave held by the Allies became smaller by the hour, the scene became ever more chaotic. Large bodies of British troops were moving steadily west towards Dunkirk, while French units were attempting to establish contact with their army in the south, and the Belgians with theirs to the north. The French' and Belgians' horse-drawn transport and artillery further confused the situation. If this was not enough, every road was further choked by thousands of refugees desperately fleeing the enemy. German aircraft constantly strafed these crowded roads, indiscriminately killing or wounding humans, horses and farm animals, and leaving a trail of smoking wreckage.

Fighting at Kemmel, 27th-28th May 1940

With the fog of war becoming ever thicker, the Staff somehow succeeded in maintaining control. Orders continued to reach units, and units still managed to react to those orders. Thus it was that by nightfall on 27th May the Battalion was concentrated east of Kemmel, a few miles south of Ypres. All the next day (28th May) the Battalion was engaged in fierce fighting and subjected to continuous artillery fire. Casualties, especially in B and D Companies, were heavy. Captain A.H.L. Farmer commanding B Company and Major J.C. Philippo Commanding D Company were killed; both were fine officers. The Carrier Platoon, together with the other two carrier platoons from 10 Brigade under command of Captain R.G. Pine-Coffin (of the Devonshire Regiment) had more than their share of excitement when, while carrying out a reconnaissance to St. Eloi, they ran into a large body of the enemy. At least seventy of these were killed, Private F.J. Williams distinguishing himself by standing up in his carrier and hurling grenades at the fleeing Germans. He was awarded the Military Medal for his bravery, but sadly lost an arm in the engagement – a wound which proved fatal.

Withdrawal to the Dunkirk Perimeter, 29th-30th May 1940

That night the Battalion withdrew from the line and marched the twenty miles north to Eikhoek, where the four platoons which had been left to hold the frontier position finally caught up after a bewildering forty-eight hours. There the footsore, weary and hungry soldiers were welcomed with a substantial meal, which the Quartermaster had somehow contrived. In the morning orders were received to destroy all equipment that could not be carried and to move by transport to the town of Furnes, four miles inland from Dunkirk, with all possible speed. Although news of the surrender of the Belgian army on 27th May had already been received, nobody till then had been prepared to face up to the desperate nature of the situation and accept defeat. Now there was no question of the outcome; the British Expeditionary Force was withdrawing to the port of Dunkirk, from which a few might possibly be saved.

The Battalion continued to be attacked from the air as it drove the final twelve miles to Furnes. Once there it was allocated a position in the extreme east of the perimeter behind the road and canal running between Nieuport and Furnes. Almost dead flat, without any sort of cover, and criss-crossed with dykes, this area could hardly have presented a less propitious defensive position. Strong barbed-wire cattle fences made movement after dark frustratingly difficult, while, perhaps worst of all, the water table was so close to the surface that in some places it was not possible to dig weapon pits.

Defence of the Dunkirk perimeter, 30th-31st May 1940

Throughout the 30th and 31st May, the Battalion lay in this uninviting countryside. Only B and C Companies managed to find marginally higher ground, which afforded reasonable fields of fire. Unfortunately farm buildings on this feature invited more than their fair share of German artillery and mortar fire. One of the most vivid memories of an officer of one of these Companies was of the almost unbelievable sang-froid of Captain the Lord Carew sitting outside the farm-house door reading *The Times*, apparently oblivious of the mortar bombs falling around him.

During 31st May Lieutenant-Colonel Rushton was detailed for duty on the beaches, and handed over command of the Battalion to Major Joslen. He was not seen again; it can only be presumed that he was among the many who were killed or drowned in the latter stages of the evacuation.

Evacuation from Dunkirk, 1st June 1940

Having received orders to withdraw to the beach at La Panne, the main body of the Battalion silently filed out of its position at midnight of 31st May, while C Company and the Carrier Platoon provided the rear-guard. Sadly, Lieutenant A. Le Grice was killed by a burst of machine-gun fire during this final withdrawal. On arrival at La Panne in the early hours of 1st June the Battalion was confronted by an awesome scene of chaos. The town was blazing, the mole destroyed and the whole area was under intense artillery fire and air attack. Evacuation from this beach was patently impossible; there was nothing for it but to continue down the coast to Dunkirk itself. These last ten miles over soft sand taxed every man to the limit. All were by now exhausted, many not having slept for the previous seventy-two hours, but Major Joslen and Regimental Serjeant-Major Hill were magnificent in keeping everybody's spirits up. Thus it was that the Battalion marched into Dunkirk, with their heads held high, still as a fighting unit, each man carrying his personal weapon. Let Regimental Serjeant-Major Hill take up the story in his own words:

> We reached the jetty at Dunkirk round about noon. Not very encouraging as the jetty had been badly bombed and almost cut in half. There was however a naval sloop – HMS *Kingfisher* – tied up at the end. The Battalion was first given the task of getting over a hundred stretcher cases on board, no mean task as two large gaps had to be crossed, one of which meant a walk in the drink. The task was eventually carried out with only minor attention from the air – no damage – several near misses, but the jetty was again badly holed. Nearly every man aboard added his bit to the ship's AA fire; rifles, Brens and even pistols having a go. Needless to state this assistance did not meet with the approval of a very irate Naval Commander who was heard to bellow from the bridge. "Get those bloody Pongos below, they are shooting away my aerial." His bellow had little effect, as every man aboard was certain that no dive-bomber was going to stop him getting away. Dunkirk left . . . with a last look at the shambles on the beaches, the bombed town, the small boats and a large column of ambulances containing badly wounded men all with their doctors, nurses, orderlies and drivers who had refused to leave them.

Thus the 2nd Battalion the Duke of Cornwall's Light Infantry steamed away from the noise, smoke and flame of Dunkirk on the afternoon of 1st June 1940 (elements of the Battalion were in fact split up between several ships, including a small party of men from C Company, and the Regimental Signallers, who embarked at Bray Dunes, having become separated in the chaos of La Panne). Few can have remembered much of the passage to England, for blessed sleep quickly enveloped those desperately weary men.

Since the start of the German onslaught on 17th May the Battalion had been almost continuously engaged in digging, marching and fighting. It had fought two major defensive battles, the River Escaut and the Dunkirk Perimeter. In both these, the odds had been overwhelming and the ground very far from ideal. Wars are not won by retreats or evacuations, and the 1939-40 campaign in Belgium and France must rate as a crushing defeat. Victory or defeat is the concern of generals, and is hardly the business of the infantry soldier. However, in defeat the calls made on him are greater; depression can take over, morale collapse and the will to carry on the fight drain away. It can be truly said that at no time did the 2nd Battalion succumb to these corrosive influences. The officers and men who boarded the ships of the Royal Navy on 1st June 1940 were physically exhausted, but they still formed a proud and robust fighting unit.

THE UNITED KINGDOM, 1940-1943

Return to England, 1st June 1940

Altogether, 338,226 men had been evacuated from Dunkirk. This vast number flooding into the Channel ports would have offered German aircraft a tempting target had not the railways laid on a highly complex operation to disperse the men as soon as each ship came in. When the bulk of the 2nd Battalion disembarked at Margate troop trains were waiting to take some to Sherborne and some to Oswestry. Cricket matches could be glimpsed as the trains rattled through the Kent villages on that sunny June afternoon. The Battalion was well and truly home.

Sherborne, 8th June 1940

By 6th June 1940 the Battalion had been concentrated at Sherborne, with a strength of 19 officers and 310 soldiers. Lieutenant-Colonel H.F. Joslen, who had previously been the Second-in-Command, assumed command in place of Lieutenant-Colonel Rushton who was missing, presumed killed. Such equipment as was available was issued and, after a forty-eight hour leave, the Battalion re-assembled, ready to take its place in the defence of the United Kingdom, once more part of 10 Infantry Brigade of the 4th Division.

Rowlands Castle & Havant, August-September 1940

After moving to Rowlands Castle between Portsmouth and Chichester, and then to Havant just west of Chichester, the Battalion was placed in reserve with a counter-attack role, should the enemy obtain a beach-head. A 'flying column' to deal with enemy parachute landings was also maintained at immediate readiness. On 12th August

1940 the Battalion relieved the 1/6th East Surreys in the forward beach area. That day it was to witness the first big air raid on Britain and have the satisfaction of capturing the crew of German aircraft shot down by the RAF. Life in those days was certainly far from dull, with almost continual alarms keeping everybody on their toes. Companies were spread out over greatly extended fronts, each of two miles or more. Sleep became a precious commodity; many observation posts were manned around the clock, while active patrolling took place throughout the hours of darkness. Through the rest of that summer and autumn of 1940 the Battalion continued the endless programme of digging defences, watching out to sea and patrolling. The rounding-up of German aircrews whose planes had been destroyed in the Battle of Britain, which raged almost continuously above their heads, provided the occasional excitement. There was almost no time for much needed training.

Southampton, October 1940

On 22nd October the Battalion marched to Southampton, where it was billeted in two schools (Taunton and Mayfield), and a large dilapidated mansion. Surely now, surrounded by shops, cinemas and pubs, there would be a chance to relax and enjoy life again. This was not to be. Occasional bombing raids on Southampton had taken place for several weeks, but just a few days after the Battalion arrived the Luftwaffe opened a devastating *blitzkrieg* on the city. All through the winter of 1940 and into the spring of 1941 the raids continued unabated. All thoughts of relaxation therefore vanished as the Battalion became more and more involved in supporting the desperately over-stretched emergency services in their heroic rescue work.

In March 1941 Lieutenant-Colonel Joslen was relieved in command by Lieutenant-Colonel R.E. Urquhart of the Highland Light Infantry. Colonel Joslen was an old soldier, commissioned in 1916, who had been a tower of strength as Second-in-Command of the Battalion during the recent campaign in France and Belgium, and as the acting Commanding Officer during the Dunkirk evacuation. However, in common with others of his age, he was ajudged to be too old for the frenetic pace of training under General Montgomery. His successor, a much younger man (later to command the 1st Airborne Division at Arnhem), quickly established himself as a hard and imaginative trainer, who demanded a high degree of physical fitness from all ranks, and who lost no time in assimilating himself into his new regiment.

The Battalion was extremely lucky not only to be commanded by an absolutely outstanding Commanding Officer but to be part of General Montgomery's V Corps. No formation in the British Army at that time was trained so hard and to such purpose. The lessons learnt in those days in the United Kingdom laid the foundation for the excellence of its performance in battle during the years that lay ahead.

Training in Scotland, March 1942

All through that and the following year the Battalion trained hard in England and Scotland and, wherever it found itself, an early priority was always the construction of an assault course. After an altogether too brief period of comparative stability in a hutted camp at Heckfield, near Reading, between August 1941 and March 1942, the Battalion moved north to Inverary on Loch Fyne, to be introduced to the mysteries of Combined Operations. This was to be the start of another intensive period of training, in which innumerable beach assaults were carried out from landing craft, wading, often chest deep, through the bitterly cold sea. When not engaged on exercises the Battalion was accommodated on board a large converted troopship, HMT *Ettrick*; a novel experience for all concerned. At the end of the month the Battalion returned to Heckfield, then moved by rail to Catterick, and from there marched 120 miles to a camp known as The Barony, eight miles from Dumfries. Everybody was thoroughly fit and in excellent spirits. There Lieutenant-Colonel E.S.D. Pentreath, MC, who was last mentioned for his bravery at the defence of the River Escaut, rejoined the Battalion, taking over command from Lieutenant-Colonel Urquhart. It would be difficult to exaggerate the contribution that Urquhart had made during his tenure of command to the efficiency of the Battalion. A unit that knows itself to be efficient usually has a correspondingly high morale; this was certainly the case with the Second.

The pace of training did not diminish. All ranks were put through the 4th Divisional Battle School at Moffat, followed by field firing exercises at Castle O'er and combined operations at Castle Toward. There then followed a short period at sea, culminating in an assault landing along the Ayrshire beaches. The name of this exercise, 'Dryshod', could not have been more inappropriate, as all ranks were required to wade ashore in four feet of seawater.

Shortly after 'Dryshod', Lieutenant-Colonel R.P.H. Burbury assumed command from Lieutenant-Colonel Pentreath. Drafts were received from the 4th and 6th Battalions, which brought the 2nd up to full establishment. The many rumours of an impending move to an operational theatre were confirmed when the vehicles were prepared for a sea voyage and leave was granted. It was not however till later that the exact destination was revealed.

On 8th November 1942 American forces landed at Safi, Casablanca, and Port Lyantey in French Morocco, while British forces landed further east at Oran in Algeria. The British force immediately set out across country to seize Tunis 400 miles away, and link up with the 8th Army. The German reaction to these landings was immediate. On 9th November airborne units were flown into Tunisia, followed by the move of large reinforcements of infantry and armour by sea. However, the winter rains started in mid November, which brought the movement of both attackers and defenders to a halt.

Back in Scotland the 2nd Battalion waited. Life became somewhat easier, but all ranks felt frustrated that while the war was being fought in Algeria they were marking time in Scotland. During November Lieutenant-Colonel Burbury had to relinquish command, due to ill health (he was later to be killed on the Normandy beaches commanding the 1st South Lancashire Regiment), and was succeeded by Lieutenant-Colonel R.B.F.K. Goldsmith. Goldsmith was an outstanding young officer, and at that time only a substantive Captain, who had come from a staff job with the recently formed 1st Airborne Division. In later years he was to become Colonel of the Duke of Cornwall's Light Infantry.

The waiting continued. The 1st Division was now on standby for a move to North Africa, and many believed that the 4th Division would not be required in that theatre. Once more rumours proliferated. Some thought that Spain might join the Axis powers, in which case a force might be landed on the Iberian Peninsula; others thought that the opening of a second front in Norway was more likely.

Orders to move overseas, March 1943

At long, long, last, at the beginning of March 1943, firm orders were received to the effect that the 4th Division was to move to an undisclosed destination.

NORTH AFRICA, 1943

The move, 11th March 1943

The Battalion despatched its transport to Glasgow for loading, and followed by rail on 11th March. There it embarked on HMT *Orion*, a pre-war luxury liner, which was packed not only with the Battalion but with many other minor units and the headquarters of both the 10th Brigade and the 4th Division: in all, about 6,500 men. *Orion* cast off that evening and steamed the few miles down the Clyde to Greenock, where a vast convoy of liners, merchantmen and warships was assembling. At dusk on 14th March the armada slipped quietly away, fanning out into five columns, each with its naval escort and strong air cover flown from the accompanying carriers.

Arrival at Algiers, 23rd March 1943

As soon as the convoy was clear of the shore, all ranks were informed of their destination. The 4th Division was to disembark at Algiers, and become part of the 1st Army. The convoy took a circuitous route to evade German submarines, so did not arrive in Algiers till the morning of 23rd March. After a certain amount of confusion as to where it was to be billeted, the Battalion set off to march the eighteen miles in the dust and sun to a tented camp. There it remained for a week, recovering its fitness after ten days cooped up in a ship. On 2nd April the Battalion was again on the move, entraining for a 400 mile rail journey to Ghardinaou. Here it met up with its transport and heavy fighting equipment, which had arrived from Scotland more or less intact.

Two days later, on 4th April 1943, the 4th Division relieved the 46th Division in a sector of the front line covering Beja, an important communication centre on the road to Bizerta. By this time the 4th Division had been re-organised into a 'mixed' division, made up of two infantry brigades (10 and 12 Brigades) and an armoured brigade (21 Army Tank Brigade, equipped with Churchill tanks). Although this organisation may have increased the tactical potential, it also meant that, with only six instead of the normal nine infantry battalions available, there was less opportunity to rest.

Djebel Munchar, 12th April 1943

The Battalion took over from the Hampshires along the rock-strewn ridge of the Djebel Munchar, which faced the enemy about a mile away. Thus, after nearly two and a half years of hard training, the 2nd Battalion was again face to face with the Germans. This time, however, the situation was very different, for it was the British who were advancing and the Germans who were being driven back.

Apart from shelling and the occasional air attack, there was little military activity visible during the hours of daylight. Indeed, local Arabs would sometimes wander into the unreal world of the forward positions, selling eggs and fruit to the soldiers resting in their weapon pits. It was only under cover of darkness that the scene came to life as water and rations were brought forward, and fighting patrols set off towards the enemy lines.

Meanwhile the 78th Division was preparing for the capture of Medjez-el-Bab, which would secure the right flank of the route forward to Tunis. The attack went in at first light and the Battalion, dug in on the high ground of Djebel Munchar, had a ringside view of the battle. Particularly impressive was the shattering effect of the entire divisional artillery putting down concentrated fire.

The following day it was the turn of the 4th Division to move forward on the left flank. The line of advance followed the valley, which runs in a north easterly direction from Beja to Mateur. The Battalion was initially in reserve, moving along the rocky slopes. Progress was painfully slow, hampered by the terrain, mines, booby traps and the increasing opposition put up by the enemy rear-guard. By dawn on 13th April the Battalion was firmly established on a high ridge overlooking the village of Sidi Nsir, where the road turns east towards Tunis. There it remained for five days. Rocks and boulders prevented the use of motor vehicles for supply purposes, so recourse had to be made to that old stalwart of the battle-field, the mule. On the night of 17th-18th April the Battalion was relieved by a combat team of the 1st U.S. Division. Used to reliefs in the line being conducted in complete silence, the Battalion was somewhat amazed when the Americans roared up in their vehicles, engines revving and headlights blazing. The subsequent hand-over must have been the shortest on record, for the Cornwalls removed themselves from the position as quickly as decency allowed, before the inevitable artillery and mortar retaliation fell about their ears.

Medjez-el-Bab, 20th April 1943

Once clear of its former position, the Battalion marched back to an area behind the Djebel Munchar, whence it was lifted by motor transport twenty miles east to Medjez-el-Bab. This was to be V Corps' assembly area for the final break through, and the capture of Tunis. The Army Commander, General K.A.C. Anderson, KCB, MC, personally briefed all officers down to Lieutenant-Colonels on the plan. The 1st and 78th Divisions were to break through the enemy line, whereupon the 4th Division was to exploit success and fight its way down the road to Tunis. He warned everybody that the enemy would almost certainly offer stiff resistance and that they must be prepared for some very fierce fighting.

On 20th April the Battalion was deployed on a steep, rocky horseshoe-shaped feature, with the open end of the horseshoe facing south west. A Company, commanded by Major A.E. Harding, occupied a strong position on four stony knolls at the top end of the horseshoe, with Battalion Headquarters, B and C Companies deployed over its right shoulder. D Company was placed in reserve, some 2,000 yards to the south west. Surprisingly, several batteries of medium artillery were dug in forward of A Company with nothing between them and the enemy but their own sentries. This risky position had been deliberately selected in order to allow the guns to make maximum use of their range in the forthcoming battle. The enemy, who remained immobile and invisible during daylight hours, was dug in about 3,000 yards to the east.

During the night of 20th-21st April, A Company was required to provide protection parties for the Royal Engineers, who were clearing routes through the minefields that lay between the antagonists. Safe approaches to the advanced gun lines were an immediate priority for the passage of Royal Artillery vehicles, which were bringing forward large supplies of ammunition to the medium guns. This left the Company severely depleted. A little before midnight heavy firing was heard from the north and east. It was quickly learnt that the platoon guarding the Gunners had been ambushed, while a determined attack had been launched on the northern-most platoon (which had been reduced by the call for protection parties to Platoon Headquarters and one section). The Platoon Commander and four men managed to make their way back to their Company Headquarters to confirm that the extreme north part of the horseshoe was now in German hands.

By daylight on 21st April the Germans were found to have advanced into the low ground, known as The Bowl, from which they were preparing to mount an attack on the southern most platoon of A Company.

Fortunately, at this moment a platoon of C Company, which had been placed under Major Harding's command, made its appearance and was able to bring down heavy fire on their assailants in The Bowl. Later that day a company of the Loyals mounted a counter attack against the surviving enemy, ably supported by A Company. For his coolness and bravery throughout this long drawn out company battle, Major Harding was awarded the MC.

Meanwhile, that night D Company, moving forward in single file through a minefield to join the rest of the Battalion, had been ambushed. A sharp fire fight developed, during which many of the

Company were killed or wounded. Amongst those killed was the Company Commander, Major D.B. Bradley, a regular officer with ten years service. This was a serious blow to Lieutenant-Colonel Goldsmith, now deprived of his reserve just as it was needed.

One must not imagine that this DCLI battle was taking part in isolation. The Germans were well aware of the impending British attack, so mounted simultaneous pre-emptive strikes all along the 4th Divisional front that were designed to disrupt the preparations. Their operation, known as '*Fliederbluhn*' (Lilac Blossom) succeeded in penetrating the British line in many places, over-running gun areas and destroying vehicles, ammunition and stores dumps. The company, platoon and even section battles which were fought with such tenacity, although perhaps appearing of minor consequence in the great overall picture, were in fact the instruments by which the German counter-thrust was contained. In spite of the damage they wrought, they failed to delay the V Corps offensive.

Just before first light on St George's Day, 23rd April, the rumble of distant gunfire to the south east could be heard. It was a sound wonderful to the ears of the men of the 1st Army, for it was the noise of the guns of the 8th Army. At last the two Armies were in audible distance, and the Germans were being squeezed between the two. A few minutes later the 1st Divisional artillery thundered into life. The final great attack to drive the Germans out of North Africa had started.

The German army was however far from beaten, and in the next fortnight fought a rear-guard action with great skill, determination and courage. Indeed, German counter attacks were launched wherever and whenever the opportunity arose and, while the 10th Brigade waited in reserve to make the final dash to Tunis, a stalemate appeared to have been reached. The key to the problem was a rocky piece of high ground known as Point 133, which dominated the main British axis of advance. The 1st Queen's Own Royal West Kent Regiment had attacked and captured this feature on 28th April, allowing the 2nd Royal Fusiliers to push ahead against heavy opposition. However, the West Kents had been driven off Point 133 by a determined counter attack, and the Royal Fusiliers had been forced to withdraw again. If mobility was to be restored to the British, it was vital that Point 133 should be recaptured. This task fell to the DCLI.

Lieutenant-Colonel Goldsmith had just been posted to the Airborne Division, newly arrived in North Africa, his place being taken by Major T. Kinnersly. This critical battle for Point 133 was to be his first test of command. He ordered a night attack to be carried out by A and D Companies (recently reinforced to bring their combined strength up to 150 men) together with a section of the Assault Pioneer Platoon, under the overall command of Major Harding. Intelligence reports initially indicated that only some fifty Germans occupied the position, but as H hour drew nearer, this estimate rose to about 130.

The battle of Point 133, 29th-30th April 1943

At 11.30 p.m. the attacking force moved forward, D Company under Captain C.S. Gill leading, followed by A Company under Lieutenant R.F.L. Jones. It was a black moonless night, and the approach march was made on a compass bearing. The plan was that immediately D Company was fired on it should go to ground, and give covering fire for A Company to carry out a right flanking movement, before assaulting the position. The attack appeared to go as planned. Suddenly at 11.45 p.m. night was turned to day as the Germans filled the sky with flares. A very fierce fire fight developed between D Company and the enemy, while A Company moved round the flank and started moving up the slope. The two D Company platoons made good progress, Lieutenant R.S. Harrowing destroying three machine-gun posts, and Lieutenant D.W. Harmer attacking from the rear. As Harrowing's platoon reached the summit it was met by fire of such intensity that every single man was killed. The other platoon fared little better, only Harmer and five men reaching the summit. They were immediately driven back, only one man surviving to bring the desperate news back to Major Harding.

A Company then inched forward up the hill against heavy fire. The stony nature of the ground made the digging of weapon pits impossible, but every man frantically gathered rocks together to build himself an improvised breastwork as he waited apprehensively for the dawn. First light revealed that the enemy had almost surrounded Major Harding's fragile position and that their strength was estimated as at least two companies closely supported by several Tiger tanks. Maximum artillery fire was directed against the enemy positions, whilst an urgent request for armoured support was made. Two Churchill tanks answered the call, but one was immediately knocked out and the second beat a hasty withdrawal, having neither armour nor a gun capable of taking on the Tigers. At about 8 a.m. a shell landed on Major Harding's headquarters, killing Lieutenant B.F. Jones, who was one of the two Artillery Forward Observation Officers, two wireless operators and two runners, and wounding the second Forward Observation Officer. At 9.30 a.m. a message was received that the artillery could no longer expend ammunition at the rate at which it had long been firing. Major Harding's force had itself run out of ammunition by this time; the only thing that was keeping the Germans back was the superb shooting of the gunners. Now, with this support threatened, the gallant survivors could only lie behind any cover they could find, with their bayonets fixed, awaiting the end. Soon after 11 a.m., just before the last wireless set was destroyed, orders were received to withdraw. The gunners deluged the hillside with smoke, allowing a withdrawal to be made down the hill straight through the encircling German positions.

The battle had lasted for almost exactly twenty-four hours, during which A and D Company groups had lost five officers and seventy-seven soldiers, most of whom were dead. They had failed to achieve their aim, but with hindsight, knowing as we do now how strong the enemy was, the two companies had been set an impossible task. They had fought to the bitter end regardless of the odds.

The battle of Point 133 must rank as one of the finest feats of bravery performed by the DCLI in the war. One aspect of this battle is indisputable – every man who survived owed his life to the gunners, particularly to the courage, determination and skill of the Forward Observation Officers.

The battle for Tunis, 5th-10th June 1943

Unknown to the weary British soldiers, who withdrew to lick their wounds, the Germans were now in a desperate situation. The full weight of the 8th Army was closing in from the east, while it was only a matter of time before the 1st Army broke through the last defensible barrier of rocky hills. The Germans were fighting for their very existence, knowing that once their line had been broken, nothing would lie between them and Tunis except flat, featureless desert across which the British would launch their armour. Previously, Field-Marshal Rommel had pleaded with Hitler to allow him to evacuate his army from Algeria, should the situation demand. However, this request had been refused, with the result that General von Arnim, now commanding the Afrika Corps, had no alternative but to fight a final hopeless battle to the bitter end.

The British plan depended on the 4th Division and 4th (Indian) Division punching a narrow breach in the German defences, allowing the 6th and 7th Armoured Divisions to exploit success, fanning out into the flat ground and attacking Tunis from the west. The attack was to open before dawn on 6th May.

On the evening of 5th May, after a short period of rest, the 2nd Battalion marched up to the concentration area. As soon as it was dark it again moved forward to the start line, and lay down to wait for zero hour. On the stroke of 3 a.m., 400 guns of all calibres opened fire on every known German position and put down a barrage in front of the advancing infantry. At the same time, Bofors guns sited on the flanks fired tracer shells to mark the axis of advance to the infantry. The 2nd Battalion advanced close to the creeping barrage and by 4.30 a.m. had consolidated on all its objectives with very few casualties. The 6th Black Watch from 12 Brigade then passed through, moving forward in perfect order 'as though taking part in a School of Infantry demonstration'. The complete success of this first phase could be judged when squadron after squadron of tanks from the 6th Armoured Division were seen driving past the Battalion position.

Capture of Tunis, 7th May 1943

On 7th May, after being relieved by the 2nd Lincolnshire Regiment, the DCLI was moved forward by motor transport to the village of Massicault. There it was learnt that the two armoured divisions had captured the town of Tunis. With the American II Corps closing in from the north west, there was now only one direction in which the Germans could retire – Cape Bon. This was a mountainous peninsula some forty-five miles long by twenty-five miles broad, which jutted out into the Mediterranean to the north east of Tunis. It was an ideal defensive position in which a last stand could be made, and speed was therefore vital in cutting off the base of the peninsula. Accordingly, on 8th May, the 6th Armoured Division was given this task. However, its tanks were held up by a strongly held German position at the seaside town of Hamman Lif, on the eastern side of the peninsula. Orders were immediately despatched to 10 Brigade to outflank the opposition to allow the armour through. The Brigadier therefore went forward with his commanding officers to carry out a reconnaissance. While this was in progress a shell burst amongst the group, killing the Commanding Officer of the supporting artillery regiment and severely wounding Lieutenant-Colonel Kinnersly and Lieutenant-Colonel K.G.J. Garner-Smith of the 2nd Bedfordshire & Hertfordshire Regiment. Major E. Remington-Hobbs of the Argyll and Sutherland Highlanders took over temporary command of the DCLI. Sadly, this reconnaissance had been unnecessary for the 6th Armoured Division was able to neutralise the opposition and pass through Hamman Lif on the night of 9th May. Early the following morning the 4th Division passed through the armour, with 12 Brigade continuing straight up the east coast, while 10 Brigade peeled off left and advanced up the west coast. A

Squadron of the Divisional Reconnaissance Regiment, followed by the 2nd DCLI, led the way. There was no opposition; instead thousands of German and Italian troops stood by the roadside waiting to give themselves up. El Haouaria, on the extreme tip of the peninsula, was occupied at 1 p.m. on 11th May. This triumphal progress was only marred by one incident when American aircraft bombed and machine-gunned the Battalion, wounding eight men.

Capture of the German & Italian Armies in North Africa, 11th-12th May 1943

At about this time General von Arnim ordered the unconditional surrender of all Axis troops in North Africa. However, on 12th May the Battalion received a signal from the Royal Navy that they were being shelled from a battery located in a fort on the coast. Lieutenant B.M. Gluckstein of D Company was ordered to sort the matter out, but no sooner had he approached the fort than his company came under heavy fire. The Commanding Officer then ordered Major Harding to take a large white flag and make contact with the enemy commander. This turned out to be no other than General Koech, the Commander-in-Chief of the Luftwaffe in North Africa, who agreed to meet Major-General J.L.I. Hawksworth, CB, CBE, DSO, commanding the 4th Division. At first General Koech was adamant that he would continue the fight but, after Major Harding had driven him over a circuitous route, which passed through vast concentrations of tanks, guns and infantry, he changed his mind and agreed to the surrender of his garrison. The 2nd DCLI was therefore instrumental in effecting the surrender of the last enemy troops in Africa.

Cape Bon, May-June 1943

For the next few weeks the Battalion was engaged in clearing up the masses of equipment discarded by the Germans. A tented camp was pitched near the sea where each company in turn was given three days much needed rest. On 17th May Major G.R.D. Musson of the King's Shropshire Light Infantry, who had been GSO 2 Operations at Headquarters 4th Division, assumed command from Major Remington-Hobbs. A sad event took place on the same day when the Battalion was required to despatch a draft of 9 officers and 277 soldiers to the 1st King's Shropshire Light Infantry, then under orders to take part in the seaborne assault of Pantellaria. It must be recorded that no reinforcement draft could have received a warmer welcome than did those men of the DCLI. The Light Infantry ethos ensured that these men were quickly and happily absorbed into their new regiment.

By this time, almost every unit in the 1st Army had acquired German vehicles and equipment. Excellent as much of this loot was, its continued use was not only impractical from the spares and maintenance point of view, but could lead to dangerous recognition problems in battle. It was therefore with certain feelings of regret that the spoils of war were handed over.

Bougie, July-December 1943

Before leaving Tunis the 2nd Battalion took part in a divisional parade for the Prime Minister, Mr Winston Churchill, and was visited by HM King George VI. At the end of June the 4th Division entrained for Bougie, a port on the Algerian coast 300 miles to the west.

There it was intended that the Division should train for the projected amphibious assault on Cortona, a port on the toe of Italy. However, almost immediately this operation was cancelled, leaving the 4th Division with the somewhat uninspiring task of cleaning up the devastation caused by the bombing of the port of Bougie. This involved very heavy manual work but life was not by any means unpleasant because, for the first time in many months, soldiers were able to relax completely when off duty and swim in the warm waters of the Mediterranean. It was during this period in Bougie that the 2nd met the 30th Battalion of the Regiment, which had recently arrived in the theatre to help work the ports.

THE ITALIAN CAMPAIGN, 1944

Move to Kabrit, Egypt, December 1943-February 1944

Large drafts arrived during October and November from the 4th and 5th Battalions of the Regiment, bringing the 2nd back to full war establishment. In mid December the Battalion embarked on SS *Llangibby Castle* for an unknown destination. Just to confuse everybody, the ship set sail heading westwards towards Gibraltar, convincing most of those on board that they were returning to Blighty. However, after a few hours she swung round and steamed due east. Arriving at Port Said on the evening of 23rd December, the Battalion disembarked over a somewhat precarious pontoon catwalk and boarded a waiting train. That night it set off south through the desert to a camp at Kabrit on the Bitter Lakes, half way between Port Said and Suez.

Christmas Eve, 1943 dawned with the 2nd Battalion in tents, looking out on the Suez Canal while in every other direction lay limitless desert. There, training started for the invasion of Rhodes. The area, consisting as it did of featureless sand, was not the easiest terrain in which to instil some feeling of the European countryside, even though mock-up structures representing houses, churches and windmills had been dotted around to provide much-needed reference points. The training was hard, and was just what was needed to integrate the new drafts from England. Reorganisation was going on at this time within the 4th Division, including the substitution of 28 Infantry Brigade from Gibraltar in place of 21 Tank Brigade, which had been with the Division for the past eighteen months. This brought the 4th Division into line with other similar formations of the army. It is of interest that 28 Brigade included a sister Light Infantry battalion, the 2nd Somerset Light Infantry.

The 2nd Battalion seemed destined to train for operations that were eventually cancelled. True to form, after two or three weeks the invasion of Rhodes was called off, leaving the 4th Division in a state of limbo. This must have been a time of frustration, for much of great consequence was taking place across the Mediterranean. On 25th July 1943 Mussolini had been removed from power; on 17th August Sicily had fallen to the Allies; and during September landings had been made on both the north and south shores of the toe of Italy, and further north at Salerno. By January 1944 the German army had withdrawn back to the well prepared 'Gustav Line', which ran across Italy following the valleys of the Garigliano and Rapido rivers. Dominating the Garigliano valley and the Liri valley (which ran north to Rome) was the towering mass of Monte Cassino, on the top of which stood the ancient Benedictine Abbey. It was to participate in the assault of this fortress that the 2nd Battalion was destined.

Move to Italy, 14th February 1944

Early in February 1944 the Battalion moved to a transit camp near Alexandria, whence on 14th February it embarked on SS *Letitia*. A week later the ship docked in Naples, the Battalion going ashore across the upturned bottom of a sunken Italian Cruiser.

* * *

Monte Ornito, 1st March-10th March 1944

The 4th Division was to take over from the 46th, holding a mountainous bridgehead across the River Garigliano. The weather could hardly have been more foul, with heavy rain, which up in the 1,000 foot mountains was very cold indeed. The 2nd Battalion took over from their old friends the Hampshires on Monte Ornito.

The relief involved a long approach, climbing up stony goat tracks while rain and sleet fell incessantly. With each man carrying full marching order with steel helmet, weapon, ammunition and two blankets, this was an experience which few ever forgot. There was no question of digging weapon pits in that ground, so rocks were piled up to form 'sangars' to give limited protection from both enemy fire and the elements. In truth, at this time, the elements were the worse enemy. Although the bodies of British and German soldiers, lying in profusion between the two lines, testified to the bitter nature of the fighting for Monte Ornito, both sides were now more or less content to man their opposing positions, and attempt to keep the bitter cold and wet at bay. However, shelling was prevalent and, to prevent the Battalion falling into a passive 'live and let live' attitude, morale-raising raids were occasionally mounted.

Sujo, 10th-18th March 1944

The Battalion remained on this rain-swept slope for ten long days, counting the hours before it would be relieved by the 6th Black Watch. On the night of 9th-10th March the 2nd Battalion made its way back down the goat tracks, and moved west along the front to their new position on the flank covering Sujo. This area was considerably more accessible than that on the Monte Ornito and somewhat safer, as the enemy were about two miles away. However, the Divisional Staff required constant intelligence of the enemy, particularly in the form of prisoners. Patrolling therefore became the most important part of the Battalion's role.

Mugnano, 18th-28th March 1944, & the battle for Monte Cassino

On 18th March the Battalion was relieved and moved back to Mugnano, north of Naples, for a very welcome period of rest. For the first time in almost three weeks men were able to dry their clothes and obtain adequate sleep. After only a few days the 2nd were again on the move north, as a result of a regrouping of the British formations in

Italy. Up to this time the 4th Division had been part of the 1st Army; now they were to be part of the 8th Army, under General Sir Oliver Lease. The first task of the Division was to relieve the 3rd Algerian Division in the mountains north of Monte Cassino. On the night of 28th-29th March the 2nd Battalion took over from a French Colonial battalion on the forward slope of Colle Belvedere, north east of Monte Cassino. Strict orders had been issued to the affect that the enemy must be given no indication of the relief, no easy task when they were occupying sangars a mere twenty yards away. However, in war, events seldom go to plan. No sooner had the Algerian soldiers spied our men toiling up the rocky slope towards them than with cries of joy they leapt out of their sangars and clattered down the hillside, making a noise to waken the dead. For what seemed an age, but cannot in fact have been more than a few minutes, the defensive position was completely unmanned. Only when the sangars had been located in the dark, and the men allotted their positions could anyone breathe easily again (strangely enough, the Germans failed to realise that any relief had taken place. A few days later they showered the DCLI position with leaflets, describing the infidelities of the Algerian wives in lurid detail!) The DCLI now found themselves facing Germans who were anything but docile, who mounted aggressive deep penetration patrols each night, leaving mines and booby traps on the approach tracks and generally making the hours of darkness decidedly unpleasant. At this time the men on Colle Belvedere had a grandstand view of the bombing raids on Monte Cassino. Spectacular as these were, the reduction of this magnificent building to rubble merely turned it into an even more formidable fortress.

Crossing of the Rapido river, 11th May 1944

General Alexander's overall plan was for the Polish Corps to attack and capture the Monte Cassino feature from the area of Colle Belvedere to the north east (so recently familiar to the DCLI), while XIII British Corps crossed the Rapido river with Monte Cassino on its right flank, made contact with the Polish Corps, and pushed on north up the River Liri valley. Meanwhile, General Clark, commanding the U.S. 5th Army, should break out of Anzio and push east, thereby cutting off the withdrawal of the retreating German 10th Army that had held the Gothic Line. All this went according to plan until General Clark, determined that U.S. troops should be the first to enter Rome, turned north east towards that city, instead of east. U.S. troops did indeed liberate Rome, but due to his disobedience of orders, General Clark allowed the German 10th Army to escape intact to fight another day.

The 2nd Battalion was soon to be committed to its first set-piece battle in Italy. Twice before, attempts had been made to capture

Monte Cassino and thus open up the only route north through the Liri valley. Twice the attacks had failed. This third attempt was to involve the 2nd Battalion in the assault crossing of the Rapido river to the south of Monte Cassino. Accordingly, the 4th Division was withdrawn from Colle Belvedere and moved back to Barracone on the Volturno river on 12th April 1944, to carry out river-crossing training. Spring had come; the miserable months of bitter cold and wet had given place to warm sun; instead of shivering in sodden great-coats men could now be seen in shirt sleeves.

The assault crossing of the Rapido river by the 4th Division was one of the most fiercely contested operations of this campaign. During the nights of the second week in May vast quantities of men, ammunition, guns and equipment were moved up towards the river, where they were concealed in carefully camouflaged positions. So vital was secrecy that men working in the forward position wore their PT plimsolls instead of boots. By 11th May all was ready, and at 11 p.m. that night the entire Divisional artillery opened up on every known German position. The noise reverberating around the steep valley was indescribable and one could have been forgiven for believing that nothing could survive this maelstrom on the far bank. After forty-five minutes of intense fire the leading assault boats were launched. B and C Companies 2nd DCLI manned the crossing, ferrying the two leading battalions (1/6th Surrey Regiment followed by 2nd Bedfordshire & Hertfordshire Regiment) across the river. D Company was given the independent task of establishing a subsidiary crossing and then linking up with the Bedfords, in order to enlarge the bridge-head. A Company remained in reserve. In spite of the very intense preliminary bombardment, the German reaction was swift and savage. The main crossing was immediately subjected to every sort of fire, which quickly sank boats and inflicted casualties. However, by 4 a.m. on 12th May both leading battalions were established in a shallow perimeter on the far bank. Meanwhile D Company under Major C.S. Gill had succeeded in getting his headquarters and two platoons across the river to the left, before being spotted by the Germans occupying a dominating feature known as Square Wood. The subsequent enemy artillery, mortar and machine-gun fire made it suicidal for any further attempt to be contemplated by the third platoon. With dawn approaching, Major Gill and his two platoons found themselves completely isolated and unable to move. Fortunately, a mist had descended on the river, allowing A Company under Major G. Rork to cross with his headquarters and two platoons. Unluckily, the mist cleared before the third platoon could join them so, like D Company, A Company was left isolated and under strength on the enemy bank.

Some progress was made towards Square Wood, but the German position was surrounded by deep barbed-wire entanglements liberally sown with anti-personnel mines.

The British position was now extremely perilous. A shallow bridge-head had been established, but it was overlooked by numerous enemy strong points, and no movement on the river was possible. If the Germans had made a concerted counter attack on 12th May there is little doubt that the isolated British units on the far bank would have been eliminated. All through the night of 12th-13th May the Royal Engineers, working heroically under heavy shelling, succeeded in building a Bailey bridge across the Rapido that was capable of carrying tanks. At dawn on 13th May the leading squadrons of the 17th /21st Lancers crossed over and made contact with the 2nd Bedfordshire and Hertfordshire Regiment. They were immediately followed by 12 Brigade, which had been held in reserve.

The battle for Point 63, 13th May 1944

At 1.15 p.m. on 13th May B and C Companies of 2nd DCLI (commanded by Major E.P. Banfield and Captain J.T.B. Notley respectively), each with a troop of Sherman tanks from 17th/21st Lancers, crossed the Rapido. Lieutenant-Colonel Musson, riding on the leading tank, led the Battalion up to the start-line for the next phase of the battle, the capture of Point 63. Point 63 was a heavily defended rocky area of high ground dominating the bridge-head. Once again, as the infantry advanced, the Divisional artillery put down a very heavy creeping barrage. Although the Germans were ensconced in caves, they had had enough of being pounded by artillery, and quickly surrendered. About a hundred prisoners were taken, who proved to have been men of the Machine-gun Battalion of the 1st Parachute Division.

With Point 63 in British hands, help could now be sent to D Company, who were still firmly pinned down by fire from Square Wood. A troop of tanks was despatched to give added fire power, allowing D Company to move forward with fixed bayonets.

For the next few days the 2nd Battalion consolidated its position on Point 63. On the morning of 17th May troops of the 78th Division passed through, to continue the advance north, leaving the 4th Division to concentrate on the clearing of Cassino town. However, once it became apparent that not only had all the defenders withdrawn but that the ruins were thickly sown with anti-personnel mines, this operation was stopped.

* * *

Rest at Piedmonte D'Alife, 19th May-7th June 1944

On the night of 17th-18th May 1944 the 2nd DCLI was withdrawn to a temporary rest area behind Monte Trocchio, about four miles from Cassino, where hot showers had been rigged up. The next day the Battalion moved back a further thirty-five miles to a camp at Piedimonte D'Alife where it could reorganise, refit and relax.

The battle for Monte Cassino had been fought and won. For six months British, Indian, Canadian, New Zealand and Polish troops had endured appalling conditions of cold and wet as they clung to their precarious mountainside positions facing this fortress that brooded above them. The Germans, fully aware of its vital tactical importance, had deployed many of their finest troops in its defence. Now it had fallen, and the way north up the Liri valley to Rome lay open. In this most terrible battle the 2nd Battalion had proved itself to be not only tough and courageous, but a thoroughly professional unit. Few awards can have been more deservedly made than that of the Distinguished Service Order to Lieutenant-Colonel Musson. The Regimental Serjeant-Major, A.E. Narborough who, although twice wounded, had continued to lead ammunition parties through heavy fire, was awarded the MC. Mention should also be made of the Medical Officer, Captain J.G. Macarthur, and his gallant band of stretcher bearers who repeatedly braved shell-fire to bring the wounded to safety.

After the war the Duke of Cornwall's Light Infantry was granted the Battle Honour 'Cassino II', which is still proudly displayed on the Queen's Colour of the Light Infantry.

Pursuit of the German Army, June 1944

The 4th Division was moved forward again during the first few days of June to join the pursuit of the withdrawing German army. On 7th June the 2nd Battalion was again in action, advancing up the Tiber valley to the east of Rome. The wooded hills offered ideal country in which to fight rear-guard actions and the Germans made full use of its potential. Bridges were destroyed and the roads liberally sowed with mines and booby traps. Progress was slow, but the Battalion experienced the unaccustomed pleasure of being welcomed as liberators by the Italian villagers.

On 12th June the 4th Division was relieved by the 8th (Indian) Division, and moved back into Corps reserve, a concentration area near Rome on the west bank of the Tiber. After four days' rest, it again advanced northwards up the Tiber valley in pursuit of the retreating German army. On 21st June the 4th Division, still being held in reserve, received instructions that it could expect to remain in the area of Viterbo for at least ten days. Leave rosters were hastily prepared, while all ranks looked forward to a period of relaxation in the surrounding Arcadian countryside. As was not unusual, this anticipation of pleasure was to be short lived. That same day a warning order was received to the effect that the Division was to be ready to move during the night, with the probability of action the following day. The reason for all this was that Field Marshal Kesselring had finally halted on a line running across Italy from Lake Trasimeno to Lake Chinsi. This consisted of ideal defensive positions, which, given time, could have been made virtually impregnable. It was therefore vital that an all-out attack should be launched without delay.

The battle of Casamaggiore, 27th June 1944

The 2nd Battalion advanced up the main road to the town of Orvieto, and thence due north towards Lake Chiusi. From this point progress was slow, as the leading troops were having to fight for every village and high feature along the route. During 27th June the 2nd Battalion, supported by a squadron of Canadian tanks, was committed to the battle. Passing through the Hampshires, C and D Companies led an attack on the heavily fortified village of Casamaggiore. D Company came under very heavy fire immediately after crossing the start line and, within a few minutes, had lost all its officers and some forty soldiers killed and or wounded. Company Serjeant-Major E.A. Manley took over from Major Gill, who was seriously wounded. Immediately reorganising the survivors of his company, he deployed them in a defensive position from which he could pass back vital information about the German deployment to Battalion Headquarters. For his cool-headed courage he was awarded the MC; sadly he died of wounds received in a subsequent action before the award was officially announced. Acting on Serjeant-Major Manley's information, Lieutenant-Colonel Musson was able to mount a second attack in which B Company passed through D Company and, with the utmost dash, established themselves on the Battalion's objective, a ridge which overlooked the town of Casamaggiore itself. During this attack the B Company Commander, Major Banfield, was badly wounded in the leg. While the DCLI held their ridge repeated attacks were put in against Casamaggiore. It was finally captured by the Surreys on the evening of 28th June.

* * *

The battle of Petrignano, 30th June-1st July 1944

The next day the advance was continued. It was slow, for almost every bridge and culvert had been blown and, as was now becoming the pattern, the route was littered with mines and booby traps. On the morning of 30th June the leading elements came up against stiff resistance at Petrignano, and the 2nd Battalion was once again called upon to carry out a set piece attack. B and C Companies led the attack. B succeeded in reaching its objective while C was pinned down by heavy mortar and machine-gun fire. Lieutenant-Colonel Musson immediately decided to exploit success, and passed A Company through B, hoping to get round behind Petrignano and cut the German line of retreat. This it very nearly did, but the enemy, conducting a rear-guard action with their normal skill, held B Company at bay until they were able to withdraw under cover of darkness. Next morning the Battalion moved cautiously into Petrignano, which had been liberally laced with booby traps. The delicate and highly dangerous work of neutralising these devices fell to Captain Bloomfield's Assault Pioneer Platoon.

Continued pursuit of the German Army, July 1944

The advance continued at an increasing pace up the Val di Chiana. All along the route there were signs of partly completed defensive positions and dumps of destroyed equipment, all bearing testimony to the hurried departure of the enemy. The withdrawal, however, certainly never became a rout, and on 4th July the British came up against yet another line of solid German resistance, which was sited along the high ground that separates the Val di Chiana from the Arno valley. For the next ten days there could be no further movement, with each side securely dug in facing each other across the valleys. However, on 15th July the New Zealand Division together with the 6th Armoured Division attacked through Arezzo, thus turning the German flank. By nightfall of 17th July the advance was again under way. The following dawn the Battalion passed through the Bedfords towards the town of Montevarchi. It was during the action to secure this objective that Serjeant-Major Manley of D Company was mortally wounded.

Rest at Montevarchi, 18th July-4th August 1944

It was at this time that the 2nd DCLI found themselves alongside the 2nd Somerset Light Infantry of 28 Brigade, the first and only occasion on which these sister battalions met during the Italian campaign. When the Somersets moved on north the 4th Division went into Corps reserve, the DCLI being billeted for a fortnight in the pleasant and largely undamaged town of Montevarchi. Not for many months had the soldiers enjoyed the luxury of sleeping under a roof, and mixing with a friendly population which welcomed then as liberators. While at Montevarchi the Battalion was visited by HM King George VI.

The battle of Incontro, 8th August 1944

Following its well earned rest the 4th Division again moved north into the battle zone. The Germans were being steadily driven back towards the River Arno, but the area was one of steep hills and ridges – each offering ideal positions to fight the type of delaying action at which they were so adept. One of the more prominent of these hills was Incontra, which dominated the surrounding countryside for many miles, and was the key to any further advance to the River Arno. On its summit was a monastery, massively built, with a nearby tower and high perimeter wall. The situation was similar to Monte Cassino on a smaller scale. The 2nd Battalion was ordered to capture this formidable fortress.

Time was allowed for meticulous planning for this attack. An intensive programme of patrolling reconnoitred all possible approach routes, while the RAF flew photographic missions, producing stereoscopic coverage of the feature. Company and platoon commanders were taken to the Battalion observation post in a farm, where they could make themselves familiar with their objective rising 800 feet above them. Large scale plans and sand models were constructed, from which all ranks were thoroughly briefed. The attack was scheduled to be launched at 4.30 a.m., and the assaulting troops were to form up on the start line before dawn on 8th August.

B and C Companies (under Captain A. Tregunno and Captain J.M. Knight) led the attack, using the south western approach. C Company was accompanied by a party from the Assault Pioneer Platoon armed with two pole charges, with which to demolish the outer wall. All through the night of 7th-8th August the guns of 22 Field Regiment pounded the hill. At 4.30 a.m. on 8th August, as B and C Companies crossed the start line, the artillery, the tanks of the North Irish Horse, the Battalion 3 in. mortars and the mortars of the 2nd Somerset Light Infantry laid down a creeping barrage. This, together with a thick morning mist, allowed the two leading companies to reach the plateau on which the monastery was constructed without suffering casualties. At about 5.30 a.m. three platoons managed to pass through the outer perimeter wall, one platoon at a breach in the south face, and two platoons in the east face. By this time, however, German resistance was hardening. The protective mist was lifting and C Company came under intense machine-gun fire from the Monastery tower while B Company, moving around the outside of the perimeter wall to attack the main entrance lodge in the north, came up against strong enemy opposition. During the ensuing fight Private K. Carter was hit in the neck and jaw, but although barely conscious, continued to deliver supporting fire. All tenuously held DCLI positions were now under concentrated artillery, mortar and machine-gun fire, the rock splinters accounting for many casualties. At 7.30 a.m. Lieutenant-Colonel Musson, seeing that the battle had lost its momentum, despatched D Company, under Major J.T.B. Notley, to take charge of all three companies and inflict the *coup-de-grace*. He arrived at B Company headquarters at about 10.30 a.m., and after some very stiff fighting took possession of the Monastery and heavily defended north gate house. The German reaction was not slow. Almost immediately the whole area was subjected to heavy artillery and mortar fire. At this point Serjeant Metcalf, who was commanding the supporting machine-gun platoon of the 2nd Northumberland Fusiliers (The 4th Division Machine-gun Battalion), observed a counter attack force forming up on the slope to the east of the Monastery. He immediately mounted his machine-guns back on their carriers, and, with great courage and *élan*, charged the enemy force, breaking it up and inflicting many casualties.

The Battalion occupied the Monastery for the next forty-eight hours, during which time it was subjected to enemy shelling. However, with this vital hill top position in British hands, the Germans were denied any freedom of movement and were impotent to offer any further effective resistance south of the Arno.

Thus ended one of the finest actions fought by any battalion of the Regiment during the whole course of the Second World War. The Battle Honour 'Incontra' is now carried on the Colours – an extremely rare example of a Battle Honour unique to a single regiment. For his skill, determination and courage, Major Notley was awarded the Distinguished Service Order; Captains Tregunno and Knight and Lieutenants H.D. Bodley and N.A. Spurdens, the MC; Private Carter, the Distinguished Conduct Medal; and Serjeant A.T. Cocks, Corporal D. James and Private S. Dyke, the Military Medal.

Field Marshal Lord Alexander later drew particular attention to this battle in his preface to the 4th Divisional History. He wrote:

The DCLI's action was a model of what a daylight attack by a battalion group on a strong position should be. It was planned in great detail, but the plan was flexible enough to allow of changes to overcome unforeseen obstacles; Lieutenant-Colonel Musson had watched the progress of the battle very closely, but had left to his company commanders those decisions which could best be made on the spot. The men of the assaulting companies had fought hard and well and had earned their notable success.

Rest at Assissi, 10th August-10th September 1944

On the night of 9th-10th August 1944 the 4th Division was relieved by the 1st Division. In pouring rain the 2nd Battalion moved back to a tented camp near Assissi, where it was to remain for a complete month.

Reorganisation of the Battalion, September 1944

The Allied situation on the Italian front was now rapidly changing. Not only were the Germans fighting in ideal terrain with continued resolution, but many British units had been withdrawn from the theatre in preparation for the Normandy invasion. Furthermore, those units which were left had received heavy casualties over the previous months, but had ceased to receive reinforcement drafts. The 2nd Battalion was reorganised on a three rifle company basis, while the Anti-tank Platoon and Mortar Platoon were both disbanded to provide a Carrier Platoon of viable strength. The 1944 Summer had been exceptionally wet, and as summer gave way to autumn the rain never seemed to stop. The operational routes degenerated into quagmires through which wheeled, and at times even tracked vehicles, became bogged down. The speed of movement became that of the infantryman on his feet, while supplies were carried forward on the backs of long-suffering mules.

Attack on the Aquilina Ridge, 18th-19th September 1944

The 4th Division came back into the battle on 18th September when the Bedfordshire & Hertfordshire Regiment led an attack across the River Ausa, a few miles south east of the port of Rimini. In this it was successful, but was then held up by heavy fire between the Ausa and a small tributary, the Budriolo, some thousand yards beyond.

The 2nd Battalion was ordered to continue the attack that night and establish a position on the Aquilina Ridge on the far side of Audriolo. This attack was notable as being the Cornwall's first experience of 'Ackford Moonlight', a technique by which searchlights were shone onto cloud over the battle-field to give reflected illumination that greatly facilitated movement. In spite of heavy defensive fire, the Battalion was half way up to Aquilina Ridge by dawn on 19th September, and by that afternoon had successfully captured Aquilina village. From there the tired soldiers were able to witness a spectacular attack by the Canadians to their right, in which the entire Corps artillery was in action together with tanks, heavy and medium bombers, and rocket-firing fighters.

The next planned operation was the assault crossing of River Marecchia. On the morning of 20th September D Company, with tank support, captured the Casa Bianchi, a feature vital to this operation. That night, however, the weather broke. Torrential rain once more turned the whole area into a sea of impassable mud, while the River Marecchia became a roaring torrent. The following day the Canadians succeeded in establishing a crossing point over to the right and establishing themselves on Route 9, the great road that runs straight up Italy to the city of Milan. The state of the weather now precluded all further mobile operations and the 2nd Battalion thus found itself billeted in Sant' Aquilana.

Change of Command, 23rd October 1944

While at Sant' Aquilana, the Battalion was dealt a hard blow. Lieutenant-Colonel Musson was posted to the Staff.*

He had assumed command at Cape Bon in North Africa on 20th May 1943 and had led the Battalion throughout the advance up Italy. The author has never met any member of the 2nd who did not hold this officer in the very highest esteem. Battle after battle

* General Sir Geoffrey Musson, in a letter to the author, made his own feelings clear on the subject of the remarkable fighting spirit of the 2nd DCLI, and its robust morale both in and out of the line. With great modesty, he inferred that the true credit for this state of affairs belonged to the officers and men of that fine Battalion. Indeed, it was a fine Battalion, which had been trained in the United Kingdom to a peak of efficiency before being tested in the bloody battles around Tunis. However, every infantry soldier will tell you that even the best material will quickly crumble in the hands of an ineffectual commanding officer. It was due to Lieutenant-Colonel Musson's tactical skill, imperturbable nature, undaunted courage, and friendliness, all adding up to superb leadership, that brought the 2nd Battalion with its head held high through the many savage battles and the cold, wet and misery of winter in the Italian mountains.

had been fought and casualties had been heavy, but every man knew that his life would not be unnecessarily sacrificed through lack of thought and careful planning. His cool judgement in times of crisis invariably remained unimpaired by the fog of war. However, it was not only Lieutenant-Colonel Musson's professionalism that endeared him to his soldiers; he had a warmth of spirit that inspired loyalty. Week after week, soaked to the skin on bleak mountain slopes, the Battalion had never lost its fighting spirit. The Regiment owes a great debt to the King's Shropshire Light Infantry for providing such an outstanding Commanding Officer at such a momentous period in its history.

Another sad loss to the Battalion was occasioned by the posting of the Medical Officer, Captain Macarthur, MC. The courage and devotion to duty displayed by officers of the RAMC in the two World Wars has become legendary; Captain Macarthur certainly lived up to that legend. He and his stretcher bearers never shirked extreme danger when there was a man's life to be saved. A soldier's great fear in battle is that he will be wounded and left to lie without succour; the knowledge that the medical team will always be close at hand is therefore a vital factor in maintaining morale. Captain Macarthur was an exceptionally brave and proficient doctor to whom many members of the 2nd Battalion owed their lives. His award of the MC could not have been more deserved.

The battle of the River Ronco, 25th-26th October 1944

Major Kerry Harding, the Second-in-Command, who probably had the longest unbroken service of any member with the Battalion, now assumed command. On 23rd October 2nd DCLI again took the field, moving with V Corps up the line of Route 9. The first battle involved the crossing of the River Ronco on the night of 25th-26th October. A Company under Major D. Ruttledge was to lead the way over a partially destroyed footbridge at 11 p.m., but the enemy shelling was so intense that the Commanding Officer delayed the operation for thirty minutes until this had died down. The weather was atrocious, with continuous driving rain that blotted out even the 'artificial moon' provided by the searchlights. A Company crossed without casualties, but almost immediately came under heavy fire from both flanks. Due to the blackness of the night and the torrential rain the Company became split up, and only one platoon and Company Headquarters reached the first objective of Casa Foschi, at almost midnight. D Company under Major Notley had meanwhile crossed the River Ronco by the same damaged bridge, and moved up into a defensive position to the right of A Company. By this time the Germans had become fully aware of the crossing, and were putting down heavy artillery fire. Shortly afterwards they counter-attacked, but were repulsed after some stiff fighting. By this time the River Ronco had become so swollen that there was no way that any further reinforcements could cross on foot. Those on the far bank therefore waited for dawn with considerable apprehension. During the night a squadron of tanks had moved forward to a pre-reconnoitred ford, and at first light the leading tank entered the river. It was immediately knocked out by an 88 mm gun which had presumably been sited to meet just such an eventuality. With the ford blocked and the river impassable, A and D Companies were now in a desperate situation. Heavy shelling was followed by counter attacks that were repulsed for about an hour. Then the Germans brought up tanks which, impervious to any fire that the two rifle companies could bring to bear, proceeded to shell them out of their positions at point blank range. The battle broke up into a series of isolated actions in which much heroism was shown in the face of overwhelming odds. The end however was inevitable. Major Notley, although seriously wounded, remained at his post exercising command as best he could. While describing the situation to the Commanding Officer, his wireless set and that of the gunner Forward Observation Officer were both knocked out, cutting off all communication to Battalion Headquarters. By this time the survivors were making their way back to the river, and at 9.30 a.m. they waded in and started the perilous swim, as the artillery blinded the enemy with smoke.

This had been the greatest set-back to the Battalion during the Italian campaign. 4 officers, including the 2 company commanders, were missing together with 124 soldiers, and a further officer and 13 wounded men had been evacuated across the river. Many of those missing were later found to have been taken prisoner.

This, the first battle fought by Lieutenant-Colonel Harding as Commanding Officer, must have been a terrible discouragement, even though no blame could be levelled either at him or any of those who crossed the river. The 60th Rifles on the right had had a very similar experience on that same night, with even heavier casualties. It was subsequently learnt that the Germans had deployed a complete division (278th Infantry Division) to oppose these two crossings. It is little wonder that just four rifle companies, unsupported by armour, had been unable to hold their ground.

The River Ronco was eventually crossed by the 1/6th Surreys on the night of 31st October. Once again torrential rain almost brought disaster, and had it not been for the heroic efforts of the Royal

Engineers in keeping a bridge open, this battalion would probably have suffered the same fate.

Attack on Forli Airfield, 5th November 1944

The next major objective was Forli airfield. Heavily defended and surrounded by deep dykes, it formed a formidable stronghold. The 2nd Battalion was tasked with securing the start line for the forthcoming attack by occupying a group of buildings known as Casa Bordi. While carrying out his reconnaissance Major Tregunno of B Company was mortally wounded, a further grievous blow to the Battalion, which had now lost three experienced company commanders in a fortnight. During the three days of occupation the buildings were systematically pounded to rubble by German artillery, and casualties were heavy. Private J. Coggins was awarded the Military Medal for repeatedly driving the armoured ambulance (a converted universal carrier) through heavy fire to bring the wounded to safety. His courageous action undoubtedly saved many lives.

On 9th November the Battalion was withdrawn for a few days rest before taking part in yet another river-crossing operation. In spite of the fact that the Germans were now withdrawing fast, their army never lost its cohesion, defending every natural obstacle with skill and determination. Although the Battalion was by now well versed in such operations, familiarity had certainly not bred contempt; all ranks now viewed each successive river crossing with grave apprehension.

Attempted crossing of the Consina stream, 21st-22nd November 1944

The Consina stream, although of no great width or depth, nevertheless constituted an obstacle that was well defended. Lieutenant-Colonel Harding planned to launch two companies across the stream, A Company (commanded by Major Phillips) on the left, leaving B Company in reserve on the near side. Both companies moved forward towards the start line on the night of 21st-22nd November. A Company successfully reached the start line in spite of sustaining casualties on *Schuh* mines which had been liberally laid along all the approaches. D Company, however, came under intense artillery fire and was pinned down. At 'H' hour, A Company advanced. German machine-guns were enfilading the stream, but by dashing across in small groups between bursts, it made the far bank without casualties. Pushing forward, it captured its first objective and took several prisoners. Shortly afterwards, however, it was subjected to heavy shelling followed by two counter attacks by tanks and infantry. These were successfully repulsed, thanks in large part to the sterling work of the supporting gunners (36th/55th Field Battery RA) and their Forward Observation Officer. However, splendidly as A Company had done, its position now looked bleak. As dawn approached it found itself entirely isolated on the far bank, for neither D Company nor the Surreys had been able to cross. Appreciating the situation, Major-General A.D. Ward, DSO (commanding the 4th Division) made the decision to withdraw A Company. This it did in good order, bringing over its haul of prisoners. Major G. Rork, who had served with the Battalion in North Africa and had taken part in every single battle in Italy, was awarded a well merited MC.

Move back to Taranto, 28th November 1944

This was to be the last operation carried out by the 4th Division. By 23rd November, as the British troops prepared for the assault crossing of the River Lamone, the 4th Division received the welcome news that it was to be relieved by the 2nd (New Zealand) Division. The 2nd Battalion were one of the last units to withdraw from the line, and it was not until the night of 27th-28th November that it made its way back towards the rest camp at Fori in the pouring rain. After handing in its vehicles, heavy equipment and anti-tank guns to the Ordnance Depôt at Pescara, it embarked on a slow and extremely uncomfortable railway train of closed goods vans, which meandered south towards Taranto. There, on 5th December, the 4th Division re-assembled in tented camps. The climate was considerably milder than that it had endured in northern Italy, and everybody looked forward to a further move by sea, which would take them right out of Italy to Palestine.

Once again, fate stepped in to frustrate the Battalion's hopes. While the 4th Division waited expectantly at Taranto for its troopships, the political situation in Greece was about to explode into civil war.

* * *

CIVIL WAR IN GREECE

During the German occupation the Greek nation, rather than uniting against the common enemy, had split up into rival factions which spent most of their energy fighting each other.

The collective title of the left-wing resistance party was Ethnikan Apelafterotikon Metopan (EAM). The military wing of EAM was known as (H)elenikos Laikos Apelefterotikos Stratos (ELAS) – a force which, on paper, could muster some 35,000 men and women controlled directly by the Communist Party of Greece, Kommunitikon Komma (H)ellados (KKE). The Athenian Corps of ELAS consisted of about 11,000 men and women, many of them riff-raff from the criminal element of Athens. Commanding Officers were generally powerless to enforce discipline, and the total lack of communication between its headquarters and units made it incapable of carrying out any co-ordinated operation; indeed, although it had fought rival left-wing guerrilla bands throughout the occupation, it had never got round to fighting the Germans. After the withdrawal of German forces in November 1944 British and Greek units of III Corps from Egypt had landed at Athens; there they had demanded the disbandment of all ELAS forces and the surrender of their weapons. This they flatly refused to countenance. On 3rd December, during a political demonstration at Constitution Square in Athens, fighting broke out, in which a number of men were killed by gunfire. In the subsequent confusion ELAS attacked and occupied police stations and other vital points in the city. By 10th December ELAS was in control of Athens, including the dominating features of the Acropolis Hill and Mount Lykavittos, and had murdered over 500 members of the civil police and gendarmerie.

The Allied situation was now somewhat perilous. III Corps Headquarters was still secure though closely besieged, and many British detachments such as hospitals, workshops and supply depôts were cut off but still holding out, though RAF Headquarters at Kifissia was in the hands of ELAS, as were the water works, power stations and telephone exchange.

Move to Athens, 13th December 1944

Meanwhile, on 9th December the move of the 4th Division to Palestine was cancelled. It was to stand by at immediate notice to reinforce III Corps in Athens, and parties were despatched post haste to collect the vehicles and heavy equipment that had so recently been handed in to the Ordnance Depôt at Pescara, 200 miles to the north. On 13th December the 2nd Battalion was packed into the bomb bays of twenty-four American Liberator bombers, in which undignified manner it was flown into Hasani airfield, about eight miles east of Piraeus. The Battalion immediately came under command of 28 Brigade, which had arrived the previous day, and was tasked with helping to secure a beach head on Salamis Bay. There, together with the 1st Durham Light Infantry, it deployed in an effective defensive perimeter. That night ELAS guerrillas mounted an attack on the left of the position, inflicting a number of casualties amongst the Durhams. The following morning the Battalion cleared the high ground just inland from Salamis Bay, driving ELAS out of a position from which they could bring small arms fire onto the beach and adjoining jetty. On 15th December the first of two ships carrying 12 Brigade, the remainder of 10 Brigade and all the Divisional heavy equipment tied up against the jetty. The following day, a third ship disembarked a battalion of Northumberland Fusiliers and four hastily assembled infantry companies formed from the Divisional artillery. With these reinforcements in place, the advance into Athens to link up with the III Corps troops could start. The 2nd Battalion, together with the rest of 10 Brigade, continued to hold the beach-head and airfield, while 12 and 28 Brigades cautiously opened the route known as Singros Avenue, which ran into the heart of the city. The advance was supported by the artillery of 4th Indian Division, the guns of destroyers anchored in the bay, and the 40th Royal Tank Regiment. It was a slow and extremely dangerous operation. ELAS snipers would fire on the advancing troops, only to melt away into the milling crowds and reappear in the rear.

By 20th December 10 Brigade was relieved of their guard duties by the Northumberland Fusiliers and the *ad hoc* gunner battalions, and joined the clearing operation in Athens. Because the street maps were hopelessly out of date, the Brigade Commander (Brigadier S.N. Shoosmith, DSO, OBE) and Lieutenant-Colonel Harding exercised command from a light aircraft. They encountered heavy small-arms fire from the ground that wounded the Brigade Commander, but did not do any great damage to the aircraft, which was able to make a safe landing.

Christmas Day was a somewhat cheerless occasion with the ever threatening danger of snipers, a dinner of bully beef and hard tack biscuits, and bitterly cold weather. On Boxing Day a column of armoured cars sped through the Battalion position. Unknown to the soldiers, they were carrying Mr Winston Churchill, Mr Anthony Eden and Field-Marshal Sir Harold Alexander, to meet representatives of ELAS. Little progress was made in these negotiations, and it fell to the revered figure of Archbishop Damaskinos eventually to lead his nation back to some sort of normality.

Island of Eubea, 31st January 1945

After some tough fighting, in which the Battalion lost two killed and five wounded, Athens was finally cleared of ELAS terrorists. They did not however give up but, following the age old pattern of guerrillas, broke up into small groups to continue the fight in rural areas. It was now vital to harass these groups without mercy. This policy was carried out with such good effect that ELAS called a truce on 11th January 1945. The previous day the Battalion had already moved north out of Athens to the area of Thebes, where it established a patrol base in the village of Vaya from which the surrounding countryside could be dominated. At the end of January the Battalion again moved, this time to the long, thin and mountainous island of Eubea which, for 110 miles, hugs the Aegean coast north of Athens. There it established itself in Khalkis, the only town on the island, harbouring a dour population of dubious loyalty. Lieutenant-Colonel Harding, seeing his task as primarily one of 'hearts and minds', addressed himself to this new problem. It was well known that the citizens of Khalkis were fanatical supporters of their local football team, Khalki Union, which had on several occasions trounced German army teams during the years of occupation. A football match was therefore arranged. A diplomatic outcome had to be discreetly engineered; to have been beaten by Khalkis Union would have destroyed the Battalion's credibility, but it was also vital that the Khalkis team did not lose face by being beaten by too great a margin. In the event, both sides played a terrific game, and the final result was 2 DCLI: 3, Khalkis Union: 2.

Everybody was delighted, and an *entente cordiale* was established to the benefit of soldiers and civilians alike.

The Agreement between the Greek Government & the EAM, 12th February 1945

On 12th February the final agreement between the legal Greek Government and the EAM was signed. The Battalion reluctantly left their friends on the island of Eubea and moved to a tented camp at Vuliagmeni, just north of Athens, for rest and refitting. Paardeberg Day, on 18th February, was celebrated for the first time in three years with a church parade and a sports meeting in the Greek Olympic Stadium.

Larissa, March 1945

In early March the Battalion were once again on the road, moving some 150 miles to the north, to a bivouac area under the mountains just outside the town of Larissa. There, each week one of the companies would set off on patrol with Greek royalist forces engaged

30. 2nd Battalion volunteers served in the reserve fleet battleship HMS *Triumph* in 1914. As a momento, Admiral Sir Thomas Jerram presented this silver model to the officers of the 2nd Battalion after the Great War.

31. 2nd Battalion volunteers embarking in HMS *Triumph*, 4th August 1914.

32. Regimental rivalry always existed in the British Army, but none more so than between the old line battalions and those that considered themselves a social élite. This cartoon by Wilmot Lunt was probably published during the second winter of the war, when goatskin coats had become a standard issue.

"Ello, matey, 'oo are you?"
"Oh, we're the Honorable Artillery Company; who are you?"
"Ho! we're the Dooks of Cornwall—'ats off, yer beggars!"

33. 3rd Battalion Recruiting March of March 1915, outside Launceston. Corporal Rendle, VC is shown on the left of the front rank.

34. 3rd Battalion Recruiting March through Cornwall, March 1915. A local appears singularly unimpressed.

35. 2nd Lt. Jessup, 6th Battalion, winning the DSO at Delville Wood.

36. 2nd Lt. Stanhope-Forbes, 1st Battalion. Painted by his father on his final embarkation leave. Four days later he was killed at Guillemont, 3rd September 1916.

37. Lady Quiller-Couch pouring tea for soldiers of the 10th Battalion in her garden at The Haven, Fowey. The officer standing at the back is probably her husband, Acting 2nd Lieutenant Sir Arthur Quiller-Couch.

38. Digging a communication trench in Delville Wood.

39. 2nd Battalion on Autumn manoeuvres, Aldershot area 1937. War was close, yet constant reduction of the Defence Budget since 1919 had deprived the army of realistic modern training.

40. The so called 'First Militia': conscripts for six months' training after the call-up in 1939. Although the were unaware of it at the time, they would remain in uniform for the next six years.

·1. Presentation of Colours to the re-formed 1st Battalion, 9th December 1942.

:. This photograph of 2nd Battalion prisoners of war was taken by a German medical officer on 11th June, '40, near Dunkirk. Nearest the camera: Sjt. Pitney; centre: Pte. Deakin, with Pte Magner (in the cap) behind m. The bare-headed man is the Battalion's French interpreter.

43. Monte Cassino, 13th May 1944. Left foreground: Sjt. Jackson, who survived the war; while on the righ is L-Cpl. Peachey, killed on 7th June.

in rounding up terrorists and bandits, who had taken to the mountains after the collapse of ELAS. Cadres were run by the Battalion for Greek officers and NCOs as a first step to building up a Greek National Army on British lines. It was during this period that news was received of Germany's unconditional surrender on 8th May 1945. The various accounts of the reaction of the Battalion are very muted. The 2nd were still operating against a ragged but dangerous enemy and Lünenberg Heath in Germany seemed far away from their bivouacs at Larissa.

Because the 2nd Battalion was disbanded in the general run-down of the British Army in 1950, its remarkable record of courageous service in the Second World War has been largely overlooked. Even before the Allied armies landed in France, operations on the Italian front had become a low priority – not only in terms of reinforcements and replacement of weapons and equipment, but in the esteem of the British public. Many soldiers felt, not without reason, that they had been forgotten, and these feelings were expressed in the ironical marching song:

We are the 'D' Day dodgers out in Italy,
Drinking all the vino, always on the spree,
Eighth Army shirkers, Yankees too,
We live in Rome that's all we do.
For we are the D Day Dodgers out in Italy.

We landed at Salerno, a holiday with pay.
Jerry brought a band down to help us on our way,
Showed us the sights and made us tea.
We all played games and the beer was free.
For we are the D Day Dodgers out in Italy.

Naples and Cassino we've taken in our stride,
We didn't go to fight there but only for the ride.
Anzio and Sangro were both a farce,
We did damn all, sat on our arse.
For we are the D Day Dodgers out in Italy.

Look around the mountains in the mud and rain,
You'll find the scattered crosses, some which bear no name.
Some hearts are breaking now they've gone,
But they're at peace and slumber on.
They are the D Day Dodgers out in Italy.

(Sung to the tune of 'Lili Marlene')

The 2nd Battalion had been one of the first units of the British Expeditionary Force to cross over to France after the declaration of war on 3rd September 1939. It had endured the frustrations and hardships of the Phoney War, before advancing into Belgium to confront the German armoured *blitzkrieg* in a type of battle for which it was ill equipped. Withdrawing back to each successive line of defence, the Battalion had acquitted itself with honour. A withdrawal is always the greatest test of a unit's self discipline, it being only too easy for withdrawal to degenerate into rout. This never happened to the 2nd Battalion. Footsore and suffering from a desperate lack of sleep, it maintained its fighting spirit to the very end. Indeed, it played a vital part in the final rear-guard action on the Dunkirk perimeter and, when finally ordered to retire to the waiting ships, did so as a formed disciplined body, embarking with each man carrying his weapon and equipment.

After a protracted period of hard training, much of it in Scotland, the 2nd Battalion was once again committed to battle in North Africa in March 1943. There, as part of the 1st Army, it had fought a succession of bitterly contested battles against a very determined enemy. The whims of public acclaim are notoriously fickle, and, although the great battles of the 8th Army are still revered by the present generation, those of the 1st Army have been almost forgotten.

The Germans having been thrown out of Africa, the 2nd Battalion crossed to Italy. There it fought a succession of savage battles over rivers and mountain ridges. It had played a full part in the bitter fighting around Cassino, and had captured another hill-top monastery in a brilliantly executed, single battalion attack. No operation had ever been easy, as was tragically demonstrated by the attempted crossing of the River Ronco, when not only the Germans but the very elements had conspired to thwart the assaulting troops. Indeed, the majority of the fighting in Italy took place in climatic conditions which tested every soldier's sticking power to the limit.

Most remember their year in 'sunny' Italy for the cold, and above all the torrential rain, which seemed to have a malice of its own.

Shortly before the end of hostilities in Europe the 2nd Battalion was moved at short notice to Athens. There it found itself taking part in a very different sort of conflict in which there was often no visible enemy, but one in which danger lurked around very street corner. The Battalion had to adapt itself quickly to a *modus operandi* which has since become familiar to every soldier, one which involved the doctrine of 'hearts and minds'. Even when the European War was over, it was still engaged in counter-terrorist operations in the Greek hinterland. The 2nd Battalion had been the first DCLI soldiers to see action in the Second World War, and was now to be the last to depart from the field of conflict.

27
The 4th Battalion (Territorial Army)

For most of the period between the two World Wars the two Territorial battalions of the DCLI were amalgamated to form the $4^{th}/5^{th}$ Battalion. Even in 1938 the tension in international affairs barely impinged on the somewhat relaxed routine, which for many years had been caused by the lack of government funding. However, by the end of the year recruiting was beginning to pick up, bringing the Battalion within two hundred of its full establishment. Indeed, this figure would have been higher had not a significant number of NCOs and men left the Territorial Army to become Regulars. The other important occurrence during this last year of peace was the belated issue of various weapons and equipment (notably the Bren light machine-gun), which had previously been confined to the Regular Army.

On 29th March 1939 the Prime Minister, Mr Neville Chamberlain, announced in the House of Commons that the Territorial Army was to be doubled in size. At that time the strength of the $4^{th}/5^{th}$ was still well below the establishment of a single battalion, so its split into two separate units was therefore not viable. However, after the Prime Minister's return from Munich few believed that war could be avoided, and recruiting immediately improved, allowing the $4^{th}/5^{th}$ to go to camp at Corfe Castle that July with over a thousand men. By 24th August the total strength was sufficient to warrant the split and the 4th Battalion was reborn again, with its recruiting area covering the western half of Cornwall. The newly appointed Commanding Officer was Lieutenant-Colonel C.J.A. Hockin. All this naturally threw a heavy strain on the permanent staff, but thanks to a draft of key personnel from the 1st Battalion in India, all went reasonably smoothly. On that first day volunteers were called for, to carry out guard duties on Falmouth docks and the wireless station at Land's End.

* * *

Mobilization at Falmouth, August 1939

On 29th August 1939 the Territorial Army was mobilised. The 4th Battalion moved down to Falmouth, where it was accommodated in the Drill Hall. Shortly afterwards it had to find a draft of 2 officers and 100 men for the 1st Battalion in India. This was a severe blow for a Territorial battalion, already under strength, which was being called upon to provide an ever increasing number of guard duties.

Roborough, October 1939

In October the 4th moved to Roborough, just north of Plymouth. The nearby open spaces of Dartmoor gave ample opportunity for training, which now started in earnest, while at the same time conscripts, mainly from London and Preston, arrived to make up the gaps left by the draft that had departed for India. This must have been somewhat of a culture shock for those Cornish Territorials whose previous voluntary service had been in a battalion consisting exclusively of their fellow Cornishmen.

Paignton & Wembury, January 1940

Early in the New Year of 1940 the Company Commanders were attached in turn to the 2nd Battalion in France, to gain active service experience. At about the same time the rifle companies were re-deployed from Roborough to Paignton and Wembury, on the South Devon coast. There they carried out guard duties. In August Lieutenant-Colonel W.W. (Max) Harrowing, DSO assumed command. Harrowing had first seen action with the 1st Battalion during the Great War but his more recent adventures in France, for which he had been awarded the Distinguished Service Order, were by any standard most remarkable. Although a digression from the history of the 4th Battalion, a brief account of Harrowing's adventures during the collapse of France deserves to be told, as it illustrates his very high qualities of leadership and his ability to make the best of available resources. When war had been declared Harrowing was medically downgraded and was not therefore able to accompany the 2nd Battalion to France; instead he was posted to the Depôt, which was in process of rapid expansion, as Second-in-Command. On 16th May 1940 he was ordered to cross to France the following day and to report to the Base Headquarters at Rouen, for onward posting to the 2nd Battalion. On arrival there, he was told that this order had been cancelled and that he was to remain at Rouen as understudy to the G2 (Operations). Two days later the General called him into his office and, much to his astonishment, informed him that, in view of the rapidly deteriorating situation in which the British Expeditionary Force found itself, he was to form a brigade of five *ad hoc* battalions made up of base troops from all arms and services. The brigade was to be known as 'Harforce'. He was to take immediate command and establish a defensive line between Morville and St Vaast in precisely forty-eight hours. For the next month Harforce was to fight a series of splendid rear-guard actions as it withdrew to Cherbourg. On the evening of 18th June Harrowing's motley but immensely proud soldiers marched onto the quay singing lustily, and embarked on a Dutch paddle steamer for England. His initiative and use of improvisation, his confident leadership in the confusion of battle, and his ability to enthuse fresh courage into exhausted soldiers had led his men to overcome the difficulties of those desperate weeks. This was the officer who took command of the 4th Battalion.

Sussex, Summer & Autumn 1940

During this period the 45th Infantry Division, with Drake's drum as its formation sign, was in the process of being formed. Both the 4th and 5th Battalions found themselves in this Division as part of 136 Brigade, together with the 9th Battalion the Devonshire Regiment. At the fall of France the Division quickly moved to the Sussex coast to construct and man sea defences. The 4th Battalion was responsible for the area around Pevensey, with Battalion Headquarters in Pevensey Castle. The two Cornish battalions provided a brigade mobile reserve consisting of a carrier platoon, a tank-hunting platoon and a motorcycle platoon. which took part in many contingency exercises.

Yorkshire, Winter 1940-1941

As autumn gave way to winter, so the threat of invasion receded. As soon as it was considered safe to do so, the 45th Division moved to Yorkshire where it had a chance to deploy its units and get on with some much-needed training. The 4th Battalion was billeted in Selby, where it was to remain till February 1941. That winter was very severe and training often had to be cancelled to release troops for clearing snow drifts from roads.

St Albans, Spring 1941

At the end of February the Division again moved south. The role of Counter Attack Brigade was allotted to 136 Brigade. The 4th was billeted in St Albans, whence it carried out fast-moving and wide-sweeping exercises. It was during one such exercise that the 4th met the 2nd Battalion, then stationed near Southampton.

Walton-on-the-Naze, Harwich & Colchester Summer 1941-Summer 1942

In the summer of 1941, 136 Brigade was relieved of its counter-attack role and returned to static beach-defence work. The three battalions took turns to be responsible for the areas of Walton-on-the-Naze, Harwich and Colchester – a stretch of the English coast which would be hard to imagine today, for in 1941-42 the civilian population had been almost entirely evacuated, leaving deserted towns and villages. At about this time the 4th said farewell to its inspirational Commanding Officer, Lieutenant-Colonel Harrowing, who was succeeded by Lieutenant-Colonel C.G. Millet. Millet was a regular officer of the DCLI who had been commissioned in 1923; he was later killed in Holland commanding the 2nd King's Shropshire Light Infantry.

Dedham, Winter 1942

By late summer of 1942 the threat of invasion had largely receded, and so it was at this time that the 4th and 5th Battalions, which had forged close bonds of comradeship over three years of war, parted company. It was a sad time for the 4th, for while the 5th became part of 214 Independent Brigade, destined for the assault on the mainland of Europe, the 4th was relegated to the role of a reserve drafting unit. Its task was to take in partially trained men from the various Infantry Training Centres and bring them up to a high standard of efficiency before despatching them to operational battalions overseas. It was certainly not one of the more exciting of war time roles, but it was one in which the enthusiasm of the permanent staff was vital, and on which depended the quality of the soldiers being sent to fight the enemy.

* * *

Northern Ireland, February 1943

In November 1942 there was a change of command, Lieutenant-Colonel Parkin taking over from Lieutenant-Colonel Millet. Much of the countryside in East Anglia had been given over to intensive agriculture to help feed the nation, leaving little land available for military training. It was therefore with a sense of anticipation that in February 1943 the whole of the 45th Division moved to Northern Ireland, where large expanses of uncultivated land allowed for realistic formation exercises to be carried out, using live ammunition. The rest of that year was occupied by hard and almost continuous training. Once more the 4th Battalion took on the shape of an efficient fighting unit, which appeared to be being groomed for a part in the forthcoming invasion of Europe.

During this period in Ireland Lieutenant-Colonel T.R. Reid, MC, of the Buffs, took over command from Lieutenant-Colonel Parkin.

England, January-June 1944

In January 1944 the Battalion was dealt a great blow when it was posted back to England to assume once more the duties of a draft training unit. As D Day approached the 4th Battalion established two transit camps in Hampshire, through which many thousands of troops staged on their way to Normandy. It must have been a melancholy task for infantrymen, recently trained in Ireland to a high pitch of operational efficiency, to be relegated to the menial tasks of pitching tents, running messes, cook-houses and canteens and carrying out innumerable guard duties for the men about to be committed to a much more dramatic role in Normandy. However, like good soldiers, they knuckled down to these humble duties, providing smoothly run organisations in which men could relax in comparative comfort before they were put to the test of battle.

D Day came on the morning of 6th June 1944. The 4th Battalion had completed its final task, and was disbanded. Lieutenant-Colonel T.V. Williams, OBE, MC, who had previously commanded the 1st Battalion in India, had the sad task of winding up this Cornish territorial battalion. The officers and men were posted to various reinforcement units. Had they known it, this was to be the beginning of their real war.

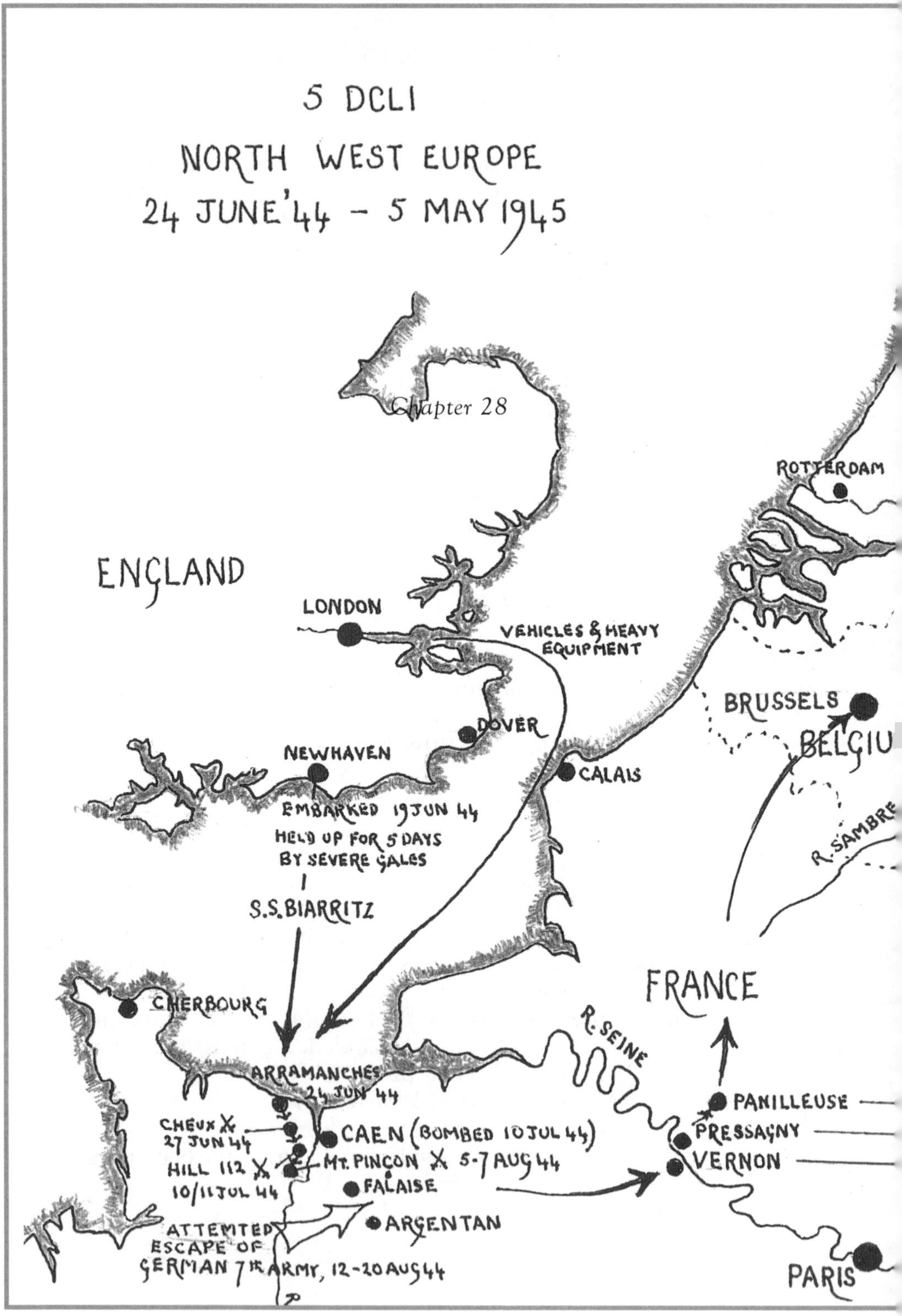
5 DCLI
NORTH WEST EUROPE
24 JUNE '44 – 5 MAY 1945
ENGLAND
LONDON
VEHICLES & HEAVY EQUIPMENT
DOVER
NEWHAVEN
EMBARKED 19 JUN 44
HELD UP FOR 5 DAYS BY SEVERE GALES
S.S. BIARRITZ
CALAIS
ROTTERDAM
BRUSSELS
BELGIU
R. SAMBRE
FRANCE
CHERBOURG
ARRAMANCHES 24 JUN 44
CHEUX 27 JUN 44
CAEN (BOMBED 10 JUL 44)
HILL 112 10/11 JUL 44
MT. PINCON 5-7 AUG 44
FALAISE
ARGENTAN
ATTEMTED ESCAPE OF GERMAN 7th ARMY, 12-20 AUG 44
R. SEINE
PANILLEUSE
PRESSAGNY
VERNON
PARIS

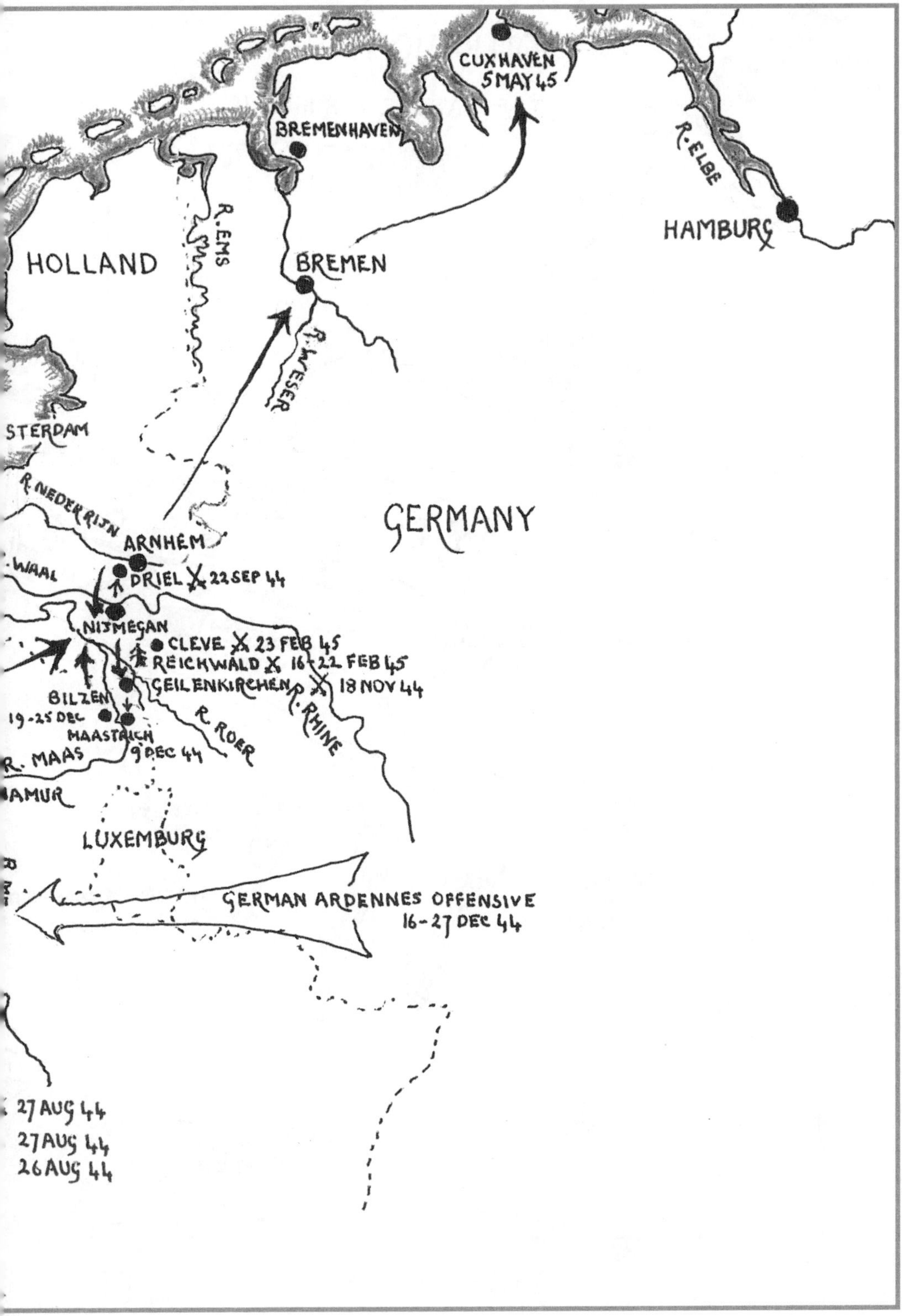
CUXHAVEN
5 MAY 45
BREMENHAVEN
R. ELBE
HAMBURG
R. EMS
HOLLAND
BREMEN
R. WESER
STERDAM
R. NEDERRIJN
GERMANY
ARNHEM
WAAL
DRIEL 22 SEP 44
NIJMEGAN
CLEVE 23 FEB 45
REICHWALD 16-22 FEB 45
GEILENKIRCHEN 18 NOV 44
R. RHINE
BILZEN
19-25 DEC
MAASTRICH
9 DEC 44
R. ROER
R. MAAS
AMUR
LUXEMBURG
GERMAN ARDENNES OFFENSIVE
16-27 DEC 44
27 AUG 44
27 AUG 44
26 AUG 44

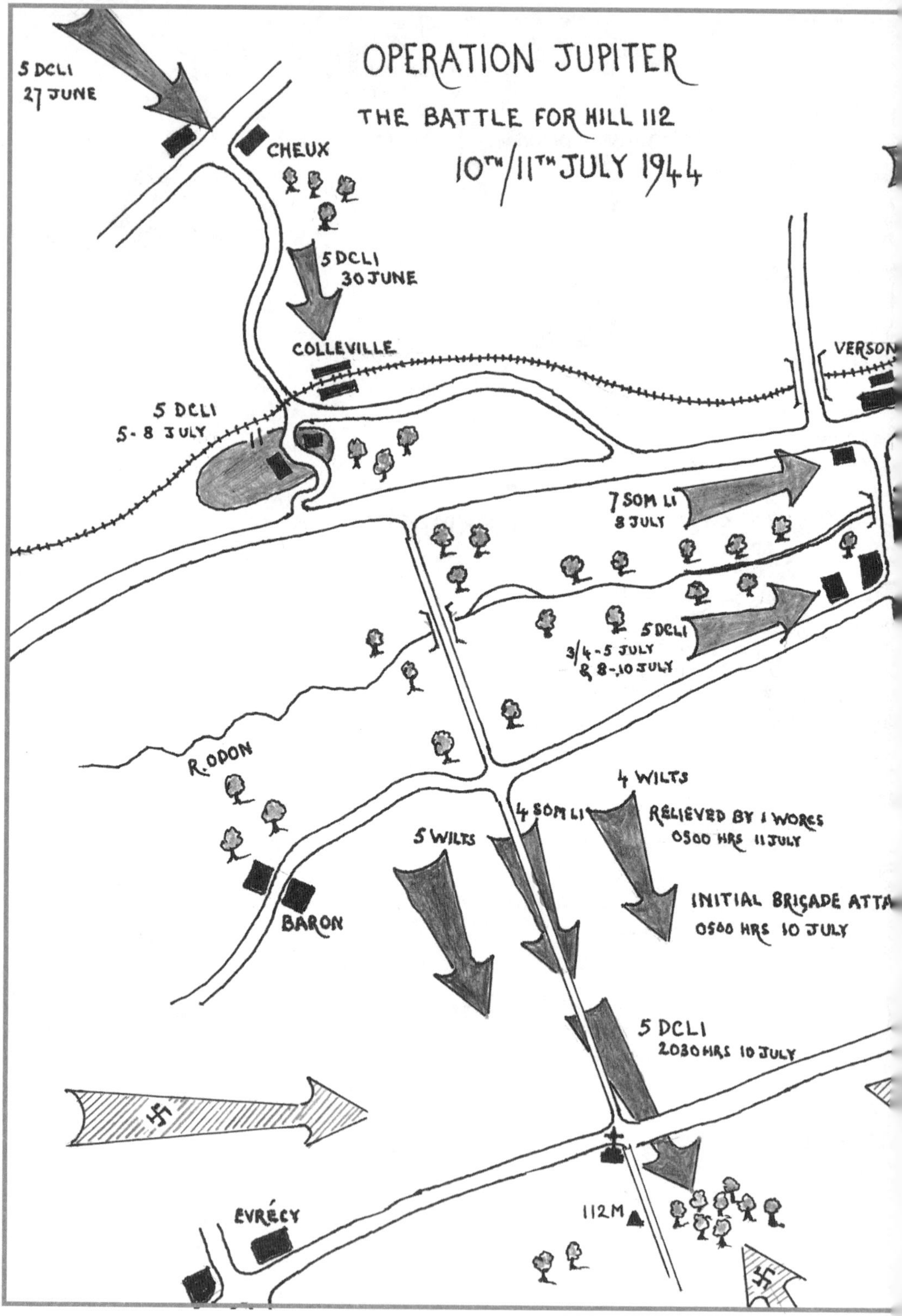
OPERATION JUPITER
THE BATTLE FOR HILL 112
10TH/11TH JULY 1944
5 DCLI
27 JUNE
CHEUX
5 DCLI
30 JUNE
COLLEVILLE
VERSON
5 DCLI
5-8 JULY
7 SOM LI
8 JULY
5 DCLI
3/4-5 JULY
& 8-10 JULY
R. ODON
4 WILTS
4 SOM LI
RELIEVED BY 1 WORCS
0500 HRS 11 JULY
5 WILTS
BARON
INITIAL BRIGADE ATTA
0500 HRS 10 JULY
5 DCLI
2030 HRS 10 JULY
EVRÉCY
112M

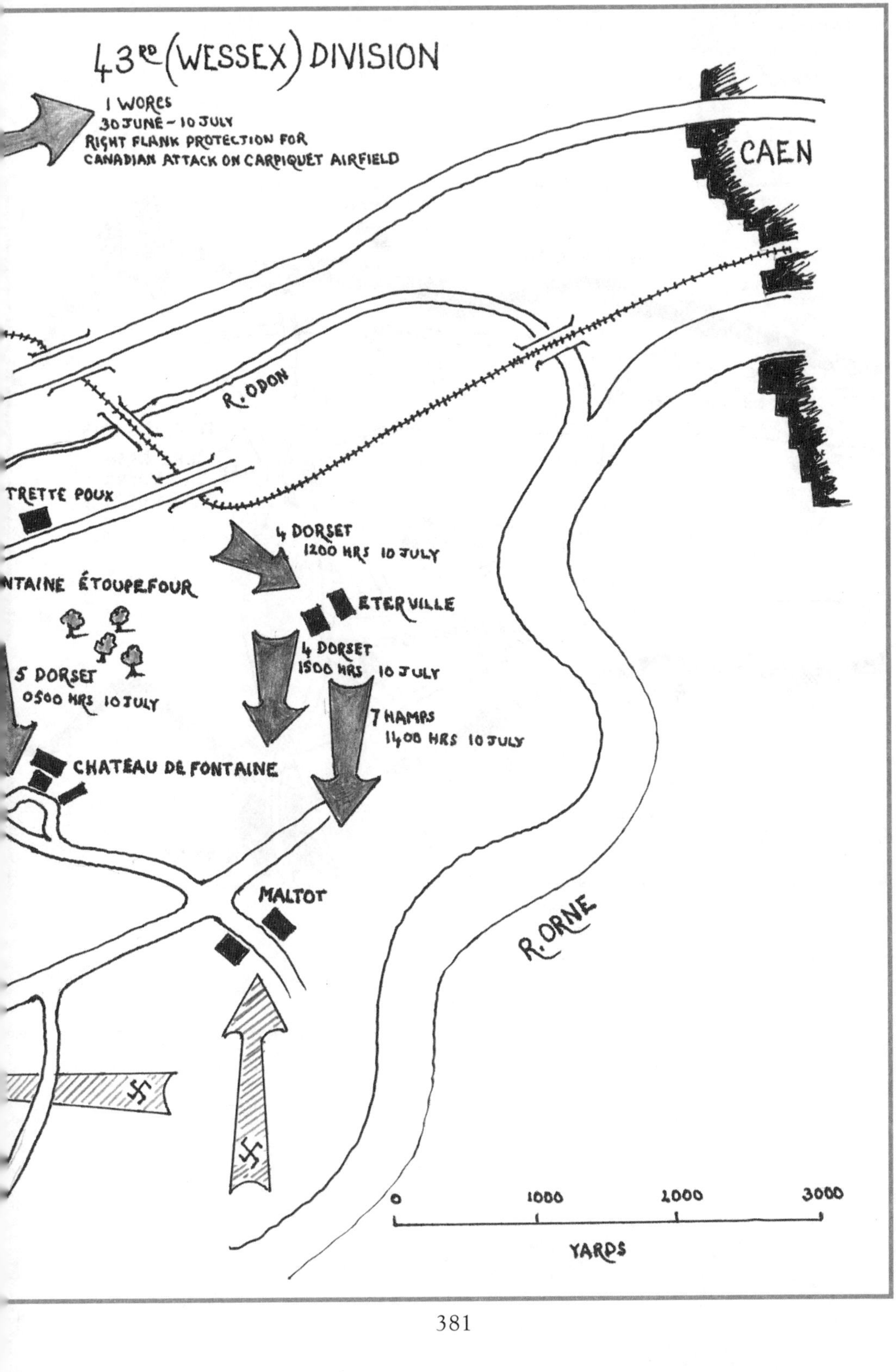
43RD (WESSEX) DIVISION
1 WORCS
30 JUNE – 10 JULY
RIGHT FLANK PROTECTION FOR
CANADIAN ATTACK ON CARPIQUET AIRFIELD
CAEN
R. ODON
TRETTE POUX
4 DORSET
1200 HRS 10 JULY
NTAINE ÉTOUPEFOUR
ETERVILLE
4 DORSET
1500 HRS 10 JULY
5 DORSET
0500 HRS 10 JULY
7 HAMPS
1400 HRS 10 JULY
CHATEAU DE FONTAINE
MALTOT
R. ORNE
0
1000
2000
3000
YARDS

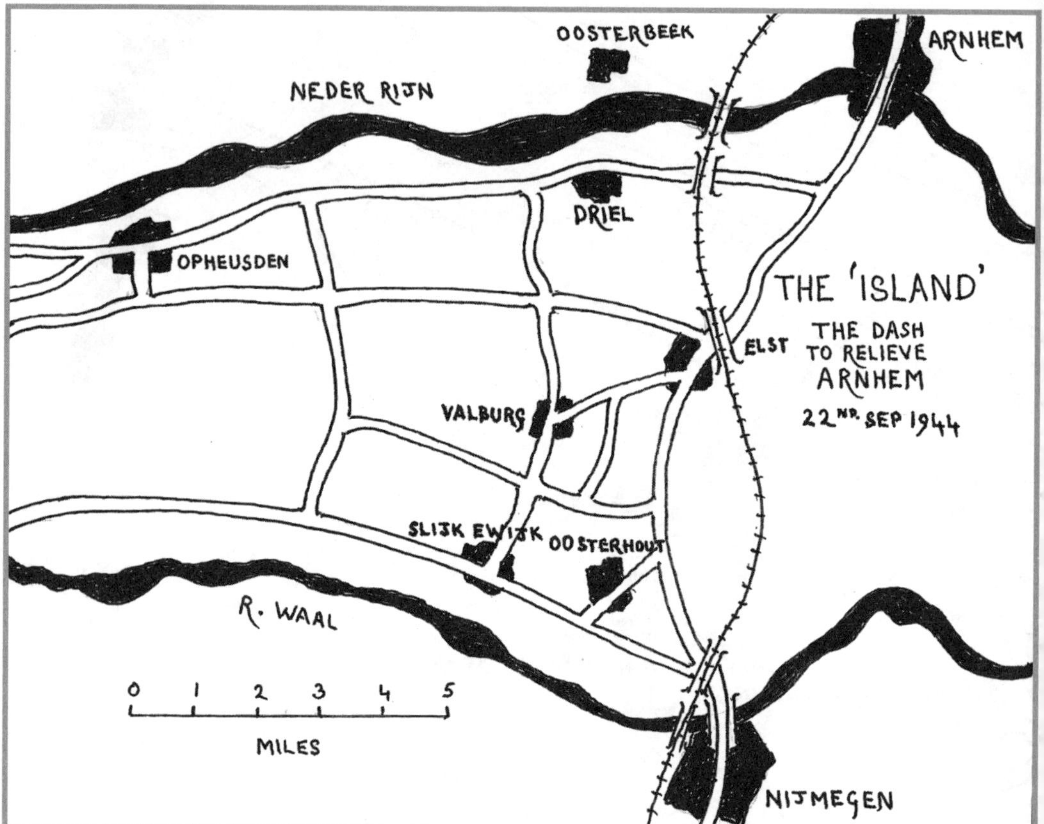
OOSTERBEEK
ARNHEM
NEDER RIJN
DRIEL
OPHEUSDEN
THE 'ISLAND'
THE DASH
TO RELIEVE
ARNHEM
22ND. SEP 1944
ELST
VALBURG
SLIJK EWIJK
OOSTERHOUT
R. WAAL
0 1 2 3 4 5
MILES
NIJMEGEN

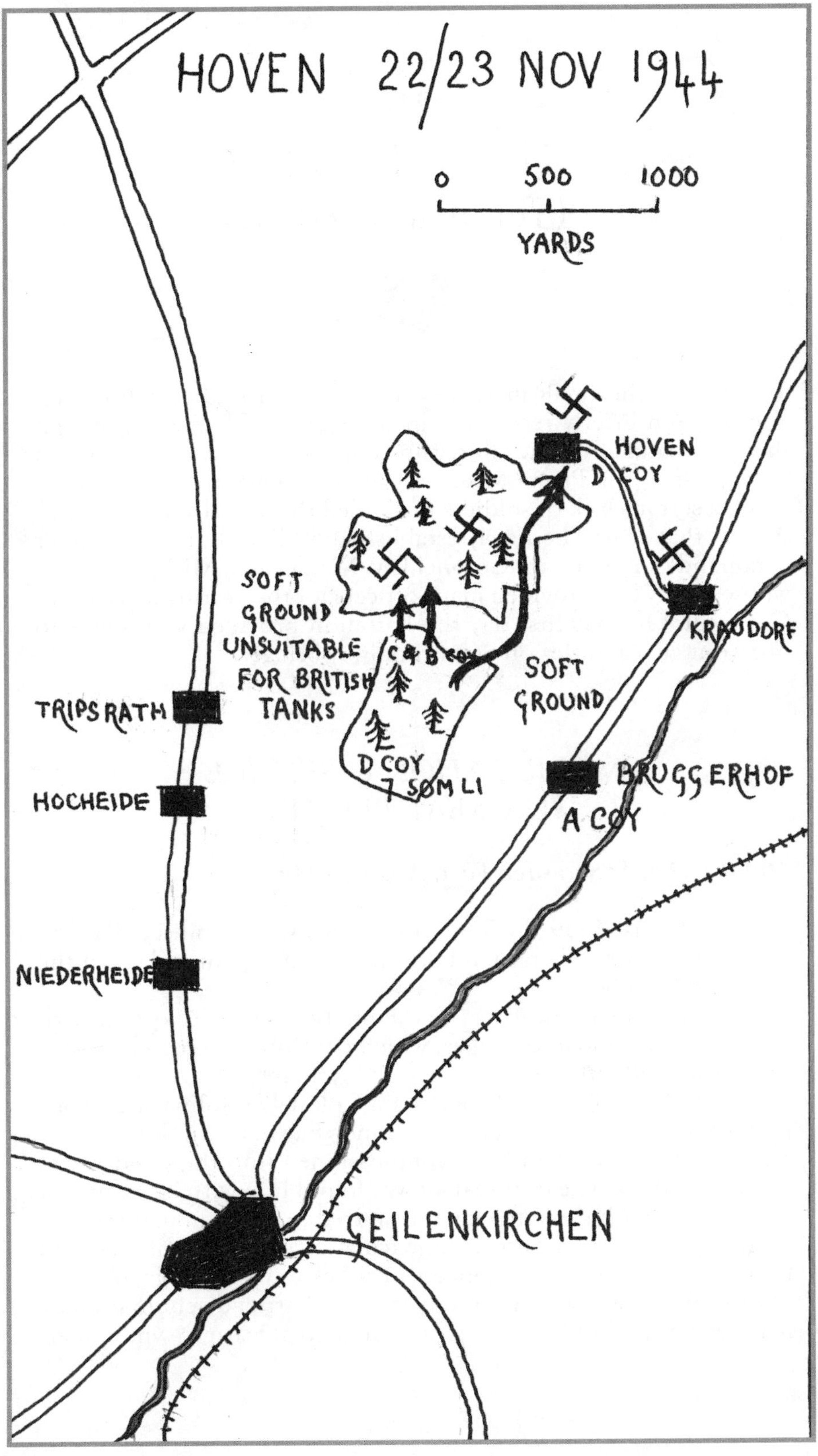

HOVEN 22/23 NOV 1944
0
500
1000
YARDS
HOVEN
D COY
SOFT GROUND UNSUITABLE FOR BRITISH TANKS
C & B COY
SOFT GROUND
KRAUDORF
TRIPSRATH
HOCHEIDE
D COY 7 SOM LI
BRUGGERHOF
A COY
NIEDERHEIDE
GEILENKIRCHEN

28
The 5th Battalion (Territorial Army)

The story of the amalgamated 4th and 5th Territorial Battalions has already been briefly recounted in the previous chapter. Although these two battalions officially regained their own individual identities as a result of the Prime Minister's announcement on 29th March 1939, a serious lack of soldiers precluded the actual split until 24th August that year. The newly established 5th Battalion came under command of Lieutenant-Colonel F.M.M. Bawden, MBE, an officer whose family had provided many officers for the Territorial Army in Cornwall. On that first day the Battalion provided volunteers to carry out guard duties on Saltash railway bridge.

MOBILIZATION & SERVICE IN GREAT BRITAIN

Mobilization & Scrasden Fort, August 1939

On 29th August 1939 the Territorial Army was mobilised. The 5th Battalion moved to Scrasden Fort on the Rame peninsula near the village of Antony.

In the split-up of the 4th/5th Battalion the 5th were lucky to inherit the complete Band and Bugles, which continued to parade in pre-war scarlet well into the summer of 1940, thereby greatly enhancing morale. In December 1939 Lieutenant-Colonel Sir John Carew Pole, Bt took over from Lieutenant-Colonel Bawden. Sir John was a regular officer who had been commissioned into the Coldstream Guards in 1923. The outbreak of war found him with his regiment in London, but he was quickly transferred to take command of the 5th DCLI. The arrival of this immaculate Coldstream officer with his rigid standards of excellence sent shock waves through all ranks of this somewhat relaxed, rural battalion. A strict disciplinarian he may have been, but he was also a man of great warmth whom men instinctively trusted and respected. Within a very short time a bond of affection had developed between him and his new battalion, and under his leadership the 5th was welded together, not only into a supremely efficient fighting unit, but also into a proud and happy one. He laid the foundations which were to sustain it through a year of the most bloody battles in North West Europe three and a half years later.

Newhaven & Seaford, May 1940

At about this time the 45th Infantry Division was in the process of being formed. Both the 4th and the 5th Battalions, together with the 9th Devons, were incorporated into 136 Brigade, which had the initial and urgent role of coastal defence. As soon as was practical the Division moved to the Sussex coast, where the 5th was allotted an area of responsibility between Newhaven and Seaford. It was a strange and somewhat surreal environment in which concrete 'dragon's teeth', pill-boxes and acres of barbed wire dominated a scene totally devoid of any civilian population, which had been evacuated inland. Invasion exercises were regularly carried out by day and night, while the 4th and 5th Battalions provided a fast moving Brigade mobile reserve in the true Light Infantry tradition.

Thorne, Winter 1940-1941

As the winter weather rendered the risk of invasion less likely, the 45th Division moved north to Yorkshire, where there was ample space to carry out advanced training. The 5th Battalion was billeted around the village of Thorne.

Welwyn Garden City, February 1940

In February the 45th Division left the snow-swept Yorkshire moors without undue regret, and again moved south to assume the role of GHQ Counter Attack Division. Training for this took the form of fast-moving exercises to oppose an assumed enemy landing on either the Norfolk or Hampshire coasts. All ranks enjoyed and benefited from this hard training, and there was general disappointment when the Division returned to the static role along the Norfolk coast.

Walton-on-the-Naze & Harwich, August 1941

The 4th and 5th Battalions rotated between beach areas around Walton-on-the-Naze and Harwich, with occasional spells in Colchester and Manningtree. Long days and nights spent in the confines of concrete pill-boxes, staring out into the bleak North Sea, was not the most inspiring sort of soldiering, particularly as the shoals and fierce tidal currents seemed to preclude any but the most foolhardy attempt at landing. In order to maintain both morale and operational efficiency, brigade exercises were held whenever opportunity arose. These, together with study days, courses and social events helped to maintain the close ties between the 4th and the 5th Battalions. Not only did a healthy rivalry develop between the two Battalions but also close bonds of friendship which were to prove of great importance when the 5th finally went to war.

Isle of Wight, Summer 1942

On 6th August 1942 the 5th Battalion received the unexpected but not unwelcome news that it was to leave its old friends in 136 Brigade and move to the Isle of Wight, where it was to become part of 214 Independent Infantry Brigade, together with the 7th Wiltshire Regiment and the 7th Somerset Light Infantry. Soldiering with this Brigade opened new visions of more aggressive active service. Coastal defence work continued to occupy much of the Battalion's time, with companies dispersed between Bembridge, Sandown and Brading, but every opportunity was taken to carry out imaginative mobile exercises under the energetic and searching guidance of the Brigade Commander, Brigadier H. Essame MC, late of the Northamptonshire Regiment. When on coastal defensive duties, the Battalion used to indulge in what was known as 'the mad minute'. This was carried out at the dawn stand to, and involved putting down one minute's rapid fire from every weapon on some imaginary enemy incursion. Although most of the civilian population had been evacuated from their seaside houses, at least one instance occurred in which a couple were rudely awakened from their sleep by a stream of machine-gun bullets passing over their bed!

Cornwall, May 1943

In May 1943 the 5th Battalion paid a hurried visit to its home county, where it was brought up to full war establishment by drafts from a number of regiments. These included the Gloucesters, Devons and Royal Sussex.

It is an aspect peculiar to the British Army, that every infantry soldier is convinced that his particular regiment is by far the finest. Loyalty to this regiment forms the bedrock on which his pride is based, and any interference with this can strike a serious blow to morale. Lieutenant-Colonel Sir John Carew Pole paid particular attention to ensure that every man coming new to his battalion was given a warm and friendly welcome. Because of their Colonel's insistence that there should be no question of 'them and us', the 5th quickly settled down into a happy and tight knit unit. This spirit was further enhanced as it became obvious to all ranks that they were earmarked for active operations.

From that moment, hard, realistic training, often using live ammunition, became the order of the day. The Brigade moved up to the Combined Operations School at Inverary to be taught the techniques of assault landings. After a month of carrying out repeated embarkation procedures, scrambles through the waist-high surf, and battle drills on the beach-head, the Brigade moved to the Northumberland coast, so rumour had it, in preparation for operations in the Azores. Whether or not there was any substance in this rumour was never established. Certainly no such operation ever took place and in October 1943, 214 Infantry Brigade lost the word 'Independent' in its title, and became a formation in the 43rd (Wessex) Division.

Kent, October 1943

The 43rd (Wessex) Division was based in Kent, and at that time was in the process of changing from its original organisation of two infantry brigades and one armoured brigade to one of three infantry brigades. Hence the need for a third infantry brigade.

214 Brigade consisted of 5th DCLI, 7th Somerset Light Infantry and 1st Worcestershire Regiment. These units were destined to remain together for the rest of the war, and in the battles that lay ahead were to become a close knit band of brothers. The Division was commanded by Major-General G.I. Thomas, DSO, MC, late of the Royal Artillery. Thomas was an officer of uncompromising standards who had taken over command in March 1942, and had since trained it to a pitch of excellence. This new brigade thus found itself with a great deal to learn in a very short time. It soon became apparent that there was to be no let up for the winter. Units were committed to ceaseless exercises, which were unmerciful to officers

and men who were often operating under the extremes of exhaustion. Neither cold, wet weather nor lack of sleep was accepted as an excuse for incompetence. Thomas welcomed the 'fog of war' on his exercises for, as he so rightly said, these would be the conditions under which the forthcoming battles would invariably be fought. The Division may have cursed him as a slave driver at the time, but later realised that no man was ever called to perform any task on the battle-field that he had not previously perfected in training. In theory the 5th Battalion was billeted in Folkstone, but in practice spent much of its time on the Stone Street training area. Who will ever forget that cold and wind-swept place? In addition, every officer, warrant-officer and serjeant was put through the rigours of the Divisional Battle School, where exercises with armour and artillery were carried out, using live ammunition. These were designed to acclimatise men not only to the noise and confusion of modern war but, not infrequently, to its dangers. During these months the Battalion became hard, fit and confident.

NORMANDY

The Invasion, June 1944

It is not known exactly when the men of the 43rd (Wessex) Division were officially told that they were to be part of the force destined to invade Europe; certainly, at the time of the divisional reorganisation in October 1943 it must have been obvious that this was to be the task for which they were being groomed. By early 1944 the stalwart commanding officers, who had so effectively transformed these amateur Territorial battalions into highly efficient fighting units, were being replaced by younger men. It was thus with the greatest sadness that the 5th DCLI said farewell to Sir John Carew Pole, who had so effectively combined the professionalism of a regular officer with the warmth and affection of a true Cornish gentleman. Sir John, like many of his contemporaries, was posted to a pool of Commanding Officers in which Lieutenant-Colonels were held at immediate readiness to replace casualties in Europe. He was later to command the 2nd Devons in France and Germany, and was to be awarded the Distinguished Service Order. Sir John was succeeded by Lieutenant-Colonel J.W. Atherton from the Dorset Regiment, who had been commanding the Divisional Battle School. At the same time the Second-in-Command, Major Sir Richard Onslow, Bt, one of the last of the old pre-war Territorial Officers, was succeeded by Major R.W. James of the Somerset Light Infantry.

In early April 1944 the Battalion moved to Crowborough. The long years of training were at an end; every operation of war had been practised, and practised again, until it had become second nature; now all that remained to be done was to check and re-check every weapon and piece of equipment to ensure that it was in perfect condition. On 6th April all leave was cancelled, letters were censored, field cashiers took the place of banks and vehicles were waterproofed. No one knew either the place or date of the forthcoming invasion, but it was obvious that the time was drawing very close when the 5th Battalion would be committed to the ultimate test of battle. Confidence in their military skill was mixed with the apprehension that gnaws at the vitals of every man who has ever awaited his baptism of fire.

At about this time the Battalion received a draft of five Canadian officers under a scheme known as Canloan. These were all splendid young men who were welcomed and quickly assimilated into the brotherhood of the 5th. Sadly, three of these officers were destined to be killed within the year.*

The Allied assault divisions landed in Normandy on 6th June 1944. The following day all available officers of the 43rd (Wessex) Division were gathered in a Hastings cinema to be briefed by Major-General Thomas on the probable tasks awaiting it in France. From that day the Battalion came into the able hands of BUCO (Build-up Control Organisation). All vehicles were despatched to London Docks, and on 14th June the 5th moved to a staging camp near Glyndbourne.

The original plan had decreed that the Battalion should be established in Normandy, complete with its transport, by 20th June. However, atrocious weather and the consequent slow turn around of shipping was causing extremely worrying delays and it was not until 19th June that the Battalion finally moved by road to Newhaven, to embark on SS *Biarritz*. The drive from Glyndbourne to Newhaven had all the elements of a triumphal progress as crowds turned out to cheer the troops through each village. Newhaven itself had briefly been the home of the Battalion in 1940, so that the welcome as they drove through the town to the docks was especially warm. There it embarked on the *Biarritz*.

That night a storm blew up, which further delayed departure. For three long days the ship lay at anchor just off Spithead, pitching and rolling in the heavy sea. The ship's name, *Biarritz*, might conjure up visions of luxury; during those days and nights soldiers,

* The Canadian officers were Lieutenant Arthur, Captain J.H.J. Gauthier, Lieutenant E. Hardy, Lieutenant M.C.P. Rush and Lieutenant B.D.J. Comolli.

together with their weapons and equipment, were packed into every available space, and luxury was not the word that sprang to mind. Those who were incarcerated in this ship remembered in years to come only the smell of sweat, self-heating soup and vomit. But all things, however unpleasant, eventually come to an end, and on the evening of 21st June the *Biarritz* weighed anchor and set off for Normandy. The following afternoon the ship approached the landing beaches. The sight was quite remarkable; never before or since has an armada been mounted on that scale. The sea was crowded with every description of warship, together with merchant ships, landing craft and naval pinnaces. Those who had been evacuated from Dunkirk almost exactly four years previously noticed one very big difference: the Luftwaffe was absent. Tactical bombing of airfields by the Royal Air Force and United States Air Force, together with constant fighter cover over the landing beaches, had ensured that no enemy dive bombing or strafing would interfere with the monumental task of landing troops, vehicles, ammunition and stores.

The *Biarritz* anchored off shore to allow the men to scramble down nets rigged along her hull into waiting landing craft. To accomplish this manoeuvre in a heavy swell without the burden of weapon and equipment would not have been easy; to do so fully accoutred and feeling extremely sick constituted a feat of gymnastic agility, particularly for the poor souls who were required to carry bicycles down the swaying nets. The language used by this latter group was never recorded, but scarcely can any bicycle ever have been the subject of such verbal abuse. Alas, these machines were found to have no discernible use in the battle area and were discarded in the concentration area at Bayeux. The construction of these army bicycles was so robust that the good citizens of Bayeux may still be riding them!

The *Biarritz* was lucky to make her approach to the beach unscathed. That same morning MT 41, *Derry Cunihy*, carrying the whole of the 43rd Reconnaissance Regiment, and its vehicles, had struck a mine as she approached the beach. The ship had been blown in half, the stern portion sinking rapidly. Casualties were heavy, 180 officers and men being drowned and a further 150 wounded (many of whom subsequently died). All the vehicles were lost. This incident and its aftermath gave a foretaste of the remarkable efficiency of the reinforcement and equipment replacement organisation, for within a very few days this unit had been brought back into the order of battle complete with men and vehicles. No such disaster struck the 5th Battalion, who were swiftly ferried ashore in the landing craft. Ashore is perhaps the wrong word, for when the bow ramps were lowered the men stepped out into chest-high water. However, so great was the relief at being safely clear of their rolling and pitching ship, and to feel firm sand beneath their submerged feet, that any discomfort barely registered. There was a great feeling of euphoria which came with the realisation that they were part of this mighty armada, and were now players in one of the most epic dramas in history.

Once on dry land, the files of men winding their way inland found themselves caught up in a remarkable scene of organised chaos. Everywhere there was frenetic activity; Pioneer Corps units laboured on the construction of steel tracking leading up from the shoreline; Royal Engineers' bulldozers and recovery tanks moved ponderously about, clearing up the detritus of former battle; Royal Military Police directed men and traffic onto their ordained routes; while everywhere vast stocks of stores, ammunition and petrol were continuously brought ashore and loaded into the waiting vehicles. In this great ant-heap of bustle and movement every man seemed to know his task, and went about it with quiet efficiency.

The 5th Battalion quickly found the route signs displaying the yellow Wyvern of the 43rd (Wessex) Division, and following them off the beach-head, made for the allotted assembly area. From there it marched a further five or six miles along rural tree-lined roads, to the Battalion concentration area amongst apple orchards, just north of Bayeux. As the soldiers rested under the trees in the dappled June sunshine, the thought must have run through many minds that, if this was war, it was certainly more pleasant than the cold bleak exercises on the Stone Street training area. Only the near continuous thump and rumble of artillery, fifteen miles to the east around Caen, indicated the reality of the situation.

Had things gone according to plan, the Battalion would have been joined by its transport, fighting vehicles and heavy equipment immediately on arrival at Bayeux. However, the storm that had delayed the marching troops on the *Biarritz* had caused a far greater dislocation of the plans for the landing of vehicles. These had sailed from London Docks on a 'Liberty' ship, but had had to wait for relatively calm weather before it was possible to lift them in slings attached to the ship's derricks and lower them into the landing craft or ferries. At last, on 24th June, the marching troops of the Fifth Battalion were once more united with their vehicles and other heavy equipment. There must have been a general sigh of relief as, up to that point, officers and men had been existing on what they carried in their fighting order. Now they claimed their packs, each containing a blanket, spare pair of boots, spare shirt and other desirable odds and ends which would make life more comfortable. More importantly, the 5th Battalion was now complete and ready for battle. The fruits of five years of training were about to be put to the test.

One must now put the arrival of the 43rd (Wessex) Division into the context of the overall Allied plan. On 6th June the British 3rd and 5th Divisions and the Canadian 3rd Division had landed on the three eastern beaches (Gold, Juno and Sword) close to the ancient city of Caen. Simultaneously, the U.S. 1st and 4th Divisions had landed on the two western beaches (Omaha and Utah), the latter facing south west across the roots of the Cherbourg peninsula. The British 6th and U.S. 82nd and 101st Airborne Divisions had secured the flanks to the east and west respectively. Field-Marshal Montgomery's overall plan was that the British and Canadian divisions should make savage and repeated thrusts to break out of the bridgehead, thereby forcing Field Marshall Rommel to commit more and more of his reserves from the 7th and 15th Armies, leaving little opposition available to face the U.S. troops when they started their advance to cut off the peninsula and then capture the port of Cherbourg. The capture of Cherbourg was absolutely vital to the continued survival of the Allied force. It represented the only deep water port in that part of the coast capable of dealing in all weathers with the massive tonnage of supplies needed to keep a modern army in the field. This plan had gone well in so much as the U.S. forces captured the port of Cherbourg on 27th June.The British and Canadian operations around Caen had however been bloody in the extreme, and, in spite of repeated hard-hitting attacks, Caen was still in German hands when the 5th DCLI joined up with its vehicles and heavy equipment on that summer day in the orchards around Bayeux on the 24th June 1944.

The Battle for Caen, June-July 1944

Action at Cheux, 25th-30th June

On 25th June a final series of battles to capture Caen was launched. The 15th (Scottish) Division took over the spear-head of the advance the following day with the 43rd (Wessex) Division following close behind, securing each objective as it was taken. Fighting was very bitter, but by that evening what remained of the village of Cheux had been captured. The weather, which up to this point had been warm and dry, now turned to rain. As the 5th Battalion moved forward to take over from the 9th Cameronians (Scottish Rifles) in

Cheux, a massive traffic jam developed on the narrow approach roads, along which the best part of two infantry brigades and two regiments of tanks were attempting to move east. At first light the next morning, 27th June, the Battalion was again able to move forward, abandoning the roads and moving through the fields, which after the heavy rain rapidly became a morass. It was now that all the training carried out in Kent was to assume such importance. In the confusion of battle the 9th Cameronians, whom the Battalion was due to relieve, had already been pulled back out of Cheux. Thus when the 5th moved forward, it found the enemy back in possession of the village. The area was alive with every sort of vehicle; even the 25 pdr guns were digging in a mere two or three hundred yards from the enemy. Under constant artillery, mortar sniping and tank fire, never did men dig in faster.

Suddenly, without warning, six large tanks rumbled down the sunken lane, passing the right flank company (B Company). Only the tops of their turrets were visible and it was assumed that they were British. As the leading tank turned a corner in the lane, it met a troop of four 17 pdr anti-tank guns being towed behind their carriers to support the Battalion. They were sitting ducks, and within seconds all four guns had been knocked out. The tanks, which proved to be Panthers, now turned into an orchard where Major J. Fry and the headquarters of D Company were dug in. Major Fry was not one to tolerate such an unwarranted incursion. Quickly organising a tank hunt, he ordered Serjeant Hicks and Corporal Ronan to take the Company Headquarters PIAT and shoot up the intrusive tanks from the rear. Meanwhile, the Company Second-in-Command, Captain T.H. Jobson, fetched the three platoon PIAT detachments, who joined in the hunt.*

Suddenly, into this scene appeared two German despatch riders, apparently unaware that they were riding straight through a British position. Major Fry and Captain Jobson quickly accounted for them, the first two Germans to be killed by the 5th Battalion.

The tanks edged forward, knocking out two of the battalion 6 pdr anti-tank guns and wounding most of the detachments. The next target was Battalion Headquarters, and soon carriers and jeeps were blazing merrily. Lieutenant-Colonel Atherton, gallantly directing the fire of another 6 pdr, was killed by a direct hit. Meanwhile the PIAT detachments were all intent on stalking the intruders. The four PIATs were registering repeated hits. One tank, hit three times, fled; Serjeant Hicks knocked one out; two more

* PIAT: Projector Infantry Anti-Tank. A crude shoulder-controlled weapon firing a hollow-charge missile.

turned away straight into the arms of Captain C.L. Blackwell of C Company, whose PIAT detachments promptly knocked out one and caused the other to withdraw so fast that it turned over. At about the same time Serjeant Wilson scored a direct hit with one of the remaining 6 pdr anti-tank guns that, to everybody's amazement, the tank brewed up. The 6 pdr anti-tank gun was not capable of penetrating the armour of the German Tiger or Panther tanks. Only a lucky hit in one of the few vulnerable spots could inflict any serious damage. Throughout this engagement Major Fry never went to ground, dodging the enemy tanks in the orchard, while all the time shouting encouragement to the PIAT detachments in his usual robust and uninhibited way. It was now only a matter of hunting and despatching the tank crews, a task which was quickly accomplished.

In its very first action the 5th Battalion had knocked out four Panther tanks and damaged a fifth in the space of half an hour. Furthermore, these were manned by SS troops, the most feared in the German army. However, the Battalion had also suffered its first casualties in this short engagement. Lieutenant-Colonel Atherton, a pre-war Territorial soldier of the highest quality, had been killed, with nineteen others killed or wounded. Major R.W. James immediately assumed command. Major James, also a pre-war Territorial officer, had earlier been seconded from the Somerset Light Infantry as Second-in-Command of the 5th DCLI. As a result of their conduct in this action, Captain Blackwell was awarded the MC, and Serjeant Hicks the Military Medal.

For the next three days the Battalion remained dug in amongst the orchards just forward of Cheux. It was a most unhealthy spot, in which the slightest movement brought down swift and accurate mortar and *nebelwerfer* fire from the Germans ensconced on Carpiquet airfield, which overlooked the whole of the Cheux area. There were many casualties, amongst whom was Captain P. E. G. Coode, commanding Support Company, who was killed by a mortar bomb. He was another pre-war Territorial, and one of the most capable and popular officers in the Battalion. Seldom however is a situation so grim that the British soldier cannot derive some humour from it. On this particular occasion, as the leading DCLI platoon cautiously crossed the railway just south of Cheux, what should they see ahead but one of those most excellent establishments of the Royal Army Ordnance Corps – a Mobile Laundry and Bath Unit. There it was, apparently quite oblivious of the enemy fire, set up beside the road well ahead of the leading infantry, belching clouds of steam. In the stress of battle, its original orders to be at that particular spot at that particular time had presumably never been countermanded.

Details of the fierce fighting that continued during those three days need not concern us here. However, in the light of events which were soon to effect the 5th Battalion in a terrible manner, it is worth noting that 29 Armoured Brigade crossed the River Odon and drove a narrow but deep wedge south through the German defences. The 8th Rifle Brigade and the 23rd Hussars had advanced with the vanguard and established themselves on the high ground commanding the crossings of the River Orne south of Caen, known as Hill 112. However, interceptions of Enigma messages, indicating that a major German counter attack was being prepared, made it vital to withdraw 29 Armoured Brigade back from its narrow corridor before it risked annihilation. Thus the British line was pulled back to the line of the River Odon, and Hill 112 was re-occupied by the enemy. On the night of 29th-30th June the 15th (Scottish) and 11th Armoured Divisions, which had taken the full brunt of the bitter fighting around Cheux, were replaced by the 43rd (Wessex) Division. The position, which became known as 'Death Valley', was subjected to almost continuous artillery and mortar fire, and was perhaps the most dangerous sector of the front at that time.

Colville & Fontaine Etoupefour, 30th June-8th July 1944

The 5th Battalion remained a further four days around the hamlet of Colville just south of Cheux, being shot at by anything the Germans could bring to bear. On the moonless night of 3rd-4th July the Battalion made its way in single file to the wrecked remains of the main Caen railway line and, turning east, picked its way painfully along the shambles of twisted rails, shattered sleepers and fallen telegraph poles with their cat's cradles of wires. After about a mile and a half, the village of Verson was reached. Here, after a short halt to collect the stragglers, the Battalion turned right and, crossing the River Odon (more of a stream than a river), moved into the deserted village of Fontaine Etoupefour on the south bank. During the original attack by the 11th (Armoured) Division, Fontaine Etoupefour had been heavily fought over. Almost every house was smashed and the detritus of war was scattered everywhere. Many corpses lay where they had fallen; of the living, either British or German, there was no sign. Now the village represented the most forward British position, and was in fact actually within the German front line. On 4th July the Canadians again attacked Capriquet airfield. Although some progress was made, the airfield itself defied capture, leaving the 5th Battalion out on a limb in Fontaine Etoupefour, in an impossibly dangerous position. As yet the Germans were unaware of the Battalion's presence in the village, but this fortunate state of affairs could not continue much longer and so, on the night of 4th-5th July, the 5th was withdrawn to its old position north of the River Odon at Colville.

On 8th July 1 (British) Corps attacked Caen from the north and north west. This was preceded on the evening of 7th July by a massive air attack on the city, in which 460 heavy bombers dropped 2,350 tons of high explosive bombs in 40 minutes – possibly the largest air support operation of the war. Lieutenant-General Sir Richard O'Connor, KCB, KBE, DSO, MC, commanding 1 (British) Corps, was called upon to make the terrible decision to destroy one of the most superb mediaeval cities in Europe. The whole strategy of the break-out in Normandy now depended on the swift capture of Caen, and General O'Connor, after agonising deliberation, became convinced that the sacrifice of a single British soldier's life in order to save beautiful buildings was not acceptable. By the evening of 8th July all but a small part of Caen was in British hands, and the 5th Battalion retraced its weary steps back across the River Odon to Fontaine Etoupefour. The following day the Canadians carried out a text-book attack on Carpiquet airfield. They took few prisoners; the defenders, Adolf Hitler Youth soldiers, preferred to fight to the death rather than surrender.

Operation 'Jupiter' & Hill 112, 10th-13th July 1944

The time had now come for the 43rd (Wessex) Division to advance across the River Orne south of Caen. The south flank was dominated by a ridge of high ground running south west between the rivers Odon and Orne. The former was merely a stream, but the latter consisted of a broad, deep waterway capable of taking small ships. To the east of the River Orne the ground rose again to a second ridge, which commanded the whole of the Orne valley. Between them, these two ridges commanded not only any crossing of the River Orne but also the approaches to Caen itself.

The ridge between the rivers Odon and Orne rises gradually from the junction of the two rivers just south of Caen to its highest point five miles to the south west, known as Hill 112. If one visits this feature, the first impression is that it can have little tactical significance. The slope rising to the south from the valley of the River Odon is barely perceptible, indeed the last 300 yards present the appearance of a flat plateau. Only on reaching the top does one realise how this hill dominates the surrounding countryside. After fording the River Odon one moves through thickly planted apple orchards for the first 1,000 yards, but after crossing the first of two metalled roads,

> which runs between Fontaine Etoupfour and Baron, these orchards give way to open cornfields. On crossing the second metalled road, which runs east to the village of Esquay, the cornfields are virtually flat for the final 300 yards to a prominent orchard standing in silhouette against the southern sky. Running straight across the feature from north to south is a dead straight, clearly defined track known as Le Chemin Guillaume (the road supposedly used by Duke William of Normandy in 1066, when he marched with his army to embark at Bayeux for the invasion of England). Where this track crosses the Esquay road stands a tall wayside crucifix. Although splattered with bullets and shell splinters it was never destroyed, and throughout the forthcoming battle provided a useful reference point. To the east of Hill 112 lie the villages of Fontaine Etoupefour and Maltot, with the Chateau de Fontaine just off the road between them. To the west lies the village of Esquay.

However insignificant Hill 112 may appear to the casual observer, its tactical importance was certainly not lost to the enemy defenders. Indeed, the German tactical doctrine laid down for the containment of the invading army was 'He who holds Hill 112 holds Normandy'. Consequently it was very heavily defended, with 10th SS Division occupying the hill itself, 277th Division to the west and a Adolf Hitler Youth battalion to the north. On the far side of the Hill lay the 102nd SS Heavy Tank Battalion waiting in the counter attack role. This battalion was equipped with 56 ton Tiger tanks. At this point in the story it is important to understand the overpowering superiority that the Germans enjoyed over the British in terms of both tanks and anti-tank guns. Their 88 mm gun had originally been developed as an anti-aircraft weapon, but it soon became apparent that its very high velocity made it an ideal anti-tank gun. When the final Second World War generations of tanks came to be designed, it seemed logical to the Germans that they should be armed with this well-proven gun. It also seemed logical that they should be sufficiently well armoured to deflect the light anti-tank shells generally used by the British. Thus the Tiger tank was produced, proof against most current British weapons, and mounting an 88 mm gun capable of punching a shell straight through one side of a British tank and out through the other at 1,000 yards. The German standard anti-tank gun continued to be this 88 mm weapon mounted on a field carriage. The British infantry was armed with the 6 pdr anti-tank gun, a weapon quite incapable of penetrating the Tigers' armour, and, although the Royal Artillery did possess a limited number of heavy 17 pdr anti-tank guns, these were inadequate in number. The majority of British tanks in Normandy were the American produced Shermans. These were reliable but woefully thinly armoured and undergunned. The standard Sherman mounted a short-barrelled 75 mm gun, which like the infantryman's 6 pdr, was incapable of penetrating a Tiger's armour. A few months before D Day this shortcoming was recognised, and an urgent programme was initiated to re-arm one in every four Shermans with a 17 pdr. These modified tanks were known as 'Fireflys', and were to prove vitally important in helping to redress the balance of anti-tank fire power. The bitter fact remained that, regardless of the gun it carried, the Sherman was woefully vulnerable to anti-tank fire. They became known by the macabre name of 'Tommy Cookers'. A Sherman would become a blazing inferno within seconds of being hit. Many brave men suffered a gruesome death trapped inside these steel coffins. The British had possessed the excellent 3.7 in. anti-aircraft gun since about 1937. Although a very similar weapon to the German 88 mm, it was seldom ever used in the anti-tank role. Why it was that the British, with their rich tradition of inventiveness, together with the Americans with their vast industrial capacity, were unable to produce a tank or to use an anti-tank gun comparable to those used by the Germans almost passes comprehension. This disparity of equipment was to have grave consequences in the battles for North West Europe.

The capture of the ridge between the river Odon and Orne by the 43rd Wessex Division was christened Operation 'Jupiter'. The key to this operation was the initial capture of Hill 112. This was to be undertaken by 129 Brigade, consisting of 4th Somerset Light Infantry, 4th Wiltshires and 5th Wiltshires. As soon as Hill 112 was secured 130 Brigade, consisting of 7th Royal Hampshires, 4th Dorsets and 5th Dorsets, was to pass through Maltot on the north east flank. Finally 4 Armoured Brigade and 214 Brigade, consisting of 7th Somerset Light Infantry, 1st Worcesters and 5th Duke of Cornwall's Light Infantry, were to pass through to the Orne and, if any bridges were found still intact, to cross and exploit success. The artillery fire plan was massive, involving the entire fire power of 15th (Scottish) Division, 43rd (Wessex) Division, 11th Armoured Division, plus two AGRAs (Army Groups Royal Artillery), together with all the mortars of 43rd (Wessex) Division and the machine-guns of 8th Middlesex.

At 5 a.m. on 10th July 129 Brigade deployed onto the start line along the Fontain Etoupefour-Baron road. The 4th Wiltshires were on the left flank, 4th Somerset Light Infantry in the centre astride the Chemin Guillaume, and 5th Wiltshires on the right flank. In spite of massive supporting fire, the German artillery had not been neutralised. The three battalions waiting on their start line were heavily shelled.

As 129 Brigade advanced it met fanatic resistance, not only from their front, but from a multitude of positions concealed in the corn, which only sprang to life after the first waves of the assault had passed. Thus the whole advance degenerated into a whole series of platoon and company battles being fought out in the rear of the leading troops. Casualties on both sides were extremely heavy. The advance came to a halt below the Maltot road, about 800 yards short of the orchard on Hill 112. There the three battalions dug in and consolidated their position as best they could.

Meanwhile on the left flank, the 5th Dorsets advanced through Fontaine Etoupefour and captured the Chateau de Fontaine and its surrounding farm buildings. As soon as this area was secure, 4th Dorsets passed through to the next village, Eterville. As the Battalion advanced it was bombed by RAF Typhoons, killing or wounding a number of men. In spite of this set-back Eterville was captured, against bitter opposition and at very heavy cost in killed and wounded. Now was the time for the 7th Royal Hampshires to pass through the Dorsets and take the village of Maltot. If this could be achieved, it would be but a short leap to the western bank of the River Orne. The 7th Royal Hampshires, with a company of the 4th Dorsets under command, advanced on Maltot, shortly afterwards reporting the village captured. In fact this was far from true. The British and German positions were merely superimposed on each other and the most savage close quarter fighting was taking place. The 4th Dorsets was now ordered to reinforce the 7th Hampshires and consolidate the British position on Maltot. Accordingly the Battalion advanced through the flat corn to its objective. Unbeknown to the 4th Dorsets, the Commanding Officer of the 7th Hampshires had been mortally wounded and his battalion had suffered 226 casualties. The order to withdraw from Maltot had been given (by whom was never established), and by the time that the the 4th Dorsets appeared on the scene, the village was again securely held by the Germans. They stood no chance whatsoever. After being pinned down in the corn under heavy fire from both Tiger tanks in Maltot itself and every sort of weapon from Hill 112, the Battalion requested maximum fire to cover its withdrawal. The entire Divisional artillery together with two AGRAs put down what was perhaps the heaviest concentrations in the whole campaign. The 10th July had been a black day for the 4th Dorsets. In a few hours of fighting it had suffered 348 casualties.

At about this time the 7th Somerset Light Infantry and the 1st Worcesters were detached from 214 Brigade and lent to the hard pressed 130 Brigade to strengthen the left flank. The 7th Somerset Light Infantry dug in alongside the 5th Dorsets at the Chateau de Fontaine with 1st Worcesters to their left, who in their turn were in contact with the 4th Wiltshires of 129 Brigade. This flank was constantly under heavy fire directed from the high ground of Hill 112.

On the night of 5th-6th July the 5th Battalion had been withdrawn from its hidden occupation of Fontaine Etoupefour, following the failure of the Canadian attack on Carpiquet airfield. Once Carpiquet had fallen, on the night of 8th-9th July the Battalion made its way back to Fontaine Etoupefour. This time, enemy shelling claimed several casualties. The launch of Operation 'Jupiter' therefore found the 5th in reserve, playing no part in the great battle. As the day wore on, and the two other battalions of 214 Brigade were committed on the left flank, the 5th DCLI became not just part of the reserve but the only reserve battalion in the Division.

The frontal assault on Hill 112 by 129 Brigade had now failed, as had the left flank attack by 130 Brigade. Casualties had been exceptionally heavy amongst every unit involved, and the Germans were still firmly ensconced on the southern slopes of Hill 112. Major-General Thomas's orders were explicit: Hill 112 must be captured. He only had a single battalion left uncommitted, the 5th DCLI. Thus it was that at about 5.30 p.m. on 10th July Lieutenant-Colonel James, who it will be remembered had only been in command for fourteen days, was ordered to pass through the 4th Somerset Light Infantry and advance up the centre line of the Chemin Guillaume to capture and hold the orchard. 'H' hour was initially ordered for 6.30 p.m. but, on the insistence of Lieutenant-Colonel James, was postponed to a more realistic start time of 8.30 p.m. (although this still left little enough time for detailed reconnaissance, the preparation of a fire plan, and the refurbishment of ammunition supplies for the guns which had been in continuous action for fifteen hours).

After a heavy artillery bombardment the 5th DCLI moved forward through the 4th Somerset Light Infantry positions at 8.30 p.m. B Company (Major G.A.L. Vaudry) led on the left, with C Company (Captain C.L. Blackwell) on the right; in support of the leading companies were A Company (Major A.W.U. Roberts) on the left, and D Company (Major J.E.E. Fry) on the right. Unfortunately the supporting tanks were late onto the start line and were unable to provide close-range fire for the assaulting companies. The two right hand companies made good progress and reached the edge of the orchard. However, the two left hand companies met heavy machine-gun fire, Major Vaudrey being killed. Major Roberts quickly deployed his reserve company and succeeded in silencing the fire, allowing B Company, now sadly reduced to about forty, to make for the orchard, advance through it and line the southern edge. Meanwhile C Company, in the smoke and din of battle had lost its sense of direction and, mistaking a small scrubby copse to the right of the orchard, had established itself there. A and D companies both reached the orchard successfully and started to dig in along a convenient ditch which ran across it. Battalion Headquarters was established between these two companies, while the survivors of B Company were pulled back from their very exposed position on the forward edge of the orchard. As the Battalion frantically attempted to dig in (their work frustrated by the mass of tree roots), enemy fire began to rain down. This was to continue almost unabated for the next nineteen hours, claiming many casualties.

At about 9.30 p.m., as the evening light began to fade, the first counter attack was launched against the DCLI. This was made by infantry without the close support of tanks. The Battalion's training now showed its value; NCOs could be heard giving out clear fire orders, audible above the maelstrom of bursting mortar bombs. So accurate was the resulting rifle and Bren fire that the attack was repulsed with heavy casualties. Very quickly a second counter attack was delivered, this time using Tiger tanks which motored up to either flank of the orchard, and raked it with machine-gun and high explosive fire as the infantry again assaulted from the front. The light was fast going, but darkness brought no cessation to the battle. Indeed, during that night, tanks penetrated the DCLI position itself, grinding around the orchard spraying the whole area with machine-gun fire. Other tanks by-passed the orchard and roamed about in the corn to the rear, cutting the fragile telephone lines and making life exceptionally dangerous for the linesmen, runners and stretcher bearers who had to operate in this area between the 5th DCLI and the 4th Somerset Light Infantry. On one occasion Lieutenant Stock and Serjeant F. Grigg were laying a line when they met a Tiger tank that was evidently lost. The commander dismounted and approached the line party, mistaking them for German infantry. He was despatched by a shot from a Verey pistol. All that night the twenty-six year old Colonel moved about this deadly arena with total disregard to his own safety, talking quietly to his men and giving them much-needed encouragement. But for his outward calm and inspirational leadership it is doubtful that these soldiers could have held on with such resolution.

As dawn broke, the northern side of the orchard was still firmly held by the 5th Battalion; a few yards away, the southern side was occupied by the enemy. Lieutenant-Colonel James therefore called forward a squadron of the Scots Greys to help clear this southern side. No sooner did their tanks appear about the crest than they were engaged by 88 mm guns. Within ten minutes five Shermans had been destroyed; the remainder therefore withdrew to hull down positions from where they could support the Battalion more effectively.

At about this time every German gun and mortar opened up on the orchard while the enemy were seen forming up just to the south. The Forward Observation Officer ordered the whole Divisional artillery to put down defensive fire. The enemy, caught out in the open corn, were annihilated. Not for the first time in this battle, the Royal Artillery had saved the situation and inflicted massive casualties on the enemy. Although there appeared to be no appreciable pauses in the ferocity of the battle, it is estimated that the Germans had launched twelve counter attacks, each one thrown back by disciplined infantry fire and by the massive concentrations put down by the Divisional artillery. However, the situation could not continue. The attrition rate of the 5th Battalion meant that it was rapidly ceasing to exist as a viable fighting unit.

At some time around 10.30 a.m. on 11th July Lieutenant-Colonel James climbed into an apple tree, the better to direct artillery fire on the constantly moving enemy in the dead ground to the south. As he shouted directions down to his signaller, Private J. Foster, in the ditch below, he was hit in the neck by a burst of machine-gun fire that nearly beheaded him. His body fell near Private Foster who, looking around, could see no officer left unwounded to take over. It was therefore with intense relief that he saw Major Fry, covered in blood but still ferociously indomitable, appear on the scene, to take over command. He quickly redeployed the survivors (then numbering about 120 men) into four groups to which he allotted fresh arcs of fire.

Suddenly from somewhere was heard the shout of "Retreat, retreat!" Nobody knew where it came from, but in their present exhausted and mind bludgeoned state, none queried it. A stream of filthy, unshaven and blood stained men started to move back the way they had come towards the 4th Somerset Light Infantry. The 4th Somersets had fought a terrible battle earlier on the previous day, and had themselves been under shell and mortar fire for twenty-four hours. They were not therefore in the most sprightly form, but the sight of these demoralised Cornishmen stumbling back through their positions made a terrible and traumatic impression. Lieutenant-Colonel C.G. Lipscombe, commanding the 4th Somerset Light Infantry, was a large man and a very great Commanding Officer. Knowing how contagious was the spirit of defeat and how retreat could quickly turn to rout, he drew his pistol and announced to all around him "I'll shoot the first Somerset who goes back". He then turned to the Cornishmen, and, by sheer personality and a magnificent display of leadership, rallied them, putting fresh courage into their exhausted bodies. One by one they turned about and made their way back through the blood-stained trampled corn to their old positions in the orchard.

In the orchard it was becoming increasingly obvious that however valiantly the Royal Artillery deluged the enemy forming-up positions with high explosive, it was only a matter of time before the survivors were overwhelmed. Major Fry requested permission to withdraw. The reply from Brigadier G.H.C. Mole was that Major Fry should go back to Brigade Headquarters to discuss the situation. This was quite contrary to accepted military practice which decrees that, in

44. Men of the 2nd Battalion resting immediately before the assault on Incontro Monastery, August 1944. Men learnt to dig in whenever possible, even for short halts – a practice that saved many lives. Note the 4th Infantry Division tac sign on the rear of the carrier.

45. Searching prisoners of war after the battle for Incontro Monastery. Foreground: RSM 'Snowy' Narborough, Background: the Battalion Intelligence Officer.

46. The Christmas card for 1940, showing a 5th DCLI soldier guarding the Sussex coast. Drawn by Sir Oswald Birley, RA, a friend of the Commanding Officer, Lieutenant-Colonel Sir John Carew Pole. The 'Drake's Drum' in the top right hand corner was the Divisional sign of the 45th Division.

47. One of the five Panther tanks knocked out by the 5th Battalion at their first engagement with the enemy at Cheux, on 27th June 1944.

48. The first Royal Tiger to be knocked out in the Normandy Campaign. Destroyed by the 5th Battalion at Le Plessis Grimault on 7th August 1944.

49. 5th Battalion advancing through corn at Hill 112, 10th July 1944.

50. The wood on Hill 112, some weeks after the battle. This shows a burnt out Sherman of the Scots Greys and one of the many temporary graves.

51. A notice erected by 5 DCLI in 1944 was replaced by the neighbouring inhabitants of Esquay, stating tha here 'the Allied Armies decided the fate of the world'. This place is still known locally as Cornwall Hill.

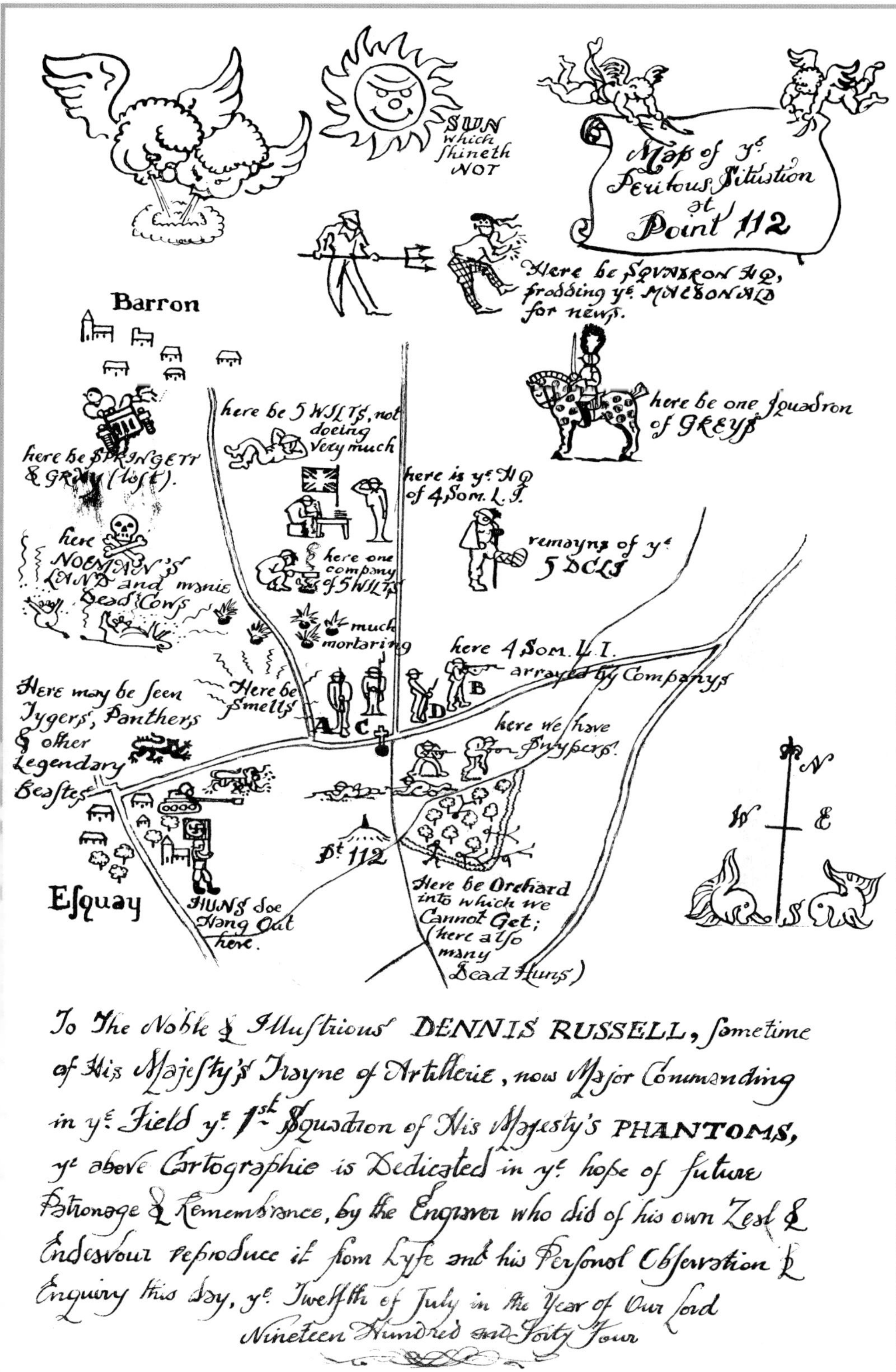

2. Phantom Patrol's situation report to Field-Marshal Montgomery, immediately after the battle for Hill 12. Montgomery was not amused. (The task of this small patrol was to provide reports from the field, when he heat of battle was disrupting communication.)

53. Field-Marshal Sir Bernard Montgomery presenting the Commanding Officer of 5th Battalion Lieutenant-Colonel G. Taylor, with the Distinguished Service Order.

54. Lieutenant-Colonel John Fry with HM the Queen Mother, 1949

5. 1st Battalion, Band and Bugles, Bermuda, 1954-55.

6. 4th/5th TA Battalion, anti-tank training near St Austell, 1959.

57. Lt.-Col. D.N.H. Tyacke, Capt. R.I. Field, MC and RSM J. Passmore leading the final parade of the DCLI in Osnabruck, 5th October 1959.

58. Col. G.T.G. Williams parades his troops out of the gates at the Depôt, Bodmin, for the last time, 16 March 1962.

battle, the senior officer should always go forward himself to access the situation, rather than order his subordinate to the rear. Major Fry felt trapped by an impossible dilemma. If he withdrew the survivors from Hill 112, he would be disobeying the original order to capture and hold that feature; if he stood firm, the survivors would be annihilated and the feature captured. He might perhaps have given the vainglorious order to fight to the last man and the last round, but what could that possibly achieve except the deaths of yet more of his soldiers? At about 3.00 p.m. Major Fry gave the order to abandon the position, at the same time requesting the heaviest artillery concentration possible, including maximum smoke on the southern edge of the orchard. The order was shouted to the sixty or so men who remained capable of walking, "We will clear out of this when the smoke comes down. Each man for himself. Keep well separated." Major Fry was the last man to leave that place of terrible carnage.

What was left of the Battalion moved back through the 4th Somerset Light Infantry and dug in near its rear Headquarters. On 13th July the 5th Battalion was relieved by the 4th Dorsets, and moved back to the village of Bas Le Mouen. In this, their first major battle, the 5th Duke of Cornwall's Light Infantry had fought up to the limits of human endurance. From 8.30 p.m. on 10th July to about 3.30 pm on the 11th July the Battalion had been subjected to heavy and almost continuous fire. It had fought off at least twelve counter attacks and lived through a night in which German tanks ranged freely through the position, often driving over the shallow weapon pits in which the Cornishmen crouched. It was reckoned that the four rifle companies and battalion tac HQ crossed the start line with some 380 officers and men. The fighting strength of the Battalion that withdrew nineteen hours later was sixty.

The majority of the German troops attacking the orchard on Hill 112 belonged to the 10th SS Panzer Division. This élite formation was so badly mauled that it was withdrawn back to Germany and was not used in action again until the battle of Arnhem more than two months later. One of its infantry units was reduced to some five or six men per company. When Hill 112 was finally evacuated by the Germans the DCLI Pioneers erected two boards, and on them painted short inscriptions in French and English, recording the Regiment's heroic stand. To this day Hill 112 is known not only to the Regiment but to the men and women of the surrounding villages as 'Cornwall Hill'.

One of the 43rd (Wessex) Division's most pressing requirements now was for Commanding Officers. It is an indication of the ferocity of the battle that the Division had lost nine Commanding Officers between 27th June and 11th July (7th Royal Hampshires, two killed; 7th Somerset Light Infantry, two killed and one wounded; 5th DCLI, two killed; 179 Field Regiment Royal Artillery, one killed and one wounded). The services of the pool of Commanding Officers waiting in the wings for just such a requirement was certainly being called upon early in the campaign.

It is impossible to overstate the part played by the Royal Artillery in this battle, and in particular to the bravery and professionalism of the Forward Observation Officers who, with their equally brave signallers, were invariably to be found with the leading platoons of infantry. The infantry held the ground and fought off the enemy at close quarters, but it was the Royal Artillery which had the muscle to smash up each succeeding counter attack and destroy its armour. At the height of the battle 179 Field Regiment had fired 1,800 rounds in fifteen minutes.

From the start General Montgomery's overall plan had been to drive a wedge towards the all important road and railway centre of Caen, thus threatening the whole German defence of Normandy and forcing Field Marshal Rommel to throw all his reserves into this battle. Once Caen had been secured General Bradley's 1st US Army would be free to break out, overrun the Cherbourg peninsula and swing round to the south east, using Caen as a firm hinge. In spite of the most determined and skilled opposition that had cost the British and Canadian formations terrible casualities, Montgomery's plan had worked. Rommel's divisions had been committed piecemeal, and had been severely mauled. Bradley was thus able to capture the deep-water port of Cherbourg on 26th June, and by 24th July had made significant advances right across his front.

Advance through Normandy, July-August 1944

Re-grouping for the next move, & back to Hill 112, 13th-21st July

When the 5th Battalion withdrew to Bas de Mouen on 13th July it had a total strength of some 200 officers and men, of whom only about sixty came from the actual fighting strength made up of Support Company and the four rifle companies. Those readers whose only service has been with the peace-time army might presume that a unit so decimated would either be pulled back for a protracted period or alternatively broken up and used as reinforcements. It is doubtful whether these alternatives were ever considered at that critical stage in the battle for Normandy.

The 5th Battalion was given six days to absorb 340 reinforcements and to make good the considerable destruction of equipment, vehicles and weapons. Many joining the 5th came from its sister Cornish battalion, the 4th DCLI. These were men who for much of the war had served alongside each other, and for them the transition was easy. There were others, however, who had to change their cap badges and lay aside proud allegiances. These had to be welcomed with special warmth by their comrades and made to feel at home amongst friends in a close-knit family. As always, much of the really hard work fell on the shoulders of the Adjutant Captain W.A.R. Gorman, the Quartermaster Lieutenant H. St G. 'Pat' Gallagher and their loyal staffs. For the next six days they barely slept as they wrestled with the detailed administrative work involved in rebuilding the Battalion into a viable fighting unit.

The new Commanding Officer was Lieutenant-Colonel G. Taylor, late of the West Yorkshire Regiment, who had up to this time been Second-in-Command of the 1st Worcesters. George Taylor possessed a combination of physical toughness and astute intellectual perception, the latter quality perhaps rare amongst officers of the pre-war regular army. An outstanding rugby player who had represented the Barbarians, Lancashire and the Army (and would have played for England but for the exigencies of the service), he was also an extremely well-read military tactician. In Bermuda, while his brother officers were enjoying the pleasures of the lively social scene, Taylor could be found in the Garrison Library studying the works of Clausewitz, Liddell Hart, Tuller and the official historians of the Great War. With him came twelve other officers including a new Second-in-Command, Major R.A.St G. Martin of the Oxfordshire and Buckinghamshire Light Infantry.

One of the first problems to be addressed by the new Commanding Officer was the place of officers in battle. This was a subject on which he held strong opinions. The 5th Battalion had lost almost twenty officers killed or wounded since its arrival in France a month before, a rate of attrition that was plainly unsupportable. Taylor was adamant that an officer should normally command from the centre of his company or platoon, where he could exercise maximum control, and not to play the hero with the leading section.

On 18th July the revitalised 5th Battalion moved back to Hill 112, taking its place, together with a squadron of tanks, as Brigade reserve for yet another attempt to capture Maltot. Counter attacks were rehearsed to cover every contingency, which proved an excellent initiation for the new arrivals. On 21st July the Battalion relieved the 7th Somerset Light Infantry facing the north flank of Hill 112. The trampled corn was alive with German snipers, and it was here that Major F. J. Colwill, commanding A Company, was killed.

* * *

Chouain, Jurques & Tiger Hill, 25th July-4th August 1944

With the slow and remorseless enlargement of the River Orne bridgehead and the continuing attrition of the enemy reserves, it was now time for the culminating phase of the Allied operation. On 25th July General Bradley unleashed his division, which punched its way through all resistance and swept around the right flank of the British positions, thus threatening the encirclement of the German army facing Caen. On the same day the 43rd (Wessex) Division was relieved by the 53rd (Welsh) Division, the former moving back to Chouain some five miles south east of Bayeux. There it looked forward to ten days of rest. As so often in war, this was not to happen. In order to counter the American thrust, General von Kluge (who had replaced Rommel, killed in an air attack on 15th July) moved the armour from the area of Caumont, west of Hill 112. General Montgomery saw his chance to launch a heavy attack through Caumont towards Mont Pincon, to the south east, in an attempt to threaten the German rear. The 43rd (Wessex) Division was hastily allotted to Lieutenant-General B.G. Horrocks's XXX Corps, which was to execute this thrust. The initial assault was to be delivered by 130 Brigade, with 214 Brigade waiting ready to pass through. Progress was very slow, partly due to the extensive mining carried out by the enemy and partly due to the very close *bocage* country which offered ideal conditions for defence.

On 2nd August the 5th Battalion was ordered to pass through the 7th Royal Hampshires and clear the opposition around the village of Jurques. Major-General H. Essame described the demeanour of the Cornishmen as they went into battle again in the following words: 'The operations now to take place bear that peculiar atmosphere of light heartedness and gallantry which throughout the campaign characterised this remarkable battalion.' What a wonderful tribute to those men who had experienced the slaughter on Hill 112, and, having survived, had imbued the newcomers with their own courageous spirit!

Lieutenant-Colonel Taylor went forward to the Hampshires' headquarters that evening but was able to obtain only the sketchiest idea of the situation ahead. He therefore ordered the Carrier Platoon under Captain G. L. Holland to push forward cautiously as far as the high ground beyond Jurques, and to report any enemy activity. The carriers passed through the rubble of the village, down into a stream valley and across a bridge that remained intact. As the leading carrier crossed, a Spandau machine-gun opened fire. Fortunately the fire went well over their heads without doing damage. The carriers moved ahead up a very steep narrow lane, their engines revving noisily. Halfway up they stopped, switched off and listened. In the bright moonlight the hedges of the close *bocage* landscape stood out sharply. There was absolute silence. Once more Captain Holland cautiously advanced. As the leading carrier reached the crest it was knocked out by an 88 mm shell. This was the signal for all hell to be loosed; grenades landed in the second carrier, flares and machine-gun fire erupted from every direction, and three or four tanks could be heard moving about on the ridge. Captain Holland succeeded in withdrawing his platoon and reported the situation to the Commanding Officer.

Initially a simple plan of attack was made in which C and D Companies were to advance on either side of the sunken lane and carry out a frontal attack, supported by the Divisional artillery, the Battalion 3 in. mortars and B Squadron 4th/7th Dragoon Guards. The attack was launched at 8.15 a.m. on 3rd August, but immediately ran into serious trouble, made worse by the fact that the armour was unable to deploy due to a mass of rocks and gullies. It therefore had to advance up the central axis of the sunken lane but, as the leading tank reached the crest, it was knocked out by an 88 mm gun, thus effectively blocking the only vehicle approach. The next chapter in the story of this battle (later to be known as Tiger Hill) concerns the personal courage and initiative of two small groups of brave men. Lieutenant-Colonel Taylor, quickly realising that a frontal attack was impractical, ordered Serjeant E. H. Long of the sniper section to take two men (Privates Nichols and Chipman) to see if there was an unguarded approach around the right flank. Using their fieldcraft skills, these three got right into the enemy position and established themselves in an unoccupied farm-house that gave excellent observation over the area. During the day these snipers killed three men of a five-man mortar detachment without disclosing their position. That evening Serjeant Long left Nichols and Chipman in the farm and made his way back to Battalion Headquarters, where he was able to give a very comprehensive report; he then returned to his two men with a wireless set. Following the successful infiltration through the right flank the Signal Officer, Lieutenant R.M. Stock, who was a fluent French speaker, was given the task of reconnoitring a route that could be used to mount a battalion flank attack. Dressed as a farm worker with a bag of ferrets, he set off around the right flank. On the way he met a Frenchman, M. Solier, who was eager to accompany him. Shortly after this, the two met a German Serjeant-Major who was lost. M. Solier persuaded the Serjeant-Major to accompany him to his house where he said a good meal would be waiting. On the way there the German was obliged to attend to the needs of nature and, to be less hampered, handed his pistol over to

Lieutenant Stock. At the farm-house the Serjeant-Major was taken prisoner, and after being escorted back to Battalion Headquarters was interrogated, and gave valuable information. For this exploit Lieutenant Stock was awarded the Military Cross. Serjeant Long was later awarded the Distinguished Conduct Medal. That night the 1st Worcesters moved up along the approach route reconnoitred by Serjeant Long, and carried out a successful attack the following morning. The approaches to the next major German defensive position on Mont Pincon were now open.

Mont Pincon & Le Plessis Grimault, 7th-8th August 1944

The German forces in Normandy now found themselves in grave danger of being cut off. The jaws of a giant trap, formed by the Americans in the south and the British and Canadians in the north, were rapidly closing shut on the town of Falaise. The Germans, fully aware of this threat, were streaming eastwards, while at the same time fighting rear-guard actions with considerable skill and tenacity. If a significant part of the German force was not to escape, speed of action by the Allies was of the utmost importance.

As mentioned above, the next German defensive position blocking the route of the 43rd (Wessex) Division was the strongly fortified hill known as Mont Pincon. During the attack and capture of this feature the 5th Battalion was in reserve and took no active part. A mile south of Mont Pincon, however, lay the village of Le Plessis Grimault, which was to be the Battalion's next objective. Two of Lieutenant-Colonel Taylor's firmly held maxims were first, that a thorough reconnaissance must always precede any attack; and second, that the enemy must, if conceivably possible, always be hit from the least expected direction. The Carrier and newly formed Scout Platoons therefore carried out detailed reconnaissance patrols around Le Plessis Grimault during the daylight hours of 7th August. As a result they succeeded in establishing the German defensive layout.

At about 10 p.m., 9 Platoon, together with a complete squadron of the 4th/7th Dragoon Guards, put in a noisy feint attack from the west. Every available weapon was fired, while three field regiments and two medium regiments of Royal Artillery laid down massive concentrations of fire. While all this was going on, the remainder of the Battalion was making its way through the scrub on the lower slopes of Mont Pincon, north of the village of Le Plessis Grimault. At 10.10 p.m. the companies wheeled right to put in the main attack. Although it was quite dark by this time, the objective was fully illuminated by the burning houses.

The Germans had been caught off balance, and all four rifle companies were able to fight their way through the ruined village without undue opposition. As he advanced Major Parker, commanding A Company, noticed two tanks standing at the cross-roads in the centre of the village. One had its hatches open and was standing alongside a lorry from which it was replenishing ammunition; the other was awaiting its turn a few yards away. Unfortunately the Company Headquarters PIAT had been destroyed earlier in the attack, but Major Parker ordered every weapon at his disposal to be directed at this group of vehicles. The very first 2 in. mortar bomb fell on the ammunition lorry, causing it to blow up. When the smoke cleared away, there was no sign of the lorry; the tank next to it was blazing, while the second tank was making a hurried departure from the scene. The tank that Major Parker's men had destroyed proved to be a Royal Tiger (a new up-armoured version of the Tiger), the first ever to be knocked out. Exactly an hour after the Battalion had crossed the start line, all the companies had consolidated on their objectives, and the success signal was fired. It had been a text-book battle. The enemy lost 31 killed, 125 prisoners and a Royal Tiger tank. The 5th Battalion casualties amounted to 1 killed and 5 wounded.

The following morning the Germans counter attacked Le Plessis Grimault, but with no success. Sadly, Major Parker, who had played such a leading part in the previous night's work, was wounded in the jaw and shoulder by a piece of 88 mm shell. That day the 50th (Northumbrian) Division took over the advance from the 43rd (Wessex) Division; the 5th DCLI were relieved by a battalion of the Durham Light Infantry in Le Plessis Grimault.

On to the River Noireau, 12th-16th August

The next task allotted to the 5th Battalion was the elimination of certain German positions which were threatening the left flank of the Allied advance. Principal amongst these were the villages of La Trulandière and Culey-le-Patry. After a careful reconnaissance by Captain G. Ruck-Keene's C Company, which located the main enemy position on the high ground to the east of the village of La Trulandière, Major Fry's D Company was ordered to carry out a wide left-flanking movement and attack the objective from the cover of orchards to the north. B Company was to pass through D as soon as it had achieved success, while A Company and the Carrier Platoon was to be held in reserve. In D Company's initial attack very heavy fire was experienced from skilfully concealed machine-guns. However, these were all knocked out with great skill and courage by Lieutenant R. Prowse's 17 Platoon, ably assisted by his section commanders, Corporals Jury, Rawle and Marden. Seeing the hold up, Lieutenant-Colonel Taylor ordered C Company to put in a feint attack from the west to draw the enemy's attention away from D Company. This ruse was entirely successful. Very quickly D Company was able to cross the road between La Trulandière and Culey-le-Patry, and drive the opposition off the high ground south of this road.

In the original plan B Company was then to pass through the first objective and attack Culey-le-Patry. However, by this time dusk was falling. Rather than risk street fighting through an unreconnoitred village at night, Lieutenant-Colonel Taylor wisely decided to consolidate his gains and continue the advance at first light.

At dawn on 13th August B Company moved forward, skirting the village of Culey-le-Patry to the south. Apart from a profusion of mines there was no sign of any enemy. The Company continued cautiously to the banks of the River Orne but found no Germans. Indeed, although Hitler did not authorise any withdrawal until 16th August, the German Army Commanders were well aware that unless they could extricate their formations from the Falaise trap, their losses would be catastrophic. Accordingly, on the night of the 12th-13th August a general enemy withdrawal had commenced.

The next operation in the race to cut off the German army involved the crossing of the River Noireau. Although the Germans were now in full retreat, their rear-guard was fighting with skill and tenacity to delay the inevitable closing of the jaws of the trap. The River Noireau ran across the line of the Allied advance, and was to be crossed by 214 Brigade in the area of the village of Berjou. The river at this point ran through a steep wooded valley; it was about twenty yards broad and three feet deep. Both the railway and road bridges had been destroyed, but the remains of the railway bridge still allowed men to cross dry shod. The plan was for the 1st Worcesters and the 7th Somerset Light Infantry to make the initial assault with the 5th Battalion in reserve. Lieutenant-Colonel Taylor considered that the Battalion must follow close on the heels of the Worcesters, in order to be ready to offer immediate assistance should it be required. This would be an entirely infantry battle for all the approaches to the fords, and the fords themselves, had been liberally sown with mines. Until these had been cleared, no tanks or anti-tank guns would be able to cross.

At about 6 p.m. on the evening of 15th August Lieutenant-Colonel Taylor and Major Fry led the Battalion across the remains of the railway bridge and then, following the track a few hundred yards to the south, shook out into its battle formation and started to climb the valley side. For about a quarter of a mile the companies advanced through woods, then the terrain changed to typical *bocage* country with small fields bounded by banks and thick hedges. It was a hot sticky evening and jackets had been left with the transport to the rear. The Worcesters and Somersets assaulted and captured the ridge with surprising ease, though the enemy still held a feature by the name of Les Bruyeres (referred to by the British as 'the Mound') about half a mile to the south east.

Three companies each of the Worcesters and DCLI proceeded to dig in along the crest, with the two remaining companies in reserve. The ground was hard and interlaced with intractable hedge roots. Digging silently under these conditions was impossible, and the clink of shovels brought immediate machine-gun fire from the enemy, dug in only eighty yards away. To add to the misery of our men, still clad in sweat-drenched shirts, the night turned bitterly cold. Although the ridge itself was now adequately held by infantry, there were still neither tanks nor anti-tank guns across the river. All awaited the inevitable dawn counter attack with trepidation.

At first light on 16th August the Germans put in two counter attacks in quick succession, supported by direct artillery fire from the Mound. Fortunately, thanks to the heroic work of the Royal Engineers, paths had been cleared of mines across the river, enabling tanks of the Nottinghamshire Yeomanry (Sherwood Rangers) and anti-tank guns to come up to the ridge. It became clear that the enemy must be quickly driven off the Mound. Accordingly the Worcesters advanced over the ridge and secured the reverse slope, allowing A Company to pass through to assault the Mound. On taking over command, Lieutenant-Colonel Taylor had made a firm policy decision that, regardless of casualties, one rifle company must always be maintained at full fighting strength in order that it could be used effectively in times of crisis. A Company was designated for this role. If a man was cross-posted to this company, he knew that although life might be slightly easier for him on account of its full strength, he would undoubtedly be called upon to take part in more than his share of danger!

The crossing of the River Noireau marked the end of the fighting in Normandy for the 5th Battalion. On the evening of 16th August the bugles sounded the 'Last Post' over the graves of the men who had died on the ridge and the Mound. It was now again time for rest and reinforcement, and for this the 5th Battalion withdrew to the high ground between Berjou and Le Hamel.

The Germans had succeeded in breaking contact and withdrawing to the far side of the River Seine. For a few happy days the 5th Battalion was allowed to enjoy a well earned rest. A concert was quickly organised, in which Captain T.H. Stokoe and Serjeant F. Grigg excelled with their irrepressible humour. A parade of the whole of 214 Brigade was laid on for the Divisional Commander, Major-General Thomas, at which he congratulated all ranks warmly for their stirling efforts in the battles for Normandy. He went on to say that there was now an urgent requirement to drive the Germans out of Northern France from where they were launching pilotless V-1 flying bombs ('doodlebugs') against London, and from which they hoped to launch an even deadlier V-2 rocket.

ACROSS THE RIVER SEINE
22 ND-27TH AUGUST, 1944

A few miles to the south of the 5th Battalion's position, scenes of terrible carnage were enacted when the German 7th Army, together with eleven panzer divisions, made desperate attempts to escape through the narrow gap between Falaise and Argentan. For five days, from 22nd to 27th August, the British and American airforces and artillery wrought destruction on the fleeing enemy. In spite of every effort by the Allies, however, the jaws of the trap never quite closed; this allowed about a third of the Germans caught in the Falaise salient to make good their escape. However, some 10,000 dead were counted after the battle and a further 50,000 prisoners were taken, while the destruction of tanks, guns, vehicles and stores was devastating by any standard. It took weeks of work to clear the roads of the charred wreckage, and, most pathetically, of the hundreds of dead and dying horses.

The scene was now set for the crossing of the River Seine by the 43rd (Wessex) Division, and by 22nd August the Division was concentrated around the town of Gacé. The part it was to play involved the establishment of a bridge-head across the River Seine at Vernon, thirty miles north west of Paris. The plan decreed that the actual assault crossing should be carried out by 129 Brigade with the 1st Worcesters under command. The remainder of the 214 Brigade was to follow up with the Royal Engineers' heavy bridging equipment. This latter column arrived at its assembly area near Vernon on the evening of 25th August, shortly before the initial assault. In order to confuse the enemy, a party consisting of a 3 in. mortar and section of the Carrier Platoon from the 5th DCLI and a 25 pdr gun from 147 Field Regiment was despatched ten miles downstream to Gaillon to simulate a crossing.

The River Seine at Vernon is fast flowing and some 200 yards wide. This alone would have made a night crossing hazardous but, to make matters worse, the air photographs were misleading and failed to show up areas of impassable mud. Far worse, however, was that the enemy were strongly entrenched on the ground rising from the river, from where they could cover the crossing with direct fire. Despite every difficulty and with great gallantry, 129 Brigade established a narrow bridge-head during that night. Immediately this was confirmed the Royal Engineers started to build a heavy bridge for, as so often in these circumstances, the infantry on the far bank were now divorced from their tanks and anti-tank guns. Speed was of the essence, as the enemy was bound to launch a counter attack within a few hours. But in spite of the bravery of the Royal Engineers, it proved impossible to build the bridge while the crossing remained under enemy observation. Accordingly, the Divisional Commander ordered the bridge-head to be extended on the left flank to Pressagny l'Orgueilleux, where a Class 40 raft capable of carrying tanks was to be launched. The far bank was to be secured by the remaining two battalions of 214 Brigade, namely the 7th Somerset Light Infantry and the 5th DCLI. It was decided that these battalions should cross the river by the wreckage of the road bridge which linked Vernon on the west bank to Vernonette on the east bank. This would have been a most precarious crossing without the attentions of the enemy, but for some unknown reason their fire abated for this critical period, and all got across unscathed. In Vernonette the infantrymen found themselves in one of those surreal situations occasionally encountered in war, for with a battle in full swing, wine, cider, flowers and kisses were pressed on the somewhat bemused soldiers. Previously the Scout Platoon under Captain Spencer had crossed the river with the task of reporting the situation on the far bank. There it had been joined by a member of the French Resistance, M. Neavilly, who offered his services as a guide. As he led the platoon up the steep wooded slopes beyond Vernonette, he suddenly came face to face with two German machine-gunners. In that split second he threw himself across the muzzles of both guns as they opened fire. He undoubtedly saved lives in the Scout Platoon, but at a cost of terrible injuries to himself. Remarkably, he survived. For this outstanding act of gallantry he was later awarded the King's Medal for Courage in the Cause of Freedom, the highest gallantry decoration that could be bestowed on a foreign civilian.

The expected counter attack on the 5th Battalion holding Pressagny failed to materialise until the early hours of 27th August. B Company were the first to feel its effect when an enemy patrol succeeded in tagging on behind a returning DCLI patrol and thus infiltrating into the heart of the Battalion position. In the darkness there was considerable confusion, and during this confusion further enemy elements managed to penetrate the defences. At dawn A Company suddenly found itself surrounded and about to be overrun. Major Parker took drastic action and ordered artillery fire to be brought down on this position, confident that his own men, well dug in as they were, would be safe. Further fierce fighting took place around D Company, in which a complete section was annihilated.

By this time the ferry had been established, and by 8 a.m. on 27th August the first tanks of the 4th/7th Dragoon Guards together with armoured cars of the 43rd Divisional Reconnaissance Regiment had crossed over to Pressagny. By that evening the Royal Engineers had completed two bridges across the River Seine linking Vernon with Vernonette. Later that morning the 5th DCLI was relieved by the 1st Worcesters and continued the advance to the next village, five miles to the north-east of Panilleuse. Most of this route ran through woods which gave good cover, but the Battalion, led by D Company, was forced to move in single file, a formation which is notoriously difficult to control. Emerging from the wood into open country, Major Fry was confronted a few hundred yards to his front by a group of farm buildings which were only too clearly occupied by the enemy. A fast dash across the intervening ground was rendered impossible by the strong barbed wire fences that bordered the small fields. Fortunately a squadron of the Nottinghamshire Yeomanry had succeeded in making its way forward through a track in the wood, and its arrival at this moment determined Major Fry to put in a quick assault. Supported by a hastily concocted artillery fire plan, and with the help of the tanks, his Company quickly succeeded in capturing its objective though, sadly, not without casualties. Lieutenant-Colonel Taylor immediately passed B Company through the farm into Panilleuse itself. The remaining Germans made a hasty withdrawal, leaving the village to a gloriously inebriated Frenchman who roared out the *Marseillaise* and flung his arms around the necks of the somewhat embarrassed soldiers.

THROUGH BELGIUM & INTO HOLLAND

Operation 'Market Garden'
14th-22nd September 1944

The next major operation was Field-Marshal Montgomery's daring plan to drive a narrow wedge through Holland into the heart of Germany. This would entail the crossing of two major canals and the great rivers of the Maas, the Waal and the Neder Rijn (the lower Rhine). The no mans land between these two was known as 'the Island'. His plan was to capture each of these crossings intact by means of airborne assaults, following up with all possible speed with ground troops. The canal crossings at Son and Veghal, together with the Maas crossing at Grave and the Waal crossing at Nijmegen, were to be secured by the American 82nd and 101st Airborne Divisions, while the British 1st Airborne Division were to capture the bridge across the Neder Rijn at Arnhem. The Guards Armoured Division, closely followed by the 43rd (Wessex) Division, would advance with all haste to link up with the airborne forces. The operation was known as 'Market Garden'.

On 14th September the 5th Battalion moved from the comfort of billets around Vernon and drove north by way of Beauvais, Albert, and through the cheering crowds in the outskirts of Brussels, to arrive in the Divisional assembly area at Diest the following day.

The airborne assaults took place as planned, while simultaneously the Guards Armoured Division advanced into Holland. After very heavy fighting the Guards succeeded in breaking through to Nijmegen, where they linked up with the American 82nd Airborne Division, together capturing both the road and railway bridges intact.

Meanwhile at Arnhem the situation had become critical. Because the road bridge was situated in the middle of the town, the airborne assault had had to be made six miles to the west. It was considered that by using the element of surprise, the British 1st Airborne Division would reach the bridge before the Germans could react. This plan might have worked had not two Panzer divisions, unbeknown to British intelligence, just moved into the area north of Arnhem to refit. These divisions were able to cut off and surround the major part of the 1st Airborne Division. In the event, only the 2nd Battalion the Parachute Regiment managed to reach the objective, holding the north side of the Arnhem bridge for the next four days with great gallantry. The Polish Parachute Brigade, which should have secured the southern side of the bridge, met unexpectedly heavy opposition and was hemmed in around their landing zone at Driel.

If the 1st Airborne Division was to be relieved and the vital bridge captured, speed was vital. With this in mind, the 43rd (Wessex) Division moved out of Diest and motored north to Hechtel, ready to make the final dash across the bridge at Nijmegen to Arnhem. There it remained at immediate readiness to advance for three frustrating days, while the fog of war became ever more opaque. One must remember that although the Guards had fought their way through to the River Waal, the corridor was dangerously narrow and the Germans were constantly attempting to cut it. Furthermore, the only three roads that led north towards Arnhem were built across the waterlogged countryside on high embankments, limiting any advance to a one tank front. As soon as the leading tank was knocked out, that particular route forward would become effectively blocked until the tank could be pushed off the road. An armoured thrust to Arnhem was therefore patently impractical. Finally, on 20th September, the order came to move with 130 Brigade in the lead. Hardly had the advance started then it came to a halt. The Germans had re-occupied Eindhoven and a major attack had to be mounted before the route could be cleared. It was not till 22nd September that the 43rd (Wessex) Division arrived immediately south of Nijmegen. There the situation was very confused.

The battle of the Island, 22nd September-6th October 1944 & the dash to relieve Arnhem

The Guards Armoured Division was now fighting a bloody battle in an attempt to push forward the final ten miles to Arnhem. As previously mentioned, the nature of the countryside with its embanked roads across marshy ground could not have been worse for tanks, rendering them unable to deploy. The Guards Armoured Division reached the village of Elst, but could advance no further. It was therefore determined that 214 Brigade should cross the River Waal by the railway bridge, swing round to the left and advance on the left flank of the Guards. First however, the village of Oosterhout had to be cleared. The 7th Somerset Light Infantry carried out this attack, supported by the Divisional artillery.

As soon as the route was cleared the 5th Battalion was ordered to pass through and advance at all possible speed to Driel. However, by this time there was only an hour of daylight remaining. There was no time to lose. Two DUKWs (heavy amphibious vehicles) loaded with vital supplies for the airborne troops reported to the Battalion which, with a minimum of orders, was launched in what was to be one of the most dramatic dashes of the whole campaign. D Company led, with a squadron of the 4th/7th Dragoon Guards and a platoon of machine-gunners from the 8th Middlesex, followed by A Company and the all important DUKWs, with the other two rifle companies and the battalion anti-tank guns, machine-guns and mortars bringing up the rear. The rapidly darkening night together was now to provide a friendly cloak under which the British could advance. German tanks, moving across from Elst, became mixed up with the 5th Battalion column and were suitably dealt with. Company Serjeant-Major R.J. Philp in the company carrier came into head-on contact with a Tiger tank, with its 88mm gun looming over his head. Unperturbed, he proceeded to kill the commander with a burst from a Bren gun and then, with the aid of C Company following behind, to destroy five other Tiger tanks waiting on the road. For this brilliant little action Serjeant-Major Philp was awarded the Distinguished Conduct Medal. Many other acts of initiative and bravery occurred during that mad dash in the darkness, with men hanging onto any available vehicle. Major Parker's A Company knocked out a further three tanks in a masterfully conceived ambush, while another two fell over the embankment into the marsh in their hurry to reverse away.

Attempts to cross the Neder Rijn, 23rd-26th September 1944

Driel was reached almost exactly thirty minutes after the first order to cross the start line had been given – a rate of advance over twelve miles that can seldom, if ever, have been equalled in war.

The 5th Battalion group had now made contact with the beleaguered Polish Parachute Brigade. Attempts were made to launch the two DUKWs into the Neder Rijn but both these clumsy vehicles slid into deep ditches bordering the road before they reached the river bank.

While all this was happening up by the Neder Rijn, the Germans had succeeded in cutting the narrow British corridor far behind at the village of Veghel, twenty miles south of Nijmegan. This effectively stopped the vital re-supply of ammunition and petrol to the American 82nd Airborne Division, the Guards Armoured Division and the 43rd (Wessex) Division, demonstrating how desperately vulnerable was this slender line of communication to Belgium.

All through the 23rd September battle raged around Driel, and during that day a decision was made to abandon the attempt to reach the bridge. Instead XXX Corps was to cross the river west of Arnhem to link up with the remains of the 1st Airborne Division. Accordingly, the 5th Dorsets took up a position to the right of the DCLI and prepared to cross as soon as it was dark, together with the Polish Parachute Brigade. The river crossing proved a disaster. The DUKWs which were to carry the Dorsets failed even to reach the river bank, while there were only sufficient assault boats for a single battalion of the Polish Division. The crossing came under very intense enemy fire, and only about two hundred men managed to make the far bank. The following morning the Corps Commander, Lieutenant-General B.G. Horrocks, CB, DSO, MC surveyed the situation from the church tower of Driel. The hard facts of the case were that the 1st Airborne Division, surrounded by a numerically superior enemy, and unable to reach the bridge, now had no military value. He therefore determined to withdraw as many as possible back across the Neder Rijn. Immediately the decision had been made an 'Orders Group' was held at

Headquarters 43rd (Wessex) Division. The plan was that the 4th Dorsets together with a battalion of Poles should be ferried across that night to establish a secure position on the north bank through which the men of the 1st Airborne Division could be evacuated. Zero hour was fixed for 10 p.m., and the crossing was to be supported by the entire Divisional artillery together with the tanks of the 13th/18th Hussars, the machine-guns of the 8th Middlesex and every weapon that the 5th Dorsets and 7th Hampshires could muster. From that moment every aspect of the operation that could go wrong did go wrong. The only redeeming feature was the rock-hard courage of all those taking part. By 10 p.m. no assault boats had arrived. In due course it was discovered that two lorries carrying boats had taken the wrong turn at Valburg and driven straight into the German positions; two had slithered off the muddy road into a dyke, whilst the last lorry did arrive but was found to be carrying no paddles. Zero hour was put back to midnight, by which time the few remaining boats had been taken away from the Poles and handed over to the 4th Dorsets. In the face of very heavy enemy fire, only about 200 men managed to consolidate on the far bank. Six more DUKWs were waiting to carry heavy weapons and ammunition across, but three of these became bogged down as they attempted to enter the river while the other three got stuck as they attempted to climb up the far side.

The advent of dawn put a stop to any thought of crossing the river that day. Artillery ammunition was becoming very scarce, and with the line of communication severed and the few roads disintegrating under their unaccustomed heavy traffic, it became vital to evacuate the 1st Airborne Division that night (25th-26th September). Orders were given for 129 Brigade to stage a feint river crossing on the west flank that afternoon, and this undoubtedly diverted valuable German forces away from Driel.

Withdrawal of survivors from the 1st Airborne Division, the night of 25th-26th September, 1944

A night of intense blackness with heavy rain offered some degree of protection as the British and Canadian Royal Engineers carried boats down to the river for the evacuation. At 9 p.m. every weapon in the Division put down rapid covering fire as the first wave of boats set off. The Germans, who were fully aware of what was happening, likewise put down all available fire. The noise was such that no orders could be heard; however, every man resolutely carried out his duty, knowing full well that the fate of the Airborne Division hung in his hands. At 9.40 p.m. the first wave returned, loaded with wounded, and all through that night the boats crossed and re-crossed under unrelenting machine-gun and artillery fire. At each crossing there were fewer boats and fewer Sappers. By dawn about 2,000 men of the Airborne Division had reached the safety of the south bank. As they landed, they made their way back to a reception area organised by the 5th Dorsets, who guided the exhausted men back to a large barn on the outskirts of Driel where they received blankets, rum, tea and hot stew. From there they were quickly evacuated back to Nijmegen by jeep, the only vehicle that could negotiate the fast-crumbling roads. Throughout that night the gallant 4th Dorsets continued to hold the far bank at a terrible price.

When the survivors of the 4th Dorsets crossed back just before dawn on 26th September it was found that the Battalion had lost 13 officers and 200 men.

In this final drama the 5th Battalion heard the sound of desperate battle but took no active part.

During the night of 24th-25th September, the 5th Battalion had been ordered to move back to help the remainder of 214 Brigade clear the village of Elst, which lay on the direct route between Nijmegen and Arnhem. On the morning of 25th September the Battalion had consolidated on the east side of the village, covering the railway line which, like the roads, ran on an embankment. Soon enemy movement was seen around a train of abandoned railway wagons. One of the anti-tank guns opened fire. The result exceeded all expectations. The train, which was carrying ammunition, blew up with an earth shattering explosion, destroying the train, the embankment and much of Elst. The farm in which Major Fry had set up his headquarters was wrecked, injuring the artillery Forward Observation Officer. Fortunately there were surprisingly few other casualties. D Company immediately moved forward and took up new positions on the remains of the railway embankment, from where it could dominate the length of the Elst-Arnhem road. This was a serious blow for the Germans, who were still roaming fairly freely around the Island. Counter attacks accompanied by heavy shelling were put in during 25th September, but in spite of casualties the 5th Battalion stood firm. Major Parker was seriously wounded in the stomach. He was a remarkable leader of men, one of those rare breed who positively enjoy the dangers of battle. He had originally enlisted as a Boy Bugler in the Oxfordshire and Buckinghamshire Light Infantry, and had already won a Military Medal before being commissioned into the DCLI. He commanded the crack A Company, and for his leadership was awarded the Military Cross. Major Fry was also slightly wounded, but while he was being attended to, the Regimental Aid Post was demolished by three direct hits from shells. Escaping from the rubble, he made his way back to his headquarters, which was promptly demolished by the explosion of the railway train. Once again he crawled out of the rubble, but Lieutenant-Colonel Taylor considered that he had done more than his fair share of fighting, and after recovering from his injuries he was posted to the Divisional staff. He was later awarded the Military Cross for his inspired leadership in every action in which the 5th Battalion had been involved.

* * *

German counter attacks on the Island, 29th September-6th October 1944

The German offensive to reoccupy the Island and drive the Allies back south of the River Waal now gained momentum. Intelligence reported the deployment of two more panzer divisions. In particular, every effort was made to destroy the bridges at Nijmegen. Their efforts included a brave attack on the night of 29th September by German frogmen, who succeeded in attaching explosive charges which rendered the railway bridge useless, but only slightly damaged the all-important road bridge.

On 1st October, the 5th Battalion was 'lent' to the Green Howards of 69 Brigade, who were being heavily attacked in the area of Bemmel, four miles to the north-east of Nijmegen. The attack was successfully stemmed.

The battle of Opheusden, 6th October 1944

On 6th October 43rd (Wessex) Division handed over responsibility for the defence of the Island to the American 101st Airborne Division. That night the whole Division, with the exception of one unit, moved back over the Nijmegen bridge for a period of rest south of the River Waal. The exception was the 5th Battalion which, as divisional reserve battalion, was ear-marked to support the Americans should the need arise. It soon did. The previous day the American 506th Regimental Combat Team had cleared the enemy out of the village of Opheusden on the south bank of the Neder Rijn, nine miles west of Driel. That night, however, the Germans had infiltrated back in, and were now firmly established in the west part of the village. The 5th Battalion was called forward to carry out a counter attack in co-operation with the No.1 Battalion 506 Parachute Infantry U.S. Army. The attack was to go in from the east with the Americans on the right flank between the Neder Rijn and the main road, which ran on an embankment through the village, and the 5th Battalion to the left of this road. This latter area was criss-crossed by numerous dykes, which although half full of very evil smelling water, gave good cover, as did the several orchards which covered much of the ground to the south of the road. D company, now under command of Captain Spencer, led the attack. It passed through the houses and advanced towards four parallel lines of drainage ditches which ran straight across the front. The first two of these were rushed, but very heavy machine-gun and mortar fire frustrated any further attempts to move further forward. Captain Spencer had been wounded, leaving D Company under command of Lieutenant F. W. Durden, who consolidated his position and ordered stretcher bearers to evacuate the wounded (the Germans ceased all firing whilst the stretcher bearers were going about their work). Meanwhile Captain Spencer was able to brief Major Hingston, commanding B Company, on the situation. Major Hingston decided to carry on the attack just north of where D Company had been stopped. On his right flank, the other side of the road, the Americans would make a further effort to advance level with the British on the north side of the road. At 4 p.m.the advance was recommenced. All might have gone well had not the Americans, with their preponderance of automatic weapons, run dangerously short of ammunition. There was nothing for it but to withdraw. Major Hingston, who had been wounded, pulled back to the survivors of D Company, where the two Companies were able to provide very heavy covering fire to allow the Americans to withdraw themselves.

While this was going on C Company, which should have been following behind B, appeared to have got lost, and found themselves engaged in a separate battle in which another American battalion with a squadron of the Scots Greys were attempting to clear a route out to the south. As darkness fell on 6th October, B, C and D Companies were in contact with the enemy. Each had suffered heavy casualties. Captain P.B. Williams, the Battalion Medical Officer, performed wonders at his hastily established Regimental Aid Post in a mill on the north edge of the village, while all the Battalion jeeps were assembled and used to ferry back the many wounded, out of the battle area. No praise can be high enough for the courage and dedication of the Medical Officer and his stretcher bearers and orderlies. The fact that every man had complete confidence in the medical team added greatly to the Battalion's morale in battle.

Some months later the 5th Battalion was gratified to read a very generous tribute for its support in this battle. Colonel Sink, who had commanded the 506th Regimental Combat Group, wrote to his superior officer, Major-General Maxwell Taylor, saying:

> On 6th October 1944, the Duke of Cornwall's Light Infantry Battalion commanded by Lieutenant-Colonel Taylor was attached to 506 RCG. In the early afternoon of October 6th this battalion was committed in an assault on the town of Opheusden to take over a portion of the attacking front of the 1st Battalion, 506th Parachute Infantry, U.S.A.
>
> These troops attacked on schedule with vigour and determination in face of withering enemy fire. The courage and ability shown by these troops was an inspiration to the 1st Battalion.
>
> The gallantry of the British officers and men was outstanding and instilled in the men of the 506 Parachute Infantry the highest regard for the fighting

ability of the British Infantry.

The undermentioned desires that Lieutenant-Colonel Taylor and his entire Battalion receive full credit for their notable work.

(Signed) Col. R. F. Sink
Commanding 506 Parachute Regiment
101 U.S. Airborne Division

The 5th Battalion could certainly be proud not merely for its part in the battle for Opheusden, but for a whole series of desperate actions fought in defence in the Island, that remarkable no man's land between the rivers Waal and Neder Rijn. Lieutenant-Colonel Taylor was awarded a bar to his Distinguished Service Order for his outstanding leadership throughout.

AS FAR AS THE FATHERLAND

After Opheusden the 5th Battalion rejoined the remainder of the 43rd (Wessex) Division in the area between the River Maas and the German frontier. It was quite different countryside to that of the Island, consisting of pleasant little villages surrounded by farm land or sandy heath. The Battalion was grouped around one such village by the name of Groesbeek, which sadly rapidly succumbed to heavy shelling. Deep patrols were carried out each night, many of them into Germany itself. Patrols would often remain hidden behind the enemy front line by day, observing troop movements and dispositions. On one occasion a returning patrol, finding its way blocked by a sentry, boldly joined a party of German soldiers carrying ration boxes forward. After another occasion, when a patrol had inflicted casualties and taken a number of prisoners, Serjeant E.F. White and Private E.C. Palambo both won Military Medals for their bravery. It was a happy time for the Battalion, for the knowledge that it was now operating across the border into Germany – something that few had even dared to think about a few months earlier – acted as a great tonic; there was now always competition to be included in these patrols.

By early November military supplies were at last coming through the liberated port of Antwerp. At the same time more and more American formations were taking their place in the Allied order of battle. A major offensive directed against Cologne was being planned. This involved XXX Corps moving south to take its place on the left flank of the two American armies. On 10th November the 43rd (Wessex) Division and the Guards Armoured Division therefore moved to their new area around Maastricht and Brunssum, close up to the German border. At the same time the American 84th Infantry Division, which was already a few miles further east, came under command of XXX Corps.

The battle of Geilenkirchen, 18th-19th November 1944

As a preliminary to the main thrust on Cologne it was necessary to capture Geilenkirchen, a small town on the River Wurm, through which ran important road and rail communications. The idea of a frontal attack held no appeal to Lieutenant-General Horrocks, who decided instead to encircle the town. The American 84th Division, already east of the River Wurm, was to push up due north behind Geilenkirchen, where they would link up with the 43rd (Wessex) Division as it advanced eastwards to the north of the town.

For the British soldiers this was to be their first battle on German soil. Throughout years of training, followed by the savage fighting in Normandy and Holland, the distant vision of marching forward into Germany itself had been the Holy Grail that had maintained every man's determination to win. Now that day had come; the 5th Battalion was about to step across the border from Holland into Germany.

Preparations for the forthcoming operation had never been more thorough. Apart from an intense programme of briefings, social evenings were held between the various messes so that the many newcomers could be welcomed into the Regimental family and made to feel the warmth of real friendship.

The spearhead of the operation was allotted to 214 Brigade (augmented by the 5th Dorsets from 130 Brigade). At 12.30 p.m. on 18th November the 7th Somerset Light Infantry and the 1st Worcesters crossed the start line. Their task was to cut the first two of the three roads leading into Geilenkirchen from the north, and capture the two villages of Tripsrath and Niederheide, which lay on the second of these roads. The 5th Battalion was then to pass through the Somersets at Niederheide at 3 p.m., and advance north, capture the village of Hocheide, and then swing east, cut the third and final road out of Geilenkirchen, and capture the village of Bruggerhof, which lay on this route. The march up towards Niederheide was uneventful, but as the Battalion approached the village it was met by a scene of confusion not uncommon in war. The road had been churned to mud, in which floundered a solid block of carriers, anti-tank guns and jeeps all trying to move forward, while innumerable demoralised prisoners were being hustled to the rear. Adding to the chaos was a continuous rain of enemy mortar fire on and around the village. By means of some choice words shouted by the Commanding Officer through a megaphone, the leading companies forced their way through the *mêlée* and deployed on the start line. They crossed on time. D Company, now commanded by Major Lonsdale, made rapid progress north, capturing the village of Hocheide without undue difficulty, in spite of the absence of their supporting tanks which had got bogged down in the mud at Niederheide. By then the evening was closing in and, with the smoke from burning buildings adding to the Autumnal mist, B company advancing on the right flank was mistaken for the enemy by their comrades in D Company, who opened fire on them. Fortunately, in the poor light the fire was inaccurate and no damage was done before the men of B Company could identify themselves by firing tracer straight up into the air, a signal which had previously been agreed upon to meet just such an emergency.

As soon as it was fully dark A Company passed through D company in Hocheide and turned left down a narrow track, which led to the village of Bruggerhof on the third and last of the roads into Gielenkirchen. No opposition was encountered, and Major Holland deployed his platoon astride this route, down which it was more than likely the German counter attack would be launched. So far it appeared that the enemy was quite unaware of the British presence, for at about 6 p.m. Serjeant Garnham's 9 Platoon heard the noise of marching boots approaching from the north. Out of the darkness appeared a platoon moving without any tactical pretence in column of threes towards Gielenkirchen. Fire was opened, killing seven, wounding others and leaving five prisoners. Now it seemed the enemy must have known of the British presence; strangely, however, they failed to react. At about 11 p.m. a horse pulling a cart loaded with ammunition passed down the road towards Gielenkirchen. A wheel passed over one of the No. 75 grenades laid by A Company; the cart blew up with a most satisfactory explosion, and the horse, by some chance unhurt, galloped off into the night. Half an hour later exactly the same thing happened to a second cart. At 1 a.m. on 19th November a reconnaissance patrol was seen cautiously moving down the road; once again fire was opened and four out of the seven were killed. Finally at 3 a.m. a Tiger tank lumbered slowly up the road from the direction of Gielenkirchen. It hit a No. 75 grenade, whereupon a couple of men climbed out of the turret and started picking up the other grenades. A burst of Bren fire persuaded them to disappear into the night, while the tank drove smartly off to the north amid a firework display of mines under its tracks.

The 5th Battalion was then left in peace for twelve hours, astride its two roads. During this time no attempt was made to dislodge the companies from their blocking positions on the roads that formed the only line of communication between Geilenkirchen and the main German front. All through the daylight hours of 19th November the sounds of heavy fighting could be heard in Geilenkirchen, as the American 82nd Division fought it way up from the south. At about 3 p.m. Germans were seen retreating out of the town, straight into the arms of the 5th Battalion. The artillery were fully prepared for such an eventuality, and with the help of the infantry weapons and the guns of the 4th/7th Dragoon Guards, great slaughter was done.

The battle of Hoven Wood, 20th-21st November 1944

After the battle on 19th November the remainder of the Division passed through the 5th Battalion, leaving it around Hochiede and Bruggerhof. Progress however was minimal. Enemy resistance was rapidly becoming ever more firm, the British line was now within range of the heavy artillery located in the concrete bunkers of the Siegfried line and, perhaps worst of all, the deep churned up mud of the battle-field was greatly hindering the movement of tanks, carriers towing anti-tank guns, and the masses of transport bringing forward ammunition, petrol and supplies. The Germans were making the most of their advantage and counter-attacking fiercely. In this critical situation the 7th Somerset Light Infantry was ordered to attack through a strip of wood nearly 2 miles long and about 600 yards wide, which ran along the left hand side of the road from Hochiede to the village of Hoven at its far end. About 800 yards from Hoven was a distinct gap in the trees. Little was known about the enemy dispositions in the wood, nor whether the saturated ground on the left flank would be passable to tanks. By nightfall on 20th November the Somersets had reached the gap. It had, however, suffered heavy casualties clearing the southern part of the wood and was in no state to tackle the northern half. Early the following morning Lieutenant-Colonel Taylor received orders to pass through the Somersets and capture the villages of Hoven and Krandorf, which lay at the far end of the wood. It was essential that these villages should be held until such time as a link up could be made with the American 84th Division, which was fighting a hard battle in the outskirts of Geilenkirchen. Lieutenant-Colonel Taylor was extremely dubious that the task represented a viable operation of war for a single, under-strength battalion, operating well ahead of the Division, with both flanks open. He took what was for him the unprecedented action of committing his reservations to paper, which he passed to the Brigade Commander. He pointed out that apart from the question of open flanks, the wet state of the ground would render tank support impossible (whereas the Tigers, with their extra broad tracks would be less affected); furthermore, he would be unable to bring his anti-tank guns forward. He again put these reservations verbally to the Brigade Commander before the 'Orders Group'. Although far from happy, he was to a certain extent placated by Brigadier Essame, who explained that the American 84th Division was pushing up from the south and would therefore be in a position to support his right flank.

The weather could not have been more foul – bitterly cold with continuous drizzle. The attack started at midday on 22nd November with C Company in the lead, while A Company moved separately up the road towards Kraudorf. Close artillery support was impossible as the height of the trees would have detonated many of the shells over the heads of the leading troops. Immediately C Company appeared in the open between the two parts of the wood, it came under very heavy fire from artillery, mortars, tanks and small arms. The rear platoon (14 Platoon) was almost wiped out, while the two leading platoons only made a few yards into the north half of the wood before being pinned down. Soldiers who had fought throughout the Normandy campaign later said that the enemy fire on this occasion was the heaviest that they had ever experienced.

Immediately that it became apparent that this first attack had failed, Lieutenant-Colonel Taylor ordered a smoke screen to be laid on the east side of the wood, and for D company to carry out a right flanking attack, and enter the wood ahead of the survivors of C Company. Meanwhile C and B Companies together with the Carrier Platoon were giving maximum fire support. Remarkably under the circumstances, D Company made excellent progress along the eastern edge of the wood, and had soon occupied the hamlet of Hoven. Now it became vital to secure the area in the wood behind Hoven, and for this task a composite company under Major Kitchen, consisting of two platoons of A Company (withdrawn from Kraudorf), one platoon of C Company and a company from the 7th Somerset Light Infantry, was ordered to form a chain of strong-points behind D Company. This they achieved with great difficulty and in spite of the rapidly decreasing afternoon light, made the more gloomy by the smoke hanging amongst the trees. However, a very determined carrying party succeeded in taking rum, hot food and ammunition to D Company in Hoven, and laying a telephone line back to Battalion Headquarters.

That night was a true test of an infantryman's stamina. The cold was bitter, battle-dresses were thick with mud and soaked by rain.

Officers and men crouched in their shallow weapon pits (digging was virtually impossible amongst the tangled tree roots), shivering uncontrollably. All through that miserable night, the battalion stretcher bearers performed epic work in evacuating the large numbers of wounded, while the enemy continued to pound the whole area with mortar and artillery fire.

Just before dawn the expected German counter attack was launched. Early in the battle a grenade destroyed the artillery Forward Observation Officer's wireless set. Shortly afterwards a German tank cut the only telephone link. D Company was now not only physically isolated, but also out of wireless and telephone communication with the rest of the Battalion (the infantry No. 18 wireless sets were not able to work through the thick rain-soaked trees). During the next few hours many deeds of great gallantry were performed by D Company in Hoven, as it fought off attack after attack, supported by tanks and self-propelled guns. Good use was made of the PIATs, which proved highly effective at close range, but it was galling for the Cornishmen to watch the German tanks with their broad tracks moving freely around their position while the British tanks floundered in the mud. Casualties were mounting, while ammunition was rapidly running out. Soon, weapons and ammunition had to be taken from the bodies of the German dead, allowing the battle to be carried on for a little longer. By the late morning the company fighting strength was down to sixteen; the buildings were blazing, and ammunition of any sort was virtually exhausted. Only then did Major Lonsdale make the decision to abandon Hoven, and break out to join Major Kitchen's composite company to his rear. This he did, together with fifteen gallant survivors of his Company. Fortunately, Major Kitchen was still in wireless contact with Battalion Headquarters and, the situation having been explained, both companies were ordered to withdraw back to the southern part of the wood from where they had started the previous afternoon. Meanwhile, in Hoven itself, the Germans rounded up the wounded survivors of D Company. As is so often the case within the brotherhood of front line soldiers, the prisoners were treated with kindness and respect by their captors.

The DCLI had fought a battle that must have equalled or surpassed the horrors of Hill 112. An officer of the 7th Somerset Light Infantry, who was well inured to the unpleasant sights of battle, has said that the sinister atmosphere of that cold, dark wood, in which lay the countless corpses of British and German soldiers, was more terrible than anything that he had ever experienced.

The Battalion had suffered grievous casualties at Hoven Wood and it was vital that it should now have time to absorb considerable reinforcement drafts of officers and men. The 43rd (Wessex) Division continued to hold the Geilenkirchen salient, but both sides were content to lick their wounds, and there was little fighting. Even when in reserve, the Battalion found life far from comfortable with day after day of cold rain. Mud continued to be the principle enemy. Virtually no movement off the roads could even be contemplated, using the standard infantry vehicles. Fortunately, this situation had been anticipated by the Divisional staff and a large number of Weasels materialised as if by magic. These maids of all work were designed for arctic warfare, their broad tracks giving them the ability to cross soft snow. They were ideal for the present muddy conditions, and it is probably true to say that without them the Division could not have continued to operate in the field. One of the few really happy aspects of this period of waiting astride the Dutch-German border was that the mining village of Brunssum could provide pithead showers with unlimited hot water. It is difficult to convey to somebody who has not been an infantryman the sheer joy of standing under a hot shower and washing the filth and sweat off one's body.

Start of the move back to Nijmegen, 19th December 1944

On 9th December snow fell and the ground froze. Once more the British army could move. XXX Corps began to hand over to XII Corps, as the former moved up north back to the Nijmegen area in preparation for an attack on the formidable obstacle of the River Maas. New pieces of equipment started to become available, including Crocodiles (flame throwers mounted on Churchill tanks) and Kangaroos (armoured personnel carriers consisting of Sherman tanks with the turret removed). The attacking of pill-boxes featured prominently in the training programme.

RETURN TO SUPPORT THE U.S. ARMY IN THE ARDENNES

The move south, as reserve behind the hard-pressed U.S. Army, 19th December 1944

On 16th December the Germans attacked in the American-held area of the Ardennes. Earlier in the war the French had made the ill-founded assumption that this closely forested country provided a sufficient barrier in itself to prohibit a major thrust from the east. Now it was the turn of the Americans to make the same mistake. Initially, little concern was shown by the Allies. The Americans, admittedly somewhat thin on the ground, but with complete air superiority, would surely be able to hold this enemy thrust. Plans to move XXX Corps northwards were not changed, and on 19th December the long column of vehicles carrying the 43rd (Wessex) Division took to the road. However, it had barely gone more than a few miles when an unexpected halt was ordered. After a brief pause it started off again, but in the opposite direction, towards the Ardennes. By that time it had become apparent that the German aim was to drive a wedge through the Ardennes forest to Liege, cross the River Meuse and advance to Antwerp, thus cutting off the British/Canadian 21 Army Group from the U.S. armies in the south. The weather was cold and foggy, which grounded the Allied air forces, allowing the Germans to make significant advances. The 43rd (Wessex) Division was immediately re-deployed along the River Meuse from Huy to Vise. The German advance was proceeding on a front of about twenty miles, but strangely this apparent set-back raised rather than lowered British morale. 21 Army Group was very different from the British Expeditionary Force which had been driven to the coast by superior German forces in 1940. Now the British had a very real chance of destroying a major part of the German army without having first to cross the formidable Siegfried Line.

During this period in reserve behind the U.S. Army, Major Lonsdale received the DSO and Major Holland the MC; and Serjeant Yeomans and Private Adams the MM, for their gallantry at the battle of Hoven.

Bilsen, Christmas Day 1944

On 23rd December the skies cleared. The Allied bombers and ground attack fighters took to the air, effectively bringing the German offensive to a halt. Christmas Day 1944 was spent in comfortable billets in Bilsen near Maastricht. The Belgians could not have been more hospitable and did everything in their power to make the festivities go with a swing. In the afternoon the DCLI football XI played the 7th Somerset Light Infantry. Wildly cheered on by both supporting battalions, the Cornwalls snatched a last minute victory, 3 - 2. The evening's celebrations were rudely interrupted by orders to move to the villages of Elsloo and Catsop in Holland, starting at 5 a.m. the following morning. The Battalion was to form part of a mobile reserve to counter the threat of a German airborne assault in this area. That morning was the coldest experienced in Holland for many years. Carrier tracks had to be unfrozen and 'oil, low, cold, test' was hastily issued for the lubrication of weapons. The Battalion saw in the New Year in this area, remaining there till 11th January. During this period additional warm clothing was issued, and 100 men per day were sent back to Brunsuum for hot showers.

ADVANCE AGAIN

Operation 'Veritable': the battles of the Reichwald, February 1945

It was now Field-Marshal Montgomery's plan to seize the initiative and destroy the German forces west of the Rhine. Known as Operation 'Veritable', the attack by XXX Corps was to take place in the area between the rivers Maas and Rhine, south east of Nijmegan, preparatory to the crossing of the Rhine itself. The attack was launched at 5 a.m. on 8th February, spear-headed by the 15th (Scottish) Division. The objective was the small town of Cleve, a couple of miles to the north east of the forest known as the Reichwald. The 43rd (Wessex) Division followed the Scotsmen, ready to pass through immediately the momentum of the attack appeared to be slowing. The Germans were now fighting for the defence of the Fatherland itself, and Hitler (now taking on personal responsibility for the conduct of the battle) had decided to throw everything available into this critical defence of the south bank of the Rhine. The extreme cold weather had given place to rain and sleet, rendering much of the ground impassable to vehicles, and to make matters worse the Germans had opened the flood sluices, inundating much of the countryside between Nijmegan and Cleve.

The battle of Goch, 9th-23rd February 1945

At 9 p.m. on the evening of 9th February the 5th Battalion took its place in the long divisional column that slowly snaked south east towards Cleve. The night was bitterly cold for the drenched infantrymen riding on the supporting tanks. Ahead of them could be heard the sounds of battle where 129 Brigade was fighting, throughout that night, in the streets of Cleve. In the darkness and the rain the situation was highly confused, and it was not till dawn on 10th February that 214 Brigade, with the 5th Battalion in the lead, were able to continue the advance. The task was to capture the village of Goch, eight miles due south of Cleve. This involved branching out across country between Cleve and the Reichwald forest, and having destroyed the enemy in the villages of Saalhof, Materborn and Hau, driving down the main road to Goch. Throughout this operation the dark, brooding mass of the Reichwald forest would lie on the Battalion's right flank. No intelligence existed to indicate whether the enemy occupied the forest. It was slow work. The Germans fought for each tactical position with great tenacity. That night D Company, supported by tanks, drove the enemy out of Saalhof, who fell back on the next village of Materborn. Materborn stood on slightly higher ground, which dominated the route south to Goch. It was obvious that it would be firmly defended. The attack was launched just after last light with two simultaneous flanking movements by C Company to the left and D Company to the right. Tanks could not operate in the soft ground, with the result that these were confined to the vulnerable metalled road leading into the village. Meanwhile B Company was despatched on a wide right flanking march to cut the road to the south. Progress was slow for the ground was sodden, and the men, who had had no sleep for forty-eight hours, were heavily laden. Wire cattle fences and water-filled ditches ran at right angles across their line of advance, and as anybody with infantry experience can vouch, these obstacles, which may appear innocuous by day, can become maddening and frustrating hazards on a dark night. The attack by C and D Companies failed. The leading tanks advancing into Materborn were destroyed by 88 mm gun fire while the two rifle companies, attempting to manoeuvre through farmland criss-crossed with wire fences and water-filled ditches, were brought to a halt by heavy mortar and machine-gun fire. Only B Company on their wide flanking march met any success, cutting the road south of Materborn and capturing a number of prisoners. By midnight it became apparent that no further progress was possible. The Battalion was regrouped back in Saalhof, where hot food and a few hours sleep raised everybody's spirits. The following day a second attack was launched against Materborn. 'H' hour was 2 p.m., and this time all went well in textbook fashion. The Battalion was supported by the 4th/7th Dragoon Guards and the entire Divisional Artillery. As soon as the village was deemed to be secure, the 7th Somerset Light Infantry swept through and continued to advance south to Goch.

For the next few days 129 and 130 Brigades carried on the fight to secure the Cleve-Goch road and capture the village of Goch. The enemy were fighting fanatically, and casualties on both sides were extremely high. By 15th February the two attacking brigades had fought themselves to the point of exhaustion. Major-General Thomas sensed that the Germans must also be in this state, and therefore ordered that 214 Brigade (reinforced by 4th Somerset Light Infantry) should mount a final attack on the afternoon of 16th February. The 1st Worcesters and 7th Somerset Light Infantry were to lead, and by 5.45 p.m. had made good progress, in spite of very heavy German defensive fire. Now was the time to launch the 5th Battalion with a squadron of the 4th/7th Dragoon Guards around the left flank. The supporting artillery fire was highly effective, enabling the rifle companies to achieve their objectives north east of Goch, effectively cutting the main Goch-Calcar road. Special mention must be made of Captain C.L. Sayer for his work in leading the anti-tank platoon forward, and placing his guns within each company area – no mean task on a pitch dark night under enemy fire. Much the same sort of problems faced the signallers, laying lines between the rifle companies and Battalion Headquarters. It must be appreciated that the 5th Battalion were somewhat out on a limb to the left flank, and there were still isolated pockets of Germans within the battalion position that were capable of putting up a spirited fight.

Meanwhile, that night the 4th Somerset Light Infantry carried out a highly successful attack on the escarpment overlooking Goch from the north. It was now only a matter of time before the important tactical village of Goch was captured. The Commander XXX Corps later described the action by 214 Brigade on the night of 16th-17th February as the turning point in the battle of the Reichwald.

On 19th February the Germans put in a heavy counter attack, which necessitated a redeployment of the 5th Battalion to face east towards the Rhine. In spite of heavy enemy artillery fire there were very few casualties, thanks to the sodden condition of the ground and the effective digging which was by then second nature to every man.

On 23rd February the 5th was relieved by a battalion of the Irish Guards. As the companies marched back to warm, dry billets in Cleve, no tears were shed for the cold, wet positions on the Goch-Calcar road.

Under Command of II Canadian Corps

The battle of Hochwald, 27th February-3rd March 1945

At about that time 43rd (Wessex) Division was put under command of II Canadian Corps, which had been given the task of breaking through the Hochwald position. This was the last defensible stronghold west of the Rhine, and it was therefore anticipated that the Germans would offer strong resistance. This assumption proved to be only too true. It was not till 4th March that after desperate fighting the Canadians succeeded in driving the enemy from the Hochwald. On the penultimate day of this great battle 214 Brigade was ordered to capture the villages of Kehrum and Marienbaum, on the north-east flank. The 7th Somerset Light Infantry led the way, mopping up German rear-guards, while the 5th DCLI followed, ready to pass through when necessary. The rain had ceased and the first sunshine of spring raised everybody's spirits. The advance was halted by a wide anti-tank ditch, beyond which was a wood. The 7th Somersets sent forward a patrol that reported the wood clear, whereupon A Company of the 5th DCLI moved through to the far edge, to provide protection for the Royal Engineers engaged in bridging the anti-tank ditch. In fact the wood was far from clear of enemy. The leading platoon found itself attacked from all sides. Artillery fire was promptly called down but in spite of this, only one section managed to make its way back: the remainder were killed, wounded or taken prisoner. Early the following morning, with bridges over the anti-tank ditch complete, a full-scale battalion attack supported by tanks and artillery was put in against Marienbaum. There was little opposition. Sixty-five prisoners and an anti-tank gun were captured, and the 5th dug in, having secured the Canadian left flank.

The Battalion was not left in peace long to enjoy the comforts of the solidly built and relatively undamaged houses in Marienbaum. Patrols had reported that the Germans had withdrawn some four miles to the little cathedral town of Xanten. It was approached by a dead straight road under observation from the Cathedral tower. The Battalion were ordered forward to regain contact with the enemy, which they did under the fortuitous cover of a morning ground mist. Xanten proved another hard nut to crack, eventually being captured by 129 Brigade. Now the west bank of the Rhine from Düsseldorf to Nijmegen was in allied hands; the 5th had been in action for twenty-eight days and were overdue a period of rest, in which the replacement of men and equipment could be carried out. It should be mentioned that during the fighting around Xanten the gallant Major Kitchen was severely wounded in the shoulder, his third wound since landing in Normandy. He was later awarded the Distinguished Service Order for his outstanding courage and leadership.

* * *

Operation 'Plunder': the crossing of the Rhine 23rd March 1945

The 5th Battalion took no active part in the XXX Corps assault crossing of the Rhine, which was carried out by the 51st (Highland) Division and the 15th (Scottish) Division during the night of 23rd-24th March between Xanten and Rees. Billeted in the shattered village of Hayan on the banks of the River Maas, the Battalion prepared for what it hoped would be the final battle of the war. In the early morning of 24th March the Cornishmen were witnesses of the vast armada of aircraft and gliders carrying a complete airborne corps to the dropping zones on the east bank of the Rhine. Two days later, on the night of 26th-27th March, the 5th Battalion left the dubious comfort of Hayan and marched to Rees, crossing by a newly erected pontoon bridge. Because the River Ijssel, running parallel to the Rhine six miles distant, had not been crossed, the bridge-head was still very shallow. Men and supplies were pouring across the many bridges constructed by the Royal Engineers, and with constant enemy shelling, the scenes were reminiscent of the Normandy beaches in the days after the initial landings.

At 3 a.m. the Battalion arrived at the village of Essenden, where after digging shell scrapes, all except the sentries lay down to sleep. The following morning the 43rd (Wessex) Division was again on the move. The countryside between the rivers Rhine and Ijssel was flat, the only prominent feature being a partly completed autobahn, which ran directly across the line of advance. This ran on a high embankment and was strongly defended by the enemy, who enjoyed superb fields of fire. The advance was led by 129 Brigade, which soon became involved in heavy fighting. As momentum was lost 214 Brigade attempted to pass through, led by the 1st Worcesters and 7th Somerset Light Infantry; meanwhile the 5th DCLI, in reserve, waited at Essenden for their Kangaroos to arrive from across the Rhine. When these appeared they were found to be fully loaded with 25 pdr gun ammunition, which had to be unloaded and stacked – an exhausting task. It was not till the early afternoon of 27th March that the 5th Battalion moved forward, with a troop of 4th/7th Dragoon Guards and a troop of Crocodile flame throwers. The objective was Meghelen, a farming village lying on the near bank of the River Ijssel on the far side of the autobahn. Fighting for the autobahn position was still far from over. Both the Worcesters and the Somersets were pinned down, unable to make further progress. Although the light was fast fading, it was imperative that the momentum of the attack should be maintained. Lieutenant-Colonel Taylor therefore decided that he would launch B Company, carried in Kangaroos, in a wide right flanking movement to get behind the autobahn, thereby bringing fire to bear on the enemy from both their front and rear. Once B Company had won this fire fight, the remainder of the Battalion would pass through the 7th Somerset Light Infantry to capture the final objective of Meghelen. It was already dusk with a fine drizzle falling from an overcast sky when the Kangaroos, driven with great skill and courage by RASC drivers, moved off. Almost immediately they came up against deep drainage ditches which forced the Kangaroos to the bridges. These were covered by *panzerfausts* (anti-tank rocket launchers), mortars and machine-guns. The leading Kangaroo was knocked out. B Company dismounted and continued on foot to the rear of the autobahn where it dug in, (the water table was only just below surface level, which meant that weapon pits were of necessity shallow). That night B Company made a slow and methodical advance towards Megehelen. The area was dotted with abandoned enemy weapon pits and dugouts, all of which had to be searched, for the German tactic of lying low while the first wave of troops passed through was well known. As dawn broke C Company moved forward through B, and occupied Megehelen without any great difficulty. The enemy retaliated with artillery but, contrary to their normal practice, made no attempt to launch a counter attack, an indication, perhaps, of the drastic straits to which the German army was being reduced.

The vital break-out from the Rhine bridge-head had been achieved, for which much of the credit must belong to the 43rd (Wessex) Division and in particular to 214 Brigade. Through the gap that had been punched in the perimeter at Megehelen now poured a seemingly endless column of tanks and wheeled vehicles, fanning out into the plains of northern Germany.

THE PURSUIT THROUGH GERMANY

30th March-4th May 1945

The enemy was now disorganised, and for the first time in the campaign was showing signs of being demoralised. Field-Marshal Montgomery fully appreciated that speed was of the essence if the break-through was to be exploited before the Germans had a chance to regroup. In his directive he said:

The operations will be conducted with speed and violence by the armoured columns; foremost commanders must always be quick to by-pass resistance with the leading troops and to push on deep into the enemy rear; if a column is held up on one route, another one must push on. This is the time to take risks and go flat out for the River Elbe. If we reach the River Elbe quickly, we win the war.

Major-General Thomas therefore re-organised the 43rd (Wessex) Division into three groups. First: the Armoured Thrust Group, consisting of 8th (Armoured) Brigade, the 12th King's Royal Rifle Corps (a motorised infantry battalion) and the 4th Somerset Light Infantry (in Kangaroos of the 1st Canadian APC Regiment); second: the Follow-up Group, consisting of one of the infantry brigades; third: the Reserve, made up of the other two infantry brigades.

The 43rd (Wessex) Division assembled in the town of Anholt on the morning of 30th March, Good Friday. The vast number of every sort of vehicle became entangled in a monumental traffic jam that sorely tried the patience and temper of all concerned. During the first days of the advance 214 Brigade was in reserve and consequently played no part in the fighting around Lingen and the crossing of the Dortmund-Ems canal. The retreating enemy had destroyed every bridge, blocked the roads by felling trees across them, mined the verges and made extensive use of booby traps. Easter Day found the 5th Battalion in the Dutch town of Hengelo. Here, most were able to enjoy comfortable billets amongst a jubilant people. There the Battalion remained for a week while the Pioneer Platoon carried out extensive work clearing the route ahead of mines and booby traps.

On 7th April 214 Brigade moved forward to take its place in the Follow-up Group, with the 5th Battalion in the lead. It was with a certain regret that the men left the comfort and warm hospitality of Hengelo to cross the frontier once more into Germany. However, all ranks were in excellent spirits, knowing that victory was now clearly in sight. The 5th Battalion crossed the River Ems at Lingen that evening. Ahead lay the town of Häselunne astride the River Häse, a tributary of the Ems. The enemy confronting the Division at this time was the 6th Parachute Division, a tough experienced formation, which, despite the hopelessness of the German predicament, was still fighting with great determination and skill. Appreciating that the river crossing at Häselunne would be strongly defended, the 7th Somerset Light Infantry and 1st Worcesters were ordered to carry out a wide left flanking movement and capture the bridge at Buckelte. Meanwhile the 5th was to distract the enemy's attention by putting in a feint frontal attack on Häselunne along the main axis. While carrying out his reconnaissance from a nearby church spire, Lieutenant-Colonel Taylor realised that the town could be approached unseen through woods on the right flank. He therefore despatched A, B and C Companies supported by a troop of the 13th/18th Hussars through the woods, while D Company put on a noisy demonstration of fire power from the front. In this the Commanding Officer was probably exceeding his mandate, which called merely for the maximum visible and audible aggression on the enemy's front rather than a slow surreptitious flanking movement aimed at capturing the town itself. Although in the long term this made no difference, the 7th Somerset Light Infantry were far from pleased to be kept waiting while the 5th Battalion carried out a complex manoeuvre that it had not been asked to undertake. This was perhaps the only time in the campaign when regimental rivalry endangered the overall outcome of a battle. In fact the Somersets caught the enemy at Buckelte entirely by surprise, finding many of them sunbathing on the banks of the river. Although the bridge had already been destroyed, the Somersets and Worcesters quickly crossed in assault boats, and proceeded to move in behind the German main position at Häselunne. Meanwhile C Company, on the extreme right of the 5th Battalion position, had found a footbridge over the River Häse which was still intact. That night D Company was moved round to the right flank, ready to pass through C Company and cross the river at first light. Making their way forward in single file, the Company found itself in a minefield. Captain J.R. Rabet, the Company Commander, was killed almost immediately. Lieutenant S.J. Wheeler, in an attempt to extricate the leading elements, was also killed. In accordance with the Field-Marshal's directive the 5th Battalion did not hang around Häselunne, but hurried after the 7th Somerset Light Infantry and 1st Worcesters, crossing the River Hase at Buckelte. By the evening of 9th April the Battalion had reached the village of Eltern, where for a short time it took over from the Divisional Reconnaissance Regiment, with the role of maintaining contact with the retreating Germans. Later that day 129 Brigade passed through to take the lead.

The battle for Cloppenburg, 13th April-14th April 1945

The 5th Battalion spent a relaxed four days in the pleasant, undamaged village of Eltern. On 13th April orders were received to advance through the town of Cloppenburg, fifty miles up the road towards Bremen, which was alleged to have been captured by the 7th Royal Hampshires. The Battalion was then to establish a firm start-line along the railway track on the far side of the town. In the event, it was found that Cloppenburg was far from clear. The enemy consisted of a battalion of sixteen-year-old potential officers known by the title of *Grossdeutschland Gruppe*. Young they may have been, but they fought with fanatical determination. They were well supplied with *spandaus* and *panzerfausts*, which they employed with great skill. Every house had to be secured and then thoroughly searched, a dangerous and time consuming operation, made ever more nerve racking as night fell. It was not till dawn on 14th April that C Company was firmly established on the railway track. The enemy still had plenty of fight, as C Company Headquarters found to its cost when a Panther tank suddenly appeared from a patch of scrub and opened fire at twenty-five yards range. At the same time a Valentine tank had a miraculous escape when an 88 mm shell passed clean through one side and out the other without harming any member of the crew.

Capture of Ahlorn, 15th April 1945

After a day of rest the 5th Battalion once more took the lead. The next objective was the large village of Ahlorn, just thirty miles short of Bremen. As the leading company approached there appeared no sign of enemy activity, but Lieutenant-Colonel Taylor was not prepared to take any chances. After a short, sharp artillery bombardment, the Battalion advanced two companies up. Those who were there remembered the attack as being reminiscent of a field firing exercise in Kent – lots of friendly fire, but nothing being returned.

Final advance to Bremen, 23rd April-26th April 1945

Once Ahlorn was captured it was time to regroup for the attack on the great city of Bremen. This was to be carried out by the 52nd (Lowland) Division from the east (which had already crossed the River Weser), and the 3rd Division and 51st (Highland) Division advancing along the west bank of the river. The 43rd (Wessex) Division was to swing west, cross the Weser at Verden, and provide the right flank protection for the 52nd (Lowland) Division. On 23rd April, after receiving a welcome draft of reinforcements, the 5th Battalion again took to the road. There was a feeling that the end of the war must now be imminent. Elation was tempered by a natural desire to survive these last few days, and at every level men became wary of taking unnecessary risks.

The countryside to the east of the Weser consisted of reclaimed marshland intersected by drainage ditches. The right flank, guarded by the 43rd (Wessex) Division, was demarcated by one such deep drainage ditch crossed by several bridges, beyond which lay the enemy.

The 5th Battalion was required to keep these under observation, and to forestall any attempted crossing.

For this purpose a mobile column consisting of a troop of tanks, two platoons of B Company in carriers, a section of mortars and a section of the Scout Platoon was quickly assembled under command of Captain G.R. Anslow. Next day a warning order was received that the 43rd (Wessex) Division was to move forward into Bremen itself. This meant that the bridges could no longer be denied to the enemy, and they were consequently blown by Royal Engineer demolition parties guarded by Captain Anslow's mobile column.

The 5th Battalion moved into Bremen on 26th April. Most of the fighting was over, but the scenes of appalling horror in the city profoundly shocked these hardened soldiers. They are best described by Major-General Essame in his history of the 43rd (Wessex) Division:

> In the rain which now began to fall, Bremen presented a scene of sordid horror almost beyond description. Great piles of rubble blocked the streets, the twisted lamp standards silhouetted grotesquely against the sky, the stench of buildings still burning offended the nostrils and the open sewers stank to heaven. The people were broken-spirited and listless. Many of them were literally green in colour, for the ventilation in the big air-raid bunkers had broken down and the sanitary arrangements inside had collapsed. They were docile, bewildered and hopeless. The fighting had released thousands of slave labourers from Eastern Europe and Russian prisoners, who broke loose and fell without restraint on the large stores of liquor in the town. Their behaviour, especially that of the Russians, can only be described as abominable. Brutal treatment by the Germans had reduced them below the level of beasts, but it is doubtful whether they ever had far to fall. Some even drank themselves to death on the commercial spirit in the docks. Fighting, rape and open murder broke out, and our troops had to intervene. None had any idea of sanitary discipline, and their huts and surroundings had reached a stage of human degradation and filth beyond the conception of any Western European. No one in the Division regretted the order to hand over the charnel-house, which had once been a great civilised city, to 52 (Lowland) Division, and to move out into the clean air of the Cuxhaven peninsula on the morning of the 28th.

The Cuxhaven peninsula, 29th April-5th May 1945

At first light on 29th April, in pouring rain, the 43rd Reconnaissance Regiment led the Division from its assembly area just south of Bremen. First it drove east across the deep drainage ditch, mentioned earlier in connection with Captain Anslow's mobile column. It will be remembered that the bridges across this obstacle had first been captured intact, and conscientiously guarded, before being blown up. Now, just three days later, the long-suffering Royal Engineers had worked through the night to rebuild them to allow the 43rd (Wessex) Division to cross. Once across, all three brigades swung north, and with 130 Brigade leading, made with all possible speed for the bridge across the Hamme at Kuhstedt. Resistance took the form of determined groups of men with *spandaus*, together with concentrated and highly accurate *nebelwerfer* fire. Afterwards, it was discovered that those responsible for the latter were instructors from a *nebelwerfer* school intent on expending their stocks of ammunition before surrendering.

The advance up the Cuxhaven peninsula did not involve the 5th Battalion in any serious fighting. All ranks were aware that the German army was rapidly crumbling into disarray, and that the end was imminent. The main battalion task was now to keep in close contact with the units to left and right, for in this fast moving advance it was becoming only too easy to get out of step with those on either flank. Failure to retain close contact could result in tragic accidents in which friend fired upon friend. At this stage every man was very aware that he had only to survive a few more days, to have survived the war.

The German Surrender, 4th May 1945

Major-General Thomas had spent most of the 5th May with 130 Brigade at the bridge-head over the Hamme Canal. On his way back to Divisional Headquarters he called in at Headquarters 214 Brigade to issue his orders for the advance to Bremerhaven, which was to be launched the following morning. At this point there was a knock on the door, which then burst open, to disclose the tall figure of Major W.J. Chalmers, the Brigade Major. Both commanders looked up with astonishment. Only an event of world-shaking importance could justify an interruption when the General was giving out his orders. "Sir," said the Brigade Major, "the BBC have just announced the unconditional surrender of the German Forces opposing Field-Marshal Montgomery in North West Europe." – " I take my orders from the Corps Commander, not the BBC," answered Major-General Thomas coldly. Major Chalmers promptly withdrew and the briefing for the operation, which both General and Brigadier knew was now of only academic interest, continued. Shortly afterwards Major Chalmers again appeared, this time carrying a signal. "A personal message to you, Sir, from the Corps Commander, timed 2115 hours." – " Read it," rapped out the General. "Germans surrendered unconditionally at 1820 hours. Hostilities on all Second Army Front will cease at 0800 hours tomorrow 5th May 45. No, repeat no advance beyond present front line without further orders from me." Without comment, the General closed his map case, climbed down from the headquarters caravan and walked over to his armoured command vehicle. Turning to the Brigadier, he said "The troops have done us damn well." There was no trace of emotion in his voice. He stepped through the steel door, clanging it shut behind him. Then, standing up in the hatch, he unsmilingly acknowledged the Brigadier's salute as the vehicle sped off into the night.

Back with the 5th Battalion, the news was received with rather more exhilaration. Battalion headquarters, situated in a farm-house, was hosting an exceptionally convivial party for the British Merchant Navy officers recently released from a nearby prison camp. In the middle of this somewhat hilarious meal, the signal announcing the German surrender was brought in and handed to the Commanding Officer. After reading it out loud, glasses were re-charged and toasts drunk. Suddenly the farm-house was filled with excited, shouting and singing soldiers who, seizing their officers, carried them shoulder high around the room and out into the night. All around, flares were arcing across the sky, no longer as warnings of danger, but as signs of jubilation.

In nearly twelve months of almost continuous battle, from Normandy to North Germany, the 5th Battalion had displayed robust courage and brilliant efficiency, which time and time again had worn down and defeated some of the finest troops of the German army.

29
The 6th & 7th Battalions & the Depôt

THE 6TH BATTALION, LATER TO BECOME THE 1ST BATTALION

Training on the Isle of Wight & at Truro, 1939-1940

From its experience of the early weeks of the Great War, in 1939 the War Office made detailed plans to accommodate the vast influx of recruits that would result from the order to mobilise. It will be remembered that in August 1914 the regimental depôts were swamped by unpredictable numbers of volunteers who flocked to the Colours. There had been inadequate accommodation, cooking facilities, uniform, equipment and, perhaps most importantly, officers and non-commissioned officers to instruct and administer these men.

Two radical changes had therefore been made to the mobilization plans. First, conscription was introduced from the first day of war (in fact, men had been conscripted for a limited period of training, under the First Militia scheme, during the weeks immediately before the declaration of war). By this means the War Office knew, with a reasonable degree of accuracy, the size and enlistment date of each new draft. Secondly, because it had become obvious in 1914 that the regimental depôts could not cope with the influx of recruits in time of major war, holding battalions were set up all over Britain. These battalions were not exclusive to a single regiment, but were each made up of men from various regiments. One such holding battalion was the 12th, stationed on the Isle of Wight. It was to the 12th that DCLI soldiers were initially sent for training.

The 12th Holding Battalion therefore included a significant contingent of DCLI recruits. However, it only existed for a few months; in early 1940 it was disbanded and the men dispersed to other larger holding battalions which had previously been established. With a certain logic that was not always evident in the workings of the War Office, the DCLI contingent from the 12th was posted *en bloc* to the 50th Holding Battalion, stationed at Truro. Quite how the numbering of these units was arrived at remains a mystery; it must certainly have perplexed enemy intelligence sources!

Coastal defence & training, 1940-1942

After Dunkirk and the capitulation of France the requirement for coastal defence units became a priority. On 9th October 1940 the 50th Holding Battalion became the 6th Battalion DCLI, responsible no longer for training but for anti-invasion operations. Lieutenant-Colonel C.J. Wood, MC, late of the Royal Irish Fusiliers, assumed command of the Battalion on 5th December 1940, while Major R.C. Cruddas (later to command the 2nd Battalion, and to rise to the rank of Major-General with a CB and a DSO and bar) became Second-in-Command, responsible for training. The Battalion Headquarters was situated in St Austell with the companies deployed around the various areas of responsibility in Cornwall. Officers and men were billeted with civilian households.

In July 1941 the 6th Battalion moved to Somerset, where it was based around Hinton St George. Because of its dispersed and operational role in Cornwall, training above platoon level had been impossible. Here in Somerset, temporarily relieved of any operational commitment, imaginative company and battalion exercises could be carried out. Because the transport had been left in Cornwall for the use of the relieving battalion, these exercises were particularly strenuous, invariably involving long marches.

At the end of the summer the Battalion returned to Cornwall, not in a fully operational role, but with the principal task of completing unit training. It moved into the newly built hutted camp adjoining the Regimental Depôt, known as Walker Lines (after the name of the late Colonel of the Regiment). While here, command changed to Lieutenant-Colonel G.J. Fletcher of the DCLI. Although Walker Lines included warm accommodation, an excellent cookhouse and NAAFI canteen, and every facility for sport and recreation, the soldiers missed their old civilian billets. They were therefore glad to hear of their next operational deployment.

On 17th October Battalion Headquarters moved to Harlyn Bay, near Padstow. The companies were deployed with a view to the defence of the many airfields in the vicinity. Exercises were frequently conducted by both day and night, in which airfields, supposedly captured by German parachute troops, were counter-attacked. At the same time, one platoon composed of men selected for their physical fitness and resolute nature was detached to a newly formed

Brigade Special Service Company billeted at Carclew, near Truro. This company was subjected to the most rigorous training of the sort later to be familiar to Commando units, in which initiative, stealth and an aggressive spirit were the order of the day. Later these platoons returned to their own battalions and continued as specialist sub-units.

On the 10th December the 6th Battalion became part of the 75th Independent Infantry Brigade, which later became Cornwall Coastal Area, establishing its headquarters in Helston. The rifle companies were billeted in Penzance, Prah Sands, Porthleven and Clowance. There the primary task consisted of constructing beach obstacles made from steel scaffolding poles, and laying acres of barbed wire entanglements. Over 600 yards of obstacles were erected across Looe Bar, and more than 2 miles between Marazion and Penzance.

When not involved in building beach defences, the Battalion took part in wide-ranging brigade counter-attack exercises across the length and breadth of the peninsula. RASC troop-carrying vehicles were attached to the Battalion on a scale which allowed every man to be carried in a single lift, thus considerably speeding up the reaction time to any threat. With such a heavy commitment of construction work and brigade exercises, it was difficult to plan the elementary training that was badly needed. This situation was made worse by the continuous turnover of men. Drafts were constantly required for posting to the other battalions of the Regiment, being replaced by men almost direct from civilian employment. For example, in January 1942 alone, 180 men were posted in, having completed just six weeks' basic training.

The problems of training were obviously appreciated by the Brigade Commander, Brigadier A. de L. Cazenove, DSO, MVO, for March was devoted entirely to individual weapon training, section and platoon training, route marching and field firing. The period concluded with an inter-platoon competition within the Brigade, which generated considerable rivalry.

In the first few months of 1942 some company locations changed. There was no longer a company in Penzance; A Company was at Trelowarren, D Company was moved from Porthleven briefly to hutted accommodation on Predannack airfield, then to billets at The Lizard, and C Company moved from Clowance to Trelanvean. Shortly after moving, C Company experienced its first taste of the ugly face of war, when it dealt with the results of bombs jettisoned on Coverack after a German air raid in Falmouth, digging the dead and injured from the wreckage of their homes.

All through that spring and early summer, training and operational duties kept the Battalion very busy. Drafts continued to be despatched to overseas battalions and to be replaced by intakes from the Infantry Training Centre at Dorchester, which was now dealing with DCLI recruits.

In May His Majesty King George VI inspected representative contingents from each of the battalions of Cornwall Coastal Area, at Falmouth. The 6th Battalion was represented by 3 officers and 90 soldiers. On 20th May the Colonel of the Regiment, General Sir Walter Venning, inspected some of the billets occupied by the Battalion and watched training at Prah Sands, Penrose and Helston.

At the end of August 1942 the 6th Battalion moved to a battle camp near St Breward on Bodmin Moor, where it lived under austere conditions in bivouacs. To add to the realism, B echelon was established in the grounds of Lanhydrock House, where all cooking was carried out under field conditions. Exercise attacks to test the efficiency of the Home Guard were carried out against the defences of Falmouth, Bodmin, Launceston and Looe. Much of the movement was carried out on foot, and during that three weeks of training the Battalion marched 225 miles.

On 17th September the 6th Battalion, less A and C Companies, marched back to Walker Lines in Bodmin. There was at that time no room for A and C Companies, which were temporarily accommodated in billets at Wadebridge, until rejoining their comrades in Walker Lines on 1st October. While in Bodmin there was an Administrative Inspection by Brigadier Cazenove, and the opportunity was taken to put every man through the complete war course at Millpool range on the Moor. Also at this time Support Company was formed by taking the Carrier and Mortar Platoons from Headquarter Company, and raising the Anti-Tank and Assault Pioneer Platoons.

The concentration of the 6th DCLI around Bodmin gave all ranks a number of chances to watch the Battalion's excellent football team playing matches against the teams of other units. Lieutenant-Colonel Fletcher, who had himself been a good amateur footballer, always encouraged a good battalion team and 6 DCLI was fortunate in having a number of very good players. In particular there was Serjeant Ramsey who, as a professional after the war, played in and later managed the England team. After England won the World Cup in 1966 he became Sir Alf Ramsey.

The New 1st Battalion, 9th December 1942

On 6th June 1942 the 1st Battalion fought the calamitous battle of Bir-el-Harmat (see p. 315 *et seq.*) To these DCLI soldiers stationed in Cornwall, the news of the destruction of the 1st Battalion in North Africa came as a terrible and traumatic shock. It seemed almost inconceivable that one of the two regular battalions of the Regiment should have been virtually annihilated in a single day's fighting, and now no longer existed as a unit in the Order of Battle.

During the autumn of 1942 rumours began to circulate concerning some possible future connection between the 6th and 1st Battalions, but it was not till November that any official announcement clarified them. A small cadre of 2 officers and 10 soldiers, survivors of the Western Desert, were to join the 6th, which would then be re-designated the 1st Battalion. By this time the 6th had left Walker Lines and returned to its old operational area on the coast around Helston. On 9th December 1942 a Part II Order was published which effectively transferred every officer and soldier of the 6th Battalion to the re-formed 1st. On the same day a ceremonial parade was held at Helston to mark this transition, at which Lieutenant-General A.N. Floyer-Acland, CB, DSO, MC (representing the Colonel of the Regiment who was on duty in America) presented Colours to Lieutenant-Colonel Fletcher and his battalion. It is perhaps of interest that the current 1st Battalion Colours were then still in India. The Quartermaster, Lieutenant W. Edwards, was therefore despatched to Bodmin to remove the 1883 stand of Colours from the Regimental Aisle of St Petroc's Church and bring them to Helston. After the ceremony they were returned to St Petroc's where they still hang today. The final story of this Battalion has been told in pp. 320-321 of this book.

Training for war, & preparations for the invasion of Normandy, December 1942-Spring 1944

Soon after assuming its new title of 1st Battalion The Duke of Cornwall's Light Infantry, the Battalion left Cornwall Coastal Area, moving from Helston to Barton Stacey Camp in Hampshire. The main body travelled by troop train from Helston Station to Andover, and from there marched to its new location. The Battalion was now in the 25th Infantry Brigade, part of the 47th (London) Infantry Division. The other battalions in the Brigade were one each from the 9th Royal Norfolks and 2nd Essex. The brigade commander was Brigadier A.H. Blest, late Essex Regiment.

The 47th Division, consisting of three brigades, was stationed in battalion locations over a large part of Hampshire and later the Isle of Wight as well. Most of the accommodation consisted of requisitioned buildings. Moves from one location to another were fairly frequent. The policy must have been not to allow units and troops generally to become too settled and static. Between December 1942 and July 1943 the Battalion spent about two months in each of four locations, namely:

Barton Stacey Camp, complete battalion
The Grange, Alresford, with two companies at Bighton
Ringwood, with two companies at Burley
Whitwell, Isle of Wight, with companies at Ventnor & Appuldurcombe

During this period the training consisted mainly of battalion and brigade exercises. Company and platoon training filled the gaps between these exercises. There was no specific defence or counter-attack role; the Battalion was part of a field formation which trained for all phases of war. This was the policy for most infantry divisions in the United Kingdom at this time.

In the summer of 1943 a large-scale embarkation exercise took place in the Southampton area, with the aim of practising the embarkation of a large British and Canadian force for an assault crossing of the Channel. The 47th Division provided troops for the organisation and staffing of the various marshalling areas through which the force would pass, where it would be broken down into craft loads in readiness for embarkation.

In order to carry out this role, the Battalion moved from the Isle of Wight to Southampton, where it was located with headquarters at Glen Eyre, with the companies deployed in camps at Basset, Taunton School and Hursley. Battalion headquarters worked closely with Movement Control; its role was monitoring the marshalling and movement process within the Battalion's area of responsibility. Once units of the embarking force were packed up and divided into craft loads, they had not only to be accommodated and fed but also given all necessary administrative assistance. Many of the procedures were new, and it was therefore a period of trial and error. The United States Army sent observers to study the organisation, a number of their officers living with the Battalion. The lessons learnt from this exercise were to prove invaluable in the planning for the invasion of Normandy the following year.

At the end of the exercise the Battalion moved back to the Isle of Wight, initially to Rookley and then to Freshwater, where it was accommodated in Golden Hill Fort and Brambles Holiday Camp.

By Christmas 1943 the Battalion found itself in Bournemouth, living in one very large requisitioned hotel. Soon after Christmas the whole of 47th Division moved to Co. Durham and North Yorkshire, in order to act with other formations as the enemy in a large exercise designed to test the formations ear-marked for the coming invasion. The Battalion was accommodated in the north western part of Co. Durham with headquarters at Hamsterley Hall, and the companies in requisitioned accommodation at Annfield Plain, Stanley and Dipton – quite a contrast from either Cornwall or Hampshire.

The exercise itself took place on the Yorkshire Wolds in the early spring of 1944. The Battalion was in a defensive position very near Sledmere, between Malton and Driffield, facing south west. Including the time spent in digging and preparing positions and filling them in after the exercise, the Battalion spent two to three weeks in the field living in bivouacs or in slit trenches. On conclusion of the exercise it returned to Co. Durham.

After this major exercise, two battalions from the Division were transferred to form part of a new independent brigade destined for the invasion. Hope, coupled with apprehension, ran high that the Battalion, which had trained so hard for so long, might also be picked for this role. This was not to be (possibly because the 5th Battalion was already committed to this force); sadly it was accepted that the 1st would be denied the opportunity to fight on the mainland of Europe.

Staffing embarkation camps, 1944

In approximately April, 1944, the Division moved south again, in order to become part of the marshalling organisation for the D Day invasion of Europe. As none of the support weapons nor a proportion of battalion transport were needed for this task, a number of Support Company and MT personnel moved to West Hartlepool, where they remained for three or four months.

The setting up of the camps and vehicle parks in the marshalling areas was no exercise; this time it was the real thing. The Battalion was stationed in an area between Southampton and Gosport with headquarters at Sarisbury. Companies provided staff for various camps in this area as well as at Sarisbury itself. These camps were mainly tented; one was in the grounds of Bay House, close to Gosport, where specialised armour was being assembled and long hessian screens were erected inside the wire perimeter fence to prevent anyone outside the camp from seeing in. Another camp was in an old fort.

The organisation and arrangements were made as they had been on the exercise at Southampton the previous year except that this time, as June approached, all outgoing mail was censored by each unit's own officers. Another difference was that shortly before the assault troops were called forward for embarkation, they were given their orders, briefings and maps. The camps were then immediately sealed. No movement in or out of the camps was permitted apart from the troops moving to the embarkation points. Not until several days after D Day were the camps unsealed.

Other units continued to pass through the camps during the build-up in Normandy. Some weeks later, with the build-up complete, the camps were closed down; the 47th (London) Division was disbanded and its units were dispersed to other formations.

Movement of officers & men, & role in training men as infantry

After moving into requisitioned accommodation at Shoreham-on-Sea for a few weeks, the 1st Battalion became part of the 55th (Lancashire) Division, at Hove.

At Hove, Support Company and the MT details which had been left at West Hartlepool rejoined the Battalion, making it complete once more. Life at Hove was a considerable improvement on that in the tented camps of the marshalling area. During this period numbers of officers and men who had been passed as fit after being wounded in Italy or Normandy were posted in the Battalion. The British order of battle was in a state of considerable flux, with many anti-aircraft units being disbanded. Many of those left without a unit found their way to the 1st Battalion, including officers and men from the 4th DCLI. At the same time that these men were joining, drafts were being despatched to France, many, but not all, to the 5th DCLI. It was a strenuous time for the Adjutant and Orderly Room staff.

The Battalion's next role was the re-training of men from Royal Artillery light anti-aircraft regiments as infantry. As a result of the Allies gaining air supremacy in North West Europe it had become possible to reduce the number of light anti-aircraft regiments in France and convert the personnel into infantry reinforcements. Under the first scheme men were flown back to England and formed into platoons badged to different regiments. After several weeks re-training complete platoons returned to France to their new infantry regiments. Later, men from a variety of units passed through the Battalion for training and re-training, and were then drafted to North West Europe.

On being posted to the British Military Mission to Ethiopia, Lieutenant-Colonel Fletcher left 1 DCLI, in March 1945. He was succeeded by Lieutenant-Colonel J.B. Peter-Hoblyn, who had been Second-in-Command since returning with the cadre from the former 1st Battalion in December 1942. Soon afterwards the 55th Division moved from Sussex to South Wales. The Battalion moved first to temporary accommodation in the grounds of Picton Castle near Haverfordwest in Pembrokeshire and then, a week or two later, to good hutted accommodation in Castlemartin Camp, the base for the Royal Armoured Corps tank ranges. For the time being there were few armoured units left in the United Kingdom so the camp and the ranges were not in use. Training of reinforcements for overseas service continued and full use was made of the excellent field firing facilities.

THE 7TH (HOME SERVICE) BATTALION, LATER TO BECOME THE 30TH BATTALION

The 7th (Home Service) Battalion, 1939-1941

Static Home Defence guard duties

The 7th (Home Service) Battalion consisted in the main of elderly reservists and volunteers who, although medically down-graded for front line service, were retained for the purpose of carrying out static guard duties.

Its origins are interesting in that they show how far from simple was the organisation of some of these home defence units. A Company was formed at Truro shortly before the outbreak of war on 24th August 1939. Although in effect DCLI, it formed part of the 10th (Home Service) Battalion the Devonshire Regiment, in which it was designated the 1st Cornish Company. It performed static guard duties at vulnerable points across Cornwall. E Company, 10th Devons was formed at Liskeard on 1st January 1940. The 5th Battalion was then temporarily stationed at Liskeard, so E Company immediately took over all that Battalion's static guard duties in the area. In May the Company moved to Falmouth, where it relieved a battalion of the Royal Ulster Rifles and took on guard duties around the docks and at St Eval airfield. In the same month H Company, 10th Devons was also formed at Falmouth. E and H Companies provided invaluable support for the disembarkation and administration of the 17,500 officers and men of the British Expeditionary Force who passed through Falmouth, having been evacuated from Cherbourg just before the fall of France. Major Cannings, commanding the two-company group, found himself showered with gifts from the grateful returning units. Consumables, which could be eaten or drunk by his men in their billets, caused no problems, but two *buckshee* Bren guns and a 30 cwt lorry (none of which was on issue to Home Defence battalions) proved more difficult to account for, and were quickly confiscated by higher authority. The two companies also provided guards for a valuable consignment of industrial diamonds passing through the port. They also stood by in case it became necessary to use force to take over a French warship lying in the docks. A fourth company was also raised in Cornwall, but as this was allocated to the 70th (Home Defence) Battalion the Gloucestershire Regiment and as it was quickly posted out of the County, its story need not concern us here.

In July 1940 E and H Companies left Falmouth, being bombed as they departed. E Company went into a tented camp at Marsh Mills, while H Company was allotted billets in Wembury (both places just outside Plymouth). There they were allotted tasks guarding Plymouth gas works, oil tanks and bridges.

By this time the 10th Devons had grown to an unwieldy size, so it was decided to split the Battalion and return the three Cornish companies to their county of origin. Accordingly, on 14th October 1940, A, E and H Companies became A, B and D Companies of the newly designated 7th (Home Service) Battalion DCLI. A fourth company, C Company, was formed by crossposting a number of men from the existing companies. Lieutenant-Colonel W.H. Liddell, MM was appointed to command the new Battalion, in which his men now wore the DCLI cap badge. The Headquarters moved from Plymouth to Camborne, with the companies dispersed across the whole of Cornwall, carrying out guard duties at vulnerable points.

In August 1941 Battalion Headquarters moved to Falmouth, and shortly afterwards Lieutenant-Colonel E.E. Mulock, MC took over command. At that time A Company was based at Land's End, B Company at Fowey, C Company at Falmouth and D Company on the Lizard. At the end of August about 150 men from the Pioneer Corps were posted in, which enabled a fifth company to be formed. This was based at Falmouth where the largest part of the workload was centred.

The 30th (Home Service) Battalion

Guard duties & counter-attack training in Cornwall

The whims of the War Office were always unpredictable, so it was with no great surprise that the officers and men of the 7th (Home Service) Battalion DCLI woke up one morning in September 1941 to learn that they now belonged to the 30th (Home Service) Battalion DCLI. The role and tasks of this newly designated battalion remained precisely as before.

To relieve the boredom of continuous guard duties, exercises were occasionally carried out. One such exercise, known as Operation 'Pilchard', involved an attack on Falmouth by the 11th Devons, stoutly resisted by the 30th DCLI. In January 1942 orders were received that the Battalion was to relieve the 30th West Yorkshire Regiment on the Isles of Scilly. In the event, only B, D and E Companies together with Battalion Headquarters moved to the islands; A and C Companies remained on the mainland at Porthcurno, with a rear headquarters established under Major C.A.G.S. Sim at Penzance. However, not long after this, Major Sim was posted to Predannack airfield as Defence Officer, his place being taken by Major W.I. Pool – a man, born and bred in Penzance. The appointment of Defence Officer is interesting. In the early years of the war, the task of guarding RAF airfields had fallen on Home Defence battalions of the army. Later however, it had been decided that soldiers were not being best used tied down to static guard duties, but should be trained in a mobile counter-attack role. The RAF were therefore instructed to make airmen available to guard their own airfields. The RAF replied that, while they could produce the airmen, they had no officers with military experience who could organise and train such a force. Accordingly, every airfield was allotted an army officer for this purpose. It is likely to have been a fairly relaxed posting. Later, the Royal Air Force Regiment was established, with its own RAFR officers.

On 6th May 1942 His Majesty the King visited Falmouth and inspected representative detachments of troops located in the South West. Lieutenant-Colonel Mulock took part in the parade with 2 officers and 37 soldiers. This was his last parade with the Battalion for on 13th June he was posted to the staff, and was succeeded by Lieutenant-Colonel H.F. Joslen. It will be remembered that he had commanded the 2nd Battalion during the evacuation from Dunkirk after Lieutenant-Colonel E. R. Rushton had been killed.

On 15th August a change of role raised hopes that the long days of guard duties might be nearing an end, and that the Battalion might go overseas. The 30th Battalion now became a counter-attack unit. 233 soldiers were drafted in from the 30th Somerset Light Infantry, and with the Battalion now well up to establishment, hard mobile training began. All ranks thoroughly enjoyed this new work, and it was good to see how the men, most of whom were medically downgraded, rose to the challenge.

Alas, this period was short-lived, and expectations were dashed when in October the Battalion reverted to its old role of static guard duties around Cornwall. Despondency was further reinforced in February 1943 by an order that every officer and soldier who was eligible for overseas service should be posted out of the 30th Battalion, and posted to the Oxfordshire and Buckinghamshire Light Infantry and to the 1st, 4th and 5th Battalions DCLI. To compensate for this loss, drafts of medically downgraded men were received from the Wiltshire Regiment, the Seaforth Highlanders, the King's Regiment, the Royal Norfolk Regiment, the Queen's Regiment and the Royal Inniskilling Fusiliers. What had once been a battalion of Cornishmen guarding Cornish soil was now a motley crew from all over the British Isles. It is to the enduring credit of Lieutenant-Colonel Joslen and his Regimental Serjeant-Major that this diverse group of men was quickly welded into a happy and efficient battalion.

At the end of April 1943, while the Battalion was involved in a change of companies between the Isles of Scilly and the mainland, an order was suddenly received to relieve the 30th Devons, then carrying out guard duties in East Cornwall and Devon. To complicate an already far from simple relief, yet more officers were posted away to other battalions of the Regiment. Scarcely had this move been effected than further orders were received on 17th June that the 30th was to mobilise for overseas service in a tropical climate. Mobilization was to be complete by 5th July. When one considers all that had to be achieved in eighteen days – medical inoculations, issue and fitting of tropical kit, handing in to Ordnance of vehicles, weapons and stores, packing of unit stores for a sea voyage, plus the entitlement of ten days' embarkation leave for every officer and soldier – one marvels at what was expected of a battalion in those days. Thankfully, the deadline was extended a further twenty days.

The 30th Battalion now became part of 42 Infantry Brigade, commanded by Brigadier P.H. Cadoux-Hudson, MC, late the Hampshire Regiment. The other battalions in the brigade were: the 30th Royal Northumberland Fusiliers, 30th Bedfordshire and Hertfordshire Regiment, 30th Royal Norfolk Regiment, 30th Green Howards and 31st Suffolk Regiment.

Algeria, August 1943-March 1944

On 13th August 1943 the Battalion left Falmouth for Glasgow in two troop trains. The trains arrived at the docks early the following morning, and the Battalion immediately embarked in HMT *Ormonde*. This ship, a pre-war luxury liner, now offered few comforts for the four infantry battalions and ancillary units packed into every available space. The *Ormonde* lay at anchor in the Clyde for three days while the convoy was assembled. At last, on the evening of 16th August, the ships put to sea, and skirting the north coast of Ireland, steamed west into the open Atlantic. Several destroyers and two aircraft carriers kept watch.

At first light on 23rd August the convoy passed through the Straits of Gibraltar, and at 6 p.m. the following day docked at Algiers. The 30th Battalion disembarked and moved by motor transport some twenty miles to a tented camp known only by the title 'Z Camp', as desolate a spot as one could ever imagine, situated in the desert near the malodorous village of Ben Zirga. All water had to be carried in bowsers from wells many miles away, and arrived warm and smelling of chlorine. In spite of the intense heat, this precious commodity was strictly rationed. Flies appeared by magic in their millions, and the hot Sirocco wind blew sand and dust into every nook and cranny. Many who had yearned for overseas service were already looking back at their days of soldiering in Cornwall with nostalgia.

The companies were widely distributed across the area, carrying out guard duties that included the Divisional workshops at Hussein Dey and a prisoner of war camp holding Italian prisoners. In September the Battalion was delighted to bid farewell to Z Camp, and move to Y Camp near Fort de L'Eau, eight miles from Algiers. Here, as the name suggests, there was adequate fresh water, and the tents were more sheltered from the dust-laden wind. At about this time Lieutenant-Colonel Joslen was admitted to hospital and his place taken by the Second-in-Command, Major H. Cantan. Lieutenant-Colonel Cantan (as he soon became) was a son of the Regiment, who had served with both the 1st and 2nd Battalions in many outlandish stations. He fully realised that however desolate the company detachments might be, it was vital that officers and men had a firm base which offered every facility for comfort, relaxation and recreation that ingenuity could devise. Winter was approaching, and the heat of the desert summer would soon give way to rain and cold. A number of Nissen huts were scrounged, which replaced the tents used as dining-rooms and canteens. A theatre, complete with stage and lighting, was built in one of these huts, and decorated by some artistically gifted Italian prisoners of war. Perhaps most importantly, Lieutenant-Colonel Cantan visited the company detachments frequently, making them feel that they were not forgotten. By these and other means, the morale of the 30th Battalion, employed as it was on dull and tedious duties in the most uncongenial surroundings, was kept up.

During March 1944 certain of the DCLI duties were taken over by the 30th Bedfordshire and Hertfordshire Regiment, giving Lieutenant-Colonel Cantan an opportunity to plan a training programme, by which each of the rifle companies would be pulled back in turn and given a refresher course in weapon training, fieldcraft and minor tactics.

A Company was the first to be put through this training, but half way through it the Battalion received orders to move.

Egypt, 1944-1946

The 30th Battalion travelled by train from Algiers to Oran, and thence by ship to Port Said. A few weeks were spent in a camp at El Tahag, near Qassassin (the scene of the 2nd Battalion battle during the Egyptian War of 1882). Here duties were few, and the opportunity was taken to despatch leave parties to the bright lights of Cairo. El Tahag, it was learnt, was only a staging post, and in June the Battalion moved to Suez where it embarked in the troopship HMT *Dilwara*. After three days of passage south down the Red Sea, the *Dilwara* arrived at the port of Massawa on the Eritrean coast. The heat was intense, far greater than that experienced in the Algerian desert the previous summer, and tropical helmets were therefore issued. The following day the Battalion set out for Asmara in ancient Italian diesel lorries. Asmara stands at 9,000 feet above sea level, surrounded by arid mountainous desert. The country had been captured from the Italians by General Wavell in 1941, with the result that there were many prisoner of war camps that had to be guarded. The Battalion was therefore dispersed over a very wide area. One of the more congenial of these camps was situated at Wadi Halfa on the River Nile. The company currently carrying out that duty was also required to provide a guard for the *Kaid* (the military commander in the Sudan). The *Kaid*, Major-General W.H.C. Ramsden, CB, CBE, DSO, MC, whose headquarters were in Khartoum, took an interest in the welfare of his DCLI soldiers, ensuring that they were made as comfortable and happy as circumstances permitted. One of his many kind gestures was to put his official launch at their disposal for recreational purposes.

In January 1945 C Company (commanded by Major P. Hodge) moved to Cartago, where political prisoners were housed in an old RAF camp. The country could hardly have been more desolate nor the job less interesting, but the accommodation was good compared with the ragged tented camps to which all ranks had become used. For no apparent reason this particular prison camp was not closed down after the surrender of Germany, and its inmates remained behind wire till late 1946. A redeployment then took place, whereby Battalion Headquarters, B, C, and D Companies were concentrated in Khartoum, leaving A Company out on a limb at Asmara. Demobilization had started soon after the German surrender. Those leaving were replaced by officers and men from the 60th Rifles, the Middlesex Regiment and various regiments of the Royal Armoured Corps. Guard duties continued, but these became less of a burden, leaving more time for recreation and sport. As can be imagined, there was an inevitable feeling of unrest; the war was over, and the thought of getting back home was naturally uppermost in everybody's mind.

Lieutenant-Colonel T. Kinnersly had assumed command on 18th May 1945. He had served with the 2nd Battalion in North Africa before being seriously wounded, and had only recently been passed fit to be posted overseas. On his shoulders fell the onerous task of maintaining morale in a dwindling unit composed of men from half the regiments in the army, who were occupied in carrying out extremely humdrum tasks.

In December 1945 the 30th Battalion (less A Company) was relieved by the 8th Royal Warwickshire Regiment. It moved by rail to Wadi Halfa and then by river steamer and barge to Shellal, which lies just south of the Aswan Dam. From there, the intention was that it should continue north by rail on the morning express. There was however insufficient space for everybody, and the Battalion became split up, some travelling on the express, some by a later slow train, and the long-suffering baggage party, who had to shift fifty tons of stores at each transhipment, travelling in a still later goods train. On the 10th January the first party pulled into Cairo station. Their tribulations were not however at an end, for on arrival they found the platform bedecked with flags and banners, and a reception party of Egyptian VIPs awaiting the imminent arrival of His Majesty King Ibn Saud. Four hundred tired, unwashed and heavily laden soldiers were definitely not what was required to increase the dignity of the occasion. The somewhat mystified men were chivvied in an undignified manner to the waiting motor transport that was to take them to their camp at Almaza, and driven through a crowded cheering throng held back by Egyptian soldiers and police. At Almaza they enjoyed the luxury of a hot shower and a good cooked meal, the first for several days.

A Company eventually rejoined from Asmara a few days later, but by this time the end of the saga was clearly in sight. Lieutenant-Colonel Kinnersly had already left for demobilization, and Lieutenant-Colonel C.V. Whiting of the Royal Welch Fusiliers, who succeeded him, formed those who were left into a single company. On 12th January 1946 the 30th Battalion DCLI held its final parade before disbandment. The majority returned home for demobilization, while the few who still had time to serve were interviewed, and given some choice as to their future posting.

The 7th Battalion, and the 30th Battalion into which it metamorphosed, did not aspire to the glamour that has traditionally been the soldier's due. It consisted of medically downgraded men who carried out duties that were for the most part intensely dull. It is, however, a remarkable fact that this Battalion, composed in the latter stages of the war of men from many different regiments and even arms, maintained a quiet pride in its achievements. Much of the credit for this must be with the robust character of its soldiers. However, without a high standard of leadership from the officers and NCOs, this state of morale could not have been maintained during these six and a half years, much of them spent in some of the least prepossessing parts of the world. Although the Battalion never fired a shot in anger, it carried out vital duties that freed front line troops to fight the enemy. The debt owed to these humble supporting units should not be forgotten.

THE DEPÔT, NO. 46 INFANTRY TRAINING CENTRE

In the latter part of 1938, as the probability of war with Germany became ever stronger, so did the number of recruits joining the Regiment increase. By late September not only was the Depôt at Bodmin full to capacity, but very obvious preparations were being made in case of air attack. Shelter trenches were dug in the adjoining fields, blast walls were constructed across ground floor windows, and blackout material was issued to all married families in quarters. In the barrack rooms, two tier bunks were introduced to double capacity, while the Quartermaster's store was reorganised with a single long counter which allowed the staff to kit out recruits far more quickly. (Part of that counter, when this book was written, was still doing duty as the ticket and shop counter in the Regimental Museum at Bodmin.)

By the end of 1938 it appeared that the Prime Minister, Mr Neville Chamberlain, might have succeeded in averting war. Once more the Depôt settled down to its routine of training, intermixed with generous periods of games and sports.

The immediate effect of the declaration of war on 3rd September 1939 was for the Depôt to become one of the many Infantry Training Centres newly established around Britain. Enlistment was immediately introduced, and if Victoria Barracks had appeared overcrowded before, it was now doubly so. A hutted camp had already been partially completed on the far side of the barrack wall to the south, but this appears not to have been used to house recruits. Instead, a tented camp was pitched nearby to accommodate the additional influx. It was not intended that this should be anything but a temporary solution as, at the same time, plans for major works services to extend the capacity of the accommodation blocks in Victoria Barracks were drawn up. It was perhaps fortunate for the preservation of the integrity of these fine Victorian buildings that this work was never executed.

Because of the immediate introduction of conscription, the incoming drafts of recruits could be anticipated with some degree of accuracy. There was therefore never the near-chaos that had overwhelmed the Depôt in the first weeks of the Great War. Much of the credit for the smooth transition from a peace-time Depôt to a wartime Infantry Training Centre must rest with Major G.H.J. Mercer (promoted to Lieutenant-Colonel as his establishment expanded), who had taken over as Depôt Commander in 1937. Amongst his many other tasks was to reorganise the training programme so that the instruction, which had previously occupied sixteen weeks, could be condensed into eight. He also became responsible for the system whereby above-average recruits were picked at an early stage for training as specialists (for example, signallers, drivers, and machine-gunners).

In June 1940 after the fall of France, every soldier, whether fully trained or not, was urgently needed to guard the coast against invasion. At that time the DCLI Infantry Training Centre (as it was initially designated) consisted of a headquarters, a headquarter company, a specialist company and two rifle companies. Headquarter Company remained in Victoria Barracks, being responsible for its defence; the remainder were deployed in defensive positions along the coast from St Austell to Mevagissey. Nights were spent in the weapon pits but after stand down each morning the recruits were withdrawn, first for a wash and shave, and then for a day of training. It was an exhausting routine, but for the young recruits a valuable experience. Back at Victoria Barracks, concrete roadblocks were erected on all approaches, and loopholes knocked through the walls of the adjoining railway station to provide additional arcs of fire.

In October the recruit companies returned to Bodmin, and from then on training proceeded without any undue interruption. Manpower was, however, organised to form a rapid reaction force, which was periodically tested, using the Home Guard as enemy.

In January 1942 the Infantry Training Centre, which up to that time had been known by the prefix DCLI, changed its name to the anonymous No. 46 Infantry Training Centre. However, by any name, its days were numbered. The United States Army had begun arriving in England, posing many problems for the Quartermaster General's department, not least of which was where they should be accommodated. In April 1942 all intakes to the Infantry Training Centre at Bodmin were suspended, and plans were made to amalgamate with the Infantry Training Centre at Dorchester. In late 1942 Victoria Barracks was handed over to the United States Army, and was occupied by the 115th Infantry Regiment, commanded by Colonel E.N. Happey, which formed part of the U.S. 29th Division. The American troops remained in Victoria Barracks till they embarked for the invasion of Normandy in June 1944.

30
The Cornwall Home Guard (formerly the Local Defence Volunteers)

The story of the Home Guard, and its metamorphosis from independent bands of ill-armed enthusiasts into a nation-wide military force with effective weapons and a proper organisation, is one of the most remarkable sagas of the Second World War.

From the earliest days it became apparent that the German army was using the tactic of dropping parachute troops well behind enemy lines. These men, trained in the arts of demolition and sabotage, were capable of inflicting severe disruption out of all proportion to their numbers. Although at this time there was no direct threat of invasion in Britain, it was fully appreciated that the nation was singularly ill prepared to counter parachute attacks of this nature.

Late on the evening of 11th May 1940, a meeting was held at the War Office to discuss the possibility of forming a citizen's defence force based in towns and villages. It was pointed out that civilians were already forming themselves into unofficial bands armed with shotguns, and that the sooner these were put on an authorised footing the better.

Matters moved fast. Two days later Mr Anthony Eden (the Home Secretary) had completed the draft of a speech calling for volunteers. This was approved by the War Office, and was transmitted over the wireless at 9.10 p.m. on 14th May 1940. It called for volunteers between the ages of sixteen and sixty-five to enrol into a force known as the Local Defence Volunteers. They would receive no pay, but would be armed with such weapons as were available. Anyone wishing to join should report to their nearest police station.

The response was overwhelming. Before Mr Eden had even stopped speaking, police stations up and down the country were being contacted by eager volunteers. By the following day an estimated 250,000 had put their names down. By the end of May there were in excess of 300,000 and by the end of June about 1,450,000 were registered.

The War Office had anticipated that between 150,000 and 200,000 men would come forward. This remarkable response caught the War Office unprepared. Not only was there an insufficiency of weapons, uniforms and equipment, but there was no adequate command structure. Furthermore, awesome events were taking place on the Continent which, although emphasising the urgent need for the Local Defence Force, rendered its birth traumatic in the extreme. Between 27th May and 4th June 1940 the British Expeditionary Force was evacuated from France. The problems confronted by the fledgling Local Defence Force became suddenly eclipsed by those faced by the regular army. Every available service rifle, recently ear-marked for the volunteers, was hurriedly issued to the regulars to replace losses incurred at Dunkirk, and the staff were thrown into the maelstrom of work involved in the post-Dunkirk deployment. The Local Defence Volunteers were largely left to use their own initiative and solve their own problems.

The original command structure, such as it was, devolved control of the Local Defence Volunteers into military areas. These areas provided the basis for all administration, and to each was attached a General Staff Officer Grade III (usually a Captain) who was responsible for all liaison between the appropriate military headquarters and the volunteer commander. The areas were split up into zones, which normally followed the police district boundaries. The areas, in their turn, were split up into groups comprising parish and village detachments.

Initially there were no military ranks in the Local Defence Volunteers. Officers were appointed by the County Lord-Lieutenants. They did not hold the King's Commission, nor did they have any authority over regular soldiers of any rank. Commanders at area, zone and group level were designated 'organisers'. These were responsible for organising their volunteers into companies and platoons.

Recruiting for the Local Defence Volunteers was carried out on a very tolerant basis. Although the official age of acceptance was between sixteen and sixty-five, no questions were asked, providing the applicant was neither geriatric nor infantile. Those whom the police pointed out as known criminals could be refused without explanation. Volunteers became subject to military law when on duty, but it would seem that officers seldom if ever resorted to the official legal process in maintaining discipline; they did however have the power to dismiss a volunteer whose conduct was seriously detrimental to the unit. Volunteers were not paid, but those using their own cars, vans or lorries for military purpose were paid a mileage allowance. Officers could obtain 3rd Class railway warrants for essential travel.

The Local Defence Volunteers initially relied almost entirely on their own resources for weapons and equipment. No uniform was issued, and men made do with khaki armbands, printed with the letters LDV. Later, denim overalls were issued to be worn over civilian clothes and the County regimental cap badge. Appeals were launched in the press and on the wireless for weapons, maps, compasses, blankets, camp beds, typewriters, heating stoves and any miscellaneous equipment that might find a use. Weapons were obviously the most urgent requirement, and a surprising collection of elderly shotguns and game rifles were handed in. Museums were stripped of their collections and defunct Boys Brigade units surrendered their old Henry-Martini carbines. However, in spite of all this, many men faced their duties armed only with a billhook or an improvised pike.

The attitude adopted by many senior officers at the War Office was that the Local Defence Volunteers were at best a sop to the nation's aggressive instinct, and at worst a menace to any military commander attempting to fight a battle. Of more immediate concern was the fear that this new force would incur a constant drain on scarce and valuable resources. It is interesting that this argument was exactly the one put forward by the military hierarchy in 1859 with regard to the formation of the Rifle Volunteers. It was largely due to the enthusiasm of the Prime Minister, Mr Winston Churchill, that the force was given fresh impetus. Not only did he change the name to the more imaginative one of Home Guard, but he identified himself with this citizen's army and was instrumental in widening its role to include more aggressive activities. In order to lend more dignity to the force, Churchill ordered that officers and men should adopt honorary military rank; thus, on 7th November Area and Zone Organisers became Lieutenant-Colonels and Majors, and Group Leaders became Captains, while those with stripes on their arms were known as Serjeants, Corporals and Lance-Corporals. He was also responsible for persuading the USA to part with many thousands of American-made P17 Enfield .300 in. rifles.

On 17th May 1940 Colonel Charles Graves was approached by the Lord-Lieutenant of Cornwall, Lieutenant-Colonel E.H.W. Bolitho, DSO, who invited him to raise a battalion of Local Defence Volunteers within the county. Between them, they decided that it should be organised into six companies, corresponding to the six police divisions. These were:

Falmouth	Lieutenant-Colonel Gooden, OBE
Land's End and Camborne	Major Watson-Smyth
St Austell	Lieutenant-Colonel Stericker, DSO
Liskeard	Vice-Admiral Wicks-Sneyd, DSO

Truro	Major Carey-Norman
Launceston	Major Colville, MC

How many battalions could boast such an august gathering of company commanders?

From the very start it became apparent that a single battalion would be unable to cope with the flood of applications; indeed, the Land's End and Camborne Company alone was over a thousand strong within a few days of formation. On 15th October the county was therefore split into two Zones (battalions), known as the North Cornwall and West Cornwall Zones. The whole of Cornwall now came under the command of Brigadier-General W.D. Croft , CB, CMG, DSO, ably assisted by Mr M. Williams who, as a Master of Foxhounds, knew every inch of the country.

Men from all classes and from all walks of life enlisted. Many were old soldiers who had seen active service in the Great War and even the South African War; many were chubby-faced boys just out of school; quite a few were well versed in the skills of poaching, an activity which required the stealth and cunning so important to the volunteers' task. All possessed an infectious enthusiasm. Both the Lord-Lieutenant and the Bishop of Truro joined, the latter demonstrating a fine example of the 'Church Militant', though never rising above the exalted rank of Private.

As has been mentioned, there was initially an almost complete lack of small arms. To make up for this deficiency a number of strange and, for the most part, highly impractical weapons were hastily conceived. What they all had in common was extreme cheapness. The first to be introduced to the Cornwall Volunteers, on 21st June 1940, was an incendiary grenade. Its construction could not have been simpler, consisting as it did of a beer bottle filled with a mixture of petrol and creosote, with a fuze made from a strip of photographic film. Lighting the fuze in wind or rain was obviously far from simple. Shortly after this, Ordnance produced a somewhat more sophisticated version, known officially as the Grenade, Self-Igniting Phosphorous, No.76, and referred to by all and sundry as the Molotov Cocktail (because they had originally been used in the Russian Revolution). The filling of these grenades now included phosphorous, which obviated the requirement for a fuze. Early in 1941 the Cornishmen received supplies of the Grenade, Anti-Tank, No.73. This consisted of a cylindrical biscuit tin full of blasting gelignite. It went off with a monumental bang, and was of almost equal danger to friend and foe. Finally, there was the Sticky Bomb or Grenade, Anti-Tank, No.74. This was perhaps the most hazardous of the lot. It had been dreamed up by boffins who did not actually have to use it, but had been vetoed by the Munitions Directorate as being far too dangerous. Churchill, who loved innovative devices, the more bizarre the better, thought otherwise and despatched a terse note to the Board of Ordnance stating 'Sticky Bomb. Make one million. WSC'.

These grenades consisted of a spherical glass flask covered with stockinette impregnated with an extremely sticky substance. The intrepid bomber had to go right up to the enemy tank and smash the bomb against the armour. Nor was this the only hazard, for once the protective metal cover had been jettisoned, the bomb had an unnerving habit of becoming irrevocably stuck to the thrower's clothing.

Three close-support weapons were also issued at about the same time. These all succeeded in combining the minimum threat to the enemy with the maximum danger to their crews: the Northover Projector, a length of steel piping from which Molotov Cocktails could be fired; the Smith Gun, which was so hazardous that even the most enthusiastic volunteers balked at its use, one Cornish battalion commander stating bluntly that it had 'a terrifying reputation for killing its crew'; and finally the Blacker Bombard, or Spigot Mortar as it was later christened, which was so inaccurate that at an early demonstration it nearly killed General de Gaulle, who was watching – an occurence that would not have improved British-Free French relations. The introduction of these was strongly championed by Churchill on the grounds that 'Each of these weapons requires three or more men to operate, and they all feel that it belongs to them and forget, for the moment at any rate, that they have not got a rifle.'

On 27th August 1940 the Royal Observer Corps was established in Cornwall and, because it was paid, took many men away from the Home Guard. In spite of this there appears to have been ample available man-power, allowing the Cornwall Home Guard to expand from two to fourteen battalions. These were designated as follows:

1st	(Stratton)	Battalion
2nd	(Coastal)	Battalion
3rd	(Castle) (Launceston)	Battalion
4th	(Wadebridge)	Battalion
5th	(St Austell)	Battalion
6th	(Liskeard)	Battalion
7th	(Falmouth)	Battalion
8th	(Helston)	Battalion
9th	(Camborne)	Battalion
10th	(Truro)	Battalion

11th	(Newquay)	Battalion
12th	(Land's End)	Battalion
13th	(Bodmin)	Battalion
14th	(Hayle)	Battalion

Sadly, no histories of these units have survived, and we do not even know exactly when they were formed. The fourteen-battalion establishment did not suddenly spring into existence but developed over a period of several months. As units became too large to be effectively administered they split, like amoeba, into two or more battalions. For instance, Truro and Newquay initially had a single battalion commanded by Major Harvey, but this later divided in two, the Newquay half being commanded by Lieutenant-Colonel T. Holman. Lieutenant-General Sir Frederick Morgan, the GOC, seems not to have entertained a high opinion of these men, writing 'those of Cornwall were nothing but a lot of damned foreigners who, as likely as not, would welcome the Germans'. For their part, the Cornishmen reckoned those of Devon to be 'a soft lot who could be relied in no way to resist the enemy.'

The 10th (Truro) Battalion appears to have acquired a launch in which detachments patrolled the Truro, Fal and Percueil rivers. Much of their energy seems to have been given over to conducting a protracted and often acrimonious correspondence with the Admiralty, demanding that their launch be allowed to fly the White Ensign. Not unnaturally, this was refused.

The 11th (Newquay) Battalion formed an Old Comrades' Association after disbandment, which published two editions of a magazine entitled *The Chough Register*, named after the chough depicted on their battalion shoulder flash. From these, a certain amount of information can be gleaned. The first thing that must strike every reader is the sheer size of the Battalion. There were 40 platoons organised into 7 rifle companies. At its first and only full battalion parade, held on Newquay golf course on 16th May 1943, there were 1,328 officers and men on parade.

The first operational call-out of the Truro-Newquay Battalion occurred at 2.30 a.m. on 26th May 1940, when it was reported that German parachute troops had landed near Dover. At that time the Battalion possessed a total of fifteen Lee-Enfield rifles, which were kept in the Police Station at Truro. These were quickly issued out, and a detachment despatched to guard the roads leading to Falmouth. Meanwhile, the Newquay Company under Major Wise sprang into action, putting a tight cordon round the town and forbidding all movement either in or out. As the morning wore on, angry words were exchanged between the general public attempting to get on with its business and the men with their LDV armbands and assortment of shotguns. Not before time the stand down was given, allowing the excited men to return home and Newquay to get on with the day's business. It was later discovered that the cause of the alarm was a German aircraft dropping parachute mines off the Dover approaches. Poor Major Wise was subjected to a considerable amount of ridicule for his all-too effective action. He resigned, his place being taken by Captain Grigg.

On the night of 7th-8th September 1940 a warning was issued to all home defence troops that the tides were suitable for a seaborne invasion. Maximum vigilance was to be maintained. That evening, Conway Home Guard was called out; nobody knew why, but even after the force had been stood down, everybody remained jittery. Later that night the Vicar of St Ives saw the lights of the fishing fleet returning to harbour. Believing this to be an approaching wave of landing craft, he had the church bells rung (the age-old signal for invasion). Immediately one set of bells was rung, the alarm was automatically spread from parish to parish, so that by the evening a large part of Britain was under arms. 'All one could hear', the *Daily Herald* reported, 'was the echoing and re-echoing of the Home Guard challenge "Halt! – who goes there?" with occasional rifle shots when the challenged party failed to stop.'

All through 1941 the Home Guard took part in exercises of increasing complexity, often acting as enemy against regular troops. On some of these occasions they came up against men of the 7th Battalion DCLI.

Even in the best trained and disciplined regular units, accidents involving firearms occasionally occur, especially when men are tired. In the Home Guard, accidents of this nature were tragically not infrequent, and Cornwall appears to have suffered its full share. In September 1941 one man was killed and two seriously injured by a single shot negligently discharged by an NCO.

In January 1942 the first large-scale formation exercise was held across Cornwall. It was organised by Brigadier Cazenove, and was designed to test co-operation between the battalions and the local Defence Committees. Although the exercise degenerated into near chaos, it taught many valuable lessons by which its faults were afterwards rectified.

In the latter part of 1942 a new National Service Bill was drafted, with the principle aim of extending the age range in which men and women could be conscripted for military service. Many of those in reserved occupations had so far evaded any call-up. Should these men be conscripted into the Home Guard and, if so, should those already in the Home Guard as volunteers henceforth become conscripts, losing their right under the so-called 'Housemaid's Clause' to resign after giving a fortnight's notice? After considerable debate, conscription to the Home Guard became law. County Appeal Boards were set up which patiently listened to every complaint against conscription, as often as not allowing dispensation. Cornwall was accused of special leniency in this respect, excusing well over half the applicants. How much the inclusion of conscripts into this previously volunteer force was detrimental to its morale cannot be gauged with any degree of accuracy. It would seem that the scheme was handled by officers and NCOs with considerable sensitivity; even the term 'conscript' was avoided, some units referring to these men as 'directees'.

Officers and men of the Home Guard were never ones to accept authority without question, or to follow any accepted military procedure in making complaints or voicing their opinions. The complete mix of classes throughout the rank structure led to strange situations that were quite alien to the orderly mind of regular officers. Looking though Hansard, one finds references to the Bishop of Truro, who was a Private in the 10th Battalion, speaking in the House of Lords on Home Guard matters. Indeed, so many elderly Peers were members of the Home Guard that the House of Lords became a valuable platform on which grievances were frequently aired, and useful suggestions made. Slowly the Home Guard became a more effective force, with a wider role than that of merely carrying out static guards. Exercises became more realistic – indeed at times too realistic, and it was in respect of this that Cornwall once again fell foul of Lieutenant-General Sir Frederick Morgan, when he found that the tin miners in the 9th Battalion, finding the authorised training pyrotechnics somewhat tame, had taken to using sticks of dynamite, which they threw about apparently with gay abandon. Although no casualty figures ever appear to have been published, those sustained on training were undoubtedly higher than is generally imagined. They seem to have had little if any effect on the morale of that robust generation. Many were miners and fishermen, who were well inured to serious accidents. Colonel Graves went so far as to say 'It is impossible to make omelettes without breaking eggs, and there have been a certain number of casualties. These, however, have added zest rather than anxiety to the average Home Guard.'

On 6th September 1944 an announcement was made over the wireless to the effect that the Home Guard would shortly be disbanded, and that with immediate effect all duties would be carried out on a voluntary basis. Although everyone had anticipated that this was inevitable, the news came as a shock. For some, particularly the conscripts, it was welcome, but for many the Home Guard had become a way of life which had provided a unique experience, forging close friendships across the social spectrum.

The final stand down took place on Saturday, 3rd December 1945 and was marked by a great ceremonial parade through the streets of London, followed by an inspection by HM The King in Hyde Park. A total of nearly 8,000 men paraded, out of which 42 were from Cornwall. The County contingent was commanded by Captain W.A. Owen and included Regimental Serjeant-Major Wills of the 14th Battalion. They travelled up to London on the Friday night, being taken by waiting lorries to their billets, the officers to the Guards Mess Annexe in Sloane Street, and the men to Chelsea Barracks. That evening an officer and soldier from each county attended a banquet given by the Lord Mayor of London at the Guildhall, Captain Owen and Private Collins representing Cornwall. The following morning the parade assembled at Chelsea Barracks. The men had been royally treated the previous evening by their hosts, who had given them the run of the Corporals' Mess, and the following morning had each been brought a cup of tea in bed.

The parade was organised into a number of battalions made up of 4 companies, each 115 strong. The Cornishmen were in No.19 Company of the 5th Battalion. The Chelsea Barracks contingent moved off after lunch and marched the three miles to the assembly area; the dress was great-coats and steel helmets with rifles and sidearms, some of the more elderly finding it a bit of a trial (perhaps in no small measure the result of the Guards hospitality the previous evening). When all was ready the whole parade set off through the streets of London, marching in sixes with sloped arms, led by the Band of the Irish Guards. Enormous crowds lined the routes, fifteen deep in places. The cheering was terrific. Looking at photographs, one cannot but be impressed by the high standard of marching, more praiseworthy in that there had been no previous rehearsal. The following morning the Cornishmen were taken by motor transport to Paddington where a coach had been reserved for them. As a final example of hospitality shown by the Brigade of Guards, each man had been provided with a haversack lunch, which included a Cornish pasty.

The Home Guard had been a unique force in the military history of Great Britain. In certain ways it mirrored the Volunteers of 1803, which had been raised in response to the threat of another European tyrant, Napoleon Bonaparte. The Home Guard, however, existed on a far greater scale, and by 1944 was far more efficiently led, trained and equipped. The early nineteenth century Volunteer Force could muster a strength of about 380,000 in mainland Britain; at its peak in March 1943 the Home Guard could boast 1,793,000 officers and men.

Although the Home Guard was disbanded on 3rd December 1944,

it is not generally realised that it was briefly reconstituted at the time of the Korean War in 1951. Although a *News of the World* poll taken in 1944 had shown that 55% of the men wished the force to continue in the post-war days, the close spirit of comradeship had long since evaporated. A target figure of 170,000 was set for the new force but, in the event, no more than 30,000 volunteered. There was no sense of purpose, no feeling that the nation was in mortal danger, and none of the spirit that had brought men from all classes together to defend their homes against a foreign foe. In any case, the new force was very different to the old. No longer did men meet each evening to take up their allotted duties; instead a volunteer was required to undertake four periods of weekend training per year. Apart from the lack of interest from the general public, there was far too much interest shown by back benchers from both parties, who were almost unanimously against the project. In particular, Mr F.H. Hayman, Labour MP for Falmouth and Camborne, argued that the threat posed by a Communist 'fifth column' was entirely illusory. It was in large measure due to the support of Churchill, forever the advocate of the unconventional, that the force was ever allowed to come back into being.

On 20th December 1955 it was announced that the Territorial Army would be drastically reduced to a mere two Divisions. These would have no overseas role, but would henceforth be solely responsible for the defence of Britain. What then was the role of the Home Guard? From that day it only existed on paper, although county headquarters continued to be manned by elderly officers who answered the occasional letter from the War Office and drank gin in their depôt officers' messes at lunch time. The final *coup de grace* did not come till 31st July 1957 when the Secretary of State for War, Mr John Hare, announced that the Home Guard would finally cease to exist. His speech generated gales of laughter from the Labour benches: thus ended what had once been a great national institution.

II. THE POST-WAR REGIMENT

* * *

31
The 1st Battalion, 1945-1950

Wales & England, May-December 1945

When Germany surrendered on 7th May 1945 the Battalion was still stationed at Castlemartin, and shortly afterwards provided the main contingent in the Victory Parade at Haverfordwest.

Some weeks later the Battalion moved to Maresfield Camp in Sussex, to become part of 61st Infantry Division, which was being re-organised as a light division to be trained for the continuing war against the Japanese in Burma.

All over Sussex units could be seen performing somewhat farcical manoeuvres, known to the cynical soldiery as JEWTs or Jungle Exercises Without Trees. The first divisional exercise involved movement along roads through the flat open country of Kent and East Sussex, pretending that they were one-way tracks through thick jungle. Umpires created hold-ups supposedly caused by enemy rear-guards on broken-down vehicles, thereby imposing delays on the advancing troops, who exerted every effort to continue moving forward.

It was during this exercise that the Royal Signals rear link operators at Battalion HQ learnt from an unauthorised transmission that Japan had surrendered. 'The war is over' one of them stated. Soon afterwards Brigade HQ issued Exercise 'Standfast', followed about half an hour later by orders for the dispersal of all units back to their normal locations. The news appears to have made little impact until, on return to camp, word spread that the Division had been granted a fortnight free from all military duties, and that the Battalion was to move to empty accommodation on the coast near Lancing. Once there, the final victory was celebrated with enthusiasm, and the days were given over to swimming, football, cricket and just lying in the sun.

Over the next few months the composition of the Battalion changed fast. Many of the old DCLI officers and soldiers were posted, pending demobilization, and their places taken by new arrivals from the various Infantry Training Centres and units disbanding in

Germany, mostly from regiments other than the DCLI. It is to the credit of the Commanding Officer, Lieutenant-Colonel J.B. Peter-Hoblyn, that these men were integrated quickly.

With the end of the war trouble was brewing again in Palestine, and by November orders were received for a move to the Middle East. On 5th December 1945 the Battalion moved to Southampton and embarked on the pre-war luxury liner HMT *Strathmore*. It was a good voyage; the weather was kind, and the many new arrivals had the opportunity to get to know their comrades and make friends. Games, sports, film shows and concerts made the time pass quickly.

Palestine via Egypt, December 1945-1948

HMT *Strathmore* docked at Port Said on 14th December 1945. The comfortable part of the journey was now over, and a train of cattle wagons waited on the quay to take the Battalion south, down the canal to the transit camp at El Quassassin. The men were crowded thirty to a wagon, the train was excessively slow, and at each of many stops was surrounded by young Egyptian boys trying to sell dubious fruit, eggs and cheap trinkets. Although El Quassassin itself was unprepossessing in the extreme – a tented camp pitched in bleak desert – spirits were kept high by the knowledge that the sojourn there was to be of limited duration. Surprisingly enough, at this stage few if any knew of their final destination. Rumours had been rife since the departure from Southampton, but it was only at the El Quassassin transit camp that word was officially received that the 1st DCLI had been selected as the Demonstration Battalion at the Middle East School of Infantry, north of Acre in Palestine. The task involved the staging of tactical demonstrations at platoon, company and battalion level, with supporting elements of other arms. Needless to say, these demonstrations had to be carefully rehearsed and faultlessly carried out in front of senior officers and highly critical students at the School of Infantry. Every soldier would be well and truly in the spotlight. Quite apart from these duties, the whole area of Palestine was a hotbed of terrorist activity, with the British Army attempting to keep the peace between Arab and Jew. As so often happens in such bitter struggles, it was the British soldier who bore much of the brunt of the murderous anger between the races. Although the Battalion would not be deployed on anti-terrorist operations except in an emergency, there was a constant and vital need for all ranks to maintain a high degree of alertness.

After enduring eight days of discomfort at El Quassassin, nobody was sorry to move to Haifa. This time the train consisted of passenger coaches, not luxurious perhaps, but infinitely more comfortable than the cattle wagons. The demonstration battalion camp was also tented, but included a few concrete buildings housing the NAAFI, dining-hall and headquarters. Lieutenant-Colonel Peter-Hoblyn was at great pains to build up a keen regimental spirit within this disparate unit whose soldiers had, until a few weeks previously, worn many different cap badges. He re-introduced Light Infantry traditions that had been put into abeyance during the war, notably the formation of a bugle section. He also firmly believed that a first class football team was one of the greatest assets to morale in peacetime, and so encouraged the continuation of the very good teams which the Battalion has possessed since the days of the 6th Battalion. Everybody was determined that the current team should beat all comers in the Middle East. Colour Serjeant Ramsey, later to become the captain of the English team, and Private Rowley, also later to become a well known professional footballer, were the mainstays of the team, which in the next year won the Palestine cup competition.

Although virtuosos on the soccer field, the 1st DCLI had been unable even to raise a rugby team for the past two years. However, as a result of the influx of new blood, fifty men put their names forward. RAF St Jean kindly lent their pitch (one of the few soft grassy grounds in the area), and the new 1st XV was soon showing considerable prowess.

The tented camp lay astride the main road running north from Haifa to Lebanon. Terrorist incidents occurred from time to time in and around Haifa, and for these occasions the Battalion was required to maintain a vehicle checkpoint, which was a tedious duty that nevertheless required ceaseless vigilance. However, life, though rough, was far from unpleasant. The School of Infantry programme of demonstrations was committed to paper weeks in advance of each course, so that every officer and soldier knew exactly what was required of him and could plan his life around the duties. Although carrying out very carefully rehearsed demonstrations can, if repeated too often, stifle the initiative of junior leaders, they undoubtedly provide a unique opportunity to transform a newly formed battalion into a working team. The close co-operation with the other fighting arms gave everybody valuable experience not easily obtained in peace-time.

During a battalion attack demonstration on 5th June 1946, approximately twelve 4.2 in. mortar bombs fell amongst a platoon, wounding Private T. Thaxter, Private H. Corby and nine other men. Despite his own severe wound and the fact that bombs were still falling, Private Thaxter, disregarding his own safety, got up and assisted Private Corby to the shelter of a rock. A further bomb, falling very close, killed Private Corby and again severely wounded Private Thaxter, causing him to lose an eye. He refused medical aid until the other nine wounded men had been attended to. He showed courage of the highest order and set a magnificent example to his platoon. For his gallantry Private Thaxter was awarded the British Empire Medal.

The Battalion's six month tour of duty at the School of Infantry finished on 25th June 1946, by which time it had, arguably, developed into the best-trained battalion in the Middle East. On that day it changed places and roles with the 3rd Coldstream Guards, so becoming part of 1 Guards Brigade in the 1st Infantry Division. The Battalion was now stationed at Megiddo Camp, an ex-RAF camp near the Jewish town of Afula, south of Nazareth. C Company was detached at Beisan, fifty feet below sea level on the River Jordan.

*

To understand the background to the terrorist campaign that was being waged between Jew and Arab at the time, it is necessary to look back thirty years to the Declaration made by Mr Arthur Balfour, the British Foreign Secretary on 2nd November 1917. The 'Balfour Declaration' stated:

> His Majesty's Government view with favour the establishment in Palestine of a national home for the Jewish people, and will use their best endeavour to facilitate the achievement of that object, it being understood that nothing shall be done which may prejudice the civil and religious rights of existing non-Jewish communities in Palestine, or the rights and political status enjoyed by the Jews in any other country.

The Jews immediately demanded that the wording, 'the establishment in Palestine of a national home', be changed to 'the reconstruction of Palestine as the national home'. Clearly, this was incompatible with British policy and would be bitterly resented by the existing Arab population in Palestine. The amendment was rejected outright by Britain, but remained an aspiration of the Jews who sincerely believed that Palestine was their promised land from which they had been driven. Thus was born the enmity between Britain, exercising her right as the rulers of Palestine, and the Jews demanding that the country should become a Jewish state. For their part, the Arabs were intent on preventing the incursion of the Jews by every means, including armed insurrection. Britain, in her attempt to reconcile Jews and Arabs, became the target of terrorist gangs from both factions. Serious Arab uprisings involving the use of British troops occurred in 1929, 1936 and 1938. The partition of Palestine was considered and rejected by both Jews and Arabs. An intractable problem had been created, which appeared to be no nearer a solution in 1946 than it had twenty-nine years previously.

*

The move of the Battalion coincided with an escalation of the terrorist war, leaving no time for it to settle in before being deployed on a series of cordon- and-search operations in Jewish settlements.

On one such operation at the village of Mizra, fifty-three men were arrested on suspected terrorist charges and search parties from the 3rd Coldstream Guards and 1st DCLI discovered a printing press and an extremely important cache of documents. Apart from these brigade operations, the Battalion was required to look after its own particular area, a piece of land some seventeen miles by six miles, occupied by Arabs. Apart from this, of course, was the need to maintain a close guard on the camp, both against terrorists and highly accomplished thieves.

There had been rumours that 1 Guards Brigade was to move to Transjordan for field training since June, but as the weeks passed and nothing further transpired, all thoughts of getting away from Afula were forgotten. Suddenly, in mid September orders were received that the Battalion was to move immediately to the area of Zerka and set up camps for the whole brigade. The Quartermaster's advance party left the following morning and motored 120 miles along indifferent tracks to the grid reference, which had been decreed as their new home. It was an area of stony, inhospitable desert over which hot winds continually blew a fine mist of fine sand. Later that day they were joined by the main body, with lorry loads of tentage and all the other stores necessary for a couple of thousand men's existence in the middle of nowhere. A detachment from the Divisional Engineers assisted with constructing such necessities as temporary drains and a waterpoint. A fortnight later the Brigade Headquarters and the two battalions of Guards arrived to find that a neat canvas town had blossomed in the arid desert. They were met by the DCLI who, deeply bronzed and hardened by heavy manual work, could not have looked fitter. During the setting up of the camps the whole project had been visited by the GOC 1st Infantry Division, Major-General R.N. Gale, CBE, DSO, OBE, MC, who had served in the 2nd Battalion of the Regiment before the war.

The Battalion, like most units at that time, was well below establishment due to the continuous release of war-time soldiers. C Company and the Anti-tank Platoon had already been disbanded, due to lack of men, while D Company was temporarily detached to Brigade Headquarters; this left the Battalion with only two rifle companies to carry out the programme of very hard field training.

At the end of October the units of 1 Guards Brigade returned to their normal locations and other brigades of the 1st Division in their turn went to Transjordan for training. On 11th November the 1st DCLI's tour of duty in 1 Guards Brigade was over and the Battalion was transferred to 3 Infantry Brigade, moving to Peninsula Barracks, Haifa, which was one of the few proper peace-time barracks in Palestine. While the accommodation was fairly basic, it seemed luxurious after the sand-swept tented camps that had been occupied since December 1945.

The joy of living in proper buildings was too good to last. Jewish terrorists threatened to blow up trains and the railway from Jerusalem to Lydda, in order to disrupt the export of citrus fruits from Palestine to Great Britain. The population at home had not enjoyed these simple luxuries in the war years, so the British Government was determined that they should enjoy them over the Christmas of 1946. The Battalion was ordered to Jerusalem at short notice in order to protect a long stretch of the railway half way to Lydda.

Headquarters, A and Support Companies were based at the Greek Orthodox Monastery of the Cross in Jerusalem, partly in the monastery itself but mainly in a tented camp outside its walls. The other companies were strung out along the railway, living in cattle trucks and tents. Day and night the line was patrolled, individual soldiers clocking up fantastic distances. For these men there were no amenities for leisure except those which they made for themselves but, like soldiers from every age, they enjoyed the feeling of independence that came from operating away from Battalion Headquarters.

The Monastery of the Cross is so called because the Crucifix is said to have been made from a tree growing nearby. The fortress-like building is of great antiquity, pre-dating Christianity, and is said to have accommodated Pontius Pilate's bodyguard at the time of the Crucifixion. The men of Headquarters Company 1st DCLI were told that they were the first troops to occupy the monastery for well over a thousand years.

During this brief tour of duty in Jerusalem, Lieutenant-Colonel Peter-Hoblyn left the Battalion. For the past eighteen months he had commanded a battalion composed of officers and men from twelve different regiments, who were not overjoyed to find themselves posted to the heat, dust and dirt of the Middle East, where they would be the 'pigs in the middle' between Jewish and Arab terrorist gangs – all of this at a time when the war was supposedly over. By force of personality Lieutenant-Colonel Peter-Hoblyn had welded this disparate unit into a highly efficient battalion with a fine morale, which lived up to the maxim 'Light Infantry are people who do everything better, quicker and with less fuss than anybody else'. A few days before the Commanding Officer's departure, the GOC Palestine had visited the Battalion. He later wrote that during his time as GOC the 1st Duke of Cornwall's Light Infantry was the best battalion that he had under his command in Palestine. Major H.J.C. Ducat-Hamersley assumed temporary command. Between 15th and 17th December 1947 the Battalion ceased its nomadic duties on the railway line and returned to Peninsular Barracks, Haifa, where Christmas was celebrated in fine style.

After Christmas the Battalion was visited by the Colonel of the Regiment, General Sir Walter Venning, GCB, CMG, CBE, MC. A short time later Major Ducat-Hamersley left and Major J.C. Liesching assumed temporary command until the new Commanding Officer, Lieutenant-Colonel H.A. Fitt, DSO, arrived. Barely had he time to be introduced to his officers before being called to Brigade Headquarters to be briefed on a 'cordon and search' operation to be carried out that night in Kafra Ata, a part of Haifa. That Sunday the Jewish 'Stern Gang' blew up the Police Headquarters. A curfew was immediately imposed, and the Battalion was turned out to enforce it for the next twelve hours. It was a cold night with heavy rain. Although the soldiers got wet they had the satisfaction of arresting some 500 curfew breakers, who were confined to a barbed wire enclosure where they got colder and wetter than their captors.

Soon after the change in command of the Battalion, a big alteration in the deployment of troops in Palestine took place. The 1st Infantry Division and 6th Airborne Division changed places, the former moving from North to South Palestine while the latter moved from South to North. 3 Infantry Brigade of the 1st Division moved to a large tented camp in which most of the brigade was accommodated, just inland from Nathanya.

On 1st March 1947 Jewish terrorists perpetrated a number of outrages, including the blowing up of the Officers' Club in Jerusalem and a noisy attack on the 2nd Foresters with mortars and machine-guns. Martial law was imposed, whereupon the Battalion deployed along the River Yarkon, which formed the northern boundary around Tel Aviv. Known as Operation 'Elephant', the companies were strung out along the cordon for the next eighteen days, maintaining a constant vigil. The only incident was a short exchange of fire in which the sole casualty proved to be a washing bowl, pierced by two bullets. A sentry of B Company reported two men sitting on the roof of a neighbouring house examining the company position through binoculars. When apprehended by a patrol they declared their innocence, saying that they were keen astronomers watching the night sky!

Cyprus, April 1947-September 1948

At midnight on 5th-6th April 1947 the 1st Duke of Cornwall's Light Infantry was relieved of all Internal Security duties, handing over to the 1st King's Own Scottish Borderers. Five days later the Battalion moved by sea in HMT *Empire Battleaxe* to Cyprus, landing at Famagusta and thence by road to Dhekelia Camp, seven miles north east of Larnaca. The accommodation consisted of a former military hospital on the seashore, which offered all ranks the luxury of once again sleeping with a roof over their heads, and unlimited swimming in the sea. Most importantly, however, was the knowledge that they were now amongst a friendly population and not surrounded by Jews and Arabs, any of whom could be terrorists intent on murdering a British soldier.

At this time shiploads of Jewish immigrants were attempting to enter Palestine. However, British policy dictated the number that could be allowed in each month, so that each person above that quota was branded as an illegal immigrant and detained in detention camps in Cyprus. The Royal Navy maintained patrols along the Palestinian coast, intercepting ships and escorting those found to be carrying immigrants to Famagusta. Once the camps had been established, the quota of immigrants to Palestine was taken periodically from those detained.

There were two detention camp complexes on the island, one at Famagusta guarded by the 1st King's Regiment and the other at Xylotymbon, close to Dhekelia, the guarding of which the 1st DCLI took over on arrival. There was a third battalion on the island, the 1st South Wales Borderers, stationed at Nicosia. The guard commitment was extremely heavy. Each guard consisted of a 24 hour element and a 12 hour night-time element. At Dhekelia, both guards were mounted at a large parade each evening. Guard duties were not confined to rifle companies; all soldiers in the Battalion bore this chore on a strict roster basis and a 'nights in bed' state was maintained by the company serjeant-majors. When this state dropped below one night in bed in four, a reinforcement company was attached from the battalion at Nicosia.

Occasionally the numbers of soldiers departing on release exceeded the numbers on incoming drafts. This occurred once in 1947 when a company of the 1st South Wales Borderers was attached to the 1st DCLI and about twice in 1948 when a company of the 1st King's was attached, the latter having by this time exchanged locations with the 1st South Wales Borderers. At times it was necessary to detach one company to Xylotymbon itself as an extra precaution. The guard battalions had no duties inside the camps and were not permitted to enter them. Certain administrative duties inside the camps were undertaken by special camp staff with their own command structure. As the number of illegal immigrants grew, so the capacity of the camp was increased and in the latter part of 1947 a third camp complex was build at Xylotbmbon.

On 3rd June Lieutenant-Colonel Fitt left to become OC Troops at Sarafand, the vast military cantonment in Southern Palestine. He handed over command to Lieutenant-Colonel R.W.M. Wetherell. At this time there was a considerable change-over of men, large numbers departing on release, but thanks to the formation of the Light Infantry Brigade their replacements came, if not from the DCLI, then at least from other Light Infantry regiments. One draft alone included 200 men from the 2nd Oxfordshire and Buckinghamshire Light Infantry, which was in the process of disbandment. Meanwhile many rumours were circulating regarding the future of the two DCLI regular battalions.

Although the soldiers bore no malice towards the men, women and children whom they were required to guard, this attitude was certainly not reciprocated by the detainees, who did all in their power to irritate the soldiers. Military training was carried out by adult internees of both sexes, which included endless drill parades, together with stalking, map reading and Morse code training. They blew bugles, raised and lowered flags, sang aggressive nationalist songs and attempted to taunt the sentries by all possible means. Slogans such as 'From Dachau to Cyprus', 'Montgomery, come and see the exploits of your Armies', or 'Punish the Murderers' were painted on large banners or the sides of huts. In spite of all the goading meted out by the internees, their guards maintained that age-old quality of the British soldier, meeting hatred with good humour and equanimity. Indeed, in spite of the poisonous atmosphere that prevailed, acts of humanity were carried out by soldiers, which were remembered far into the future by some of the internees.

Christmas 1947 was celebrated in the traditional army style on two successive days, so that those on guard duty should not be denied their share of the festivities. By now a small number of married families had joined the Battalion. They were mainly the families of officers and all lived in Larnaca in privately rented accommodation.

At this stage the organisation assisting Jews to leave Eastern Europe via the Black Sea ports for Palestine attempted to flood the whole detention camp system with much larger numbers of illegal immigrants. This was aimed at causing the whole arrangement to break down. Two 'Pan ships', SS *Pan York* and SS *Pan Crescent*, overcrowded with a total of no fewer than 15,000 immigrants in appalling conditions, were intercepted by the Royal Navy and escorted into Famagusta.

As most of those on board were to be placed in the third and newest camp complex, it fell to the Battalion to organise much of the reception arrangements and escort them to Xylotymbon. A shortage of military police women meant that there were insufficient female searchers to search the women immigrants and their belongings before they were put into the camps. Several of the DCLI wives volunteered for this unpleasant task and carried it out under military police guidance. The whole of this major operation, which could easily have degenerated into an ugly confrontation, was conducted with quiet efficiency. Shortly after this, an alert DCLI officer discovered a tunnel exit some sixty yards outside the camp perimeter. The tunnel had been cut under the double fences, mostly through solid rock, and was illuminated inside by a string of electric light bulbs.

On 15th May 1948 the British Mandate of Palestine officially came to an end. Immediately the majority of immigrants of non-military age were embarked for Palestine. When this evacuation had been completed, it was possible to concentrate the remainder of the immigrants into a single camp. Once again this potentially explosive operation was carried out peaceably. The evacuated camp, however, had been utterly vandalised by its late tenants; not a single pane of glass remained unbroken, all taps were left running and the drains were blocked with food. Most distasteful to the platoon delegated to clear up the mess was the task of shooting five maimed dogs, which had been abandoned to their fate.

During 1948 it became known that the 2nd DCLI, stationed in Greece, was to go into suspended animation. Lieutenant-Colonel C.B. Acland, its Commanding Officer, therefore flew over to Cyprus to discuss the details of who might be posted to 1st Battalion. Shortly afterwards a draft of 4 officers and about 100 NCOs and men arrived from Greece.

Rumours of the next Battalion posting had long been circulating, those 'in the know' assuring everybody that there was to be an imminent move to Malta or Asmara in Eritrea. On 20th June 1948 the advance party under Major H. B. Coxen, DSO, MC departed for Asmara. The main body was all set to follow, but no orders were received. July and August came and went without news. Then in mid September came a bolt from the blue the move to Asmara was cancelled and the Battalion was to stand by at immediate readiness to embark for an unknown destination. The few married families in Larnaca could not accompany the Battalion and were given the option of going to Malta or returning to England.

The 1st Battalion was relieved of operational duties by 40 Commando, Royal Marines on 20th September 1948, but it was not till the following day that word was received that the 'unknown destination' was to be British Somaliland. Maps were hurriedly consulted to see exactly where this country was, and what it had to offer. The short answer to the latter question seemed to be 'not much', for the maps showed little but barren desert. The troopship, appropriately for the Cornwalls named the *Empire Helford*, lay alongside in Famagusta docks. On 25th September *Empire Helford* cast off, and to the strains of the band of the 1st South Wales Borderers, turned her bows towards Egypt.

British Somaliland, October 1948-1949

As the ship sailed south, conditions became ever more hot and humid. A brief stop at Massawa allowed everybody to stretch their legs ashore in the docks. Here the advance party of the Cornwalls, who had been kicking their heels in Asmara for three months, was embarked.

On 4th October 1948 the ship hove in sight of what appeared to be a desolate scrub-covered sandy plain, backed in the distance by rocky mountains. Of signs of any life whatsoever, there was none. On approaching closer, a few huts and houses grouped amongst scraggy thorn trees could be discerned. This was Berbera, the principal port of British Somaliland, where the Battalion was to land. Even the stoutest hearts quailed at the sight of this vast area of desolation.

The whole Battalion disembarked that day by means of an aged motor launch and by lighters towed by a tug. A and D Companies moved in hired civilian transport straight to Mandera, a hutted camp in the foothills. C Company was detailed to join the baggage party, and immediately got down to the sweated labour of transferring many tons of heavy stores from ship to shore, and then into lorries. After spending an uncomfortable night in a tented transit camp the rest of the Battalion moved off to Hargeisa, 4,200ft above sea level. The journey had to be experienced to be believed. The transport consisted of ancient but remarkably robust 10 ton Italian diesel lorries, which slowly swayed and jolted up the appalling rocky tracks. The 110 miles was completed in 9 hours, but the final arrival at Hargeisa was not destined to raise the spirits of the bruised and hungry travellers. Night was falling, the cooks' lorry which was also carrying the lamps had broken down, the majority of tents lay unerected on the ground, and, to cap it all, the rain was coming down in sheets. However, by 2 a.m. the last lorries staggered in, lamps and petro-burners were lit, and within a short time the cooks had prepared a hot meal.

Daylight revealed a wild, desolate landscape dotted with thorn bushes. As the regimental journal noted, the few natives were 'very black, poor and scraggy. Only the camels appear happy, but even that is doubtful judging by the expression on some of their faces.'

The tents were pitched, but with difficulty, for it was quickly discovered that there was a shortage of tent pegs. Urgent signals were despatched to Headquarters East Africa Command in Nairobi, demanding accommodation stores, for as yet there was not a single chair, table or bed. It was indeed lucky that the Battalion had any transport of its own. The vehicles had been loaded onto a Landing Ship Tank at Famagusta before the main body left, but by some almost incredible lapse on the part of an anonymous staff officer, had been directed to Mogadiscio in Italian Somaliland. Only by the greatest good fortune had the error been noticed, and the ship diverted during passage to Berbera.

The situation is best summed up by again quoting the regimental journal:

> . . . the seemingly unnecessary facts, that our destination was only revealed to us (top secret!) shortly before embarkation, that there was a complete absence of any order or briefing as to our proposed role and conditions in our new station, and the lack of almost the barest necessities of life at our destination, have contributed to make this move what must surely have been one of the most trying and difficult to organise in the recent history of the Battalion. The fact that there have been no major mishaps has been due solely to the efforts of the Battalion itself and the cheerful spirit in which the consequent hardships and hard work have been accepted by all the ranks.

Thus it was that by early October the Battalion was established in tents at Hargeisa, less two companies at Mandera. As yet there was no firm role other than a general internal security presence, and nothing but the hard rocky ground on which to sit or sleep. There was, however, an abundance of game to implement the rations, and the less welcome presence of lions and hyenas, whose roars and howls could be heard in the stillness of the night.

Mention should be made of the ill-fated advance party – thirty-four all ranks, including Major Coxen and Regimental Quartermaster Serjeant Baker. It had sailed from Haifa to Port Said, then moved overland to Port Tewfick and thence by sea to Massawa. There they were met by transport from the 2nd Royal Berkshire Regiment (whom 1st DCLI was due to relieve) and conveyed up to Asmara. During the next weeks they prepared for the reception of the main body in the greatest detail. Suddenly they were told that all their efficient work had been done to no purpose, that they were to pack up, make the journey back to Massawa and rejoin the Battalion on its way south in the *Empire Helford*, except for Major Coxen and the RQMS who were the only two whom it was possible to fly to Hargeisa.

Early in the New Year nobody was sorry to learn that the Battalion was to move, from Hargeisa in British Somaliland to Mogadishu in Italian Somaliland. Once again very short notice was given, many thought unnecessarily so for a peace-time move. On 8th January C Company and the advance party, all under Major B. Mills, departed by road in a mixed convoy of the now familiar Italian diesel lorries and Battalion transport. While resting during the long journey, the soldiers were relieved of a considerable part of their kit by local children. Major Mills was furious, threatening all and sundry with charges of 'losing by neglect', until he found that much of his own kit was missing.

Mogadishu, January 1949-April 1950

At 9.30 a.m. on 12th January 1949 the convoy approached Mogadishu, dead on time. It was met by two lance-corporals also of the Royal Military Police, who then led it to the wrong camp.

The main body retraced its steps back to Berbera in the Italian diesel lorries. The Master of HMT *Empire Pride*, which was lying a mile off shore, had thoughtfully lowered his lifeboats to ferry the troops to the ships, a far quicker and easier means than that employed on their arrival the previous October. All ranks found conditions in *Empire Pride* to be luxurious after the privations of Hargeisa, and were most appreciative of all that the Master and ship's company did to ensure that the passage was comfortable and enjoyable. When the ship docked at Mogadishu the 1st Loyal Regiment, the battalion being relieved, was formed up on the dockside ready for embarkation.

Mogadishu was a modern Italian town with many substantial buildings, but although a far cry from the wastelands of Hargeisa, it offered little in the way of entertainment for the off-duty soldier. Drink, apart from local wine and vermouth, was prohibitively expensive, and apart from a handful of nursing sisters, there was an almost complete lack of girls. This meant that virtually all recreation had to be organised within the Battalion. Games and sports played a most important part of the daily programme, and it was with great delight that the Band was welcomed when it arrived from England, straight away taking a full part in both the ceremonial and social life of the Battalion.

As was becoming increasingly common amongst garrisons in far flung corners of the Empire, the Battalion was once again split up into company detachments – a situation welcomed by the individual Company Commanders, but not so popular with the Commanding Officer, Adjutant and Regimental Serjeant-Major, all determined that the Battalion should not fragment into a group of private armies.

Sadly, Private S. R. Stacey was washed off a rock into the sea on 21st April 1949. Without thought for their own safety and ignoring the ever present danger of sharks, Serjeant T. Cornes, Private D. J. Jones and Private T. Turner immediately dived into the sea in an attempt to rescue him. Although unsuccessful, all three soldiers received the GOC's Commendation for Gallantry. Later, Private Turner was awarded the Royal Humane Society's Bronze Medal, and Serjeant Cornes and Private Jones were each awarded the Society's Testimonial.

Return to England, 1950

In the early days of 1950 the United Nations Organisation decided that Italian Somaliland should be handed back to Italy. The 1st Battalion therefore received orders to return to England, to take over as the Light Infantry Brigade Training Battalion at Bordon from the 1st Somerset Light Infantry.

Embarkation into HMT *Empire Pride* took place on 3rd and 4th April, the ship sailing on 5th April. As England was approached the weather became progressively colder, and on arrival at Liverpool on 25th April it was as far removed from the burning heat of Somaliland as anyone could imagine. The journey south became a nightmare. The train, delayed by heavy snow on the line, did not arrive at Bordon till 10 a.m. the following morning, where Lieutenant-Colonel C.S. Howard, OBE, of the 1st Somerset Light Infantry, was waiting on the platform with his transport formed up outside the station. After handing in weapons and equipment, all ranks departed that afternoon for three weeks' leave.

32
Post-War Reorganisation

THE POST-WAR TRAINING ESTABLISHMENTS

At the end of the Second World War the unit occupying Victoria Barracks, Bodmin (the old DCLI Depôt) was known as 96 Primary Training Centre. Through it passed a continuous stream of recruits, many, but by no means all, destined for the DCLI. From Bodmin, those who had been ear-marked for the Light Infantry proceeded to 16 Infantry Training Centre at Colchester, where they were initiated into the more advanced skills of the infantryman, before being finally posted to a battalion.

Even before the Second World War many senior infantry officers had held the view that far greater flexibility could be achieved if regiments which shared a kinship, either historical or territorial, could be grouped together, and their soldiers trained together. Indeed, the Light Infantry, with its common ethos and tradition, led the way in this respect. During the war this idea had been partially implemented by arranging that the southern light infantry regiments (the Somerset Light Infantry, the Duke of Cornwall's Light Infantry and the Oxfordshire and Buckinghamshire Light Infantry) should share 16 Infantry Training Centre at Colchester. In October 1946 it was decided to carry this system further by concentrating the original two English light infantry training centres into a single unit at Cove in Hampshire. This was known at the Light Infantry Brigade Training Centre. Recruits from Cornwall initially reported to Bodmin (now re-named 32 County Primary Training Centre), where they were documented, underwent medical and aptitude examinations, were kitted out, and put through six weeks of basic training, consisting in large part of drill and PT. Those selected for the infantry then moved to Cove, where they underwent a very tough ten-week course of infantry training, carried out according to the wartime syllabus. After a short period of leave, recruits then passed to No.1 Holding Company, where they received an additional four weeks of advanced training. They were then fully fledged soldiers, having completed twenty weeks of basic and infantry training at Bodmin and then at Cove. All that now remained was for them to be crossposted to

No.2 Holding Company, a comparative rest-cure, where they were prepared for drafting to one of the twelve regular battalions of the Light Infantry. Most Cornishman found their way to one of the DCLI battalions, but the system was sufficiently flexible to allow men to be posted to any light infantry battalion, should the need arise. Thus, at the height of the Korean War and during the Malayan Emergency, many Cornishmen served with the 1st Durham Light Infantry and 1st Somerset Light Infantry respectively.

The permanent staff at Cove was selected from all the English light infantry regiments. For most of its existence the Commanding Officer was Lieutenant-Colonel W.H. Hulton-Harrap, DSO (KSLI). The DCLI Company was commanded by Captain R.G. Stevens (Somerset LI), while No. 1 and No. 2 Holding Companies were commanded by Captain A.B. Whale (DCLI) and Captain J. Edwards (KSLI) respectively.

Between 1948 and 1949 the British Army experienced very major cuts within the infantry, which involved the disbandment of most 2nd battalions. Thus at one stroke the English Light Infantry was reduced from twelve to six regular battalions. There was therefore no requirement for such a large training establishment. Cove was closed down, and a unit known as the Light Infantry Brigade Training Battalion was formed at Bordon, near Aldershot. The original plan was that each of the six Light Infantry regular battalions should take turn in running it. Initially, the 1st Somerset Light Infantry set up this establishment, handing over to the 1st DCLI under the command of Lieutenant-Colonel Wetherell.

During the 1950s the military situation was fast changing, as the cold war took an ever firmer grip across the world. With troops deployed on active service in Korea and Malaya, and the British Army of Occupation of the Rhine and the Berlin Garrison swallowing up ever more men, the army was becoming dangerously over-stretched. In August 1950 plans were submitted to bring the army's strength up to 420,000. This was implemented by increasing the period of National Service from 18 months to 2 years, and re-raising eight 2nd battalions. Indeed, the shortage of regular battalions for operational duties made it most undesirable to tie any of those units down to a purely training role. Accordingly the 1st DCLI was relieved of the duty of running Bordon, handing over to a smaller permanent staff made up from all the light infantry regiments, commanded by Lieutenant-Colonel F. H. Simpson of the Durham Light Infantry. This new unit reverted to the name of the Light Infantry Brigade Training Centre.

In 1951 Field-Marshal Sir William Slim assumed the appointment of Chief of the Imperial General Staff. Although from the Indian

Army, he had served in the Royal Warwicks throughout the Great War and had a close empathy with the British infantryman. He believed that the maintenance of morale within regiments was of paramount importance, not only for meeting the current operational challenges, but also for building a base on which future recruiting could flourish. He therefore appointed General Sir James Steele, Colonel of the Royal Ulster Rifles, to prepare recommendations for the future organisation of the infantry. He firmly believed that an infantryman's loyalty lay first and foremost with his regiment, and that it was therefore vital that every infantry recruit should, from his very first day, feel himself to be an integral part of his regimental family. The brigade training centres had proved unpopular with both permanent staff and recruits alike, for although the regiments of the Light Infantry Brigade shared a common ethos and tradition, there was little homogeneity amongst most of the other brigades. General Steele therefore recommended a return to the pre-war system, under which every infantry regiment had its own depôt situated within its recruiting area, and that the brigade training centres should be disbanded. The news was greeted with great joy. Victoria Barracks, Bodmin was re-opened in November 1951. Once more the Barrack Square echoed to the shout of drill serjeants and the crash of iron-studded boots. Newly enlisted, round-shouldered boys crept apprehensively through the barrack gate, passing out twelve weeks later as mature young soldiers proud of themselves and their Regiment, and displaying self-confidence in their bearing. Once more the Regimental Depôt took its place as the spiritual home of the Duke of Cornwall's Light Infantry. Because almost every National Service soldier now came from Cornwall, the ties between Regiment and County probably became closer than ever before. Passing out parades were great family occasions; depôt officers were welcomed into the social round; games and sports were played with local sides; and every evening, off duty soldiers in uniform could be seen among the crowds in Bodmin. Amidst jubilation at the re-opening of regimental depôts, no tears were shed for the closing of the brigade training centres. There was still, however, a requirement for units to carry out continuation training and to run NCOs' cadres. For this purpose brigade depôts were also established over and above the regimental depôts; these were normally co-located with one of the regimental depôts within the appropriate brigade. In the case of the Light Infantry Brigade Depôt this was initially formed at Strensall, alongside the Depôt of the King's Own Yorkshire Light Infantry.

The Regimental Depôt at Bodmin was at first commanded by Major E.C. Philipson-Stow. The subsequent Depôt Commanders were Major S.N. Floyer-Acland (1952-54), Major J.T.C. Howard

(1954-56), Major D. Ruttledge (1956-58) and Major G.T.G. Williams (1958-62).

This system of training recruits remained unchanged for the remaining years in the life of the Duke of Cornwall's Light Infantry. Indeed, it continued after amalgamation with the Somerset Light Infantry in 1959, when Victoria Barracks, Bodmin became the Regimental Depôt of the Somerset and Cornwall Light Infantry for a further three years.

THE POST-WAR ARMY

With the advent of peace in 1945, few could have envisaged the strain that the regular army would be called upon to bear in the latter part of the twentieth century. With the 'duration of war' soldiers demobilised, and with little desire among young men to volunteer for the restrictions of army life, when there was plenty of work available at home, it became necessary to continue conscription. This was a unique situation; never before in its history had the British Army resorted to conscription in time of peace. It might be thought that eighteen-year olds would have rebelled against such a radical curtailment of their freedom. This was not so for, after six years of war, young men had grown up in a society which regarded conscription almost as a rite of passage.

Conscription was a great leveller. Everybody, from every strata of society, enlisted in the humble rank of Recruit, and living cheek by jowl in a barrack-room ensured that men relied on each other's tolerance and support to make life bearable. New friends were quickly made, and an enduring sense of comradeship was built up in those early days of training. The vast majority of National Servicemen (as the post-war conscripts came to be known) in the Light Infantry settled down happily, determined to give of their best and make the most of whatever fate had in store for them.

Because these men came from such a variety of backgrounds, they brought with them a wide diversity of skills and interests. National Service subalterns, who harboured no ambitions of promotion, maintained a refreshing originality in their approach to the military task. It should always be remembered that the junior officers and soldiers involved in the Korean War, the Malayan Emergency, the Mau-Mau Campaign and the anti-terrorist operations in Palestine and Cyprus were for the most part National Service conscripts. These men mastered complex military skills and became tough, self-reliant soldiers. When called upon, they displayed very great courage.

National Servicemen undoubtedly looked forward to their release dates with keen anticipation. Most kept 'chuff charts' on which the months, weeks, days and finally the hours were crossed off before, with a final celebration, they returned to civilian life. This seldom affected the loyalty, determination and good humour that they displayed right up to the last day. Most took with them happy memories of the close comradeship and sense of pride which they had found in the army.

During the first fifteen years or so of the post-war era, battalions were organised, clothed and equipped much as they had been throughout the war. An infantry battalion serving in the British Army of Occupation of the Rhine consisted of a battalion headquarters, a headquarter company, four rifle companies and a support company. The support company, beside its six 3 in. mortars and six Vickers machine-guns, now for the first time had a really effective anti-tank gun: the 17 pdr. Effective it certainly was, but its massive weight did not endear it to tired rifle company soldiers who were frequently called upon to man the drag ropes and haul this great monster into its gun-pit. The .303 in. No.4 Lee-Enfield rifle and Bren light machine-gun continued to give thoroughly reliable service. At platoon level, the crude and heavy PIAT provided close protection against tanks until superseded by the American 3.5 in. rocket launcher; while at section level the energa grenade, fired with a ballistite cartridge from an adaptor attached to the muzzle of a rifle, gave additional anti-tank fire power. These close range weapons all relied on a projectile with a 'hollow charge' warhead that could burn through about 5 in. of armour plate, providing the target was hit squarely. The platoon was also equipped with a simple and robust 2 in. mortar capable of firing high explosive, smoke or parachute illuminating bombs to a range of 525 yards. The crude, unpopular and potentially dangerous Sten sub-machine-gun underwent various modifications before being superseded by the far superior weapon known as the Sterling. The old No.36 high explosive grenade, dating back to the early days of the Great War, continued to give good service, together with the No.80 phosphorous smoke grenade. Last but perhaps not least, every man carried either a pick or shovel. The one enduring memory of every infantryman of this period must be the never-ending toil of digging weapon pits, which experience had shown to be of such vital importance if unnecessary casualties were to be avoided.

The post-war soldier continued to wear khaki battle dress, iron-studded ankle boots and 1937 pattern web equipment, which was required to be blancoed and have its many brass fittings polished. To save expense, 'denims' were worn for most exercises and for training in barracks. Officers had always worn collars and ties with battle-dress, but this practice was extended to all ranks in 1950.

> Uniform changes which specifically affected the DCLI at that time included the substitution of yellow-on-green shoulder titles for the old white-on-red ones, together with the issue of a dark green beret to all ranks, to replace the khaki 'Cap General Service', an unattractive and unpopular head-dress which had been introduced as a cheap war-time measure. By far the most visible change of uniform was the introduction of No.1 Dress, the first dress uniform to be worn by all ranks since 1914. Before the Second World War 'blue patrols' had been worn by officers and those warrant officers, NCOs and soldiers who were prepared to buy them. In 1950 a start was made in the long process of clothing the whole army in a similar uniform known as No.1 Dress. In the case of all light infantry regiments, this consisted of a dark green jacket with stand collar and white metal buttons and collar badges, blue trousers with a 1 in. dark green stripe, and a dark green forage cap with a black patent leather peak and chin strap. Officers, who continued to buy their own uniform, wore either a Sam Browne belt, sword in a leather-

covered scabbard, and brown leather gloves in 'undress', or alternatively in the 'dress' version, a crimson silk net waist sash, silver lace shoulder cords and sword slings, sword in a nickel plated steel scabbard and white gloves. Other ranks wore a white buff belt, bayonet frog and rifle sling, and white gloves, while their specialist and rank badges were in silver lace. The production of this new clothing was a slow affair, and it was not till near the end of the Regiment's existence that a complete battalion could parade in this dress.

The majority of junior subalterns in the immediate post-war period were commissioned National Servicemen. They were initially selected during the early days of their recruit training, and sent away to attend a War Office Selection Board. If successful, they were posted to an Officer Cadet School where they were put through a tough and very concentrated course designed to turn them into officers in the shortest possible time. Commanding Officers often maintained that the young National Service subaltern was of more use than his Regular counterpart. The former, although possessing only a limited military knowledge, at least knew the rudiments of commanding a platoon, while the latter, wise in arcane matters of higher tactics, had little conception of how to care for thirty young soldiers.

Trooping to distant parts of the still far-flung British Empire was carried out by sea. The troop ships, designated HMT (Hired Military Transport) were leased from the major shipping companies, and varied in the degree of comfort they provided. In the early post-war days officers enjoyed cabin accommodation (albeit cramped) and excellent service, while the soldiers usually had to make do with double tier bunks or even hammocks. In some of the older ships men slept and ate in the confines of the same cramped and fetid troop decks – no wonder that many preferred to sleep on deck. By the end of the sea-trooping era in 1963, a new generation of ships was providing very much more civilised accommodation for all ranks. However, even before this date, the concept of air trooping had been accepted as a viable alternative. The aircraft used were either leased from civilian airlines or supplied by the RAF. Many types were appropriated for this service, offering a wide variety of speed and comfort. While undoubtedly providing a faster and cheaper form of transport, something was lost when battalions no longer trooped by sea. Old soldiers remember with pleasure the hours spent watching flying fish curfetting in the bow wave, and the new sights, sounds and smells of distant ports. However, it was not just nostalgia that made many regret the passing of the troopers. Those days of relaxation in the warm sunshine were not wasted, for they provided a rare opportunity for a battalion to shake itself out and forget the frenetic pressures of modern soldiering. Boredom was kept at bay by such modest training as could be conducted in the confines of a ship (which included Bren and rifle shooting from the poop-deck at balloons), physical training and sports, film shows and concerts. After the very considerable hassle of packing up and preparing for a move, a sea voyage provided a welcome period of relaxation in which everybody could draw breath before plunging into the duties of the new posting.

In the post-war period neither battalion of the Duke of Cornwall's Light Infantry was engaged in any of the wars or counter-insurgency campaigns waged by the British Army. It did, however, send sizeable drafts to the 1st Somerset Light Infantry in Malaya. It also provided a platoon of twenty-five Cornishmen for the 1st Durham Light Infantry in Korea. This later draft was not dispersed around their new battalion, but was kept together within a single company commanded by a fellow Cornishman, Major J.A. Tresauna, DSO (subsequently killed in action). In the same war another DCLI officer, Lieutenant P.K.E. Curtis, while on secondment to the 1st Glosters was awarded a posthumous Victoria Cross for his gallantry at the battle of the Imjin River.

Although not involved in the campaigns that hit the headlines and captured popular imagination in the years following the Second World War, the Regiment was actively engaged in the bitter post-war operations in Palestine, aimed at formulating some sort of peace between Arab and Jew. The terrorist campaign of 1945-50 has since been largely overshadowed by a terrible escalation of violence in that unhappy country, with the result that the part played by our soldiers in the early days has now been largely forgotten. In this vicious chapter of the long-running history of hatred between Arab and Jew, there could be no winners. As so often the British soldier stood between the two factions, the target for the murderous spleen of both. All internal security duties require a very special standard of self-discipline, a discipline that makes a man stand firm in the face of the most intense provocation by those whom he is required to protect.

The post-war history of the DCLI covers Palestine, Cyprus, Eritrea, England, and Germany, the West Indies and, finally, a second tour in Germany. Few regiments can have soldiered in such diverse terrains, or been required to perform such a wide variety of roles. In its final years, the Regiment maintained the very highest standards of professionalism and discipline. Whether operating against Middle Eastern terrorists, carrying out garrison duties in remote desert outposts or prestigious islands, training recruits in England, or exercising on the North German plain, the Cornishmen (for at this time, virtually every man came from

Cornwall) ensured that, as amalgamation approached, the DCLI would be one of the most efficient, best administered and happiest infantry regiments in the Army.

THE LIGHT INFANTRY BRIGADE TRAINING BATTALION, QUEBEC BARRACKS, BORDON

May 1950-February 1951

In order to give flexibility to the posting of officers and soldiers, the infantry was at this time grouped into 'brigades'. These had nothing to do with tactical field formations of that name, but consisted of groups of up to six regiments, so formed because they shared a geographical or historical base. Although many of these 'brigades' were composed of regiments that had little in common, the Light Infantry Brigade, with its six regiments, all shared a tradition that had for many years bound them together both in war and peace.

In 1950 all recruits carried out their basic training with their brigade training battalion. This training role was made the responsibility of one of the regular battalions in the 'brigade', each battalion carrying out the duty in succession. When the First Battalion arrived home from Somaliland, the 1st Somerset Light Infantry was the resident training battalion at Bordon. The DCLI were next in line, and took over the role in May 1950.

Quebec Barracks was a fine pre-war brick built complex – a welcome change for those who had lived under canvas for the best part of four years. It was surrounded by sandy heathland, studded with woods of pine and silver birch, which provided excellent training areas and ranges. Although the actual village of Bordon offered little for the off-duty soldier, the towns of Farnham and Aldershot were only a few miles away, accessible by way of the 'Bordon Bullet' – a train that became familiar to the DCLI soldiers. The area was heavily populated with military units, which made for a full sporting programme throughout the year.

The Battalion was reorganised into a headquarter company, three rifle companies and a holding company. Each of the rifle companies was responsible for training the constant intakes of recruits. Having completed twelve weeks, these men were granted leave before returning to join H (Holding) Company. There they were prepared for drafting to one of the six regular battalions of the Light Infantry. As far as was possible, men were posted to a battalion of their own county regiment, but the system was sufficiently flexible to allow men to be switched to wherever they were most needed. H Company also ran a FARELF (Far East Land Forces) cadre, where those about to be posted to operational battalions in the Far East – notably the 1st King's Own Yorkshire Light Infantry and 1st King's Shropshire Light Infantry – received additional training. The command of H Company, with its continually changing and floating population, was no easy task. Occasionally there would be as many as a thousand men in strength; sometimes as few as two hundred.

AMALGAMATION OF THE 1ST & 2ND BATTALIONS, 9TH JUNE 1950

Quite apart from the training commitment, rehearsals for the ceremonies marking the amalgamation of the 1st and 2nd Battalion, which were due to take place in June, kept everybody more than busy. With the rapid peace-time run-down of the British Army, most infantry 2nd battalions had already been disbanded. In keeping with this policy, the 2nd Duke of Cornwall's Light Infantry had been reduced to a small representative cadre on 4th June 1948. On that day, at Aliki Camp in Greece, it had paraded for the last time in the presence of HM King Paul of Greece. Now, almost exactly two years later, on 9th June 1950, the Colours of the two battalions were to be finally trooped before being laid up in the Parish Church of Bodmin, and new Colours were to be presented to the 1st Battalion.

The parade took place at Bordon on a blazing hot summer's day under a cloudless sky. General Sir Daril Watson, GCB, CBE, MC, the Colonel of the Regiment, presented the new Colours. In his speech he was at pains to point out that although the battalion was to be known as the 1st Battalion, it was in fact an amalgamation of the 1st and 2nd and must maintain the great traditions of both the 32nd and 46th. The old Colours were finally paraded at the Depôt in Bodmin on 13th August, and laid up in the Parish Church. At this service the screen in the north aisle, a memorial to all those members of the Regiment who died in the Great War, was dedicated by the Bishop of Truro, Dr J.W. Hunkin. Later that same day, the new addition to the War Memorial commemorating the dead of the Second World War outside the Depôt barrack gates was also dedicated by the Bishop.

33
The 1st Battalion, 1951-1959

Bulford, February-December 1951

In early 1951, because of the acute shortage of infantry battalions to undertake Britain's commitments, a policy decision decreed that the existing brigade training battalions should cease to exist, and should from thence be manned by a reduced staff made up of officers and men from the appropriate 'brigade'. Lieutenant-Colonel Wetherall handed over to Lieutenant-Colonel F.J. Simpson of the Durham Light Infantry on 26th February, the new unit becoming the Light Infantry Brigade Training Centre. On that day the Battalion moved by road to its new barracks in Bulford on Salisbury Plain, there to become part of 61 (Lorried Infantry) Brigade in the 6th Armoured Division.

By this time, the Battalion was seriously depleted. Apart from A Company – the only rifle company – none of the other sub-units was in any way up to strength. In Headquarter Company the WRAC (Women's Royal Army Corps) cooks departed (doubtless to the regret of many of the soldiers) to be replaced by members of the Army Catering Corps; the Signal Platoon had just been re-formed, but had received no equipment as yet. Support Company had likewise been re-formed, but like the signallers was still without equipment. On arrival at Bulford, the Battalion was presented with a formidable training programme to prepare it for its new role as part of a lorried infantry brigade, but with little equipment and fewer men this was easier said than done. On top of this, warning orders were received that the Battalion was shortly to receive a large number of far from enthusiastic 'Z' Reservists, and would also be required to provide staff for the running of cadet summer camps.

Lieutenant-Colonel Wetherall handed over command to Lieutenant-Colonel J.C. Liesching on 26th May 1951. Few peace-time commanding officers can have led their battalions through a more widely varied succession of roles. These had included the guarding of Jewish illegal immigrants in Cyprus, garrison duties in both British and Italian Somaliland, training of recruits in England, and finally taking its place in a lorried infantry brigade. In spite of a constantly changing supply of man-power, and several major unit moves undertaken at minimal notice, which threatened to degenerate into chaos brought about by appalling staff work from above, the Battalion had invariably retained its sense of proportion and performed its many and varied tasks with cheerful and robust efficiency. Credit for this must rest with Lieutenant-Colonel Wetherall.

With the gradual arrival of men and equipment, the Battalion expanded to its full establishment of Headquarter Company, Support Company and three rifle companies. There was much to be learnt in the new role, and training proceeded apace, leading up to Exercise 'Surprise Packet', the 1st Corps autumn manoeuvres.

Shortly after 'Surprise Packet', news was received that the Battalion was to move to Minden in Germany, where it was to be part of a Lorried Infantry Brigade in the 6th Armoured Division. Before this, however, two large drafts were despatched, one to the 1st Durham Light Infantry in Korea, and one to the 1st Somerset Light Infantry in Malaya. The move of the main body by air and sea took place on 12-13th December 1951. Everybody was generous in their praise for the practised efficiency of the Royal Engineers Movements Control staff, particularly those who shepherded the Battalion through the embarkation port of Harwich onto the *Empire Parkstone*. How very different this was to the nightmare journeys that many of the old hands could remember from their days in the Middle East.

Minden, December 1951-December 1953

Clifton barracks in Minden, taken over from the 1st Royal Hampshire Regiment, was typical of those excellent establishments built for the Wermacht in the 1930s. Commodious as was the accommodation, few had much time to enjoy a peace-time existence. Training, training and yet more training was the order of the day.

For all those soldiers who served in the British Army of Occupation of the Rhine (BAOR) the names of Sennelager, Putlos, Borkenberg and Lüneberg Heath became so familiar that maps became almost superfluous. The Sennelager training area, complete with its complex of barracks and railway sidings, had been set up in the nineteenth century. Many generations of German soldiers had manoeuvred across its sandy heathland, watched over by senior staff officers from the top of a specially built tower. Not only did it provide wide tracts of land over which large-scale exercises could be held, but it included imaginative field firing-ranges of a quality unknown in the United Kingdom at that time. Support weapon concentrations were conducted at Putlos on the Baltic coast; platoon and company training was carried out at Borkenberg, where a tented camp stood amidst trees on a lakeside (a site previously enjoyed by Aryan youths as a 'Health through Joy' camp); last but not least, as far as an armoured division was concerned, was Lüneburg Heath. This area (where the capitulation of the German Armies Northern Group had taken place) offered wide-open spaces in which tanks could be deployed. Exercises followed one after another, culminating in the SHAPE manoeuvres involving British, Canadian, Belgian and Dutch formations. Throughout this period there was a constant turnover of the National Service element. By Christmas 1952 over 200 soldiers had departed to civilian life, and during the next four months they were followed by a further 180. Their reliefs, fresh from the Depôt at Bodmin, were of necessity often thrown straight into major exercises, which placed a great responsibility on the junior leadership of the Battalion. Scarcely had the New Year of 1953 dawned, than the endless annual training cycle was renewed. Lesson 1 on the rifle was once more solemnly drummed into the newest joined soldiers and the hoary veteran alike, as was every page in the manuals for the rifle, bayonet, Bren, sten, grenades, PIAT and 2 in. mortar. Nobody could claim ignorance of whatever personal weapon he was given. In the spring each company in turn made the pilgrimage back to Sennelager, where every officer and soldier had to put his marksmanship to the test in the annual classification. Simultaneously, field training progressed through the stages of individual, section, platoon, company, battalion and brigade, until once again the time came round for the great BAOR manoeuvres.

In the spring of 1953 the 1st Battalion Coronation party, complete with the Colours, was despatched to England under the command of Major G.T.G. Williams. With them went the Band, which had the great honour of being selected to march in the procession. The remainder of the Battalion took part in the Minden Garrison Coronation parade; unlike the heavy rain experienced by those in London, the weather in Germany could not have been better.

That summer, news was received that the Battalion was destined for the West Indies in the forthcoming year. Not since the 2nd Battalion had been stationed in Bermuda in 1907 had the Regiment served in that part of the world, and its return was eagerly anticipated.

Exercise 'Grand Repulse', Autumn 1953

In the autumn of 1953 the Battalion took to the field for the last time in its tour. Exercise 'Grand Repulse' was a NATO (North

Atlantic Treaty Organisation) exercise conducted on a truly vast scale. Thousands of tanks, armoured cars, guns and assorted vehicles, and tens of thousands of men from the USA, Great Britain, France, Holland, Belgium and West Germany were concentrated in a comparatively small area. The sight was awesome, and few who took part will ever forget the experience. For this exercise the Battalion enjoyed the role of umpire staff. Umpiring such a polyglot force required great diplomatic skills. Not only was there a language problem, but the rivalry between nations on opposing sides could easily erupt into somewhat greater aggression than the Directing Staff intended.

On 18th October 1953 the Battalion was stood down from all training in order to start preparations for its move. A large number of men who were ineligible for posting to the West Indies by virtue of their limited remaining service were despatched to the 1st Battalion of the King's Shropshire Light Infantry, the King's Own Yorkshire Light Infantry and the Oxfordshire & Buckinghamshire Light Infantry.

Move to England, 2nd December 1953

The advance party of the relieving unit, the 1st Green Howards, arrived at Clifton Barracks in mid November 1953 and the final hand-over took place on 2nd December. A great gathering of friends, together with the band of the 1st South Staffordshire Regiment, had gathered on Minden railway station to bid the Cornwalls farewell. Soon afterwards the train halted briefly at Osnabrück, where everybody was delighted to see many officers and men of the 1st Oxfordshire & Buckinghamshire Light Infantry with their band assembled on the platform, to cheer a sister battalion on its way. The embarkation at the Hook of Holland and disembarkation at Harwich went like clockwork, and thirty-six hours after leaving Minden the train drew into Plymouth, North Road Station.

Plymouth, December 1953-February 1954

Plumer Barracks

After a couple of days spent in sorting out men and stores at Plumer Barracks, Crownhill, all ranks dispersed for five weeks leave. However, during those two days, the opportunity was taken to dine out Lieutenant-Colonel Lieching. Lieutenant-Colonel P.D. Daly, DSO,

MBE (who had been with the Battalion as Second-in-Command since the previous October) assumed command.

On return from leave everybody had a further five-week period in which to prepare for embarkation. Up till this point the Battalion had been chronically short of soldiers, and indeed, at one stage had been reduced to two rifle companies. Now an influx of some 300 men from the various Light Infantry depôts and a further 40 NCOs from other Light Infantry battalions (many of the latter with active service experience in Korea) brought the total strength to just above 700 all ranks. This necessitated the establishment of a fifth rifle company. It was a busy period, particularly for the Adjutant and Quartermaster. Stores were packed, men were inoculated and fitted with tropical kit, and the Orderly Room worked flat out to prepare the documentation required for a major sea move, complete with wives and children. A farewell church parade, attended not only by the 1st Battalion but by the 4th/5th Battalion and a very large contingent of Old Comrades, was taken by the Honorary Regimental Chaplain, the Rev. Canon G.W.S. Harmer.

The Caribbean, 1954-1955

Move to the Caribbean, February 1954

On the evening of 19th February 1954, in pouring rain, the Battalion entrained at Plymouth, North Road Station for Liverpool. It was still raining next morning as the train pulled into the docks alongside the troopship, HMT *Empire Clyde*. *Empire Clyde* proved to be the reconditioned *Cameronia* and very much the new look, with four-berth cabins and cafeteria feeding for all, in place of the old cramped troop decks.

The ship sailed on the afternoon of 20th February, with everybody happily settled in and looking forward to the warmth of the Caribbean.

Arrival in the Caribbean, February-March 1954

The disposition of the Battalion in the Caribbean was to be as follows:

Battalion Headquarters, HQ Company	Up Park Camp, Jamaica
A Company	Prospect, Bermuda
B Company	Up Park Camp, Jamaica

C Company	Newcastle, Jamaica
D Company	Newcastle, Jamaica
E Company	Airport Camp, British Honduras

Empire Clyde steamed into Bermuda harbour on the evening of 28th February 1954. Bermuda had not been garrisoned by British troops for years, so the arrival of the Battalion was not a routine unit relief but the happy return of the British Army after a long absence.

In preparation for the following morning's ceremony, all ranks of A Company were wearing their best battle dress and highly polished best boots. *Empire Clyde* was too large a ship to secure alongside, so the process of disembarking A Company with all its baggage and the Band and Bugles (which were to take part in the forthcoming ceremony) had to be effected by the use of a somewhat antique river steamer. To further complicate matters, it being a Sunday night, no dock labour was available. The heavy crates had therefore to be manhandled by soldiers from ship to river steamer, from river steamer to quay, from quay to civilian lorries and from these lorries to their final destination at Prospect. Laboriously polished boots were certainly not the best footwear in which to carry out baggage fatigues! It was not till 2 a.m. on 29th February that everybody managed to get to bed. The following morning A Company marched into Prospect behind the Band and Bugles, where they were received by a guard of honour mounted by the Bermuda Rifles with their Band. A large crowd had assembled to watch the ceremony, and numerous television and film cameras were there to record this historic event for posterity. HE The Governor, Lieutenant-General Sir Alexander Hood, inspected the parade; the Bishop said a prayer; the Union Flag and the Regimental Flag were raised; and the new garrison marched past the Governor. A Company could now relax, and start to clean up and repair their camp which had been empty for so long.

The Band and Bugles then re-embarked, and *Empire Clyde* continued her passage to Jamaica. She steamed into Kingston harbour on the afternoon of the 4th March, but, due to strong cross-winds, it was not till 7 p.m. that evening that she was able to secure alongside the quay. HE the Governor, Sir Hugh Foot, immediately came aboard and was received by a guard of honour paraded on the upper deck together with the Band and Bugles. Sir Hugh, himself a Cornishman, said how delighted he was to welcome so many fellow Cornishmen to Jamaica.

Battalion HQ and HQ, B, C, D and Support Companies disembarked that night, C Company motoring the hour's drive up the winding roads to its mountain quarters at Newcastle, the remainder moving to Up Park, a short distance from Kingston. In each case the outgoing battalion, the 1st Royal Welch Fusiliers, welcomed their reliefs with great hospitality, ensuring that every single man received a good hot meal before going to bed in the early hours of 5th March.

Empire Clyde was now left with just E Company on board, together with the families which could not take over their new quarters till later. It was ironic that the Company Commander, Major J.E.E. Fry, MC, perhaps the most confirmed bachelor in the British Army, should find himself in charge of eighty-six wives and an un-numbered gaggle of children for the final leg of the voyage. That evening the ship pulled away from the dockside and headed for British Honduras, the destination of E Company. She arrived there on the morning of 8th March but, because of shallow water, had to move fifteen miles off shore. This complicated the relief of the Royal Welch Fusiliers Company, which had to be carried out by means of two lighters towed by launches.

Up Park, Jamaica

Up Park Camp in Jamaica, where all but two companies were quartered, lay close to the foothills north east of Kingston. It was a large camp occupying a pleasant area of lush green grassland, studded with bougainvillaea and other flowering shrubs, some two miles long by a mile broad. Within its wire perimeter lay the Area Headquarters, the Officers' Club, the Families' Club, a NAAFI, hospital, church, married quarters, and of course the barracks occupied by the resident unit. Apart from a couple of cinemas and innumerable rum shops, Kingston itself offered little for the soldiers. The Commanding Officer was therefore determined that as much recreation and entertainment should be available within the bounds of the camp.

Newcastle, Jamaica

The camp at Newcastle, occupied by C Company, was perched on the top of a 3,500 foot spur running south from the main mountain ridge. What it lacked in amenities was made up for by its beautiful setting and bracing climate. From the camp one could see for many miles across the islands, to Kingston and the South Atlantic Ocean beyond.

* * *

Airport Camp, British Honduras

E Company lived at Airport Camp, just outside Belize, the capital of British Honduras. At that time few had ever heard of this remote outpost of the Empire, and fewer still had any idea of exactly where it was, or what it looked like. In fact, British Honduras lies on the west coast of that part of South America north of the Panama Isthmus and south of Mexico. Its neighbour, Guatemala, ever covetous of this British territory, was wont to make incursions across the ill-defined border – hence the need for a military presence. British Honduras is about the size of Wales, and consists almost entirely of tropical jungle. The north and the south of the Colony are cut off from each other by the jungle-covered Maya Mountains. Much of the country is unmapped. Belize, the capital and only port (if port it can be called, for no ocean-going ship can even approach it) lies on a piece of coastal ground barely a foot above sea level. A few modern European-type buildings were mixed somewhat incongruously with the more usual native huts elevated on stilts. The camp occupied by E Company consisted of wooden huts raised, like their native counterparts, above ground level. The local population, made up of British, Spanish and Creoles, were one of the most friendly, cheerful and well mannered peoples imaginable – the several races living together in harmony without any trace of colour bar. As can be imagined, British Honduras offered a perfect training ground for jungle warfare and, to the joy of the E Company Commander, it was 750 miles from Battalion Headquarters.

Prospect, Bermuda

Bermuda is not part of the Caribbean islands, lying as it does 1,200 miles north east of Jamaica – a pinpoint in the vast expanse of the Atlantic Ocean. It is indeed a small island, so small that one can get from the capital, Hamilton, to any part of its beautiful coastline by bicycle. Bermuda could not have presented a greater contrast to British Honduras. At that time it was not perhaps such a sophisticated holiday resort for the rich that it has since become, but could certainly provide all that was needed to make it an idyllic posting for the peace-time soldier. From the day that A Company arrived, the Bermudians started to show in practical form how pleased they were to see the British Army back again. Invitations poured in for every conceivable form of recreation. As can be imagined, much of the military activity revolved around the provision of guards of honour and the laying on of a multitude of ceremonial parades.

Barrack-square soldiering can however become very debilitating, so to counter this, each platoon in turn was put through Exercise 'Tiddy Oggi', in which it was required to fight its way across the island, pitted against another platoon – hard work, but great fun, particularly as each evening a truce was called to allow everybody to go swimming. Apart from these exercises, each platoon carried out a fortnight's tour at Warwick Camp, laying on demonstrations for the Bermuda Rifles, Bermuda Militia and Cadet Force, while NCOs' cadres were also run for these units.

Meanwhile, in Jamaica the main part of the Battalion found time to carry out some strenuous battalion and company training in the Moneague area, in the centre of the island. The countryside here is refreshingly English, with rolling grassy hills, hedges, farm tracks and pleasant country houses. Ceremonial, however, filled much of the soldiers' time, and the standard achieved was high. Guards of Honour were provided for the State visits of HE President Tubman of Liberia; HE The President of Haiti, General Magloire; and HRH The Princess Alice and the Earl of Athlone. Most memorable was the visit of HRH The Princess Margaret in the Royal Yacht, HMY *Britannia*, on 19th February 1955. On her arrival at Port Royal the Battalion mounted a guard of honour with the Queen's Colour, and that evening provided the bar staff and waiters at a reception held at King's House for 3,000 guests – proving that a Light Infantryman can turn his hand to anything! The Commanding Officer later received a letter from the Private Secretary, who wrote 'Princess Margaret wishes me to tell you how greatly impressed she was by the fine bearing of All Ranks in Jamaica. The high standard of the Guard of Honour mounted by the Duke of Cornwall's Light Infantry was indeed outstanding.'

The Band

In all these events in the West Indies the Regimental Band, under the Bandmaster WOI P.W. Parkes, and the 1st Battalion Bugles, under the Bugle Major Colour Serjeant W. Allen, played a prominent part. This was exemplified by the visit of the light fleet carrier HMS *Triumph* on 13th February 1955. On this occasion the ship's company and many invited guests were entertained to a brilliant ceremony of retreat on the flight deck, in which the performers made their entry and exit by means of an aircraft lift. Certainly, the Band and Bugles must have completed more sea miles on HM ships than anyone else in the British Army, having carried out a month's tour to the islands of Dominica, St Lucia and the Caymans, and to British Honduras by courtesy of HMS *Burghead Bay*. In each of these territories they received a rapturous welcome.

Hurricane relief, Haiti, 13th-18th October 1955

At 11.30 p.m. on 13th October, men of the Anti-Tank Platoon and Assault Pioneer Platoon were suddenly ordered to pack their kit and move with all possible speed the seventeen miles to Port Royal and embark in HMS *Vidal*. The reason for the extreme urgency of this call-out was that Hurricane 'Hazel' had struck the island of Haiti, inflicting very considerable damage to property. HMS *Vidal* was not expecting the arrival of the soldiers till 3 a.m. at the earliest, so were greatly surprised when they turned up at the dockside at 12.30 a.m., exactly an hour after being called out – such was the speed with which light infantry soldiers could react to a crisis. All that night stores and medical supplies were loaded, and early on the morning of 14th October HMS *Vidal* sailed for Haiti, 200 miles to the east. For the next three days she steamed around the coast providing succour for the injured and homeless, and co-operating with helicopter crews from USS *Saipan* to evacuate casualties. The DCLI detachment, having completed its work, returned to Jamaica in HMS *Vidal* on 18th October, bringing with it a refugee dog from the convent at Dame Marie, which had been acquired by the Anti-Tank Platoon, and appropriately named Vidal.

Move of D Company to British Guiana, April 1956

On 7th April 1956 D Company relieved the 2nd Black Watch in British Guiana, which was due to return to Scotland for disbandment. The Company left Jamaica on the troopship HMT *Dilwara*, disembarking at Trinidad, and from there completing the journey in five flights of Viking and Viscount aircraft. Flying was a new experience to most of the soldiers, who thoroughly approved of this method of transport, and particularly of the air hostesses who welcomed them aboard with a cheerful smile.

Immediately on arrival, the Company was thrown into a tight programme of rehearsals for the Queen's Birthday Parade, which was due to take place at Georgetown only a fortnight away. This proved to be an exceptionally complex affair, as it included the British Guiana Volunteer Force, who marched at heavy infantry pace; D Company, which of course stuck to its 140 to the minute; and the Mounted Police, whose horses were not too worried about keeping in any particular step. In the event, the parade was a success, the Light Infantrymen being warmly applauded by the local population.

The Company was based at Atkinson Field, an airstrip bulldozed out of the jungle. It had very few amenities. The country, which is about 500 miles long and 300 miles deep, lies a few degrees north of the equator. The climate is hot and extremely humid; the land, apart from a cultivated coastal strip, is for the most part covered by thick equatorial jungle. Georgetown, the capital, is clean and well laid out, but the fact that it lay twenty-seven miles away down a rough unmetalled road meant that its bright lights were seldom seen by the soldier. All this, together with the fact that the company was now 1,500 miles from Battalion Headquarters, ensured that everybody became more resourceful. The boundless stretches of jungle provided an ideal area in which to teach platoon and section commanders to be self-reliant.

Honours and Awards: Captain R.I. Feild, MC

While the 1st Battalion was stationed in the West Indies, an officer of the Regiment had been distinguishing himself many thousands of miles away across the Atlantic in Kenya, where operations against the terrorist organisation known as the *Mau Mau* were taking place. Captain Feild was awarded the Military Cross for one of the most imaginative and potentially hazardous intelligence operations of the campaign. His citation reads as follows:

> He built up an intelligence organisation in Kenya, and in March last (1954) led a mixed European and African police patrol deep into the Mount Kenya forest. He and the patrol were disguised as Mau Mau gangsters. They managed to enter a Mau Mau camp in daylight without detection by sentries in view forty yards away. A meeting was being held within the camp and the European part of the patrol was able to advance to within ten yards of the meeting before opening fire, killing three *Mau Mau* and severely wounding six others, and to capture a quantity of arms, ammunition and documents.
>
> The hazards of an operation of this kind in broad daylight are obviously immense, and success depends largely on the iron nerve, courage and coolness of the leader. The slightest mistake by this small force would have meant instant death for all concerned.

* * *

Return to England, March 1957

All good things must come to an end, and it was with a certain feeling of apprehension that the Battalion viewed its future back on the plains of northern Germany. Soldiering in the British Army of Occupation of the Rhine would be a new experience to the National Servicemen, but for most of the Regulars the anticipation of more endless exercises on the over-familiar training areas held little joy.

The Caribbean tour literally finished with a bang, as a most impressive earthquake hit Jamaica just as the Battalion was about to leave. Fortunately this did not affect the departure in the troopship HMT *Dilwara*. On the way home the Band and Bugles and the Colours were disembarked at Bermuda, where they, with A Company, were to take part in the various ceremonies at the forth-coming Bermuda Conference. Sadly, in the tight economic climate of that time, the powers that be had decided that the Bermuda Garrison could no longer be afforded. A Company 1 DCLI, and the Band and Bugles, were therefore the last British troops to do duty on this idyllic island. After the conference was finished they departed on the troopship HMT *Captain Cook*, with what appeared to be the entire population of Bermuda crowding the quay to wish them *bon voyage*.

The main body arrived in Southampton on 17th March 1957. Nobody could be in any doubt that this was England when it was found that the civilian workforce responsible for cleaning the ship was on strike. However, the following letter was subsequently received from Major-General R. W. Ewbank, the Director of Movements, which read:

> I recently visited the *Dilwara* after her voyage to Bermuda. As you know, owing to the strike, we were unable to get any shore labour for cleaning; but, owing to the excellent behaviour of the unit carried (the 1st Battalion The Duke of Cornwall's Light Infantry), the ship, on arrival at Southampton, was in spotless condition. I have never seen a ship arrive in better shape. This reflects the highest credit on the unit and the permanent staff, and I would be most grateful if you would pass on to them my congratulations and appreciation.

The following day the Battalion (less A Company and the Band and Bugles) travelled by two troop trains to Bodmin. The trains halted briefly at Plymouth, where all ranks were delighted to see the officers and the Band and Bugles of the 1st Somerset Light Infantry assembled on the platform to welcome them back into the West Country. At Bodmin General Station they were again welcomed by the Mayor and Mayoress of Bodmin, who were waiting for them in the cold March drizzle. From there, it was only a few hundred yards to Walker Lines, adjoining the Regimental Depôt. Kit was deposited in stores, and the Battalion quickly departed on leave. During these brief few hours in Walker Lines, Lieutenant-Colonel Daly handed over command to Lieutenant-Colonel D.N.H. Tyacke, who was no stranger to the Battalion, having held the appointment of Second-in-Command during the Caribbean tour. Lieutenant-Colonel Daly had been required to meet the challenges of commanding a battalion whose companies were spread out over 3,000 miles, encompassing the playground of rich Americans in Bermuda to the steaming jungles of British Guiana. It would have been only too easy for a lesser man to have allowed the companies to degenerate into private armies existing in a state of blissful indolence. From the very first, this was not allowed to happen. The Battalion met its various tasks with enthusiasm, maintained a high state of discipline, and kept fit, while at the same time being always ready to carry out ceremonial duties under the full glare of the media.The exemplary behaviour, cheerfulness and enthusiasm of the Battalion was long remembered in the West Indies.

Walker Lines, Bodmin, March-July 1957

Walker Lines consisted of a wooden hutted camp adjoining the south-eastern wall of the Regimental Depôt. It had lain empty for many months, and looked peculiarly uninviting when the Battalion arrived there in the cold rain on 18th March. This was the first time that the 1st Battalion had ever been co-located with the Depôt. Whether this was due to prescient staff work or was merely the luck of the draw, it was certainly fortuitous, for it brought the whole Regiment together to celebrate the Centenary of the Defence of Lucknow. The celebratory week, starting on 24th May, included dances, dinners, lunches, a cricket match and a church parade. The weather throughout was perfect, and the Sunday church parade included the 1st Battalion with its Band, Bugles and Colours, the 4th/5th Battalion (TA) with its Band, Bugles and Colours, a contingent from the Cornwall Combined Cadet Force, a contingent from the Cornwall Army Cadet Force, and over 350 Old Comrades (of whom 61 were from the London Branch). This parade was marred by a tragic accident when Marlene Meade, daughter of Private and Mrs Meade, was killed by a passing car while waiting to see the parade on its return from church.

During the Battalion's brief residence in Walker Lines, the opportunity was taken to despatch the Band and Bugles on a goodwill tour of Cornwall. This included visits to Truro, Falmouth, Saltash,

Penzance, Wadebridge, Helston, Redruth, Camborne, Launceston, Looe, Bude, Newquay and Fowey. In each of these towns the ceremony of Retreat was performed, together when possible, with a march through the streets and a concert. They also took part in the SSAFA Tattoo held in the White City Stadium, London, with the massed bands of the Light Infantry Brigade.

Move to Germany, 9th July 1957

All too soon it was time to leave Cornwall and renew acquaintance with the British Army of Occupation of the Rhine. The Battalion entrained at Bodmin General station on 9th July 1957. Over the past half-century tens of thousands of soldiers had arrived and departed by way of its single platform, so conveniently situated a hundred yards from the barrack gate. This was to be the last time that a formed military unit would use the station. A certain confusion over the quantity of baggage necessitated a hasty shedding of the less urgent crates before the train was able to depart for Harwich. Even so, further pruning of non-essentials had to be carried out on the dockside, amid loud and indignant protests, before it could be stowed aboard the ship.

This was a time of military retrenchment and radical cost cutting. For two years it had been known that in 1959 the Regiment was to amalgamate with the Somerset Light Infantry. It was therefore with a pang of sorrow that all those involved in this move realised that the 1st Battalion the Duke of Cornwall's Light Infantry was embarking on its last voyage from the shores of Britain. When the Battalion eventually returned, it would be part of a new regiment.

Arrival at Osnabrück, 10th July 1957

The Battalion formed part of 12 Brigade of the 4th Infantry Division and was quartered in Mercer Barracks, Osnabruck, which it shared with the 3rd Carabiniers. The accommodation was luxurious beyond all expectations, while the local training areas of Achmer and Vorden offered considerable scope for platoon and company exercises. Little time, however, was to be enjoyed in barracks, for soon the Battalion became immersed in the constant round of exercises that was for ever the lot of BAOR units. Few of those then serving had ever worked with tanks, and complete familiarity with these beasts and the men who operated in them became a priority. The Battalion was lucky in sharing its barracks with a cavalry regiment, so that personal friendships at all levels were quickly established. The first major exercise with the 3rd Carabiniers, held at Borkenberg, was remarkable chiefly for the almost incessant rain, which descended on friend and foe alike. The autumn of 1957 continued to be an exceptionally wet season, which tried the stamina of the infantry involved in the subsequent brigade, divisional, and Rhine Army exercises. A conversation overheard on one particularly cold and miserable night in the field between a Cornish and a Somerset soldier went something like this (the Cornishman spoke first):

"Freezin', isn' it, John."
"Too right, boy."
"I bet 'e isn't like this 'ere 'ome."
"Course 'tis. 'Tis always freezin' in Cornwall."
"No, 'e isn't. Down P'nzance 'e's warm like summer all the year round."
"Aw, 'ow's P'nzance so different?"
"Well, we got the Persian Gulf for keepin' warm!"

Celebration of the 100th Anniversary of the Relief of Lucknow, 15th November 1957

Although the Centenary of the Defence of Lucknow had already been observed as part of the Regimental Week festivities back in Cornwall, it was determined that the actual date of the final relief, 17th November, should be celebrated by the Battalion in suitable style. Accordingly, over the fortnight leading up to this date parties of many sorts were organised throughout the Battalion, leading up to the traditional Serjeants' Mess Ball on the eve of the Relief. The fortnight culminated with a church parade the following morning. Apart from these events, the British Forces Network was kind enough to give time on the air on 15th November for a live 'Lucknow' broadcast. The hard preparatory work put in by the cast, all from the Battalion, was vindicated by the professional result.

Scarcely had these celebrations died down than everybody turned to cleaning, blancoing, scrubbing and pressing in preparation for the annual Administrative Inspection. This was held on 26th November, and was carried out by Major-General R.H. Hewetson, CBE, DSO, Commander 4th Infantry Division.

The idyllic environment of Mercer Barracks was rudely shattered the following year by the arrival of German contractors preparing the site for a large-scale building programme of married quarters. Families of the future might well appreciate these facilities, but for the Battalion, watching the bulldozers churning the surrounding pleasant fields and woods into a quagmire, the reaction was the the somewhat different.

The routine of hard field-training on the now familiar areas of north Germany continued unabated throughout the last full year of the Regiment's existence. At that time the possibility of war with Soviet bloc forces still posed a very real threat. It is said that tacticians always look back to the previous war for inspiration, but in the case of the nuclear battle there was no precedent. Theories had to be put to the test under the most realistic possible conditions, which for the units in BAOR, meant countless exercises.

The Carabiniers, who had welcomed the Battalion into Mercer Barracks in 1957, departed, their place being taken by the 16th/5th Queen's Royal Lancers. The sharing of a barracks with a unit from another arm often leads to acrimony, but such was the natural friendliness of the Cornish soldiers that from the first, the DCLI and their new cavalry compatriots lived and worked in harmony.

AMALGAMATION WITH THE SOMERSET LIGHT INFANTRY, 6TH OCTOBER 1959

The 6th October 1959 was the date decreed for the amalgamation of the Duke of Cornwall's Light Infantry with the Somerset Light Infantry. So much reorganisation has since taken place in which regiments and battalions have been amalgamated or disbanded, that it is perhaps difficult to understand what a deeply traumatic experience this first round of cuts was to all those concerned. If asked, an infantryman will seldom say that he is in the army; he will tell you that he belongs to a certain regiment. His regiment is a close-knit family group in which every member claims kinship quite regardless of rank or service. His regiment is the bed-rock on which his pride and loyalty are anchored, and it is this pride, loyalty and sense of kinship, nurtured from his first day in uniform, that sustains him on the battle-field, and gives him the determination never to let his comrades down. The destruction of this bedrock has the potential to do untold damage to the cohesion and happiness of a regiment, and ultimately to the fighting efficiency of its battalions. It was therefore vital that the Somersets and the Cornwalls should come together in a spirit of mutual friendship.

From the start, one thing stood out clearly: the similarities between the two regiments were far greater than the differences. They shared the same traditions and ethos of the Light Infantry, wearing almost identical uniforms and using the same drill. Most importantly, the officers and men from both regiments were West Countrymen whose attitude to life was broadly similar. Of course there was great sadness at the forthcoming demise of the Duke of Cornwall's Light Infantry, but there was also a strong resolve that the new Regiment, the Somerset and Cornwall Light Infantry, should be the finest in the army.

In preparation for the amalgamation, Major W. Hine-Haycock was crossposted to the 1st Somerset Light Infantry, then performing the duties of demonstration battalion at the School of Infantry, Warminster. In return, Captain R.B. Robertson was posted to the 1st Duke of Cornwall's Light Infantry. Both these officers proved excellent ambassadors.

On 21st September 1959 the Commander of 12 Infantry Brigade wrote to the Commanding officer of the Battalion to express his appreciation of it and regret at its imminent demise. The text of his letter was published in Part One Orders a few days later:

> As you know only too well, amalgamation is a beastly business; unfortunately, it is also a fact of life. Before the crime, and I use the word advisedly, is perpetrated, I want you to know how much 12 Infantry Brigade Group as a whole, and I myself in particular, regret what is to happen.
>
> The DCLI, in my experience, have always been one of those Regiments who are known to be first class, who are always charming, who are a pleasure to serve with, an inspiration to fight with and an honour to command. Whatever you do is done quite admirably; whatever the task, it is performed to the letter; no job is too difficult, no duty to dull or irksome. In man-management, in bearing and turnout, in discipline and sheer efficiency, the best and only the best is acceptable.
>
> To reach such a standard requires much effort by all ranks over a period of years. It thus becomes tradition. To maintain such a tradition requires as much, perhaps even more hard work, but tradition is not a thing that lies easily. Accordingly, I am confident that when amalgamation becomes fact, your tradition and your standards will continue in the new Regiment. No commander could ask for more.

The final, emotional farewell to the 1st Battalion the Duke of Cornwall's Light Infantry was ceremonially enacted at Mercer Barracks in the still of an autumn evening on 5th October 1959 before the Colonel of the Regiment, Major-General R.B.F.K. Goldsmith, CB, CBE. The Band and Bugles, resplendent in their dark green No.1 Dress and white buff belts were drawn up in the centre of the barrack square, around which were seated many hundreds of spectators. There they played a selection of music to accompany successive re-enactments depicting some of the key chapters in the Regiment's history. The effect on the audience of the sudden floodlighting of these scenes was dramatic. Suffice it to say that the spectators were awarded a *son et lumière* saga, performed by soldiers in period dress, in which was compounded a respectful scanning of the past, a last lingering glance at the present, and a glimpse into the future. As the lights went out in the final re-enactment, the whole arena was floodlit for the march-on of the hundred-strong guard in No.1 Dress, escorting the Queen's and Regimental Colours. The Band and Bugles played 'Abide With Me' and then 'Evening Hymn with Last Post', followed by 'Retreat'. There can have been few dry eyes as the silvery-strident notes of this last call sounded in the still evening air, and the Regimental flag was lowered for the last time.

As the bugles died away, the command rang out: "Cornwall Light Infantry, Farewell Salute, Present Arms!" Then the Band and Bugles, guard and Colour party shouldered arms for their ultimate march past the Colonel of the Regiment.

34
The 4th/5th Battalion (Territorial Army)

RE-ESTABLISHMENT OF THE BATTALION 1 MAY 1947

After the final disbandment of the war-time 5th Battalion at Sharnhorst Barracks, Minden, on 26th November 1946, there followed a period in which the Territorial Army ceased to exist. However, with Germany defeated, the forces of the Soviet Republic now posed a threat which the West could only at its peril ignore. Even with the continuation of compulsory National Service, the vast military man-power requirements needed to maintain a viable army in Germany, while at the same time meeting the threat of insurgency in the Colonies, left little for the defence of the home base.

Throughout the winter of 1946-47 the Government deliberated this problem, and debated the possibility of re-raising the Territorial Army. Every factor seemed to testify against such a course. First, because the nation was exhausted by six years of war, those who had played their part in the conflict were disinclined to get back into uniform. This factor was particularly relevant as, unlike the years immediately following the Great War, there was at that time almost unlimited employment available. Secondly, the entire age group from eighteen and a half to twenty years, from which the pre-war Territorial Army had largely recruited, was already bespoke for National Service. Like their fellows who had fought in the war, they looked forward to consigning their khaki to the bin and returning to home, family and a job.

After considerable debate, the Territorial Army was reconstituted under the National Service Act of March 1947. Under this Act, the Territorial Army was not to be a purely voluntary force; from henceforth all National Servicemen enlisted into the army were required to complete eighteen months with the Colours, followed by a further four years in the Territorial Army. This was changed in 1950 to two years with the Colours and three years in the Territorial Army. During their reserve service with the Territorial Army, National Servicemen were required to complete a total of sixty days training, plus a fifteen-day camp each year. Those who volunteered to become Territorials were liable to thirty hours training per year, plus the annual camps. If they volunteered for an additional thirty hours per year, they received a bounty. National Service was abolished in 1960, the last soldiers being discharged from the Colours in May 1963, and from the Territorial Army in 1966.

From the inception of the Territorial Army on 1st May 1947, the constant cry was for more men. Looking at the strength figures in those early days, one can only marvel at the tenacity of those loyal officers and NCOs who kept an almost pathetically small battalion going under the most difficult circumstances. The man-power shortage was further aggravated by the fact that Cornwall was required to recruit a Heavy Anti-Aircraft Regiment, Royal Artillery (TA) and an Engineer Squadron, Royal Engineers, (TA) beside the 4th/5th Battalion. Each of these units had their own clearly defined recruiting areas from which poaching was not encouraged.

On 1st May 1947 when recruiting opened for Volunteers, the first to sign up were Lieutenant-Colonel Sir John Carew Pole, DSO, Major G.B. Drewitt, Major P.C. Buchanan, MC, Captain P. Stericker, Lieutenant J.B. Brewer, and CSM R.J. Philp, DCM. By December the numbers had grown to 10 officers and 27 other ranks. Looking into the future, Lieutenant-Colonel Sir John Carew Pole was determined to accept only high quality material, for he realised that this initial cadre would be required to provide the leadership for the National Servicemen who were to arrive in due course. By 1948 the strength had increased to 19 officers and 50 other ranks, but of these only 10 officers and 23 other ranks were able to attend the annual camp. However, by this time, National Servicemen who had completed their eighteen months with the Colours were now reporting to start their reserve service with the Territorial Army. To the delighted surprise of all concerned, more than half of these National Servicemen became Volunteers with the 4th/5th Battalion. In the 1940s and early 1950s few working men possessed motor-cars, so that it was necessary to maintain a large number of drill halls which were easily accessible on foot, bicycle or public transport. These were located at Bude, Bugle, Camelford, Delabole, Launceston, Liskeard, Looe, Newquay, Penzance, Saltash, St Austell, St Columb, Truro and Bodmin. Battalion Headquarters were located in the old C.S.D. building in Coldharbour Lane, Bodmin.

It was difficult at this stage to carry out anything but individual training, but all the notes in the *One and All* tell of a lively social life. This was actively encouraged, both to allow all ranks to get to know each other (so necessary for Territorials who only meet occasionally), and to encourage outsiders to join an organisation which enjoyed such conviviality.

On 23rd March 1948 Lieutenant-Colonel H.M. Sainthill, DSO, late Coldstream Guards, assumed command from Lieutenant-Colonel Sir John Carew Pole. Sir John had enjoyed a long and distinguished military career. Originally commissioned into the Coldstream Guards in 1923, he had taken command of the 5th DCLI

(TA) in 1939. Having trained the Battalion to a peak of efficiency, he had handed over to a younger man shortly before D Day, and been posted to the reserve pool of Commanding Officers. Casualties amongst Commanding Officers in Normandy were very high, and he soon found himself posted to the 2nd Battalion Devonshire Regiment. While in command he was awarded an immediate Distinguished Service Order and was Mentioned in Despatches. Finally he had raised the post-war 4th/5th DCLI (TA) and nursed the Volunteer cadre through its fledgling days.

When Lieutenant-Colonel Sainthill handed over command to Lieutenant-Colonel G.B. Drewitt in March 1951, much had been achieved. The Battalion strength, thanks largely to the influx of National Servicemen, had risen to over 400 all ranks. This gave much greater scope for imaginative training, particularly deep penetration patrolling, carried out on Bodmin Moor and Dartmoor. One of the greatest problems lay in the difficulty of recruiting suitable young officers in Cornwall; indeed, of the fifteen subalterns on strength, only two lived in the County, enabling them to take part in routine evening training.

The Battalion provided two parties for the Coronation of HM Queen Elizabeth II on 6th June 1953. The processional party was commanded by the Second-in-Command, Major P.C. Buchanan, MC, TD, and included Regimental Serjeant- Major K.F. Broom, Colour-Serjeant R. Williams, Corporal A. Holdroff and Private G. Jasper. The street-lining party was commanded by Lieutenant K.F. Baker (with the Queen's Colour) and included Company Serjeant-Major L. Yates, Serjeant F. Lean, Corporals D. McCabe and R. Jones, Lance-Corporal Calters, and Privates W. Deigan, H. Gibson, J. Caselton, R. Aunger, M. Cawrse, R. Gregory, W. Hammond, G. Lean, R. Peters, I. Dodd, M. Johns, G. Drew and A. Ridgement. Both parties paraded in London in dark green No. 1 Dress with white belts, slings and bayonet frogs.

The following year Lieutenant-Colonel Drewitt was succeeded by Lieutenant-Colonel P.C. Buchanan, MC, TD. An inducement for young men to join the Territorial Army remained the top priority. National Servicemen were still carrying out their statutory obligation of sixty days training plus the annual camps, but these sixty days, which were spread over three years, were insufficient to maintain any satisfactory continuity in the training cycle. A *cri de coeur* in the *One and All* notes:

> A few NCOs still provide a band of 'faithfuls', but as each year passes, retirement is brought nearer and replacements are not forthcoming. The spirit of selflessness which inspired these few invaluable volunteers is not being carried on in the younger generation.

In 1954 the National Service contribution, which was so vital to the continued efficiency of the whole Territorial force, was severely cut. From then until the final abolition of National Service a man was only required to attend camp and carry out five additional days' training each year. It needs little imagination to understand how almost impossible it was to arrange a progressive training programme under these conditions. On 4th September 1954 the Battalion provided a Guard of Honour with the Regimental Colour on the occasion of the unveiling of the 43rd (Wessex) Divisional war memorial on Rough Tor by General Sir Ivor Thomas, GCB, KBE, DSO, MC, who had commanded the Division throughout the North West Europe campaign. Major T.H. Jobson, who had fought with the 5th Battalion on Hill 112, commanded the Guard which included some of the few remaining NCOs and men who had served with this valiant band of brothers.

By the end of that year the Battalion strength stood at 33 officers and 547 men. This was a considerable achievement, which represented a great deal of hard work by those responsible for recruiting. However, it still seemed meagre compared to the two other battalions in the Brigade, the 4th Devons and the 4th/5th Somerset Light Infantry, each of which could boast over 1,000 all ranks.

In 1955, as a result of cutbacks in the Territorial Army, 456 (Cornwall) Heavy Anti-Aircraft Regiment, Royal Artillery, (TA) was disbanded. This had the three-fold effect of opening up additional recruiting areas in Cornwall, welcoming ex-anti-aircraft gunners keen to remain in the Territorial Army, and absorbing extra National Servicemen who would previously have been allotted to 456 Regiment. The immediate effect was highly encouraging. Eight officers and eighty other ranks – mainly NCOs – were rebadged DCLI, bringing the total strength up to 730. These ex-gunners were soon put to the test, which must have come as a rude shock after the comforts of a heavy anti-aircraft camp, for the Battalion took part in a Divisional exercise on Salisbury Plain, which involved digging a defensive position and remaining in it for three days and nights. Exciting it was not, but cold and very wet it most certainly was. In spite of the worst that the elements could summon up, everybody, including the ex-gunners, emerged with their spirits far from broken.

In July the first 100% call out took place. The Battalion concentrated in Pencarrow woods before making an advance to the Naval ranges on the coast north of Delabole, where a notional enemy force had landed. Here a great quantity of live ammunition was discharged seawards, not only by the rifle companies but by the mortar and machine-gun platoons. The weather was perfect throughout, the enemy was annihilated, and everybody went home feeling a sense of real achievement.

At about the same time, building work started on a new TA Centre at Cold Harbour, adjoining the north-east corner of the Depôt barracks. The architect was the late Commanding Officer, Lieutenant-Colonel G.B. Drewitt.

The Suez crisis of 1956 did not affect the 4th/5th Battalion and, although the Reservists lived in fearful anticipation, none from the Regiment was called back to the Colours. The TA did, however, receive a serious blow which reduced its available man-power very considerably. It must be remembered that up to this time the majority of men turning up for training had been National Servicemen. In 1956 an edict was issued, absolving National Servicemen from their entire commitment except for the fourteen days' annual camp. Apart from this, they were merely names on paper, so that the Battalion nominal roll of 818 all ranks bore no relation to the effective parade state of only 360. Also at this time, the role of the Territorial Army was being seen more in terms of aid to the civil power in the event of a nuclear attack or natural disaster, and less as a fighting force. The good news was that the 43rd (Wessex) Division was designated as one of only two Territorial divisions which were not to undergo complete reorganisation.

Before the Second World War the Mount Charles Band had doubled up as the 4th/5th Battalion Band, exchanging their Mount Charles uniforms for the scarlet of the DCLI on ceremonial occasions and for social engagements. Since the war, while the other battalions in the Brigade had been able to brag about the excellence of their respective bands, the 4th/5th had to admit rather sheepishly that in their own County, famed for its musical talent, they were unable to follow suit. In 1956, all this was to change. The twenty-two adults and four boys of the Lostwithiel Band were signed up as members of the Battalion. The Bandmaster, Mr Chapman, had qualified at the Royal Military School of Music, Kneller Hall, and was in every way an outstanding man for this job. Members who had once served with the 1st Battalion in Lahore remembered him well as the Bandmaster of the Punjab Police Band and the leader of the very popular dance band in Faletti's Hotel.

In 1958 Lieutenant-Colonel S.E. Bolitho, MC, late of the Grenadier Guards, assumed command vice Lieutenant-Colonel Buchanan. That year saw the Golden Jubilee of the Territorial Army. It was marked at national level by a Review held in London on 22nd June, at which men and women from every Territorial unit in the United Kingdom paraded for inspection by HM The Queen. Major G.V. Bennetts and a party of twenty-five all ranks represented the

4th/5th DCLI, with Captain J. Hickling and Lieutenant F.W. Drake carrying the Queen's and Regimental Colours respectively. The weather could scarcely have been worse, torrential rain soaking participants and spectators alike. On 6th July a somewhat drier ceremony was held, when the Battalion marched to Truro Cathedral for a commemoration service.Second Lieutenant J. Morgan and Second Lieutenant P.J. Phillips carried the Colours.

Ever since news of the forthcoming amalgamation of the Duke of Cornwall's Light Infantry with the Somerset Light Infantry had been announced the previous year, there had been much speculation concerning the future of the two Territorial battalions, many fearing that the two counties would provide only a single battalion. To the joy of all concerned, it was now confirmed that each would retain its own battalion with an unchanged establishment. The two battalions were to be known as the Somerset Light Infantry and the Duke of Cornwall's Light Infantry respectively, and, since they were the only battalions bearing these names, the designating battalion numbers would be dropped. Of great importance to morale was the decision that the two Territorial battalions should retain their old cap badges and not the new Light Infantry badge adopted by the Regular battalion. All this was put into effect on 6th October 1959.

Up to 1960 the official establishment of a Territorial infantry battalion was fixed at 991 all ranks, but that year it was reduced to a figure of 774. At the same time it was announced that any unit which failed to achieve an actual strength of two-thirds the establishment would be vulnerable for disbandment.

The drastic implications of this ruling were certainly not lost on anybody in the DCLI, which could only muster a total of 33 officers and 298 other ranks. It was therefore absolutely vital that yet ever greater efforts should be aimed at recruiting.

With the threat of disbandment hanging over the very existence of the Battalion, Lieutenant-Colonel T.H. Jobson took over command from Lieutenant-Colonel Bolitho on 30th June 1960. Lieutenant-Colonel Jobson had been a pre-war regular officer who had served with the 1st Battalion in India, Iraq and the Western Desert. He had been captured at the ill-fated battle of Bir-el-Harmat on 6th June 1942 and taken, with most of the survivors, to a prisoner of war camp in Italy. Taking advantage of the brief period when the camp lay unguarded as a result of the Italian surrender, he escaped with Captains G.T.G. Williams and E. Pryke of the DCLI, and Captain I. Shaw of the Green Howards. The four of them walked some 600 miles south to cross into the British lines thirty-five days later. After recuperating from his experiences, Captain Jobson had been posted to the 5th Battalion, crossing with it to France on 24th

June 1944. He was wounded when leading his company at the battle of Hill 112. After a period in hospital, and further recuperation, he had been posted back to his original battalion, the First, which was then involved in anti-terrorist operations in Palestine. Since then, he had held the appointments of both Adjutant and Training Major of the 4th/5th Battalion. He was, therefore, not only a very experienced operational soldier, but one who already had a good understanding of Territorials in war and peace.

The last great ceremonial occasion involving Lieutenant-Colonel Jobson's Battalion was the provision of a Royal Guard of Honour, on the opening of the Tamar Road Bridge by HM The Queen Mother on 26th April 1962. TA soldiers were not all issued with No.1 Dress, and it had been a nightmare for the Quartermaster and his small staff to fit out a hundred men. In the event, the guard made a brave showing as it marched onto the bridge in perfect spring weather, behind their newly established band from Lostwithiel, which was taking part in a major ceremony for the first time. The Guard was commanded by Major R.W. Potts, and the Queen's Colour was carried by Lieutenant A.S. Webber.

Lieutenant-Colonel Jobson retired in 1962, his place being taken by Lieutenant-Colonel G.T.G. Williams. Quite apart from being a born-and-bred Cornishman, Lieutenant-Colonel Williams had held the appointment of Training Major with the 4th/5th from 1953 to 1956, so already had an excellent knowledge and understanding of the Territorial soldier. Furthermore, he had commanded the Regimental Depôt during its final days from 1958 to 1962, so merely had to move across the road to the newly built TA Centre. Lieutenant-Colonels Williams and Jobson were old friends, having been commissioned on the same day in 1939. They had both been captured at Bir-el-Harmat, had escaped, and had made the marathon trek down the spine of Italy to rejoin the British forces in the south.

The regimental journal noted that, with the Depôt gone, much of its former role of maintaining a high regimental profile in the county would have to be taken on by the Territorial Battalion. It was therefore fortuitous that Lieutenant-Colonel Williams was already famed for his running of the Depôt mess, in which his standards of hospitality, food and drink were high. Now it was the turn of the TA mess to benefit from his dedication to civilised living.

However, let it not be thought that life in the Duke of Cornwall's Light Infantry was entirely concerned with the good life. Imaginative exercises, including field firing, were carried out on the training areas of Bodmin Moor and Dartmoor, and the Anti-Tank Platoon, which at this stage had only one gun, succeeded in disposing of thirty-five rounds, most of them begged or borrowed from units which had been befriended. Recruiting drives were now rewarded by great success, so much so that recruit training weekends had to be initiated, and there was even talk of operating a more selective approach.

Remembrance Sunday had a special significance in 1963, for the Territorials were given the honour of carrying the old DCLI Colours of the 1st and 3rd Battalions to St Petroc's Church, where they were to be laid up. The 1st Battalion Colour Party was made up of Lieutenants Broad and Hooper, Company Serjeant-Major Love, and Serjeants Elmer and Harding (all ex-members of 1st DCLI). The 3rd Battalion Colour Party consisted of Captain Webber, Lieutenant Phillips, Company Serjeant-Major Jones, Colour-Serjeant Cummins and Serjeant Edney. The Colours were received before the high altar by the Colonel of the Regiment, Major-General R.F.K. Goldsmith, CB, CBE.

The annual camp of 1963 was held at Sennybridge. As every soldier knows to his cost, this training area has the unenviable reputation of being perhaps the wettest place in the United Kingdom. It is said that if you can see the mountain tops it is going to rain, and if you cannot see the mountain tops it is raining. This particular May, the weather managed to exceed its usual beastliness, and the regimental journal shows photographs of cascades of storm water pouring down the hillsides, while men smile ruefully from the swathes of their groundsheets (a garment, if it can be so called, singularly useless in keeping the wearer dry).

Indeed, 1963 appears to have been a particularly wet year. The *One and All* shooting challenge cup was fired under conditions of almost impenetrable mist and drizzle at Millpool range, while for the annual patrol competition on the Lizard the elements conspired to produce both gale force winds and torrential rain. The competition was won by C Company. Their team not only had to contend with the weather but found themselves, at the dead of night, traversing a knacker's yard littered with the grizzly skeletons of cows, sheep and horses; not an experience for the faint hearted. Thanks to the morale of the Battalion, all ranks appeared to maintain their sense of humour, and did not hand in their resignations *en bloc*.

The 1964 annual camp was held at Plasterdown camp on Salisbury Plain, where the Battalion was split up into cadres which were each put through a cycle of elementary training, before being launched into an ambitious long-range patrol exercise over a course of twenty-eight miles. As followers of these TA activities could have foretold, it rained hard from beginning to end. Nor was that all, for thick fog covered most of the Plain.

The Battalion strength at this time was 485 all ranks; still under two thirds of the authorised 774 establishment which would render it invulnerable to disbandment, but a continued improvement towards that total.

On 5th June 1965 Lieutenant-Colonel 'Toots' Williams handed over command to Lieutenant-Colonel A.N.L. Thom, who came from the Ministry of Defence where he had been looking after cadet forces. In the three years under Lieutenant-Colonel Williams the Battalion had trained hard, its morale unaffected by a deplorable run of weather. New recruits were still exceeding the wastage, and the present strength had passed the 500 mark. That autumn Captain P.J.B. Michell took the 'Ever-Readies' over to join the 1st Battalion Somerset and Cornwall Light Infantry at Sennelager in Germany, where they were able to make good use of all the excellent training facilities available. For the bulk of the Battalion, however, summer camp consisted of fire-fighting instruction at the Army Home Defence Centre at Devizes, where it learnt to handle the various complex equipments available.

The great event of 1965 was the Battalion's shooting team triumph at Bisley, where it won the China Cup. The competition requires the participation of two teams each of three riflemen, with one Bren pair. The DCLI teams were:

Rifle team 1	Major Miller, Captain Broad and Lance-Corporal Dodge (Score, 148 points)
Rifle team 2	Serjeant Castle, Corporal Smith and Private Skelton (Score 145, points)
Bren pair	Company Serjeant-Major Philp and Corporal Coppin (Score, 221 points)

Not only was the DCLI score of 514 points the highest for many years, but it was the only one to exceed 500 at that meeting.

The China Cup itself is a monumental piece of silver almost four feet tall, heavily ornamented with dragons and other Chinese symbols, which was acquired by British volunteers who fought alongside the regular troops in the Boxer Rebellion of 1900. In its wooden case the cup proved to be too big a load for the one-ton truck, and a three tonner had to be hastily summoned. This was the first time that the Regiment had won this most prestigious award. Apart from winning the China Cup, Captain Broad achieved second place in Class A (Officers) of the Queen Mary's individual competition, while Company Serjeant-Major Philp, DCM and Corporal Smith both finished the meeting in the Territorial Army Fifty and took third place in the Quartet Cup.

Even before the end of 1964, rumours had been circulating that there might be swingeing cuts to the Territorial Army. It was not until 1966, after Lieutenant-Colonel R.H. Potts had taken over command from Lieutenant-Colonel Thom, that the severity of the blow became apparent. In the event, Cornwall was lucky that in proportion to its small population it was allowed to retain more than many other counties, but to understand what happened it is necessary to look at the new structure of the reorganised Reserve Forces.

THE ARMY VOLUNTEER RESERVE

The Army Volunteer Reserve (as it was originally known) was, with effect from 1st April 1967, to be divided into four classes. These were as follows:

AVR I

The 'Ever Readies', which composed a comparatively small group, liable to call-out at any time to reinforce the Regular Army anywhere in the world.

AVR II

Similar to the old Territorial Army. It was only liable to call-out following the proclamation of a National Emergency. It was to be used to reinforce the Regular Army anywhere in the world.

AVR III

Liable for call-out only for home defence within the United Kingdom.

AVR IV

Only applicable to Territorial Army bands, which were to be drastically cut.

Cornwall was warned that it would be called upon to provide one company for a Light Infantry AVR III battalion. The Battalion, which was to be known as the Light Infantry Volunteers, was to have its headquarters and headquarter company in Shrewsbury, with rifle companies in Truro, Wakefield, Hereford and Durham. The Truro company was designated as A Company (Cornwall) the Light Infantry Volunteers. As it was essentially a sub-unit of the Light Infantry Brigade with no direct link to the Duke of Cornwall's Light Infantry, it need concern us no further.

The existing TA battalion, the Duke of Cornwall's Light Infantry, was to become an AVR III unit on 1st April 1967. It consisted of a Headquarters and Headquarter Company (Signals, Assault Pioneers and Reconnaissance platoons) at Bodmin, with two rifle companies, one at Bodmin and one at Truro. The total establishment was to be 220 all ranks. Vehicles, clothing and equipment were to be cut to the bare minimum, and it was announced in Parliament that the total cost of AVR III nation-wide was not to exceed £3 million per year. Never can a reserve army have been run on such a slender budget. The Colonel of the Light Infantry, Major-General C.L. Firbank, CB, CBE, DSO was to write in the Regimental Journal: 'Last year the Territorial Army was practically annihilated by the major reorganisation that was forced upon it.' This summed up the situation most succinctly.

In spite of disappointment in the Battalion, morale remained surprisingly high. The new role of home defence required new skills to be learnt, and close relationships to be established with the Police, Fire Brigade, Civil Defence and Royal Observer Corps. If anybody had thought that the pace of life was going to slacken, they were soon given a rude awakening. On 1st April 1967, the first day of the Battalion's existence, it was called out to deal with the oil spillage caused by the wreck of the tanker MV *Torey Canyon*. Transport was begged and borrowed from Regular units and two parties, one from Bodmin and one from Truro, were quickly on the North Cornwall beaches. Oil cleaning was something entirely new to soldiers, putting the newest recruit on the same level of experience as the oldest, gnarled veteran. The work continued for three weeks, at the end of which all ranks were becoming extremely professional. During this oil clearance operation the soldiers featured prominently on television and in the press, both local and national; excellent PR for a Battalion emerging from a major reorganisation.

Suddenly, on 16th January 1968, without any prior warning, the Government announced that all AVE III battalions were to be disbanded. A cadre of all ranks was to be formed to represent each battalion, on 'a care and maintenance basis'. This bomb-shell, coming out of the blue, caused considerable disgust and anger. Over the previous year the loyalty of soldiers had been strained to the limit. They had joined the Territorial Army to be soldiers, but had seen their fighting role emasculated till they were merely acting as an emergency labour force for the civil authorities. Their numbers had been halved, their transport and equipment reduced to a bare minimum, they had forfeited their support weapons, and their budget had been cut to a totally unrealistic figure that had resulted in the cancellation of annual camps. Throughout this period the officers and men had shown a determination to achieve the highest possible standards. Now, at the stroke of the pen, all this hard work and loyalty was to be destroyed. It is no wonder that there was a feeling of great bitterness amongst all ranks.

The Cadre consisted of Major W.K. Launder, Captain J.J. Hooper, Lieutenant J.A. Coode, Serjeant-Major H. Bate, Colour-Serjeant

L.T. Tonkin, Corporal P. Coppin and Private R. Cole. Major P.J.B. Michell took over from Major Launder later that year. This Cadre was in existence for a period of eighteen months before its final demise. It is only fair to say that its members were the last ever to wear the DCLI cap badge and as such deserve their place in history; however they had no *raison d'etre* and no equipment to carry out any task that might conceivably be required of them. Training was meant to be carried out – but training for what? And how do you train a cadre of four officers, a warrant officer, two NCOs and a private soldier? It must be admitted that the whole concept was a joke in poor taste. One 'camp' was held when five members of the Cadre were attached to the 2nd Light Infantry for a fortnight. There was little for them to do, and Major Michell recounted how he was reduced to cleaning the officers' mess silver in order to keep himself occupied. Another story that illustrates the somewhat surrealistic world in which this cadre existed concerns the tale of a substantial quantity of non-existent small arms ammunition. Lieutenant Coode received a demand for the return of several thousand rounds of 7.62 mm. As the unit, since its inception, had held no weapons, never mind ammunition, this order seemed unreasonable. However, as an officer blessed with initiative, his thoughts immediately turned to the 1st Argyll and Sutherland Highlanders, then stationed down the road at Plymouth. This Battalion was about to be disbanded under the latest cuts; they might well have *buckshee* ammunition which they might be prepared to 'lose'. Enquiries were made, and a deal quickly established. With only a few weeks of their existence left, nobody in the Battalion showed any concern for the niceties of service accounting, with the result that Lieutenant Coode was offered all the ammunition he required, with any other stores he could take away. He declined the offer of the latter but gratefully accepted the gift of ammunition, which was then returned to Ordnance to everybody's mutual satisfaction.

APPENDICES

APPENDICES

* * *

1
The Somerset & Cornwall Light Infantry

Amalgamation, Osnabrück, 1959

The 1st Battalion the Duke of Cornwall's Light Infantry amalgamated with the 1st Battalion the Somerset Light Infantry (Prince Albert's) on 6th October 1959. At the time of amalgamation the Cornwalls were occupying Mercer Barracks, Osnabrück, while the Somersets had just completed a tour as demonstration battalion at the School of Infantry, where they had been quartered in Knook Camp, Warminster. On the afternoon of 6th October the troop train carrying the Somerset half of the newly formed battalion pulled into Eversburg station, to the strains of the Band and Bugles of their Cornish brothers. The Somerset and Cornwall Light Infantry had been born.

The Colonels of the two former Regiments had let it be known that any acrimony or recrimination between the two halves would not be tolerated. It was natural that the past should be remembered with pride and affection, but times had moved on, and it was now up to every member of the new Regiment not to dwell in the past, but to look to the future, and ensure that the Somerset and Cornwall Light Infantry would be the finest regiment in the army. Past amalgamations had sometimes provided sad examples of regiments failing in this respect. Officers' and serjeants' messes had remained split; cliques had been formed, with jealousy taking the place of social harmony. This atmosphere of antipathy had quickly spread from the messes to the barrack rooms, resulting in a long period of in-fighting and unhappiness which had inevitably had a serious effect on military efficiency. It was vital that this attitude must not poison relations within the Somerset and Cornwall Light Infantry.

Lieutenant-Colonel W.R. Lawson, MBE, late Somerset Light Infantry, was appointed the first Commanding Officer, while Major J.T.C. Howard, MC, late DCLI, was his Second-in-Command. Perhaps most importantly that splendid Cornish soldier, W.J. 'Jan' Passmore became the Regimental Serjeant-Major. Jan represented all that was best and most loyal in a West Country warrant officer. He possessed a deep understanding of soldiers and, while accepting only the highest standards, was not the screaming martinet of popular conception. Instead, he relied on good humoured praise or admonishment delivered in his wonderfully rich Cornish voice. Above all, he presided over a happy Serjeant's Mess in which all 'tribalism' was banished. For this alone, Jan deserves to be recognised as the man, perhaps more than anyone, who ensured that soldiers from Somerset and Cornwall came together in harmony. The amalgamation augured well from its first inception and, with a few exceptions, was carried through without rancour. The reasons were two-fold: first, both halves were of Light Infantry stock and shared common traditions, not merely the visible distinctions of drill and dress, but the less easily defined Light Infantry ethos rooted in the teaching of Sir John Moore. Secondly, the character of men born and bred in the West of England tended to be similar, so that soldiers from Somerset and Cornwall mixed easily and quickly developed new friendships.

Whatever the causes, there is no doubt that the 1st Battalion the Somerset and Cornwall Light Infantry was a happy and efficient unit from the start. One of the proofs of complete absorption of the two parts was that within a short time it was difficult to remember whether an individual came from Somerset or Cornwall. In matters of dress, the new Regiment adopted customs previously granted to its two forebears. From the Somersets came the somewhat dubious tradition of officers and serjeants wearing their sashes knotted on the right hip (dubious, because although the subject of many myths, no evidence exists concerning its origin). The Cornwalls felt strongly that their tradition of wearing a red backing to the cap badge (celebrating the victory at Paoli in 1777) should be perpetuated. A submission to this effect was made to the MoD Dress Committee, but was refused on the grounds that the infantry now wore brigade badges, and that a firm decision had been made that no individual regiment would be permitted to modify its brigade badge in any way. A word is necessary to explain the new system of badging the infantry. Each brigade now had its brigade cap badge, while each regiment within the brigade was identified by its own individual regimental badge being worn on the collar. In the case of the SCLI, the regimental badge consisted of the traditional Light Infantry stringed bugle horn, surmounted by the mural crown (symbolic of the Somersets' heroic defence of Jellalabad in 1842). As the Regiment was refused the right to wear the red backing in its cap badge, it sought approval to place the backing behind the collar badge. This was agreed. Thus, the tradition of the Paoli backing was perpetuated. Of necessity, the SCLI wore the red behind their collar badges, but this was the only time that any Light Infantry regiment wore it in any place but the head-dress.

To enable the newly formed battalion to play a full part within 12 Infantry Brigade Group, training became an immediate and urgent priority. However, this did not mean that sports were neglected. Before 1959 drew to a close the soccer team had won nine of the ten matches in the Army Cup and Garrison League; the rugby team had won four of the five matches in the Army Cup; and the hockey team (with its traditional hard core from the Band) had won the first three rounds of the Army Cup. Nor were other interests abandoned, as the Journal notes for the Mortar Platoon - written by Lieutenant M.St.C. Baddeley, one of the Battalion's more colourful officers - suggests:

A recent visit to Osnabrück Zoo was a great success. Since his visit the Platoon Commander has come to know the Superintendent well, and there is a rumour that, should we visit the zoo again, we may be permitted to enter the lion's cage! The rabbits on Achner training area have provided us with good sport, and it is hoped for even better in the future because the platoon is shortly to acquire a mascot, Camilla by name, and a ferret by nature.

On 3rd April 1969 Lieutenant-Colonel W. Hine-Haycock assumed command of the Battalion at very short notice. He was an ideal choice, for not only had he seen previous service with the DCLI in Osnabrück, but he had also held the appointment of Second-in-Command of the Somersets at Warminster.

Plymouth, June-August 1961

The Battalion left Osnabrück for Plymouth on 12th June 1961, crossing the Channel in HMT *Empire Parkestone.* Seaton Barracks, Plymouth was merely a staging post for the forthcoming move to Gibraltar that August, but these three months were exceptionally busy. Not only was there the usual activity of packing up preparatory to a sea voyage, but the opportunity was taken to exercise the Freedoms of the former Regiments at Wells, Taunton, Bodmin and Truro, and accept them on behalf of the new Regiment. Also during this all-too-brief spell at Plymouth, the opportunity was taken to hold a very large reunion at Seaton Barracks, attended by many hundreds of Old Comrades, some of whom had seen service as far back as the South African War and some as recently as the last tour in Germany. In all these events the Territorials played a large part, reminding the public that the Regiment, be it Regular or Territorial, was firmly rooted in the two counties.

The move to Gibraltar, in HMT *Devonshire*, was the last undertaken by sea.

Gibraltar, 1961-1963

The tour of duty in Gibraltar lasted from August 1961 to August 1963. Fortunately at that time the border with Spain was open, although subject to certain restrictions; the British Government's imminent refusal to honour the promise of its predecessor – to sell naval vessels to Franco's regime – had not yet become the catalyst for the Spanish Government's imposition of numerous restrictions, which would have made service on the Rock much less agreeable, and were to inconvenience the inhabitants of the Colony for decades to come.

Little military training was possible on the Rock itself, the soldier's life being largely devoted to ceremonial duties, which included guards on the Convent (the Governor's Residence) and the Four Corners (the border with Spain), the Ceremony of the Keys, the firing of gun salutes to visiting warships and numerous guards of honour. It was therefore fortunate that one company at a time was detached to Tobruk, where the vast desert spaces gave full scope to imaginative training and field firing. The highlight of the tour was the presentation of new Colours by Field-Marshal Lord Harding of Petherton, GCB, CBE, DSO, MC. Many weeks of hard work had gone into ensuring that the event should be of the highest standard. The weather was perfect right up to the final dress rehearsal but, on the night before the parade, a gale blew up: the sea crashed over the Europa Point cliffs, and torrential rain turned the unmetalled surface of the barrack square into a sea of mud. Dawn revealed a scene of chaos, with every tent blown down and the carefully arranged lines of chairs scattered around Europa Point. There was no alternative but to carry on and, with the wind dropping, every available man was put onto repairing the damage. The whole ceremony then proceeded with precision, the only concession to the weather being that chinstraps were ordered to be worn down; perhaps the only time that this has occurred on a grand ceremonial occasion. The artist, David Shepherd, captured the scene brilliantly, but with some artistic licence, showing the rain clouds breaking up prematurely.

On 3rd July 1962 Lieutenant-Colonel J.T.C. Howard, MC assumed command vice Lieutant-Colonel Hine-Haycock. To relieve the monotony of ceremonial duties, as many as possible were sent off on adventure training in the mountains of Morocco while sports of every sort, including such novel activities as whaler racing, pot holing and riding, were encouraged. Lieutenant A.I.H. Fyfe represented Gibraltar in the 3 Miles at the Commonwealth Games.

Towards the end of 1962 the last of the National Servicemen departed, leaving the Battalion to fend for itself as far as recruiting was concerned.

In August 1963 the Gibraltar tour finished, for the first time the Battalion moving back to England not by troopship but by air.

Berlin, 1963-1965

The Battalion moved from Gibraltar in August 1963, some by way of MoD-hired civilian aircraft and others in their own private cars, assembling again at Brooke Barracks in Berlin on 24th October. There was no staging post in England, every soldier being trusted to take his leave and report for duty at the right time and place. The SCLI were stationed at Brooke Barracks, in Charlottenburg, one of the most prosperous residential areas of the city, with families allotted quarters, including various perks, in up-to-date housing built by the Germans as part of the war reparations.

West Berlin, garrisoned by brigade groups from the British, American and French armies, was once again a station in which high profile ceremonial duties played a major part. An Allied Forces Day Parade took place, with American and French allies, through the centre of the Western Zone of the City, and a Queen's Birthday Parade was held at the old Olympic Stadium. Guards of Honour, prestigious parades, and guards on Spandau Prison and the Russian War Memorial (which by some illogical quirk was situated in the British sector) all ensured that the SCLI retained its Gibraltar reputation for smartness. However, the Battalion also trained hard to meet its operational role which, surrounded as it was on all sides by the Russian army, was not to be taken lightly. Frequently, at night and without warning, Exercise 'Rocking Horse' caused the Battalion to turn out of its beds, in a matter of minutes, to take up defensive positions in case of attack. Allied exercises occurred, when on at least one occasion the Battalion played its part and returned to barracks, while the Americans consulted their instruction manuals and the French failed to put in an appearance at all. In the summer the Battalion exchanged positions with another British unit from West Germany, for six weeks' exercise. Another periodic duty was guarding the military train that ran from Berlin to Brunswick, which entailed co-operating with the Russians watching the train. However, most movement was by road, along the corridor through East Germany, on which strict protocols had to be observed, to avoid the ignominy of arrest and detention by the East German police. Guarding the Russian soldiers, who guarded their War Memorial, because of the tension between Russian and West Berliner, was especially hard on cold winter nights when temperatures were many degrees below freezing. SCLI soldiers shivered in their standard British Army kit, while the Russians were snug in sheepskin hats, coats, gloves, and boots – until Clark's, manufacturers of sheepskin goods at Street in Somerset, kindly donated some warm clothing.

In addition to the usual sports that could be played on the many excellent sites left by the Nazis, in winter tobogganing could be enjoyed on the range of hills in the process of being constructed by the West Berliners from the rubble left after the destruction of their city, and in the summer there were water sports, including sailing, on the broad reaches of the River Havel. In order to keep alive treaty rights given by the Russians at the end of the war, men and their families were encouraged to visit East Berlin for sight-seeing and cultural events such as operas and concerts.

The opportunities for enjoyment made a marked contrast to the remaining evidence of the grim events that culminated in 1945, such as the shell-pocked and denuded façades of street buildings, the appearance of notorious addresses where the premises had been left shuttered and boarded up, the remaining ruins, and the frequent uncovering of human remains, when barracks construction works were being carried out. The realities of the present repressive regime across the wall in East Berlin were also brought home by obvious surveillance, such as anonymous telephone calls; the evidence of one's eyes; and through contact with local people, all too many of whom had tragic stories to tell.

During this period in Berlin, Lieutenant-Colonel I.G. Mathews took over command from Lieutenant-Colonel Howard.

Gravesend, 1965

The Battalion moved to Milton Barracks at Gravesend in October 1965. However, the role, that of the Allied Mobile Force (Land), ensured that little time was spent at home. Cold weather exercises were conducted in Canada and Norway, where training took place in temperatures of –38°C, to prepare the Battalion for its role in the rapid reaction force. The principle threat to NATO was then considered to be an outflanking attack by the Soviet army across the north of Norway. For this reason the Allied Mobile Force had to be prepared to deploy at very short notice and be capable of fighting in conditions of extreme arctic cold. In January 1966 a company group under Major R.I. Feild, MC was despatched to northern Canada where, with the help of superb Canadian equipment and clothing, it learnt to live and operate in sub-zero temperatures. Meanwhile the other companies carried out equally hard, but less spectacular, training in Scotland and Northumberland. In February the whole Battalion flew to Bardufoss in Northern Norway to take part in Exercise 'Winter Express', the largest NATO exercise ever carried out in the Arctic. Memories of that exercise were not particularly happy for, unlike the Canadian clothing, the British equivalent failed to keep out the extreme cold.

Interlude in Aden, 1966

However, all was about to change. Even as the Battalion was shivering in the Arctic wastes, plans were well advanced to undertake an emergency tour in Aden. In February 1966 Her Majesty's Government had announced that Britain would withdraw from

Aden by 1968. With victory in their grasp, the two terrorist organisations (the National Liberation Front, and the Front for Liberation of South Yemen), financed by Egypt and supported by the USSR, stepped up their fight to speed the departure of the British. From that moment the previous sporadic acts of terrorism escalated to an all out campaign of extreme violence. Few of the officers or men then in the Battalion had ever heard a shot fired in anger, but during the next six months all would have ample opportunity to experience the dubious joys of being targets for rockets, grenades, mortars and small arms. For outstanding work in the theatre, Captain R. Vyvyan-Robinson (the Intelligence Officer) was made an MBE, while Serjeant R. Bogan (commanding one of the Special Branch squads) was awarded the BEM. It had been a testing time for the Battalion. Living in discomfort and shot at by an often invisible enemy, the various Companies had displayed a high degree of professionalism, under great provocation in a regrettable chapter of British Colonial history.

Back to Gravesend, 1967-1969

The Battalion returned to Milton Barracks, Gravesend, reassuming its role as part of the Allied Mobile Force (Land) on 3rd January 1967. In May of that year it took part in what was to be the final exercise of its brief existence. Exercise 'Polar Express', which took place in Northern Norway, involved units from Italy, America, Canada, Belgium, Holland and Norway. It was the biggest exercise of its kind ever to take place in that area (exceeding 'Winter Express' in terms of numbers taking part), and perhaps formed a fitting grand finale for the Somerset and Cornwall Light Infantry. The Battalion moved to Norway by sea and air. The exercise itself was a much happier experience than that of the previous year. Clothing and equipment had been vastly improved, making the arctic conditions more tolerable and allowing the Battalion to show its true worth.

Since the Government Defence White Paper of April 1967, everyone had been fully aware that a major reorganisation of the Infantry was inevitable. The following month the Colonels of every infantry regiment were summoned to the Ministry of Defence to be briefed by the Chief of the General Staff, General Sir James Cassels, GCB, KBE, DSO. They were informed that a decision had been made that the Infantry of the Line (less the Parachute Regiment) was to be reorganised into five new Divisions by grouping together the existing Brigades. These were to known as: the Queen's, King's, Prince of Wales's, Scottish and Light Divisions. This last was to consist of the Light Infantry and the Royal Green Jackets. So far so good; the new organisation would not affect the existing regimental system, and this official confirmation of the already close relationship between Light Infantrymen and Green Jackets would not only give greater man-power flexibility, but would actually strengthen the individual elements by binding them together more closely. However, this announcement had a sting to its tail. The CGS put a hypothetical question to the Colonels, asking them for their recommendations in the event of each Brigade being required to lose one battalion. The answer was to be given by 15th June. Although posed as a hypothetical question, there was no doubt in anybody's mind that the proposal for this new cut was already a *fait accompli*. The four Light Infantry Colonels immediately carried out a consultation with a wide cross section of their respective regiments, and met on 5th June to formulate their reply. They reported back to the CGS as follows:

> . . . if the Light Infantry were ordered to lose a battalion, a large Regiment should be formed pooling the resources and property of all four Regiments . . . The Colonels hope that this reorganisation will mitigate the effect of losing a Battalion and will enable the traditions and spirits of all four Regiments to be combined in a new Regiment.

Major-General C.L. Firbank, CB, CBE, DSO, DL, Colonel of The Somerset and Cornwall Light Infantry, striving to maintain morale, stated that it was the intention to preserve the connections with the counties of Somerset and Cornwall, and to maintain a presence in these counties; he went on to say:

> . . . we shall do our utmost to foster these associations in the future. It is vital to us that the people of our counties should understand that, though the county names are being dropped from our title, and individual regular battalions will not be affiliated to any particular county, we are none the less their Regiment, relying on their help and support as much as we ever did in the past.

The date on which the old regiments would be consigned to history and the new Regiment formed was given as 10th July 1968.

In Gravesend this news was received with resigned sadness. Practically every officer and soldier came from either Somerset or Cornwall, and the prospect of losing the county titles to become merely an anonymous battalion of a much larger Regiment did not fill anyone with great enthusiasm. Nevertheless, life was too busy to allow time to brood. Hardly had news of the pending reorganisation been received than the Battalion moved to a temporary camp at Crookham, nine miles from the Royal Military Academy, Sandhurst. It had been tasked with providing the support for a tri-service demonstration of weapons and equipment that was to be presented by the Chief of the Defence Staff at Sandhurst from July to September 1967. It was without doubt the greatest exercise of this type ever held. The Battalion's duties included everything from meeting and hosting VIPs from NATO and the Commonwealth to guarding the vast complex of expensive and often secret hardware. Not, one would think, the most exciting of tasks but, because the Battalion took centre stage in an extremely high profile operation, everyone enjoyed the change from soldiering at Gravesend.

On 29th September 1967, soon after its return to Gravesend, Lieutenant-Colonel Mathews handed over to Lieutenant-Colonel C.D.C. Frith. He was destined to be the last Commanding Officer of the 1st Battalion the Somerset and Cornwall Light Infantry.

Winter warfare training was renewed in January 1968, when A Company Group together with the Recce and Anti-Tank Platoons were deployed to Fort Wainwright in Canada, for Exercise 'Frozen Jump'. Meanwhile B Company flew to Voss in Northern Norway, followed the following month by C Company with the ubiquitous Recce and Anti-Tank Platoons. Soldiering in the Arctic may not have been all that pleasant, but was generally preferred to the rain and general misery of Salisbury Plain, which was frequented by the companies not currently involved in Canadian or Norwegian exercises.

On 3rd July 1968 the Colours of the Somerset and Cornwall Light Infantry were trooped at Milton Barracks for the last time. The following day the Colour Party, Escort to the Colours, and Band and Bugles travelled to Truro, where the Regiment exercised its right, as freemen of the City, to march through the streets with Colours flying. The march finished at Truro Cathedral, where, at a very moving service, the Colours were received by Field-Marshall Lord Harding of Petherton, who passed them to the Dean of Truro Cathedral for safe keeping.

On the afternoon of 6th July 1969 the complete Battalion paraded at Milton Barracks before Field-Marshal Lord Harding. In his address he said:

> There is always a feeling of sadness when you come to the end of a chapter, but there is also a feeling of challenge and hope at the beginning of a new one. Change is the order of life. To refuse to change is to live in the past and so to die. What is important is that when changes take place, as they must, all that has been of true value in the past is carried forward into the future.

Thus a proud Regiment of the Line, bearing the name of Cornwall in its title, passed into the pages of history. On 10th July 1969 officers and men became members of a 'large regiment'. Known as the Light Infantry, it incorporated the four former regiments: the Durham Light Infantry, King's Own Yorkshire Light Infantry, King's Shropshire Light Infantry, and Somerset and Cornwall Light Infantry. It had originally been intended that the four battalions should bear their county titles which, it was considered, were so vital to the retention of goodwill within the recruiting areas. However, over a year before this reorganisation was due to take place, the Ministry of Defence had announced further cuts, whereby each new large regiment was to lose one of its battalions by 1970. This was reluctantly accepted by the Council of Colonels, with the important proviso that the choice of which battalion was to be disbanded should be made by the Regiment and not the Ministry of Defence. It therefore came as a shock when, on 11th July 1968, the Ministry of Defence, without prior consultation, issued the following statement: 'The Brigade (Light Infantry) intends to form a large regiment. The Regiment will reduce by one battalion, the Fourth Battalion, which is now the 1st Battalion the Durham Light Infantry.'

Not only had the wishes of the Council of Colonels been ignored, but the one thing that the Council had so assiduously sought to avoid – the nomination of a specific battalion for disbandment – had been imposed on the Light Infantry Brigade in an insensitive way.

Since the inception of the Light Infantry Brigade, County Durham had not only manned its own regiment but provided tough and loyal soldiers for every other regiment in the Brigade. To have told this fine regiment, whose motto was 'Faithful', that it was to be disbanded in two years time was crass in the extreme. A working party, headed by the Council of Colonels was immediately convened to formulate a damage limitation policy. Meeting on 24th July, it was agreed that, whatever else happened, the Durham Light Infantry *per se* must not face disbandment. To achieve this, the battalions of the new Regiment must not bear county titles as originally planned; traditions and customs must be standardised throughout the four battalions; property including paintings and silver must be re-distributed; and the policy of crossposting officers and men between regiments must be stepped up. By these means it was hoped that, soon after the formation of the large Regiment, such a degree of homogeny would have been achieved that battalions would cease to identify themselves with their parent county. This was undoubtedly a fudge. For many years to come battalions retained the *mores* of their former selves, and nobody was under any delusion that one of the finest fighting regiments in the army had been sacrificed to Whitehall parsimony, purely on account of its being the most junior Light Infantry regiment in the Line (the 68th). It was the cause of great bitterness.

Thus it was that the Somerset and Cornwall Light Infantry became the 1st Battalion the Light Infantry, and that, for the first time since 1778, its title carried no indication of its county affiliation. For better or for worse it was now part of a larger regiment that stretched from Durham to Cornwall and, in spite of a Regimental Office being established in the old DCLI Depôt barracks in Bodmin, and however much recruiting teams might reiterate the official line that the Light Infantry was Cornwall's county regiment, the County itself showed itself reluctant to embrace the new Regiment. Now, in 2005, it is forty-seven years since the Duke of Cornwall's Light Infantry ceased to exist as an element of the regular army, but still it is this regiment that captures the imagination of Cornishmen. Three hundred years of history culminating in the two greatest wars which this nation has ever fought is too deep an experience to be discarded in a single lifetime.

2
The British Light Infantry
Its History, Dress & Drill

A BRIEF HISTORY

1748

Following the reduction of the British Army as a result of the Treaty of Aix-la-Chapelle, 4,000 soldiers with their wives and families were given free passage to Canada, and granted land on which the city of Halifax now stands.

To protect these families, three companies of 'Rangers' were raised locally from hunters and woodsmen. They were organised on the lines of the *Jägers* and *Chasseurs* of Europe, and can thus claim to have been the first corps of British Light Infantry.

1755

General Braddock landed in Canada with 1,400 British regular soldiers. He was defeated at the battle of Monongahela river by a very much smaller force.

As a direct result of the lessons learnt at the Monongahela river, a regiment was raised, named the 60th Royal Americans. This was to be the forebear of the 60th (King's Royal Rifle Corps), which today forms part of the Royal Green Jackets.

See pp. 108-109.

1757-1758

Colonel Lord Howe arrived in Canada in Command of the 55th Foot.

The year following Lord Howe's arrival and use of 'forest warfare' tactics, Colonel Gage was ordered to raise the 80th Regiment of Light Armed Foot. It had a chequered career, being disbanded in 1776, reformed in 1778, disbanded in 1784, and finally reformed as a regiment of foot in 1794. See pp. 109-110.

A major milestone in the history of Light Infantry was the appointment of General Jeffrey Amherst to command the British forces operating against the French in North America.*

Amherst's name has now been largely forgotten, eclipsed perhaps by that of General Wolfe, whose death in the hour of victory ensured his place in the halls of fame. However, Lord Amherst was without doubt one of the most brilliant soldiers of the eighteenth century, some would say a near equal of his mentor the Duke of

*Amherst was ennobled in 1780 on his appointment as Commander-in-Chief at Horse Guards. He was Colonel of the 32nd Foot from 1775 to 1781, and retired in 1795 with the rank of Field-Marshal.

Marlbrough, under whom he had served in the European campaigns. When Amherst assumed command in North America light infantry soldiers were in danger of becoming a law unto themselves. Many considered that, providing they could shoot straight, they were not subject to tactical discipline. Amherst was perhaps the first officer to realise that the training and discipline of light troops was absolutely crucial to their effective employment in battle. He revolutionised their tactics, formulated new drills and set about training them until they could truly claim that they were the élite of the British Army. He made great use of his light troops in his masterly operations, which culminated in the capture of Louisburg on 26th July 1758.*

After Major-General Lord Howe's death that year, General Wolfe described him as 'the best soldier in the British Army'. Had he lived he would undoubtedly have risen to the very top of his profession.

1759
General James Wolfe continued to implement Amherst's policy with regard to the training and employment of light infantry. He was a humanitarian who insisted that true discipline could only be instilled by officers who knew the nature and feelings of their individual soldiers (not necessarily a common attribute of the eighteenth century officer).

1760
A small force under a Colonel Montgomery was making its way up a densely wooded river valley when it was attacked by a vastly superior number of American Indians. The situation was very similar to that which had confronted General Braddock at Monogahela river five years earlier, but this time the result was to be quite different. Using their carefully rehearsed light infantry skills, Montgomery's men counter-attacked, routing the Indians with great slaughter. Due to the imaginative thinking and drive of a number of distinguished officers, the tactics of the British Army in North America had been transformed. These new tactics, which relied on speed of movement, accurate shooting, intelligent use of cover and a high standard of junior leadership, had evolved to meet a specific threat; however, forward looking officers believed that important lessons had been learnt in North America that could be adapted for use in any theatre. Sadly, their views were ignored in England where the old dogma of rigid shoulder-to-shoulder formations, which manoeuvred by beat of drum at a ponderous seventy-five paces to the minute, continued to hold sway for many years.

1770
Light companies had been introduced into the organisation of battalions as far

*One of Amherst's major changes to British infantry battle drills was the substitution of the traditional three-deep line with the two-deep line. Eighteenth century battle drills were immensely complicated; suffice it to say that all future light infantry movements depended for their rapid execution on the new two-deep line. He also revolutionised the drills for delivering fire at an advancing foe, which ensured that at least one third of the muskets would be loaded at any one time. His battle drills laid the basis for the devastating fire power of British infantry in the late eighteenth and early nineteenth centuries.

back as 1745. During the North American Wars, which had lasted intermittently from 1740 to 1763, these companies had been grouped together to form *ad hoc* light battalions in which their skills could be employed to best effect. No sooner had relative peace come to North America than light companies were abolished. Over twenty years of experience was lost. In 1770, as a result of the rapidly worsening political situation in America, light companies were re-introduced. Initially these companies were seen by commanding officers as a convenient dumping ground for their worst characters, and were regarded within the army as little more than penal settlements, until reorganisation in 1774.

See p. 110.

1775

During the War of American Independence, the training and employment of light infantry once more became vital to British operations. Much had been forgotten since 1763, and in 1775 the battle of Lexington was lost and the battle of Bunker Hill only won at the cost of heavy and unnecessary casualties. The following year General Howe again organised all the light companies into light infantry battalions, which he proceeded to train up to a high standard of proficiency. A classic example of a highly successful light infantry operation was the night attack by one such battalion at Paoli on 20th-21st September 1777, when a small force of six light companies was led by a fanatic of light infantry tactics, Major-General Sir Charles Grey.*

See p. 112.

1780

Although perhaps not strictly relevant to the history of British Light Infantry, mention must be made of two remarkable officers: Captain Banistier Tarleton of the 78th Foot, and Captain John Sincoe of the 40th Foot. Tarleton is still well known for his aggressive tactics, remarkable speed of operation, appalling ruthlessness and for the dashing image which he cultivated by wearing glamorous light cavalry uniforms of his own design. Sincoe was a more modest man, but probably the sounder officer of the two. Both were imaginative leaders of what were essentially mounted light infantry. In spite of Tarleton's uniforms, their soldiers were trained to fight on their feet, and to make use of surprise to hit an unprepared enemy force (often far superior in numbers) a devastating blow. To achieve this vital element of surprise they used horses, which gave them the ability to cover great distances at speed. As an example of this, in the summer of 1780 Tarleton, with 160 men, surprised an enemy column of 800 strong. He killed 150, captured a further 200 together with 2 field guns and a large quantity of stores, and released 100 British prisoners; all this for the loss of 1 officer killed and 15 men wounded.

The concept of mounted infantry was not entirely new. In 1706 the Earl of Barrymore's Regiment of Foot (later the Somerset Light Infantry) had been reconstituted in the field as dragoons, i.e. mounted infantry. As far as is known, this experiment was never repeated until Tarleton and Sincoe's irregular units were raised seventy-four

*The American casualty figures at Paoli vary considerably according to different sources. That of 460 is taken from the journal of an officer who was present at the engagement. The number of enemy dead was certainly extremely high, and to this day a monument marks the field of 'The Paoli Massacre'.

years later. The outstanding success achieved by these young officers was again largely forgotten until the latter part of the nineteenth century, when every infantry battalion was required to maintain a platoon, trained and ear-marked for mounted infantry duties. In the South African War these platoons were formed into battalions, which more than proved their worth in the vast spaces of the South African veldt. Indeed, Tarleton and Sincoe can be considered the fathers of Second World War units like the Special Air Service Regiment and the Long Range Desert Group, which created havoc to the enemy in the North African desert out of all proportion to their size.

1781

On the disastrous conclusion of the American War of Independence, light companies reverted back to their parent regiments. For the time being little more was heard of light infantry battalions, although the concept was kept alive by a few officers. Prominent amongst these was an experimental light infantry corps raised in the West Indies by Major-General Grey in 1794. Although disbanded later that year, a provisional rifle battalion was raised for a short time at Swindle Camp near Horsham.

1803

In 1790 a certain Captain Johann Ewald, who had served under Lord Howe in America with the Hessian Infantry Regiment, wrote a treatise on the training and employment of light infantry. His book, *Abhundlung vom Dienst derleichten Truppen*, was translated into English in 1803. It had an immediate and profound effect on British military thinking. Ewald's opening paragraph reads:

> In a military system where it is wished that light troops should be made less necessary, the only way would be to instruct the troops of the line to perform these particular duties. Why should not the troops of the line be taught to practice the same duties, being (as they are) made up of the same sort of men, and clothed and armed alike? The difference of the name alone cannot constitute a different kind of troop.

In other words, Ewald was looking far ahead of his time when every infantry soldier should be capable of operating in the light infantry role.

One of those who doubtless read and agreed with Ewald's treatise was Major-General John Moore. Moore had been born into a well-educated and cultivated Scottish family. As a young boy he had travelled widely in Europe with his mentor, the Duke of Hamilton, learning to speak fluent French, German and Italian and being introduced to Field-Marshal Sporken of the Prussian army. Sporken had arranged for a serjeant to instruct the boy in field drills, and soon had him firing the regulation five rounds per minute. Already Moore's burning ambition was to be a soldier. In 1776, when he was still only fifteen, the Duke of Argyle procured him an Ensigncy in the 51st Foot (later the King's Own Yorkshire Light Infantry). While serving with this regiment in Minorca he was offered and accepted a Lieutenancy in the 82nd Foot, which was in process of being raised for service in America. There, in 1779, he finally realised his ambition of leading men in battle, while at the same time learning the tactical importance of light infantry. In 1783, following the end of the American war, the 82nd Foot was disbanded and Moore found himself rusticated to half-pay. Never one to idle away his time, he accepted an offer by his old friend the Duke of Hamilton to secure him a seat in Parliament.

In 1787, doubtless as a result of his previous active service in America and his known vigorous support of light infantry tactics, Moore was promoted to the rank of Major and attached to the 60th (Royal American) Regiment, to help organise a newly raised battalion. Having completed this assignment with enthusiasm, he returned to the 51st Foot, then stationed in Cork. His Commanding Officer was a John Jacques, whose principal boast seems to have been a total ignorance of all military matters. It is said that he thanked God that his regiment had never been a good one and prayed that it should never be one so long as he was in command. Jacques and Moore could not have been two officers more totally opposed. However, in 1790 the 51st Foot was warned for active service, whereupon Jacques immediately resigned his commission, allowing Moore to purchase the Lieutenant-Colonelcy.

When Moore had originally joined the Regiment it had been one of the finest in the army. Now, after eight years of misrule it had become little short of a rabble. Moore was forced to impose iron discipline, at the same time getting rid of many officers. So great were his powers of command that by the time the 51st embarked for Gibraltar, two years later, it was again generally considered to be an outstanding corps. His subsequent active service in Corsica and the West Indies confirmed Moore as an officer of enormous potential.

The establishment of Major-General Sir John Moore's training camp at Shorncliffe in 1803 marks perhaps the most important point in the evolution of modern light infantry. Whether or not Moore was a great field commander is arguable; what is certain is that he was one of the greatest trainers of men that the British Army has produced. His brief from The Duke of York was simple: to take three regiments of the line and turn them into highly motivated and superbly trained light infantry. The first regiment to be selected was the 52nd Foot (later to become the 2nd Battalion Oxfordshire and Buckinghamshire Light Infantry). A few months later it was joined by the 43rd Foot (later to become the 1st Battalion Oxfordshire and Buckinghamshire Light Infantry). Finally the 95th Foot (later to become the Rifle Brigade) joined the trio, which was to form the original Light Brigade of Peninsular fame.

Although one of the greatest proponents of loose skirmishing formations, Moore never ignored the vital necessity for battalions to achieve perfection in their close order drills. Only by the use of these could men remain immune from enemy cavalry and deliver the devastating fire power against attacking infantry for which the British were justifiably held in awe. He encouraged initiative, yet made it clear that individual action must be guided by a clearly understood sense of discipline.*

He was a hard task master, never accepting standards that were less than perfect. He made the officers drill with their men in the ranks so that they became totally

*A fine example of this ability to use initiative occurred in the last great crisis of the battle of Waterloo, when the French Imperial Guard was flung into a final desperate attack against the British line. The Imperial Guard advanced in close column just to the left of Colonel Colborne's 52nd Light Infantry. The Colonel, seeing his opportunity but with no time to seek approval for his action, wheeled his battalion through 90° out of the line, so that it lay parallel to the enemy advance. From there he was in a position to deliver volley after volley into the flank of the hapless Imperial Guard. Had he waited for orders, the outcome of the whole battle might well have been very different.

conversant with the evolutions that they themselves would be required to teach. As can be imagined, this sort of soldiering was anathema to the ideas of many early nineteenth century officers who deemed it a privilege of their social position to relax in the mess room while the Serjeant-Major got on with the job of drilling the battalion. Moore was ruthless in his demands for excellence and, backed by The Duke of York, he soon had any officer removed who failed to meet his exacting standards.

1808

This new Light Brigade, commanded by Colonel Robert Craufurd (Black Bob), was one of the few formations to maintain its fighting spirit and discipline in the terrible winter conditions of Moore's retreat to Corunna in 1808-09.

1809

In the second Peninsular Campaign, General Sir Arthur Wellesley had the benefit of a complete Light Division which came into official existence on 1st March 1810. It was initially commanded by that supremely tough and unyielding officer, Major-General Robert Craufurd. With a strength of just over 4,000 all ranks, it was smaller in numbers than the other seven divisions, and was made up as follows:

1st Light Brigade (Lieutenant-Colonel T. S. Beckwith, 95th Rifles)
- 43rd Light Infantry
- 3rd Caçadores (a Portuguese light infantry battalion)

2nd Light Brigade (Lieutenant-Colonel R. Barclay, 52nd Light Infantry)
- 52nd Light Infantry
- 1st Caçadores
- Four companies of 95th Rifles

Artillery
- Ross's Battery

Cavalry
- 1st Hussars, King's German Legion

Major-General Craufurd was mortally wounded at the storming of Ciudad Rodrigo on 19th January 1812. A great infantry commander and an inspiring leader who never concerned himself with either his safety or personal comfort, he was deeply loved by his soldiers, in spite of his quick temper and often caustic tongue. It is said that, at his funeral, there was not a dry eye in the Light Division. Rifleman Harris of the 95th Rifles wrote 'I do not think I ever admired any man who wore the British uniform more than I did General Craufurd.'

Craufurd was succeeded by Major-General Baron Charles Alton, a Hanoverian who had served with the King's German Legion.

By the end of the Peninsular campaign, the Light Division had been increased by the inclusion of:

68th Light Infantry
(later to become the 1st Battalion Durham Light Infantry)
71st Highlanders
(later to become the 1st Battalion Highland Light Infantry)

1814

After the signing of the Treaty of Paris on 30th April 1814, Wellington's superb Peninsular army was quickly dispersed, and the Light Division disbanded. However, each battalion retained its light company which continued to be trained in the skills of skirmishing.

1815

There was no Light Division in the British order of battle at Waterloo, although the 3rd (British) Brigade, commanded by Major-General Sir Frederick Adam, was in effect a Light Brigade, consisting as it did of the following:

52nd Light Infantry
71st (Highland) Light Infantry
Six companies of 2nd/95th Rifles
Two companies of 3rd/95th Rifles

The practice of concentrating light companies together in battle was typified by the gallant defence of Hougoumont Farm which, in the initial stages, was held by the light companies of the First Guards, the Coldstream Guards and the Third Guards.

1854

The Light Division, commanded by Lieutenant-General Sir George Brown, that accompanied the British Expeditionary Force to the Crimea, was 'Light' in name only. Although it included the 2nd Battalion Rifle Brigade, the other six battalions were all heavy infantry.

1858

Up to this date regiments styled as Light Infantry were selected and trained to perform a specific role which was peculiar to these corps. However, following the defence of Lucknow by the 32nd Foot in 1857, this regiment was accorded the title of Light Infantry the following year, not as a description of its future function in battle, but as a very great honour to be bestowed only on a small élite within the infantry.

1859

By the end of the 1850s every infantry soldier in the British Army was armed with the Enfield rifle, a superb weapon by mid nineteenth century standards, which was sighted to 1,000 yards. Although close order battle drills were to be used against 'savage' tribes for many years to come, the introduction of an accurate rifle by every European nation sounded the death knell for such tactics. It is interesting that the *Field Exercise Manual* of 1859 devoted a large part of its content to light infantry battle drills. Indeed, it is most significant that the second paragraph of the introduction to this section reads as follows:

> All Regiments to be instructed in Light Infantry Movements. Although a certain number of regiments are styled 'light infantry', it is necessary that every corps of infantry shall be fully instructed in this important *branch of its duty.*

1867

The conversion of the Enfield rifle to breech loading, by the introduction of the hinged Snider breech, allowed the individual soldier to re-load his weapon from the lying position without undue movement. This important advance in small-arms design hastened the process by which the whole infantry became, in effect, light infantry. It was further confirmed by the introduction of the Martini-Henry rifle in 1871, the Lee-Metford magazine rifle in 1880, and smokeless powder in 1892.

1899

If the future concept of infantry tactics was ever in any doubt, the painful lessons of the South African War of 1899-1902 left the British with a very clear vision of the future. In the Preface to the *Infantry Training Manual* of 1902, Field-Marshal Lord Roberts wrote:

> Not only must the superior officer possess the tactical skill conferred by practice and professional zeal; but the subordinate leader must be so accustomed to responsibility as to be capable, when necessary, of using his own judgement to further the general plan; the soldier of acting with intelligence and resolution when thrown on his own resources; and the whole animated by the discipline which arises from the precise execution of all duties.

Is not this the essence of the Light Infantry ethos throughout the ages?

1902

It is interesting that in the *Infantry Training Manual* mentioned above, it is laid down that the old close order battle drills were still to be taught for use in operations against 'savages'. The opening paragraph of the relevant chapter reads as follows:

> SAVAGE WARFARE
>
> Necessity for special drill.
>
> Against an enemy armed with the breech-loader, close order formations are applicable only for assembly, for marches and during the preparatory stages of the fight.

> Attacks by savages armed with spears and swords must, however, usually be met in close order, and for warfare against such an enemy, movements in line, in echelon and in square will be practised.

1914

By 1914 the British infantry, as far as field tactics were concerned, had become light infantry. Movement within range of enemy fire was invariably carried out in widely dispersed formations; men were taught the use of cover; and junior leaders were strongly encouraged to use their initiative. Twenty years previously, a battalion would have been rigidly controlled in battle by the Commanding Officer himself. Now the *Infantry Training Manual* of 1914 laid down:

> Battalion commanders should never trespass on the proper sphere of action of their subordinates. Any attempt to exercise personal control over all portions of the force must inevitably lead to the neglect of other duties.

It is interesting that the German military attaché had watched British infantry exercises in the years immediately preceding the Great War, and had reported his observations back to the General Staff. They were of the opinion that, although soldiers might well be taught to carry out these skirmishing type tactics in peace time, cohesion would quickly be lost if they were attempted under fire. In the early stages of the Great War, German infantry frequently attacked in close order, and sustained terrible casualties in the face of disciplined British rifle fire.

In both the First and Second World Wars, certain formations were composed either exclusively or predominately of Light Infantry or Rifle regiments. They were grouped in this manner, not because their tactical training differed in any way from the rest of the infantry, but because they had developed a common ethos which provided firm bonds of friendship and trust.

1933

The close-knit family nature of a British infantry regiment meant that the transfer of an officer from one to another was often an experience accompanied by great personal trauma. The Colonels of the seven Light Infantry regiments, having witnessed these problems, and realising that the effective employment of officers in the future would require even greater flexibility, determined to build up a spirit of mutual friendship amongst the officers of all Light Infantry regiments. Accordingly, the Light Infantry Club was formed on 6th December 1933.

It must be emphasised that although the membership consisted of serving and retired Light Infantry officers, it was in no way military in its affairs, but was a club solely devoted to sporting and social activities aimed at promoting understanding and friendship across the individual regiments.

These activities originally consisted of cricket and squash matches, point-to-pointing and an annual dinner in London. When in 1946 the Army Council considered the grouping of infantry regiments into brigades, the Colonels of the Light Infantry were able to argue that, because a strong *rapport* already existed between their regiments, it would be logical to group them into a Light Infantry Brigade rather than into diverse brigades dictated by territorial considerations. In the event, the six English Light Infantry regiments were brigaded together, while the Highland Light Infantry opted for inclusion in the Highland Brigade. Thus the formation of the Club had a profound effect on the future of the English Light Infantry regiments.

DRESS

The story of light infantry dress is far from an exact science. This is partly due to the fact that, by their nature, light units were constantly having to adapt to changing conditions; it is also undoubtedly the result of the independent spirit enjoyed by light troops, who considered themselves an élite to whom the niceties of dress regulations need not apply. The water-colour by C.C.P. Lawson depicting a soldier of the Light Company, 46th Foot *c.*1777 is probably pretty accurate (we know that he went to great lengths to achieve authenticity). As Lord Howe had suggested in 1757, the skirt has been cut off his coat and the brim off his hat. One can immediately see that, in the forest, this was a far more practical dress than the official uniform. Whether or not light troops (apart from rifle regiments) ever wore green coats is open to argument. Perhaps there was no need for this, for it must be remembered that until 1871 the British infantry rank and file did not wear scarlet coats, but ones of cloth that was described as being 'brick red'. Many contemporary observers noted that, after months in the field subjected to sun and rain, the soldier's coat faded to a dull russet.

Officers and soldiers of the flank companies (the grenadier and light companies) were distinguished from those of the battalion companies by the wearing of 'wings' in place of epaulettes. These were moon-shaped pieces of stiff cloth attached along the shoulder seam. Light company wings were decorated with a bugle horn badge (of which more later). As the years went by, officer's wings became more and more elaborate and expensive, until, by the time of their abolition in 1855, they represented superb works of the gold bullion embroiderers' art.

Another excellent water-colour by C.C.P. Lawson shows a Light Company officer of the 32nd Foot in 1802 wearing a Tarleton helmet. This was a head-dress worn by Colonel Tarleton's mounted infantry (see p. 536) in the American wars, which consisted of a stiff leather cap surmounted by a bearskin crest. By the early nineteenth century this had become the standard head-dress for Light Dragoons but was not, as far as can be ascertained, ever authorised for light companies. One can only assume that this was an example of light troops adopting glamorous items of uniform as a statement of their élite status.

From the introduction of the 1829 coatee, officers of light infantry regiments and light companies wore a silver whistle secured by a chain attached to a lion's head ornament on the front of their white buff sword belts. Serjeant-majors, colour-serjeants and serjeants wore a similar lion, chain and whistle on the buff cross belt. The origin of these was undoubtedly practical, for by this time much of the manoeuvering of skirmishers was controlled by whistle blasts. With the demise of the coatee and the introduction of the tunic in 1855, officers carried their swords on waist-belts, the old cross belt becoming obsolete. There was thus nowhere for them to wear their whistles, and the custom was dropped. However, other ranks continued to wear a white buff cross belt over the left shoulder to which was attached a padded pouch containing percussion caps for the Enfield rifle. The lion, chain and whistle was transferred to this new belt. In 1871, with the introduction of the Martini-Henry rifle, there was no longer a requirement for a percussion cap pouch; the shoulder belt was therefore not included in the design of the new equipment. It seemed that the authorised wearing of the lion, chain and whistle had finally run its course. However, regimental dress distinctions often bear little relation to any dress regulations and the army, with good sense, tends to turn a blind eye to these infringements. Sometime after 1871 the serjeants of certain Light Infantry regiments started wearing the lion, chain and whistle attached to their red shoulder sashes. As far as can be ascertained the practice was never officially authorised, nor was it adopted by all the regiments of Light Infantry. Furthermore, those that did adopt it were, with the exception of the Durham Light Infantry, irregular in its use. There is no evidence that the Duke of Cornwall's Light Infantry ever wore the lion, chain and whistle on their serjeant's sashes; however, photographs exist which prove that both the Somerset Light Infantry and the King's Shropshire Light Infantry both adopted this custom (though not apparently on a regular basis) and continued its use till about 1917.

Officers of Light Infantry regiments and light companies adopted a distinctive pattern of waist sash (probably in 1829), which they continued to wear till the abolition of the coatee in 1855. Whereas the standard infantry sash consisted of a length of crimson silk 'patent netting' terminating in tassles, which was passed twice round the waist and tied on the left hip, the light infantry version was a more elaborate affair which incorporated two crimson silk cords, each three feet long ending in tassles. The cords were designed to hang in a large loop across the right hip, with the ends hooked onto the right hand bottom button of the coatee, allowing the tassles to hang just below the waist. However, paintings of officers of the 13th Light Infantry and the Light Company 46th Foot made in 1840 show the cords hooked onto a button high up on the chest (doubtless worn this way to avoid the encumbrance of the low hanging cords which would have been too easily caught up in undergrowth). The light infantry sash appears to have had no practical purpose, and to have been designed purely for show.

Although it is very doubtful whether Light Infantry troops ever wore green before the introduction of green No. 1 Dress in 1950, dark green became a colour associated with light troops from an early age. In particular, head-dresses were either embellished with green plumes or ball tufts, or covered in green cloth. (However, the light company of the 46th Foot wore red plumes or ball tufts in recognition of its part in the engagement at Paoli in 1777.) Over the years more and more items of light infantry uniform assumed the dark green colour. Amongst these were whistle cords, bugle cords, hose-tops, battle-dress shoulder titles, backings to badges of rank, and stable belts.

It is often assumed that dark green was adopted by Rifle regiments as a form of camouflage. Whether this was indeed the original concept is not known; there is however no doubt that, under normal daylight conditions, few colours stand out more clearly or offer a better aiming mark. In 1800 a certain Lieutenant-Colonel Haviland Smith, late 27th Foot, carried out an experiment to evaluate the comparative vulnerability of men wearing various colours in battle. He had three targets painted rifle green, red and light iron-grey respectively. Then, using men of the 6/60th Rifles who had recently returned from the Helder campaign (in which they had worn light iron-grey uniforms), he ordered them to fire a total of 108 rounds from rifled muskets at each of the targets. The results were remarkable. The rifle green target was completely shot to pieces; the red suffered somewhat less; while the iron-grey was hardly hit at all. The soldiers remarked that, after the first few rounds, the iron-grey targets became almost invisible in the smoke. No action was taken on Smith's report, but fifty-four years later, Colonel Ardant du Picq noted that, especially at dusk, the Russians in their grey great-coats melted into the background. A painting of Lieutenant-Colonel Lord Mark Kerr's 13th Light Infantry at the battle of Azimghur, in the latter stages of the Indian Mutiny, shows the soldiers dressed in loose fitting, light grey uniforms. A very similar dress was worn by General Cameron's troops in the New Zealand War of 1863. The Germany army continued to wear 'field grey' throughout both World Wars.

Above all else, the bugle-horn came to be the recognised symbol of light troops. Both Light Infantry and Rifle regiments incorporated it in their badges, wearing it in their head-dress, on their wings and skirt ornaments.

In 1814 this practice, which had undoubtedly been in unofficial use for many years, was finally authorised by a Horse Guards memorandum which stated:

> His Royal Highness the Prince Regent having been pleased to command that the Caps of the Rifle and Light Infantry Corps and the Rifle and Light Infantry Companies of Regiments shall have a Bugle Horn with the number of the Regiment below it instead of the Brass Plate worn by the rest of the Infantry. The Commander-in-Chief has directed that the same shall be established throughout the several Companies and Corps of Riflemen and Light Infantry in His Majesty's Service.

This original bugle-horn that was authorised to be worn on the chaco was similar to that later adopted by the Oxfordshire and Buckinghamshire Light Infantry, that is to say a 'stringed' bugle-horn, with its mouth-piece to the right, over which the strings or cords were shown looped up into a 'crow's foot'. At a later date, the King's Own Yorkshire Light Infantry, the Highland Light Infantry and the majority of Rifle Volunteer regiments adopted the French horn as a basis for their badges in preference to the simple bugle-horn.*

Arcane regimental dress distinctions are sacrosanct institutions in the British Army, and the abolition or alteration of some minor detail can generate strong emotions incomprehensible to an outsider. It is therefore understandable that no moves were made to standardise dress within the six English Light Infantry regiments until the major reorganisation of the infantry into brigades in 1951. It then became apparent that the crossposting of officers and men between Light Infantry regiments would become increasingly common, and that to save expense and provide continuity in pride of uniform it was important that standardisation within the six regiments was essential. The most visible application of this policy was probably the abolition of the old 'blue patrol' uniform and the substitution of a dark green No. 1 Dress with silver buttons. Regimental cap badges continued to be worn and minor distinctions, such as the methods of wearing the whistle cord and the various patterns of NCOs' chevrons, remained unaltered. Because officers' service dress was not

*A bugle is a breed of mid-European cow. Its curved horns provided the instruments that had long been used by German hunters. They could produce two, or possibly three, somewhat mournful notes.

then an authorised parade uniform, this also remained unaltered, allowing the Oxfordshire and Buckinghamshire Light Infantry to retain their unique 'Regimental Belts' in place of the standard Sam Browne, and the vestigial gorget on their collars.

There is no doubt that only two of the new infantry brigades really worked happily and efficiently from the start. These were both made up of light troops: the Light Infantry and the Green Jackets. Both these brigades shared a common ethos, had gone to great trouble to standardise dress and, in the case of the Light Infantry, had already established a strong cohesion between its officers through the Light Infantry Club, formed with such foresight eighteen years before.

The Defence White Paper of 1957 foreshadowed a drastic reduction of the infantry, and in 1959 the Somerset Light Infantry amalgamated with the Duke of Cornwall's Light Infantry to form the Somerset and Cornwall Light Infantry. The Oxfordshire and Buckinghamshire Light Infantry had departed for the Green Jackets the previous year, leaving only four remaining English Light Infantry regiments. There was never any doubt at this stage that the policy was for brigades to evolve into new 'large regiments'. Some of the brigades deliberately dragged their feet, but in the Light Infantry there was a determination to face up to the inevitable, work towards the formation of a 'large regiment', and ensure that its eventual birth would be achieved with the minimum of pain. Brigade badges were in process of replacing the old regimental badges. For most of the infantry their design proved highly contentious, and the results, determined by disparate committees, were most unpopular. Once again, the Light Infantry found itself in an enviable position, for there was never any doubt in anybody's mind that the new brigade badge should consist of the bugle horn. As mentioned previously, the standard design of bugle horn was that worn by the Oxfordshire and Buckinghamshire Light Infantry. As this regiment was no longer part of the current Light Infantry Brigade, it was felt that some slight change should be made in the design of the new badge. The result was that the depiction of cords was replaced by one of ribbons tied at the base of the 'crow's foot' with a tasselled cord. The Somerset and Cornwall's Light Infantry's request for a red backing behind the Brigade cap badge was refused, but it was to be replaced behind the new Somerset and Cornwall Light Infantry collar badges.

See p.526.

The evolutionary process towards the 'large regiment' moved inexorably forward. On 9th May 1967, in response to a directive issued by the Chief of the General Staff the previous day, the Colonels of the four regiments met in London to consider the future of the Light Infantry. This annexure merely concerns dress, so it is unnecessary to delve into the soul searching and vehement discussion that took place at this and subsequent meetings. It is enough to say that it was agreed that the four regiments should merge into a single regiment and that, upon the merger taking place, they should be known simply as the 1st, 2nd, 3rd and 4th Battalions, the Light Infantry. This merging (or vesting as it became known) took place on 10th July 1968.

With the old regiments gone and the old battalions now being part of a single new regiment, it was important that, for the corporate image of the Light Infantry, regimental dress should be standardised. This was merely the consumation of a process which had been gradually taking place since 1951. During the intervening years mess dress, No 1 Dress, badges of rank, sword knots, cap badges, and many other small details had been made standard throughout the Brigade. Now was the time to take the final step and produce comprehensive dress regulations, which would be applicable to every Light Infantry officer or soldier, regardless of where he was serving. It was considered that, in order to maintain continuity between the old regiments and the new, as many of the former dress distinctions as possible should be adopted by the Light Infantry. Thus, for example, the officers and serjeants were to knot their sashes on the right hip (Somerset Light Infantry); the red backing was to be reinstated behind the cap badge (Duke of Cornwall's Light Infantry); the sword scabbard was invariably to be hooked up on the Sam Browne belt (King's Shropshire Light Infantry); and the lion's head chain and whistle were again to be worn by the serjeants on their sashes (Durham Light Infantry).

This, however, was not to be the end of the matter. The Light Infantry (now only three battalions since 1959) was but one of two regiments in the newly formed Light Division, the other being the Royal Green Jackets (also of three battalions). As the army shrank, flexibility was maintained by crossposting officers and men, not merely within their own regiment, but across their division. Henceforth it became ever more common for Light Infantry officers and men to find themselves serving in Royal Green Jacket battalions, and *vice versa*. In order to provide uniformity on parade without involving individuals or the public in additional expense, it was agreed that sweeping changes should be made to ensure that parade uniforms could be simply and cheaply altered to meet the requirements of either regiment. As it happened, it was the Light Infantry that made the greater changes, assuming many of the traditional characteristics of Royal Green Jackets' dress.

It is interesting to take a quick look at the origins of the uniform worn by Rifle regiments, the vestiges of which became part of Light Infantry parade dress. In 1797, Baron de Rottenburg, an *émigré* from Austria-Hungary, raised the 5th Battalion of the 60th Royal American Regiment. It was to be the first true Rifle battalion in the British army, and was originally made up of an amalgamation of two battalions of German and Austrian soldiers in the service of Britain. The 5/60th were from the start dressed in dark green, the traditional colour of mid-European *Jäger* troops. However, de Rottenburg had originally served with a Hungarian Hussar regiment which had worn the heavily frogged short jacket (the *dolman*), the fur lined *pelisse*, the *sabretache*, the pouch belt and the fur cap. All these he introduced into his new battalion, laying down that officers should dress as Hussars, albeit in the more sober colour of dark green with black frogging and lace, traditional to the *Jägers*. Thus it was that the 60th Rifles, and subsequently the Rifle Brigade, adopted the distinctive and glamorous Hussar uniform.

Most of these splendid accoutrements were swept away in the radical Dress Regulations of 1855, which decreed that uniform should henceforth be more practical and less expensive. A few of the Rifle idiosyncracies did however survive, notably the black leather pouch belt with its silver ornaments, sword slings and waist belt. It was these that were assumed by the Light Infantry in 1974 as immediately recognisable symbols of the Light Division. At the same time Light Infantry buglers and bandsmen were issued with the Rifle Cap, which owed its origin to the fur head-dress once worn by mid-European Hussars. These were made from nylon mock sealskin, the genuine article being deemed unacceptable to modern sensibilities.

It is a strange quirk of tradition that articles of dress, once worn by wild horsemen roaming the steppes of Hungary, should have become the visible symbols of the Light Infantry and the Royal Green Jackets.

The policy which had led to Light Infantrymen becoming almost indistinguishable from Riflemen is open to argument. There was never any tradition of Light Infantrymen wearing black belts or sealskin caps, and the adoption of these items of dress laid the Light Infantry open to the accusation of attempting to emulate a distinguished Regiment with which it never had genuine links. On the other hand, these black belts and sealskin caps, however spurious, undoubtedly gave the Light Infantry a clearly identifiable corporate image which it previously lacked; they gave their soldiers a pride in standing out from the common herd; they thus helped recruiting; they cut down on the expenses incurred by officers on crossposting between the two Regiments; and, on the purely practical side, they reduced the burden of cleaning to a minimum (important to busy officers in times when they are denied the services of batmen). To the initiated, there were still many points of difference between the two regiments. Among the more obvious were the Light Infantry bright metal buttons, serjeant's sashes and the custom of other ranks (less the RSM) wearing berets in parade dress.

DRILL

Today, drill is performed on a flat barrack square for purely ceremonial purposes. It must however be realised that throughout the eighteenth and much of the nineteenth centuries, drill was synonymous with field evolutions which were designed to be performed in battle across broken ground.

Throughout the eighteenth century the influence of Frederick the Great of Prussia (1712-1786) had a profound effect on all European armies. His tactics, which had proved eminently successful in the Seven Years War, relied on extreme precision in the execution of complex movements by bodies of troops massed in shoulder to shoulder formations. Such bodies could deliver devastating volleys at close range (the Prussian infantryman was trained to fire five rounds per minute), while the close proximity of comrades, all performing well-rehearsed drills, must have been a major factor in maintaining the courage and determination of every individual soldier. Having broken the enemy line by musket fire, Frederick's men would then close with the bayonet. This was however no wild charge, but was carried out in strictly regimented lines with the drums beating out the stately time of seventy-five paces to the minute. In the minds of eighteenth century tacticians, it stood to reason that the side that could hurl the greatest quantity of lead at their foe would ultimately prove victorious. Disruption by fire power followed by destruction by the bayonet was the keystone to all infantry tactics. Little thought was given to the employment of light troops.

We have seen how, in the forests of North America, the use of these close formations was not practical, and that highly effective light infantry tactics had evolved. However, these came about as a result of experience gained in a specific theatre of operations, and were not authorised or indeed accepted by the diehards at Horse Guards in London. The British army that returned from America, beaten and disillusioned, rapidly fell into decline. Without a modern drill book, or indeed any tactical guide lines, commanding officers trained (or more often failed to train) their soldiers according to their own individual ideas. The inevitable result was that battalions, without any common doctrine, soon became incapable of working together. The army was fast ceasing to be an integrated fighting force when a staff-officer at the Headquarters in Dublin appeared on the scene. Colonel David Dundas had attended the last full scale manoeuvres held by Frederick the Great, and was so impressed by the perfection of Prussian drill that, in 1788, he published a manual entitled *Principles of Military Movement Chiefly Applied to Infantry*. Dundas, an officer not endowed with any great imagination, was of the old school who believed implicitly in close order drill carried out with rigid discipline. Right or wrong, his work did at least give commanding officers clear guidelines on which to base the training of their battalions. In 1792 Dundas, now a Major-General at the Horse Guards, published his great work, *Rules and Regulations for the Formations, Field Exercises and Movements of His Majesty's Forces*. Whereas his 1788 manual had merely outlined his own personal views, that of 1792 was published by the authority of Horse Guards, and as such became the official directive for the army. The book, closely printed on 458 quarto-sized pages, went into immense detail covering every conceivable aspect of military field training, from the teaching of the recruit to stand up straight, to the manoeuvring of large formations in battle. What is of special interest to us is that, for the first time, nine pages were devoted exclusively to the employment of light infantry. In spite of his reactionary instincts Dundas realised that light troops performed a vital service in the field, and that their tactics should be regularised so that light companies and battalions could work together. He laid down that light troops, when manoeuvring on their own, should move in quick time (108 paces to the minute), or when necessary in double time (180 paces to the minute); that they should work in pairs, firing alternately so that one would always have a loaded weapon; that they should be capable of loading and firing from the lying position; that they should make best use of all available cover; and that they should carry their muskets 'sloped' or 'trailed', as opposed to heavy infantry who invariably carried theirs at 'the shoulder' (butt supported in the palm of the left hand, trigger guard to the rear and stock rested vertically against the shoulder). Contemporary illustrations tend to show light troops carrying their muskets either at the trail or laid diagonally across the body, supported in the crook of the right arm.

No further authorised drill manual was produced till 1824, when the Adjutant-General, Major-General Sir Henry Torrens, published *Field Exercises of the Army*. Here at last was a concise drill book, which would be clearly recognisable today. In a smaller format publication of 217 pages, Torrens devoted forty-three pages to light infantry manoeuvres. He described in detail: firing from the lying position; loading while on the move; skirmishing; the rapid forming of square from widely extended order, when attacked by cavalry; and the use of standardised bugle calls (this is the first official mention of the use of buglers by light troops). Finally, Torrens laid down that young officers should never be allowed to drill soldiers till they themselves had perfected their own skills by being drilled in squads by a field officer; something that General Moore had insisted upon at Shorncliffe many years previously.

From the advent of the rifled musket in 1851 the specialised role of light troops began to be assumed by all infantrymen; indeed, as has already been mentioned, the Light Division in the Crimean War was 'light' in name only, and in 1858 light companies were abolished. During the late nineteenth and for the first part of the twentieth century, the manuals contained no reference to any peculiarities of light infantry drill. That these peculiarities existed however is beyond dispute, though they seem to have been carried out at the personal whim of commanding officers. Lieutenant-Colonel Lord Mark-Kerr of the 13th (Prince Albert's) Light Infantry took great delight in practising traditional light infantry drills on major ceremonial occasions (although one suspects that this may have been mainly to anger senior officers, whom he generally detested). Paintings of the Crimea period show his battalion marching with rifles at the trail. On one famous occasion, when marching past General Simpson at a grand review, Mark-Kerr was ordered to fix bayonets and shoulder arms. Ignoring the order, he shouted over his shoulder "Fix fiddlesticks!" whereupon the men gave a raucous cheer. We also know that the Duke of Cornwall's Light Infantry (and probably the other Light Infantry regiments) doubled past on ceremonial occasions. The 2nd Battalion performed this evolution at Alexandria in 1883 on the occasion of the presentation of the Khedive Stars by the Khedive himself. Unfortunately the Stars were only loosely pinned on, and many fell off. That evening witnessed the undignified sight of hundreds of soldiers crawling over the dusty parade ground, searching for their lost awards.

It is very difficult to ascertain the exact nature of the drill carried out by the various Light Infantry battalions during this period. Whatever peculiarities were practiced, they were certainly frowned on by senior officers. Quite apart from the fact that any movement not authorised by the drill manual was forbidden, a single Light Infantry battalion could cause chaos on a brigade or divisional parade if it insisted on performing its own drill movements.

In 1928, thanks largely to the interest taken by the Adjutant-General, General Sir Walter Braithwaite, late of the Somerset Light Infantry, official recognition was given to Light Infantry regiments marching past at the trail in quick time. Two years later Major-General Deedes, Colonel of the King's Own Yorkshire Light Infantry, was appointed Director of Personal Services, and so dealt with matters of drill. As a result of his efforts the position of the trail was approved for use by Light Infantry at all times in quick and double time.

The *Infantry Drill Manuals* for 1896, 1902 and 1914 make no mention whatsoever of light infantry movements; hence perhaps the reluctance of senior officers to allow any deviation. It is only when we read *The Manual of Ceremonial, 1935* that we find any official indication is given to English Light Infantry regiments not fixing bayonets on certain occasions, and marching at the trail. Even at this stage, photographs show a wide divergence of the drill used by different Light Infantry regiments, and even by different battalions of the same regiment. In 1935 the 1st Battalion Duke of Cornwall's Light Infantry appear always to have marched past at the trail, while the 2nd Battalion still marched past at the slope with fixed bayonets. In truth, it would seem that some Light Infantry battalions were more 'Light' than others, and that this depended to some extent partly on historical links, and partly on the caprice of the commanding officer.

During the Second World War recruits from a variety of regiments were trained together at Primary Training Centres. It was thus impossible to maintain a separate drill for those who were badged as Light Infantrymen, and as a result Light Infantry drill was put into abeyance for the duration of the war.

In 1946 the Army Council considered a 'grouping' system whereby the existing infantry regiments would be grouped according to territorial or traditional links. Thanks largely to General Sir Daril Watson, Colonel of the Duke of Cornwall's Light Infantry, who was then Quarter-Master-General, it was agreed that the six English Light Infantry regiments should be grouped together, and that a Light Infantry Training Centre should be established at Cove, near Aldershot. With all

Light Infantry recruits now training together, it was essential that a common drill should be established. A meeting was therefore held on 22nd January 1947, chaired by General Deedes, at which details of a common drill were formulated.

Needless to say, although recruits were taught a standard drill during their basic training at Cove (and later at Bordon), individual battalions continued to practice their traditional idiosyncrasies. These were too numerous to itemise comprehensively, but as examples: the bugle drill of each regiment varied considerably; the King's Own Yorkshire Light Infantry (as befitted a regiment which had fought with the original Light Division in the Peninsula) doubled onto the battalion markers at the start of ceremonial parades; and the Somerset Light Infantry carried out all movements outside the ranks in double time. Further variations crept in when the 1st and 2nd Battalions were amalgamated in 1950 for, as previously mentioned, individual battalions were jealous of their distinctions.

In 1957 the loosely integrated Light Infantry 'group' was formally designated the Light Infantry Brigade. With this change came a greater degree of standardisation in matters of drill, although the individual regiments clung tenaciously to their old traditions. However, even at this stage it was becoming evident that it was the intention of the Army Council that these 'brigades' should evolve into 'large regiments'. Indeed, an 'Infantry Reorganisation Committee' was established by the Army Council under the chairmanship of Lieutenant-General Sir Roger Bower, late of the King's Own Yorkshire Light Infantry, to consider how this could be best achieved. His remit included the thorny subject of regimental tradition, custom and drill.

On 10th July 1968 the four remaining English Light Infantry regiments (the Oxfordshire and Buckinghamshire Light Infantry had transferred to the Green Jackets in 1957 and the Somerset Light Infantry and the Duke of Cornwall's Light Infantry had amalgamated in 1959) were finally merged to become battalions of a large regiment: the Light Infantry. A further grouping then took place whereby pairs of these new large regiments were allotted to 'divisions'. As was natural, the Light Infantry became partners with the Royal Green Jackets (as this regiment had now become), thus forming the Light Division. Within each 'division', officers and soldiers now came onto a common roll which gave great flexibility, allowing crossposting, not merely within the large regiments, but within the divisions. In most divisions there was little, if any homogeny; crosspostings could therefore be an unpopular and traumatic experience. The Light Division, however, shared a common ethos and tradition which made for a happy interchange between Light Infantrymen and Riflemen. A brand new Light Division Depôt was built just outside Winchester at which all recruits were trained together. Naturally this called for yet a further standardisation of drill.

Light Infantry and Rifle drill already had much in common, both having evolved from the same tactical needs. Thus, both marched at 140 paces to the minute in quick time, employed double time as a parade ground movement, marched at the trail, carried out all movements from the 'at ease' position, did not fix bayonets on parade, and generally carried out drill evolutions with the minimum words of command. In this last respect, the Rifle Regiments (now the Royal Green Jackets) had refined their drill to an even greater degree than the Light Infantry. As an example of this, regiments of heavy infantry needed four separate words of command to turn a body of troops standing in line and set it off marching to its flank; the Light Infantry used two; but the Royal Green Jackets just one: 'to the right (or left), quick march!' A smart reaction to this extreme exercise in brevity required every man to be able to think for himself and to be thoroughly alert; in fact to portray the classical attributes of light troops through the ages.

The layman might well query the sense in spending many valuable hours of a soldier's training programme to teach him arcane drill movements that lost any functional purpose well over a century ago. It is difficult to explain to somebody who has never taken part in a well-executed parade the extraordinary thrill derived from carrying out complex drill movements in absolute harmony. It is perhaps akin to the pleasure felt and experienced by rowers when they work in perfect unison. Drill, when executed with skill, epitomises the total physical unity of a body of troops, and is, without any doubt, an exercise which inspires personal and corporate pride. During the North West Europe campaign of 1945, 'Rocky' Knight (ex Welsh Guards) found himself as the Regimental Serjeant-Major of the 7th Somerset Light Infantry. Brought up in the traditions of Caterham and Wellington Barracks, he had no doubt about the morale value of well performed drill, believing that it was every bit as important on active service as in peace-time. When the Battalion came out of the line and moved into billets, he allowed the men a day to clean themselves up and get some much needed sleep; he would then take each company in turn and give it three-quarters of an hour of brisk drill. At first the soldiers grumbled, murmuring that they had not come to France to be messed about by some guardsman (or words to that effect!), but the results were electric. Twenty-four hours before, these men had come out of battle haggard with exhaustion, unshaven, filthy and despondent. Suddenly they were men again, standing up straight with their chests out – not just ordinary men, but supermen proud of being soldiers in the finest battalion of the finest regiment in the British army. Any soldier of the 7th Somerset Light Infantry will tell you that 'Rocky' Knight did more to maintain fighting spirit than perhaps any other man in that battalion.

3

Notes on a Recent Visit to the Trenches [in France], May 1915

By a Commanding Officer, Lieutenant-Colonel Stokoe

The country is as flat as a billiard table. The soil is clayey and very heavy. Hedges are only placed round small gardens and are impenetrable until cut down. Small dykes full of water, just jumpable, cover the country. The fields are all ploughed and ready for sowing. From the roof of any house a clear view can be obtained for two miles in any direction. Sometimes a few poplars skirt the roads. All houses within two miles of the firing line are destroyed, but yet are occupied by troops. All church spires and any point from which a good view can be obtained are at once knocked down by artillery.

Form of the trenches

In the sections visited by me the trenches were within a few yards of a road, just outside the remains of a straggling village. Headquarters was about 300 yards behind in a ruined house on a road running to the rear. The two companies in support were in more ruined houses another 200 yards in rear of headquarters. Reserves were three miles in rear in a partly destroyed village. A dressing station was placed within 400 yards of the firing line. Many trenches were placed half a mile or more in rear. These were dug by civilian labour under the supervision of Royal Engineers, but nobody seemed to know quite where they were or who should occupy them. This was a noticeably weak spot in the plan of defences. Some guns were close up but completely concealed. The trenches were daily rising more and more above ground on account of the waterlogged condition of the soil. They were much broader than the Witley ones and were of the engineering book pattern. The Officers all said they would prefer the trenches to be much narrower but the difficulty of communication, relieving, removal of wounded and bringing up supplies of ammunition and food compelled them to increase the width. The communication trenches could not be compared with those dug by the Brigade at Witley. The diggers were handicapped of course, by the state of the soil. They had only dug a few feet into the ground and had thrown the excavated earth on either side. Trestles and planks had been placed in position to keep the men above water level. These trenches were dangerous, and all who passed along them had to stoop very much. The enemy were 100 yards in front, entrenched apparently in a similar manner, but strongly covered by cheveaux-de-frise. We had little wire and very few cheveaux-de-frise – not nearly enough. Although it looks very risky as a matter of fact there is not very much danger in carrying out these cheveaux-de-frise at night and placing them in position. If the workers lie down when the star shells go up they never get hit. Practically the only wire entanglement in use besides the cheveaux-de-frise is the low wire entanglement made according to book pattern, the wire having a width of at least 10 yards, cheveaux-de-frise are easily damaged by artillery fire.

Dug-outs are not very plentiful, again because of the wetness of the soil. Undercutting was not resorted to and no funk holes were seen in the trenches. Boxes had been let into the parapet to hold ammunition, log books, bully beef tins and odds and ends. Between each traverse one or two loop-holes had been constructed, but were only used for odd shots in the daytime. Diagonal loop-holes were rather favoured. When a trench is attacked the loop-holes are not used, all firing taking place over the parapet. The loop-hole is bad in that it is difficult to withdraw the rifle and bayonet quickly and the field of fire is very restricted. The loop-holes are all made of wood and of one pattern, and are constructed away in the rear. They were built into the parapet and about two feet of earth placed upon them. Sandbags are extensively used and both parties make no attempt to conceal them.

Trench fighting

Nearly all the casualties in the trenches occur through carelessness – a man leaning against the parapet with a loop-hole behind him, or having a peep over the top, etc. The sentries need not look out all the time. A glance every minute is quite enough. The battalions at the front have just been issued with two telescope sights apiece, and it is reported that the number is to be brought up to 20 per battalion when available. Rifle fire goes on intermittently all day and night, but increases very much at night. In the advanced posts each sentry fires about 200 rounds. For bombs, iron cylinders about the size and shape of our sham bombs and weighting about 1½ lbs. are mostly in use. They are set alight by twisting the projecting fuse. When smoke appears the bomb is thrown by hand. The fuze burns for about six seconds before the explosion takes place. The British throw these bombs well up to 30 yards. The Germans seem unable to throw any distance, probably owing to the fact that they are less adept at games than our men.

When a sap is discovered the head should be silently rushed at night and bombed or the workers shot from above. The attackers should not jump in as a machine-gun is generally trained to fire down the sap or communication trench. Another effective plan to stop a sap is to counter-sap from two points in the parapet right and left of it and directed at the trench in the enemy's side of the sap head. The workers are thereby cut off or are in too dangerous a position to work. A third apparently effective plan is to aim the counter-sap at the sap head and place maxims to fire down them. When the saps meet the enemy can make no further progress.

The particular Brigade visited might be described as a weak one, consisting of one Regular, one Territorial, and two Gurkha battalions. It was impossible not to be struck by the absence of any organized plan of offensive action of the section occupied by them. Everything was purely defensive. Everyone was cheerful and confident of keeping the Germans off – that's all. This attitude is not to be taken as at all typical of that adopted along the whole British line.

Supplies and messing

The messing for officers should be done by battalion messes. By this means officers feed alike; they see one another daily, and the Commanding Officer sees them. They can talk and discuss matters with one another, can thus gain experience and do not become obsessed with the idea that their platoons are the only units in the force. A mess cart is sanctioned, but has to be purchased by the officers. The Government provides the horse. It would be a good thing if these carts could be purchased in England and taken over with the unit. Possibly permission might be obtained to do this. The Mess Sergeant superintends the officer's messing arrangements, and by means of officers' servants sends the food into the firing line and the supports.

When the battalion is in reserve the cooking for the men is done by the Master-Cook. When it is in the trenches the company cooks prepare the meals as near the firing line as possible. Water is taken as close to the trenches as possible in a service water cart or in a large barrel fixed on a connecting cart. It is drawn off into camp kettles or empty rum jars in order to be carried into the trench itself. Empty rum jars have proved invaluable for conveying water. A certain number of candles are provided by Government, but the supply needs to be augmented. Within three miles of the firing line no shops are open with the exception of wine shops.

The system of supply is simple. The railway carries the supplies to within ten or fifteen miles of the front. From there it is transferred into motor lorries by the ASC [Army Service Corps] and taken to the rendezvous for supply, which may be about four or five miles in rear of the firing line. There the regimental carts are loaded by five or six men from the unit for whom the supplies are destined. (These men are chosen from those who are of little use in the firing line. One of these men should go forward and return with each cart). The carts are then taken to the Brigade rendezvous and handed over to the Quartermaster, who distributes them to the companies, etc. The carts at once return to the rendezvous for further supplies. The carts bear no flags. If each cart were distinguishable by means of a small flag showing the company letter and name of the regiment endless confusion would be saved.

No blankets are taken when going on front line duty. The blankets are all left with second line transport until the battalion returns to the reserve. Blankets were found to make the men too slow in turning out. The soldier carries an extra bandolier of ammunition and everything else he possibly can on his back when the battalion moves into the front line. The amount of clothing some men carry is excessive. It consists of one great-coat, one British warm coat, a sheep-skin coat, and a mackintosh cape which reaches to the knees. The small Indian mule cart carries forward a supply of 150 gum boots and the food. The Brigadier arranges as to whether battalions take their own picks and shovels into the trenches, or whether the relieving battalion takes over the tools of the old guard. The small entrenching tool is not much used.

Strenuous efforts are required to counteract the tendency to waste in various directions. For instance, wounded men's rifles should always be brought back from the firing line. It is common to see abandoned stores of many kinds – for instance you see bicycles lying in ditches.

* * *

Relieving of trenches

The Commanding Officer and the Company Officer of the relieving battalion should proceed round the whole of the trenches the day previous to that on which the relief takes place. It would probably be advisable for the battalion of the New Armies on the occasion of their first taking over trenches from the old Army actually to enter the trenches on the day previous and to have the first 24 hours with the old guard. In this time they would learn all the tips picked up by the long experience of the old Army. When relieving the Commanding Officers meet at some pre-arranged spot probably the same headquarters, and the new Commanding Officer receives over the reports, log books, sketches, plans, etc., of the old battalion. The Commanding Officer of the old battalion should therefore have all these papers ready, and the utmost care must be taken that nothing is lost, forgotten, or destroyed. A full discussion must take place as to the proposals of advances or retirements (whether they may be intentional or compulsory). Every eventuality must be thought of, and Commanding Officers of the flank battalions must also confer as soon as they possibly can. The relieving of the . . . s by the . . . s was carried out in a manner very similar to that practiced at Witley. A guide from every platoon of the . . .s met the companies of the . . . s at a cross-roads (a bad place) three quarters of a mile in rear of the firing line, and at once took off their corresponding platoons into their positions. Companies arrived at the point of assembly at intervals of ten minutes. The Commanding Officer remained at headquarters while reliefs went on and each company commander reported when company relief was complete. Total relief took two hours. Firing should die down while relieving is taking place in order to allow it to proceed as peacefully as possible. Heavy firing always draws corresponding heavy fire from both rifles and guns. Incidentally it may be noted that the Germans relieved their trenches about the same time that we relieved ours.

The Commanding Officer and second-in-command visited all trenches daily, one taking the mornings and the other the afternoons.

Sanitary problems

The sanitary state of the billets and surrounds of the particular brigade visited appeared little less than disgraceful.The excuse was made that battalions changed places daily and that therefore none took any interest in the matter, also that the Indian regiments were responsible for the state of affairs. Human excreta and refuse covered the ground and was thick on the floors of the rooms. No provision had been made by the brigade authorities for working parties or for any kind of supervision. The battalion sanitary squads had ceased to exist, and each company scratches the earth where it liked and called it a urinal. Only the most strenuous measures can now prevent fever from breaking out in this area when warm weather comes. The stench is horrible.

The battalion sanitary squad must be kept up. Rears must be deep and filled in daily, and should be so placed as to be convenient, and on some plan, and not scattered over the whole area. I think it would be advisable for each company to have a small yellow flag to mark the position of these trenches.

Discipline

The cleanliness of the men on the last day of their being in reserve was excellent. Their bodies were clean as a result of baths which had been instituted under battalion arrangements. They were well shaven and their hair was kept short. (Clippers are most valuable for this purpose). Buttons and fittings had been rubbed up, equipment cleaned as well as possible and boots well dubbed. The most noticeable point was the excellent saluting by all soldiers; but from want of thorough teaching in this matter it was easy to distinguish the old Army from the new recruits. Drinking houses are under no restrictions, are always open and are everywhere up to within two miles of the firing line. The wine is made of beetroot and is very potent, two glasses being sufficient to make a man drunk. Punishment is given by Field Punishments Nos. 1 and 2. There is practically no imprisonment. Defaulters are put on to all the worst and dirtiest jobs. They have no rest. The men when in trenches were always accoutred. Those in support 300 or 400 yards in rear had their kits handy. In billets three or four miles in rear men wore no accoutrements whatever. Sock uppers covered the butts of the rifles; but care must be taken that they do not become wet in that position or the bolts will rust.

It was strongly impressed on me that cheerfulness is the most valuable asset in an Officer, N.C.O. or Man. Let the officer rag, let the men rage, let them sing and play when possible, but stop grousing and moping.

A SELECT GLOSSARY

Army, British, nomenclature. The British system of designation is so idiosyncratic that one might be tempted to believe that it was deliberately designed to mislead enemy intelligence. The fact is that like much of our heritage, it was never designed as a whole but evolved over the centuries.

The following table may be of some help to the uninitiated:

At unit level

Cavalry/Armour	Artillery	Infantry	Royal Engineers	
Troop	Troop		Platoon	Troop commanded by a subaltern an ensign or lieutenant
Squadron	Battery	Company	Squadron	commanded by a captain or major
Regiment	Regiment	Battalion	Regiment	commanded by a lieut-colonel or in the early days sometimes by a colonel

Above unit level the designation of formations becomes more logical:
Brigade, generally consisting of three or four Regiments/Battalions commanded by a Brigadier-General or Brigadier.
Division, generally consisting of three or four Brigades commanded by a Major-General.
Corps, generally consisting of two or more Divisions commanded by a Lieut-General.
Army, consisting of two or more Corps commanded by a General or Field-Marshall.

However, to confuse matters the infantry has from its inception been formed into regiments. An infantry regiment has never been a fighting unit as such, but more of a close-knit family to which officers and men have owed their main allegiance. Up to 1881, most infantry regiments consisted of a single battalion, with the result that the terms regiment or battalion came to be used as synonymous alternatives. It was only after this date, when every infantry regiment had at least two battalions, that the two terms became distinct.

As a further confusion, two regiments, the King's Royal Rifle Corps & Rifle Brigade which now form part of the Royal Green Jackets, had these misleading titles. They were similar in organisation to any other infantry regiment, and their names had nothing to do with the higher formations known as Corps or Brigades.

Ballistite. A special cartridge, which does not incorporate a bullet, used to propel a missile from a rifle or mortar.

Battle Honour. An honour accorded to a regiment that has taken part in an important battle or has fought with particular valour in a minor engagement. At least the headquarters and half the strength must have been present. First awarded retrospectively in 1816, regiments displayed all such honours on their Regimental Colour (qv). So many battle honours were awarded in the Great War (qv) that regiments were invited to choose the ten most significant. The same procedure was adopted after the Second World War. All battle honours dating from the Great War onwards are displayed on the Queen's (or King's Colour) (qv).

Black Powder. See Gunpowder.

Blanco. A substance used for cleaning web equipment.

Blitzkrieg. An intense military campaign by land or air intended to bring about a swift victory (German).

Bocage. Countryside in France made up of small fields, sunken lanes and substantial hedgerows.

Bodega. A large barn-like building in which sherry is manufactured in Spain. Also loosely used as a Spanish wine ship.

Boer. A South African of Dutch descent. For the period covered by the two Boer Wars, the Boers occupied the Republic of Transvaal and the Orange Free State.

Brevet Rank. Initially an honorific promotion for brave or skilful conduct. Latterly, especially between the two World Wars, a promotion to a rank for which there was no vacancy on the establishment. In neither case did brevet rank carry any increase of pay. Discontinued in 1939.

Brew Up. Soldiers term to make tea, usually in a mess tin (qv).

Broad Sword. A heavy straight sword with a basket hilt peculiar to the Highlands of Scotland. Often misnamed as the Claymore.

Bugle Horn. A crude instrument made from a cow's horn used by Jäger troops. Latterly a formalised horn was used as the badge of Light Infantry.

Cartridge. In the days of muzzle loaded small arms, cartridges consisted of a paper tube at one end of which was incorporated the bullet. Paper cartridges proved impractical for breech loaded weapons and were quickly replaced with ones of brass.

Cavalry.

Horse and Dragoons. The British cavalry originally consisted of Regiments of Horse. Quite apart from these, there were Regiments of Dragoons. The former were true cavalry; the latter were mounted infantry who fought on foot, merely using their horses to achieve rapid mobility.

Dragoon Guards. In 1746 the cavalry was reorganised, the 2nd, 3rd and 4th Regiments of Horse being relegated to the status of Dragoons. To ameliorate this blow to their pride, they were re-designated Dragoon Guards and permitted to continue to carry standards (as opposed to the guidons authorised for Dragoons).

Light Dragoons. In 1759, regiments of Light Dragoons were established with the primary role of reconnaissance. In an era of social unrest, they also proved themselves of great value at home by their ability to move at speed to meet widely dispersed threats of civil disturbance.

Hussars. Certain Light Dragoon regiments were re-named Hussars in 1806. Hussars owed their origin to the Hungarian cavalry, and as such were clothed in the traditional very glamorous Hungarian uniform of frogged jacket and pelisse.

Lancers. Throughout the Napoleonic wars, Continental armies, particularly those of Poland, had employed light cavalry armed with the lance. In skilled hands, this could prove an exceptionally deadly weapon. Because of their undoubted success, three British Light Dragoon regiments were re-equipped as Lancers in December 1815. The lance was carried by mounted cavalry of every nation throughout the Great War. British Lancers continued to wear the square topped Polish czapka as their distinctive head-dress up to the abolition of full dress. On ceremonial occasions their lance pennants are still red and white, the traditional Polish colours.

Chaco. Shako (qv) a stiff military head-dress, usually of cylindrical shape, worn by soldiers of most armies throughout most of the nineteenth century.

Cheveaux-De-Frise. A defensive entanglement made from felled trees with the

branches (often sharpened) pointing towards the enemy.
Classification. Usually used to describe the test undertaken annually by every officer and soldier in an infantry battalion, by which his small arms shooting proficiency is graded.
Coatee. A military jacket cut to waist length at the front with 'tails' at the back. Worn by the British Army from the end of the eighteenth century to 1858, when it was superseded by a loose fitting tunic copied from the French Army.
Colours. The battle flags of an infantry battalion. Until the introduction of smokeless powder, the battlefield quickly became wreathed in a dense cloud of white smoke, which could cut down visibility to a few yards. The Colours thus became a vital rallying point. In the early eighteenth century an infantry battalion had ten Colours; in 1751 these were reduced to the present issue of two: the King's (or Queen's) and the Regimental. The former took the form of the Union Flag; the latter was the colour of the regimental facings (qv), and bore the regiment's battle honours (qv). Up to 1855 infantry Colours measured some 6ft square (the exact dimensions varied according to successive orders). The size was reduced to 3ft 9in x 3ft. The last recorded instance of Colours being carried in battle was by the 58th Foot in 1881. In 1882 the infantry was advised that it need not take Colours on active service. After the Great War, the large number of Battle Honours awarded made it necessary that a selected number of these should in future be emblazoned on the Regimental Colour (there being no further space on the King's Colour). Rifle Regiments do not carry Colours. Cavalry carry Standards or Guidons (qv).
Djebel. A hill (Arabic).
Dragoons. See Cavalry.
Drift. A shallow crossing place on a river at which it could be forded. South African.
Dubbed. Impregnated with dubbin – a greasy concoction for keeping boots waterproof and supple.
Durum dalluh. See Sammee.
Echelon. An infantry battalion is divided into three echelons: F echelon contains the men, vehicles and equipment needed to fight the battle; B echelon contains the immediate administrative requirements of the leading troops; C echelon contains those administrative elements not needed in battle.
Ensign. The junior commissioned rank in the infantry. The term was abolished in 1870 when Ensigns became known as Sub-Lieutenants. Ten years later they were again re-named Second Lieutenant, a rank that remains in use today.
Epaulettes. Ornamental shoulder straps terminating in a fringe that fell over the point of the shoulder. In the eighteenth century the wearing of either a single epaulette or a pair, together with the length of the fringe, denoted an officer's rank. They became increasingly elaborate and expensive until their abolition in 1855.
Field Punishment No. 1. A punishment that was authorised to take the place of flogging (abolished in 1881). A soldier sentenced to Field Punishment No. 1 was tied by his wrists and ankles to a gun or wagon wheel for a period depending on the seriousness of his offence. This degrading punishment was much used in the Great War but was abolished in 1919.
Forward Observation Officer. A junior Royal Artillery officer who, together with his signaller, works alongside the leading infantry sub-units in order to direct artillery fire onto targets as they occur in the battle.
French Horn. A type of hunting horn in which the tube is coiled into a complete

loop. Adopted as a badge by the King's Own Yorkshire Light Infantry, the Highland Light Infantry and numerous Rifle regiments.

Frogging. An often elaborate arrangement of decorative horizontal cords and toggles across the chest of a dress uniform, particularly by Hussars and Rifle Regiments, in emulation of Hungarian troops.

Fusiliers. Regiments originally raised to guard the Train of Artillery. Fusiliers were some of the first troops to be armed with flint-lock fusils (hence their name) as the more common match-lock musket represented a hazard in the presence of large quantities of gunpowder.

Ghee. Clarified butter (Hindustani).

Glacis. A smooth sloping area of ground, devoid of cover, which is deliberately sited in front of a fortification to allow the defenders to rake any attacking force with fire. Much used in the eighteenth and nineteenth centuries.

Grape Shot. An artillery projectile used in the days of muzzle loaded guns, which consisted of a number of iron balls (each about the size of a golf ball) contained in a canvas bag.

Gunpowder. The explosive used both as a propellant and bursting charge up to the introduction of nitro-glycerine based explosives in the latter part of the nineteenth century. Gunpowder or Black Powder (qv) produces large clouds of white, oily smoke when exploded.

Heliograph. A signalling instrument that uses a movable parabolic mirror to direct a concentrated beam of sunlight over considerable distances. Morse code can be transmitted by the movement of the mirror.

Hollow Charge. An explosive charge, the front of which is hollowed out to a parabolic shape, which directs the explosive force to a single point. It can thus melt a hole through a considerable thickness of armour plate.

Horse Guards. A regiment of the Household Cavalry. Also the building in Whitehall occupied by the Commander-in-Chief and his staff, up to the abolition of that office by Cardwell in 1881.

Hose Tops. Woollen footless stockings (similar to today's leg warmers) worn in tropical dress with boots and puttees. Often in regimental colours.

Howitzer. A short barrelled field piece designed to fire a heavy shell at a high angle so that walled fortifications or reverse slope positions (qv) can be engaged

Kepi. A light, low crowned chaco (qv) made from a variety of materials. Adopted by the British Army from the French after the Crimean War.

Land Port. A fortified gate approached from land (as opposed from water) in the defensive walls of a fortress built on the edge of a sea or river.

Lascar. Originally a native soldier in the East India Company Artillery who carried out menial duties. The term was extended to Indians who accompanied an army on the march as tent-pitchers. Latterly an Indian, often from the Madras area, employed as a seaman or steward on a ship.

Liberty Ship. A class of cheap but robust merchant ships, most of their structure pre-fabricated, which were mass-produced by the U.S.A. during the Second World War.

Limber. A two-wheeled vehicle often used to carry artillery ammunition. When used by the Royal Artillery, a field piece was frequently hooked on behind.

Mess Tin. A light cooking container carried by all ranks in the field for cooking food or drink. Originally kidney shaped, but for many years rectangular; issued in

pairs, the small fitting into the larger.
Mess. Originally merely a room (often in an inn) where officers or warrant officers and NCOs (qv) could eat and relax in privacy. In barracks, messes have become increasingly elaborate, incorporating sleeping quarters together with an anteroom and dining room in which the regimental Colour, silver and pictures can be displayed.
Mortar. A short-barrelled artillery piece with a proportionately large bore compared to its length, capable of lobbing a heavy shell at a steep angle. Latterly used as a term to describe a light tube used by both the artillery and infantry, from which bomb shaped shells can be rapidly discharged.
NCO. Non-commissioned officer.
Netherlands. Used today as an alternative name for Holland. Originally a collection of minor states in N. W. Europe. United to include Belgium in 1815, which remained part of the Netherlands till 1838.
Nullah. A dry watercourse especially in India. (Hindustani)
Oil Low Cold Test. Oil that freezes at a very low temperature, used to lubricate weapons.
Picquet, piquet. In the field, a group of soldiers deployed forward of the main position to warn of an enemy approach. In barracks, a group detailed for a specific duty, e.g. fire piquet.
Picquet, piquet, sentry. A sentry detailed to guard a particular place, object or area (as opposed to the main gate sentry).
Pole Charge. A high explosive demolition charge attached to a long pole.
RASC. Royal Army Service Corps ('Royal' included after 1918), from 1889 to 1965 responsible for supply of transport above unit level. Also supplied clerks. Originated in the Corps of Waggoners of 1794. Reorganised as the Royal Corps of Transport in 1965, and finally the Royal Logistics Corps in 1993.
Rears. Slang term for latrine.
Red Indians. See Red Skins.
Red Skins. Red Indians. Colloquial name applied to the native North American tribes.
Regimental Facings. Originally the colour shown by the folding back of the coat tails, by which regiments were identified. Latterly the colours displayed in full dress on the collar and cuffs.
Reverse Slope. A slope on the far side of high ground to that of the enemy. Troop dispositions on a reverse slope are thus hidden from enemy observation and direct fire.
Rifle Cap. A pattern of full-dress busby originally worn by Rifle Regiments. Those of officers were made of black Persian lambskin; soldiers of sealskin. Now worn by bandsmen and buglers of the Light Division, and very obviously made of nylon fur.
Sam Browne. A pattern of leather equipment to which the sword, revolver, binoculars, etc. could be attached. Invented by General Sir Samuel Browne, VC, GCB, KCSI who, having lost an arm in battle, found the existing method of carrying his sword and pistol impractical. No longer worn in the field.
Sammee. Also known as a dhurum dalluh (qv). A defensible building outside the walls of a fortress that provided a firm base, in which the outlying picquets (qv) were housed when not on duty (Hindustani).
Sangar. A protective breastwork built of rocks.
Sap. A trench dug at right angles to the defensive line towards the enemy.

Schuh Mine. A German anti-personnel mine used in the Second World War.
Self Heating Soup. Soup contained in a special tin which incorporates a heating element.
Sepoy. From the Persian word Sipah meaning a soldier. A term used by the East India Company and later by the Indian Army as the native rank equivalent to the British Army Private.
Shell. In the era of muzzle-loaded artillery, a shell consisted of a hollow cast iron spherical projectile packed with gunpowder and incorporating a simple fuze which, when ignited by the propellant, exploded the shell a few seconds later. From the introduction of breech-loaded artillery, cylindrical shells of increasing sophistication (and cost) have been introduced into service.
Soyer Stove. A cooking boiler for use in the field, designed by M. Soyer in the latter part of the Crimean War. Originally consisting of a substantial cast iron body incorporating the fire-box, into which fitted an iron pot holding about ten gallons, Soyer stoves are now made of lighter sheet steel, and are still in service.
Staff. During most of the time bracket of this book, the Staff was organised into three branches: The General Staff, (G), responsible for the employment of the fighting troops, and with all matters connected with the actual execution of military operations; the Quartermaster General's Staff, (Q), responsible for the equipping, clothing, feeding and housing of all troops; the Adjutant General's Staff, (A), responsible for the provision of manpower, for discipline and welfare of all troops.
Subaltern. An officer below the rank of Captain. Its use probably dates from 1870 when the ranks of Ensign (qv) and Cornet were replaced by that of Sub-Lieutenant.
Verey Pistol. A signal pistol, usually of 1in. bore, which can fire coloured or white flares.
Vital Ground. Ground, which if taken by the enemy, would render a defensive position untenable.
Water Canteen. A container, which has always formed an important part of every soldier's equipment, in which water is carried. Originally constructed of wood in the shape of a flat barrel, it has since been made from a wide variety of materials.
Weapon Pit. A trench to provide protection for two or three men from which they can use their weapons. In the latter stages of its construction, often includes a minimal covered rest period.
Z Reservist. A soldier who, having completed his original engagement with the Colours, opts to remain on the Reserve. In exchange for an annual payment, such a soldier remains liable for recall.

BIBLIOGRAPHY

Dates are given for editions consulted by the author.

General History

Cannon, Richard. *Historical Records of the 46th Regiment*. 1836
Godfrey, E.G. *The Duke of Cornwall's Light Infantry, 1939-1945*. 1966
Swiney, G.C. *Historical Records of the 32nd (Cornwall) Light Infantry*. 1893
Wyrall, Everard. *The Duke of Cornwall's Light Infantry, 1914-1919*. 1932
Regimental Journals:
One and All, 1886-1959 (1st Battalion, DCLI)
The Cornish Chough, 1906-192 (2nd Battalion, DCLI)
The Red Feather, 1914-1916 (6th Battalion, DCLI)
The Light Bob, 1960-1968 (SCLI)

1702 - 1839

Bond, Peter. *Three Hundred Years of British Gibraltar*. 2003
Cumming, William P & Rankin, Hugh. *The Fate of a Nation: the American Revolution through Contemporary Eyes*. 1975
Drinkwater, John. *A History of the Late Siege of Gibraltar*. 1786
Gleig, G.R. *Battle of Waterloo*. 1848
Harvey, Maurice. *Gibraltar: A History*. 1996
Hibbert, Christopher. *Corunna*. 1961
Hibbert, Christopher. *Redcoats and Rebels: the War for America, 1770-1781*. 1990
Houlding, J.A. *Fit for Service: the Training of the British Army, 1715-1795*. 1981
Jackson, Sir William, G.J. 'The Rock of Gibraltarians: a History of Gibraltar'. 1957
Longford, Elizabeth. *Wellington: the Years of the Sword*. 1969
Mann, Michael. *A Paticular Duty: the Candian Rebellions*, 1837-1839. 1986
Monro, C.C. 'Notes on Gibraltar'. 1928
Muir, Rory. *Salamanca, 1812*. 2001
Napier, W.P.F. *History of the War in the Peninsula*. 1832
Nicholas, Paul Harris. *Historical Record of the Royal Marine Forces*. 1845
Paget, Julian. *Wellington's Peninsular War*. 1990
Pericoli, Ugo; Glover, Michael; & Longford, Elizabeth. *The Armies at Waterloo*. 1973
Robinson, C.W. *Wellington's Campaigns, 1808-1815*. 1908
Ross-Lewis, Harry. *With the 32nd in the Peninsula*. 1834

The Crimean War

Anon. Robins, Colin, ed. *The Murder of a Regiment: a Crimean War Officer's Journal*. 1994
Campbell, Frederick. *Letters from the Crimea*. 1894

Dallas, George Frederick. Mawson, Michael Hargreaves, ed. *Eyewitness in the Crimea.* 2001
Dunscombe, Nicholas. Robins, Colin, ed. *Captain Dunscombe's Diary.* 2003
Hamley, Edward. *The War in the Crimea.* 1910
Massie, Alastair. *The National Army Book of the Crimean War.* 2004
Palmer, Alan. *The Banner of Battle: the Story of the Crimean War.* 1987
Pemberton, W Baring. *Battles of the Crimean War.* 1962
Woodham-Smith, Cecil. *The Reason Why.* 1953

The Second Sikh War & Indian Mutiny

Anon. *A Lady's Diary of the Siege of Lucknow.* 1857
Anon. *The Defence of Lucknow.* 1858
Anon. Hutchinson, G. ed. *Narrative of Events in Oude, 1857.* 1857
Brydon, Corlina. *The Lucknow Siege Diary.* 1858
Case, Adelaide. *Day by Day at Lucknow.* 1858
Dunlop, John. *Mooltan.* 1849
Edwardes, Michael. *A Season in Hell.* 1973
Germon, Maria. *Journal of the Siege of Lucknow.* 1858
Hibbert, Christopher. *The Great Mutiny.* 1978
Inglis, Julia. *The Siege of Lucknow.* 1892
Lang, Arthur Moffat. *Lahore to Lucknow.* 1992
Metcalfe, Robert. Tuber, Francis, ed. *The Chronicle of Private Henry Metcalfe.* 1953
Rees, L.E. *Siege of Lucknow.* 1858
Thomson, Mowbray. *The Story of Cawnpore.* 1859
Waterfield, Robert. Swinson, Arthur; & Scott, Donald, eds. *The Memoirs of Private Waterfield.* 1968

From the Late Nineteenth Century to 1914

Barthorp, Michael. *The Anglo-Boer Wars.* 1991
Carver, Michael. *The National Army Museum Book of the Boer War.* 1998
Evans, Martine, Marix. *The Boer War.* 1999
Jackson, Tabitha. *The Boer War.* 1999
Pakenham, Thomas. *The Boer War.* 1979
Pemberton, W. W. *Battles of the Boer War.* 1964
Philp, John. *Reminiscences of Gibraltar, Egypt and the Egyptian War.* 1893
Rose, A.W. White, Hugo, ed. *The Diary of 2874 Lance-Corporal A.W. Rose, 2nd DCLI.* 1999
Wilson, H.W. *With the Flag to Pretoria.* 1901

The Great War

Ascoli, David. *The Mons Star.* 1981
Bloem, Walter. *The Advance from Mons.* 1930
Coombs, Joan. *A Fowey Jig-Saw.* 2000
Doyle, A. Conan. *The British Campaign in France/Flanders, 1916.* 1918
Dunn, J.C. *The War the Infantry Knew.* 1938

Edmonds, J. E. *The Official History of the Great War, 1914*. 1922
Edmonds, J.E. The *Official History of the Great War, December 1915-July 1916*. 1932
Falls, Cyril. *Military Operations, Egypt & Palestine from June to the End of the War*. 1930
Farrar-Hockley, A.H. *Ypres, 1914: Death of an Army*. 1967
Gliddon, Gerald. *When the Barrage Lights: a Topographical History of the Battle of the Somme*. 1987
Lake, Harold. *In Salonika with our Army*. (Date of publication unknown)
Liddle, Peter. *Passchendaele in Perspective*. 1997
MacDonald, Lyn. *Somme*. 1983
MacDonald, Lyn. *They called it Passchendaele*. 1978
Matthews, E.C. *With the Cornwall Territorials on the Western Front*. 1921
McWilliams, J, & Steel, R.J. *Gas: the Battle for Ypres, 1915*. 1985
Mitchinson, K. W. *Pioneer Battalions of the Great War*. 1997
Pitt, Barrie. *1918: the Last Act*. 1962
Prior, R. & Wilson, T. *Passchendaele*. 1996
Schwink, Otto. *Ypres, 1914*. 1917
Steel, N., & Hart, P. *Passchendaele*. 2000
Teraine, John. *The Road to Passchendaele*. 1977
Terraine, John. *Mons*. 1960
Warner, Philip. *Passchendaele*. 1987
The War Diaries of the 1st, 2nd, 1/4th, 1/5th, 6th, 7th, 8th, & 10th Battalions DCLI, 1914-1919

The Second World War

Atkin, Ronald. *Pillar of Fire: Dunkirk, 1940*. 1990
Butler, E. & Bradford, J.S. *Dunkirk*. 1955
Churchill, Winston. *The Second World War*. 1948
Collier, Richard. *The Sands of Dunkirk*. 1961
Delaforce, Patrick. *The Fighting Wessex Wyverns*. 1994
Docherty, Richard. *Normandy, 1944*. 2004
Ellis, John. *Cassino: the Hollow Victory*. 1984
Elstob, Peter. *Battle of the Reichwald*. 1970
Essame, H. *The 43rd (Wessex) Division at War, 1939-1945*. 1952
Ford, Ken. *Assault Crossing of the River Seine*. 1988
Ford, Ken. *Assault on Germany: the Battle of Geilenkirchen*. 1989
Hastings, Max. *Overlord and the Battle for Normandy*. 1984
How, J.J. *Hill 112*. 1984
How, J.J. *Normandy: the British Breakout*. 1981
Lord, W. *The Miracle of Dunkirk*. 1982
Majdalany, Fred. *Cassino: Portrait of a Battle*. 1957
Parker, Matthew. *Monte Cassino*. 2003
Saunders, Tim. *The Island: Nijmegan to Arnhem*. 2002
Taylor, George. *Infantry Colonel*. 1990
Williamson, Hugh. *The Fourth Division, 1939-1945*. 1951

INDEX

for pages 1 (Introduction) to 533 (Appendix 1)

M